Hutchinson
POCKET
Encyclopedia

Hutchinson
POCKET
Encyclopedia

Hutchinson

London Melbourne Auckland Johannesburg

First published in 1987 by Century Hutchinson Ltd,
Brookmount House, 62-65 Chandos Place, London WC2N 4NW

Century Hutchinson Group (Australia) Pty Ltd
16-22 Church Street
Hawthorn
Melbourne
Victoria 3122

Century Hutchinson Group (NZ) Ltd
32-34 View Road
PO Box 40-086
Glenfield
Auckland 10

Century Hutchinson Group (SA) Pty Ltd
PO Box 337
Bergvlei 2012
South Africa

Set in Times and Univers by Saxon Printing Ltd, Derby

Printed and bound in Great Britain

ISBN 0-09-172300-0

How to Use This Book

Because the new Hutchinson Pocket Encyclopedia is so different from ordinary encyclopedias, please take a moment to read this page to be sure that you know how to get the most from this book.

The new Hutchinson Pocket Encyclopedia is more than a handy reference guide to people and places, dates, facts, and figures – it is also a compact, up-to-date, subject-by-subject guide to politics and world affairs, science and technology, art, music, literature, sport, and much more.

The Hutchinson Pocket Encyclopedia is arranged thematically, by subject area, rather than alphabetically. Within each subject area – Society, The Arts, Science and Technology – each individual section, such as Economics, Music, or Computing, is specially designed to provide an overview of a particular topic, prepared by an expert in that field. Each section contains the background to the subject – the important terms, ideas, and concepts, with concise definitions – as well as the essential names, dates, facts and figures. This means that within each section you will be able to see at a glance the context as well as the information. So, for example, all the computing terms and programming languages are grouped together, rather than scattered throughout the alphabet as in an ordinary encyclopedia. The final section is a Gazetteer, with concise information on all the countries of the world.

Because it can be used in two ways – both for an overview of a subject, and for quick reference like an ordinary A–Z encyclopedia – the Hutchinson Pocket Encyclopedia contains both a table of contents, arranged by subject, and an A–Z index listing every main entry.

The TABLE OF CONTENTS, at the beginning of the book, is the subject guide to all the major topics covered in the Pocket Encyclopedia.

The A–Z INDEX, at the end of the book, lists every entry in alphabetical order with the page number on which it appears, for quick reference when you want to look up a specific name or term.

EDITORS

Editorial Director
Michael Upshall

Project Editor
Bonnie Falconer

Consultant editors
Lionel Bender BSc, ChBiol, MIBiol
Steve Parker BSc

Text editors
Jane Anson
Susan Baker
Genevieve Clarke
Jane Farron
Edith Harkness
Erica Ison
Alison Kepple
Mike March
Bodie Mauger

Design
Grant Bradford

Typography
Gwyn Lewis

Typesetting
Ian Laing, Saxon Printing

CONTRIBUTORS

David Armstrong MSc, PhD
John Ayto MA
Brendan P Bradley MA, MSc, PhD
Hans Brill MA
Suzanne Brill MA
John O E Clark BSc
Anne Cordwent BA, Cert Ed
David Cotton BA, PhD
Nigel Davis MSc
Alan J Day MA
Ian D Derbyshire MA, PhD
J Denis Derbyshire BSc, PhD, FBIM
Peter Dews PhD
Dougal Dixon BSc, MSc
Robin Dunbar BA, PhD
Elizabeth Fenwick MA
Linda Gamlin BSc, MSc
Hildi Hawkins BSc
Jane Insley MSc
Roz Kaveney BA
Robin Kerrod FRAS
Chris Lawn BA
Miren Lopategui BA
Tom McArthur MA, MLitt, PhD
Karin L A Mogg BSc, Msc
Bob Moore BA, PhD
Ian Morrison
Gerald Norris
Maureen O'Connor
Elizabeth Porges Watson MA, BLitt
Ian Ridpath
Kate Salway BA, DFA
Marian Short
Tim Shreeve BSc, MSc, PhD, FRES
Martin Slattery BA, MSc
Angela Smith BA
John Stidworthy MA
Graham Storrs BA, MBCS
Stephen Webster BSc, MPhil
Elizabeth L Whitelegg BSc

Contents

Society

The study of society and human behaviour has a long history. All the great thinkers, in all the major civilizations, have asked questions about how and why people behave the way they do, as individuals and in groups. Western thought about society has been particularly influenced by the ideas and insights of such great theorists as Plato and Aristotle, Machiavelli, Rousseau, Hobbes, and Locke. The modern study of society, however, can be traced to the great intellectual period of the 18th century called the Enlightenment, and to the industrial and political revolutions of the 18th and 19th centuries, to the moral philosophy and political economy of such key figures as Adam Smith, David Hume, and David Ricardo. With the development of positive philosophy or positivism, the French thinker Auguste Comte (1798--1857), using the term social science, attempted to establish the study of society as a scientific discipline, capable of precision and prediction in the same way as natural science.

The modern academic social sciences are generally listed as sociology, economics, anthropology, political science, and psychology, but their area of study overlaps extensively with such subject areas as history, geography, law, philosophy, and even biology. And although some thinkers – such as Marx – have attempted to synthesise the study of society within one theory, none has yet achieved what Einstein has done for physics or Darwin for biology.

This part of the Pocket Encyclopedia focusses on various aspects of human society and the study of it, providing an overview of selected topics. It contains sections on History, Economics, Education, Language, Philosophy, Politics and Government, Psychology, Religion and Mythology, Resources, Sociology, Sport, and Women in Society.

History

The history of the world encompasses all the people who have ever lived, together with all the things they have ever done. As a result, any survey of world history, even one dealing only with powerful people and major events – monarchs and statesmen, wars and battles – has to be highly selective.

This section aims to provide a concise overview of some of the important people and events in world history by presenting them as a series of topics, from the ancient world to modern times, complemented by biographical entries, tables, and chronologies. It begins with a chronology of *The Ancient World*, followed by biographical notes on *Leaders of the Ancient World*. This is followed by a similar chronology and biographical notes for *The Medieval and Early Modern World*. *Wars and Battles* begins in the ancient world and continues to the present day, outlining the major conflicts, and indicating how they affected the course of world history. Next, *Revolutions* looks at the impact which certain rapid political and economic changes, key people, and institutions have had on the societies in which they occurred, and also on the world at large. Then there are outlines on the *Emergence of the Third World* and the *Search for Peace*, which highlight these two important, long-term processes in contemporary history. Finally, there are tables of rulers, monarchs, and heads of state, and biographical notes on *Leaders of the Modern World*, including leaders and statesmen from the last two centuries who have done most to influence the structure of the world as we know it today. The history of individual countries is covered in the separate Gazetteer section, and information on forms of government, along with a chronology of important political events, appears in the section on Politics and Government.

The Ancient World

14 million BC Africa, which is considered the 'cradle-continent', probably produced the first human-like creatures
3–5 million direct line of descent of modern humans established from E Africa
c. 60000 American Indians entered N America from Asia
15000 agriculture first practised in Egypt
10000–2000 the originally fertile Sahara became a barrier desert between northern and southern Africa
9000 Marmes man in N America, earliest human remains
5450–2500 era of Saharan rock and cave paintings, as in the Tassili
c. 3000 first dynasties of Mesopotamia: King Gilgamesh; Bronze Age civilizations: Minoan, Mycenaean
2800–2205 Sage kings in China, earliest Chinese dynasty; civilization spread to all of China
2500–1500 Indus valley civilization
1950 first Babylonian Empire established
625 birth of Buddha
550 birth of Confucius
246 Shi Huangdi, Emperor of China, succeeded to the throne of Qin. He had reunited the country as an empire by 221, and built the Great Wall of China

Egypt
5000 BC Egyptian culture already well established in the Nile Valley
3200 Menes united Lower Egypt (the Delta) with his own kingdom of Upper Egypt to form the Egyptian state
2800 Imhotep built step pyramid at Sakkara
c. 2600 Old Kingdom reached the height of its power and the kings of the 4th Dynasty built the pyramids at Gīza
c. 2200–1800 Middle Kingdom, under which

the unity lost towards the end of the Old Kingdom was restored
1730 invading Asiatic Hyksos established their kingdom in the Delta
c. 1580 New Kingdom established by the 18th Dynasty, following the eviction of the Hyksos, with its capital at Thebes; high point of Egyptian civilization
c. 1321 19th Dynasty
1191 Ramses III defeated the Indo-European 'Sea Peoples', but after him there was decline and eventual anarchy
8th–7th centuries brief interlude of rule by kings from Nubia
666 the Assyrians under Ashurbanipal occupied Thebes
525 after a brief resurgence of independence, Egypt became a Persian province following conquest by Cambyses
332 conquest by Alexander; on the division of his empire, Egypt went to Ptolemy, whose descendants ruled until Cleopatra's death in 30 BC
30 conquest by the Roman Emperor Augustus: Egypt a province of the Roman and Byzantine empires
641 AD conquest by the Arabs, so that the Christianity of later Roman rule was replaced by Islam

Greece
c. 1600–1200 BC Mycenean civilization
c. 1180 Siege of Troy
c. 1100 Dorian invasion, and the rise of the Greek city states, of which the greatest were Athens and Sparta
750–550 trading colonies founded round the Mediterranean, Black Sea, and elsewhere
5th century Persian Empire sought to establish its rule over the Greeks
490 Persians defeated at Marathon
480 The Spartans defended Thermopylae to the death against a fresh invasion by Xerxes, but the Persians were defeated at sea (Salamis 480) and on land (Plataea 479)
461–429 Pericles attempted to convert the alliance against the Persians into the basis of a Greek empire

431–404 Peloponnesian War prompted by Sparta's suspicion of Pericles's ambitions, with the resultant destruction of the political power of Athens
378–371 Sparta, successor to Athens in the leadership, overthrown by Thebes
358–336 Philip II of Macedon seized his opportunity to establish supremacy over Greece
334–331 Philip's son Alexander the Great defeated the decadent Persian Empire, and went on to found his own
3rd century Greek cities formed the Achaean and Aetolian Leagues to try and maintain their independence against Macedon, Egypt, and Rome
146 Greece annexed by Rome
330 AD capital of Roman Empire transferred to Constantinople
529 closure of the University of Athens by Justinian ended Greek cultural dominance

Persia
550 BC Cyrus II became king of the Medes and Persians, founding the Persian Empire, which at its height was to include Babylonia, Assyria, Asia Minor, Egypt, Thrace, and Macedonia
521 Darius I became king of Persia
499 revolt of the Ionian Greeks against Persian rule
490 Darius I defeated by the Greeks at Marathon
480 Xerxes I victorious at Thermopylae, which Leonidas, king of Sparta, and 1,000 men defended to the death against the Persians; Athens captured but Greek navy victorious at Salamis
479 Greeks under Spartan general Pausanias victorious at Plataea, driving the Persians from the country
334–326 conquest by Alexander the Great

Rome
753 BC traditional date for the foundation of Rome
510 the Etruscan dynasty of the Tarquins was expelled, and a republic was established, governed by two consuls, elected annually by the popular assembly, and a council of elders or

senate. The concentration of power in the hands of the aristocracy aroused the opposition of the plebeian masses
390 Rome sacked by Gauls
367 the plebeians secured the right to elect tribunes, the codification of the laws, and the right to marry patricians; it was enacted that one consul must be a plebeian
338 the cities of Latium formed into a league under Roman control
343–290 the Etruscans to the north were subdued during the 5th and 4th centuries, and the Samnites to the south east
280–272 the Greek cities of the south were conquered
264–241 first Punic War, ending in a Roman victory and the annexation of Sicily
238 Sardinia seized from Carthage and became a Roman province
226–222 Roman conquest of Cisalpine Gaul (Lombardy); conflict with Carthage, which was attempting to conquer Sicily
218 Hannibal invaded Italy and won a brilliant series of victories
202 victory over Hannibal at Zama, followed by surrender of Carthage and relinquishing of its Spanish colonies
148 three wars with Macedon were followed by its conversion into a province
146 after a revolt Greece became in effect a Roman province. In the same year Carthage was annexed. On the death of the king of Pergamum, Rome succeeded to his kingdom in Asia Minor
133 Tiberius Gracchus put forward proposals for agrarian reforms and was murdered by the senatorial party
123 Tiberius's policy was taken up by his brother Gaius Gracchus, who was likewise murdered
109–106 the leadership of the democrats passed to Marius
91–88 Social War: a revolt of the Italian cities compelled Rome to grant citizenship to all Italians
87–84 while Sulla was repelling an invasion of Greece by Mithridates, Marius seized power
82 on his return Sulla established a dictatorship

and ruled by terror

70 Sulla's changes were reversed by Pompey and Crassus

66–62 defeat of Mithridates and annexation of Syria and the rest of Asia Minor

60 Pompey formed an alliance with the democratic leaders Crassus and Julius Caesar

51 Gaul conquered by Caesar as far as the Rhine

49 Caesar's return to Italy (crossing the Rubicon) led to civil war between Caesar and Pompey

48 defeat of Pompey at Pharsalus

44 Caesar's dictatorship ended by his assassination

32 the Empire divided between Caesar's nephew Octavian in the west, and Antony in the east; war between them

31 defeat of Antony at Actium

30 with the deaths of Antony and Cleopatra Egypt was annexed

27 Octavian took the name Augustus; he was by now absolute ruler, although in title only *Princeps* (first citizen)

43 AD Augustus made the Rhine and the Danube the frontiers of the Empire; Claudius added Britain

96–180 under the Flavian emperors Nerva, Trajan, Hadrian, Antoninus Pius, and Marcus Aurelius the Empire enjoyed a golden age

115 Trajan conquered Macedonia; peak of Roman territorial expansion

180 death of Marcus Aurelius. A century of war and disorder followed, during which a succession of generals were placed on the throne by their armies

284–305 Diocletian reorganized the Empire as a centralized autocracy

324–37 Constantine I realized the political value of Christianity and became a convert

330 Constantine removed the capital to Constantinople, and the Empire was divided

410 the Goths overran Greece and Italy, sacked Rome, and finally settled in Spain. The Vandals conquered Italy

451–2 the Huns raided Gaul and Italy

476 the last Western emperor was deposed

Leaders of the Ancient World

Alexander the Great 356–323 BC. King of Macedonia and conqueror of the Persian Empire. Son of Philip II of Macedon, he was tutored by Aristotle, and made his mark as a boy by taming the great horse Bucephalus. In 336 BC he succeeded to the throne on his father's assassination and immediately established his rule in Macedonia and Greece. In 334 BC he crossed the Dardanelles to what is now Asiatic Turkey, and began his assault on the Persian Empire, defeating Darius at Issus in 333 BC, and treating the Persian king's wife, mother, and children humanely. Making a detour to Syria and Egypt, he founded Alexandria, and then resumed his pursuit of Darius. In 331 BC he defeated Darius again at Arbela on the Tigris with 47,000 men against a Persian army of half a million (which included an 'armoured division' of scythed chariots and elephants). He continued his trail of conquest in a great arc into N India as far as the Sutlej, where he was only deterred from going on to the Ganges by the revolt of his weary soldiers. Turning back, he attempted to consolidate his empire by intermarriage between his followers and his new subjects, himself marrying one of Darius's daughters in addition to his wife Roxana (daughter of a chieftain in the Hindu Kush). He died in Babylon, his intended capital. He lives on in modern legend because of his powerful personality, strategic skill, intellectual stature (he always travelled with a copy of the *Iliad*, and sponsored exploration and scientific experiment), and his vision of a humanely civilized empire.

Amenhotep the name of four Egyptian pharaohs, including: *Amenhotep III c.*1400 BC, who built great monuments at Thebes, including the temples at Luxor. Two portrait statues at his tomb were known to the Greeks as the

Colossi of Memnon – one was cracked, and when the temperature changed at dawn gave out a weird sound, then thought supernatural. His son *Amenhotep IV* changed his name to Ikhnaton.

Augustus Gaius Julius Octavianus 63 BC–14 AD. First Roman emperor. He was the adopted son of his great-uncle, Julius Caesar, and, following the latter's murder, formed (with Mark Antony and Lepidus), the triumvirate which divided the Roman world among them, and proceeded to eliminate the opposition. On his return to Rome in 29 BC, he was in sole command (Antony a suicide and Lepidus in retirement); he restored the forms of the republic, but exercised a 'presidential rule' himself, backed by a 'kitchen cabinet' including Agrippa, Maecenas, and his second wife, Livia. Virgil and Horace were the 'poets laureate' and 'public relations' men of the new regime. Empire frontiers were established on defensible lines; a sound administration was created; and a professional army was formed with fixed pay and length of service, as well as a permanent fleet. Rome was given an adequate water supply, a fire brigade, a police force, and fine public buildings. The title Augustus 'venerable', was awarded to him by the populace in 27 BC. Having no male heir, he married his profligate daughter Julia to his unwilling stepson Tiberius, with disastrous results. In 6 BC a serious revolt in Pannonia (modern Yugoslavia) took his stepsons two years to subdue, and brought the threat of invasion to Rome itself. The three finest Roman legions were annihilated by Varus in 9 AD, so that Augustus died a broken man, saying: 'Varus, give me back my legions!'

Caesar Gaius Julius c. 102–44 BC. Roman statesman and general. A patrician, he allied himself with the popular party, and when elected Aedile in 65 BC nearly ruined himself with lavish amusements for the Roman populace. Although a free thinker, he was elected chief pontiff in 63 BC, and in 61 BC was appointed governor of Spain. Returning to Rome in 60 BC, he formed, with Pompey and Crassus, the first triumvirate, but as governor

of Gaul was engaged in its subjugation 58–50 BC, defeating the Germans under Ariovistus, and selling thousands of the Belgic tribes into slavery. In 55 BC he crossed into Britain, with a further campaigning visit in 54 BC. A revolt by the Gauls in 52 BC, under Vercingetorix, was crushed in 51 BC. His own Commentaries on the campaigns have a mastery worthy of fiction, as does his account of the ensuing Civil War. His governorship of Spain was to end in 49 BC, and, Crassus being dead, Pompey was now a rival. Declaring 'the die is cast', Caesar crossed the Rubicon (the small river separating Gaul from Italy) to meet the army raised against him. In the ensuing Civil War, he followed Pompey to Epirus in 48 BC, defeated him at Pharsalus, and chased him to Egypt, where he was murdered. Caesar stayed some months in Egypt, where he had a son (Caesarion) by Cleopatra, then executed a lightning campaign in 47 BC against King Pharnaces in Asia Minor, which he summarized: *Veni vidi vici* ('I came, I saw, I conquered'). By his final victory in Spain at Munda in 45 BC over the sons of Pompey, he established his position, having been awarded a ten-year dictatorship in 46 BC. On 15 Mar 44 BC, however, he was stabbed to death at the foot of Pompey's statue in the senate house. As statesman, general, author, Caesar was unparalleled but fell victim to the weakness of those whom he ruled and for whom he came to have contempt.

Cambyses reigned 529–522 BC. Emperor of Persia. He succeeded his father Cyrus the Great, assassinated his brother Smerdis and conquered Egypt in 525, outraging its religious customs. He died on his homeward journey in Syria, although it is unclear whether this was by suicide or accident.

Claudius 10 BC–54 AD. Nephew of Tiberius, made Roman emperor by his troops in 41, after the murder of Caligula, though more inclined to scholarly pursuits and the writing of histories. In 43 he took part in the invasion of Britain. He was long dominated by his third wife, Messalina, and is thought to have been poisoned by his fourth (Agrippina the Younger).

Cleopatra c. 68–30 BC; Queen of Egypt 51–48 BC and 47–30 BC. She succeeded her father jointly with her younger brother Ptolemy XIII, whom she married according to Pharaonic custom. When Julius Caesar arrived in Egypt in 49 BC, he restored her to the throne from which she had been ousted in favour of her brother. She became his mistress, returning with him to Rome until his assassination, and bore him a son, Caesarion. In 41 BC she met Mark Antony who, after returning to Rome in 40 BC to marry Octavia (sister of the future Augustus), settled with Cleopatra in Egypt, where she bore him three sons. In 32 BC open war broke out with Augustus, and after Actium in 31 BC, Antony and Cleopatra were besieged in Alexandria. Cleopatra killed herself with an asp after Antony's suicide. By descent she was Macedonian, not Egyptian. Caesarion was put to death by Augustus.

Constantine the Great c. 274–337 AD. First Christian emperor of Rome, and founder of Constantinople. Son of Emperor Constantius (ruler of the Western Empire 305–6), who died at York in 306, he was acclaimed by the troops there as his successor. He defeated his rival Maxentius in 312, and then, by defeating Licinius in 324, established his rule over the Eastern Empire. In 313 he recognized Christianity as one of the legal religions of the Empire by the Edict of Milan, summoned and presided over the first general council of the church at Nicaea 325, and with the aid of the church established a close-knit network of autocratic authority. He died on an expedition to defend the Euphrates frontier against the Persians.

Crassus Marcus Licinius c. 108–53 BC. Roman general who crushed the Spartacus rising in 71 BC. In 60 BC he joined with Caesar and Pompey in the first triumvirate and in 55 BC obtained command in the East. Invading Mesopotamia, he was defeated by the Parthians, captured, and put to death.

Cyrus the Great died 529 BC. Founder of the Persian Empire. King of Persia, originally as vassal to the Medes, whose empire he overthrew in 550 BC, he captured Croesus in 546 BC,

and conquered all Asia Minor, adding Babylonia (including Syria and Palestine) to his empire in 539 BC. The exiled Jews were allowed to return to Jerusalem. He died fighting in Afghanistan.

Darius I the Great c. 558–465 BC. King of Persia from 512 BC, he inscribed his conquests on a mountain rock-face at Behistun, but is chiefly remembered for his defeat by the Greeks at Marathon.

Diocletian (Gaius Valerius Diocletianus) 245–313 AD. Roman emperor 284–305, when he abdicated in favour of Galerius. He reorganized and sub-divided the Empire, with two joint and two subordinate emperors, and in 303 initiated severe persecution of the Christians.

Hadrian 76–138 AD. Roman emperor, adopted by his kinsman, the Emperor Trajan, whom he succeeded in 117. He abandoned Trajan's conquests in Mesopotamia, and adopted a defensive policy.

Hamilcar Barca c. 270–228 BC. Carthaginian general, father of Hannibal, who harassed the Romans in Italy 247–241, and died heading a battle expedition to Spain.

Hannibal 247–182 BC. Carthaginian general from 221, son of Hamilcar Barca. His siege of Saguntum (modern Sagunto, near Valencia) precipitated the second Punic War. Following a brilliant campaign in Italy (after crossing the Alps in 218 with 57 elephants), Hannibal was the victor at Trasimene in 217 and Cannae in 216, but failed to take Rome. In 203 he returned to Carthage to meet a Roman invasion, but was defeated at Zama in 202, and was exiled in 196 at Rome's insistence. He fled first to Syria, then to Bythinia (on the Black Sea). The Romans persistently sought his extradition until he took poison to prevent himself falling into their hands.

Hasdrubal died 207 BC. Carthaginian general, brother of Hannibal, who left him in command in Spain in 218, to fight against the Scipios. In 208 he marched to Italy to relieve Hannibal, and was defeated and killed to the north-west of Ancona.

Marcus Aurelius Antoninus 121–180 AD. Stoic philosopher (author of *Meditations*) and

Roman emperor from 161, when he succeeded his uncle Antoninus Pius. He persecuted the Christians (as politically divisive), and spent much of his reign combatting Germanic invasions. He died in Pannonia, where he had gone to fight off the Marcomanni.

Marius Gaius 155–86 BC. Roman general. Consul in 107 BC, he was appointed to defeat Jugurtha (who actually surrendered to Sulla), was again consul 104–100 BC, and defeated the Germanic tribes attacking Gaul and Italy in 102 and 101 BC. Incensed at the appointment of Sulla to the command against Mithridates, he had himself substituted by 'popular demand', until Sulla reversed the situation by marching on Rome. Marius fled, returned in 88 BC, after Sulla had gone east, attained a final consulship, and started a general massacre of his enemies, ended by his death.

Mark Antony (Marcus Antonius) 83–30 BC. Roman soldier-statesman, who served under Julius Caesar in the later campaign in Gaul, fought with him at Pharsalus, and as consul in 44 BC tried to secure for him the title of king. After Caesar's assassination, he formed a triumvirate with Octavius and Lepidus, and in 42 BC helped defeat Brutus and Cassius at Philippi. Touring the eastern provinces in 41 BC, Antony fell in love with Cleopatra, securing Egypt for his share when the triumvirs shared the Empire among them. By 37 BC Antony had left his wife Octavia (sister of Octavius) for Cleopatra, and by 33 BC relations between the two men had altogether broken down. The senate declared war on Cleopatra in 32 BC, and Antony committed suicide after being defeated by Octavius at Actium.

Menes traditionally the first king of the 1st Dynasty of ancient Egypt in c. 3400 BC, alleged founder of Memphis and of organized worship of the gods.

Nerva (Marcus Cocceius Nerva) c. 35–98 AD. Roman emperor. A senator, he was proclaimed emperor on Domitian's death in 96, and introduced state loans for farmers, family allowances, and allotments of land to poor citizens.

Pericles c. 490–429 BC. Athenian states-

man, who dominated the city's politics from 461 BC (as leader of the democratic party), and under whom Greek culture reached its climax. He created a confederation of cities under the leadership of Athens, but the disasters of the Peloponnesian War led to his overthrow 430 BC. Although quickly reinstated, he died soon after.

Philip II of Macedon 382–336 BC. King of Macedonia from 359 BC. He seized the throne from his nephew, for whom he was regent, conquered the Greek city states and formed them into a league whose forces could be united against Persia. He was assassinated just as he was planning this expedition, and was succeeded by his son Alexander the Great. His tomb was discovered at Vergina, N Greece, in 1978 and, his skeleton having been identified by traces of an earlier eye injury from an arrow, his one-eyed head was reconstructed at Manchester University for exhibition in the city's museum in 1984.

Pompey the Great (Gnaeus Pompeius Magnus) 106–48 BC. Roman soldier-statesman. Originally a supporter of Sulla and the senatorial party, he joined the democrats when he became consul with Crassus in 70 BC. He defeated Mithridates of Pontus, and annexed Syria and Palestine. In 60 BC he formed the first triumvirate with Caesar (whose daughter Julia he married) and Crassus, and when it broke down after 53 BC he returned to the senatorial party. On the outbreak of civil war in 49 BC he withdrew to Greece, was defeated by Caesar at Pharsalia in 48 BC, and was murdered in Egypt.

Ptolemy name of dynasty of Macedonian kings who ruled Egypt over a period of 300 years; they included *Ptolemy I* (died 283 BC), king of Egypt from 304 BC, who was one of Alexander's generals, and possibly his half-brother. He established the library at Alexandria. *Ptolemy XIII* 63–47 BC was joint ruler of Egypt with his sister-wife Cleopatra; she put him to death.

Ramses name of 11 kings of ancient Egypt including: *Ramses II* reigned c. 1300–1225 BC. The son of Seti I, he campaigned successfully against the Hittites, and built two rock temples at Abu Simbel in Upper Egypt (the larger commemorates himself and the other his wife Nefertari). Threatened with submersion when the Aswan High Dam was built in 1966, the temples were reconstructed above the water line. *Ramses III* reigned c. 1200–1168 BC. He won a naval victory over the Philistines and other barbarian peoples, and asserted his suzerainty over Palestine.

Solon c. 638–558 BC. Athenian statesman. As one of the chief magistrates c. 594 BC he carried out the revision of the constitution which laid the foundations of Athenian democracy.

Sulla Lucius Cornelius 138–78 BC. Roman soldier-statesman, a leader of the senatorial party. Forcibly suppressing the democrats in 88 BC, he departed for a successful campaign against Mithridates of Pontus. The democrats seized power in his absence, but on his return Sulla captured Rome and massacred all opponents. As dictator, his reforms, which strengthened the senate, were backward-looking and shortlived. He retired in 79 BC.

Thuthmose name of four Egyptian kings of the 18th Dynasty: *Thuthmose I* reigned c.1540–1501 BC and founded the Egyptian Empire in Syria. His grandson *Thutmose III* reigned c. 1500–1446 BC and extended the Empire to the Euphrates, and conquered Nubia.

Tiberius Claudius Nero 42 BC–37 AD. Roman emperor, adopted son of Augustus and his successor from 14 AD. Under his conscientious rule the Empire prospered.

Trajan (Marcus Ulpius Trajanus) c. 52–117 AD. Roman emperor from 98, adopted heir of Nerva. Born in Seville, he was a just and conscientious ruler, corresponded with Pliny about the Christians, and conquered Dacia (approximately modern Romania) 101–107 and much of Parthia. Trajan's Column, Rome, commemorates his victories.

Tutankhamen king of Egypt of the 18th dynasty c. 1360–1350 BC. A son of Ikhnaton or of Amenhotep III, he was probably about 11 at his accession. In 1922 his tomb was discovered by Lord Carnarvon and Howard Carter in the Valley of the Kings at Luxor, almost untouched by tomb robbers. The contents included many works of art and his solid gold coffin.

Xerxes c. 519–465 BC. King of Persia from 485 BC, when he succeeded his father Darius, and, after several years' preparation, continued the Persian invasion of Greece. In 480 BC at the head of an army of some 400,000 men, supported by a fleet of 800 ships, he crossed the Hellespont over a bridge of boats. He defeated the Greek fleet at Artemisium and, having stormed the pass of Thermopylae, captured and burnt Athens. But Themistocles annihilated the Persian fleet at Salamis and Xerxes was forced to retreat. He spent his later years on a grandiose extension of the capital Persepolis and was eventually murdered in a court intrigue.

Medieval and Early Modern

300–1500 AD period of the great medieval states in Africa: Ghana, Mali, Songhai, Benin, Ife
320–550 Gupta dynasty in India
4th century Christianity became the established religion of the Roman Empire
4th–6th centuries Western Europe overrun by Anglo-Saxons, Franks, Goths, and Lombards
570 birth of Muhammad
7th–8th centuries Islamic expansion began in N, E, and Central Africa. Christendom threatened by Moorish invasions
800 Charlemagne given title of Emperor by the Pope
c. 1000 Leif Ericsson traditionally reached N America
1073 Gregory VII began 200 years of conflict between the Empire and the Papacy
1096–1291 the Crusades were undertaken to recover the Holy Land from the Muslims
1192 first Muslim kingdom of India established
12th century setting up of German, Flemish,

and Italian city states in Europe, which in the 14th and 15th centuries fostered the Renaissance

12th–14th centuries height of Moundbuilder and Pueblo cultures in N America

12th–15th centuries era of Arab travellers in Africa, such as Ibn Batuta, and of trade (for example Kilwa)

1280 Kublai Khan became emperor of China

1395 Tamerlane defeated the Golden Horde, the invading Mongol-Tartar army which had terrorized Europe from 1237

1398 Tamerlane captured Delhi

1453 Constantinople captured by the Turks

1488 Diaz rounded the Cape of Good Hope

1492, 12 Oct Columbus first sighted land in the Caribbean

16th century arrival of Europeans in S America, with the Spanish (Pizarro) and Portuguese conquest. American Indians were either killed, assimilated, or, where unsuitable as slave labour, replaced by imported slaves from Africa

1526 Babur established the Mogul Empire in India

1565 first Spanish settlements in N America

16th–17th centuries Europe dominated by rivalry of France and the Hapsburgs, the Protestant Reformation, and the Catholic Counter-Reformation

1607 first permanent English settlement in N America at Jamestown, Virginia

17th century beginnings of the British East India Company in India. Era of absolute monarchies in Europe (notably Louis XIV)

18th century War of Austrian Succession and Seven Years' War ended in loss of French colonial empire to Britain and the emergence of Prussia as a leading European power. Height of the Atlantic and Indian Ocean slave trade

1789–95 French Revolution and the overthrow of Louis XVI

Leaders

Babur title, meaning 'tiger', of Zahir ud-din Mohammed, 1483–1530. The first Great Mogul of India, he was a grandson of Tamerlane, and inherited Turkestan from his father when he was 12. By 1526 he had taken Delhi and established a dynasty which nominally lasted until 1858.

Borgia Cesare 1476–1507. Italian soldier, illegitimate son of Pope Alexander VI. Made a cardinal at 17 by his father, he resigned the honour to become captain-general of the papacy, campaigning successfully against the city republics of Italy. Ruthless and treacherous in war, he was an able ruler (the model of Machiavelli's *The Prince*) of conquered territory, but his power crumbled on the death of his father. He was a patron of artists, including Leonardo da Vinci.

Charlemagne or *Charles the Great* 742–814. King of the Franks 768–814 and Holy Roman Emperor 800–814, son of Pepin the Short. He campaigned against the Saxon tribes and the Lombards, and in N Spain, where the great warrior Roland was killed by the Basques at Roncesvalles. As ruler of Western Christendom, he introduced legal reforms; standardized coinage and weights and measures; organized and reformed the church; and initiated the Carolingian Renaissance by attracting the English scholar and poet Alcuin to his court at Aachen in 781. He had himself collected old heroic poetry, and after his death became the hero of a cycle of medieval romances.

Charles V 1500–58. Holy Roman Emperor 1519–56. Son of Philip of Burgundy and Joanna of Castile, he inherited the Netherlands from his father in 1506, then Spain, Naples, Sicily, Sardinia, and the Spanish dominions from his maternal grandfather (Ferdinand V) in 1516, and from his paternal grandfather (Maximilian) the Hapsburg dominions in 1519, when he was elected emperor. Such vast possessions led to rivalry from Francis I, whose alliance with the Turks brought Vienna under siege in 1529 and 1532. From 1517 the Empire was split by the rise of Lutheranism, Charles making unsuccessful attempts to reach a settlement at Augsburg in 1530, and being forced by the Treaty of Passau to give in to most of the Protestant demands. He abdicated in favour of his son, Philip II, in the Netherlands 1555 and Spain 1556, and yielded the imperial crown to his brother Ferdinand.

Columbus Christopher 1451–1506. Italian navigator. Sponsored by Ferdinand and Isabella of Spain to find a new route to the East, he set sail on 3 Aug 1492, and on 12 Oct sighted Watling Island (now San Salvador), later sighting Cuba and Haiti (site of his wrecked flagship, the *Santa Maria*, off Hispaniola, located in 1968). He made a second voyage 1493–96, discovering more West Indian islands, and a third in 1498, in which he discovered S America and the Orinoco. His colonists complained about him, however, and he was sent home in chains. Recovering favour, he made a fourth voyage 1502–4, still trying to find a passage to India. He died in poverty, and is buried in Seville Cathedral. The cost of his initial voyage was queried, until it was pointed out that it cost the same as one banquet for Isabella.

Elizabeth I 1533–1603. Queen of England. Daughter of Henry VIII and Anne Boleyn, she was born at Greenwich. Under Queen Mary her Protestant sympathies required that she live in retirement at Hatfield until she became queen in Nov 1558. Securing her throne by making a broad religious settlement, she refused to endanger her position by marriage or naming a successor, but she had several favourites (Leicester, Raleigh, Essex) and royal suitors. Mary Queen of Scots, who arrived in England in 1568 and whom Elizabeth imprisoned, was a focus of revolt and foreign intrigue, especially by Spain, until her execution in 1587. Open war with Spain and the despatch of the Armada followed, but neither this, nor growing Puritan discontent, nor growing assertiveness by Parliament, endangered Elizabeth's hold on the country. A rebellion by Essex in 1601 failed hopelessly.

Galileo Galilei 1564–1642. Italian mathematician, astronomer, and physicist, who revolutionized the scientific thinking of his time and ultimately changed the way people looked at their world. His observations and arguments were an unwelcome refutation of the ideas of Aristotle taught at the (church-run) universities, especially because they made plausible for the first time the heliocentric (sun-centred) theory of Copernicus. Galileo's persuasive *Dialogues on the Two Chief Systems of the World* 1632 was banned by the church authorities in Rome, while its author was made to recant by the Inquisition and put under house arrest for his last years.

Genghis Khan 1162–1227. Mongol conqueror (original name Temujin), who established his supremacy over all Mongol tribes by 1206, and assumed the name Genghis ('perfect warrior'). At his death he ruled an empire reaching from the Yellow Sea to the Black Sea.

Gustavus Adolphus 1594–1632. King of Sweden from 1611, he waged successful wars with Denmark, Russia, and Poland, and in the Thirty Years' War championed the Protestant cause. He was mortally wounded in the Battle of Lützen in 1632, when he defeated Wallenstein.

Hapsburg or *Habsburg* former imperial house of Austria-Hungary. The name comes from the family castle in Switzerland. The Hapsburgs held the title Holy Roman Emperor 1273–91, 1298–1308, 1438–1740, and 1745–1806. They ruled Austria from 1278, under the title of Emperor 1806–1918.

Innocent III 1161–1216. Pope from 1198, he asserted papal power over secular princes, especially over the succession of Holy Roman Emperors, and made King John of England his vassal. He promoted the fourth Crusade, and crusades against the pagan Livonians and Letts, and Albigensian heretics.

Kublai Khan 1216–94. Mongol emperor of China from 1259, grandson of Ghengis Khan. In 1281 he attempted to invade Japan, but his

4,400 ships were dispersed in battle.

Louis XIV 1638–1715. King of France (the 'Sun King') from 1643, though until 1661 the country was ruled by Mazarin. The policy of Louis as ruler was summed up in his saying 'L'Etat c'est moi' ('I am the State'). Greatest of his ministers was Colbert, whose work was undone by Louis' military adventures. Louis attempted 1667–8 to annex the Spanish Netherlands, but was frustrated by an alliance of Holland, England, and Sweden. Having detached England from the alliance, he invaded Holland in 1672, but the Dutch stood firm (led by William of Orange) and despite the European alliance formed against France, achieved territorial gains at the Peace of Nijmegen in 1678. When war was renewed 1688–97 between Louis and the Grand Alliance (including England), formed by William of Orange, the French were everywhere victorious on land, but the French fleet was almost destroyed at La Hogue in 1692. The acceptance by Louis of the Spanish throne in 1700 (for his grandson) precipitated the War of the Spanish Succession, however, and the Peace of Utrecht (1713) ended French supremacy in Europe. In 1660 Louis married the Infanta Maria Theresa of Spain, but his mistresses who included Louise de La Vallière, Mme de Montespan, and Mme de Maintenon, were also a significant influence on him.

Machiavelli Niccolò 1469–1527. Florentine politician, who was imprisoned and then exiled in 1513 by the Medici. His influential work *Il Principe/The Prince* 1513, a guide to the ruthless exercise of power for the future prince of a unified Italian state, gave rise to the term 'Machiavellian' (to mean cynical and manipulative), but reflects the actualities of contemporary statecraft.

Magellan Ferdinand c. 1480–1521. Portuguese navigator, sponsored by Spain to sail to the E Indies by the western route. Starting from Seville, he sailed through the Strait of Magellan, crossed the Pacific, which he named, and in 1521 reached the Philippines, where he was killed in battle. Other members of the expedition completed the return voyage under Del Cano, but Magellan and his Malay slave, Enrique de Malacca, were the first circumnavigators of the globe, since they had originally sailed from the Philippines to Europe.

Maria Theresa 1717–80. Austrian empress, daughter of Emperor Charles VI, whom she succeeded as archduchess of Austria and queen of Hungary and Bohemia in 1740. As a woman, her right to the crown was challenged by Charles of Bavaria (emperor from 1742), and Frederick of Prussia occupied Silesia. After the consequent War of the Austrian Succession, she retained most of her inheritance, though not regaining Silesia, and her husband (her cousin Francis of Lorraine, whom she had married in 1736) became emperor (1745–65). Intent on recovering Silesia, she allied with France and Russia against Prussia in the Seven Years' War (1756–63), which exhausted Europe and left the territorial position unchanged. Henceforward she concentrated on internal reforms. Though ruling despotically, she encouraged education, codified the law, and abolished torture. She was assisted by her son Joseph II (emperor from 1765), who succeeded her in the Hapsburg domains.

Mazarin Jules 1602–61. Italian-born French statesman, born at Piscina. He passed from the papal diplomatic service to that of Richelieu in 1639, was created cardinal in 1641, and succeeded Richelieu as chief minister in 1642. His attack on the power of the nobility led to the Fronde, a series of revolts against his administration, and his temporary exile, but his diplomacy achieved a successful conclusion to the Thirty Years' War, and, in alliance with Cromwell, he gained victory over Spain.

Medici family founded in Florence by Giovanni 1360–1429, businessman and banker, politically influential as a supporter of the popular party. His eldest son Cosimo 1389–1464, regarded as the embodiment of Macchiavelli's *Prince*, dominated the government from 1434, and was succeeded by his inept son Piero 1416–69, and grandson Lorenzo the Magnificent 1449–92, who was also a poet and, like his grandfather, a munificent patron of the arts. Lorenzo's son Giovanni 1475–1521, became pope in 1513 as Leo X.

Philip II of Spain 1527–98. Son of Emperor Charles V, on whose abdication (1556) he inherited Spain, the Netherlands (whose people he drove to revolt), and Spanish America; he annexed Portugal in 1580. In 1554 he married Queen Mary of England, and would have wished to marry Elizabeth I, but became involved in war with England instead and also with France from 1589. His reign marked the decline of Spanish power.

Richelieu Armand Jane du Plessis de 1585–1642. French cardinal from 1622 and chief minister (through the influence of Marie de' Medici) from 1624. He made the monarchy absolute by crushing the nobility and destroying Huguenot power (though leaving them religious freedom), and ensured French supremacy in Europe by backing Gustavus Adolphus and the German Protestant princes against Austria, and bringing France into the Thirty Years' War in 1635.

Saladin or *Sala-ud-din* 1138–93. Sultan of Egypt from 1175, in succession to the Atabeg of Mosul on whose behalf he had conquered it 1164–74. A Kurd, he conquered Syria 1174–87, and by his recovery of Jerusalem from the Christians in 1187, precipitated the third Crusade. Saladin, who was renowned for knightly courtesy, made peace with Richard I of England in 1192.

Savonarola Girolamo 1452–98. Italian reformer, a Dominican friar whose eloquent preaching won him popular influence. In 1494 he led a revolt in Florence which expelled the Medicis and established a democratic republic. However, his denunciations of Pope Alexander VI led to his excommunication in 1497, and in 1498 he was burned for heresy.

Tamerlane or *Timur i Leng* 1336–1405. Mongol ruler of Samarkand from 1369, who conquered Persia, Azerbaijan, Armenia, Georgia; defeated the Golden Horde 1395; sacked Delhi 1398; invaded Syria and Asia Minor, and captured the sultan at Ankara 1402. He died while invading China.

14

Wars and Battles

In the history of the world there have been many conflicts between peoples and between states. These have led to innumerable wars and battles in all parts of the globe. Represented here, in chronological order, are those conflicts which appear to have done most to shape the world as we know it today.

Peloponnesian War 431–404 BC. War between Athens and Sparta and their allies, originating in suspicions of 'empire-building' ambitions of Pericles. It ended in the destruction of the political power of Athens.

Punic Wars 264–146 BC. Series of wars between Rome and Carthage:
First 264–241 BC resulted in the cession of Sicily to Rome
Second 218–210 BC. Hannibal invaded Italy, defeating the Romans at *Cannae* but finally being defeated himself by Scipio at *Zama*
Third 149–146 BC ended in the destruction of Carthage, and her possessions becoming the Roman province of Africa

Actium Battle of 31 BC. Naval battle in which Octavian defeated the combined fleets of Antony and Cleopatra.

Rome Sack of 410 AD. The invasion and capture of the city of Rome by the Goths. Generally accepted as marking the effective end of the Roman Empire.

Crusades 1096–1291. A series of wars undertaken by various European rulers to recover the Holy Land from the Muslims. Motivated by religious zeal and the desire for more land – together with the trading ambitions of the major Italian cities – the Crusades were very varied in the effect they had and in the degree of success they achieved.
1st Crusade 1095–99 motivated by occupation of Asia Minor and Jerusalem by the Seljuk Turks. Crusade succeeded in recapturing Jerusalem

and establishing a series of Latin kingdoms on the Syrian coast

2nd Crusade 1147–49 led by Louis VII of France and Emperor Conrad III – a complete failure

3rd Crusade 1189–92 led by Philip Augustus of France and Richard I of England. Failed to recapture Jerusalem seized by Saladin in 1187

4th Crusade 1202–4 directed against Egypt but diverted by the Venetians to sack and divide Constantinople

5th Crusade 1218–21 captured and then lost Damietta

6th Crusade 1228–29 led by Frederick II – recovered Jerusalem by negotiation with the Sultan of Egypt. City finally lost in 1244

7th and 8th Crusades 1249–54, 1270–72 both led by Louis IX of France. Acre, the last Christian fortress in Syria, was lost in 1291.

Hundred Years' War 1337-1453. The name given to the struggle between England and France that began with the claim of Edward III, through his mother, to the crown of France. At the outset the English were victorious at the naval battle of *Sluys* in 1340 and on land at *Crécy* in 1346 and *Poitiers* in 1356. After 1369 the tide turned in favour of the French, and when Edward III died in 1377 only Calais, Bordeaux, and Bayonne were in English hands. A state of half-war continued for many years until Henry V invaded France in 1415 and won a victory at *Agincourt*. After his death his brother Bedford was generally successful until Joan of Arc raised the siege of *Orléans* in 1429. Even after her capture and death the French continued their successful counter-offensive, and in 1453 only Calais was left in English hands.

Thirty Years' War 1618–48. A major war in central Europe, beginning as a conflict between Protestants and Catholics, it gradually became transformed into a struggle to determine whether the Hapsburgs would gain control of all Germany. After the defeat of a Bohemian revolt against Austrian rule 1618–20, some Protestant princes continued the struggle against Austria, with the aid of Denmark 1625–27. From 1630 Gustavus Adolphus of Sweden intervened on the Protestant side,

overrunning N Germany before his death in 1632. When the Swedes were defeated at *Nordlingen* 1634, Richelieu brought France into the war to inflict several defeats on Austria's Spanish allies. The *Treaty of Westphalia* 1648 gave France S Alsace, and Sweden certain Baltic provinces, the emperor's authority in Germany becoming only nominal. The mercenary armies of Wallenstein, Tilly, and Mansfeld devastated Germany.

Mohács Battle of 1687. An Austro-Hungarian defeat of the Turks which effectively marked the end of Turkish expansion into Europe. Also the site of an earlier Turkish victory in 1526.

Spanish Succession War of 1701–14. A war between Britain, Austria, the Netherlands, Portugal and Denmark (the Allies) and France, Spain, and Bavaria. Caused by Louis XIV's acceptance of the Spanish throne for his grandson, Philip – a violation of the *Partition Treaty* of 1700, by which the crown would have passed to Archduke Charles of Austria. The war produced a series of notable battles:

1704 French marched on Vienna to try and end the war but were defeated by John Churchill of Marlborough and Eugène of Savoy at *Blenheim*

1705 Allies invaded Spain, twice occupying Madrid but failing to hold it

1706 Marlborough victorious over French (under Villeroi) at *Ramillies* 23 May in Brabant, Belgium

1708 Marlborough and Eugène defeated French (under Duke of Burgundy and Vendôme) at *Oudenaarde* (near Ghent, Belgium) 30 Jun–11 Jul

1709 Marlborough and Eugène again defeated French (under Villars) at *Malplaquet* 11 Sept

The Treaties of *Utrecht* 1713 and *Rastatt* 1714 gave Philip recognition as king of Spain but Gibraltar, Minorca and Nova Scotia ceded to Britain, and Belgium, Milan and Naples to Austria.

Seven Years' War 1756–63. The war between Britain and Prussia on the one hand, and France, Austria, and Russia on the other. Its military interest centres on the successful struggle of Frederick II of Prussia against great odds. Britain's part in the war, under the direction of Chatham, was mainly confined to operations at sea, notably the victory of Quiberon Bay 1759, and in the N American and Indian colonies.

American Independence Wars of 1775–83. The revolt of the British N American colonies which resulted in the establishment of the USA. It was caused by colonial resentment at the contemporary attitude that commercial or industrial interests of any colony should be subordinate to those of the mother country, and the unwillingness of the colonists to pay for a standing army. It was preceded by:

1773 a government tax on tea which led citizens disguised as N American Indians to board the ships carrying the tea and throw it into the harbour (the *Boston Tea Party*).

1774–75 the *First Continental Congress* held in Philadelphia to call for civil disobedience in reply to British measures

1775 19 Apr hostilities began at Lexington and Concord, Massachusetts, the first shots being fired when British troops, sent to seize illegal military stores, were attacked by the local militia. The first battle was *Bunker Hill* Massachusetts, 17 Jun 1775, in which the colonists were defeated; George Washington was appointed colonial commander soon afterwards

1775–76 the *Second Continental Congress* on 4 Jul 1776 issued the *Declaration of Independence*

1776 27 Aug at *Long Island* Washington was defeated, forced to evacuate New York and retire to Pennsylvania, but re-crossed the Delaware to win successes at *Trenton* (26 Dec) and *Princeton* (3 Jan 1777)

1777 a British plan, for Sir William Howe (advancing from New York) and General Burgoyne (from Canada) to link up, miscarried. Burgoyne surrendered at *Saratoga* (17 October), but Howe invaded Pennsylvania, defeating Washington at *Brandywine* (11 Sept) and *Germantown* (4 Oct), and occupying Philadelphia; Washington wintered at Valley Forge 1777–78

1778 France and Spain entered the war on the

American side

1780 12 May capture of *Charleston,* the most notable of a series of British victories in the American south, but they alienated support by attempting to enforce conscription

1781 19 Oct Cornwallis, besieged in *Yorktown* by Washington and the French fleet, surrendered

1782 peace negotiations opened

1783 3 Sept *Treaty of Paris* American independence recognized

French Revolutionary Wars 1792-1862. A series of wars between France and the combined armies of England, Austria, Prussia, and others.

1791 Emperor Leopold II and Frederick William II of Prussia issued the *Declaration of Pillnitz* inviting the European powers to restore Louis XVI to power

1792 France declared war on Austria, who formed a coalition with Prussia, Sardinia, and (from 1793), Britain, Spain, and the Netherlands; victories for France at *Valmy* and *Jemappes*

1793 French reverses until the reorganization by Carnot

1795 Prussia, the Netherlands, and Spain made peace

1796 Sardinia forced to make peace by Napoleon's Italian campaign

1797 Austria compelled to peace under the *Treaty of Campo-Formio*

1798 Napoleon's fleet, after its capture of Malta, was defeated by Nelson in Egypt at the *Battle of the Nile* (Aboukir Bay), and he had to return to France without his army; William Pitt organized a new coalition with Russia, Austria, Naples, Portugal, and Turkey

1798–99 Coalition mounted its major campaign in Italy, but dissension led to the withdrawal of Russia

1799 Napoleon, on his return from Egypt, reorganized the French army

1800 14 Jun Austrians defeated by Napoleon at *Marengo* in NW Italy, and again on 3 Dec (by Moreau) at *Hohenlinden* near Munich

1801 Austria made peace under the *Treaty of Lunéville*; Sir Ralph Abercromby defeated the

French by land in Egypt at the **Battle of Alexandria**, but was himself killed

1802 Peace of Amiens truce between France and Britain, followed by the Napoleonic Wars.

Napoleonic Wars 1803–15. A series of wars which followed the Revolutionary Wars.

1803 British renewed the war, following an appeal from the Maltese against Napoleon's seizure of the island

1805 Napoleon's planned invasion of Britain from Boulogne ended by Nelson's victory at **Trafalgar**; coalition formed by Britain, Austria, Russia, Sweden. Austria defeated at **Ulm**; Austria and Russia at **Austerlitz**

1806 Prussia, latest member of the coalition, defeated at **Jena**; Napoleon instituted an attempted blockade, the **Continental System**, to isolate Britain from Europe

1807 Russia defeated at **Eylau** and **Friedland** and on making peace with Napoleon under the **Treaty of Tilsit** changed sides, agreeing to attack Sweden, and was forced to retreat

1808 Napoleon's invasion of Portugal, and habit of installing his relatives as puppet kings, led to his defeat in the Peninsular War

1809 revived Austrian opposition to Napoleon was ended by defeat at **Wagram**

1812 the Continental System finally collapsed on its rejection by Russia, and Napoleon made the fatal decision to invade; he reached Moscow but was defeated by the Russian resistance, and by the bitter winter as he retreated through a countryside laid waste by the retreating Russians (380,000 French soldiers died)

1813 Britain, Prussia, Russia, Austria, and Sweden formed a new coalition, defeated Napoleon at the **Battle of the Nations** and he abdicated and was exiled to Elba

1814 Louis XVIII became king of France, and the **Congress of Vienna** met to conclude peace

1815 Napoleon returned to Paris. 16 Jun Wellington defeated Ney at **Quatre Bras** (in Belgium, SE of Brussels), and after a hundred days Napoleon was finally defeated at **Waterloo** S of Brussels, 18 Jun. Wellington had 68,000 troops (24,000 British, the rest German, Dutch and Belgian) and Napoleon 72,000; in the last stage Wellington was supported by the Prussians under Blücher. The Congress resumed with Napoleon more securely incarcerated at St Helena.

Peninsular War 1808–14. War caused by Napoleon's invasion of Portugal and Spain. Portugal was occupied by the French in 1807, and in 1808 Napoleon placed his brother Joseph on the Spanish throne. Armed revolts followed all over Spain and Portugal. A British force under Sir Arthur Wellesley was sent to Portugal and defeated the French at **Vimeiro**; Wellesley was then superseded, and the French were allowed to withdraw. Sir John Moore took command and advanced into Spain, but was forced to retreat to Corunna, when his army was evacuated. Wellesley took a new army to Portugal in 1809, and advanced on Madrid, but after defeating the French at **Talavera** had to retreat. During 1810–11 Wellesley (now Viscount Wellington) stood on the defensive; in 1812 he won another victory at **Salamanca**, occupied Madrid, and forced the French to evacuate S Spain. The victory at **Vitoria** 1813 drove the French from Spain, and in 1814 Wellington invaded S France. The war was ended by Napoleon's abdication.

Mexican War 1846-48. War between the USA and Mexico, begun when General Zachary Taylor invaded New Mexico. Mexico City was taken in 1847, and under the **Treaty of Guadaloupe-Hidalgo**, Mexico lost Texas, New Mexico, and California (half its territory) to the USA for $15 million compensation.

Crimean War 1854-56. The war arose nominally from a disagreement over the custody of the Holy Places at Jerusalem, actually from British and French mistrust of Russia's ambitions in the Balkans. Hostilities began in 1853 with a Russian invasion of the Balkans (whence they were compelled to withdraw by Austrian intervention) and the sinking of the Turkish fleet at **Sinope**. Britain and France declared war on Russia in 1854, and were joined in 1855 by Sardinia. The main military operations were the invasion of the **Crimea**, the siege of **Sevastopol** (Sept 1854–Sept 1855), and the battles of the **Alma**, **Balaclava** (including the Charge of the Light Brigade), and *Inkerman*, fought in 1854. The French lost 62,500 men, the British 19,600 – 15,700 of them by disease, a scandalous state of affairs that led to the organization of proper military nursing services by Florence Nightingale. Conflict was settled by the *Treaty of Paris*, Feb 1856.

American Civil War 1861–65. War between the Southern or Confederate States (South Carolina, Mississippi, Florida, Alabama, Georgia, Louisiana, and Texas; joined later by Virginia, Arkansas, Tennessee, and North Carolina), and the northern or Federal States. The southerners wished to maintain their 'state rights', in particular the institution of slavery, and claimed the right to secede from the Union; the northerners fought to maintain the Union.

1861 seven southern states set up the Confederate States of America (president Jefferson Davis) on 8 Feb; Fort Sumter, Charleston, captured 12–14 Apr; Lee (Confederate) was victorious at the first *Battle of Bull Run* 21 Jul

1862 Battle of Shiloh 6–7 Apr was indecisive. Grant captured New Orleans in May, but the Confederates were again victorious at the second *Battle of Bull Run* 29–30 Aug. Lee's advance was then checked by McClellan at *Antietam* on 17 Sept

1863 the *Emancipation Proclamation* was issued by Lincoln on 1 Jan, freeing the slaves; *Battle of Gettysburg* (Union victory) on 1–4 Jul marked the turning point of the war; Lincoln delivered the *Gettysburg Address* at the dedication of the national cemetery on 19 Nov; Grant overran the Mississippi states, capturing *Vicksburg* on 4 Jul

1864 Battles of Cold Harbor near Richmond, Virginia; in the first, on 27 Jun 1862, Lee defeated McClellan, and by the second Grant was delayed in his advance on Richmond. Sherman marched through Georgia to the sea, taking *Atlanta* on 1 Sept and *Savannah* on 22 Dec

1865 Lee surrendered to Grant at Appomattox Court House on 9 Apr; Lincoln was assassinated on 14 Apr; last Confederate troops surrendered on 26 May. There were 359,528

Union dead and 258,000 Confederate dead. The war, and in particular its aftermath, when the South was occupied by Northern troops, left behind lasting bitterness. Industry prospered in the North while the economy of the South continued to decline.

Seven Weeks' War 1866. War between Austria and Prussia, engineered by Bismarck over the Schleswig–Holstein question. The *Battle of Sadowa* (Königgrätz) was the culmination of von Moltke's victories. By the *Treaty of Prague*, Prussia took both Holstein, previously seized by Austria, and Schleswig.

Franco-Prussian War 1870–71. War provoked by Franco-Prussian rivalry. Bismarck used the candidature of a German for the Spanish throne to provoke Napoleon III into a declaration of war. After trouncing him at Sedan, the Prussians successfully besieged Paris. The *Treaty of Frankfurt* in May 1871 brought Prussia Alsace and Lorraine, plus a large French indemnity, and established Prussia as Europe's leading power.

Pacific War 1879–83. War between an alliance of Bolivia and Peru against Chile. Chile (by seizing Antofagasta and the rest of the Bolivian Pacific coast) rendered Bolivia completely landlocked, and also annexed the Peruvian coastline (from Arica to the mouth of the Loa). Bolivia has since tried to regain Pacific access, either by a corridor across her former Antofagasta province or by a twin port with Arica at the end of the rail link from La Paz. Brazil supports the Bolivian claims which would facilitate her own transcontinental traffic.

Spanish-American War 1898. War by Cuban revolutionaries (with US backing) against Spanish rule. The *Treaty of Paris* ceded Cuba, the Philippines, Guam and Puerto Rico to the USA.

Russo-Japanese War 1904-5. War brought about by Russian penetration in Manchuria, culminating in the lease of Port Arthur in 1896, and the occupation of the Amur province in 1900. In 1904 diplomatic relations were broken off by the Japanese, who then without warning attacked the Russian fleet at Port Arthur. The outstanding events of the subsequent fighting were the siege and surrender of the Russian garrison in *Port Arthur* (May 1904–Jan 1905) and the destruction of the Russian Baltic fleet in the *Tsushima Straits* (May 1905). Peace was concluded at Portsmouth, USA, in 1905. Russian rights in Port Arthur passed to Japan, together with the Manchurian railway; Korea became a Japanese sphere of influence, and Sakhalin was divided between Russia and Japan.

World War I 1914-18. War between the Central European Powers (Germany, Austria-Hungary and allies), against the Triple Entente (Britain and the British Empire, France, and Russia), together with the USA, and their allies.

outbreak on 28 Jun 1914 the heir to the Austrian throne was assassinated at Sarajevo; on 28 Jul Austria declared war on Serbia; as Russia mobilized, Germany declared war on Russia and France, taking a short-cut in the west by invading Belgium; on 4 Aug Britain declared war on Germany

1914 Western Front the German advance reached within a few miles of Paris, but an Allied counter-attack at *Marne* drove them back to the River Aisne; the opposing lines then settled to trench warfare

Eastern Front Hindenburg halted the Russian advance at the *Battle of Tannenberg*

Africa on 16 Sept all Germany's African colonies were in Allied hands

Middle East on 1 Nov Turkey entered the war

1915 Western Front several offensives on both sides resulted in insignificant gains. Haig became British commander-in-chief

Eastern Front Mackensen and Hindenburg drove back the Russians and took Poland

Middle East British attacks against Turkey in *Mespotamia* (Iraq), the *Dardanelles*, and at *Gallipoli* were all unsuccessful

Italy declared war on Austria; Bulgaria joined the Central Powers

war at sea Germany declared all-out U-boat war, but the sinking of the liner *Lusitania* (with Americans among the 1,198 lost) led to demands in the USA to enter the war

1916 Western Front German attack on the Verdun salient, countered by the Allies on the *Somme* and at *Verdun*

Eastern Front Romania joined the Allies but was soon overrun by Germany

Middle East Kut was taken from the British by the Turks

war at sea the indecisive *Battle of Jutland*

1918 Eastern Front on 3 Mar Russia signed the *Treaty of Brest-Litovsk* with Germany

Western Front Germany began a final offensive. In Apr the Allies appointed Foch supreme commander, but by Jun (when the first US troops went into battle) the Allies had lost all gains since 1915, and the Germans were on the Marne. The battle at Amiens marked the launch of the victorious Allied offensive

Italy at *Vittorio Veneto* the British and Italians finally defeated the Austrians. German capitulation began with naval mutinies at Kiel, followed by uprisings in the major cities. Kaiser Wilhelm II abdicated, and on 11 Nov the armistice was signed

1919 18 Jun, *Peace Treaty of Versailles*.

Spanish Civil War 1936–39. War following attempted military revolt (pronouncement) by Spanish Army officers including Francisco Franco. His insurgents (Nationalists, who were supported by Fascist Italy and Nazi Germany) seized power in the S and NW, but were suppressed in Madrid, Barcelona, etc. by the workers' militia. The loyalists (Republicans) were aided by the USSR and the volunteers of the International Brigade, including George Orwell.

1937 Bilbao and the Basque country were bombed into submission by the Nationalists

1938 Catalonia was cut off from the main Republican territory

1939 Barcelona fell in Jan and Madrid in Apr, and Franco established a dictatorship.

World War II 1939-45. War between Germany, Italy, and Japan (the Axis powers), and Britain, the Commonwealth, France, the USA, USSR, and China.

1939 Sept German invasion of Poland; Britain and France declared war on Germany; USSR invaded Poland from the east; fall of Warsaw

(Poland divided between Germany and USSR) *Nov* USSR invaded Finland. On the Western front, the 'phoney war' with both sides entrenched behind defensive lines lasted until May 1940

1940 Mar Soviet peace treaty with Finland

Apr Germany invaded Denmark and Norway. In Britain, a coalition government was formed under Churchill.

May Germany outflanked the Maginot defensive line by invading the Netherlands, Belgium, and Luxembourg

May-Jun British evacuation of Dunkirk

Jun Italy declared war on Britain and France; Germans entered Paris; Pétain signed the armistice with Germany

Jul-Oct Battle of Britain between British and German air forces

Sept Japanese invasion of French Indo-China

Oct abortive Italian invasion of Greece

1941 Apr Germany overran Greece and Yugoslavia

Jun Germany invaded USSR; Finland declared war on USSR

Jul Germans entered Smolensk

Dec Germans within 40 km/25 mi of Moscow, with Leningrad under siege. First Soviet counter-offensive. Japan attacked *Pearl Harbor*, and declared war on USA and Britain. Germany and Italy declared war on USA

1942 Jan Japanese conquest of Philippines

Jun naval battle of *Midway*, the turning point of the Pacific War

Aug German attack on Stalingrad

Oct-Nov Battle of Alamein, first major victory for the Western Allies

Nov Russian counter-offensive on Stalingrad

1943 Jan Casablanca conference; German surrender at Stalingrad

Mar Russians drove Germans back to the River Donetz

May end of Axis resistance in N Africa

Aug beginning of campaign against Japanese in Burma

Sept Italy surrendered to Allies; Allied landings at Salerno; Russians retook Smolensk

Oct Italy declared war on Germany

Nov–Dec Tehran conference

1944 Jan Allied landing at Anzio

Mar end of German U-boat campaign in the Atlantic

May fall of *Monte Cassino*

Jun D-Day: Allied landings in Normandy

Jul bomb plot against Hitler

Aug Romania joined Allies

Sept Battle of Arnhem; Soviet armistice with Finland

Oct Tito and Russians entered Belgrade

Dec German counter-offensive, *Battle of the Bulge*

1945 Feb Russians reached German border; Yalta conference; Allied bombing campaign over Germany: Americans landed on *Iwo Jima*

Apr Hitler committed suicide

May German surrender to the Allies

Jul Potsdam conference

Aug atom bombs dropped on *Hiroshima* and *Nagasaki* Japan surrendered

An estimated 55 million lives were lost, 20 million of them citizens of the USSR.

Arab-Israeli Wars 1948- .Wars between members of the Arab League and Israel, caused by conflict between Zionist aims in Palestine from 1913, furthered by the Balfour Declaration, and Arab opposition. From 1920 there were anti-Zionist riots under Britain's League of Nations mandate in Palestine, and in 1936 an Arab revolt led to a British Royal Commission which recommended partition (approved by the United Nations in 1947, but rejected by the Arabs).

First Arab-Israeli War 14 Oct 1948–13 Jan/ 24 Mar 1949. This followed the British surrender of the mandate, when the Arabs attacked the new state, and it resulted in the enlargement on all fronts of the original Israeli boundaries.

Second Arab-Israeli War 29 Oct–4 Nov 1956. Coincident with the Suez crisis, it resulted in the Israelis capturing Sinai and the Gaza Strip, from which they withdrew after the entry of a United Nations force.

Third Arab-Israeli War 5–10 Jun 1967, the 'Six Day War'. This resulted in the Israeli capture of the Golan Heights from Syria; Old Jerusalem and the West Bank from Jordan;

and, in the south, occupation of the Gaza Strip and Sinai Peninsula as far as the Suez Canal.

Fourth Arab-Israeli War 2–22/24 Oct 1973, the 'Oct War' or 'Yom Kippur War'. So-called because the Israeli forces were taken by surprise on the Day of Atonement. It resulted in the recrossing of the Suez Canal by Egyptian forces and initial gains, though there was some later loss of ground by the Syrians in the north. The Arab cause was adopted by the USSR and the Israeli by the USA; terrorist outrages by Arab extremist groups and retaliation by Israelis continued. In 1978 the *Camp David Agreements* brought Egypt–Israeli peace, but this was denounced by other Arab countries. Israel withdrew from Sinai 1979–82, but no final agreement on Jerusalem and the establishment of a Palestinian state on the W Bank was reached.

Fifth Arab-Israeli War from 1978 the presence of Palestinian guerrillas in Lebanon led to alternate Arab raids on Israel and Israeli retaliatory incursions, but on 6 Jun 1982 Israel launched a full-scale invasion. By 14 Jun Beirut was encircled, and PLO and Syrian forces were evacuated (mainly to Syria) 21–31 Aug, but in Feb 1985 there was a unilateral Israeli withdrawal from the country without any gain for losses incurred. This, however, has not prevented Israeli incursions, making the withdrawal more nominal than actual.

Korean War 1950–53. War between North Korea (supported by China) and South Korea, aided by the United Nations (including the UK, though the troops were mainly US). North Korean forces invaded the South 25 Jun 1950, and the Security Council of the United Nations, owing to a walk-out by the USSR, voted to oppose them. After a 'concertina' campaign up and down the peninsula, which ended in the restoration of the original boundary on the 38th parallel, an armistice was signed with the North, although South Korea did not participate.

Vietnam War 1954–75. War following the division of Indo-China under the 1954 Geneva Convention into the separate states of North and South Vietnam. Within S Vietnam the Communist Vietcong, supported by N Vietnam and China, attempted to seize power. The USA provided military aid to support the S Vietnamese and following the Gulf of Tonkin incident 1964, when N Vietnamese torpedo boats allegedly attacked two US destroyers, the USA intervened directly and sent troops. Several large-scale invasion attempts by N Vietnam were defeated by indigenous and US forces, but the unpopularity of the war within the USA led to US withdrawal fron 1973. A peace treaty was signed between N and S Vietnam 1973 but S Vietnam was invaded by N Vietnam in March 1975, and the country was reunited as the Socialist Republic of Vietnam in 1976. Although US forces were never militarily defeated, Vietnam was undoubtedly the most humiliating political defeat the USA has ever suffered..

Iran-Iraq war or **Gulf War** 1980– . War between Iran and Iraq, claimed by the former to have begun with the Iraq offensive of 21 Sept 1980, and by the latter with the Iranian shelling of border posts 4 Sept 1980. Occasioned by dispute over the Shatt al'Arab waterway, it fundamentally arose because of Iran's encouragement of the Shi'ite majority in Iraq to rise against their Sunni government. Among Arab states, Iran was supported by Syria and Libya, the remainder supporting Iraq. By 1985 stalemate had led to a willingness to compromise, notably in Iran's abandonment of a demand for the resignation of President Saddam Hussein of Iraq; but in 1987 fighting continues with Iranian advances into Iraqi territory and Iraqi bombing of Iranian cities.

Revolutions

Revolution is a term that can be used to describe any rapid, far-reaching or violent change in the political, social or economic structure of society. It has usually been applied to different forms of political change: the American Revolution (War of Independence), where colonists broke free from their colonial ties and established a sovereign, independent state; the French Revolution, where an absolute monarchy was overthrown by opposition from inside the country and a popular rising; and the Russian Revolution, where a repressive monarchy was overthrown by those seeking to institute widespread social and economic changes in line with a socialist model. While political revolutions are often associated with violence, there are other types of change which often have just as much impact on society. Most notable is the Industrial Revolution, a process which has imposed massive changes on economies and societies since the mid-18th century. In the 1980s, a new 'silicon' revolution can be identified, involving the increasing use of computers to undertake tasks formerly done 'by hand'.

Industrial Revolution the sudden acceleration of technical development which occurred in Europe from the late 18th century, and which transferred the balance of political power from the landowner to the industrial capitalist, and created an organized industrial working class. The great achievement of the first phase (to 1830) was the invention of the steam engine in Britain, originally developed for draining mines, but rapidly put to use in factories and in the railways. In the second phase, from 1830 to the early 20th century, the Industrial Revolution enlarged its scope from Europe to the world, with some initial exploitation of 'colonial' possessions by European

powers as a preliminary to their independent development. The internal combustion engine and electricity were developed, and in 1911 Rutherford split the atom at Manchester, opening up the prospect of nuclear power. Electronic devices were developed which made automation possible, with the eventual prospect of even managerial decision-making being in the hands of 'machines'.

French Revolution 1789-99. The forcible abolition of the *Ancien Régime* 'old order of things' (feudalism and absolute monarchy).
1789 5 May the *States General* (an assembly of the three 'estates', nobles, clergy, and commons) met at Versailles, bent on establishing a new constitution; 17 Jun *National Assembly* formed by the *Third Estate* (commons); 14 Jul Bastille was taken by the mob when Louis XVI attempted repressive moves
1791 20 Jun flight of the royal family to Varennes; 14 Sept Louis, brought back as a prisoner, accepted the new constitution
1792 20 Apr war declared on Austria, which threatened to suppress the revolution; 10 Aug royal palace stormed by the French mob; 21 Sept *First Republic* proclaimed
1793 21 Jan Louis XVI executed; 2 Jun overthrow of the moderate Girondists by the Jacobins; rule of the dictatorial *Committee of Public Safety*; 5 Sept the mass executions of the *Reign of Terror* began
1794 27 Jul (9 Thermidor under the Revolutionary calendar) fall of Robespierre and end of the Terror; the *Directory* (a body of five directors) established to hold a middle course between Royalism and Jacobinism. It ruled until Napoleon seized power in 1799.

Bastille a fortress prison in Paris, stormed by the mob at the beginning of the revolution on 14 Jul 1789, when it was found to contain only seven prisoners. The governor and most of the garrison were killed and the building razed.

Commune of Paris 1789-94. First body which took this name. It acted as the municipal government of Paris from the storming of the Bastille to the fall of Robespierre.

Jacobins extremist republican club founded at Versailles in 1789, which later used a former

Jacobin (Dominican) friary as its headquarters in Paris. It was led by Robespierre and closed after his execution in 1794.

Girondins right-wing republicans of the French Revolution whose leaders came from the Gironde departement of France.

Robespierre Maximilien. François Marie Isidere de 1758-94. French politician,'the Sea Green Incorruptible'. As Jacobin leader in the *National Convention*, he supported the execution of Louis XVI and the overthrow of the Girondins, and as dominant member of the Committee of Public Safety instituted the Reign of Terror in 1793. His extremist zeal made him enemies on both left and right, resulting in his overthrow and death by guillotining in Jul 1794.

Danton Georges Jacques 1959-94. French lawyer and leading revolutionary. Influential in the early years of the revolution in Paris, he was instrumental in organizing the rising of 10 Aug 1792 which overthrew the monarchy. He also helped to instigate the revolutionary tribunal and the Committee of Public Safety in 1793. He led the Committee until Jul 1793 but was then superseded by Robespierre. An attempt to reassert his power failed and he was guillotined in 1794.

Marat Jean Paul 1743–93. French revolutionary leader and journalist. He was the idol of the Paris revolutionary crowds, and was elected in 1792 to the National Convention, where he carried on a long struggle with the Girondins, ending in their overthrow in May 1793. In Jul he was murdered by Charlotte Corday.

Revolutions of 1848 A series of revolts in various parts of Europe against monarchical rule. While some of the revolutionaries had republican ideas, many more were motivated by economic grievances. The revolution began in France and then spread to Italy, the Austrian Empire, and to Germany where the short-lived Frankfurt Parliament put forward ideas about German political unity. None of the revolutions enjoyed any lasting success, and most were violently suppressed within a few months.

Indian Mutiny 1857–58. The revolt of the Bengal Army against the British in India. The movement was confined to the North, from Bengal to the Punjab, and Central India. Most support came from the army and recently dethroned princes, but in some areas it developed into a peasant rising or general revolt. Outstanding episodes were the seizure of *Delhi* by the rebels, and its seige and recapture by the British, and the defence of *Lucknow* by a British garrison. The mutiny led to the end of rule by the East India Co. and its replacement by direct Crown administration.

Paris Commune 1871. The second body to bear this name. A provisional government of Socialist and left-wing Republicans, elected in Mar 1871 after an attempt by the right-wing National Assembly at Versailles to disarm the Paris National Guard, it held power until May, when the Versailles troops captured Paris and massacred at least 20,000 people. It is famous as the first Socialist government in history.

Chinese Revolution 1911-49. A series of major political upheavals which began in 1911 with a Nationalist revolt which overthrew the Manchu dynasty in 1922. Led by Sun Yat-sen (1923–25) and then by Chiang Kai-shek (1925–49), the Nationalists came under increasing pressure from the growing Communist movement. The 6,000-mile *Long March* of the Chinese Communists 1934–35 to escape from the Nationalist forces saw Mao Zedong emerge as leader. After World War II, the conflict expanded into open civil war 1946–49 with the Nationalists finally being defeated at *Nanking*. This effectively established Communist rule in China under the leadership of Mao.

Sun Yat-sen or *Sun Zhong Shan* 1867–1925. Chinese revolutionary, founder of the Nationalist Guomindang, and moving spirit behind the revolution. He was briefly president 1912, but the reactionaries gained the ascendant, and he broke away to try to establish an independent republic in S China based on Canton. He lacked organizational ability, but his three 'people's principles' of nationalism, democracy, and social reform were influential.

Chiang Kai-shek or *Jiang Jie Shi* 1887-1975. Chinese statesman. He took part in the revolution, and after the death of Sun Yat-sen was made commander-in-chief of the Guomindang armies in S China in 1925. The initial collaboration with the Communists, broken in 1927, was resumed following the Xi An incident, and he nominally headed the struggle against the Japanese invaders, receiving the Japanese surrender in 1945. Civil war then resumed between Communists and Nationalists, and ended in the defeat of Chiang in 1949, and the limitation of his rule to Taiwan.

Mao Zedong or *Mao Tse-Tung* 1893–1976. Chinese statesman, the 'Great Helmsman'. Born in Hunan, he became the leader of the Communists in 1927. After the rupture with the Nationalists, led by Chiang Kai-shek, Mao Zedong and his troops undertook the 6,000-mile 'Long March' 1934–35 from SE to NW China, the prelude to his ascent to power. Again in nominal alliance with Chiang against the Japanese 1937–45, he subsequently defeated him, and proclaimed the People's Republic of China in 1949. As Chairman of the Communist Party, he provided the pattern for the development of the country through the Great Leap Forward of 1959, and the Cultural Revolution of 1966 based on his thoughts contained in the 'Little Red Book'. His reputation plunged after his death, but was later somewhat restored.

Russian Revolution 1917. The name given to the two revolutions of Mar and Nov 1917 which began with the overthrow of the Romanov Imperial dynasty and ended with the the establishment of a state run by Lenin and the Bolsheviks. The revolution of Mar 1917 arose in part from the repressive nature of Tsarist government but primarily as a result of the mismanagement of the war after 1914. Riots in St Petersburg led to the abdication of Tsar Nicholas II and the formation of a provisional government under Kerensky. This ruled until Oct 1917 but found its power increasingly undermined by the soldiers' and workers' soviets in Petrograd (St Petersburg) and Moscow. During this period the Bolsheviks, under Lenin's guidance, had concentrated on gaining control of the soviets and advocating

an end to the war and land reform. Under the slogan 'All power to the soviets' they staged a coup on the night of 6–7 Nov which overthrew the government. The second All-Russian Congress of Soviets, which met the following day, proclaimed itself the new government of Russia. The Bolshevik seizure of power led to peace with Germany through the *Treaty of Brest-Litovsk*, but also to civil war as anti-Bolshevik elements within the army attempted to seize power. The war lasted until 1920, when the Red Army, organized by Trotsky, finally overcame 'white' opposition.

Lenin Pseudonym of Vladimir Ilich Ulyanov 1870–1924. He was converted to Marxism in 1889 and exiled to Siberia in 1895 as a result of subversive activity. After 1900, he spent most of his time in Western Europe, emerging as the leader of the more radical Bolshevik section of Russian Social Democracy. Returning to Russia in Apr 1917 with German help, Lenin assumed control of the Bolshevik movement and was instrumental in organizing the coup of 6–7 Nov. From then until his death in 1924, he effectively controlled Russia, establishing Bolshevik rule and the beginnings of Communism.

Trotsky Leon 1879–1940. Born 7 Nov at Yanovka. Communist theorist, agitator, and collaborator with Lenin after the two met in exile in London in 1902. Trotsky was a leading member of the Bolshevik movement in 1917 and helped overthrow the provisional government. He was instrumental in building up the Red Army so that it could win the civil war and acted as Commissioner for Foreign Affairs until 1924. He was ousted during the power struggle which followed Lenin's death, but remained active in opposing Stalin's rule until he was assassinated in Aug 1940.

Cuban Revolution 1959. Name given to the overthrow of the Batista regime in Jan 1959 by Castro and the 26 Jul Movement. Having led abortive coups in 1953 and 1956, Castro succeeded in overthrowing Batista with a force of only 5,000 men. Politically non-aligned, Castro was increasingly forced to seek Eastern Bloc help for government as a result of US opposition – opposition which culminated in the abortive *Bay of Pigs* invasion of 1961 sponsored by the CIA. The missile crisis of 1962 highlighted Russian involvement in Cuba. Between 1959 and 1974, Cuba, led by Castro, his brother Raúl and initially Che Guevara, adopted economic and social policies based on the principles of Marxism-Leninism and relied almost exclusively on Communist help. After 1974, in an attempt to stabilise the economy, Castro reintroduced incentives into society with the maxim that each 'should receive according to his work' rather than according to his need.

Castro Ruz Fidel 1927– . Cuban prime minister. Of wealthy parentage Castro was educated at Jesuit schools and, after studying law at the University of Havana, he gained a reputation through his work for poor clients. He strongly opposed the Batista dictatorship, and with his brother Raúl took part in an unsuccessful attack on the army barracks at Santiago de Cuba in 1953. After spending some time in exile in the US and Mexico, Castro attempted a secret landing in Cuba in 1956 in which all but 11 of his supporters were killed. He eventually gathered an army of over 5,000 which overthrew Batista in 1959 and became prime minister a few months later. He became president in 1976, and in 1979 also president of the Non-Aligned Movement. His brother Raúl was appointed Minister of Armed Forces in 1959.

Guevara Ernesto 'Che' 1928–67. Revolutionary. Born in Argentina, he was trained as a doctor, but in 1953 left the country because of his opposition to Peron. In effecting the Cuban revolution of 1959, he was second only to Castro and his brother, but in 1965 moved on to fight against white mercenaries in the Congo, and then to Bolivia, where he was killed in an unsuccessful attempt to lead a peasant rising.

Chilean Revolution 1970–73. Name given to the period of Salvador Allende's presidency, the world's first democratically elected Marxist head of state. Allende was brought to power in 1970 as the head of the Popular Unity alliance of Socialists, Communists, and radicals. He was committed to extensive social and economic reforms to be carried out within the existing political structure, but nationalization of key industries and increased contacts with Eastern Bloc countries strained Chile's traditional economic relations with the USA and the West. His failure to stabilize the economy created widespread opposition, culminating in a military coup in Sept 1973, when the Allende regime was overthrown and replaced by a four-man junta led by General Pinochet .

Allende Gossens Salvador 1908– . Born in Valparaiso, Chile, Allende became a Marxist activist in the 1930s and rose to prominence as a left-wing presidential candidate in 1952, 1958, and 1964. In each election he had the support of the Socialist and Communist movements but was defeated by the Christian Democrats and Nationalists. Eventually elected in 1970, Allende never succeeded in keeping the electoral alliance together in government, and the 1973 coup brought about his death and that of many of his supporters.

Nicaraguan Revolution 1978-79. The revolt led by the FSLN (Sandinist National Liberation Front named after Augusto Cesar Sandino, killed by the National Guard in 1934) against the dictatorship established by the father of the president Anastasio 'Tacho' Somoza. The dictatorship of the Somoza family had been underwritten by US support but this was of little help in 1978–79 when the Sandinistas mounted a full scale challenge to the regime and the hated National Guard. Somoza was forced into exile and assassinated in Paraguay in 1980. Since the revolution, the Sandinistas have taken political control of the country, introducing socialist policies and receiving help from Eastern Bloc countries as US aid dried up. The Sandinista government has had to contend with severe economic problems and also the activities of a counter-revolutionary movement, the Contras, operating in the north of the country with US monetary and technical support.

Emergence of the Third World

One of the major political changes to have taken place in recent years has been the break-up of the European overseas empires. Apart from the Spanish colonies in South and Central America which achieved their independence in the early 19th century, nearly all of this decolonization has taken place since the end of World War II, either by negotiation or by force. This has created many new, independent, sovereign states in South and Central America, Africa and Asia – all of whom share the experience of having been colonized as part of the Third World (where the USA and USSR form the First World, and the industrialized European states together with Canada and Japan the Second World). While the term Third World may indicate a colonial past, it also indicates the present economic situation of those coun-

tries; industrially less developed and dependent on the developed world for many essential products. This relationship between the industrialized nations and the Third World has created a severe debt crisis for many of the less developed nations where they are now having to raise loans internationally merely in order to pay off existing debts, rather than for industrial or agricultural development projects. There are well over one hundred Third World states and in recent years they have tried to exert some political influence in world affairs through the creation of the non-aligned movement within the United Nations; and economic influence through the creation of the 'Group of 77' (1964), an organization designed to bring pressure on the developed world to provide aid and monetary assistance. A series of selective tables over the following pages outlines the colonial origins of some of the more important Third World states and their recent political history. They are grouped according to the European country by which they were originally colonized and, within these groups, listed chronologically according to their date of independence.

BELGIUM

Current name	Colonial Names and History	Colonized/ Independent	Recent Events
Zaire	Belgian Congo	1885/1960	Republic of Congo 1960-71 under P Lumumba; J D Mobutu after coup 1965

FRANCE

Current name	Colonial Names and History	Colonized/ Independent	Recent Events
Kampuchea	Cambodia to 1970	1863/1953	Led by Prince Sihanouk except Khmer Republic 1970-75, Pol Pot regime 1976-78; invaded by Vietnam 1978
Laos	French Indo-China (protectorate)	1893/1954	Civil war until Vientiane Agreement divided country 1973; Communists in power from 1975
Vietnam	Tonkin, Annam, Cochin-China to 1954; N&S Vietnam 1954-76	1858/1954	Led by Ho Chi Minh to Vietnam War 1954-75; Socialist Republic from 1976

Current name	Colonial Names and History	Colonized/ Independent	Recent Events
Burkina Faso	Upper Volta to 1984	1896/1960	Military coups 1966, 1980, 1982, 1983; Captain Thomas Sankara president 1983-
Central African Republic	Ubangi-Shari	19th cent./ 1960	Republic 1960-76, 1979- ; Central African Empire 1976-79 led by Jean Bokassa
Chad	French Equatorial Africa	19th cent./ 1960	Continuing civil war with Libyan and French support
Côte d'Ivoire	Ivory Coast to 1986	1883/1960	Félix Houphouët-Boigny president of one-party state from 1960
Madagascar		1896/1960	Malagasy Republic 1960-75; Madagascar, under Didier Ratsiraka, 1975-
Mali	French Sudan	19th cent./ 1960	Moussa Traoré president from 1969; one-party state from 1974
Niger		1912/1960	Under Colonel Seyni Kountché since military coup 1974
Algeria	Colonized in 19th cent.; incorporated into France 1881	c.1840/1962	Led by Mohamed Ben Bella until overthrown by Huari Boumédienne 1965; Benjedid Chadli president of one-party state 1979-

GREAT BRITAIN

Current name	Colonial Names and History	Colonized/ Independent	Recent Events
India	British E India Co. 18th cent.-1858	18th cent./ 1947	Republic conceived by Mohandas K Gandhi, led by Pandit Nehru 1947-64, Indira Gandhi 1966-77, 1980-84, and Rajiv Gandhi 1984-
Pakistan	British E India Co. 18th cent.-1858	18th cent./ 1947	Republic established by Mohammad Ali Jinna, led by Zulfikar Ali Bhutto in 1970s, now under General Zia-ul-Haq since military coup 1977
Sri Lanka	Portuguese, Dutch 1602-1796; Ceylon 1802-1972	16th cent./ 1948	Led by Solomon Bandaranaike 1956-59, then his wife Sirimavo; republic from 1972, now under Junius Jayawardene
Ghana	Gold Coast	1618/1957	Several coups since Kwame Nkrumah deposed 1966; now under military rule

Current name	Colonial Names and History	Colonized/ Independent	Recent Events
Nigeria		1861/1960	Federal republic from 1963, led by Yakubu Gowon 1966-75; Biafran War 1967-70; now under military rule after several coups
Cyprus	Turkish to 1878, then British rule	1878/1960	Led by Archbishop Makarios 1960-77; divided into Greek and Turkish states from 1975
Sierra Leone	British protectorate	1788/1961	Made republic 1971; one-party state from 1978
Tanzania	German E Africa to 1921; British mandate from League of Nations/ UN as Tanganyika	19th cent./ 1961	Joined with Zanzibar 1964 to form Tanzania under Julius Nyerere 1962-85
Jamaica	Spanish to 1655	16th cent./ 1962	Led by Michael Manley 1972-80; in opposition to Edward Seaga from 1980
Trinidad & Tobago	Spanish 1532-1797; British 1797-1962	1532/1962	Republic under Ellis Clarke from 1976
Uganda	British protectorate	1894/1962	Led by Milton Obote 1962-71, 1980-85; Idi Amin 1971-79
Kenya	British colony from 1920	1895/1963	Led by Jomo Kenyatta 1963-78; Daniel Arap Moi 1978-
Malaysia	British interests from 1786; Federation of Malaya 1957-63	1874-1963	Federal republic led by Mahmud Iskander from 1984
Malawi	British protectorate of Nyasaland 1907-53; Federation of Rhodesia & Nyasaland 1953-64	1891/1964	One-party state under Hastings Banda from 1966
Malta	French 1798-1814	1798/1964	Led by Dom Mintoff to 1984; Mifsud Bonnici 1984-
Zambia	N Rhodesia – British protectorate; Federation of Rhodesia & Nyasaland 1953-64	1924/1964	Led by Kenneth Kaunda from 1964; one-party state from 1972
The Gambia		1888/1965	Led by Dawda K Jawara from 1965
Singapore	Federation of Malaya 1963-65	1858/1965	Led by Lee Kuan Yew from 1959
Guyana	Dutch to 1796; British Guiana 1796-1966	1620/1966	Led by Forbes Burnham to 1985; Desmond Hoyte 1985-
Botswana	Bechuanaland – British protectorate	1885/1966	Led by Seretse Khama to 1980; Quett Masire 1980-

28

Current name	Colonial Names and History	Colonized/ Independent	Recent Events
Lesotho	Basutoland	1868/1966	Monarchy under Moshoeshoe II from 1966
Bangladesh	British E India Co. 18th cent.-1858; British India 1858-1947; E Pakistan 1947-71	18th cent./ 1971	Led by Lt-General Ershad from 1982 after several coups; martial law ended 1986
Zimbabwe	S Rhodesia from 1923; UDI 1965-79 under Ian Smith	1895/1980	Led by Robert Mugabe from 1980

THE NETHERLANDS

Current name	Colonial Names and History	Colonized/ Independent	Recent Events
Indonesia	Netherlands Indies	17th cent./ 1949	Military rule of Dr Sukarno to 1966; General Suharto 1967- ; incorporated Dutch New Guinea 1963, E Timor 1976
Suriname	British colony 1650-67	1667/1975	Led by Lt-Col Desi Bouterse from 1982 after several coups

PORTUGAL

Current name	Colonial Names and History	Colonized/ Independent	Recent Events
Brazil		1532/1822	Military coup 1964; civilian rule from 1985
Uruguay	Province of Brazil	1533/1828	Military coup 1976; civilian rule from 1985
Mozambique		1505/1975	Led by Frelimo leader Samora Machel to 1986
Angola		1491/1975	Continuing civil war between dos Santos government and Jonas Savimbi

SPAIN

Current name	Colonial Names and History	Colonized/ Independent	Recent Events
Paraguay	Viceroyalty of Buenos Aires	1537/1811	Military rule under Alfredo Stroessner from 1954

Current name	Colonial Names and History	Colonized/ Independent	Recent Events
Argentina	Viceroyalty of Buenos Aires	16th cent./ 1816	Military rule 1976-83; Raul Alfonsín president 1983-
Chile		1541/1818	Led by General Pinochet since military coup overthrew Allende 1974
Costa Rica		1563/1821	Led by Oscar Arias Sanchez 1986-
Mexico	Viceroyalty of New Spain	16th cent./ 1821	Federal republic under Miguel de la Madrid Hurtado 1982- and Institutional Revolutionary Party
Peru		1541/1824	Civilian rule since 1980 after several coups
Bolivia		16th cent./ 1825	Civilian rule under Dr Victor Paz Estenssoro 1985-
Ecuador	Greater Colombia 1822-30	16th cent./ 1830	Civilian rule from 1979; led by Febres Cordero 1984-
Venezuela	Captaincy-General of Caracas to 1822; Greater Colombia 1822-30	16th cent./ 1830	Led by Dr Jaime Lusinchi 1984-
Honduras	Federation of Central America 1821-38	1523/1838	Civilian rule under Roberto Suazo 1982-85, José Azcona del Hoyo 1985- , after long military rule
El Salvador	Federation of Central America 1821-39	16th cent./ 1839	Continuing conflict between guerrilla forces and government of José Duarte
Guatemala	Federation of Central America 1821-39	16th cent./ 1839	Civilian rule from 1985 after long military rule
Dominican Republic	Hispaniola to 1821; ruled by Haiti to 1844	16th cent./ 1844	Civilian rule from 1966, under Joaquin Balaguer 1986-
Cuba		1512/1898	Led by Castro from 1959; Bay of Pigs incident 1961
Colombia	Viceroyalty of New Granada to 1819; Greater Colombia to 1830	16th cent./ 1903	Led by Virgilio Barco Vargas 1986-
Panama	Part of Colombia to 1903	16th cent./ 1903	Panama-US treaty on canal 1977
Philippines	Spain 1565-1898; US 1898-1946	1565/1946	Led by Ferdinand Marcos 1963-86; Corazón Aquino 1986-

The Search for Peace

Europe in 1815 until the end of the 18th century, the idea of states making war against each other was regarded as an acceptable, and even a normal, way of settling international disputes. Following the catastrophic political and economic effects of the French Revolutionary and Napoleonic Wars, many leading statesman recognized the need, not only to reconstruct Europe politically, but also to develop some machinery for ensuring a lasting peace and the settlement of international disputes by negotiation. This change of attitude was reinforced by the belief that an equilibrium existed in which the aims and objectives of all European states could be made compatible. Towards the end of the war, the victorious powers, Russia, Prussia, Austria, and Britain arranged a peace conference in Vienna.

Congress of Vienna international congress held 1814–15 to discuss the reconstruction of continental Europe. National representatives included Prince Metternich (Austria), Alexander I (Russia), Castlereagh and Wellington (Britain). The settlement created the basis for the Quadruple Alliance of the Victorious Powers – transformed in 1818 into the Quintuple Alliance with the inclusion of France. The congress also produced other attempts at international co-operation.

Holy Alliance a 'Christian Union of Charity, Peace and Love' initiated by Alexander I of Russia in 1815 and signed by every crowned head in Europe. Although apparently an attempt to facilitate European co-operation through Christian principles, the alliance became associated with Russian attempts to preserve autocratic monarchies at any price and an excuse to meddle in the internal affairs of other states. The Idea of an international army acting in the name of the alliance were rejected by Britain and Austria in 1818 and again in 1820.

Congress system developed from the Congress of Vienna. A series of international meetings at Aix-la-Chapelle 1818, Troppau 1820, and Verona 1822. British opposition to the repressive intentions of the congresses effectively ended them as a system of international arbitration, although congresses continued to meet into the 1830s.

International co-operation in the 19th century the period 1815–53 saw much internal political disruption in many European states but it was not until mid-century that a series of wars, most notably the Crimean, Seven Weeks', and Franco-Prussian, led to changes in the European order. New nation states were created in Italy and Germany, the Austrian empire was divided and France weakened. This also created a new impetus towards international co-operation.

Geneva Convention an international agreement regulating the treatment of the wounded in war, reached at a conference in 1864, and later extended to cover the treatment of the sick and prisoners, and protection of civilians in wartime. The rules were revised at conventions held in 1906, 1929, 1949, and 1977.

Red Cross international agency founded to assist the wounded and prisoners of war. Prompted by war horrors experienced by the Swiss Henri Dunant, the Geneva Convention laid down principles ensuring the safety of ambulances, hospitals and personnel distinguished by the emblem of the red cross. Red Cross societies were established in most western states and a parallel Red Crescent organization was created in Muslim countries.

Conference system a system of international conferences promoted principally by Bismarck to ease the integration of a new powerful German state into the 'Concept of Europe'. The conferences were intended to settle great power disputes, mainly related to the Balkans, the Middle East and the designation of colonies in Africa and Asia. Most important of these was the congress of Berlin 1878 which determined the boundaries of the

Balkan states after the Russo-Turkish War. The system fell into disuse with the retirement of Bismarck and the pressures of new European alliance blocks.

Alliance system and 'balance of power' the failure of both the congress and conference systems to produce any lasting machine led to an increasing reliance on individual alliances and the creation of hostile European blocks. The most important of these alliances were:

Three Emperors League (Dreikaiserbund) 1872 an informal alliance between the emperors of Russia, Germany and Austria. Effectively at an end by 1879.

Triple Alliance 1882 an alliance formed between Germany, Austria-Hungary and Italy which formed the basis of central power involvement in World War I (Italy remaining neutral and then joining allied powers).

Dual Entente 1893 an alliance between France and Russia which lasted until the Bolshevik Revolution of 1917.

Anglo-French Entente (Entente Cordiale) 1904 an alliance based on the need to settle colonial differences. Similar treaty with Russia in 1907 led to:

Triple Entente 1907–17 alliance of Britain, France and Russia. In 1911 this became a military alliance and formed the basis of the allied cause in World War I.

The failure of the alliance system to create a stable balance of power, coupled with universal horror of the carnage created by World War I, led to further attempts to create a new international order.

The League of Nations international organization suggested in President Woodrow Wilson's 'Fourteen Points' 1917 as part of the peace settlement for World War I. The league covenant was drawn up by the Paris Peace Conference in 1919 and incorporated into the Versailles and other peace treaties. Established in Geneva in 1920, the league included representatives from states throughout the world, but was severely weakened by the US decision not to become a member. The states which did become members undertook to preserve the territorial integrity of all, and to

submit international disputes to the league or to arbitration. The league enjoyed a good deal of success in the humanitarian field (international action against epidemics, drug traffic and the slave trade) and also established a number of important subsidiary organizations. Most notably:

International Labour Organization (*ILO*) based in Geneva and concerned primarily with working conditions and social welfare. Formed in 1919, the ILO continued to exist as an affiliated body of the United Nations.

High Commission for Refugees (Nansen Office) an organization created to assist refugees, primarily from Russia and eastern Europe. Built on the work of Norwegian explorer Fridtjof Nansen as first High Commissioner, the high commission declined in importance after his death and the entry of the USSR to the league. Formed the basis for post-1945 refugee work by the United Nations.

Permanent Court of Justice court created in The Hague in 1921, based on ideas for some form of international court put forward at The Hague Congress of 1907.

The league also achieved some success in organizing population exchanges after the Paris peace conferences had established new national boundaries, and in deferring arguments over disputed territories and former German colonies by mandating a league member to act as a caretaker administration for a specified period of time, or until a permanent solution could be found. Mandates were created for Palestine (Britain), SW Africa (S Africa), and Danzig. In the political and diplomatic field, the league was permanently hampered by internal rivalries and the necessity for unanimity in the decision-making process. No action was taken against Japan's aggression in Manchuria 1931; attempts to impose sanctions against Italy for the invasion of Ethiopia 1935–36 collapsed; no actions were taken when Germany annexed Austria and Czechoslovakia, nor when Poland was invaded. Japan (1932) and Germany (1933) simply withdrew from the league and the expulsion of Russia in 1939 had no effect on the Russo-Finnish War.

Long before the outbreak of World War II, diplomacy had abandoned international security and reverted to a system of direct negotiation and individual alliances.

Alliance, aggression and appeasement the period 1936–39 saw a series of alliances and treaties ostensibly to guarantee the security of individual states.

Rome-Berlin Axis the sometimes uneasy alliance of Nazi Germany and fascist Italy. The axis was formed in 1936 when Italy was threatened with 'sanctions' because of the invasion of Ethiopia, and became a full military and political alliance in May 1939. A ten-year alliance between Germany, Italy and Japan (Rome, Berlin, Tokyo Axis) was signed in Sept 1940 and was later joined by Hungary, Bulgaria, Romania, Slovakia and Croara. The axis collapsed with the fall of Mussolini in 1943.

Munich Agreement the agreement between Britain, France, Germany and Italy signed by Chamberlain, Daladier, Hitler and Mussolini at Munich on 29 Sept 1938. Its main provision was to cede Sudeten areas of Czechoslovakia to Germany. Although the signatories all guaranteed the new Czechoslovak frontiers, Hitler seized the rest of the country in Mar 1939. Britain and France did not respond immediately, leading Hitler to assume that they would not intervene anywhere in Eastern Europe. Nevertheless, Hitler's violation of the agreement did create a change in attitude and further guarantees to Poland.

Hitler-Stalin Pact agreement signed in August 1939 between Nazi Germany and the USSR by Ribbentrop and Molotov. The treaty provided for the partition of Poland between the two states.

International peace and security since 1945 at the end of World War II, an attempt was made to re-establish an organization for international security, as a successor to the discredited League of Nations.

United Nations (UN) an association of states pledged to maintain international peace and security, and to promote international co-operation. Its charter, which was drawn up by the San Francisco Conference in 1945, is based

on proposals drafted at the Dumbarton Oaks Conference. Its six principal organs are:

General Assembly of representatives of all member states, which meets regularly once a year, and may discuss any matter within the scope of the charter, but may not make recommendations on anything already being dealt with by the Security Council. Decisions on important questions are made by a two-thirds majority of members voting, and on other questions by a simple majority, each member having one vote.

Security Council consisting of five permanent members (UK, USA, USSR, France, and Communist China), and six others elected for two years by the General Assembly. Its decisions must be supported by at least seven of its members, including all permanent members, who thus exercise the right of veto. Taking cognizance of disputes, it may undertake investigations into the circumstances and make recommendations to the parties concerned, and may call on all members to take economic or military measures to enforce its decisions.

Economic and Social Council consisting of representatives of 18 member states, elected for three years by the General Assembly, which initiates studies of international economic, social, cultural, educational, health and related matters, and may make recommendations to the General Assembly. It operates largely through specialized commissions of international experts on economics, transport and communications, human rights, status of women, etc. It also co-ordinates the activities of such specialized inter-governmental agencies as the United Nations Educational, Scientific and Cultural Organization (UNESCO 1946) to combat illiteracy, raise living standards through education, and so on; International Labour Organization; Food and Agriculture Organization (FAO 1945), to help the nations improve food and production and distribution, raise nutritional standards, and so on; International Atomic Agency (IAEA 1957), to develop the peaceful uses of atomic energy; World Health Organization (WHO 1946), to prevent the spread of, and eliminate, such diseases as malaria and tuberculosis; International Monetary Fund and International Bank for Reconstruction and Development, which promote international economic co-operation, and so on.

Trusteeship Council consisting of members administering Trust Territories (territories under UN trusteeship), other permanent members of the Security Council, plus sufficient other elected members to balance the administering powers.

International Court of Justice at The Hague, the United Nation's principal judicial organ: the 15 judges are elected by the General Assembly and the Security Council, and the United Nation members are pledged by the charter to comply with the decisions of the court in cases to which they are a party.

Secretariat the administrative body, consisting of the Secretary General, appointed by the General Assembly on the recommendation of the Security Council for five years, and an international staff.

Members contribute according to their resources, an apportionment being made by the General Assembly, with the addition of voluntary contributions from some governments to the funds of the United Nations. These finance the programme of assistance carried out by the United Nations, intergovernmental agencies, the United Nations Children's Fund (UNICEF), the United Nations refugee organizations, and the United Nations Special Fund for less developed countries. There are six offical working languages: English, French, Russian, Spanish, Chinese, and Arabic. The preponderance of influence in the United Nations, originally with the Allied States of World War II, is now more widely spread. Although part of the value of the United Nations lies in recognition of member states as sovereign and equal, the rapid increase in membership of minor, in some cases minute, states was causing concern by 1980 (154 members) as lessening the weight of voting decisions. Taiwan (Nationalist China), formerly a permanent member of the Security Council, was expelled 1971 on the admission of Communist China. The United Nations also suffers from the lack of adequate and independent funds and forces, the latter having been employed with varying success, for example, in Korea, Cyprus, and Sinai, and the intrusion of the Cold War which divides members into adherents of the East or West and the uncommitted. In spite of its many successes, the United Nations and its subsidary organizations have failed to prevent the rebuilding of defensive alliances. Even before the end of World War II, relations between the USSR and the Western powers became strained leading to the Cold War and the creation of the two huge defensive alliances – one based round the USSR and the other round the USA.

North Atlantic Treaty Organization (NATO) defensive alliance created by the North Atlantic Treaty, signed in Washington DC on 4 Apr 1949 by Belgium, Canada, Denmark, France, Iceland, Italy, Luxembourg, the Netherlands, Norway, Portugal, the UK, and the USA. The signatories agreed that 'an armed attack against one or more of them in Europe or North America shall be considered an attack against them all'. Greece and Turkey acceded in 1952, and Germany in 1955. The chief body of the North Atlantic Treaty Organization is the Council of Foreign Ministers which holds periodic meetings and also functions in permanent session through the appointment of permanent representatives. The unified international secretariat has its headquarters at Brussels (until 1967 in Paris) as does a military committee consisting of chiefs of staff (until 1967 in Washington). The military headquarters are called the Supreme Headquarters Allied Powers, Europe (SHAPE) and moved from Rocquencourt, France, to Chièvres-Casteau, near Mons, in 1967. The Supreme Allied Commanders, Europe and Atlantic, are Americans, but there is also an Allied Commander, Channel – a British admiral. France withdrew from the organization, but not from the alliance, 1966, and Greece withdrew militarily, but not politically, in 1974 over the Cyprus issue, rejoining in 1981.

Warsaw Pact a pact signed on 14 May 1955 by Albania (excluded in 1962), Bulgaria, Czechoslovakia, East Germany, Hungary, Poland, Romania, and the USSR; extended in 1985 for a further 20 years. It established an alliance on NATO lines known as the Warsaw Treaty Organization.

Cold War a state of economic and political hostility that lasted for more than 20 years before the two superpowers began discussions on disarmament and other matters of mutual concern – thus beginning a process which has become known as détente.

Strategic Arms Limitation Talks (SALT) were suggested by US President Johnson in 1967 for the mutual limitation and eventual reduction of strategic nuclear weapons. They were delayed by the Soviet invasion of Czechoslovakia but began in 1969. SALT I operated from 1972 to 1977. SALT II was mainly negotiated before 1976 but signed by Brezhnev and Carter at Vienna in 1979, though the Soviet invasion of Afganistan prevented ratification.

Helsinki Conference international conference in 1975 at which 35 countries including the USSR and the USA supposedly reached agreements on co-operation in security, economics, science, technology and human rights. Often regarded as marking the end of the Cold War.

Further progress in relations between the two major powers has been hampered by Soviet actions in Afghanistan and US involvement in Central America. Arguments have centred on the supposed balance of forces (in Europe and elsewhere) being upset by the deployment of Pershing, Cruise and Trident missiles by the USA and USSR SS20 missiles. More recently, the issue has been further complicated by President Reagan's adoption of the so-called Strategic Defence Initiative (SDI) or 'Star Wars'. The Soviet willingness to make concessions at the Rekjavik summit between Reagan and Gorbachev in 1986 suggest they are anxious to forestall this apparent extension of the arms race into space.

Peace Movement the peace movements of the 1980s can trace their origins back to the pacifists of the 19th century, conscientious objectors during World War I and peace campaigners during the inter-war years. Since World War II, the campaign has concentrated on opposing the spread, and even the existence, of nuclear weapons. Thus it has attracted not only pacifists but also those opposed to all uses of nuclear power. Peace movements now exist in many Western and non-aligned countries.

CHINESE DYNASTIES

Dynasty	Date	Major Events
Xia (Hsia)	c.2000-c1500 BC	agriculture, bronze, first writing
Shang (Yin)	c.1500-c.1066 BC	first major dynasty; first Chinese calendar
Zhou (Chou)	c.1066-c.221 BC	developed society using money, iron, written laws; age of Confucius
Qin (Ch'in)	221-206 BC	unification after period of Warring States, building of Great Wall began, roads built
Han	206 BC-220 AD	first centralized and effectively administered empire; introduction of Buddhism
San Kuo (Three Kingdoms)	220-280	division into three parts, prolonged fighting and eventual victory of Wei over Chu and Wu; Confucianism superseded by Buddhism and Taoism
Western Jin (Chin)	265-316	beginning of Hun invasions in the north
Eastern Jin (Chin)	317-439	
Southern and Northern	386-581	
Sui	581-618	reunification; barbarian invasions stopped; Great Wall refortified
Tang (T'ang)	618-907	centralised government; empire greatly extended; period of excellence in sculpture, painting and poetry
Wu Tai (Five Dynasties	907-960	economic depression and loss of territory in northern China, central Asia, and Korea; first use of paper money
Song (Sung)	960-1279	period of calm and creativity; printing developed (movable type); central government restored; northern and western frontiers neglected and Mongol incursions began
Yuan	1279-1368	beginning of Mongol rule in China, under Kublai Khan; Marco Polo visited China; dynasty brought to an end by widespread revolts, centred in Mongolia
Ming	1368-1644	Mongols driven out by native Chinese, Mongolia captured by 2nd Ming emperor; period of architectural development; Beijing flourished as new capital
Manchu or Qing (Ch'ing)	1644-1911	China once again under non-Chinese rule, conquered by nomads from Manchuria; initially, trade and culture flourished, but conservatism led to a decline, culminating in the dynasty's overthrow by revolutionaries led by Sun Yat-sen.

Pinyin spellings are given here, following official adoption of the *Pinyin* system in 1979, with the older romanized forms in brackets.

HOLY ROMAN EMPERORS

Carolingian Kings and Emperors

Charlemagne, Charles the Great	800-14
Louis I, the Pious	814-40
Lothair I	840-55
Louis II	855-75
Charles II, the Bald	875-77
Charles III, the Fat	881-87
Guido of Spoleto	891-94
Lambert of Spoleto (co-emperor)	892-98
Arnulf (rival)	896-901
Louis III of Provence	901-5
Berengar	905-24
Conrad I of Franconia (rival)	911-18

Saxon Kings and Emperors

Henry I, the Fowler	918-36
Otto I, the Great	936-73
Otto II	973-83
Otto III	983-1002
Henry II, the Saint	1002-24

Franconian (Salian) Emperors

Conrad II	1024-39
Henry III, the Black	1039-56
Henry IV	1056-1106
Rudolf of Swabia (rival)	1077-80
Hermann of Luxembourg (rival)	1081-93
Conrad of Franconia (rival)	1093-1101
Henry V	1106-25
Lothair II	1126-37

Hohenstaufen Kings and Emperors

Conrad III	1138-52
Frederick I Barbarossa	1152-90
Henry VI	1190-97
Otto IV	1198-1215
Philip of Swabia (rival)	1198-1208
Frederick II	1215-50
Henry Raspe of Thuringia (rival)	1246-47
William of Holland (rival)	1247-56
Conrad IV	1250-54
The Great Interrugnum	1254-73

Rulers from Various Noble Families

Richard of Cornwall (rival)	1257-72
Alfonso X of Castile (rival)	1257-73
Rudolf I, Hapsburg	1273-91
Adolf I of Nassau	1292-98
Albert I, Hapsburg	1298-1303
Henry VII, Luxembourg	1308-13
Louis IV of Bavaria	1314-47
Frederick of Hapsburg (co-regent)	1314-25
Charles IV, Luxembourg	1347-78
Wenceslas of Bohemia	1378-1400
Frederick III of Brunswick	1400
Rupert of the Palatinate	1400-10
Sigismund, Luxembourg	1411-37

Hapsburg Emperors

Albert II	1438-39
Frederick III	1440-93
Maximilian I	1493-1519
Charles V	1519-56
Ferdinand I	1556-64
Maximilian II	1564-76
Rudolf II	1576-1612
Matthais	1612-19
Ferdinand II	1619-37
Ferdinand III	1637-57
Leopold I	1658-1705
Joseph I	1705-11
Charles VI	1711-40
Charles VII of Bavaria	1742-45

Hapsburg-Lorraine Emperors

Francis I of Lorraine	1745-65
Joseph II	1765-90
Leopold II	1790-92
Francis II	1792-1806

ENGLISH SOVEREIGNS FROM 900

Dynasty	Name	Date	Title
West Saxon Kings	Edward the Elder	901	son of Alfred the Great
	Athelstan	925	son of Edward I
	Edmund	940	half-brother of Athelstan
	Edred	946	brother of Edmund
	Edwy	955	son of Edmund
	Edgar	959	brother of Edwy
	Edward the Martyr	975	son of Edgar
	Ethelred II	978	son of Edgar
	Edmund Ironside	1016	son of Ethelred
Danish Kings	Canute	1016	son of Sweyn
	Hardicanute	1040	son of Canute
	Harold I	1035	son of Canute
West Saxon Kings (restored)	Edward the Confessor	1042	son of Ethelred II
	Harold II	1066	son of Godwin
Norman Kings	William I	1066	
	William II	1087	son of William I
	Henry I	1100	son of William I
	Stephen	1135	son of Adela (daughter of William II)
House of Plantagenet	Henry II	1154	son of Matilda
	Richard I	1189	son of Henry II
	John	1199	son of Henry II
	Henry III	1216	son of John
	Edward I	1272	son of Henry III
	Edward II	1307	son of Edward I
	Edward III	1327	son of Edward II
	Richard II	1377	son of the Black Prince (son of Edward III)
House of Lancaster	Henry IV	1399	son of John of Gaunt
	Henry V	1413	son of Henry IV
	Henry VI	1422	son of Henry V
House of York	Edward IV	1461	son of Edward III
	Richard III	1483	brother of Edward IV
	Edward V	1483	son of Edward IV
House of Tudor	Henry VII	1485	son of Edward III
	Henry VIII	1509	son of Henry VII
	Edward VI	1547	son of Henry VIII
	Mary I	1553	daughter of Henry VIII
House of Stuart	Elizabeth I	1558	daughter of Henry VIII
	James I	1603	great-grandson of Margaret
The Commonwealth	Charles I	1625	son of James I
House of Stuart (restored)	Charles II	1660	son of Charles I
	James II	1685	son of Charles I

Dynasty	Name	Date	Title
	William III and Mary	1689	son of Mary (daughter of Charles I)/daughter of James II
	Anne	1702	daughter of James II
House of Hanover	George I	1714	son of Sophia (granddaughter of James I)
	George II	1727	son of George I
	George III	1760	son of Frederick (son of George II)
	George IV	1820	son of George III
	William IV	1830	son of George III
	Victoria	1837	daughter of Edward (son of George III)
House of Saxe-Coburg	Edward VII	1901	son of Victoria
House of Windsor	George V	1910	son of Edward VII
	Edward VIII	1936	son of George V
	George VI	1936	son of George V
	Elizabeth II	1952	daughter of George VI

FRANCE

Valois Kings

Philip VI	1328-50
John	1350-64
Charles V	1364-80
Charles VI	1380-1422
Charles VII	1422-61
Louis XI	1461-83
Charles VIII	1483-98
Louis XII	1498-1515
Francis I	1515-47
Henry II	1547-59
Francis II	1559-60
Charles IX	1560-74
Henry III	1574-89

Bourbon Kings

Henry IV	1589-1610
Louis XIII	1610-43
Louis XIV	1643-1715
Louis XV	1715-74
Louis XVI	1774-93

ITALY

Vittorio Emanuele II	1861-78
Umberto I	1878-1900
Vittorio Emanuele III	1900-46
Umberto II	1946
	(*abdicated*)

AUSTRIA

Emperors

Franz II and I	1804-35
Ferdinand I	1835-48

Emperors of Austria-Hungary from 1867

Franz Josef	1848-1916
Karl	1916-18
	(*abdicated*)

RUSSIAN TSARS/TSARINA (EMPERORS/EMPRESSES) 1721-1917

Ivan IV ('the Terrible')	1547-84
Fyodor (Theodore) I	1584-98
(Regent: Boris Gudunov 1584-98)	
Irina (widow of Fyodor I)	1598
Boris Gudunov	1598-1605
Fyodor (Theodore) II	1605
Dmitri (Dimitri) III	1605-6
Vasily (Basil) IV	1606-10
Mikhail (Michael) Romanov	1613-45
Aleksei (Alexis)	1645-76
Fyodor (Theodore) III	1676-82
Pyotr I ('Peter the Great')/Ivan V (brothers)	1682-96
(Regent: Sophia Aleksevna 1682-89)	
Pyotr I ('Peter the Great'), Tsar	1689-1721,
Emperor	1721-25
Ekaterina (Catherine)I, (widow of Pyotr I)	1725-27
Pyotr (Peter) II	1727-30
Anna Ivanovna	1730-40
Ivan VI	1440-41
(Regents: Ernst Biron 1740; Anna Leopoldovna 1740-41)	
Elisaveta (Elizabeth)	1741-62
Pyotr (Peter) III	1762
Ekaterina II ('Catherine the Great'), (widow of Pyotr III)	1762-96
Pavel (Paul) I,	1796-1801
Aleksandr (Alexander) I	1801-25
Nikolai (Nicholas) I)	1825-55
Aleksandr (Alexander) II	1855-81
Aleksandr (Alexander) III	1881-94
Nikolai (Nicholas) II	1894-1917

BRITISH PRIME MINISTERS

Sir Robert Walpole	(Whig)	1721
Earl of Wilmington	(Whig)	1742
Henry Pelham	(Whig)	1743
Duke of Newcastle	(Whig)	1754
Duke of Devonshire	(Whig)	1756
Duke of Newcastle	(Whig)	1757
Earl of Bute	(Tory)	1762
George Grenville	(Whig)	1763
Marquess of Rockingham	(Whig)	1765
Duke of Grafton	(Whig)	1766
Lord North	(Tory)	1770
Marquess of Rockingham	(Whig)	1782
Earl of Shelburne	(Whig)	1782
Duke of Portland	(Coalition)	1783
William Pitt	(Tory)	1783
Henry Addington	(Tory)	1801
William Pitt	(Tory)	1804
Lord Grenville	(Whig)	1806
Duke of Portland	(Tory)	1807
Spencer Perceval	(Tory)	1809
Earl of Liverpool	(Tory)	1812
George Canning	(Tory)	1827
Viscount Goderich	(Tory)	1827
Duke of Wellington	(Tory)	1828
Earl Grey	(Whig)	1830
Viscount Melbourne	(Whig)	1834
Sir Robert Peel	(Conservative)	1834
Viscount Melbourne	(Whig)	1835
Sir Robert Peel	(Conservative)	1841
Lord J Russell	(Liberal)	1846
Earl of Derby	(Conservative)	1852
Lord Aberdeen	(Peelite)	1852
Viscount Palmerston	(Liberal)	1855
Earl of Derby	(Conservative)	1858
Viscount Palmerston	(Liberal)	1859
Lord J Russell	(Liberal)	1865
Earl of Derby	(Conservative)	1866
Benjamin Disraeli	(Conservative)	1868
W E Gladstone	(Liberal)	1886
Benjamin Disraeli	(Conservative)	1874
W E Gladstone	(Liberal)	1880
Marquess of Salisbury	(Conservative)	1885
W E Gladstone	(Liberal)	1886
Marquess of Salisbury	(Conservative)	1886

W E Gladstone	(Liberal)	1892
Earl of Rosebery	(Liberal)	1894
Marquess of Salisbury	(Conservative)	1895
A J Balfour	(Conservative)	1902
Sir H Campbell-Bannerman	(Liberal)	1905
H H Asquith	(Liberal)	1908
H H Asquith	(Coalition)	1915
D Lloyd George	(Coalition)	1916
A Bonar Law	(Conservative)	1922
Stanley Baldwin	(Conservative)	1923
Ramsay MacDonald	(Labour)	1924
Stanley Baldwin	(Conservative)	1924
Ramsay MacDonald	(Labour)	1929
Ramsay MacDonald	(National)	1931
Stanley Baldwin	(National)	1935
N Chamberlain	(National)	1937
Sir Winston Churchill	(Coalition)	1940
Clement Attlee	(Labour)	1945
Sir Winston Churchill	(Conservative)	1951
Sir Anthony Eden	(Conservative)	1955
Harold Macmillan	(Conservative)	1957
Sir Alec Douglas-Home	(Conservative)	1963
Harold Wilson	(Labour)	1964
Edward Heath	(Conservative)	1970
Harold Wilson	(Labour)	1974
James Callaghan	(Labour)	1976
Margaret Thatcher	(Conservative)	1979

PRESIDENTS OF THE UNITED STATES OF AMERICA

Name	*Party*	*Took Office*
1. George Washington	(Federalist)	1789
2. John Adams	(Federalist)	1797
3. Thomas Jefferson	(Democratic Republican)	1801
4. James Madison	(Democratic Republican)	1809
5. James Monroe	(Democratic Republican)	1817
6. John Quincy Adams	(Democratic Republican)	1825
7. Andrew Jackson	(Democratic)	1829
8. Martin Van Buren	(Democrat)	1837
9. William Henry Harrison	(Whig)	1841
10. John Tyler	(Whig)	1841
11. James Knox Polk	(Democrat)	1845
12. Zachary Taylor	(Whig)	1849
13. Millard Fillmore	(Whig)	1850
14. Franklin Pierce	(Democrat)	1853
15. James Buchanan	(Democrat)	1857
16. Abraham Lincoln	(Republican)	1861
17. Andrew Johnson	(Democrat)	1865
18. Ulysses Simpson Grant	(Republican)	1869
19. Rutherford Birchard Hayes	(Republican)	1877
20. James Abram Garfield	(Republican)	1881
21. Chester Alan Arthur	(Republican)	1881
22. Grover Cleveland	(Democrat)	1885
23. Benjamin Harrison	(Republican)	1889
24. Grover Cleveland	(Democrat)	1893
25. William McKinley	(Republican)	1897
26. Theodore Roosevelt	(Republican)	1901
27. William Howard Taft	(Republican)	1909
28. Woodrow Wilson	(Democrat)	1913
29. Warren Gamaliel Harding	(Republican)	1921
30. Calvin Coolidge	(Republican)	1923
31. Herbert C Hoover	(Republican)	1929
32. Franklin Delano Roosevelt	(Democrat)	1933
33. Harry S Truman	(Democrat)	1945
34. Dwight D Eisenhower	(Republican)	1953
35. John F Kennedy	(Democrat)	1961
36. Lyndon B Johnson	(Democrat)	1963
37. Richard M Nixon	(Republican)	1969
38. Gerald R Ford	(Republican)	1974
39. James Earl Carter	(Democrat)	1977
40. Ronald Reagan	(Republican)	1981

Adenauer Konrad 1876–1967. Chancellor of West Germany 1949–63, known as the 'Old Fox'; with de Gaulle he achieved the postwar reconciliation of France and Germany.

Allende Gossens Salvador 1908–73. Chilean statesman. Elected president in 1970 as the candidate of the Popular Front alliance, Allende never succeeded in keeping the electoral alliance together in government. His failure to solve the country's economic problems or to deal with political subversion allowed the army to stage the 1973 coup which brought about Allende's death, and those of many of his supporters.

Amin Dada Idi 1926– . President of Uganda 1971–79. He led the coup which deposed Obote in 1971, expelled the Asian community in 1972, and exercised a reign of terror over his own people. He fled when 'rebel' Ugandan and Tanzanian troops invaded his country in 1979.

Andropov Yuri 1914–84. Soviet statesman. As ambassador to Hungary, he was involved in the suppression of the revolt in 1956, but is alleged to have opposed the invasion of Czechoslovakia in 1968 while head of the KGB 1967– May 1982. In Nov 1982 he succeeded Brezhnev as General Secretary of the Soviet Communist Party, becoming president in Jun 1983.

Aquino Maria Corazón ('Cory') 1933– . Philippine stateswoman, who became president 1986 after the overthrow of the Marcos régime.

Asquith Herbert Henry, 1st Earl of Oxford and Asquith 1852–1928. British Liberal statesman. He was Home Secretary in Gladstone's 1892–95 government, Chancellor of the Exchequer 1905–8 (when he introduced old age pensions), and prime minister from 1908. Forcing through the radical budget of his Chancel-

lor (Lloyd George) led him into two elections in 1910, which resulted in the Parliament Act of 1911, limiting the right of the Lords to veto legislation. His endeavours to pass the Home Rule for Ireland Bill almost caused civil war. Unity was re-established by the outbreak of World War I, and a coalition government was formed in May 1915. In Dec 1916 he was replaced by Lloyd George.

Baldwin Stanley, 1st Earl Baldwin of Bewdley 1867–1947. British Conservative statesman. As Chancellor under Bonar Law, he achieved a settlement of war debts with the USA, and succeeded him as prime minister in 1923. He lost his clear majority after the general election of Dec 1923, and resigned on his defeat in the Commons in Jan 1924. During his second premiership, Oct 1924 to 1929, he weathered the General Strike 1926, but was badly defeated in the general election of May 1929. During his third premiership 1935–37, he handled the abdication crisis of Edward VIII, but was later much criticized for his failure to resist popular desire for an accommodation with Hitler and Mussolini, and failure to rearm more effectively.

Balfour Arthur James, 1st Earl of Balfour 1848–1930. British Conservative statesman. In 1902 he succeeded Salisbury as prime minister. His cabinet was divided over Joseph Chamberlain's Tariff Reform proposals, and at the 1905 elections he suffered a crushing defeat. Balfour retired from the party leadership in 1911. In 1915 he joined the Asquith coalition as 1st Lord of the Admiralty, and he was Foreign Secretary 1916–19; as such he issued the 'Balfour Declaration' of 1917 in favour of a national home in Palestine for the Jews and signed the Treaty of Versailles.

Banda Hastings Kamuzu 1905– . Malawian statesman. Once a student and medical practitioner in Britain, he led his country's independence movement, and was prime minister of Nyasaland from 1963, and first president of Malawi from 1966.

Bandaranaike Sirimavo 1916– . Sri Lankan stateswoman who succeeded her husband Solomon Bandaranaike to become the world's first woman prime minister 1960–65, 1970–77, but was expelled from parliament in 1980 for abuse of her powers while in office.

Bandaranaike Solomon West Ridgeway Dias 1899–1959. Sri Lankan statesman. An ardent nationalist he founded in 1951 the Sri Lanka Freedom Party and in 1956 became prime minister, pledged to a socialist programme and a neutral foreign policy. He failed to satisfy extremists and was assassinated by a Buddhist monk.

Begin Menachem 1913- . Israeli statesman, born in Poland. He was a leader of the extremist Irgun Zvai Leumi organisation in Palestine from 1942; he was prime minister of Israel 1977-83, as head of the right-wing Likud, and in 1978 shared a Nobel peace prize with Sadat for work on the Camp David Agreement.

Ben Bella Ahmed 1916- . Algerian leader of the National Liberation Front (FLN) from 1952; he was prime minister of independent Algeria 1962–65, when he was overthrown by Boumédienne and detained till 1980. He founded a new party, Mouvement pour la Démocratie en Algérie 1985.

Beneš Eduard 1884–1948. Czech statesman. President of the Republic from 1935 until forced to resign by the Germans, he headed a government-in-exile in London during World War II. Returning home as president in 1945, he was again forced to resign when the Communists gained control in 1948.

Ben Gurion David 1886–1973. Israeli statesman, the country's first prime minister 1948–53, 1955–63.

Bevan Aneurin 1897–1960. British Labour statesman. Son of a Welsh miner, and himself a miner at 13, he became member of parliament for Ebbw Vale 1929–60. As Minister of Health 1945–51, he inaugurated the National Health Service, and was Minister of Labour Jan–Apr 1951, when he resigned (with Harold Wilson) on the introduction of Health Service charges, and led a faction against the government.

Bevin Ernest 1881–1951. British Labour statesman. Chief creator of the Transport and General Workers' Union, he was its General

Secretary 1921–40, when he entered the War Cabinet as Minister of Labour and National Service. He organized the 'Bevin boys', chosen by ballot to work in the coal mines as war service, and was Foreign Secretary in the Labour government 1945–51.

Bhutto Zulfikar Ali 1928–79. Pakistani statesman, who was president 1971–73, and then prime minister until the 1977 military coup. In 1978 he was sentenced to death for conspiracy to murder a political opponent, and was hanged. His followers, led by his daughter *Benazir Bhutto,* continue in opposition to the new regime.

Bismarck Otto Eduard Leopold, Prince von Bismarck 1815–98. German statesman. Ambitious to establish Prussia's hegemony inside Germany and eliminate the influence of Austria, he became Foreign Minister in 1862. He secured Austria's support for his successful war of 1863–64 against Denmark, then in 1866 went to war against Austria and her allies, his victory forcing Austria out of the German Bund, and unifying the N German states in the N German Confederation under his own chancellorship in 1867. He then defeated France, under Napoleon III, in the Franco-Prussian War of 1870, proclaimed the German Empire in 1871, and annexed Alsace-Lorraine, He tried to secure his work by a Triple Alliance 1881 with Austria and Italy, but ran into difficulties at home with the Roman Catholic church and the socialist movement, and was dismissed by William II in 1890.

Bokassa Marshal Jean Bédel 1921- . Central African Republic politician. As army commander-in-chief 1963-79, he took power in a military coup 1965, and was both presidents 1966-79 and prime minister 1966-75. In 1976 his country's name was changed to the Central African Empire and he was proclaimed Emperor Bokassa I. Self-crowned in 1977, at a ceremony widely criticized for its extravagance, he was overthrown in a coup in 1979, and the country resumed the name Central African Republic. Sentenced to death in his absence, he lives in exile in France.

Boumédienne Houari. Adopted name of

Algerian statesman Mohammed Boukharouba 1925–78, who brought Ben Bella to power by a revolt in 1962, and superseded him as president 1965–78 by a further coup.

Brandt Willy 1913– . German statesman, an anti-Nazi active in the resistance movement, he became mayor of West Berlin, and was Federal Chancellor 1969–74, when one of his aides was found to be an East German spy. His Ostpolitik led to treaties with the USSR and Poland and a 'Basic Treaty' between East and West Germany, and he won a Nobel peace prize in 1971. He became chairman of the 'Brandt Commission' on international development in 1977, publishing reports on relations between the rich Northern Hemisphere and the poor South in 1980 and 1983, calling for urgent action. He was a Euro-MP 1979-83.

Brezhnev Leonid Ilyich 1906-82. Russian statesman. President of the USSR 1960-64, he ousted Kruschev, succeeding him as Secretary of the Soviet Communist Party, in Oct 1964, and from 1977 was the first to combine both offices.

Callaghan (Leonard) James 1912– . British Labour statesman. He was Home Secretary 1967–70, and as Foreign Secretary 1974–76 renegotiated Britain's entry to the Common Market. Succeeding as prime minister on Wilson's resignation in 1976, he entered into a pact with the Liberals in 1977 to maintain his government in office, but lost the election in May 1979, and in 1980 resigned the party leadership under left-wing pressure.

Carter 'Jimmy' (James Earl) 1924– . Democratic president of the USA 1977–81. Born in Plains, Georgia, he served in the navy, studied nuclear physics, and after a spell as a peanut farmer entered politics as a Democrat in 1953. In 1976 he narrowly wrested the presidency from Ford. Features of his presidency were the Panama Treaty, the Camp David Agreements, and the Iranian seizure of American Embassy hostages. He was defeated by Reagan in 1980.

Castro Ruz Fidel 1927– . Cuban revolutionary and statesman. He gathered an army of over 5,000 which overthrew the dictator Batista in 1959 and became prime minister of Cuba a few months later. He became president in 1976, and in 1979 also president of the Non-Aligned Movement. His brother Raúl was appointed Minister of Armed forces in 1959.

Cavour Camillo Benso, Count 1810–61. Italian statesman. Prime Minister of Piedmont 1852–59 and 1860–61, he enlisted the support of Britain and France for the concept of a united Italy, achieved in 1861.

Chamberlain (Arthur) Neville 1869–1940. British Conservative statesman. He succeeded Baldwin in the premiership in 1937, and attempted to 'appease' the demands of the dictators in Europe. When in 1938 he returned from Munich, having negotiated with Hitler the settlement of the Czechoslovak question, he claimed to have brought 'peace with honour'. Soon, however, he agreed that he had been tricked, and when Britain declared war on 3 Sept 1939, he summoned the people to fight the 'evil things' that Hitler stood for.

Chernenko Konstantin 1911–85. Soviet statesman, a specialist in political propaganda, and protégé of Brezhnev. Defeated in the immediate power struggle after Brezhnev's death, he succeeded Andropov as party leader Feb 1984–Mar 1985, the briefest ever tenure of the leadership.

Chiang Kai-shek or *Jiang Jie Shi* 1887-1975. Chinese statesman. He took part in the Revolution of 1911, and after the death of Sun Yat-Sen was made commander-in-chief of the Guomindang armies in S China in 1925. He nominally headed the struggle against the Japanese invaders, receiving the Japanese surrender in 1945. Civil War then resumed between Communists and Nationalists, and ended in the defeat of Chiang in 1949, and the limitation of his rule to Taiwan.

Chirac Jacques 1932– . French statesman. Prime minister under Giscard d'Estaing 1974–76, he resigned after differences with him, and was a presidential candidate himself in 1981. He again became prime minister in 1986 under Mitterrand.

Churchill Sir Winston Leonard Spencer

1874–1965. British Conservative statesman. Entering parliament in 1900, he was Home Secretary 1910–11, and First Lord of the Admiralty 1911–15. His sponsorship of the Gallipoli operation led to his exclusion from the first coalition government of 1915, but he was Minister of Munitions under Lloyd George in 1917, when he was concerned with the development of the tank. As Secretary for War 1918–21 he was active in support of White opposition to the Bolsheviks in Russia, then as Chancellor under Baldwin 1924 he returned Britain to the gold standard and was prominent in the defeat of the General Strike of 1926. He was out of office from 1929 until he returned to the Admiralty on the outbreak of World War II, and on 10 May 1940 succeeded Chamberlain in the premiership, making his historic 'blood and tears, toil and sweat' speech to the Commons on 13 May. His coalition government conducted the war in alliance with the USSR and USA, but was defeated in the general election of 1945. He returned to power 1951–55.

de Gaulle Charles 1890–1970. French statesman. In 1940 he refused to accept Pétain's truce with the Germans, and became leader of the Free French in England. In 1944 he entered Paris in triumph and was briefly head of the provisional government before resigning in protest at the defects of the new constitution of the Fourth Republic in 1946. When bankruptcy and civil war loomed in 1958 he was called to form a government, promulgated a constitution subordinating the legislature to the presidency and in 1959 became president (re-elected 1965). He quelled the student-worker unrest of 1968, but in 1969 resigned after the defeat of the government in a referendum on constitutional reform.

Disraeli Benjamin Earl of Beaconsfield 1804–81. British Conservative statesman. Born a Jew, he was baptized a Christian at 13. He was Chancellor of the Exchequer, under Derby as prime minister, in a series of minority governments 1852, 1858–9, and 1866–8, taking over as prime minister just before the Conservative electoral defeat of 1868. In opposition, he established the Conservative Central

Office, the prototype of the modern party organization. In 1874 he became prime minister with a landslide majority, bought a controlling interest in the Suez Canal in 1875, made Queen Victoria Empress of India in 1876, brought home 'peace with honour' from the Congress of Berlin in 1878, and 'duelled' with Gladstone on foreign policy; he retired on his electoral defeat in 1880. He established the Conservative Party as one for which the working man, whom he enfranchised in 1867, might vote.

Dubček Alexander 1921– . Czech statesman. As First Secretary of the Communist Party 1967–69, he launched a liberalization campaign. He was arrested by invading Soviet troops, and expelled from the party in 1970.

Eden Anthony, 1st Earl of Avon 1897–1977. British Conservative politician. In 1935 he became Foreign Secretary, resigning in Feb 1938 in protest against Chamberlain's decision to open conversations with Mussolini. He was Foreign Secretary again Dec 1940–45 and 1951–Apr 1955, when he succeeded Churchill as prime minister. He negotiated an interim peace in Vietnam 1954. His military intervention in Suez led to his resignation in Jan 1957.

Eisenhower Dwight David ('Ike') 1890–1969. Republican president of the USA 1953-61, born in Denison, Texas. In World War II he was sent to England in Jun 1942 as US Commander, European theatre; became commander-in-chief of the American and British forces for the invasion of N Africa Nov 1942; commanded the Allied invasion of Sicily Jul 1943, and announced the surrender of Italy on 8 Sept 1943. In Dec he became commander of the Allied invasion of Europe, and from Oct 1944 commanded all the Allied armies in the West. He resigned from the army in 1952 to campaign for the presidency as a Republican; he was elected, and re-elected in 1956.

Farouk 1920–65. Last king of Egypt, son of Fuad; compelled to abdicate by a military coup in 1952, his little son Fuad was briefly proclaimed in his stead.

Franco Bahamonde Francisco 1892–1975. Spanish dictator. Born in Galicia, he became chief of staff in 1935, but in 1936 was demoted to governor of the Canary Islands, and so plotted an uprising (with German and Italian assistance) against the Republican government. As leader of the insurgents (Nationalists) during the Spanish Civil War, he proclaimed himself *Caudillo* (leader) of Spain, and the defeat of the Republic in 1939 brought all Spain under his rule. During World War II he observed a cautious general neutrality, and as head of state for life from 1947 slightly liberalized his regime. In 1969 he nominated as his successor and future king of Spain, Juan Carlos; he relinquished the premiership in 1973, and by his death had presided over considerable economic growth.

Gandhi Indira 1917–84. Indian stateswoman and prime minister of India 1966–77, 1980–84. A daughter of Nehru, she married in 1942 Feroze Gandhi (died 1960), not related M K Gandhi, and had two sons, *Sanjay Gandhi* 1946–80, who died in an air crash, and Rajiv andhi. She became leader of the Congress Party and prime minister in 1966. In 1975 her election to parliament was declared invalid and she declared a state of emergency. During this time her son, Sanjay, was implementing a social and economic programme (including a ruthless family planning policy) which led to her defeat in 1977, though he masterminded her return to power in 1980. She was assassinated by members of her Sikh bodyguard, resentful of her use of troops to clear malcontents from the temple at Amritsar.

Gandhi Mohandas Karamchand 1869–1948. Indian leader, called Mahatma ('Great Soul'). Born in Porbandar, he studied in London, and then led the Indian community in South Africa in opposition to racial discrimination. Returning to India in 1915, he led the struggle for Indian independence by 'non-violent non-cooperation' (*satyagraha*, defence of and by truth), which included several 'fasts unto death'. He was several times imprisoned by the British authorities, was influential in the Congress (nationalist) Party, and in the independence negotiations in 1947. His fasts were less effective against his fellow countrymen, and he

was assassinated by a Hindu nationalist in the violence which followed Partition.

Gandhi Rajiv 1945– . Indian statesman, son of Indira Gandhi. He was an airline pilot, but became political adviser to his mother on the death of his brother Sanjay. He entered parliament in 1981, and in 1984 succeeded his mother as prime minister. In 1985 he reached a political settlement with the moderate Sikhs.

Garibaldi Giuseppe 1807–82. Italian soldier. A follower of Mazzini, he fled abroad after condemnation to death for treason. Returning during the revolution of 1848, he served with the Sardinians against the Austrians, and led the army of the Roman Republic in defending the city against the French. In 1860, at the head of his 1,000 Redshirts, he conquered Sicily and Naples for the new kingdom of Italy.

Giscard d'Estaing Valéry 1926 . French Independent Republican statesman, Minister of Finance under de Gaulle 192-66 and Pompidou from 1969, succeeding the latter as president 1974-81, when he was defeated by Mitterrand.

Gladstone William Ewart 1809–98. British Liberal statesman. He was Chancellor of the Exchequer 1852–55 and 1859–66. As prime minister 1868–74 he carried through the disestablishment of the Church of Ireland, the Irish Land Act, the abolition of the purchase of army commissions and of religious tests in the universities, the introduction of elementary education and of vote by ballot. Returning to office in 1886, Gladstone introduced his Irish Home Rule Bill, which was defeated by the secession of the Liberal Unionists, and he thereupon resigned. He formed his last government in 1892, resigning after the Lords' rejection of his second Home Rule Bill.

González (Márquez) Felipe 1942- . Spanish statesman. A lawyer, he joined the Spanish Socialist Party in 1964 and opened the first labour law office to deal with workers' problems in 1966. He became prime minister of Spain in 1982.

Gorbachev Mikhail Sergeievich 1931– . Soviet statesman, born in the N Caucasus. A

Moscow law graduate, he became a Komsomol official, and was in charge of agriculture 1978–84. A Politburo member from 1980, he was groomed for power by Andropov, and became Chairman of the Foreign Affairs Committee in 1984. He succeeded Chernenko as party leader in 1985, becoming known for his policy of *glasnost*, or openness.

Gowon Yakubu 1934– . Nigerian head of state, by a military coup, 1966–75. After the Biafran Civil War 1967–70, he reunited the country with a policy of 'no victor, no vanquished'.

Heath Edward Richard George 1916– . British Conservative statesman. He succeeded Home as leader of the party in 1965 (the first elected leader), and though defeated in 1966 achieved a surprise victory in the general election of 1970. A miners' strike, resulting from his attempt to control inflation (including wages), led to his narrow inconclusive defeat in Feb 1974, and defeat by a larger margin in Oct 1974. This resulted in his replacement in the leadership by Margaret Thatcher.

Hitler Adolf 1889–1945. German dictator, born at Braunau-am-Inn, Austria. He served in World War I, founded the Nazi Party in 1921, and after a failed rising in 1923 (Munich Putsch), spent nine months in prison, writing *Mein Kampf/My Struggle*. Supported by the industrialists from 1930, Hitler became chancellor in 1933, and succeeded Hindenburg as Head of State (with the title of *Führer*) in 1934. In 1936 he occupied the Rhineland; 1937 allied himself with Mussolini; 1938 annexed Austria and secured the Sudetenland (under the Munich Agreement); 1939 annexed the rest of Czechoslovakia in Mar, signed a non-aggression pact with Russia in Aug, and invaded Poland (with resultant declaration of war by Britain and France) in Sept. Hitler narrowly escaped assassination in 1944 in a bomb plot by high-ranking officers and on 29 Apr 1945 married Eva Braun and committed suicide with her in a Berlin bunker as the Russians took the city.

Ho Chi Minh 1892-1969. North Vietnamese statesman. He headed the Communist Viet-

minh from 1941, campaigned against the French colonial rulers 1946–54, and became president of North Vietnam on its independence.

Home Alex Douglas-Home, Baron Home of the Hirsel 1903– . British Conservative statesman. Foreign Secretary 1960–63, when he succeeded Macmillan as prime minister, he renounced his peerage (as 14th Earl of Home) to fight (and lose) the general election of 1964; he resigned as party leader in 1965. He was again Foreign Secretary 1970–74, when he received a life peerage.

Honecker Erich 1912– . East German statesman, a security specialist, who became first secretary of the East German Communist Party in 1971, and chairman of the Council of State (that is, head of state) in 1976.

Jinnah Mohammed Ali 1876–1948. Indian statesman, president of the Muslim League from 1916, who insisted in 1946 on the partition of British India into Indian and Muslim states. He became first governor-general of Pakistan 1947–48.

Johnson Lyndon Baines 1908–73. Democratic President of the USA 1963–69; born in Texas. He stood as vice-president in 1960, so bringing crucial Southern votes to Kennedy, then succeeded him. After the Tonkin Gulf incident, he made the first escalation of the Vietnam War, which eventually dissipated the support won by his Great Society legislation (civil rights, education, alleviation of poverty), so that he declined the presidential nomination in 1968 after failing to end the war.

Kaunda Kenneth David 1924– . Zambian statesman. Imprisoned in 1958 as founder of the Zambia African National Congress (released 1960), he became in 1964 first prime minister of N Rhodesia, then first president of Zambia. From 1973 he introduced one-party rule.

Kennedy John Fitzgerald 1917–63. Democratic President of the USA 1961-63. In 1960 he defeated Nixon for the presidency, the first Roman Catholic and the youngest man to be elected, and surrounded himself with the academics and intellectuals of the New Frontier.

In foreign policy he carried through the unsuccessful Bay of Pigs invasion of Cuba, and in 1963 secured the withdrawal of Soviet missiles from the island. His programme for reforms at home was posthumously executed by Lyndon Johnson. He married Jaqueline Lee Bouvier (1929–) in 1953. Kennedy was assassinated 22 Nov 1963, on a visit to Dallas, by Lee Harvey Oswald, who was in turn shot dead by Jack Ruby. Kennedy's sensational death when still young helped to accord him legendary status.

Kenyatta Jomo. Name assumed by Kenyan politician Kamau Ngengi c. 1889–1978, *Kenyatta* meaning 'beaded belt'. A Kikuyu, he spent some years in Britain, and in 1946 returned to Kenya as president of the Kenya African Union, agitating for independence. In 1953 he was sentenced to seven years' imprisonment for his management of the Mau-Mau uprising, though some doubt remains on his complicity. In 1963 he became prime minister (president 1964–78) of independent Kenya.

Khomeini Ayatollah Ruhollah 1900– . Shi'ite Muslim leader, born in Khomein. Exiled for opposition to the Shah from 1964, he returned in 1979 to establish a fundamentalist Islamic republic.

Khrushchev Nikita Sergeyevich 1894–1971. Soviet statesman. As Secretary-General of the official party 1953–64, he denounced Stalinism in a secret session of the Soviet Communist Party in Feb 1956, initiating the 'thaw' in attitudes; many 1930s purge victims were released or posthumously rehabilitated. However, the Hungarian revolt of Oct 1956 was ruthlessly suppressed. Having ousted Bulganin, he also took over as prime minister 1958, and pursued a policy of peaceful co-existence and competition with capitalism. However, he developed a feud with Mao Zedong of China. In 1963 he despatched nuclear missiles to Cuba which had to be withdrawn under US pressure. He was consequently compelled to resign in 1964.

Kissinger Henry 1923– . American politician. He was Nixon's assistant for National Security Affairs from 1969 (Secretary of State 1973–77). His secret missions to Peking and Moscow led to détente and Nixon's visits to both countries; and he shared a Nobel prize with Le Duc Tho for his Vietnam peace negotiations. He also actively pursued solutions to the Arab-Israeli, Angola, and Rhodesia crises, and in 1983 Reagan appointed him to head a bipartisan commission on Central America.

Kohl Helmut 1930– . West German statesman. Leader of the CDU (Christian Democratic Union)/CSU (Christian Social Union) from 1976, he succeeded Schmidt as chancellor in 1982, and was confirmed in office in the 1983 election. In 1986 he became West Germany's first chancellor to be under investigation while in office, for allegedly accepting bribes; the charges were later dropped.

Lee Kuan Yew 1923– . Singaporean politician. A third generation Straits Chinese, he studied law at Cambridge, became a founder member of the left-wing People's Action Party (PAP), and prime minister of Singapore from 1959, which he led out of the Malaysian Federation in 1965.

Lenin Pseudonym of Vladimir Ilich Ulyanov 1870–1924. Russian Marxist revolutionary leader. After 1900, he spent most of his time in Western Europe, emerging as the leader of the more radical Bolshevik section of Russian Social Democracy. Returning to Russia in Apr 1917 with German help, Lenin assumed control of the Bolshevik movement and was instrumental in organizing the coup of 6–7 Nov. From then until his death in 1924, he effectively controlled Russia, establishing Bolshevik rule and the beginnings of Communism. In addition he modified traditional Marxist doctrine to fit the objective conditions prevailing in Russia, a doctrine known as Marxism-Leninism, which became the basis of Communist ideology.

Lincoln Abraham 1809–65. Republican president of the USA 1861-65, born in Kentucky. Self-educated, he became a practising lawyer from 1837 at Springfield, Illinois, joined the new Republican Party, and was elected in 1860 on a minority vote. His refusal to evacuate Fort Sumter, Charleston, precipitated the war, in which his chief concern was the preservation of the Union from which the slave states had seceded. In 1863 he proclaimed the freedom of the slaves in Confederate territory, and made the Gettysburg Address, declaring the war aims of preserving a 'nation conceived in liberty, and dedicated to the proposition that all men are created equal' and ensuring that 'government of the people, by the people, for the people, shall not perish from the earth'. Re-elected 1864, he advocated a reconciliatory policy towards the south 'with malice towards none, with charity for all'. Five days after Lee's surrender, he was assassinated by a Confederate fanatic, John Wilkes Booth.

Lloyd George David, 1st Earl Lloyd-George 1863–1945. Welsh Liberal statesman. As Chancellor of the Exchequer 1908–15, he introduced old age pensions in 1908 and health and employment insurance in 1911. His 1909 budget (with graduated direct taxes and taxing land values) provoked the Lords to reject it, and resulted in the Act of 1911 limiting their powers. He was Minister of Munitions 1915–16, and succeeded Kitchener as War Minister in Jun 1916. In Dec there was an open breach between him and Asquith, and he became prime minister of a coalition government. As one of the 'Big Three', with Wilson and Clemenceau, he had a major role in the Versailles peace treaty which ended World War I. In the 1918 elections he achieved a huge majority over Labour and Asquith's followers, but high unemployment, intervention in the Russian Civil War, and use of the 'black and tans' in Ireland, eroded his support. Creation of the Irish Free State in 1921, and his dangerous pro-Greek policy against the Turks, led to withdrawal of the Conservatives and collapse of the coalition in 1922. He had become largely distrusted within his own party, and never regained power.

Louis Philippe 1773–1850. King of France 1830–48. Son of the Duke of Orleans (he was known, like him, as Philippe Egalité, from his early support of the 1792 Revolution). He fled into exile 1793–1814, but became king after the 1830 Revolution with the backing of the rich bourgeoisie. Corruption discredited his regime, and after his overthrow he escaped to England and died there.

Lumumba Patrice 1926–61. Congolese statesman, active in the independence movement, and first prime minister of independent Congo (now Zaïre) in 1960. He was deposed in a coup, and murdered.

MacDonald (James) Ramsay 1866–1937. British Labour statesman, son of a labourer. He helped to found the Labour Party, and was prime minister Jan–Oct 1924, when he was forced to resign on withdrawal of Liberal support. He again headed a minority government 1929–31, and, when this collapsed under the impact of the economic crisis, left the Labour Party to lead a National government with Conservative and Liberal backing. He resigned in 1935.

Machel Samora 1933–86. Mozambican leader from 1966 of the Frente de Libertação de Moçambique (Frelimo) against Portuguese rule, and president of Mozambique from 1975. He was killed in an air crash.

Macmillan (Maurice) Harold, Earl of Stockton 1894–1987. British Conservative statesman. He was Minister of Housing 1951–54, Defence 1954, Foreign Secretary 1955, and Chancellor 1955–57. He took over as prime minister on Eden's resignation after Suez, and by his realization of the 'wind of change' advanced the independence of former colonies in Africa. In 1959 he led the party to electoral victory with the slogan 'You have never had it so good' (in context a warning rather than a congratulation) but in 1962 dismissed seven cabinet colleagues in a re-shuffle, and was blocked by de Gaulle in an attempt to enter the Common Market in Jan 1963. In Jun the government was rocked by the Profumo affair, but a Nuclear Test Ban treaty was achieved in Aug before the Prime Minister's resignation in Nov owing to ill-health.

Makarios III 1913-77.Cypriot Orthodox archbishop 1950–77. Exiled by the British to the Seychelles 1956–57 for supporting armed action to achieve union with Greece, he was president of the Republic of Cyprus 1960–77 (briefly deposed by a Greek military coup Jul–Dec 1974).

Manley Michael 1924– . Jamaican statesman and prime minister 1972–80. The son of Norman Manley 1893–1969, founder of the Peoples National Party and prime minister 1959–62.

Mao Zedong or *Mao Tse-Tung* 1893–1976. Chinese statesman, who proclaimed the People's Republic of China in 1949. As Chairman of the Communist Party, he provided the pattern for the development of the country through the Great Leap Forward of 1959, and the Cultural Revolution of 1966 based on his thoughts contained in the 'Little Red Book'.

Marcos Ferdinand 1919– . Filipino statesman. Born on Luzon, he was convicted while a law student in 1939 of murdering a political opponent of his father, but eventually secured his own acquittal. In World War II he was a guerrilla fighter, survived prison camps of Bataan, and became president in 1965. His regime, backed by the USA, became increasingly repressive, with the use of 'secret marshals', anti-crime squads executing those only suspected of offences. Overthrown and exiled in 1986.

Mazzini Giuseppe 1805–72. Italian nationalist, born in Genoa and founder of the 'Young Italy' movement. Returning to Italy (after having been condemned to death in his absence by the Sardinian government) on the outbreak of 1848 Revolution, he headed a republican government established in Rome, but was forced into exile again on its overthrow. He acted as a focus for the concept of Italian unity.

Meir Golda 1898–1978. Israeli Labour (*Mapai*) politician. Foreign Minister 1956–66, and prime minister 1969–74, she resigned following criticism of Israeli unpreparedness in the 1973 Arab-Israeli War.

Mitterrand François 1916– . French socialist politician, who organized a joint left-wing front against de Gaulle and Giscard d'Estaing, defeating the latter in the presidential election of 1981. In office his policies were modified (the Communists left the government), and in 1985

his introduction of proportional representation was allegedly to weaken the growing opposition from left and right.

Mobutu Seso-Seko-Kuku-Ngbeandu-Wa-Za- nga (formerly Joseph-Désiré) 1930– . Zaïrean general who assumed the presidency by coup in 1965, and created a unitary state under his centralized government. He replaced secret voting in elections in 1976 by a system of acclamation at mass rallies.

Moi Daniel Arap 1924– . Kenyan statesman, president (following Kenyatta) from 1978.

Mugabe Robert Gabriel 1925– . Zimbabwean statesman. Under detention in Rhodesia for nationalist activities 1964–74, he then carried on guerrilla warfare from Mozambique (in alliance with Joshua Nkomo from 1976), and in 1980 became prime minister of independent Zimbabwe. In 1985 he postponed the introduction of a multi-party state for five years.

Mussolini Benito 1883–1945. Italian dictator. He founded the *fasci di combattimento* in 1919 (violently nationalist and anti-socialist) which attracted popular support, as well as that of landowners and industrialists. His Blackshirt followers were forerunners of Hitler's Brownshirts. In Oct 1922 he became prime minister with the backing of the king and the army, and having assumed dictatorial powers in 1925, *Il Duce* ('the leader') began a series of military ventures. In 1935–36, he successfully invaded Ethiopia; intervened in the Spanish Civil War to support France 1936–39; conquered Albania in 1939; and in Jun 1940 entered World War II in support of Hitler. Defeated in N Africa and Greece, and with Sicily invaded by the Allies, he was compelled to resign in Jul 1943 by his own Fascist Grand Council. German parachutists released him from prison in Sept, and set up a 'Republican Fascist' government in N Italy, but he was captured and hung upside down in Milan.

Napoleon III 1808–73. Emperor of the French. Son of Louis Bonaparte and Hortense de Beauharnais, brother and step-daughter respectively of Napoleon I, he led two unsuccessful revolts (Strasbourg 1836, Boulogne

1840). Imprisoned, he escaped to London in 1846, was elected president of the Republic in Dec 1848, and in 1852 proclaimed emperor. To strengthen his repressive regime, he joined in the Crimean War, fought Austria 1859 (winning the battle of Solferino near Lake Garda) and attempted to found a vassal empire in Mexico in 1863–67. In 1870 he was manoeuvred into war with Prussia, surrendered at Sedan, and went into exile in England.

Nasser Gamal Abdel 1918–70. Egyptian statesman. The driving power behind the Neguib coup in 1952 which ended the monarchy, he was prime minister in 1954–56 and president from 1956. He nationalized the Suez Canal.

Nehru Jawaharlal 1889–1964. Indian statesman. Born at Allahabad, and educated at Harrow and Cambridge, he led the Socialist left wing of the Congress Party, and was second only in influence to M K Gandhi. Nine times imprisoned 1921–45 for his political activities. He was prime minister from the creation of the Dominion (later Republic) of India in Aug 1947 until 1964, and originated the theory of non-alignment. He was the father of Indira Gandhi.

Nixon Richard Milhous 1913– . Republican president of the USA 1968–74, born in California. In 1948, as a member of the Un-American Activities Committee, he pressed for the investigation of Alger Hiss. He was vice-president to Eisenhower 1953–60, failed to defeat J F Kennedy for the presidency in 1960, but in a 'law and order' campaign defeated Vice-President Humphrey in 1968. He was re-elected in 1972 in a landslide victory and ended the US Vietnam commitment in 1973. In 1974 he was forced to resign, the first US president to do so, following the threat of impeachment on three counts: obstruction of the administration of justice in the investigation of Watergate; violation of constitutional rights of citizens; and failing to produce 'papers and things' as ordered by the Judiciary Committee. He was granted a controversial free pardon by President Ford.

Nkrumah Kwame 1909–72. Ghanaian statesman. He agitated for self-government, and was imprisoned in 1950, but became prime minister of the Gold Coast 1952–57, of Ghana 1957–60, and first president of the republic from 1960 until his dictatorial rule led to his deposition and exile in 1966. From 1973 he was 'rehabilitated'.

Nyerere Julius Kambarage 1922– . President of Tanganyika from 1962, and of Tanzania 1962–85. A Christian and dedicated socialist, he campaigned for independence from 1954, but led his country into financial difficulties. On resigning the presidency, he remained chairman of the ruling party.

Obote (Apollo) Milton 1924– . Ugandan statesman who led the independence movement from 1961. He became prime minister 1962, and was president 1966–71 and 1980–85, being overthrown successively by Amin and Okello.

Palme (Sven) Olof 1927-86. Swedish politician. A Social Democrat, he was prime minister 1969-76 and again from 1982 until his assassination in a Stockholm street in Feb 1986.

Pérez de Cuellar Javier 1920- . Peruvian diplomat. A delegate to the first UN General Assembly 1946-47, he held several ambassadorial posts and was appointed Secretary-General of the UN in 1982.

Perón Juan Domingo 1895–1974. Argentine leader of the Labour party and presidential dictator from 1946 to 1955, when he was deposed. He returned from exile to the presidency 1973, and was succeeded as president, until her overthrow in 1976, by his third wife *Maria Estela Isabel(ita)* 1930– .

Primo de Rivera Miguel 1870–1930. Spanish soldier-statesman, who effectively became dictator of Spain in 1923 with the support of Alfonso XIII, and instituted a number of reforms 1925–30.

Reagan Ronald 1911- . Republican president of the USA from 1981- . Governor of California 1967–74, he lost to Nixon in 1968 and Ford in 1974 in bids for the presidential nomination, but won a landslide victory against Carter 1980, and an even greater one against Mondale in 1984. He was wounded in an

assassination attempt in 1981, adopted an active policy in Central America, especially Nicaragua, and intervened in Lebanon and Grenada. His Strategic Defence Initiative (SDI) proved increasingly controversial.

Roosevelt Franklin D(elano) 1882–1945. Republican president of the USA 1933-45. He served as Governor of New York 1929–33, and in 1932 was elected president by a decisive margin in the midst of the Depression. His New Deal recovery programmes did not fully extract the country from the Depression, the number of jobless remaining high until World War II, but his introduction of Social Security, stock market regulation, minimum wage, insured bank deposits, etc., modified American life. He inculcated a new spirit of hope by his skilful 'Fireside Chats' on the radio to the nation, and his inaugural address statement, 'the only thing we have to fear is fear itself'. He achieved a sweeping victory in the presidential election of 1936, and broke a long-standing precedent by achieving a third term in 1940. He introduced 'lease-lend' for the supply of war materials to the Allies, making the USA the 'arsenal of democracy', and in 1941 drew up with Churchill the Atlantic Charter and defined the Four Freedoms. Following the Japanese attack on Pearl Harbor in Dec 1941, he devoted himself entirely to the war effort, and participated in the conferences of Casablanca, Quebec, Cairo, Tehran, and Yalta. He was re-elected for a fourth term in 1944, but died in office.

Sadat Anwar 1918-81. Egyptian statesman. Succeeding Nasser as president in 1970, he restored morale by his handling of the Egyptian campaign in the 1973 war against Israel. In 1977 he visited Israel to reconcile the countries, and shared a Nobel peace prize with Begin 1978. He was assassinated by the Islamic fundamentalists.

Schmidt Helmut 1918– . West German Social Democratic statesman, who succeeded Brandt as chancellor 1974–82. An 'Atlanticist', he supported NATO, but also pursued a modified Ostpolitik.

Smith Ian Douglas 1919– . Prime minister of Rhodesia (now Zimbabwe) 1964–79. He made a unilateral declaration of independence from Britain (UDI) 1965, maintaining it despite United Nations pressure and sanctions.

Stalin adopted name, meaning 'steel', of Russian statesman Joseph Vissarionovich Djugashvili 1879–1953. A Georgian, he became a Marxist and was many times exiled to Siberia under the Tsar. He became associated with Lenin and in 1917, as editor of *Pravda*, joined with him in the carrying out of the 'October Revolution'. Lenin, alarmed by Stalin's rapid consolidation of a powerful following (including Molotov), died before being able to remove him from the General-Secretaryship of the Communist Party. Stalin, who wanted to create 'Socialism in one country', now clashed with Trotsky, who denied the possibility of Socialism inside Russia until revolution had occurred in Western Europe. Stalin won this ideological struggle by 1927, and a series of five-year plans was launched to collectivize industry and agriculture from 1928. All opposition was eliminated by the Great Purge 1936–38, supposedly triggered by the assassination of Kirov, by which Stalin disposed of all real and fancied enemies. During World War II, Stalin became Chairman of the Council of People's Commissars and intervened in the military direction of the campaigns against Nazi Germany. After the war, he maintained a one-man rule of single-minded intensity. His rule was denounced after his death by Khrushchev.

Suharto 1921- .Indonesian general. He ousted Sukarno to become president in 1966, and was re-elected for the fourth time in 1983. He ended confrontation with Malaysia, invaded East Timor in 1975, and reached a co-operation agreement with Papua New Guinea 1979.

Sukarno Achmed 1901–70. Indonesian nationalist, who co-operated during World War II in the local administration set up by the Japanese, replacing Dutch rule. In 1945 he became president of the new Indonesian Republic, assuming the presidency for life 1966; he was ousted by Suharto 1967.

Thant U 1909–74. Burmese diplomat, Secretary-General of the United Nations 1962–71. He helped to resolve the US-Soviet crisis over the Soviet installation of missiles in Cuba, and made the controversial decision to withdraw the United Nations peacekeeping force from the Egypt-Israel border 1967 during Arab-Israeli Wars.

Thatcher Margaret 1925– . British Conservative politician. She entered parliament in 1959, was Minister of Education 1970–74, defeated Heath for the Conservative leadership in 1975, and became prime minister in 1979, her government being re-elected in 1983 and 1987. Landmarks of the administration include the independence of Zimbabwe, the Falklands conflict, reduction of inflation, large-scale privatization, the Anglo-Irish Agreement of 1985, but also a large rise in unemployment.

Trotsky Leon Davidovitch. Assumed name of Russian revolutionary Lev D Bronstein 1879–1940. Russian Communist theorist, agitator, and collaborator with Lenin after the two met in exile in London in 1902. Trotsky was a leading member of the Bolshevik movement in 1917 and was instrumental in building up the Red Army to the point where it could win the Civil War. He was ousted in 1924 during the power struggle which followed Lenin's death, but he remained active in opposing Stalin's rule until he was assassinated in 1940.

Truman Harry S 1884–1972. Democrat president of the USA 1945–53. In Jan 1945 he became vice-president to Roosevelt, succeeding him in the presidency in Apr, and in 1948 was elected for a second term in a surprise victory over Thomas Dewey. He used the atom bomb against Japan to shorten World War II; launched the Marshall Plan to restore West Europe's economy; nurtured the European Community, NATO (including the rearmament of W Germany), an independent Israel, and the lines of 'containment' in Europe and Asia (called the Truman Doctrine). In Korea, he intervened when the South was invaded, but sacked General Macarthur when the General's policy threatened to start World War III.

Truman's decision not to enter Chinese territory, betrayed by Kim Philby, led to China's entry into the war.

Ulbricht Walter 1893–1973. East German statesman. An exile in the USSR during the Nazi era, he was from 1950 First Secretary of the Socialist Unity Party in East Germany and as Chairman of the Council of State 1960–73, built the Berlin Wall in 1961 and established East Germany's economy and recognition outside the E European bloc.

Waldheim Kurt 1918– . Austrian diplomat. He was Foreign Minister 1968–70, and in 1971 succeeded U Thant as Secretary-General of the United Nations. Elected president of Austria 1986.

Weizmann Chaim 1874–1952. First president of Israel, born in Russia. As a Zionist, he negotiated the Balfour Declaration, becoming first president of Israel 1948–52.

Wilson (James) Harold, Baron Wilson 1916– . British Labour statesman. In 1963 he succeeded Gaitskell as Labour leader. He was prime minister 1964–70 (increasing his majority in 1966) and (following elections) formed a minority government in Feb 1974 and achieved a majority of three in Oct 1974. He resigned in 1976, to be succeeded by Callaghan. His premiership was dominated by the issue of UK admission to EEC membership, the Social Contract, and economic difficulties.

Wilson (Thomas) Woodrow 1856–1924. Democratic president of the USA 1913–21, born at Staunton, Virginia. He was forced to declare war on Germany by the U-boat campaign in 1917 (calling it the 'war to end war'), and in Jan 1918 issued 'Fourteen Points' as a basis for peace, his plan for a League of Nations being incorporated into the Treaty of Versailles, but failed to get the Senate to accept the twin package. His aim was 'open covenants, openly arrived at'.

Zia-ul-Haq Mohammad 1924– . Pakistani general and statesman. Chief martial law administrator in 1977 (president from 1978), following the overthrow of Bhutto. He had Bhutto executed, and introduced a fundamentalist Islamic regime.

Economics

Economics seeks to understand how, in a given society, choices are made on the allocation of resources to produce goods and services for consumption, and what mechanisms and principles govern this process. It seeks to apply scientific method to construct theories about the economic process and to test them against what actually happens. Within this broad framework, economics has two central concerns: the efficient allocation of available resources, and the problem of reconciling finite resources with a virtually infinite desire for goods and services. Economics investigates efficient allocation by analysing the ingredients of economic efficiency in the production process, and the implications for practical policies. The economic problem of reconciling scarce resources (for all resources are by definition scarce unless they cost nothing, which virtually nothing does) and limitless demand is studied by examining the conflicting demands and the consequences of whatever choices are made, whether by individuals, enterprises, or governments. Crucial to economics is the concept of opportunity cost, which defines the cost of a particular choice not in terms of money but rather in terms of the value of those options not chosen.

This section contains an introduction to the major *Spheres of Economics*, brief biographies of some of the *Great Economists*, an outline of some important *Economic Institutions*, and short definitions of *Terms*.

Spheres of Economics

divisions of economics the subject is usually divided into the disciplines of *microeconomics*, studying individual producers, consumers or markets, and *macroeconomics*, studying whole economies or systems. These spheres often overlap, but in practice it is useful to distinguish between the two main levels at which economic phenomena are studied.

Straddling both spheres is the sub-discipline of *econometrics*, which analyses economic relationships using mathematical and statistical techniques. Increasingly sophisticated econometric methods are today being used for such topics as economic forecasting.

Economics aims to be either *positive*, presenting objective and scientific explanations of how an economy works, or *normative*, offering prescriptions and recommendations on what should be done to cure perceived ills. However, it is important to remember that however objective the aim, value judgements are usually involved when economists present particular formulations.

microeconomics the study of individual decision-making units within an economy: a consumer, firm, or industry. It looks at how individual markets work and how individual producers and consumers make their choices and with what consequences. This is done by analysing how relevant prices of goods are determined and the quantities that will be bought and sold.

The operation of the market is therefore a central concern of microeconomics. For simplicity, microeconomics begins by analysing a market in which there is perfect *competition*, a theoretical state which exists only when no individual producer or consumer can influence the market price. In the real world, there is always imperfect competition for various reasons (monopoly practices, barriers to trade, and so on), and microeconomics examines what effect these have on wages and prices.

Underlying these and other concerns of microeconomics is the concept of *optimality*, first advanced by Vilfredo Pareto in the 19th century. Pareto's perception of the most efficient state of an economy, as being when there is no scope to reallocate resources without making someone worse off, has been extremely influential.

macroeconomics the study of whole (aggregate) economies or systems, including such aspects as government income and expenditure, the balance of payments, fiscal policy, inflation, and unemployment. It seeks to understand the influence of all relevant economic factors on each other and thus to quantify and predict aggregate national income.

Modern macroeconomics takes much of its inspiration from the work of Keynes, whose *The General Theory of Employment, Interest and Money* 1936 proposed that governments could prevent financial crises and unemployment by adjusting demand through control of credit and currency. *Keynesian macroeconomics* thus analyses aggregate supply and demand and holds that markets, especially the labour market, do not continuously 'clear' (quickly attain equilibrium between supply and demand) and may require intervention if objectives such as full employment are thought desirable.

Keynesian macroeconomic formulations were generally accepted well into the post-war era and have been refined and extended by the *neo-Keynesian* school, which contends that in a recession the market will clear only very slowly and that full employment equilibrium may never return without significant demand management (by government). At the same time, however, *neo-classical* economics has experienced a recent resurgence, using microeconomic tools to challenge the central Keynesian assumption that resources may be under-employed and that full employment equilibrium requires state intervention.

Another important school is **new classical** economics, which seeks to show the futility of Keynesian demand management policies and stresses instead the importance of **supply-side economics**, believing that the principal factor influencing growth of national output is the efficient allocation and use of labour and capital. A related school is that of the **Chicago monetarists** led by Milton Friedman, who have revived the old idea that an increase in money supply leads inevitably to an increase in prices rather than in output; however, whereas the new classical school contends that wage and price adjustment is almost instantaneous and so the level of employment at any time must be the natural rate, the Chicago monetarists are more gradualist, believing that such adjustment may take some years.

Great Economists

Friedman Milton 1912– . American economist, professor of economics at the University of Chicago since 1948, and Nobel prizewinner 1976. The foremost exponent of monetarism, he argues that a country's economy, and hence inflation, can be controlled through its money supply, although governments lack the 'political will' to control inflation by cutting government spending and thereby increasing unemployment.

Galbraith John Kenneth 1908– . Canadian political economist whose major works include *The Affluent Society* 1958 and *Economics and the Public Purpose* 1974. In the former he argued that advanced industrialized societies like the USA were suffering from private affluence accompanied by public squalor.

Keynes John Maynard, 1st Baron Keynes 1883–1946. British economist, whose *The General Theory of Employment, Interest, and* *Money* 1936, proposed the prevention of financial crises and unemployment by adjusting demand through government control of credit and currency. Keynes is regarded as the most important economist of the 20th century, responsible for that part of economics now known as macroeconomics. His ideas are today often contrasted with those of monetarism.

Lucas Robert 1937– . US economist, leader of the Chicago University school of new classical macroeconomics which contends that wage and price adjustment is almost instantaneous and that the level of unemployment at any time must be the natural rate (it cannot be reduced by government action except in the short term and at the cost of increasing inflation).

Malthus Thomas Robert 1766–1834. British cleric and economist, whose *Essay on the Principle of Population* 1798 and 1803 argued for population control, since people increase in geometric ratio, and food only in arithmetical ratio. He later suggested 'moral restraints' (delaying marriage and sexual abstinence before it) could keep numbers from increasing too quickly, a statement seized on by later birth-control pioneers (the 'neo-Malthusians').

Marshall Alfred 1842–1924. British economist, professor of economy at Cambridge University 1885–1908. A founder of neo-classical economics, he stressed the power of supply and demand to generate equilibrium prices in markets, introducing the concept of elasticity of demand relative to price. His *Principles of Economics* 1890 remains perhaps the most influential textbook of neo-classical economics.

Marx Karl Heinrich 1818–83. German philosopher, economist and social theorist, whose philosophical system, also known as 'dialectical materialism', proposes that social and political institutions progressively change their nature as economic developments transform material conditions, so that the succession of feudalism, capitalism, and socialism is inevitable. His three-volume *Das Kapital/Capital* 1867–94 is the fundamental text in Marxist economics.

Pareto Vilfredo 1848–1923. Italian economist and political philosopher. He produced the first account of society as a self-regulating and interdependent system which operates independently of human attempts at voluntary control. A founder of welfare economics, he put forward a concept of optimality which contends that optimum conditions exist in an economic system if no one can be made better off without at least one other person becoming worse off. A vigorous opponent of socialism and liberalism, Pareto justified inequality of income on the grounds of his empirical observation (Pareto's law) that income distribution remained constant whatever efforts were made to change it.

Pigou Arthur Cecil 1877–1959. British economist whose notion of the 'real balance effect' (the 'Pigou effect') contended that employment was stimulated by a fall in prices, because the latter increased liquid wealth and thus demand for goods and services.

Ricardo David 1772–1823. British economist, widely regarded as the greatest of the classical economists after Adam Smith. After making a fortune on the London Stock Exchange, he published in 1817 *Principles of Political Economy*, in which 'laws' of rent, value, and wages, long generally accepted, were clearly enunciated, including the important concept of comparative advantage (that countries can benefit by specializing in goods they produce most efficiently and trading internationally to buy others). Ricardo was one of the first to state the law of diminishing returns – that continued increments of capital and labour applied to a given quantity of land will eventually show a declining rate of increase in output.

Schumpeter Joseph A(lois) 1883–1950. Vienna-born US economist and sociologist. In *Capitalism, Socialism and Democracy* 1942 he contended that Western capitalism, impelled by its very success, was evolving into a form of socialism because firms would become increasingly large and their managements increasingly divorced from ownership, while social trends were undermining the traditional motives for entrepreneurial accumulation of wealth.

Smith Adam 1723–90. Scottish economist and philosopher, regarded as the founder of modern political economy. His *The Wealth of Nations* 1776 defined national wealth in terms of labour, as the only real measure of value, which is expressed in terms of wages. The cause of wealth is explained by the division of labour – dividing a production process into several repetitive operations, each carried out by different workers. Smith advocated the free working of individual enterprise, and especially the necessity of 'free trade' rather than the protection offered by the mercantile system.

Walras Léon 1834–1910. French economist, first holder of the chair of political economy at Lausanne University (Switzerland). In his *Éléments d'économie politique pure* 1874–77, he made a pioneering attempt to develop a unified model for general equilibrium theory (a hypothetical situation in which demands equal supply in all markets). He also originated the theory of marginal utility of a good (the increased value to a person of consuming some more of a product).

Economic Institutions

Bank of England UK central bank originally founded by Act of Parliament in 1694. It was entrusted with note issue in 1844, and nationalized in 1946. Known by its London site as the 'Old Lady of Threadneedle Street', it is banker to the UK government and assists in implementing the latter's financial and monetary policies.

Brandt Commission officially the Independent Commission on International Development Issues, established in 1977 under the chairmanship of former West German chancellor Willy Brandt. Consisting of 18 eminent persons acting independently of governments, the Commission examined the problems of developing countries in the world economic system and sought to identify corrective measures that would command international support. Its main report, published in 1980 under the title *North-South: A Programme for Survival*, made detailed recommendations for accelerating the development of poorer countries (involving the transfer of resources to the latter from the rich countries). Little government action was taken on the report, however, and the Commission was disbanded in 1983, after producing a second report called *Common Crisis*.

Comecon *(Council for Mutual Economic Co-operation)* established in 1949 in opposition to the Marshall Plan, links the USSR with Bulgaria, Czechoslovakia, Hungary, Poland, Romania, East Germany (from 1950), Mongolia (from 1962), Cuba (from 1972) and Vietnam (from 1978), with Yugoslavia as an associated member. It seeks to promote economic co-operation and development, but has no real central organization and no free trade between members.

European Community an organization which comprises the European Coal and Steel Community 1952; European Atomic Energy Community/Euratom 1957; and European Economic Community/EEC/popularly 'Common Market', both the last-named created under the two *Treaties of Rome* signed there March 1957. Since 1967 they have shared the institutions of the *Commission,* which initiates action (president Jacques Delors from 1986); the Council of Ministers, which decides on the Commission's proposals (both with headquarters in Brussels); *European Parliament*; and *European Court of Justice* (headquarters Luxembourg), which interprets the Rome Treaties. Original members were Belgium, France, West Germany, Italy, Luxembourg, Netherlands; subsequently Denmark, Republic of Ireland, UK 1973 (Norway withdrew its application 1972); Greece 1981; Spain

and Portugal 1986.

European Free Trade Association an organization established 1960, currently consisting of Austria, Finland, Iceland, Norway, Sweden, and Switzerland. There are no import duties between members. Of the original members, Britain and Denmark left (end 1972) to join the European Community, as subsequently did Portugal (end 1985).

Federal Reserve System *(Fed)* US central banking system and note issue authority, established in 1913 to regulate the country's credit and monetary affairs and to contribute to its economic well being. The Fed consists of the twelve federal reserve banks and their 25 branches and other facilities throughout the country; it is headed by a board of governors in Washington, appointed by the US President with Senate approval.

International Monetary Fund *(IMF)* specialized agency of the United Nations, established under the 1944 Bretton-Woods agreement and operational since 1947. It seeks to promote international monetary co-operation, the growth of world trade and smooth multilateral payments arrangements among member states. IMF stand-by loans are available to members in balance-of-payments difficulties (the amount being governed by the member's quota), usually on the basis of acceptance of instruction on necessary corrective measures. The Fund also operates other drawing facilities, including several designed to provide preferential credit to developing countries with liquidity problems. Having previously operated in US dollars linked to gold, since 1972 the IMF has used the special drawing right (SDR) as its standard unit of account, valued in terms of a weighted 'basket' of major currencies. Since the 1971 Smithsonian agreement permitting wider fluctuations from specified currency parities, IMF rules have been progressively adapted to the increasing prevalence of fully floating-exchange rates.

Organization for Economic Co-operation and Development *(OECD)* Paris-based intergovernmental organization of 24 industrialized countries active in co-ordinating member states' economic policy strategies. It super-seded the Organization for European Economic Co-operation (established 1948 to promote European recovery under the Marshall Plan) in 1961, when the USA and Canada became members and its scope was extended to include development aid. The OECD's subsidiary bodies include the International Energy Agency, set up in 1974 in the face of a world oil crisis.

Organization of the Petroleum Exporting Countries *(OPEC)* 13–nation body established in 1960 to co-ordinate the price and supply policies of oil-producing states. Its concerted action in raising crude oil prices sharply in the 1970s triggered worldwide recession, and generated huge revenues for OPEC members, some of these sums being donated or recycled to poorer developing countries. In the 1980s OPEC's dominant position was undermined by reduced demand for oil in industrialized countries and by rising non-OPEC production, notably from the North Sea. These factors and others caused a sharp fall in world oil prices, forcing OPEC to institute production cutbacks.

Paris Club an international forum dating from the 1950s for the rescheduling of debts granted or guaranteed by official bilateral creditors; it has no fixed membership nor an institutional structure. In the 1980s it has been closely involved in seeking solutions to the major debt crisis affecting many developing countries.

Securities and Exchange Commission *(SEC)* official US agency created in 1934 to ensure full disclosure to the investing public and protection against malpractice in the securities and financial markets (such as insider trading).

Stock Exchange institution for the buying and selling of stocks and shares (securities). London's is the oldest stock exchange, opened 1801. The former division between brokers (who bought shares from jobbers to sell to the public) and jobbers (who sold them only to brokers on commission, the 'jobbers' turn') was abolished in 1986. The major stock

exchanges are London, New York (Wall Street) and Tokyo.

World Bank popular name for the *International Bank for Reconstruction and Development,* established in 1945 under the 1944 Bretton-Woods agreement which also created the International Monetary Fund. The World Bank is a specialized agency of the United Nations which borrows in the commercial market and lends on commercial terms. The International Development Association is an arm of the World Bank.

Terms

balance of payments the difference between debits and credits in the buying and selling of goods and services between one country and other countries (usually the rest of the world). A balance-of-payments crisis usually means that more is leaving the country (in paying for imports) than is coming in (in payments for exports).

bank a financial institution which uses funds deposited with it to extend loans to companies or individuals, and also provides financial services to its customers. A central bank issues currency for the government, in order to provide cash for circulation and exchange.

big bang popular term for the major changes instituted in late 1986 to the organization and practices of the City of London as Britain's financial centre. Facilitated in part by computerization and on-line communications, the changes included ending the distinction between jobbers and brokers on the Stock Exchange, allowing non-members of the Stock Exchange to own member firms and opening up the charging of commissions to competition.

capital commonly signifies accumulated or inherited wealth held in the form of assets (such as stocks and shares, property, and bank deposits); in economics, capital is defined as the stock of goods (themselves produced) used in the production of other goods, and may be fixed capital (such as plant and machinery) or circulating capital (raw materials and components). The creation of all forms of capital requires the forgoing of consumption at some point.

comparative advantage law of international trade first elaborated by David Ricardo showing that trade becomes advantageous if the cost of production of particular items differs as between one country and another. At a simple level, if wine is cheaper to produce in country A than in country B, and the reverse is true of cheese, A can specialize in wine and B in cheese and they can trade to mutual benefit.

consumption the purchasing and using of goods and services. In economics, it means the total expenditure, in a given economy and over a given period, on goods and services (including expenditure on raw materials). In Britain consumption accounts for about 80 per cent of the national income, the remainder going to investment.

cost of living the cost of goods and services needed for an average standard of living. In Britain the first cost-of-living index was introduced in 1914 and based on the expenditure of a working-class family of man, woman, and three children; the standard is 100. Known from 1947 as the Retail Price Index (RPI), it is revised to allow for inflation, etc. Supplementary are the Consumer's Expenditure Deflator (formerly Consumer Price Index) and the Tax and Price Index (TPI).

crawling peg also known as a 'sliding party', a method of achieving a desired adjustment in a currency exchange rate (up or down) by small percentages over a given period, rather than by a major one-off revaluation or devaluation.

credit means by which goods or services are obtained without immediate payment. The three main forms are *consumer credit* (usually extended to individuals by retailers), *bank credit* (such as overdrafts or personal loans)

and *trade credit* (common in the commercial world both within countries and internationally).

crowding out situation in which an increase in government expenditure, by generating price rises and thus a reduction in the real money supply, results in a fall in private consumption and/or investment. Crowding out has been used in recent years as a justification for privatization of state-owned services and industries.

currency the particular type of money in use in a country. The currency of the United Kingdom is pounds sterling (£).

debt crisis generally any situation in which an individual, company or country owes more to others than they can repay or service when required; more specifically, the term refers to the massive indebtedness of many developing countries which became acute in the 1980s, threatening the stability of the international banking system as many debtor countries became unable to service their debts. The best-known example is Brazil, which in 1987 again 'rescheduled' (announced its incapacity to pay) its debts.

depreciation the decline or erosion of the value of a currency in relation to other currencies; also, the fall in value of an asset (such as factory machinery) resulting from age, wear and tear, or other factors.

deregulation action to abolish or reduce state controls and supervision over private economic activities, as with the deregulation of the US airline industry in 1978. In Britain the major changes in the City of London in 1986 (the big bang) were in part deregulation.

devaluation the lowering of the value of a currency in the international market or against specific other currencies, which makes exports cheaper and imports dearer. It is usually intended that devaluation should improve a country's balance of payments. *Revaluation* is the opposite process.

development aid financial and other assistance given by richer, usually industrialized, countries to developing states. Official development aid (ODA) may be given for idealistic, commercial, or political reasons, or a combination of the three.

disinvestment the practice of withdrawing investment from a country for political reasons. Most generally applied to the removal of funds from South Africa in recent years by such multinational companies as General Motors and Barclays Bank. Disinvestment may be motivated by fear of loss of business in the home market caused by adverse publicity, or by fear of loss of foreign resources if the local government loses power.

exchange rate the price at which one currency is bought, sold or valued in terms of other currencies, gold or accounting units such as the special drawing right of the International Monetary Fund. Exchange rates may be fixed by international agreement or as a matter of government policy, or they may be wholly or (more commonly) partly allowed to 'float' (i.e. find their own level) in world currency markets, as has been the case with most major currencies since the 1970s.

export credits loan, finance, or guarantees provided by government or financial institutions enabling companies to export goods and services in situations where payment for them may be delayed or subject to risk. In Britain the Export Credits Guarantee Department, established in 1930, issues insurance cover in respect of such risks.

exports goods and services produced in one country and sold to another; they may be visible (goods which are physically exported) or invisible (services such as tourism or insurance, provided in the exporting country but paid for in another country).

Financial Times (FT) Index customarily signifying the FT industrial ordinary index measuring the daily movement of 30 major industrial share prices on the London Stock Exchange (1935 = 100). Other FT indices cover government securities, fixed-interest securities, goldmine shares, and Stock Exchange activity.

fiscal policy the range of measures by which government revenue is raised (notably by taxation) and the priorities and purposes governing its expenditure. Post-war British governments have customarily made frequent adjustments to fiscal policy in order to regulate the level of economic activity (although under the post-1979 Conservative administration greater emphasis has been given to monetary policy).

game theory a group of mathematical theories, first developed in 1944 by Oscar Morgenstern and John von Neumann, which seeks to abstract from invented game-playing scenarios and their outcome the essence of situations of conflict and/or co-operation in the real political, business, and social world. A feature of such games is that the rationality of a decision by one player will depend on what the others do; hence game theory has particular application to the study of oligopoly.

gilt-edged stock securities issued by the British government to raise funds and traded on the Stock Exchange. A relatively risk-free investment, gilts bear fixed interest and are usually redeemable on a specified date.

hyperinflation rapid and uncontrolled increases in prices, usually associated with political and/or social instability (as in Germany in the 1920s).

imports goods and services which one country purchases from another for domestic consumption. If an importing country does not have a counterbalancing value of exports, it may experience balance-of-payments difficulties and accordingly consider restricting imports by some form of protection (such as an import tariff or by imposing import quotas).

income tax direct tax levied on personal income, mainly wages and salaries, but which may include the value of receipts other than in cash. In Britain income tax was first introduced in 1799 and has been a permanent fiscal feature since 1842. Indirect taxes are duties payable whenever a specific product is purchased; examples include VAT and customs duties.

incomes policy government-initiated exercise to curb inflation by restraining rises in incomes, on either a voluntary or a compulsory basis; often linked with action to control prices, in which case it becomes a prices and incomes policy. In Britain incomes policies have been applied at various times since the 1950s with limited success. An alternative to incomes policy, employed by the post-1979 Conservative government in Britain, is *monetary policy*, which attempts to manage the economy by controlling the quantity of money in circulation.

inflation a rise in the general level of prices, caused by an excess of demand over supply (*cost-push inflation* such as the world price rise in oil in 1974), and related to an increase in the supply of money (*demand-pull inflation*). *Deflation* is the reverse, a fall in the general level of prices.

insider dealing illegal use of privileged information in trading on the stock exchanges, for example when a company takeover bid is imminent. Insider dealing is in theory detected by the *Securities and Exchange Commission (SEC)* in the USA, and by the *Securities and Investment Board (SIB)* in the UK. Neither agency, however, has any legal powers other than public disclosure.

investment commonly used to signify the purchase of any asset with the potential to yield future financial benefit to the purchaser (such as a house, a work of art, stocks and shares, or even a private education); more strictly, it denotes expenditure on the stock of capital goods or resources of an enterprise or project, with a view to achieving profitable production for consumption at a later date.

laissez-faire theory that the state should refrain from all intervention in economic affairs, originating with the motto of the 18th-century French Physiocrats: *laissez-faire et laissez-passer*, that is 'leave the individual alone, and let commodities circulate freely'. The degree to which intervention should take place is still one of the chief problems of modern economics, both in capitalist and in communist regimes.

monetarism economic policy, advocated by the economist Milton Friedman and others, which proposes control of a country's money supply to keep it in step with the country's ability to produce goods, with the aim of

curbing inflation. Cutting government spending is advocated, and the long-term aim is to return as much of the economy as possible to the private sector, allegedly in the interests of efficiency. Additionally, credit is restricted by high interest rates, and industry is not cushioned against internal market forces or overseas competition (with the aim of preventing 'over-manning', 'restrictive' union practices, 'excessive' wage demands, and so on) Unemployment results, but, monetarists claim, less than eventually occurs if Keynesian methods are adopted. The theory was ineffectively applied against Edward Heath in the UK in the early 1970s, and from 1979 the Thatcher government attempted a more complete application of monetarism.

monetary policy an approach by governments which sees control of the money supply and of liquidity as essential to the achievement of desired objectives and thus places less emphasis on tools such as fiscal policy and incomes policy. A monetary policy may not fully embrace all the doctrines of monetarism, but use of it usually indicates that the practitioner gives a higher priority to price stability and balance-of-payments equilibrium than to low unemployment and consumption.

money any common medium of exchange acceptable in payment for goods or services or for the settlement of debts. Today money is usually coinage (first used in the West of Lydia but invented by the Chinese in the second millennium BC) or paper notes (used by the Chinese about 800 AD to avoid imperial messengers being weighed down by coin when pursued by bandits). More recent developments such as the cheque and credit card fulfil many of the traditional functions of money.

money supply term used to denote the amount of money present in an economy at a given moment. In Britain there are several definitions of money supply, none of them totally satisfactory. The **M1** definition encompasses notes and coin in circulation plus current account deposits; **M2**, now rarely used, covers the M1 items plus deposit accounts; and the officially preferred **M3** definition covers M1 and M2 items plus all other deposits held by UK citizens and companies in the UK banking sector.

monopoly in the UK, originally a royal grant of the sole right to manufacture or sell a certain article. In modern commerce, the domination of a particular industry by a cartel or trust (a group of firms) which is large enough to restrict competition against itself and keep prices high.

multinational corporation company or enterprise operating in several countries, often defined as one which has 25 per cent or more of its output capacity located outside its country of origin. Such enterprises, many of them US-based, are seen in some quarters as posing a threat to individual national sovereignty and as exerting undue influence to secure favourable operating conditions.

multiplier theoretical concept, formulated by J M Keynes, of the effect on national income or employment by an adjustment in overall demand. Thus investment by a company in new plant will stimulate new income and expenditure, which will in turn generate new investment, and so on, so that the actual increase in national income may be several times greater than the original investment.

national debt the total amount of money borrowed by the central government of a country, on which it pays interest. In Britain the national debt is managed by the Bank of England, under the control of the Treasury.

newly-industrialized country (*NIC*) term used to denote a former less-developed country which has made a breakthrough into manufacturing and rapid export-led economic growth. The prime examples are South Korea, Singapore, Brazil and Mexico, which on average expanded their gross domestic product (GDP) twice as fast as the older industrialized countries during the 1970s, partly by rapidly increasing the share of manufactured goods in their exports.

oligopoly situation in which a small group of companies controls a large proportion of a particular market and concerts its actions to perpetuate such control. Oligopolies are usu-

ally opposed by governments as being against the general interest.

privatization the selling or transfer into private hands of state-owned assets and services (notably nationalized industries). Privatization of services takes place by the contracting out to private firms of the rendering of services previously supplied by public authorities. The policy has been pursued by several governments in recent years, particularly the post-1979 Conservative administrations in Britain.

profit-sharing a system whereby an employer pays his workers a fixed share of his profits. It originated in France in the early 19th century, and under the influence of the Christian Socialists was widely practised for a time within the co-operative movement.

quantity theory of money theory dating originally from the 17th century and elaborated by the US economist Irving Fisher (1867–1947) to show, in essence, that an increase in the amount of money in circulation will cause a proportionate increase in prices. The quantity theory of money forms the theoretical basis of modern monetarism.

reserves a country's holdings of internationally acceptable means of payment (major foreign currencies or gold); central banks also hold the ultimate reserve of money for their domestic banking sector. On the asset side of company balance sheets, undistributed profits are listed as reserves.

saving the reservation, by individuals or companies, of a portion of income for future needs. Seldom the massing of a money hoard in modern times, because of dangers of fire and theft, but tending to be synonymous with investment.

Say's Law the 'law of markets' enunciated by Jean-Baptiste Say (1767–1832) to the effect that supply creates its own demand and that resources can never be under-used. Widely accepted by classical economists, the 'law' was regarded as erroneous by J M Keynes in his analysis of the depression in Britain during the 1920s and 1930s.

stagflation the condition (experienced in

Britain in the 1970s) in which rapid inflation is accompanied by stagnating, even declining, output and by increasing unemployment. Its cause is often sharp increases in costs of raw materials and/or labour.

stocks and shares broad term for investment holdings in private or public undertakings. Although distinctions have become blurred, in Britain stock usually means fixed-interest securities, especially those issued by central and local government. Shares represent a stake in the ownership of a trading company and, if they are ordinary shares, yield to the owner dividends reflecting the success or otherwise of the company. In the USA the term stock generally signifies what in Britain are ordinary shares.

Treasury bill in Britain, borrowing by the government in the form of a promissory note to repay the bearer 91 days from the date of issue; such bills represent a flexible and relatively cheap way for the government to borrow money for immediate needs.

unemployment the involuntary lack of paid employment. Unemployment is generally subdivided into *frictional* unemployment (the inevitable temporary unemployment of those moving from one job to another); *cyclical* unemployment, caused by a downswing in the trade cycle; *seasonal* unemployment, in an area where there is high demand only during holiday periods, for example; and *structural* unemployment, where changing technology or other long-term change in the economy results in large numbers without work, particularly in certain regions.

Education

In its widest sense, education begins at birth. In the more restricted sense of imparting knowledge and literacy, education has today become almost worldwide. Although highly developed systems of learning emerged early in China, formal education as we know it today is largely of European origin. The earliest known European educational systems are those of ancient Greece, though they were only for the privileged few. Medieval monastic schools gradually admitted other pupils and learning was spread. Compulsory attendance at primary schools was first established in the mid-18th century in Prussia. By the middle of the 20th century, education was free and compulsory in most countries of the world from about six to 16.

This section deals mainly with the British education system, but includes comparisons with education in other countries. It outlines the various *Stages of Education* – pre-school, primary, secondary, post-school – in an international context, and their aims, such as basic literacy, vocational objectives, graduate and post-graduate work. Then it touches on *Recent Changes* in UK education over the last 20 years – the switch to comprehensive secondary education, the expansion of higher and further education, and the response to the falling birth-rate in the 1970s, again in an international perspective. It then looks at the major *Areas of Debate* in the mid-1980s. Finally there is a glossary of *Terms* used in education.

Stages of Education

Education is compulsory and free of charge in the UK from the age of five until the age of 16, but in common with most industrialized countries, educational services are provided in various forms from the age of three to the stage of post-doctoral research in universities and other higher education colleges, by which time students may be in their mid-20s. Education up to the age of 18 is provided almost exclusively by local education authorities in schools which are administered by a locally based education committee. The Department of Education and Science, the arm of government responsible for education, only has general oversight of school policy, and direct control of the universities, teacher training, and some research. There is also a private fee-paying school sector which attracts 6.5% of school pupils.

pre-school education the UK lags behind many of its industrial neighbours in provision of pre-school education. Only 43% of three- and four-year olds are provided for in maintained nursery and infants' schools and classes. Another 450,000 children are catered for in playgroups run on a voluntary basis.

school education is divided into *primary* (5 to 11) and *secondary* (11 to 18) sectors. There is a large voluntary sector of schools run co-operatively by the churches and local authorities together, accounting for one-third of primary schools and a smaller proportion of secondary schools. A few local authority areas maintain middle schools, which take children from the ages of 8 or 9 to 12 or 13. School transfer in the private sector often also takes place at 13.

education after 16 beyond school-leaving age students have a choice of remaining in school sixth forms, which generally specialize in the A Level courses which lead to entrance to higher education, or colleges of further education which specialize in vocational courses, or the Youth Training Scheme which offers a combination of work experience and training. The UK has a very low proportion of 16- to 19-year-olds, at just under 40%, remaining in full-time education compared to its industrial competitors.

degree level education is divided between 45 universities, which are funded directly by the government through the University Grants Committee, and the public sector of polytechnics and colleges of higher education, which are funded in part by the local education authorities. Participation in full-time higher education beyond the age of 19 stands at 13%. Higher education course fees are paid in full for UK students, and there is a system of maintenance grants, on a parental means test basis, to cover students' living expenses while they are studying.

Recent Changes

Education in the UK is going through a period of rapid change which has already continued throughout the last 20 years. Structural change has been complicated by first a rapid increase in the child population in the 1960s followed by a sharp drop in the birth-rate in the 1970s which will reduce the school population by one-third by the time it has worked its way through the system.

comprehensive schools the 1960s and 1970s saw a slow but major reform of secondary education, in which the majority of local authorities replaced selective grammar schools taking only the most academic 20% of children and secondary modern schools for the remainder, with comprehensive schools capable of providing suitable courses for children of all abilities. By 1985 only 3.2% of secondary pupils were still in grammar schools. Scotland

and Wales have switched completely to comprehensive education, while Northern Ireland retains a largely selective system.

expansion of higher education during the 1960s, on the recommendation of the Robbins Report, university education expanded rapidly with the establishment of seven new 'green field' universities and the 'promotion' of the Colleges of Advanced Technology to university status. In 1970 a further major expansion was presaged by the designation of 30 polytechnics which were to retain their local authority connections and provide degree level education with a vocational bias. The number of students in higher education in the UK reached a record 885,600 in 1984.

falling rolls during the 1970s a period during which local education authorities had great difficulty in providing enough schools was rapidly succeeded by one when pupil numbers, particularly in inner cities experiencing a general loss of population, fell dramatically. Between 1976 and 1985 primary school numbers in England fell from 4,800,000 to 3,700,000. Secondary pupils reached a peak in 1979 of 3,800,000 and by 1985 had dropped to 3,500,000 with further losses still to come. As a result local authorities instituted a major programme of school closures and amalgamations which reduced the number of schools in England from a peak of 30,700 in 1977 to 18,500 in 1985, with more closures in the pipeline.

Areas of Debate

The educational debate has moved in new but no less contentious directions in the mid-1980s. The following are some of the main areas of continuing debate:

central, local, or parental control the Thatcher government has twice strengthened the involvement of parents in the running of the schools by first insisting on the election of parents to governing bodies (1980 Education Act) and then by strengthening that representation and by providing for an annual report by governors to parents (Education Act 1986). It has given parents greater freedom to select schools within the state system, and to opt into the independent sector, by means of the Assisted Places Scheme. In 1986 Mr Kenneth Baker announced plans to set up a limited number of new independent City Technology Colleges, to widespread local authority opposition. The government has also taken greater powers centrally to influence and fund parts of the curriculum and examination system. The local education authorities fear that the government is engaged in a process of centralization of the education service which could end local political involvement completely.

vocational and technical education the Manpower Services Commission (MSC) has funded a major expansion of technical and vocational education for students over 14 in schools and colleges (TVEI). TVEI funding was originally provided in pilot schemes which reached roughly three per cent of secondary school children, but it was announced in 1986 that funding would be extended, at a significantly less generous level, to all secondary schools. The MSC has also become involved with the further education colleges as the Youth Training Scheme for unemployed young people has expanded, but only a minority of YTS trainees attend college.

a 'national curriculum' growing concern about the low proportion of 14- and 16-year-olds opting to study maths, science and technology, with a particularly low take-up rate amongst girls, has strengthened moves towards a 'core curriculum' for all school students at least up to the age of 16. The 'core' is generally assumed to include maths, English, science, and technology, religious education, and physical education. Worries are expressed about the potential threat to studies in the humanities and the arts. There are also acute difficulties in staffing maths, science, and CDT (craft, design and technology) courses.

examination reform the Conservative government since 1979 has initiated a major reform of the public examination system. After a long debate, it authorized the amalgamation of the two 16–plus examinations to create the GCSE, to be introduced in 1988, and initiated reforms leading to the new CPVE and AS level examinations, and a major review of vocational qualifications. These changes have been undertaken with some support from teachers. More contentious will be new discussions on the A Level examinations, which it is argued need to be reformed in order to accommodate the GCSE reform, and to broaden the traditional three A Level sixth-form programme of study. The government has also encouraged the development of new forms of assessment, such as records of achievement, which assess young people over a longer period of time and a wider range of activities rather than in an all-or-nothing final examination.

higher education 1986 saw a record number of students in higher education, in spite of cuts in university funding which reduced student numbers in the universities after 1981. The extra numbers in higher education are accounted for by the fact that public sector colleges and polytechnics were accepting surplus applicants, with minimal extra funding, as the universities contracted. In 1987 the government conceded that higher education numbers should expand by about four per cent by 1990. But plans to rationalize courses, and concentrate on science, technology, and business studies, at the expense of the humanities and social sciences, were confirmed.

Terms

---

admission to school legally, in the UK, at the beginning of the term after a child's fifth birthday, but an increasing number of schools now admit children earlier.

A Level General Certificate of Education examinations usually taken in no more than four subjects at the age of 18 after two years' study. Two A Level passes are required for entry on to a degree course.

AS Level Advanced Supplementary GCE examinations introduced in 1988 as the equivalent to 'half an A Level' as a means of broadening the sixth form curriculum.

assessment the means of measuring performance by way of examinations, tests, or classwork marking.

Assisted Places Scheme a scheme established in 1980 by which the government assists parents with the cost of fees at private schools, on a means-tested basis.

Baccalauréat the French school-leaving certificate and qualification for university entrance, also available on an international basis as an alternative to A Levels.

banding the division of school pupils into broad streams by ability. Banding is used by some local authorities to ensure that comprehensive schools receive an intake of children spread right across the ability range. Banding is used internally by some schools as a means of avoiding groups of very wide mixed ability.

boarding school school offering board and lodging as well as tuition. Most boarding education in the UK is provided in the private sector, but there are a number of state schools with boarding facilities.

Bullock Report *A Language for Life*, the report of a committee of inquiry, published in 1975, on the teaching of English.

class size the number of children in a class: a factor regarded by many teachers and parents as crucial to the quality of education.

co-education the education of boys and girls together in one institution. There has been a marked switch away from single sex education and in favour of co-education over the last 20 years, although there is some evidence to suggest that girls perform better in a single sex institution, particularly in maths and science.

college of higher education college controlled by the local education authorities in which a large proportion of the work undertaken is at degree level or above.

community schools/education the philosophy which asserts that educational institutions are more effective if closely integrated with, and opened up to all members of, the surrounding community.

comprehensive school a secondary school which admits pupils without regard to their ability and therefore without any selection procedure. Secondary education in the United States and the USSR has always been comprehensive, but most western European countries, including France and the UK, have switched from a selective to a comprehensive system within the last 20 years.

computer literacy the ability to understand the functions and role of and make use of computer technology in an everyday context.

CPVE *Certificate of Pre-vocational Education* a qualification introduced in 1986 for students over 16 in schools and colleges who want a one-year course of preparation for work or further vocational study.

credits the system whereby a qualification from one institution is accepted by another. Credit transferability is common in higher education in the United States but is only just beginning to be developed between institutions in the UK. At school level, the equivalence between an O Level pass and a Grade 1 pass at CSE, and between a BTEC diploma and A Levels is a long-standing one.

CSE *Certificate of Secondary Education* the examinations taken by the majority of secondary school pupils, who were not regarded as capable of GCE O Level, before the introduction of the common secondary examination system, GCSE, in 1988.

curriculum the range of subjects offered within an institution or course. The only part of the school curriculum prescribed by law in the UK is religious education. General responsibility for overseeing the curriculum in England and Wales rests with the local education authority and school governors, although

there are accelerating moves to increase central control of the curriculum to ensure that all young people study certain basic subjects such as maths and science.

Department of Education and Science (DES) the government department responsible for education policy making in England, and for the universities throughout the UK.

Education Acts (UK) the foundation for much education policy is still the reforming 1944 Education Act. This has been revised by two further acts in 1980, which repealed previous legislation enforcing comprehensive re-organization, and gave new rights to parents, by the 1981 Education Act which made new provisions for the education of children with special needs, and by legislation in 1986 giving further powers to school governors and in 1987 on the remuneration of teachers.

Eleven Plus examination the test designed to select children for grammar school education at the time when local authorities provided separate grammar, secondary modern, and occasionally technical schools for children over the age of eleven. The examination became defunct on the introduction of comprehensive schools in Scotland, Wales, and most of England during the 1960s and 1970s.

finance the funding of education. Education in the UK is funded in two ways: 1. By the local education authorities who, by a combination of government rate support grant and rates directly charged on the local community, support schools, further education, and, through a national pool, parts of higher education such as the polytechnics. 2. By direct grant from the DES to the universities, some other colleges of higher education, and for a limited number of specific projects in the schools, and via the Manpower Services Commission, to vocational education in colleges and schools.

further education colleges colleges for students over school-leaving age which provide courses of a vocational or pre-vocational nature and some of general education at a level below that of a degree course.

GCE *General Certificate of Education* the public examination usually taken at the age of

16 at Ordinary Level (O Level) and at 18 at Advanced Level (A Level). The GCE O Level examination, which was aimed at the top 20% of the ability range, will be superseded in 1988 by the General Certificate of Secondary Education.

GCSE *General Certificate of Secondary Education* the new examination for 16-year old pupils, which will supersede both GCE O Level and CSE, and offer qualifications for up to 60% of school leavers in any particular subject. The GCSE is intended to be more practically biased than O Level and is organized in the light of National Criteria laid down by the Secondary Examinations Council.

governor member of a institution's governing body. Education Acts of 1980 and 1986 have increased elected parental and teacher representation on school governing bodies in England and Wales, and reduced the influence of governors appointed by the local education authorities.

grant allowance made to students to cover the cost of course fees and, in higher education, maintenance costs during term-time. The National Union of Students campaigns for a 'living grant' for all students in further and higher education over the age of 16, with a removal of the present obligation upon parents to contribute on a means tested basis.

health education most secondary schools offer pupils teaching and advice on healthy living, including nutrition, sex education, and advice on drink, drugs and other threats to health. Health education is often included within a course of personal and social education, or alternatively integrated into subjects such as biology, home economics or physical education. School governors were given specific responsibility for the content of sex education lessons in the 1986 Education Act.

higher education education beyond the age of 18 leading to a degree or similar qualification, provided in the UK mainly in universities, polytechnics and colleges of higher education, and by distance learning through the Open University.

independent school school run privately without direct assistance from the state. Just over 6% of children in the UK attend private fee-paying schools. The sector includes most boarding education in the UK. Although a majority of independent secondary schools operate a highly selective admissions policy for entrants at the age of 11 or 13, some specialize in the teaching of slow learners or difficult children and a few follow particular philosophies of progressive education.

inspectors there are two systems of inspection for schools and colleges in the UK. Her Majesty's Inspectors of Schools are a national body, independent of the Department of Education and Science, with a wide remit to visit institutions, survey particular areas of study, comment on standards and levels of provision, and advise the government. Local education authorities also employ their own inspectors, often now called advisers, to advise schools and colleges on their performance at a local level.

integrated studies a course which combines two or more subjects which are usually studied separately. For instance, integrated humanities may include elements of history, geography, social studies, and English; integrated science would normally include elements of physics, chemistry, and biology.

intelligence test test which attempts to measure innate intellectual ability, rather than acquired knowledge. Intelligence tests were widely used as part of the Eleven Plus procedures, in the early days of which it was assumed that inborn intelligence was unalterable. It is now generally believed that children's ability to score at a particular level in an intelligence test can be affected by their environment and teaching. There is also considerably more scepticism now about the accuracy of intelligence tests than there was when they were first introduced in the 1930s, but they are still widely used as a diagnostic tool when children display learning difficulties.

IQ intelligence quotient: the score achieved as the result of an intelligence test, with a score of 100 being regarded as average ability.

Ivy League a collective term for the long-established East Coast universities in the United States.

literacy the ability to read and write at a level to enable an adult to function in the society in which he or she lives. The level at which functional literacy is set rises as society becomes more complex and it becomes increasingly difficult for an illiterate person to find work and cope with the other demands of everyday life.

local education authorities the education committees of metropolitan or county councils which have responsibility for providing educational services locally. There is one directly elected education authority in England, the Inner London Education Authority, and in Northern Ireland the responsibility for education is held by the Education and Library Boards.

mixed ability teaching the practice of teaching children of all abilities in a single class. Mixed ability teaching is normal practice in British primary schools but most secondary schools begin to divide children according to ability, either in sets or, more rarely, streams, as they approach public examinations at 16.

modular course course, usually leading to a recognized qualification, which is divided into short and often optional units which are assessed as they are completed. An accumulation of modular credits may then lead to the award of a qualification such as a degree, a BTEC diploma or a GCSE pass. Modular schemes are increasingly popular as a means of allowing students to take a wider range of subjects.

O Level the GCE examination usually taken at 16 plus by the most able children and superseded by the GCSE in 1988.

open learning teaching which is available to students without pre-qualifications by means of flexible attendance at an institution and very often including teaching by correspondence, radio, television, or tape.

Open University an institution established in 1969 to enable mature students without qualifications to study to degree level without regular attendance. OU teaching is based on a mixture of correspondence courses, TV and radio lectures and demonstrations, personal tuition organized on a regional basis, and summer schools.

Open College an open learning initiative launched by the Manpower Services Commission to enable people to gain and update technical and vocational skills by means of distance teaching.

Oxbridge generic term for Oxford and Cambridge universities, the two oldest foundations in the UK and still distinctive because of their ancient collegiate structure, their idiosyncratic entrance procedures and their high proportion of students from private schools.

parent teacher association (PTA) group attached to a school consisting of parents and teachers who support the school by fund raising and educational activities amongst the parent body. PTAs are organized into a national federation, the National Confederation of PTAs, which increasingly acts as a pressure group for maintained schools.

parent governors the 1980 Education Act made it mandatory for all maintained schools to include elected parent representatives on their governing bodies, in line with the existing practice of some local education authorities. The 1986 Education Act increased parental representation.

play-group a voluntary, usually part-time pre-school group, run either by parents or sometimes by charitable organizations, to provide nursery education for children from three to five. Play-groups sprang up in the 1960s in response to a national shortage of places in maintained nursery education. By the 1980s they were catering for 450,000 children annually, and training and advice services were organized nationally by the Pre-School Playgroups Association.

preparatory schools fee-paying private school catering for children up to the age of 13.

primary education the education of children between 5 and 11 in the maintained school system in England and Wales, up to 12 in Scotland.

progressive methods a generic term for

teaching methods which take as their starting point children's own aptitudes and interests and encourage them to follow their own investigations and lines of enquiry.

racial disadvantage term used to describe a condition in which children from ethnic minority groups perform less well than they should. There is evidence that this is the case in British Schools. The Swann Report 1986 recommended methods of combatting racial disadvantage in schools and local authorities are increasingly adopting anti-racist policies and attempting to give their curricula a multi-cultural dimension.

religious education (RE) the formal teaching of religion in schools. In England, RE is the only compulsory subject. In voluntary aided church schools, RE syllabuses are permitted to follow the specific teachings of the church concerned; in other maintained schools the syllabus is agreed between representatives of the local churches and the education authority. The law allows parents to withdraw their children from RE on conscientious grounds.

remedial education special classes, or teaching strategies, which aim to help children with learning difficulties to catch up with children of the normal range of achievement.

school leaving age pupils may leave school in the year in which they reach the age of 16 in the UK, but precise regulations, which differ between England and Wales and Scotland, govern the precise date at which an individual can leave school, depending on his or her birthday.

secondary education education from the age of 11 (12 in Scotland) until school-leaving at 16 or later.

secondary modern school the secondary school which normally takes children who have failed to gain a grammar school place, in those few areas of the UK which retain selection at 11 or 12.

setting the practice of dividing pupils into ability groups for each subject.

sixth form inclusive term used for pupils staying on for one or two years of study beyond school-leaving age in order to gain A Level or other post-15 qualifications. In some areas, sixth form education is concentrated in sixth form colleges.

special education education, often in separate 'special schools', for children with specific problems or disabilities: that is, the blind, deaf, or maladjusted. The 1981 Education Act encouraged local authorities to integrate as many children with special needs into mainstream schools as was practicable but did not recommend the complete closure of special schools.

streaming the practice of dividing pupils for all classes according to an estimate of their overall ability, with arrangements for 'promotion' and 'demotion' at the end of each academic year. Rigid streaming is unusual in secondary education in the 1980s and has disappeared from primary education.

teacher training in the UK teachers are trained by means of the four year Bachelor of Education degree, which integrates professional training and the study of academic subjects, or by means of the one year Post Graduate Certificate of Education which offers one year of professional training to follow a normal degree course in a specialist subject.

tertiary college a college for students over 16 which combines the work of a sixth form and a further education college.

TVEI the Technical and Vocational Education Initiative, funded by the Manpower Services Commission, and intended to provide secondary schools with equipment and teaching expertise to allow them to expand their vocational and technical courses for 14- to 18-year-olds. Initially available in only 3% of schools, it has now been extended to cover all secondary schools.

vocational education education relevant to a specific job or career and extending from further education courses in craft skills to medical and legal education in the universities.

Language

Language is the general name for human communication through speech or writing, or both, while 'a language' is any expression of language used by one or more communities for everyday purposes (the English language, the Japanese language, and so on). Natural human language has a neurological basis centred on the left hemisphere of the brain and is expressed through two distinct mediums in most present-day societies: through sound, or the phonic medium, and through writing, or the graphic medium. It appears to develop in every normal child under normal circumstances, crucially between the ages of one and five years, and as a necessary interplay of innate and environmental factors. Any human child can learn any human language, under the appropriate conditions.

This section contains an overview of the principal *Languages of the World*, both ancient and modern; notes on *Grammar and Usage*, including parts of speech and punctuation; and definitions of *Terms* people use in the study of language today.

Languages of the World

Afrikaans along with English, an official language of the Republic of South Africa. Spoken mainly by the Afrikaners, descendants of Dutch and other 17th-century colonists, it is a variety of the Dutch language, modified by circumstance and the influence of German, French, and other immigrant and local languages. It became a standardized written language about 1875.

Anglo-Saxon the group of dialects spoken by the Anglo-Saxon peoples who in the 5th to 7th centuries invaded and settled in Britain (in what became England and Lowland Scotland). Anglo-Saxon is traditionally known as Old English.

Arabic a Hamito-Semitic language of W Asia and N Africa, originating among the Arabs of the Arabian peninsula. Arabic script is written from right to left. A feature of the language is its consonantal roots; for example *s-l-m* is the root for *salaam*, a greeting that implies peace, *Islam*, the creed of submission to God and calm acceptance of His will, and *Muslim*, one who submits to that will (a believer in Islam). The *Quran*, the sacred book of Islam, is 'for reading' by a *qari* ('reader') who is engaged in *qaraat* ('reading'). The 7th-century style of the Quran is the basis of *Classical Arabic*. The language has spread as far west as Morocco and as far east as Malaysia, Indonesia and the Philippines. Forms of *Colloquial Arabic* vary in the countries where it is the dominant language: Algeria, Bahrain, Egypt, Iraq, Jordan, Kuwait, Lebanon, Libya, Mali, Mauretania, Morocco, Oman, Sudan, Syria, Tunisia, the United Arab Emirates, and the two Yemens. It is also a language of religious and cultural significance in such other countries as Bangladesh, India, Indonesia, Iran, Malaysia, Pakistan, the Philippines and Somalia.

Aramaic a Hamito-Semitic language of W Asia, the everyday language of Palestine in the time of Christ. In the 13th century BC Aramaean nomads set up states in Mesopotamia, and over the next 200 years spread into N Syria, where Damascus, Aleppo and Carchemish were among their chief centres. Aramaic spread throughout Syria and Mesopotamia, becoming one of the official languages of the Persian Empire under the Achaemenids and serving as a lingua franca of the day. Aramaic dialects survive among small Christian communities in various parts of W Asia.

Aryan languages either the languages of the Aryan peoples of India, or a 19th-century name for the Indo-European languages.

Bantu languages a group of related languages spoken widely over the greater part of Africa south of the Sahara, including Swahili, Xhosa and Zulu. Meaning 'people' in Zulu, the word *Bantu* itself illustrates a characteristic use of prefixes: *mu-ntu*, 'man', *ba-ntu*, 'people'. The Bantu-speaking peoples probably originated in N Central Africa. Until 1978, the black people of the Republic of South Africa were officially designated *bantu(s)*, and the official 'homelands' of the various black ethnic groups were known as *bantustans* ('Bantu lands').

Basic English a simplified form of English devised and promoted by C K Ogden in the 1920s and 1930s as an international auxiliary language, a route into Standard English for foreign learners, and a reminder to the English-speaking world of the virtues of plain language. Its name derives from the letters of *B*ritish, *A*merican, *S*cientific, *I*nternational, *C*ommercial. Basic has a vocabulary of 850 words (plus names, technical terms, etc.), only 18 of which are verbs or 'operators'. *Get* therefore replaces 'receive', 'obtain' and 'become', while *buy* is replaced by the phrase 'give money for'.

Basque a language of W Europe known to its speakers, the Basques, as *Euskara*, and apparently unrelated to any other language on earth. It is spoken by some half a million people in N Spain and SW France, around the Bay of Biscay ('the Basque bay'), as well as by emigrants in both Europe and the Americas. Although officially discouraged in the past, Basque is now accepted as a regional language in both France and Spain, and is of central importance to the Basque nationalist movement.

Bengali a member of the Indo-Iranian branch of the Indo-European language family, the official language of Bangladesh and of the state of Bengal in India.

Bretone a member of the Celtic branch of the Indo-European language family, the language of Brittany in France, related to Welsh and Cornish, and descended from the speech of Celts who left Britain as a consequence of the Anglo-Saxon invasions of the 5th and 6th centuries. Although subject to official neglect for centuries, Breton is now a recognized language of France and has since 1985 received some encouragement from the central government. The Breton Liberation Movement claims equal status in Brittany for Breton and French.

Castilian a member of the Romance branch of the Indo-European language family originating in NW Spain, in the provinces of Old and New Castile. It is the basis of present-day standard Spanish and is often seen as the same language, the terms *castellano* and *español* being used interchangeably in both Spain and the Spanish-speaking countries of the Americas.

Catalan a member of the Romance branch of the Indo-European language family, an Iberian language closely related to Provençal in France. It is spoken in Catalonia in NE Spain, the Balearic Isles, Andorra and a corner of SE France. Since the end of the Franco regime in Spain in 1975, Catalan nationalists have vigorously promoted their regional language as co-equal in Catalonia with Castilian Spanish.

Celtic languages a branch of the Indo-European family, further divided into two groups: the *Brythonic* or *P-Celtic* (Welsh, Cornish, Breton, and Gaulish) and the *Goidelic* or *Q-Celtic* (Irish, Scottish and Manx Gaelic). As their names suggest, a major distinction between the two groups is that where Brythonic has 'p' (as in Old Welsh *map*, 'son'), Goidelic has a 'q' sound (as in Gaelic *mac*, 'son'). Celtic languages once stretched from the Black Sea to Britain, but have been in decline for centuries, and are now limited to the so-called 'Celtic Fringe' of W Europe. Gaulish is the long-extinct language of ancient Gaul, Cornish died out as a natural language in the late 18th century and Manx in 1974. All surviving Celtic languages have experienced official neglect in recent centuries and have suffered from emigration; currently, however, governments are more inclined than in the past to encourage their use.

Chinese depending upon definition, a language or group of languages of the Sino-Tibetan family, spoken in China, Taiwan, Hong Kong, Singapore and Chinese communities throughout the world. Varieties of spoken Chinese differ greatly, but share a written form using thousands of ideographic symbols which have changed little in 2,000 years. Because the writing system has a symbolic form (rather like numbers and road signs) it can be read and interpreted regardless of the reader's own dialect. Nowadays, *putonghua* ('common speech'), based on the educated Peking dialect known as 'Mandarin' Chinese, is promoted throughout China as the national spoken and written language. The Chinese dialects are tonal (that is, they depend upon the tone of a syllable to indicate its meaning, *ma* with one tone meaning 'mother', with another meaning 'horse'). The characters of Chinese script are traditionally written vertically and read from right to left but are now commonly written horizontally and read from left to right, using 2,000 simplified characters. A variant of the Roman alphabet has been introduced and used in schools to help with pronunciation. Called *Pinyin*, this is prescribed for international use by the People's Republic of China, for personal and place names; for example, Beijing rather than Peking. It is not accepted by the Taiwan government.

77

Coptic a member of the Hamito-Semitic language family and a minority language of Egypt. It is descended from the language of the ancient Egyptians and is the ritual language of the Coptic Christian church. It is written in the Greek Alphabet.

Cornish an extinct member of the Celtic language, branch of the Indo-European language family spoken in Cornwall until 1777. Written Cornish first appeared in 10th-century documents. Some religious plays were written in Cornish in the 15th and 16th centuries, but later literature is scanty, mainly folk-tales and verses. Members of the Cornish nationalist movement have in recent years 'revived' the language for social purposes and for its symbolic value.

Creole languages pidgin languages which have ceased to be simply trade jargons in ports and markets and have become the mother tongues of particular communities. The name 'creole' derives through French from Spanish and Portuguese, in which it originally referred both to children of European background born in tropical colonies and to house slaves on colonial plantations. The implication is that such groups picked up the pidgin forms of languages like Portuguese, Spanish, Dutch, French and English as used in and around the Caribbean, in parts of Africa, and in island communities in the Indian and Pacific Oceans. Having begun with the characteristics of pidgin languages (crudely, the vocabulary of the dominant community arranged in accordance with the syntax or grammar of the dependent groups), many creoles have developed into distinct languages with incipient literatures of their own, such as Jamaican Creole, Haitian Creole, Krio in Sierra Leone, and Tok Pisin in Papua New Guinea.

Danish a member of the N Germanic group of the Indo-European language family, spoken in Denmark and Greenland and related to Icelandic, Faroese, Norwegian and Swedish. As one of the languages of the Vikings, who invaded and settled in parts of Britain during the 9th to 11th centuries, Old Danish had a strong influence on English. *They*, *their* and

them as well as such *sk-* words as *sky*, *skill*, *skin*, *scrape* and *scrub* are among the language gifts of the Danelaw, along with such place-name endings as *by* (a farm or town) as in Derby, Grimsby and Whitby.

Dutch a member of the W Germanic branch of the Indo-European language family, often referred to by scholars as Netherlandic and taken to include not only the standard language and dialects of the Netherlands (excluding Frisian) but also Flemish (in Belgium and N France) and, more remotely, its off-shoot Afrikaans in S Africa. Many, however, regard Flemish and Afrikaans as distinct languages. Dutch is also spoken in Surinam in S America and the Netherlands Antilles in the S Caribbean.

English a member of the W Germanic branch of the Indo-European language family, traditionally described as having passed through four major stages over about 1,500 years: *Old English* or *Anglo-Saxon* (about 500–1050), *Middle English* (about 1050–1550), *Early Modern English* (about 1550–1700), and *Late Modern English* (from about 1700 onwards). The ancestral forms of English were dialects brought from the NW coastlands of Europe to the island of Britain by Angle, Saxon and Jutish invaders who gained footholds in the SE in the 5th century and over the next 200 years extended and consolidated their settlements from the Channel to the Firth of Forth. Scholars distinguish four main early dialects: of the *Jutes* in Kent, the *Saxons* in the south, the *Mercians* or *S Angles* in the Midlands, and the *Northumbrians* or *N Angles* north of the Humber. For several centuries English was in competition with other languages: first the various Celtic languages of Britain, then Danish (9th–11th centuries), then Norman French after the Conquest of 1066, and Latin as the language of the Catholic church. In 1362 English replaced French as the language of the law courts of England, although the records continued for some time to be kept in Latin. When William Caxton set up his printing press in London in 1477 the new hybrid language (vernacular English mixed with courtly French and learned

Latin) became increasingly standardized, and by 1611, when the Authorized Version of the Bible was published, the educated English of the Home Counties and London had become the core of what is now called 'Standard English'. By the end of the 16th century, English was firmly established in England, Scotland, Wales and Ireland, and with the establishment of the colonies in N America in the early 17th century took root in what are now the United States, Canada and the Caribbean islands. Sea-faring, exploration, commerce and colonial expansion took the language to every corner of the world. By the time of Johnson's *Dictionary* in 1755 and the American Declaration of Independence in 1776, English was recognizably the language we use today. Current English has absorbed material from many other tongues, and is used in varieties from British English, American English, Canadian English, Indian English through to Singapore English and Nigerian English and many pidgins and creoles. It is spoken by more than 300 million 'native speakers', and between 400 and 800 million 'foreign users'. It is the official language of aircraft and shipping, the leading language of science, technology, computers and commerce, and a major medium of education, publishing and international negotiation. For this reason scholars frequently refer to its latest phase as 'World English'.

Erse originally a Scottish form of the word 'Irish', a name applied by Lowland Scots to Scottish Gaelic and also sometimes used as a synonym for Irish Gaelic.

Esperanto an artificial language devised in 1887 by Dr Ludwig L Zamenhof, a Warsaw oculist (1859–1917), as an international auxiliary language. For its structure and vocabulary it draws upon various European languages. Esperantists refer to Esperanto as a 'planned language' and to the natural languages of the world as 'ethnic languages'. Its spelling is phonetic, its accents varying according to the ethnic backgrounds of its users. For its centenary in 1987, Esperantists have claimed some 10 to 15 million users worldwide, and say that

Esperanto estas tre facile lernebla lingvo ('Esperanto is a very easily learnable language').

Finnish a member of the Finno-Ugric language family, the national language of Finland and closely related to neighbouring Estonian, Livonian, Karelian and Ingrian languages. At the beginning of the 19th century Finnish had no official status, Swedish being the language of education, government and literature in Finland. The publication of the *Kalevala*, a national epic poem, in 1835, contributed greatly to the arousal of Finnish national and linguistic feeling.

Finno-Ugric a group or family of more than 20 languages spoken by some 22 million people in scattered communities from Norway in the west to Siberia in the east and to the Carpathian mountains in the south. Speakers of these languages tend to live in enclaves surrounded by Germanic, Slavonic and Turkish speakers, all of whom exercise influence upon the local Finno-Ugric varieties. The best-known members of the family are Finnish, Lapp, and Hungarian.

Flemish a member of the W Germanic branch of the Indo-European language family, spoken in N Belgium and the Nord department of France. It is closely related to Dutch.

French a member of the Romance branch of the Indo-European language family, spoken in France, Belgium, Luxembourg and Switzerland in Europe, Canada (especially the province of Quebec) in N America, such islands as Haiti and Martinique in the Caribbean, Reunion and Mauritius in the Indian Ocean, New Caledonia in the Pacific, and the Francophone (French-speaking) countries of N and W Africa (for example, Mali, Côte d'Ivoire and Senegal). French developed from the Latin spoken in Gaul and was established as a distinct language by the 9th century. Varieties used north of the river Loire formed the *Langue d'oil* (*oui*) while those to the south formed the *Langue d'oc*, according to their word for 'yes'. However, by the 13th century the dialect of the Ile de France was supreme and became in 1539 the official medium of the courts and administration of France. Its literary form still serves as the basis of *le bon français* ('correct French'), which is officially protected by the Académie Française (founded in 1635 at the behest of Cardinal Richelieu) and by occasional legislation in both France and Quebec.

Gaelic a member of the Celtic branch of the Indo-European language family, spoken in Ireland, Scotland and (until 1974) the Isle of Man. It is, along with English, one of the national languages of the Republic of Ireland, with over half a million speakers, and is known there as both Irish and Irish Gaelic. In Scotland, speakers of Gaelic number around 90,000 and are concentrated in the Western Isles, in parts of the NW coast and in the city of Glasgow. Gaelic has been in decline for several centuries, subject until quite recently to neglect within the British state. There is a small Gaelic-speaking community in Nova Scotia, Canada.

German a member of the W Germanic branch of the Indo-European language family, the national language of W Germany, E Germany and Austria, and an official language of Switzerland. There are many spoken varieties of German, the best known distinction being between High German (*Hochdeutsch*) and Low German (*Plattdeutsch*). 'High' and 'low' refer to geography rather than social status, Hochdeutsch originating in the central and southern highlands of Germany, Austria and Switzerland, Plattdeutsch being used in the lowlands of N Germany. However, modern standard and literary German is based on High German, in particular on the Middle German dialect used by Martin Luther for his translation of the Bible in the 16th century. Low German is closer to English in its sound system, the verb 'to make' being *machen* in High German but *maken* in Low German. Such English words as *angst, blitz, frankfurter, hamburger, poltergeist, sauerkraut* and *schadenfreude* are borrowings from High German.

Germanic a branch of the Indo-European language family, divided into *East Germanic*

(Gothic, now extinct), *North Germanic* (Danish, Faroese, Icelandic, Norwegian and Swedish), and *West Germanic* (Afrikaans, Dutch, English, Flemish, Frisian, German and Yiddish). The Germanic languages differ from the other Indo-European languages most prominently in the consonant shift known as Grimm's Law. In it, the sounds *p, t, k* became either (as in English) *f, th, h* or as in Old High German *f, d, h*. Thus, the typical Indo-European of the Latin *pater* is *father* in English and *Fater* in Old High German. In addition, the Indo-European *b, d, g* moved to become *p, t, k*, or in Old High German *f, ts, kh*; compare Latin *duo*, English *two*, and German *zwei* ('tsvai').

Greek a well-documented member of the Indo-European language family which has passed through at least five distinct phases since the second millennium BC: *Ancient Greek*, including Mycenaean, around the 14th to 12th centuries BC; *Archaic Greek*, which included the language of the Homeric epics, coming to an end around 800 BC; the *Classical Greek* of Athens (Attic Greek), Sparta (Doric Greek) and Ionia (Ionian Greek), until around 400 BC; the *Hellenistic Greek* or *Koine* ('common language') of Greece, Asia Minor, W Asia and Egypt from around the 4th century BC to the 4th century AD, first spread by the campaigns of Alexander the Great; *Byzantine Greek*, the language of the Eastern Roman or Byzantine Empire, 5th to 15th centuries AD; and *Modern Greek*, with a variety of dialects but most noticeably divided into the general vernacular (*Demotic Greek* or *Demotiki*) and the so-called 'pure' language of education and traditional literature (*Katharevousa*). In its earlier phases Greek was spoken mainly in Greece proper, the islands, the W coast of Asia Minor and in colonies in Sicily, the Italian mainland and S France. Hellenistic Greek was an important language not only in the Near East but also in the Roman Empire generally, and is the form also known as *New Testament Greek* (in which the Gospels and other books of the New Testament of the Bible were first written). Byzantine Greek was the medium of the Greek Orthodox Church. Modern Greek, in both its forms, is spoken in Greece and in Cyprus, as well as wherever Greeks have settled throughout the world (especially Canada, the United States and Australia). Classical Greek word-forms continue to have a great influence in the world's scientific and technical vocabulary, and make up a large part of the technical vocabulary of English.

Gujarati or **Gujerati** a member of the Indo-Iranian branch of the Indo-European language family, spoken in and around the state of Gujarat in India. It is written in its own script – a variant of the Devanagari script used for Sanskrit and bindi.

Hamito-Semitic languages a family of languages spoken widely throughout the world but commonly associated with N Africa and W Asia. It has two main branches, the *Hamitic* languages of N Africa and the *Semitic* languages originating in Syria and Mesopotamia, Palestine and Arabia but now found from Morocco in the west to the Arabian or Persian Gulf in the east. The Hamitic languages include ancient Egyptian, Coptic and Berber, while the Semitic languages include the most numerous – Arabic, and such other culturally significant languages as Hebrew, Aramaic and Syriac. The scripts of the two best known Hamito-Semitic languages, Arabic and Hebrew, run from right to left.

Hebrew a member of the Hamito-Semitic language family spoken in W Asia by the ancient Hebrews, sustained for many centuries as the liturgical language of Judaism, and revived and developed in the 20th century as Modern Israeli Hebrew, the national language of the State of Israel. It is the original language of the Old Testament of the Bible. Such English words as *bar-mitzvah*, *cherub*, *Hanukkah*, *Jehovah/Yahweh*, *kosher*, *rabbi*, *seraph* and *shibboleth* are borrowings from Hebrew. The Hebrew alphabet is written from right to left.

Hindi a member of the Indo-Iranian branch of the Indo-European language family, the official language of the Republic of India, although resisted as such by the Dravidian-speaking states of the south. Hindi is a north Indian language with many varieties. Hindi proper is used by some 30 per cent of Indians, in such northern states as Uttar Pradesh and Madhya Pradesh. Bihari, Punjabi and Rajasthani, the dominant language varieties in the states of Bihar, Punjab and Rajasthan, are claimed by some to be varieties of Hindi, by others to be distinct languages. Hindi has close historical and cultural links with Sanskrit, the classical language of Hinduism, and is written (from left to right) in Devanagari script.

Hindustani a member of the Indo-Iranian branch of the Indo-European language family, closely related to Hindi and Urdu and originating in the bazaars of Delhi. It serves as a lingua franca in many parts of the Republic of India, and was the contact language during the British Raj between many of the British in India and their servants, shopkeepers, etc. It is sometimes known as Bazaar Hindi.

Hungarian a member of the Finno-Ugric language group, spoken principally in Hungary but also in Czechoslovakia, Romania and Yugoslavia. Known as *Magyar* among its speakers, Hungarian is written in a form of the Roman alphabet in which *s* corresponds to English *sh*, and *sz* to *s*. Like the Turks, the Magyars originated in NE Asia; the term 'Hungarian' appears to derive from the Turkish *on ogur* ('ten arrows'), describing their ten tribes, which may also be the origin of the English 'ogre'.

Icelandic a member of the N Germanic branch of the Indo-European language family, spoken only in Iceland and the most conservative in form of the Scandinavian languages. Its early literature is largely anonymous and seems to have originated in Norse colonies in the British Isles (around 9th–10th centuries). This literature consists mainly of the two Eddas and the more numerous Sagas. Despite seven centuries of Danish rule, Icelandic has remained virtually unchanged since the 12th century, being assured survival by the existence of written law and Bishop Gudbrand's vernacular Bible of 1584. After independence in 1918, Icelandic has experienced a revival, as well as governmental protection against such outside linguistic influences as English-language broadcasting. Halldor Laxness (1902–), writing about Icelandic life in the style of the Sagas, was awarded a Nobel prize in 1955.

Indian languages traditionally, the languages of the subcontinent of India; since 1947, the languages of the Republic of India. These number some 200, depending on whether a variety is classified as a language or a dialect, and divide into five main groups, the two most widespread of which are the *Indo-European* languages (mainly in the north) and the *Dravidian* languages (mainly in the south). The Indo-European languages include the two classical languages, Sanskrit and Pali, and such vernaculars as Bengali, Hindi, Gujarati, Marathi, Oriya, Punjabi and Urdu. The Dravidian languages include Kannada, Malayalam, Tamil and Telugu. A wide range of scripts are used, including Devanagari for Hindi, Arabic for Urdu, and distinct scripts for the various Dravidian languages. The Sino-Tibetan group of languages occurs widely in Assam and along the Himalayas.

Indo-European languages a family of languages whose members are now distributed throughout every inhabited continent of the world but which were once located along a geographical band from India through Iran into NW Asia, E Europe, the northern Mediterranean lands, N and W Europe and the British Isles. When first described in the 19th century this family was known as the Aryan and then the Indo-Germanic language family. However, because of an unwelcome association with ideas of 'Aryan' racial purity and superiority and with the ideology of Nazi Germany, both titles have been abandoned by scholars in favour of the neutral 'Indo-European'. The family includes some of the world's leading classical languages (Sanskrit and Pali in India, Zend Avestan in Iran, and Greek and Latin in Europe) as well as several of the most widely spoken languages of the modern world (English worldwide; Spanish in Iberia, Latin America and elsewhere; and the Hindi group of languages in N India). Eastern Indo-European languages are often called the *satem* group (Zend, 'a hundred') while western Indo-European languages are the *centum* group (Latin, 'a hundred'); this illustrates a split that occurred over 3,000 years ago, between those which had an *s*-sound in certain words and those which had a *k*-sound. Scholars have reconstructed a Proto-Indo-European ancestral language by comparing the sound systems and historical changes within the family, but continue to dispute the original homeland of this ancient form, some arguing for N Europe, others for Russia north of the Black Sea.

Irish Gaelic first official language of the Irish Republic, but much less widely used than the second official language, English.

Irish a common name for Irish Gaelic. At one time, especially in the form 'Erse', also a name for the Gaelic of Scotland.

Italian a member of the Romance branch of the Indo-European language family. Its development parallels the integration of the Italian peninsula and the plains south of the Alps into a cultural and national unity. The standard language originates in the Tuscan dialect of the Middle Ages, particularly as used for literary purposes by Dante Alighieri. With a strong infusion of Latin for religious, academic and educational purposes the written standard has tended to be highly formal and divorced from the many regional dialects (often mutually unintelligible) that are still largely the everyday usage of the general population. Italian has provided English with much of the vocabulary of music (*adagio, arpeggio, cello, crescendo, diminuendo, mezzosoprano, pianoforte*), Italian cuisine (*lasagne, macaroni, pasta, pizza, ravioli, spaghetti, tagliatelle*), and an assortment of social comment (*extravaganza, graffiti, imbroglio, mafia, seraglio*).

Japanese a traditionally isolated language of E Asia, spoken almost exclusively in the islands of Japan. It may be related to Korean. Japanese has a well-defined structure of syllables generally ending with a vowel (*dojo, judo, hiragana, samurai, Honshu, kimono,*

Mitsubishi, teriyaki). Culturally and linguistically influenced by Mandarin Chinese, Japanese is written in a triple system that has evolved from Chinese ideograms: its *Kanji* ideograms are close to their Chinese originals, while the *Hiragana* system is a syllabary for the general language, and *Katakana* a syllabary for foreign borrowings. In print, the three systems blend on the page in a manner comparable to the distinct typefaces of the Roman alphabet. Japanese has an extensive religious and secular literature, including such terse poetic forms as haiku. English words adapted into Japanese belong in *gairaigo*. the foreign vocabulary expressed in the syllable signs of Katakana: *fairu* ('file') *ereganto* ('elegant'), and *purutoniumu* ('plutonium'). Shorter forms are common: *fainda* ('viewfinder') and *wapuro* ('word-processor').

Korean the language of Korea, written from the 5th century AD in Chinese characters until the invention of an alphabet by King Sejong in 1443. This alphabet was, however, discouraged as 'vulgar letters' (*onmun*) and banned by the colonizing Japanese. However, after World War II it has been revived as 'top letters' (*hangul*). The linguistic affiliations of Korean are unclear, but it appears to be distantly related to Japanese.

Lallans a variant of 'lowlands' and a name for Lowland Scots, whether conceived as a language in its own right or as a northern dialect of English. Because of its rustic associations, Lallans has been known since the 18th century as the 'Doric', in contrast with the 'Attic' usage of Edinburgh ('the Athens of the North').

Latin an Indo-European language of ancient Italy, named after the Latini, the inhabitants of Latium ('the broad plain'), the territory around the river Tiber and the city of Rome. Latin has passed through four influential phases: as the language of Republican Rome, the Roman Empire, the Roman Catholic church, and W European culture, science, philosophy and law during the Middle Ages and the Renaissance. It is the parent form of the Romance languages, noted for its highly inflected grammar and conciseness of expression; thus, one word *amabunt* expresses the three English words 'they will love', and *amabuntur* means 'they will be loved'. The influence of Latin in Europe is still considerable, and indirectly both the language and its classical literature still affect many modern languages and literatures. Latin vocabulary has entered English in two major waves: as religious vocabulary from Anglo-Saxon times until the Reformation, and as the vocabulary of science, scholarship and the law from the Middle Ages onwards. In the 17th century the makers of English dictionaries deliberately converted Latin words into English, enlarging the already powerful French component of English vocabulary into the language of education and refinement, placing *fraternity* alongside 'brotherhood', *feline* beside 'cat-like', and so on. Many 'Latin tags' are in regular use in English: *habeas corpus* ('you may have the body'), *ipse dixit* ('he said it himself'), *non sequitur* ('it does not follow'). Nowadays, with fewer students studying Latin in schools and universities, there is a tendency to make Latin words more conventionally English; for example, 'cactuses' rather than *cacti*. There is also some uncertainty about usage, for example whether words like 'data' and 'media' are singular or plural.

Latvian the language of Latvia, one of the two surviving members of the Baltic branch of the Indo-European language family, the other being Lithuanian.

lingua franca any language that is used as a means of communication by groups who do not themselves normally speak that language at home and cannot otherwise do business; for example, English is a lingua franca used by Japanese doing business in Finland, or Swedes in Saudi Arabia. The term derives from Italian (*la lingua franca* 'the Frankish tongue'), referring to French as used around the Mediterranean shores in the Middle Ages. Many of the world's lingua francas are pidgin languages, such as Bazaar Hindi (Hindustani), Bazaar Malay, and Melanesian Pidgin English (also known as Tok Pisin), the official language of

Papua New Guinea.

Lithuanian an Indo-European language spoken by the people of Lithuania that through its geographical isolation has retained many ancient features of the Indo-European language family. It acquired a written form in the 16th century, and is currently spoken by around three to four million people.

Malay a member of the Western or Indonesian branch of the Malayo-Polynesian language family, used in the Malay peninsula and many of the islands of Malaysia and Indonesia. The dialect of the S Malay peninsula is the basis of both standard Malay in Malaysia and Bahasa Indonesia, the official language of Indonesia. Bazaar Malay is a widespread pidgin variety used for trading and shopping. The Malaysian and Indonesian varieties officially employ slightly different versions of the Roman alphabet but are also sometimes written in the Jawi form of Arabic script.

Malayo-Polynesian also known as Austronesian, a family of languages spoken from Malaysia through the Indonesian archipelago, parts of Indo-China, Taiwan, Madagascar, and the Melanesian islands to Polynesia (excluding Australia and most of New Guinea). The group contains some 500 distinct languages, some spoken by only a few hundred people, others the standard languages of millions. The family includes Malay in Malaysia, Bahasa Indonesia, Fijian, Hawaiian and Maori.

Maori a member of the Polynesian branch of the Malayo-Polynesian language family, spoken by the Maori people of New Zealand. Of the approximately 300,000 Maoris today, not more than one third use the language, but efforts are being made to strengthen it after a long period of decline and official indifference. In Maori, New Zealand is *Aotearoa* ('land of the long white cloud') and European settlers are *Pakeha*, a term often used by white New Zealanders when contrasting themselves with the Maori.

Norse generally, the older forms of the Danish, Icelandic, Norwegian and Swedish languages; more particularly, the older common form of Norwegian and Icelandic, in

which the Sagas and Eddas were written in the 12th to 14th centuries.

Norwegian a member of the N Germanic branch of the Indo-European language family, spoken in Norway. It is divided into two distinctive but mutually intelligible forms: *Dano-Norwegian* (Bokmal or Riksmal) and *New Norwegian* (Nynorsk). The first arose during the union with Denmark (1380-1814), while the second was created in the 19th century by Ivar Aasen from various rural dialects, to revive the tradition of Old Norse. Both varieties are used in government and education, but Dano-Norwegian dominates the media and literature.

Pali an ancient Indo-European language of N India, related to Sanskrit and a classical language of Buddhism.

Persian a member of the Indo-Iranian branch of the Indo-European language family and the official language of the state once known as Persia but now officially called Iran. Persian is known to its own speakers as *Farsi*, the language of the province of Fars (Persia proper). It is written in the Arabic script, from right to left, and has a large admixture of Arabic religious, philosophical and technical vocabulary. Words in English which derive from Persian include *balcony*, *bazaar*, *paradise*, *sherbet* and *turban*.

Pidgin English commonly and loosely used to mean any kind of 'broken' or 'native' version of the English language, pidgin English proper began as a trade jargon or contact language between the British and the Chinese in the 19th century. *Pidgin* is believed to have been a Chinese pronunciation of the English word 'business' (whence the expression, 'This isn't my pigeon'). There have in fact been many 'pidgin Englishes', often with common elements because of the wide range of contacts made by commercial shipping. The original pidgin English of the Chinese ports combined words of English with a rough-and-ready Chinese grammatical structure, while Melanesian Pidgin English (also known as Tok Pisin) tends to combine English and the syntax of local Melanesian languages. Thus, instead of the

English pronoun 'we', Melanesian pidgin English has both *yumi* (you and me, speaking to each other) and *miffela* (me and fellow, excluding you).

pidgin languages trade jargons, contact languages or lingua francas arising in ports and markets where people of different linguistic backgrounds meet for commercial and other purposes. Generally, a pidgin comes into existence to answer short-term needs, for example Korean Bamboo English as used during the Korean War. Unless there is a reason for extending the life of such a hybrid form (in the case of Korean Bamboo English combining elements of English, Korean and Japanese), it will fade away when the need passes. Usually a pidgin is a rough-and-ready blend of the vocabulary of one (often more dominant) language with the syntax or grammar of one or more other groups (usually in a dependent position). Pidgin English in various parts of the world, *français petit nègre*, and Bazaar Hindi or Hindustani are examples of pidgins which have served long-term purposes, to the extent of being acquired by children as one of their everyday languages.

Polish a member of the Slavonic branch of the Indo-European language family, spoken mainly in Poland. Polish is written in the Roman and not the Cyrillic alphabet and its standard form is based on the dialect of Poznan, in W Poland.

Portuguese a member of the Romance branch of the Indo-European language family, the national language of Portugal, closely related to Spanish and strongly influenced by Arabic. It is also spoken in Brazil, Angola, Mozambique and other ex-Portuguese overseas possessions.

Prakrit a general name for the ancient Indo-European dialects of N India, contrasted with the sacred classical language Sanskrit. The word is itself Sanskrit, meaning 'natural', as opposed to *Sanskrit*, which means 'perfected'. The Prakrits are considered to be the ancestors of such modern N Indian languages as Hindi, Punjabi and Bengali.

Provençal a member of the Romance branch of the Indo-European language family and spoken in and around Provence in SE France. It is now regarded as a dialect or patois but during the Middle Ages was in competition with French, was the language of the troubadours, and had a strong literary influence on such neighbouring languages as Italian, Spanish and Portuguese. Since the 19th century attempts have been made to revive it as a literary language.

Punjabi a member of the Indo-Iranian branch of the Indo-European language family, spoken in the Punjab provinces of India and Pakistan. It is considered by some to be a variety of Hindi, by others to be a distinct language.

Romance languages the branch of the Indo-European languages descended from the Latin of the Roman Empire ('popular' or 'vulgar' as opposed to 'classical' Latin). The present-day Romance languages with national status are French, Italian, Portuguese, Romanian and Spanish. Romansh (or Rhaeto-Romanic) is a minority language of Switzerland which is nevertheless one of the four official languages of the country, while Catalan and Gallego (or Galician) in Spain, Provençal in France and Friulian and Sardinian in Italy are recognised as distinct languages with strong regional and/or literary traditions of their own.

Romanian a member of the Romance branch of the Indo-European language family, spoken in Romania, Macedonia, Albania and parts of N Greece. It has been strongly influenced by the Slavonic languages and by Greek. The Cyrillic alphabet was used until the 19th century, when a variant of the Roman alphabet was adopted.

Romansh a member of the Romance branch of the Indo-European language family, spoken by some 50,000 people in the eastern cantons of Switzerland and accorded official status alongside French, German and Italian in 1937. It is also known among scholars as Rhaeto-Romanic.

Russian a member of the Slavonic branch of the Indo-European language family. The people of Russia proper refer to it as 'Great

Russian', in contrast with Ukrainian (which they call 'Little Russian') and the language of Byelorussia ('White Russian'). It is written in the Cyrillic alphabet and is the standard means of communication throughout the Soviet Union. Words in English which derive from Russian include *apparatchik*, *commissar*, *cosmonaut*, *czar/tsar*, *pogrom*, *samovar* and *vodka*.

Sanskrit the dominant classical language of the Indian subcontinent, a member of the Indo-Iranian group of the Indo-European language family, and the sacred language of Hinduism. The oldest form of Sanskrit is *Vedic*, the variety used in the Vedas and Upanishads (around 1500–700 BC). *Classical Sanskrit* was systematized by Panini and other grammarians in the latter part of the first millennium BC and became fixed as the spoken and written language of culture, philosophy, mathematics, law and medicine. It is written in Devanagari script and is the language of the two great Hindu epics, the *Mahabharata* and the *Ramayana*, as well as many other classical and later works. Sanskrit vocabulary has not only influenced the languages of India, Thailand and Indonesia but has also enriched several European languages, including English, with such words as *bhakti*, *guru*, *karma*, *kundalini*, *mahatma*, *pundit*, *swami* and *yoga*, all relating to Hindu religion and philosophy.

Scots the form of the English language as traditionally spoken and written in Scotland, regarded by some scholars as a distinct language. It is also known as *Inglis* (now archaic, and a variant of 'English'), *Lallans* ('Lowlands'), *Lowland Scots* (in contrast with the Gaelic of the Highlands and Islands), and *the 'Doric'* (as a rustic language in contrast with the 'Attic' or 'Athenian' language of Edinburgh's literati, especially in the 18th century). It is also often referred to as 'Broad Scots' in contrast to the anglicized language of the middle classes. Scots derives from the Northumbrian dialect of Anglo-Saxon or Old English, and has been spoken in SE Scotland since the 7th century. During the Middle Ages it spread from the Central Lowlands northeastwards to Aber-

deenshire and to the far north, where it blended with the Norn dialects of Orkney and Shetland (once distinct varieties of Norse). Scots has been a literary language since the 14th century, with a wide range of poetry, ballads and prose records, including two national epic poems, Barbour's *Bruce* and Blind Harry's *Wallace*. With the transfer of the court to England upon the Union of the Crowns in 1603 and the dissemination of the King James Bible, Scots ceased to be a national and court language in the 17th century, but has retained its vitality among the general population and in various literary and linguistic revivals. In Scotland a wide range of traditional Scots usage intermixes with standard English, such as *advocate* (barrister), *close* (entrance to a staircase of tenement flats), *kirk* (church).

Slavonic or Slavic languages a branch of the Indo-European language family spoken in central and E Europe, the Balkans and parts of N Asia. The family divides into three groups: the *southern group* (Serbo-Croat, Slovene and Macedonian in Yugoslavia, and Bulgarian in Bulgaria); the *western group* (Czech and Slovak in Czechoslovakia, Sorbian in E Germany, and Polish and its related dialects); and the *eastern group* (Russian, Ukrainian, and Byelorussian, in the Soviet Union). There is such a high degree of uniformity among the Slavonic languages that scholars speak of a 'dialect continuum' in which the users of one variety understand tolerably well much of what is said in other varieties. Some Slavonic languages, like Polish, are written in the Roman alphabet while others, like Russian, are written in Cyrillic.

Spanish a member of the Romance branch of the Indo-European language family, traditionally known as Castilian and originally spoken only in NE Spain, in the kingdoms of Castile and Aragon. As the language of the court it has been the standard and literary language of the Spanish state since the 13th century, but has never succeeded in supplanting such regional languages as Basque, Gallego or Galician, and Catalan. Because of the long Muslim dominance of the S Iberian peninsula,

Spanish has been strongly influenced by Arabic. Spanish is now a world language, spoken in all South American and central American countries (save Brazil, Guyana, Surinam and French Guiana), as well as in Mexico and the Philippines. Words in English of Spanish origin include *bronco*, *cargo*, *galleon*, *mosquito*, *ranch* and *sherry*.

Swahili a language of Bantu origin and strongly influenced by Arabic, a widespread lingua franca of E Africa and the national language of Tanzania (1967) and Kenya (1973).

Swedish a member of the N Germanic branch of the Indo-European language family, spoken in Sweden and Finland and closely related to Danish and Norwegian. Words in English of Swedish origin include *ombudsman*, *smorgasbord* and *tungsten*.

Syriac an ancient Semitic language, originally the Aramaic dialect spoken in and around Edessa (now in Turkey) and widely used in W Asia from around 700 BC to 700 AD. From the 3rd to 7th centuries it was an important Christian liturgical and literary language.

Tamil a Dravidian language of SE India, spoken principally in the state of Tamilnadu (formerly, Madras state) and also in N Sri Lanka. It is written in its own distinctive script. Words in English of Tamil origin include *catamaran*, *cheroot*, *mulligatawny* and *pariah*.

Turkish a language of central and W Asia, best known as the national language of Turkey. Originally written in Arabic script, the Turkish of Turkey has since 1928 been written in a variant of the Roman alphabet. Varieties of Turkish are spoken in NW Iran and several of the Asian republics of the Soviet Union, and all have been influenced by Arabic and Persian. Words of Turkish origin in English include *divan*, *coffee*, *cossack*, *horde*, *kiosk* and *yoghourt/yogurt*.

Ukrainian a member of the Slavonic branch of the Indo-European language family, spoken in the Ukraine, a republic of the Soviet Union. It is closely related to Russian and is sometimes referred to by Russians as 'Little Russian', a description which Ukrainians generally do not find appropriate.

Urdu a member of the Indo-Iranian branch of the Indo-European language family, related to Hindi but written not in Devanagari but in Arabic script. Strongly influenced by Persian and Arabic, Urdu is the official language of Pakistan and a language used by Muslims in India.

Welsh a member of the Celtic branch of the Indo-European language family, spoken by over half a million people in Wales out of a total population of just under three million. Among its own speakers it is known as *Cymraeg*. Modern Welsh, like English, is not a highly inflected language, but British, the Celtic ancestor of Welsh, was like Latin and Anglo-Saxon a highly inflected form. The continuous literature of Welsh, from the 6th century onwards, contains the whole range of change from British to present-day Welsh. Although the spoken language is the strongest of the surviving Celtic languages it has been in retreat in the face of English expansion since the accession of the Welsh Henry Tudor (as Henry VII) to the throne of England. Nowadays, few Welsh people speak only Welsh; they are either bilingual or only speak English.

Yiddish a member of the W Germanic branch of the Indo-European language family, deriving from Rhineland German and spoken by Polish and Russian Jews, who have carried it to Israel, the United States and many other parts of the world. In the United States, Yiddish has had a powerful impact on English, especially in the city of New York and in the national media. Such words and expressions as *bagel*, *chutzpa(h)*, *kibbitz*, *mensh*, *nosh*, *schlemiel*, *schmaltz* and *schmuck* are currently acquiring international status in English. Isaac Bashevis Singer (1904–), born in Poland, US citizen 1943, who writes in Yiddish, won the Nobel Prize for Literature in 1978.

THE INDO-EUROPEAN LANGUAGES

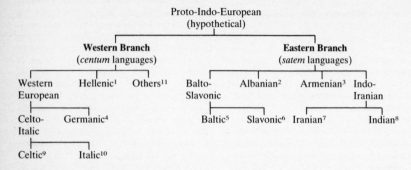

1 Hellenic: Greek (including *Ancient, *Archaic, *Classical, *Koine, *Byzantine and the modern forms *Demotiki* and *Katharevousa*)

2 Albanian: Albanian

3 Armenian: Armenian

4 Germanic: Afrikaans, *Anglo-Saxon, (Old English), Bavarian, Danish, Dutch/Flemish, English/Scots, Faroese, Frisian, German (Low, High, Swiss, etc), *Gothic, Icelandic, Luxemburgish, *Old Norse, *Old High German, Norwegian, Swedish, Yiddish

5 Baltic: Latvian, Lithuanian, *Old Prussian

6 Slavonic: Bulgarian, Byelorussian, Croatian, Czech, Kashubian, Macedonian, Polish,
(or Slavic)   Pomeranian, Russian, Serbian, Slovak, Slovene, Sorbian, Ukrainian

7 Iranian: *Avestan (Zend or Zand), *Bactrian, Baluchi, Kurdish, *Median, Ossetic, *Pahlavi, *Parthian, Pashto, Persian (Farsi), Tadzhik

8 Indian: Assamese, Bengali, Bhili, Bihari, Gujarati, Hindi, Kashmiri, Konkani, Marathi, Oriya, Pahari, *Pali, Punjabi, Rajasthani, *Sanskrit, Sindhi, Sinhalese, Urdu

9 Celtic: Breton, *Brythonic, *Cornish, Gaelic (Irish, *Manx and Scottish), *Gaulish, *Goidelic, Welsh

10 Italic: (1) *Latin, *Oscan, *Umbrian
                 (2) Romance: Catalan, French, Gallego (Galician), Italian, Portuguese, Provençal, Romanian (Rumanian), Romansh, Spanish (Castilian)

11 others   *Anatolian (including Hittite), *Tocharian

The Indo-European languages An outline diagram of the historical relationships among the Indo-European languages, followed by lists of languages in each branch of the family tree. Extinct languages are marked with an asterisk (*).

Grammar and Usage

grammar as an aspect of language and the study of language, grammar has traditionally been seen as dealing with the rules of combining words into phrases and clauses, phrases and clauses into sentences, and sentences into paragraphs.

'good grammar', in this view, is the result of an adequate education in one or more classical language, in the mother tongue, in one or more foreign languages, or a combination of these. As a consequence, people with 'bad grammar' have tended to be seen as uneducated, poorly educated, inattentive while being educated, and/or inclined towards sloppy thinking and slovenly style.

classical approach this widespread view has emerged out of 2,500 years of educational procedures and social attitudes relating to the classical Greek *grammatike tekhne* ('art of letters'). This original 'grammar' was an analytical approach to writing, intended to improve the understanding and the skills of scribes, philosophers and litterateurs. Because of a traditional emphasis on writing and (since the 15th century) on the standardizing impact of print, spoken or colloquial language has often been perceived as less grammatical than written – especially literary – language. In addition, when compared with Latin, English has also been widely regarded as having 'less' grammar or at least a simpler grammar; it would be truer, however, to say that English and Latin have *different* grammars, each complex in its own way.

linguistics is the contemporary study of language, in which grammar or syntax is generally understood to refer to the arrangement of the elements in a language, for the purposes of acceptable communication in speech, writing and print. All forms of a language, standard or otherwise, have their grammars or grammatical systems, which children acquire as they mature into that language; indeed, a child may acquire several overlapping systems within one language (especially a non-standard form for everyday life and a standard form linked with writing, school and national life).

natural grammar not even the most comprehensive grammar book (or grammar) of a language like English, French, Arabic or Japanese completely covers or fixes the implicit grammatical system that people use in their daily speech. The rules and tendencies of natural grammar operate largely in non-conscious ways, but can, for many social and professional purposes, be studied and explicitly developed as conscious as well as inherent skills.

part of speech the grammatical function of a word, described in the grammatical tradition of the Western world, based on Greek and Latin. The four major parts of speech are the noun, verb, adjective and adverb; the minor parts of speech vary according to schools of grammatical theory, but include the article, conjunction, preposition and pronoun. In languages like Greek and Latin the part of speech of a word tends to be invariable (usually marked by an ending or inflection); in English, it is much harder to recognise the function of a word simply by its form. Some English words may have only one function (for example, *and* as a conjunction). Others, however, may have several functions (for example, *fancy*, which is a noun in the phrase 'flights of fancy', a verb in 'fancy that', and an adjective in 'a fancy hat').

noun the grammatical part of speech that names (or stands for) such classes of words as persons (*John*), animals (*cat*), places (*London*), things (*hat*), qualities (*love*), actions (*arrest*), ideas and abstractions (*idea, abstraction, reality, Communism, Roman Catholicism*), and so on. *Types of noun* A *common noun* does not begin with a capital letter (*child, cat*), while a proper noun does, because it is the name of a particular person, animal, place, etc (*John, Rover, London*). A *concrete noun* refers to things which can be sensed (*dog*, *box*), while an **abstract noun** relates to generalizations 'abstracted' from life as we observe it (*love*, *illness*). A countable noun can have a plural form (*book*: *books*), while an uncountable noun or mass noun cannot (*dough*). Many English nouns can be used both countably and uncountably (*wine*: 'Have some wine; it's one of our best wines'). A **collective noun** is singular in form but refers to a group (*flock*, *committee*), and a **compound noun** is made up of two or more nouns (*blackbird*, *coffee jug*). A **verbal noun** is formed from a verb (*run*: *running*; *build*:*building*; *regulate*: *regulation*) and in English many simple words are both noun and verb (*crunch*, *jump*, *rain*). Adjectives are often used as nouns (a *local* man: one of the *locals*; a *regular* soldier: an *Army regular*).

verb the grammatical part of speech for what someone or something does (*to go*, *to imagine*), experiences (*to live*, *to die*), or is (*to be*, *to exist*). In the sentences 'They *saw* the accident', 'She *is working* today', and 'He *should have been trying to meet* them', the words in italics are verbs and, in the last case, two verb groups together; these sentences show just how complex the verbs of English can be. Verbs involve the grammatical categories known as number (singular or plural: 'He *runs*; they *run*'), voice (active or passive: 'She *writes* books; it *is written*'), mood (statements, questions, orders, emphasis, necessity, condition, and so on), aspect (completed or continuing action: 'She *danced*; she *was dancing*'), and tense (variation according to time: simple present tense, present continuous/progressive tense, simple past tense, and so on). *Types of verb* A **transitive** verb takes a direct object (he saw *the house*), while an **intransitive verb** has no object ('She laughed'). An **auxiliary** or **helping verb** is used to express tense and/or mood ('He *was* seen'; 'They *may* come'), while a **modal verb** or **modal auxiliary** generally shows only mood; common modals are *may/might*, *will/ would*, *can/could*, *shall/ should*, *must*. The infinitive of the verb usually includes 'to' (*to go*, *to run*, and so on), but may be a bare infinitive (for example, after modals, as in 'She may *go*'). A **regular verb** forms tenses in the normal way (*I walk: I walked: I have walked*); **irregular verbs** do not (*swim:swam:swum*; *put:put:put*, and so on). Because of their conventional nature, regular verbs are also known as weak verbs, while some irregular verbs are strong verbs with special vowel changes across tenses, as in *swim:swam:swum* and *ride:rode:ridden*. A **phrasal verb** is a construction in which a particle attaches to a usually one-syllabled verb for certain grammatical and idiomatic purposes (for example, *put* becoming *put up*, as in 'He put up some money for the project', and *put up with*, as in 'I can't put up with this nonsense any longer'). Verbs are formed from nouns and adjectives by adding affixes (prison: *imprison*; light: *enlighten*; fresh: *freshen (up)*; pure: *purify*). Some words function as both nouns and verbs (*crack*; *run*), both adjectives and verbs (*clean*; *ready*), and as nouns, adjectives and verbs (*fancy*).

adjective the grammatical part of speech for words that describe nouns (for example, *new* and *enormous*, as in 'a new hat' and 'an enormous dog'). Adjectives generally have three degrees (grades or levels for the description of relationships): the **positive** degree (*new*; *enormous*), the **comparative** degree (*newer*; *more enormous*), and the **superlative** degree (*newest*; *most enormous*). Some adjectives, however, because of their meanings, do not normally need comparative and superlative forms; one person is not normally 'more asleep' than someone else, a lone action is unlikely to be 'the most single-handed action ever seen', and many people dislike the expression 'most unique', because something unique is supposed to be the only one that there is. However, for purposes of emphasis or style these conventions are often set aside ('I don't know who is more unique; they are both remarkable people'). Double comparatives such as 'more bigger' are unnecessary and not grammatical in Standard English, but Shakespeare is on record as using a double superlative ('the most unkindest cut of all'). Some adjectives may have both of the comparative and superlative forms (*commoner* and *more common*; *commonest* and *most common*), while occasionally shorter words may be given the forms for longer words ('Which of them are the *most clear*?') for emphasis or other reasons. When an adjective comes before a noun it is attributive; if it comes after noun and verb (for example, 'It looks *good*'), it is predicative. Some adjectives can only be used predicatively ('The child was asleep', but not 'the asleep child'). The participles of verbs are regularly used adjectivally ('a *sleeping* child', 'boiled milk') and often in compound forms ('a *quick-acting* medicine', 'a *glass-making* factory', 'a *hard-boiled* egg', '*well-trained* teachers'). Adjectives are often formed by adding suffixes to nouns (sand: sand*y*; nation: nation*al*).

adverb the grammatical part of speech for words that modify or describe verbs ('She ran *quickly*'), adjectives ('a *beautifully* clear day'), and adverbs ('They did it *really* well'). Most adverbs are formed from adjectives or past participles by adding *-ly* (*quick: quickly;*), or *-ally* (*automatic: automatically*). Sometimes they are formed by adding *-wise* (*like: likewise*, and *clockwise*, as in 'moving clockwise'; in 'a clockwise direction', *clockwise* is an adjective). Some adjectives have a distinct form from their partnering adjective, as with good/well ('It was *good* work; they did it *well*'). Others do not derive from adjectives (*very* in 'very nice'; *tomorrow* in 'I'll do it tomorrow'), and some are unadapted adjectives (*pretty*, as in, 'It's pretty good'). Sentence adverbs modify whole sentences or phrases: '*Generally*, it rains a lot here'; '*Usually*, the town is busy at this time of year'. Sometimes there is controversy in such matters. *Hopefully* is universally accepted in sentences like 'He looked at them hopefully' (in a hopeful way), but some people dislike it in, 'Hopefully, we'll see you again next year' (We hope that we'll see you again next year).

article a grammatical part of speech, of which there are two in English: the *definite article* 'the', which serves to specify or identify a noun (for example, 'This is the book I need'), and the *indefinite article* 'a' or 'an (before vowels), which indicates a single unidentified noun ('They gave me a piece of paper and an envelope'). Some people use the form 'an' before *h* ('an historic building'); this practice dates from the 17th century, when an initial *h* was often not pronounced (as in '*h*onour'), and is nowadays rather grandiose and unnecessary.

conjunction a grammatical part of speech that serves to connect words, phrases and clauses; for example *and* in 'apples and pears' and *but* in 'we're going but they aren't'.

participle a form of the verb, in English either a *present participle* ending in *-ing* (such as 'work*ing*' in 'They were working', 'working men', and 'a hard-working team') or a *past participle* ending in *-ed* in regular verbs (such as 'train*ed*' in 'They have been trained well', 'trained soldiers', and 'a well-trained team'). In irregular verbs the past participle has a special form (such as drive/*driven*; light/*lit*, burn/*burned, burnt*). The participle is also used to open such constructions as 'Coming down the stairs, she paused and...', and 'Angered by the news, he...'. Such constructions, however, are not always logically formed, with amusing or ambiguous results. 'Driving along a country road, a stone broke my windscreen' suggests that the stone was driving along the road. This illogical usage is a *misrelated participle*. A *dangling* or *hanging participle* has nothing at all to relate to: 'While driving along a country road there was a loud noise under the car'. Such sentences need to be completely re-expressed, except in some well-established usages where the participle can stand alone (as in 'Taking all things into consideration, your actions were justified').

inflection or **inflexion**. In grammatical analysis, an ending or other element in a word which indicates its grammatical function, (whether it is plural or singular, masculine or feminine, and so on). In a highly inflected language like Latin, nouns, verbs and adjectives have a whole battery of inflectional endings (for example, in the word *amabunt* the base *am* means 'love', and the complex *abunt* indicates the kind of verb, the future tense, indicative mood, active voice, third person and plurality). English is not a highly inflected language, but does have inflections for plural and for certain forms of the verb, (as in the *s* in 'He runs', indicating the third person singular, while in 'the books' it indicates plurality).

preposition a grammatical part of speech coming before a noun or pronoun in order to show a location ('in', 'on'), time ('during'), or some other relationship (such as figurative relationships in phrases like 'by heart' or 'on time'). In the sentence 'Put the book on the table' *on* is a preposition governing the noun 'table' and relates the verb 'put' to the phrase 'the table', indicating where the book should go. Some words of English that are often prepositional in function may, however, be used adverbially, as in the sentences, 'He picked the book up' and 'He picked up the book', in which the ordering is different but the meaning the same. In such cases *up* is called an *adverbial particle* and the form 'pick up' is a *phrasal verb*.

pronoun a grammatical part of speech that is used in place of a noun, usually to save repetition of the noun (such as 'The people arrived around nine o'clock. *They* behaved as though we were expecting *them*'). Words like *they*, *them*, *he*, *she*, and so on, are *personal pronouns* (because they represent people), words like *this/these* and *that/those* are *demonstrative pronouns* (because they demonstrate or point to something : this book and not that book and so on), words like *that* and *who* can be *relative pronouns* in sentences like 'She said that she was coming' and 'Tell me who did it' (because they relate one clause to another), and words like *myself* and *himself* are *reflexive pronouns* (because they reflect back to a person, as in 'He did it himself').

punctuation the system of conventional signs (*punctuation marks*) and spaces by means of which written and printed language is organized so as to be as readable , clear and logical as possible. It contributes to the effective layout of visual language; if a work is not adequately punctuated there may be problems of ambiguity and unclear association among words. Conventions of punctuation differ from language to language and there are preferred styles in

the punctuation of a language such as English. While some people prefer a fuller use of punctuation, others punctuate more lightly; comparably, the use of punctuation will vary according to the kind of passage being produced, a personal letter, a newspaper article and a technical report all being laid out and punctuated in distinctive ways.

period a punctuation mark (.). The term 'period' is universally understood in English, and is the preferred usage in N America; the term 'full stop' is the preferred form in Great Britain, while the term 'point' is casually used but is not generally considered a technical term. Traditionally, the period has two functions: to mark the end of a properly formed sentence, and to indicate that a word has been abbreviated. In present-day practice these functions continue, but in such contexts as fictional dialogue and advertising, periods often follow phrases and incomplete sentences in order to represent speech more faithfully or for purposes of emphasis. In addition, such abbreviations as acronyms are unlikely to have periods (NATO rather than N.A.T.O.) and certain abbreviations may or may not have periods, according to the stylistic preference of the writer (for example, 'Mr Greene' or 'Mr. Greene'.

comma a punctuation mark (,), intended to provide breaks or pauses inside a properly formed sentence; commas may come at the end of a clause, after a phrase, or in lists (as in apples, pears, plums, and pineapples; or, apples, pears, plums and pineapples). Uncertain where sentences properly end, many occasional writers use a comma instead of a period (or full stop), writing *We saw John last night, it was good to see him again*, rather than *We saw John last night. It was good to see him again*. The meaning is entirely clear in both cases. One solution in such situations is to use a *semicolon* (;), which combines period and comma and serves well in bridging the gap between the close association of the comma and the sharp separation of the period.

colon punctuation mark (:), intended to direct the reader's attention forward, usually because what follows explains or develops what has just been written, for example, *The soldiers carried a variety of weapons: rifles, hand-guns, several machine-guns and an anti-tank weapon.*

semicolon a punctuation mark (;) with a function halfway between the sharp separation of sentence from sentence by means of a period (.) and the gentler separation provided by a comma (,). Although semicolons are not as commonly used as formerly, they provide a useful half-way stage between commas and periods. Rather than the sharpness of *We saw John last night. It was good to see him again*, and the more casual (and often condemned) *We saw John last night, it was good to see him again*, the use of the semicolon both reflects the close link between the two parts of the statement and is traditionally considered correct and good style: *We saw John last night; it was good to see him again.*

exclamation mark or exclamation point. A punctuation mark (!), used to indicate emphasis or strong emotion ('What a surprise!'). Usually the emphasis or emotion is built directly into the text, as part of a story, dialogue, and so on, but the exclamation can also be placed in brackets to indicate that the writer is surprised by something, especially by something in a quotation. Although the exclamation mark is a natural part of imaginative or emotional writing, its use is generally kept to a minimum in serious prose and technical writing.

question mark a punctuation mark (?), used to indicate enquiry or doubt. When indicating enquiry, it is placed at the end of a *direct question* ('Who is coming?') but never at the end of an *indirect question* ('He asked us who was coming'.). When indicating doubt, it usually appears between brackets, to show that a writer or editor is puzzled or uncertain about a statement or quotation.

apostrophe a mark used in the written presentation of English ('). It serves primarily to indicate a missing letter or number (as in *don't* for 'do not' and *'47* for '1947'). It also often precedes the plural *s* used with numbers

and abbreviations (as in *the 1970's* and *a group of P.O.W's*); it is possible, however, to do without the apostrophe in such usages (as in *the 1970s*, *a group of POWs*). The use of an apostrophe to help indicate a plural (as in a shopkeeper's *Apple's* and *Tomato's*, followed by their prices) is nonstandard and regarded by many as semi-literate. Grammatically, the apostrophe indicates possession (as in *the gentleman's hat*, *the gentlemen's hats*, *the lady's hat*, *the ladies' hats*). In the case of certain words ending with *s*, usage is split, as between *James's book* and *James' book*. In current English, the possessive apostrophe is often omitted from such usages as *in ten months' time/in ten months time* and such titles as *Chambers Dictionary*. Many people otherwise competent in writing have great difficulty with the apostrophe, which has never been stable at any point in its history, and some authorities argue that its use will decline over the next few decades, especially as a marker of possession.

asterisk a star-like punctuation mark (*) used to link the asterisked word with a note at the bottom of a page, to mark that certain letters are missing from a word (especially a taboo word such as *f**k*), or to indicate that a word or usage is nonexistent (as in 'In English we say three boys and not **three boy*').

hyphen a punctuation mark (-) with two functions: to join words, parts of words, syllables, and so on, for particular purposes, and to mark the break in a word continued from the end of one line to the beginning of the next line. The hyphenation of compound words in English is by no means clearcut; the same writer may in one article write, for example, *world view*, *worldview* and *world-view*. Broadly speaking, conventional hyphenation is a first stage in bringing two words together; if their close association is then generally agreed, the two words are written or printed as one (*teapot*, as opposed to *tea-pot* or *tea pot*), or are kept apart for visual and aesthetic reasons (*coffee pot* rather than *coffee-pot* or **coffeepot*). Practice does, however, vary wildly. There is a growing tendency in the use of prefixes towards omitting the hyphen.

Terms

accent a way of speaking that identifies a person with a particular country ('a New Zealand accent'), region ('a Northern Irish accent'), language ('a French accent'), social class ('an upper-class accent'), linguistic style ('a Country and Western accent'), or some mixture of these ('a French-Canadian accent'; 'a working-class Glasgow accent'; 'a middle-class south-east of England accent'). People often describe only those who belong to groups other than their own as having accents ('She spoke with a funny accent'; 'He had a harsh foreign accent'), and may give them special names, such as an Irish brogue or a Northumbrian burr.

acronym a word formed from the initial letters and/or syllables of other words, intended as a pronounceable abbreviation, such as *NATO* (*N*orth *A*tlantic *T*reaty *O*rganization), *radar* (*ra*dio *d*etecting *a*nd *r*anging), and *Asda* (*As*sociated *Da*iries). Many acronyms are so successfully incorporated into everyday language that their original significance is widely overlooked.

acrostic a number of lines of writing, especially verse, whose initial letters (read downwards) form a word, phrase or sentence. A *single acrostic* is formed by the initial letters of lines only, while a *double acrostic* is formed by both initial and final letters. In the original Greek, acrostic means 'at the extremity of a line or row'.

alphabet a set of conventional symbols for the purpose of writing, so-called from *alpha* and *beta*, the names of the first two letters of the classical Greek alphabet. Alphabetic writing began in W Asia during the second millennium BC among the northern Semitic peoples, and now takes many forms, including the Arabic script, written from right to left, the

Devanagari script of the Hindus, in which the symbols 'hang' from a line common to all the symbols, and the Greek alphabet, with the first clearly delineated vowel symbols. Each letter of the alphabets descended from Greek represents a particular sound or sounds, usually described as *vowels* (*a*, *e*, *i*, *o*, *u*, in the English version of the Roman alphabet), *consonants* (*b*, *p*, *d*, *t*, and so on) and *semi-vowels* (*w*, *y*). Letters may operate in special arrangements to produce distinct sounds (for example *a* and *e* together in words like *tale* and *take*, or *o* and *i* together to produce a 'wa' sound in the French *loi*), or may have no sound whatsoever (for example the silent letter *gh* in 'high' and 'through').

antonymy near or precise oppositeness between or among words. 'Good' and 'evil' are antonyms, 'good' and 'bad' are also antonyms, and therefore 'evil' and 'bad' are synonyms in this context. Antonymy may vary with context and situation; in discussing the weather, 'dull' and 'bright' are antonymous, but when talking about knives and blades the opposite of 'dull' is 'sharp'.

dialect a variety of a language, either as spoken in a particular area ('Yorkshire dialect'), by a particular social group ('the dialect of educated Standard English'), or both ('the black American dialects of English'). The term is used both neutrally, as above, and in a judgemental and often dismissive way ('the locals have a harsh, ugly dialect; few of them have been properly educated'). In the latter case, the standard language of a community is not seen as a dialect itself, but as the 'proper' form of that language, dialects being considered in some way corrupt. This is a matter of social attitude, not of scientific study.

dictionary a book that contains a selection of the words of a language, with their pronunciations and meanings, usually arranged in alphabetic order. The first dictionaries of English (in the 17th century) served to explain 'hard' Latin and Greek words in everyday English. Samuel Johnson's dictionary of 1755 was one of the first dictionaries of standard English, to which Noah Webster in 1828 offered an American alternative. The term dictionary is also applied to any usually alphabetic work of reference containing specialized information about a particular subject, art or science, such as a dictionary of music.

etymology the study of the origin and history of words within and across languages. It has two major aspects: the study of the *phonetic* or the written forms of words, and the *semantics* or meanings of those words. Etymological research has been particularly successful in tracing the development of words and word elements within the Indo-European language family. Standard dictionaries of a language like English usually contain etymological information within square brackets at the end of each entry.

homonymy an aspect of language in which, through historical accident, two or more words may sound and look alike (*homonymy* proper, as in a farmer's bull and a papal bull), may sound the same but look different (*homophony*; as in *air* and *heir*; *gilt* and *guilt*), and may look the same but sound different (*homography*, as in the wind in the trees and roads that *wind*). Homonyms, homophones and homographs seldom pose problems of comprehension, because they usually belong in different contexts. They may, however, be used to make puns (such as talking about a papal bull in a china shop).

jargon language usage that is complex and hard to understand, usually because it is technical or occupational, more technical and complicated than necessary, used in the wrong contexts, or intended to impress or confuse ('technical jargon'; 'writing in pseudoscientific jargon'; 'using a meaningless and barbarous jargon'). Jargon is often also known as *gobbledygook/gobbledegook* and *bafflegab*, and is sub-categorized as *bureaucratese* and *officialese* (the usage of bureaucrats and officials), *journalese* (the languages of newspapers), *medicalese* (the often impenetrable usage of doctors), and so on. In writing, jargon may be highly formal, while in speech it often contains slang expressions.

rhetoric traditionally, the art of the orator (in Greek, *rhetor*) or of public speaking and debate. Rhetorical skills are valued in such occupations as politics, the law, preaching and broadcasting. Accomplished rhetoricians need not be sincere in what they say; they should, however, be effective, or at least entertaining. Nowadays, 'rhetoric' is often a pejorative term ('Cut the rhetoric and tell us what you really think!').

rhetorical question a question, often used by public speakers and debaters, which either does not require an answer or for which the speaker intends to provide his or her own answer ('Where else in the world can we find such brave young men as these?').

slang extremely informal language usage that often serves to promote a feeling of group membership. Slang is not usually accepted in serious, formal speech or writing, and includes expressions that may be impolite or taboo in conventional terms. Some types of slang are highly transient; others may last across generations, and gain currency in the standard language. Because slang is often vivid, suggestive and linked with such subjects as defecation, urination, sex, blasphemy, and getting drunk, many people find it offensive. It is, however, pervasive in its influence and effects. Thus, the standard French *tête* ('head') derives from *testa* ('nutshell' or 'pot'), probably the slang of the Roman legions. It can be compared with the English expression 'Use your nut'.

synonymy near or identical meaning between or among words. There are, however, very few strict synonyms in any language, although there may be many near-synonyms, depending upon the contexts in which the words are used. Thus, 'brotherly' and 'fraternal' are synonyms in English, but a 'brotherhood' is not exactly the same as a 'fraternity'; people talk about the brotherhood of man but seldom if ever about the 'fraternity of man'. *Brotherhood* and *fraternity* are not therefore strictly synonymous.

Philosophy

Philosophy, from the Greek 'love of wisdom', is a difficult subject to define, since unlike biology or history, for example, it does not possess a specific object of enquiry. Rather, philosophy is concerned with fundamental problems which arise in every area of human thought and activity, and which cannot be resolved by a specific method. In thinking about morality, for example, we are likely to wonder whether human beings are responsible for their actions, or whether everything which we do is determined. Similarly, in considering the development of science, we may be led to ask whether there can be any final scientific truth. In the past there have been many philosophical systems which attempt to give a comprehensive account of the world and of the place of human beings within it. Contemporary philosophers, however, are more inclined to think of philosophy as an activity – an investigation of the fundamental assumptions which govern our ways of understanding and acting in the world.

This section begins with a table of *Great Philosophers*, from the ancient Greeks to the present day, followed by brief individual accounts of each philosopher and his leading ideas. This is inevitably selective, but an attempt has been made to include those philosophers who are most representative of historical periods and major trends in philosophy. The section concludes with a glossary of the most frequently encountered philosophical *Terms*.

GREAT PHILOSOPHERS

name	dates	nationality	representative work
Heraclitus	c.544–483 BC	Greek	*On Nature* (fragments)
Parmenides	c.510–c.450 BC	Greek	fragments
Socrates	469–399 BC	Greek	———
Plato	428–347 BC	Greek	*Republic*
			Phaedo
Aristotle	384–322 BC	Greek	*Nicomachean Ethics*
			Metaphysics
Epicurus	341–270 BC	Greek	fragments
Lucretius	c.99–55 BC	Roman	*On the Nature of Things*
Plotinus	205–270 AD	Greek	*Enneads*
Augustine	354–430	N African	*Confessions*
			City of God
Aquinas	c.1225–1274	Italian	*Summa Theologica*
Duns Scotus	c.1266–1308	Scottish	*Opus Oxoniense*
William of Occam	c.1285–1349	English	*Commentary of the Sentences*
Nicholas of Cusa	1401–1464	German	*De Docta Ignorantia*
Giordano Bruno	1548–1600	Italian	*De la Causa, Principio e Uno*
Bacon	1561–1626	English	*Novum Organum*
			The Advancement of Learning
Hobbes	1588–1679	English	*Leviathan*
Descartes	1596–1650	French	*Discourse on Method*
			Meditations on the first Philosophy
Pascal	1623–1662	French	*Pensées*
Spinoza	1632–1677	Dutch	*Ethics*
Locke	1632–1704	English	*Essay Concerning Human Understanding*
Leibniz	1646–1716	German	*The Monadology*
Vico	1668–1744	Italian	*The New Science*
Berkeley	1685–1753	Irish	*A Treatise Concerning the Principles of Human Knowledge*
Hume	1711–1776	Scottish	*A Treatise of Human Nature*
Rousseau	1712–1778	French	*The Social Contract*
Diderot	1713–1784	French	*D'Alembert's Dream*
Kant	1724–1804	German	*The Critique of Pure Reason*
Fichte	1762–1814	German	*The Science of Knowledge*
Hegel	1770–1831	German	*The Phenomenology of Spirit*
Schelling	1775–1854	German	*System of Transcendental Idealism*
Schopenhauer	1788–1860	German	*The World as Will and Idea*
Comte	1798–1857	French	*Cours de philosophie positive*
Mill	1806–1873	English	*Utilitarianism*
			On Liberty
Kierkegaard	1813–1855	Danish	*Either Or*
			Concept of Dread

name	dates	nationality	representative work
Marx	1818–1883	German	*Economic and Philosophical Manuscripts* *The German Ideology*
Dilthey	1833–1911	German	*The Rise of Hermeneutics*
Peirce	1839–1914	American	*How to Make our Ideas Clear*
Nietzsche	1844–1900	German	*Thus Spake Zarathustra* *Beyond Good and Evil*
Bergson	1859–1941	French	*Creative Evolution*
Husserl	1859–1938	German	*Logical Investigations* *Ideas*
Russell	1872–1970	English	*Principia Mathematica*
Lukács	1885–1971	Hungarian	*History and Class Consciousness*
Collingwood	1889–1943	English	*An Essay on Philosophical Method* *The Principles of Art*
Wittgenstein	1889–1951	Austrian	*Tractatus Logico–Philosophicus* *Philosophical Investigations*
Heidegger	1889–1976	German	*Being and Time*
Gadamer	1900–	German	*Truth and Method*
Sartre	1905–1980	French	*Being and Nothingness* *Critique of Dialectical Reason*
Merleau-Ponty	1908–1961	French	*The Phenomenology of Perception* *The Visible and the Invisible*
Quine	1908–	American	*Word and Object*
Foucault	1926–1984	French	*The Order of Things*

Great Philosophers

Aquinas St Thomas c.1225–74. Italian Dominican scholastic philosopher, monk, and theologian, known as the 'Angelic Doctor'; canonized in 1323. His *Summa Contra Gentiles* (1259-64) argues that reason and faith are compatible. His unfinished *Summa Theologica*, begun 1265, deals with the nature of God, morality, and the work of Christ. His works embodied the world view taught in universities up to the mid-17th century, and include scientific ideas derived from Aristotle. In 1879 they were recognized as the basis of Catholic theology by Pope Leo XIII, who had launched a modern edition of his works.

Aristotle 384–322 BC. Greek philosopher, pupil of Plato, founder of the Lyceum, and tutor to Alexander the Great. Aristotle turned away from Platonic mysticism, placing great emphasis on classification and knowledge through the experience of the senses. He is responsible for pioneering work in natural science, metaphysics, logic, ethics, politics, and literary criticism. His notion of the Unmoved Mover was to have a profound effect upon subsequent thinkers and the idea was incorporated into Christian theology.

Augustine 354–430. Christian saint, theologian, and a Father of the Church. He wrote about 230 works as well as many sermons and pastoral letters. Augustine's most famous writings are his *Confessions*, his spiritual autobiography, and the influential *De Civitate Dei/ City of God* vindicating the Christian Church and Divine Providence in 22 books.

Bacon Francis 1561–1626. English philosopher, who became Lord Chancellor and later Viscount St Albans. Bacon's most significant contribution to philosophy was a new conception of science which broke away from Aristotle. In the *Novum Organum* 1620 he redefined the task of natural science, seeing it as a means of empirical discovery and a method of increasing human power over nature. He laid the foundations for scientific induction and the British empiricism of the 18th century.

Bergson Henri 1859–1941. French philosopher. He was professor of philosophy at the Collège de France (1900–21), and in 1928 was awarded the Nobel Prize for Literature. For Bergson time, change, and development were the essence of reality and he considered that time was not a succession of distinct and separate instants, but a continuous process in which one period merged imperceptibly into the next. In *Creative Evolution* 1907 he expressed his dissatisfaction with the materialist account of evolution popularized by such thinkers as Herbert Spencer, and attempted to prove that all evolution and progress are due to the working of the *élan vital* or life-force.

Berkeley George 1685–1753. Irish philosopher, who became Bishop of Cloyne. He is best known for his immaterialism, the belief that there is no such thing as material substance. This is not a denial that things exist, merely that they lack substantiality. For Berkeley, everyday objects are collections of ideas or sensations, hence the dictum *esse est percipi* ('to exist is to be perceived').

Bruno Giordano 1548–1600. Italian philosopher. He became a Dominican in 1563, but his sceptical attitude to Catholic doctrines forced him to flee from Italy in 1577. After visiting Geneva and Paris, he lived in England 1583–85, where he wrote some of his finest works. After returning to Europe, he was arrested by the Inquisition in 1593 in Venice, and burned at the stake for his adoption of Copernican astronomy and his heretical religious views.

Collingwood Robin George 1889–1943. English philosopher, professor of philosophy at Oxford. Collingwood stressed the importance of 'doing philosophy historically'. In effect this meant that any philosophical theory or position could only be properly understood within its own historical context and not from the point of view of the present. He is also significant for his aesthetic theory, outlined in

The Principles of Art 1938.

Comte Auguste 1798–1857. French philosopher, one of the first to consider the development of science in a historical perspective. He argued that human thought passed through three stages: theological, metaphysical, and positive. In the first, events were explained by reference to deities, and in the second by reference to occult forces. In the positivist phase, science relies only on the correlation of observed facts. He announced the emergence of sociology as the culmination of this development.

Descartes René 1596–1650. French philosopher, who exposed the doubtful nature of commonly accepted 'knowledge' (such as that acquired through the senses). He then attempted to rebuild human knowledge using as his foundation *Cogito ergo sum* ('I think, therefore I am'). The 'thinking thing' (*res cogitans*) or mind, Descartes identified with the human soul or consciousness; the body, though somehow interacting with the soul, was a physical machine, secondary to, and in principle separable from the soul.

Diderot Denis 1713–84. French philosopher of the Enlightenment and editor of the celebrated Encyclopaedia. He exerted an enormous influence on contemporary social thinking with his materialism and anti-clericalism. His materialism, most articulately expressed in *D'Alembert's Dream*, sees the natural world as nothing more than matter and motion. He gave an account of the origin and development of life which is purely mechanical.

Dilthey Wilhelm 1833–1911. German philosopher, a major figure in the tradition of hermeneutics. He argued that the 'human sciences' (*Geisteswissenschaften*) could not employ the same methods as the natural sciences, but must use the procedure of 'understanding' (*Verstehen*) to grasp the inner life of an alien culture or past historical period. Thus Dilthey extended the significance of hermeneutics far beyond the interpretation of texts to the whole of human history and all of human culture.

Duns Scotus c.1266–1308. Franciscan monk, born in Scotland, and an important figure of medieval scholasticism. On many points he turned against the orthodoxy of Aquinas; for example, he rejected the idea of a necessary world, favouring a conception of God as absolute freedom capable of spontaneous activity. In the medieval controversy over universals he advocated nominalism.

Epicurus 341–270 BC. Greek materialist philosopher of the Hellenic period. He believed the world was made up of atoms moving in empty space; the unpredictability of the movement of the atoms accounted for chance and human freedom. In ethics he advocated ataraxia, a blissful state of peace, which came about through the avoidance of suffering. For Epicurus, the purpose of knowledge was to free people from ignorance and superstition.

Fichte Johann Gottlieb 1762–1814. German philosopher, pupil of Kant, who later taught at the universities of Jena and Berlin. Fichte criticized the Kantian doctrine of the thing-in-itself as dogmatic, and developed a comprehensive form of subjective idealism, expounded in his *The Science of Knowledge* 1794. For Fichte, the absolute ego posits both the external world (the non-ego) and the finite self. Morality consists in a striving of this finite self to rejoin the absolute.

Foucault Michel 1926–84. French philosopher, one of the generation that came to maturity in the 1950s, and who rejected phenomenology and existentialism. His work is concerned with how forms of knowledge and forms of human subjectivity are constructed by specific institutions and practices, and is largely historical in character. Foucault was deeply influenced by Nietzsche, and developed a novel analysis of the operation of power in modern society using Nietzschean concepts.

Gadamer Hans-Georg 1900– . German philosopher, a major contributor to the tradition of hermeneutics in the 20th century. In his masterpiece, *Truth and Method* 1960, he argued that 'understanding' is fundamental to human existence, and that all understanding

101

takes place within a tradition. The relation between text and interpreter can be viewed as a dialogue, in which the interpreter must remain open to the truth of the text. The historical nature of this dialogue excludes the possibility of a definitive interpretation.

Hegel Georg Wilhelm Friedrich 1770–1831. German philosopher, author of *The Phenomenology of Spirit* 1807, *Encyclopaedia of the Philosophical Sciences* 1817, and *Philosophy of Right* 1821. He was professor of philosophy at Heidelberg 1817–18, and at Berlin 1818–31. Hegel conceived of consciousness and the external object as forming a unity, in which neither factor can exist independently. Mind and nature are two abstractions of one indivisible whole. Thus the world is the unfolding and expression of one all-embracing absolute idea, an organism constantly developing by its own internal necessity so as to become the gradual embodiment of reason. Each system by its own development brings about its opposite (antithesis), and finally a higher synthesis unifies and embodies both.

Heidegger Martin 1889–1976. German philosopher, one of the most influential of the 20th century. In his major work, *Being and Time* 1927, he used the methods of Husserl's phenomenology to develop an account of the concrete structures of human existence, *Dasein*. Throughout his work, he argued that Western philosophy had forgotten the basic question of the 'meaning of being', and in his later writings meditated on the fate of a world dominated by science and technology.

Heraclitus c. 544–483 BC. Greek pre-Socratic philosopher, who saw everything in the universe as fire. Fire was the fundamental material which accounted for all change and motion in the world; it also explained the contradictory, ever-changing, nature of things. Nothing in the world ever stays the same, hence the famous dictum 'one cannot step in the same river twice'.

Hobbes Thomas 1588–1679. English philosopher, best known for his political philosophy, notably his notion of the social contract. In the state of nature man is in a state of

perpetual war of all against all. The social contract is enacted to bring about civil peace; the state comes into existence as a result of the individual's voluntary submission to established power. Without the state the life of the individual would be 'solitary, poor, nasty, brutish and short' (*Leviathan* 1651).

Hume David 1711–76. Scottish moral and political philosopher, a figure of the Enlightenment, whose indifferently-received philosophical work *A Treatise of Human Nature* 1740 has proved to be a lasting stimulus. He shared many of the beliefs of the British Empiricist school, especially those of Locke.

Husserl Edmund Gustav Albrecht 1859–1938. German philosopher, founder of phenomenology, one of the most influential movements in 20th-century philosophy. His aim was to grasp the essence of phenomena through a close descriptive analysis of the structures of experience. In order to achieve this the philosopher must carry out a 'transcendental reduction', a suspension of all accepted beliefs, including the belief in a world independent of consciousness.

Kant Immanuel 1724–1804. German philosopher. In his *The Critique of Pure Reason* 1781 he argued that our knowledge of the world cannot be the mere aggregate of impressions impinging on our consciousness from our senses (roughly the view of Locke), but that it is dependent upon the conceptual apparatus of the human understanding – which is not itself derived from experience. In ethics, Kant stressed that the right action is objectively determinable and must conform to a moral law he called the 'Categorical Imperative'; feelings and inclinations are not a basis for moral decisions.

Kierkegaard Soren Aabye 1813–55. Danish philosopher, usually considered to be the founder of existentialism. He was a consistent opponent of Hegel's philosophy, arguing that no system of thought could explain the unique experience of the individual. He defended Christianity, suggesting that God cannot be known through reason, but only through a 'leap of faith'.

Leibniz Gottfried Wilhelm 1646–1716. German philosopher and mathematician. In his metaphysical works (such as *The Monadology* 1714) he argued that the world (that is, the totality of everything there is) consisted of innumerable units – 'monads'. Each monad's properties determined its past, present, and future, and were selected by God so that monads, though independent of each other, interacted predictably; this meant that Christian faith and scientific reason need not be in conflict, and that 'this is the best of all possible worlds'.

Locke John 1632–1704. English philosopher. His great works are *Treatises on Government* (from a Whig viewpoint) and *Essay Concerning Human Understanding*, both 1690. The former, influential also in America and France, supposed governments to derive authority from popular consent (regarded as a 'contract'), so that a government may be rightly overthrown if it infringes such fundamental rights of the people as religious freedom. The latter maintained that experience was the only source of knowledge (empiricism), and that 'we can have knowledge no farther than we have ideas' prompted by such experience.

Lucretius (Titus Lucretius Carus) c. 99–55 BC. Roman poet and Epicurean philosopher, whose *De Rerum Natura/On the Nature of Things* envisaged the whole universe as a combination of atoms, and had some concept of evolutionary theory: animals were complex but initially quite fortuitous clusters of atoms, only certain combinations surviving to reproduce.

Lukács Georg 1885–1971. Hungarian philosopher, generally considered to be the founder of the tradition of Western Marxism, a philosophical current opposed to the Marxism of the official communist movement. In his book *History and Class Consciousness* 1923 he emphasized the Hegelian aspects of Marxism, arguing that the working class was both subject and object of history, and could therefore grasp society as a 'totality'. However, Lukács himself repudiated the book, and spent much of the rest of his life as an orthodox communist.

He also made major contributions to Marxist aesthetics and literary theory.

Marx Karl 1818–83. German philosopher and social theorist, whose account of change through conflict is known as historical materialism. The theory demonstrates the material basis of all human activity: 'Life is not determined by consciousness, but consciousness by life' (*German Ideology* 1845). Marx also developed a powerful critique of capitalist society, which he saw as giving rise to alienation, and as ultimately a self-destructive system. The collapse of capitalism would usher in a period of socialism and eventually communism. Marx's philosophical work owes much to the writings of Hegel.

Merleau-Ponty Maurice 1908–61. French philosopher, one of the most significant contributors to phenomenology after Husserl. He attempted to move beyond the notion of a pure experiencing consciousness, arguing in *The Phenomenology of Perception* 1945 that perception is intertwined with bodily awareness and with language. In his posthumous work, *The Visible and the Invisible* 1964, he argued that our experience is inherently ambiguous and elusive, and that the traditional concepts of philosophy are therefore inadequate to grasp it.

Mill John Stuart 1806–73. English philosopher, celebrated for his work in logic, economics, political theory, and ethics. He is identified with the ethical theory known as utilitarianism, formulated in his book *Utilitarianism* 1863, which puts forward the 'greatest happiness' principle. This states that actions are right if they bring about happiness and wrong if they bring about the reverse of happiness. Mill's *On Liberty* 1859 is often seen as the classic philosophical defence of liberalism.

Nicholas of Cusa 1401–64. German philosopher, important in the transition from scholasticism to the philosophy of the modern period. He argued that knowledge is learned ignorance (*docta ignorantia*), since God, the ultimate object of knowledge, stands above the opposites in terms of which human reason grasps the objects of nature. Nicholas also asserted that the universe is boundless and that it has no circumference, thereby breaking with the cosmology of the Middle Ages.

Nietzsche Friedrich Wilhelm 1844–1900. German philosopher whose thought is a sustained attack on the illusions of metaphysics and religion, and on the moral values upheld by these forms of thought. He argued that 'God is dead', and that man is therefore free to create his own values. Nietzsche claimed that knowledge is never objective, but always serves some interest or unconscious purpose. His insights into the relation between thought and language have had an important influence on contemporary philosophy.

Parmenides c. 510–c. 450 BC. Greek philosopher, head of the Eleatic School (so called after Elea in S Italy). Against Heraclitus's doctrine of becoming Parmenides presented the world in a state of being. He saw the world as immobile and dense with matter. Motion was impossible because it implied a contradiction. Parmenides saw speculation and reason as more important than the evidence of the senses.

Pascal Blaise 1623–62. French philosopher-mathematician. He contributed to the development of hydraulics, the calculus, and the mathematical theory of probability. After a mystical experience 1654, he took refuge in the Jansenist monastery of Port Royal and defended the Jansenists against the Jesuits in his *Lettres Provinciales* 1656. His influential *Pensées* 1670 was part of an unfinished defence of the Christian religion.

Peirce Charles Sanders 1839–1914. American philosopher, the founder of pragmatism, who argued that genuine conceptual distinctions must be correlated with some difference of practical effect. He wrote extensively on the logic of scientific enquiry, suggesting that truth could be conceived of as the object of an ultimate consensus. His writings on the theory of signs have also had an influence on 20th-century developments in this area.

Plato 428–347 BC. Greek philosopher, pupil of Socrates and founder of the educational

establishment, the Academy. He was the author of more than 20 philosophical dialogues on such topics as metaphysics, ethics and politics. Central to his teaching is the notion of forms: located outside the everyday world, these are timeless, motionless, and absolutely real. True knowledge can only be knowledge of the forms; the senses can only give us opinion or illusion. Plato and his pupil Aristotle were the most influential thinkers of the ancient world.

Plotinus 205–270. Greek philosopher, who was born in Egypt and lived in Rome. He was the founder of Neo-Platonism, a revival of Plato's teaching which placed strong emphasis upon mysticism. In his principal work, the *Enneads*, Plotinus expounded the notion of the three realities, a religious reworking of Plato's form of the Good.

Quine Willard Van Orman 1908– . American philosopher and logician, professor of philosophy at Harvard. In his important paper *Two Dogmas of Empiricism* 1951, Quine argued against the analytic/synthetic distinction. In *Word and Object* 1960, he put forward the thesis of radical untranslatability, the view that a sentence can always be regarded as referring to many different things.

Rousseau Jean Jacques 1712–78. French philosopher, born in Geneva. He published an examination of the *Origin and Foundations of Inequality Amongst Men* 1754 and *Emile* 1762, outlining a new theory of education to elicit the unspoilt nature and abilities of children. His revolutionary *The Social Contract* 1762, which saw governments as given authority by the people, who could also withdraw it, was immensely influential.

Russell Bertrand Arthur William 1872–1970. English philosopher and mathematician, who contributed greatly to the development of modern mathematical logic. He is also significant in the early 20th-century revival of British empiricism. In later life, Russell moved away from technical philosophy, writing works on education, ethics and the dangers of nuclear war.

Sartre Jean-Paul 1905–80. French philosopher, one of the leading proponents of existentialism in post-war philosophy. His first major work, *Being and Nothingness* 1943, propounds a radical doctrine of human freedom. Our awareness of our own freedom takes the form of anxiety, and we therefore attempt to flee from this awareness into what Sartre terms 'bad faith'. In his later work, Sartre became more sensitive to the social constraints on our action, and in *Critique of Dialectical Reason* 1960 he tried to produce a monumental synthesis of existentialism and Marxism.

Schelling Friedrich Wilhelm Joseph 1775–1854. German philosopher, who began as a follower of Fichte, but moved away from subjective idealism towards a 'philosophy of identity' ('Identitätsphilosophie'), in which subject and object are seen as united in the absolute. His early philosophy influenced Hegel, but in his later work he became one of the first critics of Hegel, arguing that *being* necessarily precedes *thought*.

Schopenhauer Arthur 1788–1860. German philosopher, whose chief work *The World as Will and Idea* 1818 expounded an atheistic, pessimistic theory akin to Buddhism. The driving force of irrational will in human beings results in an ever-frustrated cycle of desire, from which the only escape is a contemplative existence inspired by the arts, and eventual absorption into nothingness. This theory struck a responsive chord in Nietzsche, Wagner, Thomas Mann, and Hardy.

Socrates 469–399 BC. Greek philosopher, who wrote nothing but was immortalized in the dialogues of his pupil, Plato. In his desire to combat the scepticism of the sophists, Socrates asserted the possibility of true knowledge. In the sphere of morality he put forward the view that the good person never knowingly does wrong. True knowledge emerges through dialogue and an abandoning of uncritical claims to knowledge. The effect of Socrates's teaching was disruptive and he was executed by the Athenian authorities.

Spinoza Benedict or Baruch 1632–77. A

Dutch philosopher, who abandoned Judaism for a rationalistic pantheism that owed much to Descartes. He taught that all that we know, mind and matter, is a manifestation of the all-embracing substance that is God, good and evil being relative. His *Ethics* 1677 is his chief work.

Vico Giambattista 1668–1744. Italian philosopher, usually considered to be the founder of the modern philosophy of history. He argued that history develops according to inner laws, and that society passes through a cycle of three phases: the divine, the heroic, and the human. He was critical of Descartes' emphasis on the mathematical and natural sciences, and argued that we can understand history more adequately than nature, since it is we who have made it. This is expressed in his celebrated dictum *verum et factum convertuntur* ('the true and the made are convertible').

William of Occam c. 1285–1349. Medieval English theologian, scholastic philosopher, and critic of Aquinas. A tutor at Oxford university, he was accused of heresy and escaped from prison to Bavaria. On the matter of universals he was, like Duns Scotus, an advocate of nominalism. His abiding contribution to philosophy is a principle of simplicity and economy, known as Occam's razor. This states that 'entities are not to be multiplied beyond necessity'.

Wittgenstein Ludwig 1889–1951. Viennese philosopher, who taught at Cambridge in the 1930s and 1940s and whose work has been very influential. *Tractatus Logico-Philosophicus* 1922 was a detailed working out of a 'picture theory' of language: a sentence must be analysable into 'atomic propositions' whose elements stand for elements of the real world; otherwise, the sentence is not stating any fact. Wittgenstein's later philosophy as presented, for example, in *Philosophical Investigations*, published in 1954, developed a quite different, anthropological, view of language: words are used according to different rules in a variety of human activities – different 'language games' are played with them.

Terms

aesthetics that branch of philosophy which deals with the nature of beauty, especially in art. Aesthetics only emerged as a distinct branch of enquiry in the mid-18th century, the term first being used by the German philosopher Baumgarten (1714–62).

alienation in Hegel's philosophy, a term describing the process whereby consciousness becomes 'lost' to itself through taking on an objective form. Marx denied that alienation was purely a matter of consciousness, and employed the term to describe the condition of the worker in capitalist society.

analytic a term derived from Kant's philosophy: the converse of synthetic. In an analytic judgement the subject is contained in the predicate, and the judgement therefore provides no new knowledge. For example: 'All bachelors are unmarried'.

a posteriori a Latin term meaning 'from what comes after'. A posteriori propositions are true or false in relation to known and established facts of experience.

a priori a Latin term meaning 'from what comes before'. An a priori proposition is one that is known to be true, or false, without reference to experience.

category a fundamental concept applied to being, which cannot be reduced to anything more elementary. Aristotle listed ten: substance, quantity, quality, relation, place, time, position, state, action, passion. Kant derived a table of 12 categories that are applied in experience, although they do not derive from it.

deduction a form of argument in which the conclusion necessarily follows from the premises: it would be inconsistent to accept the premises but deny the conclusion.

dialectic a Greek term, originally associated with Socrates's method of argument through dialogue and conversation. The word was taken over by 19th-century German thinkers, notably Hegel and Marx. For Hegel, dialectic refers to thought which develops through contradiction.

determinism the view that denies human freedom of action, arguing that because everything in the natural world is strictly governed by the principle of cause and effect, human action is no exception.

dualism the belief that reality is essentially dual in nature. Descartes, for example, refers to thinking and material substance. These entities interact, but are fundamentally separate and distinct. Dualism is contrasted with monism.

emotivism a position in the theory of ethics which came to prominence during the 1930s, largely under the influence of A J Ayer's *Language, Truth and Logic* 1936. Emotivists deny that moral judgements can be true or false: they merely express an attitude or an emotional response.

empiricism a long-established tradition in British philosophy, frequently contrasted with rationalism. The principal tenet of empiricism is the belief that all knowledge is ultimately derived from sense experience. It is only through experience that we can come to understand the world.

Enlightenment a broad intellectual movement, reaching its high point in the 18th century. Enlightenment thinkers were believers in social progress and in the liberating possibilities of science. They were often critical of existing society and were hostile to religion, which they saw as keeping the human mind chained down by superstition. Leading representatives of the Enlightenment are Voltaire (1694–1778), Lessing (1729–81), and Diderot (1713–84).

epistemology the study of knowledge. It examines the nature of knowledge and attempts to determine the limits of human understanding. How knowledge is derived, how it is to be validated and tested are central issues in epistemology.

ethics the area of philosophy concerned with human conduct, also referred to as moral philosophy. As well as investigating the meanings of moral terms, ethics studies theories of conduct and goodness.

existentialism a trend in modern philosophy, whose origins are usually traced back to Kierkegaard. Existentialists argue that philosophy must begin from the concrete situation of the individual in the world, and that this situation cannot be comprehended by any purely rational system.

hermeneutics a philosophical tradition concerned with the nature of understanding and interpretation. From its origins in problems of biblical interpretation, hermeneutics has expanded to cover many fields of enquiry, including aesthetics, literary theory, and social science. Dilthey, Heidegger, and Gadamer are influential contributors to this tradition.

idealism a philosophical theory which states that what we ordinarily refer to as the external world is fundamentally immaterial and a dimension of the mind. Objects in the world exist but, according to this theory, they lack substance.

induction by examining and observing particular instances of things, induction derives general statements and laws. It is the opposite of deduction which moves from general statements and principles to the particular. The principle of induction was criticized by Hume because it relied upon belief rather than valid reasoning.

intentionality the property of consciousness whereby it is directed towards an object, even when this object does not exist in reality (such as 'the golden mountain'). Intentionality is a key concept in Husserl's philosophy.

irrationalism a feature of many philosophies rather than a philosophical movement. Irrationalists deny that the world can be comprehended by conceptual thought, and often see the human mind as determined by unconscious forces.

logic a branch of philosophy which studies the structure and principles of valid reasoning and argument. It is also the study of those relations by virtue of which one thing may be said to follow from or be a consequence of another.

materialism the theory that there is nothing in existence over and above matter and matter in motion. Such a theory excludes the possibility of deities. It also sees mind as an attribute of the physical, denying idealist theories which see mind as something independent of body, for example, Descartes' theory of 'thinking substance'.

mediation a technical term in Hegel's philosophy, and in Marxist philosophy influenced by Hegel, describing the way in which an entity is defined through its relations to other entities.

metaphysics a branch of philosophy that deals with first principles, especially 'being' and 'knowing', and which is concerned with the ultimate nature of reality.

monad a technical term deriving from the philosophy of Leibniz, suggesting a soul or metaphysical unit which has a self-contained life. In Leibniz the monads were independent of each other, but were co-ordinated by a 'pre-established harmony'.

monism the theory that reality is made up of one, and only one, substance. This view is usually contrasted with dualism, which divides reality into two substances, matter and mind. Spinoza (1632–77), the celebrated monist, saw the one substance as God or Nature.

Neo-Platonism a school of philosophy which flourished during the declining centuries of the Roman Empire (3rd–6th centuries AD). Neo-Platonists argued that the highest stage of philosophy is attained not through reason and experience, but through a mystical ecstasy. Many later philosophers, including Nicholas of Cusa, were influenced by Neo-Platonism.

nominalism a philosophical position which argues that universals have no objective reality, and that all that truly exists are particular things. William of Occam was a leading medieval exponent of nominalism.

ontology that branch of philosophy concerned with the study of being as such. In the 20th century, Heidegger distinguished between an 'ontological' enquiry (an enquiry into being) and an 'ontic' enquiry (an enquiry into a specific kind of entity).

phenomena a technical term in Kant's philosophy, describing things as they appear to us, rather than as they are in themselves.

phenomenalism a philosophical position which argues that statements about objects can be reduced to statements about what is perceived or perceivable.

phenomenology an influential tradition in 20th-century philosophy, founded by Husserl. Phenomenology attempts to describe the nature of experience from the standpoint of the experiencing subject, without any metaphysical assumptions. It has been practised by Heidegger, Sartre, and Merleau-Ponty.

positivism a theory, frequently associated with Comte and empiricism, which confines genuine knowledge within the bounds of science and observation. The theory is especially hostile to theology and metaphysics which oversteps this boundary. In the 20th century 'logical positivism' was influential through the work of A J Ayer (1910–   ).

pragmatism a philosophical tradition which interprets truth in terms of the practical effects of what is believed, and in particular the usefulness of these effects.

rationalism in the most common sense of the term, the philosophical view that knowledge of the world is derived from reason, not dependent upon perception and experience.

realism in the medieval philosophy known as scholasticism, the theory that the only truly real things are 'universals'; it is thus opposed to nominalism. In modern philosophy, the doctrine that what is experienced through the senses has an independent existence. As such it is opposed to idealism.

relativism a philosophical position which denies the possibility of objective truth, independent of some specific social or historical context or conceptual framework.

scepticism an ancient philosophical view which doubts the possibility of genuine knowledge. Its most radical form is known as solipsism; the solipsist sees himself/herself as the only real person, assuming other people to be a reflection of their own consciousness.

scholasticism the name given to medieval philosophy, as studied in the schools or universities. Principally scholasticism sought to integrate Christian teaching with Platonic and Aristotelean philosophy.

sophists an assortment of Greek teachers and philosophers, contemporaries of Socrates. They were noted for their bogus reasoning, sophistry being more to do with winning arguments than establishing truth.

structuralism a 20th-century movement which has also been influential in linguistics and literary criticism. Inspired by the work of the Swiss linguist, Ferdinand de Saussure (1857–1913), structuralists believe that objects should be analysed as systems of relations, rather than as positive entities.

syllogism a set of statements devised by Aristotle in his pioneering work on logic. Its purpose is to establish the conditions under which a valid conclusion follows or does not follow from given premises: 'All men are mortal, Socrates is a man, therefore Socrates is mortal,' is a valid syllogism.

synthetic a term employed in Kant's philosophy, and subsequently, to describe a judgement in which the predicate is not contained within the subject, for example: 'The flower is blue'.

thing-in-itself *ding-an-sich* a technical term in the philosophy of Kant, employed to denote the unknowable source of the sensory component of our experience. Later thinkers, including Fichte and Hegel, rejected this concept.

universal a property which is instantiated by all the individual things of a specific class: for example, all red things instantiate 'redness'. Many philosophical debates have centred on the status of universals, including the debate between nominalism and realism.

utilitarianism a theory of ethics, associated with Bentham (1748–1832) and Mill (1806–73). According to utilitarianism, an action is morally right if it has consequences which lead to happiness, and wrong if it brings about the reverse of happiness.

Politics and Government

Until relatively recently the study of politics was almost exclusively concerned with three things: the reasons why people should choose to associate together in communities which accepted common governments and rules; the nature and most appropriate form of such associations; and the precise meaning of terms such as freedom, democracy, and justice that were constantly employed in political dialogue. In the last 50 years the study of politics has widened to embrace such matters as the formal and informal processes of politics, with terminology, concepts, and theories being borrowed from many other disciplines, including sociology, anthropology, and economics.

The six parts of this section comprise an introduction to the *Language of Politics*, which defines some of the most frequently used expressions in politics; brief biographies of the 14 most important *Political Thinkers* since Plato; a section defining some of the most commonly used expressions in *International Politics*, a discussion of the principal *Political Ideologies* of 20th-Century politics; an outline of the *Process of Government*, which considers the ways in which governments may be classified, the main voting systems currently in operation, and the machinery of government in two of the leading Western democracies, Britain, and the USA, and a *Chronology of Major Political Events*, which reviews some of the decisive political developments since the ancient Greeks. Political systems of individual countries are treated in the Gazetteer section and a historical approach to world political events can be found in the History section.

The Language of Politics

authority the capacity to take and enforce decisions within a political system. The nature, sources, and limitations of political authority have been much debated questions since the ancient Greeks.

coalition an association of political groups, usually for some limited or short term purpose, such as fighting an election or forming a government where one party has failed to secure a majority in a legislature following an election.

communication the circulation of information and attitudes within a political system. The importance of mass media such as television has led some thinkers (such as Marshall McLuhan) to develop sophisticated theories of communication.

corporatism the belief that the state in modern capitalist democracies should intervene to a large extent in the economy in order to ensure social harmony.

elite the most influential individuals and groups in a political system. Also called 'the establishment' or 'the governing circles', their identification, selection, and methods of operation have been much discussed issues.

hegemony from Greek 'leadership', in modern political thought it refers to the Marxist approach of thinkers such as Gramsci that sees the state as a means of maintaining the predominance of bourgeois values and ideas over other classes.

ideology a system of basic values, ideas about the nature of the world, and beliefs about ultimate human purposes. All political activity has an ideological base but in some groups, such as Marxists, this is more explicit or self-conscious than in others.

justice a goal of political activity and a subject of political inquiry since Plato. The term has been variously defined as fairness, equity, rightness, the equal distribution of resources and positive discrimination in favour of underprivileged groups.

legitimacy the justification of a ruling group's right to exercise power. Principles of legitimacy have included divine right, popular approval and, in the case of Communist parties, an insight into the true meaning of history.

mandate the right of a government to carry out a programme of policies to which the people are assumed to have given their consent by electing the government to office.

nationalism any movement aimed at strengthening national feeling, especially when aimed at unification of a nation or its liberation from foreign rule. Stimulated by the French Revolution, such movements were widespread in Europe in the 19th century, and subsequently became potent in Asia and Africa.

nationalization policy of bringing essential services and industries under public (government) ownership (as pursued in the UK especially under the Labour government 1945–51) and also taking over assets in the hands of foreign governments or companies. In recent years the trend towards nationalization has slowed and in some countries (Britain, France, and Japan) reversed.

obligation the duty of individuals to obey the laws of their state and, generally, to accept the authority of its government. The basis of political obligation has been depicted as a contract between ruler and people or as arising from the state's ability to provide for the welfare of its citizens.

opinion poll attempt to measure public opinion as a whole by taking a survey of the views of a small, representative sample of the electorate. The first accurately sampled opinion poll was carried out by George Gallup during the US presidential election of 1936. Opinion polls have encountered criticism on the grounds that they may actually influence the outcome of an election, rather than simply predicting it.

order a pattern of behaviour by the members of a society that is conducive to stability and coexistence. Normally associated with some system of rules, as implied by the phrase 'law and order'. Like justice, it has been one of the major concerns of political analysis, but in practice order and justice may sometimes be conflicting goals.

pluralism the view that decision making in contemporary liberal democracies is the outcome of competition among several interest groups in a political system characterized by free elections, representative institutions and open access to the organs of power. This conception is opposed by corporatist and other approaches that perceive power to be centralized in the state and its principal elites.

pressure group (also called 'interest group' or 'lobby') group which puts pressure on parties or governments to ensure laws and treatment favourable to its own interest. Pressure groups have played an increasingly prominent role in contemporary Western democracies. In general they fall into two types: groups concerned with a single issue, such as nuclear disarmament, and groups attempting to promote their own interests, such as oil producers.

privatization reconversion of nationalized services and industries to private ownership, as under the Conservative governments in the UK from 1953, especially the Thatcher government from 1979, and in France since 1986.

propaganda literally the spreading of information, used particularly with reference to the promotion of a religious or political doctrine. This century the word has acquired pejorative connotations because of its association with the use of propaganda by Nazi Germany.

rights an individual's automatic entitlement to certain freedoms and other benefits, usually, in liberal democracies such as the UK, in the context of the individual's relationship with the government of the country. The struggle to assert political and civil rights against arbitrary government has been a major theme of Western political history.

rule of law the doctrine that no individual, however powerful, is above the law. The principle had a significant influence on attempts to restrain the arbitrary use of power by rulers and on the growth of legally enforceable human rights in many Western countries. It is often used as a justification for separating legislative from judicial power.

separation of powers an approach to limiting the powers of government by separating governmental functions into the executive, legislative, and judiciary. The concept has its fullest practical expression in the constitution of the USA.

social contract the idea that government authority derives originally from an agreement between ruler and ruled in which the former agrees to provide order in return for obedience from the latter. Social contract theories are associated particularly with the work of Hobbes, Locke, and Rousseau.

sovereignty absolute authority within a given territory. The possession of sovereignty is taken to be the distinguishing feature of the state, as against other forms of community. The term has an internal aspect, in that it refers to the ultimate source of authority within a state such as Parliament or a monarch, and an external aspect, where it denotes the independence of the state from any outside authority.

Political Thinkers

Aquinas Saint Thomas 1225–74. Italian theologian and political philosopher, born of aristocratic parentage, and canonized in 1323. His *Summa Contra Gentiles* 1259–64 and the incompleted *Summa Theologica* 1266–73 are designed to show that reason and faith are compatible. His works embodied the world view taught in universities up till the mid-17th century, and include scientific ideas derived from Aristotle. In politics he insisted that government should be morally directed and subject to law.

Aristotle 384–322 BC. Greatest of Greek philosophers. He studied under Plato, and became tutor to Alexander the Great. He stressed the value of reason. Amongst his many contributions to political thought were the first systematic attempts to distinguish between different forms of government, ideas about the role of law in the state and the purpose of political activity, an early discussion of social classes and, in general, the very conception of a science of politics.

Bentham Jeremy 1748–1832. British philosopher and legal reformer. His *Fragments on Government* 1776 and *Principles of Morals and Legislation* 1789 outline his Utilitarian philosophy that laws should be 'for the greatest happiness of the greatest number' and he later contended that 'utility' was best served by allowing each individual to pursue their own interests unhindered by restrictive legislation.

Gandhi Mohandas Karamchand 1869–1948. He led the struggle for Indian independence using his philosophy of nonviolence. He proposed that Third World countries like India should develop their own village based, non-capitalist economic system rather than pursuing Western-style industrialization, but this idea has few adherents today.

Hegel Georg Wilhelm Friedrich 1770–1831. German philosopher, author of *The Phenomenology of Mind* 1807, *Encyclopedia of the Philosophical Sciences* 1817, and *Philosophy of Right* 1821. As a 'rightist' he championed religion, the Prussian state and the existing order, but 'leftist' followers include Marx, who used Hegel's dialectic to attempt to show the inevitability of radical change and attacked both religion and the social order.

Hobbes Thomas 1588–1679. English political philosopher, tutor to the exiled Prince Charles. The first thinker since Aristotle to attempt to develop a comprehensive theory of nature, including human behaviour. His political thinking was much influenced by the anarchic age in which he lived and he is best remembered for *The Leviathan* 1651, in which he advocates absolutist government as the only means of ensuring order and security.

Lenin pseudonym of Vladimir Ilyich Ulyanov 1876–1924. Russian statesman who after 1893 devoted himself entirely to revolutionary propaganda. In *What is to be Done* 1902, he maintained that the revolution must be led by a disciplined party of professional revolutionaries; at the 1903 Social Democratic Party congress in London this theory was accepted by the majority of the delegates, who hence became known as the Bolsheviks (Russian: 'majority'). He later attacked those socialists who supported World War I, which in his view was a purely 'imperialist' struggle, as expounded in his most important book, *Imperialism* 1917. He led the Bolsheviks to power on 7 November 1917.

Locke John 1632–1704. English philosopher. His *Two Treatises on Government* 1690 supply the classical statement of Whig theory and enjoyed great influence in America and France. He maintains that governments derive their authority from the people's consent, and that they may overthrow any government threatening their fundamental rights. Among these rights he includes freedoms, although he would deny toleration to Catholicism and atheism as dangerous to society.

Machiavelli Niccoló 1469–1527. Italian statesman and author whose name is now synonymous with cunning and ruthless statesmanship. In his most important political works, *The Prince* 1513 and *The Discourses* 1531, he discusses ways in which rulers can advance the interests of their states (and themselves) through an often cynical and amoral manipulation of other people.

Mao Zedong 1893–1976. Chinese statesman, founder member of the Chinese Communist Party. He led it to victory in 1949 after a long civil war, and was the effective ruler of China until his death. He is credited with having developed Marxism-Leninism and applied it to the circumstances of a poor Third World country with a huge peasant population but small industrial working class. The Cultural Revolution of 1966–76, which he inspired, was an attempt to keep alive revolutionary fervour, but the disruption and hardship caused by his attempts to put his theories into practice are now strongly criticized in China.

Marx Karl Heinrich 1818–83. German philosopher and socialist. In 1844 he began his lifelong collaboration with Friedrich Engels, with whom he developed the Marxist philosophy, first formulated in their joint works *The Holy Family* 1844 and *German Ideology* 1846 and Marx's *Poverty of Philosophy* 1847. Both joined the Communist League, a German refugee organization, and in 1847–48 they prepared its programme, 'The Communist Manifesto'. In 1849 he settled in London, where he wrote *Class Struggles in France* 1849, *The 18th Brumaire of Louis Bonaparte* 1852, *Critique of Political Economy* 1859 and his monumental work *Das Kapital (Capital)* 1867. His systematic theses on class struggle, history and the importance of economic factors in politics have exercised an enormous influence on later thinkers and political activists.

Mill John Stuart 1806–73. British philosopher and economist. In his most important work, *On Liberty* 1859, he moved away from the Utilitarian notion that individual liberty was necessary for economic and governmental efficiency and advanced the classical defence of individual freedom as a value in itself and the mark of a mature society. He sat in parliament as a Radical 1865–8 and introduced a motion for women's suffrage. His feminist views inspired his *On the Subjection of Women* 1869.

Plato 428–c348 BC. Athenian philosopher, disciple of Socrates and teacher of Aristotle. In his major political works, *The Republic* and *The Laws*, he discusses theories of justice and conceptions of the ideal state, arguing in favour of a state governed by a special class of 'philosopher kings' specially trained for that purpose.

Rousseau Jean Jacques 1712–78. French philosopher. His *Discourses on the Origins of Inequality* 1754 denounced civilized society and made him famous but his most important work was the *Social Contract* 1762, which emphasized the rights of the people over those of the government and was a significant influence on the French Revolution.

International Politics

alliance an agreement between two or more states to come to each other's assistance in the event of war. Alliances were criticized after World War I as having contributed to the outbreak of war but NATO and the Warsaw Pact have been major parts of the post 1945-structure of international relations.

arms control attempts to limit the arms race between the superpowers by reaching agreements to restrict the production of certain weapons, as in the Strategic Arms Limitation Talks (SALT) of the 1970s and the Geneva and Helsinki negotiations of the 1980s.

balance of power the theory that the best way of ensuring international order is for power to be so distributed among states that no single state is able to achieve a preponderant position. The term, which may also refer more simply to the actual distribution of power, is one of the most enduring conceptions in international relations. Since the development of nuclear weapons, it has been asserted that the balance of power has been replaced by a balance of terror.

Cold War expression used to portray the state of relations between the USA and the USSR since 1945: one of underlying conflict that is 'neither war nor peace'.

collective security a system for achieving international security by an agreement among all states to unite against any aggressor. Such a commitment was embodied in the post-World War I League of Nations and also in the United Nations Organization, although neither body was able to live up to the ideals of its founders.

détente relaxation of tension in relations between the superpowers.

deterrence the underlying conception of contemporary nuclear strategy: the belief that a potential aggressor will be deterred from

113

launching a 'first strike' nuclear attack by his adversary's possession of an assured 'second strike' capability. This doctrine is widely known as that of 'Mutual Assured Destruction, (MAD).

diplomacy the process by which states attempt to settle their differences through peaceful means such as negotiation or arbitration.

European Community consists of the European Coal and Steel Community 1952, European Economic Community (EEC, popularly called the Common Market 1957), and the European Atomic Energy Community (Euratom, 1957). These three shared from 1967 the following institutions: The Commission of 13 members, pledged to independence of national interests, who initiate Community action; The Council of Ministers, which makes decisions on the Commission's proposals; the European Parliament, directly elected from 1979, which is mainly a consultative body but can dismiss the Commission; and the European Court of Justice, which safeguards interpretation of Rome Treaties (1957) that established the Community. The original six members, Belgium, France, West Germany, Italy, Luxembourg and the Netherlands were joined by Britain, Denmark and the Irish Republic in 1974, Greece 1981 and Spain and Portugal 1985.

imperialism the attempt by one country to dominate others. In the 19th century this was synonymous with the establishment of colonies but contemporary leftist thinkers believe that the role of Western (especially American) finance capital in the Third World constitutes a form of imperialism.

international law rules that states have agreed amongst themselves to regulate their relations in such areas as diplomacy, rights of passage at sea, the rights of aliens, and title to territory. In the absence of an international legislature to enact law, international law is mainly derived from long established custom and from treaties and other agreements between states.

International Monetary Fund (IMF) estab-

lished by the 1944 Bretton Woods Conference with the aim of providing the international financial base necessary for a liberal trading system that would prevent the sort of protectionist policies which contributed to the economic depression of the 1930s. Part of the IMF system broke down in the 1970s when states opted for floating instead of fixed exchange rates, but the IMF is still an important source of finance for international trade.

neutrality the legal status of a country that decides not to take part in a war. Certain states, notably Switzerland and Austria, have opted for permanent neutrality. Neutrality always has a legal connotation whereas the term 'nonalignment' is normally used in a political sense to signify non-membership of the major post-war alliance systems.

North Atlantic Treaty Organization (NATO) established in 1949 to provide for the collective defence of the major Western European and North American states against the perceived threat from the Soviet Union. Its military headquarters is called Supreme Headquarters Allied Powers Europe (SHAPE). It has encountered numerous problems since its inception over such issues as the hegemonial position of the USA, the presence in Europe of American nuclear weapons, burden sharing, and standardization of weapons. France withdrew from the organization but not the alliance in 1966.

Organization of African Unity (OAU) Pledged to eradicate colonialism, emancipate still dependent territories, and improve conditions in the economic, cultural, and political spheres throughout Africa by its charter, adopted in 1963. It has helped to co-ordinate African policies on the South African and other questions.

Organization of the Petroleum Exporting Countries (OPEC) established in 1960 to co-ordinate the interests of oil producing states worldwide and also to improve the position of Third World states by forcing Western states to open their markets to the resultant products. Its concerted action in raising prices in the 1970s triggered worldwide recession but also lessened demand so that its influence was reduced by the mid-1980s.

Star Wars popular term for the Strategic Defence Initiative (SDI) announced by US President Reagan in 1983. This was a decision to seek to develop a space-based defensive system capable of destroying Soviet missiles soon after launching by using advanced laser and particle beam technology. Its critics argue that it is impractical and will destabilize the balance of power between the USA and USSR.

superpower after the Napoleonic Wars the term 'great power' was used to describe the five leading states of that time (Austria, Britain, France, Prussia, and Russia). By the end of World War II the US and USSR had emerged as significantly stronger than all other countries and the term 'superpower' was coined to describe this status.

United Nations Organization (UNO) formed in 1945 at the San Francisco Conference. The original intention was that the UN's Security Council would preserve the wartime alliance of the USA, USSR and Britain (with France and China also permanent members) in order to maintain the peace. This never happened because of the outbreak of the Cold War, but the UN has played a role in many other areas such as refugees, development assistance, disaster relief, and cultural cooperation.

Warsaw Pact established in 1955 between the Soviet Union and the Eastern European communist states as a response to the admission of West Germany into NATO.

Political Ideologies

anarchism a term derived from the Greek *anarkhos* ('without ruler'). It does not mean 'without order', since most theories of anarch-ism imply an order of a very strict and symmetrical kind, but they maintain that such order can be achieved by cooperation, claiming that other methods of achieving order, which rely on authority, are both morally reprehensible and politically unstable. The religious type of anarchism, claimed by many anarchists to be exemplified in the early organization of the Christian church, has found expression in modern times in the social philosophy of Tolstoy and Gandhi. The theory of anarchism is best expressed in the works of Peter Alexeivich Kropotkin 1842–1921.

communism the revolutionary socialist movement basing its theory and practice on the teachings of Marx. At its heart is a theory which combines with a belief in economic determinism to form the central communist concept of 'dialectical materialism'. According to this, human society has passed through successive stages - primitive society, slavery, feudalism and capitalism. Each phase was at first progressive, but later hindered progress and had to be superseded by a higher phase through the taking of power by a new class. Marx believed that capitalism, progressive in its earlier stage, had become a barrier to progress and needed to be replaced by a dictatorship of the proletariat (working class), which would build a socialist society. The movement was increasingly dominated after the Bolshevik Revolution 1917 by Stalin's Russia but, beginning in 1948 with the development of a distinctive approach to socialism in Yugoslavia, a number of divergent paths to socialism emerged in China, Romania and Hungary and among 'Euro-Communist' parties in France, Italy, Spain and elsewhere.

conservatism an approach to government and economic management identified with a number of Western political parties such as the British Conservative, West German Christian Democratic and Australian Liberal parties. It tends to be explicitly non-doctrinaire and pragmatic but its central themes may be identified as an emphasis on the importance of national traditions, a belief in free enterprise capitalism, a minimalist approach to governmental intervention in the economy, and a stress on law and order.

fascism the totalitarian nationalist movement founded in Italy by Mussolini. It was essentially a product of the economic and political crisis of the years after World War I. It protected the existing social order by its forcible suppression of the working class movement and by providing scapegoats for popular anger in the Jew, the foreigner or the black person; it also provided the machinery for the economic and psychological mobilization of the nation for war. Its ideology denied all rights to the individual in his relations with the state, personified in the infallible 'leader' (*Duce, Führer*). The atrocities committed by Nazi Germany and other fascist countries discredited fascism but small neofascist groups still exist in many Western European states.

Islam one of the great world religions (Arabic 'submission', that is, to the will of Allah). The Oneness of God is emphasizsed as are his omnipotence, beneficence and inscrutability. Beliefs are drawn from a succession of scriptures, including parts of the Old and New Testaments of the Christian bible. The ultimate and perfect revelation is the Koran of Muhammad (c. 570–632). Islam is a major force in the Arab world and is also a focus for nationalism among the peoples of Soviet Central Asia. It is also a significant factor in Pakistan, Indonesia, Malaysia and parts of Africa. Since World War II a resurgence of fundamentalist Islam, often fanatically opposed to the ideas of the West, has become a potent factor in modern politics in Iran, Libya, Pakistan, and elsewhere.

liberalism the political and social theory associated with the Liberal party in Britain and similar parties elsewhere. Liberalism developed during the 17th to 19th centuries as the distinctive theory of the industrial and commercial classes in their struggle against the power of the monarchy, the church and the feudal landowners. In politics it stood for parliamentary government, freedom of the press, speech and worship, and the abolition of class privileges; economically it was associated with laissez faire, a minimum of state interference in economic life and international free trade. These ideas were modified in the late 19th and early 20th centuries by the acceptance of a certain amount of state intervention in order to ensure a minimum standard of living and to remove extremes of poverty and wealth.

socialism a movement aiming at the establishment of a classless society through the substitution of common for private ownership of the means of production, distribution and exchange. The term is used both to cover all movements with this aim, such as communism and anarchism, and more narrowly for evolutionary socialism or democracy. In general the tendency since 1917 has been for a clear distinction, if not opposition, to exist between parties governed by Marx's revolutionary, 'scientific' socialism and the gradualist, reforming approach of the British Labour party and Western European Social Democratic party.

The Process of Government

classification of governments political theorists have made many attempts to divide governments (and political systems generally) into different types. Such endeavours have seldom been completely satisfactory because few, if any, societies have conformed exactly to the 'ideal type'; such typologies are inadequate and simplistic as means of describing where power is located in any society; and many of the words used (dictatorship, tyranny, totalitarian, democratic) have acquired negative or positive connotations which makes it difficult to use them in any objective fashion. Aristotle was the first to attempt a systematic classification of governments. His main distinctions were between government by one person, by few and by many (monarchy, oligarchy and democracy), although the characteristics of each may vary between states and each may degenerate into tyranny (rule by an oppressive elite in the case of oligarchy or by the mob in the case of democracy). Later writers attempted a refinement of Aristotle's definitions, including the French philosopher Montesquieu 1689–1755 who distinguished between constitutional governments – whether monarchies or republics – which operated under various legal and other constraints, and despotism, which was not constrained in this way. A more modern distinction is between liberal democracies, totalitarian states and autocracies.

'liberal democracy' was a term coined to distinguish Western types of democracy from the many other political systems that claimed to be 'democratic'. Its principal characteristics are the existence of more than one political party, open processes of government and political debate and a separation of powers.

totalitarian is a more disputed term. It has been applied to both fascist and communist states and denotes a system where all power is centralized in the state, which in turn is controlled by a single party deriving its legitimacy from an exclusive ideology.

autocracy describes a form of government that has emerged in a number of Third World countries, where state power is in the hands either of an individual or of the army; normally ideology is not a central factor, individual freedoms tend to be suppressed where they may constitute a challenge to the authority of the ruling group and there is a reliance upon force.

Other useful distinctions are between *federal* governments (where important powers are dispersed among various regions which in certain respects are self-governing) and *unitary* governments (where powers are concentrated in a central authority); and between *presidential* (where the head of state is also the directly elected head of government, not part of the legislature) and *parliamentary* systems (where the government is drawn from an elected legislature which can dismiss it).

voting systems Western democracies

employ many different voting systems of which the many variants are:

1 Where the electorate is divided into constituencies, each of which elects one member of the legislature, with the candidate who receives the largest number of votes winning, (Britain and the USA).

2 Similar to the above except that a second ballot may be held, with those receiving the lowest number of votes eliminated, in order that one candidate may receive an absolute majority of votes cast (France).

3 A single member constituency system but with the electorate entitled to list all candidates in order of preference so that the votes of the weaker candidates may be distributed among the stronger until one candidate receives an absolute majority, (Australia).

4 Proportional representation, which may take many forms but essentially involves systems where legislative seats are distributed among parties in such a way as to correspond to the votes cast for each party. Some countries also make use of a referendum on specific issues. This is the procedure whereby a decision on proposed legislation is referred to the electorate for settlement by direct popular vote. It is most frequently employed in Switzerland but has also been used in Canada, Australia, New Zealand and certain states of the USA. It was used for the first time in the UK in 1975 on the issue of British membership of the European Community.

machinery of government in Britain and the US, government policy is decided and laws are made through bodies called the cabinet (UK and US), Congress (US), and Parliament (UK).

Cabinet in Britain the committee of ministers holding the most important executive offices who decide the government's policy. Cabinet policy is a collective one, and a vote of censure on one minister usually involves the whole Cabinet. In the USA a Cabinet system developed early, the term being used from 1793, though it is not responsible as in Britian for initiating legislation. Members are selected by the President and, again contrary to British

117

practice, may neither be members of Congress nor speak there, being responsible to the President alone.

Congress national legislature of the USA, consisting of a House of Representatives (435 members, apportioned to the States of the Union on the basis of population, and elected for two-year terms) and the Senate (100 Senators, two for each state, elected for six years, one third elected every two years). Both representatives and senators are elected by direct popular vote. Congress meets at Washington in the Capitol. An Act of Congress is a bill or resolution that has been passed by the Senate and the House of Representatives and has received the President's assent. Even if the President vetoes it, it may become an Act of Congress if it is returned to Congress again and passed by a majority of two-thirds in each House.

Parliament the supreme legislature of Great Britain comprising the House of Commons and the House of Lords. Parliament originated under the Norman kings as the Great Council of royal tenants-in-chief, to which in the 13th century representatives of the shires were sometimes summoned. De Montfort's parliament (1265) set a precedent by including representatives of the boroughs as well as the shires. Under Edward III the burgesses and knights of the shires began to meet separately from the barons, thus forming the House of Commons. By the 15th century Parliament had acquired the right to legislate, vote and appropriate supplies, examine public accounts and

impeach royal ministers. The powers of Parliament were much diminished under the Yorkists and Tudors but under Elizabeth I a new spirit of independence appeared. The revolutions of 1640 and 1688 established parliamentary control over the executive and judiciary, and finally abolished all royal claim to tax or legislate without parliamentary consent. During these struggles the two great parties appeared and after 1688 it became customary for the king to choose his ministers from the party dominant in the Commons. The duration of parliaments was fixed at five years in 1911 but any parliament may extend its own life, as happened during both world wars. The House of Lords comprises the temporal peers (all hereditary peers and all life peers: both the Law Lords and those created under the Life Peerage Act of 1958) and the spiritual peers (the two archbishops and 24 of the bishops). Since the Parliament Act of 1911 the powers of the Lords have been restricted in that they may delay a bill passed by the Commons but not reject it. The Lords are presided over by the Lord Chancellor, and the Commons by the Speaker. A public bill is given a preliminary first reading and discussed in detail at the second reading; it is then referred to a select or standing committee, after which it is considered by a committee of the whole House. After the third reading it is sent to the Lords, whose procedure is similar. If it passes both Houses, it receives the royal assent and so becomes law.

479 BC   Greeks defeated Persians at battle of Plataea: beginning of golden age of Athenian democracy under Pericles (c 490–429 BC).

431–404   Peloponnesian War, ending in the defeat of Athens by Sparta.

207   Unification of China under the Han dynasty.

49–46   Civil war in Italy ended with victory of Julius Caesar and his establishment as dictator, effectively marking the end of the Roman Republic and the start of the Imperial era.

330 AD   Byzantium renamed Constantinople (after Constantine the Great) and declared the Christian capital of the Roman Empire, as distinct from the non-Christian Rome.

634–643   Omar, the great Caliph (successor to Muhammad) conquered the whole Middle East and imposed the Islamic religion upon it.

800   Charlemagne (768–814) declared first Holy Roman Emperor by Pope Leo III.

878   Alfred the Great, King of Wessex, defeated the Danes at the battle of Edington.

980   Dynastic struggles in Russia ended with the victory of Prince Vladimir, who established Christianity there.

1066   Battle of Hastings ended in the imposition of Norman rule under William the Conqueror upon England.

1073–85   Gregory VII (Hildebrand) became pope. Asserted the authority of Church over Emperor, beginning a long struggle for primacy between secular and religious heirs of Roman Empire.

1206   Temujin chosen to be Genghis Khan ('supreme king') of the Mongolian people. Beginning of Mongol conquests of China, Central Asia and Eastern Europe

1215   King John I of England forced to sign the Magna Carta, the most famous of a number of charters of liberties that appeared in Europe at this time. With such affirmations by the King as 'To no one will we sell, to no one will we deny, or delay right or justice' it laid the foundations for the protection of political and civil rights.

1378– 1415   The Great Schism in the Roman Catholic church, when two and later three popes were in existence at the same time. This marked the effective end of the dreams of a universal European order under the pope and the beginning of the modern European states system.

1517   Martin Luther (1483–1546) nailed his 95 theses criticizing certain practices of the papacy to the church at Wittenburg, unleashing the Protestant Reformation.

1534   Act of Supremacy of Henry VIII (1491–1547) declared the king to be 'the only supreme head in earth of the Church of England'.

1555   Peace of Augsburg established principle that each German state should adopt the religion of its ruler.

1640   Establishment of Long Parliament in England.

1642   Outbreak of English Civil War.

1648	Peace of Westphalia ended Thirty Years War and established the sovereign equality of states as the basic principle of the international order, finally discarding the special political role of the papacy.
1649	Charles I executed. English Commonwealth established.
1653	Oliver Cromwell (1599–1658) Lord Protector of the United Kingdom.
1660	Restoration of monarchy in England.
1661– 1715	Louis XIV of France (1638–1715), king since 1643, assumed absolute power. Period of French ascendancy.
1679	Habeas Corpus act established freedom from arbitrary arrest in England.
1688	William of Orange landed in England, displacement of James II in the 'Glorious Revolution'.
1689	English Bill of Rights laid down the political and civil rights achieved by the 'Glorious Revolution'.
1689– 1725	Rise of Russia to major power status under Peter the Great (1672–1725).
1707	Union of England and Scotland.
1776	American Declaration of Independence asserted the basic rights of all to 'life, liberty and the pursuit of happiness': the first affirmation of human rights of the modern era.
1787	Constitution of the United States of America established the basic features of the American political system: the first modern democracy.
1789	French Revolution began. Declaration of the Rights of Man (liberty, equality and fraternity).
1791	Adoption of French constitution (constitutional monarchy with guarantees of human rights).
1804	Napoleon Bonaparte (1769–1821) emperor of France.
1815	Defeat of Napoleon.
1832	First Reform Bill in England extended franchise.
1848	Nationalist and liberal revolutionary movement throughout Europe.
1861–5	American Civil War.
1868	Beginning of Meiji Restoration which transformed Japan into a major power within thirty years.
1911	Establishment of Chinese Republic
1914–18	World War I.
1917	Russian Revolution.
1933	Adolf Hitler (1889–1945) Chancellor of Germany.
1939–45	World War II.
1945	First use of atomic bomb against Japan. Establishment of United Nations Organization.

1947   Indian independence marked the start of decolonization and the emergence of the 'Third World'.

1948   Proclamation of State of Israel. Yugoslavia expelled from Cominform (the Soviet dominated alliance of communist parties).

1949   Communist victory in China.

1958   European Economic Community (EEC) came into being.

1959   Fidel Castro established communist government in Cuba.

1960   Many African states gained independence.

1964   Major civil rights bill passed in USA aimed at implementing programme of equal rights for black people.

1965   Crisis in the EEC caused by French opposition to relinquishing sovereign powers to Community institutions.

1966   Outbreak of 'Cultural Revolution' in China, which aimed at restoring ideological purity to the country and sanctifying the 'Thought' of Mao Zedong.

1968   Violent unrest in France; Britain announced a policy of ending its role as a world power; USSR invaded Czechoslovakia to stamp out liberal reforms.

1970   Moscow Treaty between West Germany and USSR renounced force and recognized the inviolability of all existing European borders.

1972   US President Nixon's visit to China ended more than 20 years of Sino-American hostility; Britain entered EEC.

1974   Nixon forced to resign over Watergate affair.

1977   Historic meeting of Israeli and Egyptian leaders, Menachim Begin and President Sadat after nearly 30 years of conflict.

1979   Margaret Thatcher became first woman prime minister of Britain; Islamic Republic declared in Iran.

Psychology

The scope of psychology is large, and attempts to define it have been varied. For example, William James saw psychology as the 'science of mental life', while J B Watson regarded it as the study of human and animal behaviour. Differing views of psychology are reflected in the diverse areas of study and application.

This section comprises an overview of the main *Areas of Study* and the main *Areas of Application* of psychology; definitions of *Terms and Concepts* used in psychology; *Biographies* of key people who have made important contributions to psychology; and a *Chronology* of major events in the development of psychology.

Areas of Study

experimental psychology emphasizes the application of rigorous and objective scientific methods to the study of mental processes and behaviour. This covers a wide range of fields of study including:

human and animal learning in which learning theories describe how new behaviours are acquired and modified.

cognitive processes the study of cognition covers a number of functions; for example, perception, attention, memory and language.

physiological psychology relates the study of cognition to different regions of the brain.

artificial intelligence refers to the computer simulation of cognitive processes, such as language and problem-solving.

developmental psychology is the study of development of cognition and behaviour from birth to adulthood.

social psychology concerns the study of individuals within their social environment; for example, within groups and organizations. This has led to the development of occupational and organizational psychology.

Areas of Application

clinical psychology concerns the understanding and treatment of health problems, particularly mental disorders. The main problems dealt with include anxiety, phobias, depression, obsessions, sexual and marital problems, drug and alcohol dependence, childhood behavioural problems, psychoses (such as schizophrenia), mental handicap and brain damage (such as dementia). Other areas of work include forensic psychology (concerned with criminal behaviour) and health psychology. The main approaches include:

assessment procedures which assess intelligence and cognition, for example, in detecting the effects of brain damage. Assessment procedures usually involve the use of psychometric tests.

behavioural approaches are methods of treatment which apply learning theories to clinical problems. *Behaviour therapy* helps clients change unwanted behaviours (such as phobias, obsessions, sexual problems) and to develop new skills (such as improve social interactions). *Behaviour modification* relies on operant conditioning, and makes selective use of rewards (such as praise) to change behaviours. This is particularly useful for children, the mentally handicapped and for patients in institutions, such as mental hospitals.

cognitive therapy is a new approach to treating emotional problems, such as anxiety and depression, by teaching clients to change negative thoughts and attitudes.

counselling, developed by Rogers, is widely used in order to help clients to solve their own problems.

psychoanalysis, as developed by Freud and Jung, is little used by clinical psychologists today. It emphasizes childhood conflicts in leading to adult problems.

educational psychology concerns work primarily in schools, including the assessment of children with achievement problems and advising on problem behaviours in the classroom.

occupational psychology studies human behaviour at work. It includes dealing with problems in organizations, advising on management difficulties and investigating the relationship between humans and machines (as in the design of aircraft controls). Another important area is the use of psychometric assessment procedures to assist in selection of personnel.

Terms and Concepts

anxiety an emotional state of fear or apprehension. Normal anxiety is a response to dangerous situations. Abnormal anxiety can either be free-floating, when the person may feel anxious much of the time in a wide range of situations, or it may be phobic, when the person is excessively afraid of an object or situation.

behaviour therapy the application of behavioural principles, derived from learning theories, to the treatment of clinical conditions such as phobias, obsessions, sexual and inter-personal problems. For example, in treating agoraphobia the person is taken into the situation which he or she is afraid of, in gradual steps. Over time, the fear typically reduces, and the problem improves.

behaviourism an influential approach, first systemically described by Watson. It concentrates on observable behaviour in human and other animals.

brain damage this can be caused by trauma (for example, accidents) or disease (such as encephalitis), or it may be present at birth. Depending on the area of the brain which is affected, language, movement, sensation, judgement, or other abilities may be impaired.

cognition a general term covering the functions involved in dealing with information, for example, perception (seeing, hearing, etc.) attention, memory and reasoning.

cognitive therapy a treatment for emotional disorders, particularly depression and anxiety, developed by Professor Aaron T Beck in the USA. This approach encourages the client to challenge the distorted and unhelpful thinking that is characteristic of these problems. The treatment includes behavioural methods, and has been particularly helpful for people suffering from depression.

conditioning there are two major principles of conditioning. In *classical conditioning*, described by Pavlov, a new stimulus can evoke an automatic response by being repeatedly associated with a stimulus that naturally provokes that response. For example, a bell repeatedly associated with food will eventually trigger salivation, even if presented without food. In *operant conditioning*, described by Thorndike and Skinner, the frequency of a voluntary response can be increased by following it with a reinforcer or reward. For example, children will be more likely to say 'Thank you' if they have been repeatedly praised for doing so when given something.

counselling an approach in which clients are encouraged to solve their own problems with support from a counsellor. The importance of qualities of the counsellor, such as empathy, warmth and genuineness, was emphasized by Rogers.

dementia a progressive loss of mental abilities such as memory and orientation. Typically a problem of old age, it can be accompanied by depression.

depression an emotional state characterized by sadness, unhappy thoughts, apathy and dejection. Sadness is a normal response to important losses (bereavement, unemployment, and other major losses). However, clinical depression, which is prolonged or unduly severe, often requires treatment, such as anti-depressant medication, cognitive therapy or in some cases, electro-convulsive therapy (ECT), in which an electrical current is passed through the brain.

drug and alcohol dependence individuals can become dependent on addictive drugs such as alcohol, nicotine (in cigarettes), tranquillizers, heroin, or solvents (as in for example, glue sniffing). Such substances can alter mood or behaviour. When dependence is established, sudden withdrawal from the drug can cause an unpleasant reaction, which can be dangerous for some drugs.

extraversion a personality dimension described by Jung and later by Eysenck. The typical extravert is sociable, impulsive and

125

carefree. The oppositie of extraversion is introversion; the typical introvert is quiet, inward-looking and reliable.

health psychology a new development within clinical psychology which applies psychological principles to promote physical well-being. For example, people with high blood pressure can learn methods such as relaxation, meditation, and life-style changes.

intelligence a general concept that summarizes the abilities of an individual in reasoning and problem solving, particularly in novel situations. These consist of a wide range of verbal and non-verbal skills and therefore some psychologists dispute a unitary concept of intelligence.

learning theories these describe how an organism acquires new behaviours. Two main theories are classical and operant conditioning.

mental handicap impairment of intelligence which can be very mild, but in the more severe cases is associated with social problems and difficulties in living independently. Individuals may be born with mental handicap or may acquire it through brain damage. Mental handicap is also known as pervasive learning difficulty.

neurosis a general term referring to emotional disorders, such as anxiety, depression and obsessions. The main disturbance tends to be one of mood, whereas contact with reality is relatively unaffected, in contrast to psychosis.

neuroticism a personality dimension described by Eysenck. People with high neuroticism are worriers, emotional and moody. The opposite to neuroticism is emotional stability.

obsession repetitive unwanted thought that is often recognized by the sufferer as being irrational, but which nevertheless causes distress. It can be associated with a compulsion where the individual feels an irresistible urge to carry out a repetitive series of actions. For example, a person excessively troubled by fears of contamination by dirt or disease may engage in continuous hand-washing for four or five hours every day.

personality an individual's characteristic way of behaving across a wide range of situations. Two broad dimensions of personality are extraversion and neuroticism. A number of more specific personal traits have also been described, including psychopathy (anti-social behaviour).

phobia excessive irrational fear of an object or situation, for example, agoraphobia (fear of open spaces and crowded places), acrophobia (fear of heights), claustrophobia (fear of enclosed places). Behaviour therapy is one form of treatment.

psychoanalysis a theory and treatment method for neuroses, developed by Freud. It emphasizes the impact of early childhood sexuality and experiences which are stored in the unconscious and can lead to the development of adult emotional problems. The main treatment method involves the free association of ideas, and interpretation. Treatment typically is expensive and prolonged and there are serious doubts about its effectiveness. Modern approaches, drawing from Freud's ideas, are briefer and problem-focussed.

psychometrics the measurement of mental processes. This includes intelligence and aptitude testing to help in job selection and in the clinical assessment of cognitive deficits resulting from brain damage.

psychosis a general term for a serious mental disorder where the individual commonly loses contact with reality and may experience hallucinations (seeing or hearing things that do not exist) or delusions (fixed false beliefs). For example, in a paranoid psychosis, an individual may believe that others are plotting against him or her. A major type of psychosis is schizophrenia.

psychotherapy treatment approaches for mental problems which involve talking rather than physical methods such as drugs. Examples of such approaches include behaviour therapy, cognitive therapy and psychoanalysis.

schizophrenia one of the psychoses which is of unknown origin. This may develop in early adulthood and can lead to profound changes in personality and behaviour. Modern treatment approaches use drugs, and can include family therapy, stress reduction and rehabilitaion.

stress a wide range of situations or events which can tax the individual's physical or mental coping abilities. Examples of stress include excessive noise, marital conflict and overwork. Individual reactions to stress are varied, including irritability, fatigue, anxiety or physical health problems, such as stomach ulcers, high blood pressure. Stress is now treated by health psychology.

unconscious an absence of awareness. In psychoanalysis it refers to part of the personality of which the individual is unaware. This contains impulses or urges which are held back, or repressed, from conscious awareness. Emotional problems and irrational actions are believed by psychoanalysts to stem from unconscious conflicts.

Biographies

Eysenck Hans 1916–. German-born British psychologist who was appointed Professor of Psychology at London University's Institute of Psychiatry in 1955. He promoted behaviour therapy, attacked psychoanalysis, and devised scientific measures of extraversion and neuroticism, key dimensions of personality.

Freud Sigmund 1856–1939. Austrian psychiatrist who developed psychoanalysis. He held that the repression of infantile sexuality caused adult neuroses. His treatment involved making the patient aware of unconscious conflicts. Books include *Studies in Hysteria*, and *The Interpretation of Dreams*.

James William 1842–1910. American psychologist and philosopher; brother of the novelist Henry James. He published *Principles of Psychology* an influential early text. He emphasized the physiological aspects of memory and emotion and advocated a scientific approach.

Jung Carl 1875–1961. Swiss psychiatrist who collaborated with Freud until their disagreement in 1912 about the importance of sexuality in causing psychological problems. He studied religion and dream symbolism and saw the unconscious as a source of spiritual insight. He also distinguished between introversion and extraversion.

Pavlov Ivan 1849–1936. Russian physiologist who studied conditioned reflexes in animals. His work greatly influenced behavioural and learning theory.

Piaget Jean 1896–1980. Swiss psychologist who studied the development of thought, concepts of space and movement, logic and reasoning in children. He wrote *The Child's Construction of Reality* and *The Child's Construction of Intelligence*.

Rogers Carl 1902– . US psychologist who developed the client-centred approach to counselling and psychotherapy. This stressed the importance of clients making their own decisions and developing their own potential (self-actualization).

Skinner Burrhus 1903– . American radical behaviourist who rejects mental concepts, seeing the organism as a 'black box' (internal processes are not important in predicting behaviour). He studied operant conditioning and stresses that behaviour is shaped and maintained by its consequences. His radical approach rejected almost all previous psychology; his text *Science and Human Behaviour* contains no references and no bibliography.

Watson John B 1878–1958. American founder of behaviourism. He rejected introspection (observation by an individual of his or her own mental processes) and regarded psychology as the study of observable behaviour, within the scientific tradition.

Wundt Wilhelm 1832–1920. German physiologist who regarded psychology as the study of internal experience or consciousness. His main psychological method was introspection; he also studied sensation, perception of space and time, and reaction times.

1897	Wilhelm Wundt founded the first psychological laboratory, in Leipzig.
1890	William James published the first comprehensive psychology text, *Principles of Psychology*.
1895	Freud's first book on psychoanalysis was published.
1896	The first clinical psychology clinic was founded by Witner at the University of Pennsylvania.
1903	Pavlov reported his early studies on conditioned reflexes in animals.
1905	Binet and Simon developed the first effective intelligence test.
1908	A first textbook of social psychology was published by William McDougall.
1913	J B Watson published his influential work *Behaviourism*.
1926	Jean Piaget presented his first book on child development.
1947	Eysenck published *Dimensions of Personality*, a large scale study of neuroticism and extraversion.
1953	Skinner's *Science of Human Behaviour*, a text of operant conditioning, was published.
1957	Chomsky's *Syntactic Structures*, which stimulated the development of psycholinguistics, the study of language processes, was published.
1963	Milgram's studies of compliance with authority indicated conditions under which individuals behave cruelly to others when instructed to do so.
1967	Neisser's *Cognitive Psychology* marked renewed interest in the study of cognition after years in which behaviourism had been dominant.
1972	Newell and Simon simulated human problem solving abilities by computer, an example of artificial intelligence.

Religion and Mythology

The term religion is probably derived from the Latin *religāre*, 'to bind', and is used to describe people's attitude towards the gods or God. In original Buddhism, there is no Deity; yet Buddhism, like atheistic Jainism, and Confucianism, which is primarily a code of good behaviour, is always included in a list of the world's religions. A great many prominent thinkers have attempted to define religion: as a belief in spiritual beings; as morality touched with emotion; as a feeling of harmony between oneself and the universe; or as a feeling of awe or reverence for an Unseen Power.

In addition to the main religions of the world, there are also a great many 'new religions' and offshoots. In some parts of the world, for example Africa and North America, indigenous religions still survive despite contact with modern westernized society.

Religion and mythology are closely linked. When we talk about, for example, Greek or Roman mythology, we are talking of what was once the sacred history of a living religion. The stories of mythology often concern themselves with the great religious questions, such as 'How did everything begin?' and 'What happens after death?', and try to answer them in terms familiar to the hearer.

This section contains an overview of living ***Religions of the World*** and their tenets; details of ***Rites of Passage*** in various religions; a look at the ***Holy Books*** of different religions; biographies of major ***Religious Figures***; a list of ***Holy Places*** in different religions; and the main religious ***Festivals*** with a table. Finally, ***Mythological Figures*** looks at the gods, goddesses, and other main figures of ancient religions.

Religions of the World

African religions there is a wide variety of belief and practice in African religion. Most indigenous African religions are basically polytheistic (believing in a number of gods), but there is often a concept of one High God, generally a creator who has withdrawn from interaction with the world. There are also many spirits, which are present in all natural objects: water is seen as a particularly powerful force. Dead ancestors are very important in African religions, and are consulted before major undertakings. If offended, they can cause natural disasters and sterility, so they must be placated with offerings. In society, healers are regarded highly, since they deal with supernatural powers, as do diviners, but the most powerful human figure is the chief-king, who is surrounded by prohibitions because he is so dangerous: he is the life of the tribe incarnate, though because of this he may be required to sacrifice himself to preserve the health of his people.

American Indian religions these form a wide variety, but have some features in common, especially a belief that everything in nature is alive and contains powerful forces which can be helpful or harmful to humans. If the forces are to be helpful, they must be treated with respect, and so hunting and other activities require ritual and preparation. Certain people are believed to be in contact with or possessed by the spirit world and so to have special powers; but each individual can also seek power and vision through ordeals and fasting.

Baha'i religion forshadowed by the teachings of Iranian Mirza Ali Muhammad 1819–50 known as the Bab, 'the Gate'. His claim that Islam was not God's final revelation ended in his being shot by the government at Tabriz.

Another of his countrymen, Husayn Ali, known as Baha'u'llah, 'God's Glory' proclaimed himself as the prophet the Bab had foretold. The most important principle of his message was that all great religious leaders, including the Bab and Baha'u'ullah, are manifestations of the unknowable God; therefore all founders of religions are to be honoured and all scriptures are sacred. Baha'is are expected to work towards world unification, and great stress is laid on equality regardless of religion, race or gender. Drugs and alcohol are forbidden, as is monastic celibacy. Marriage is strongly encouraged; there is no arranged marriage, but parental approval must be given. Baha'is are expected to pray daily, but there is no set prayer. From 2nd to 20th March, adults under 70 fast from sunrise to sunset. There is no priesthood: all Baha'is are expected to teach, and administration is carried out by an elected body, the Universal House of Justice.

Buddhism one of the great world religions, which originated in India. It derived from the teaching of Buddha, who is regarded as one of a series of such enlightened beings, the next incarnation being due c. 3000 AD. *scriptures* The only complete canon of the Buddhist scriptures is that of the Sinhalese (Sri Lanka) Buddhists, in Pali, but other schools have essentially the same canon in Sanskrit. The scriptures are known as Pitakas or 'baskets'. They are three divisions: *Vinaya* or Discipline, listing offences and rules of life; *Sutta* or Discourse or *Dhamma* or Doctrine, the exposition of Buddhism by Buddha and his disciples; *Abhidhamma* or Further Doctrine, later discussions on doctrine. The most important belief doctrine is that of *karma*, good or evil deeds meeting an appropriate reward or punishment either in this life or (through transmigration or rebirth) in a long succession of lives. The self is not regarded as permanent, and the aim of the Noble Eightfold Way is to break the chain of karma, and achieve dissociation from the body by attaining *Nirvana* 'blowing out', the eradication of all desires, either in annihilation, or by absorption of the self in the infinite. There are no gods, but great reverence is accorded to

Buddha, and other such advanced incarnations.

divisions: Theraveda Buddhism, the School of the Elders, which is also known as *Hinayana* or Base Career, prevails in southern Asia (Sri Lanka, Thailand, and Burma), and its scriptures are written in *Pali* an Indo-Aryan language with its roots in N India; *Mahayana* or Great Career, which arose at the beginning of the Christian era, exhorts the individual not merely to attain Nirvana as an individual, but to become a trainee Buddha (or Boddhisattva), and so save others. This prevails in northern Asia (China, Korea, Japan, and Tibet). The form established in Tibet, *Lamaism,* dates from 750 AD when the Dalai Lama became both spiritual and temporal ruler; its outward forms include prayer wheels and it had strong magical elements. In India itself Buddhism was replaced by Hinduism, but still has five million devotees, and is growing. *Zen* originated with a Mahayana monk, Bodhidharma, c. 520 AD, in China, and from the 12th century was adopted in Japan; it is characterized by anecdotes giving rise to exchanges between master and pupil which result in sudden enlightenment. Japan is also noted for such lay organizations as *Soka Gakkai* (Value Creation Society), founded 1937, which equates absolute faith with immediate material benefit, and by the 1980s was followed by more than seven million households.

Christianity world religion derived from the teaching of Jesus Christ in the first third of the first Christian century; overall membership c. 944 million. Belief in an omnipotent God the Father is the fundamental concept, together with the doctrine of the Trinity, that is the union of the three Persons of the Father Son and Holy Spirit in one Godhead. Like Buddhism and Islam it is a universal religion, and has always had a missionary element. In the late 20th century it is spreading most rapidly in Africa and South America. The chief commandment is love of God, and of one's neighbour as of oneself.

divisions:

Roman Catholicism which acknowledges the supreme jurisdiction of its head the Pope, infallible when he speaks *ex cathedra* 'from the throne', a tenet which remains the chief stumbling block in attempted reunion with other churches; the doctrine of the Immaculate Conception (which states that the Virgin Mary was conceived without the original sin which all other human beings are born with), and an allotment of a special place to the Virgin Mary (the mother of Jesus) is also at issue. The final split between Eastern and Western churches was in 1054, and a further schism came with the Reformation in the 16th century, to which the Counter-Reformation provided only a partial answer. An attempt to update its doctrines in the late 19th century was condemned by Pope Pius X in 1907, and more recent moves have been stifled by Pope John Paul II. Membership 585 million.

Eastern Orthodox a federation of self-governing churches (some founded by the Apostles and their disciples). There is elaborate ritual and singing (no instrumental music) in services, and in the marriage service the bride and groom are crowned. There is a married clergy, except for bishops; the Immaculate Conception is not accepted.

Protestantism originating with the Reformation, and named from the protest of Luther and his supporters at the Diet of Spires 1529 against the decision to reaffirm the Edict of the Diet of Worms against the Reformation. The chief sects are the Anglican Communion, Baptists, Christian Scientists, Lutherans, Methodists, Pentecostal Movement, Presbyterians, Unitarians. Membership c. 320 million. There has been a move this century to reunite various Protestant sects and, to some extent, the Roman Catholic church, for example the World Council of Churches 1948. In the 1970s and 80s there has been a revival of interest in Christianity among young people which is not necessarily connected to the established churches, for example the so-called Jesus Freaks and Children of God.

Confucianism the body of beliefs and practices that are based on the Chinese classics and are supported by the authority of Confucius, although he himself maintained that he was a transmitter rather than a creator. For some 2,500 years Confucianism has been the religion of the great masses of Chinese. The scriptures of Confucius are the five Chinese classics or canonical books, namely the *Shu King*, or book of historical documents; the *Shih King*, or ancient poems; the *Li Ki*, or book of rites and ancient ceremonies and institutions; the *Yi King*, or book of changes; and the *Annals* of *Lu*, otherwise known as Spring and Autumn. Only the last may be attributed with any confidence to Confucius's authorship, but the material in the other books may owe something to his editing. From these scriptures the Chinese in countless generations have derived their ideas of cosmology, political government, social organization, and individual conduct. The origin of things is seen in the union of *Yin* and *Yang*, the negative and positive principles. Human relationships follow the patriarchal pattern; until 1912 the emperor was regarded as the father of his people, appointed by heaven to rule. The Superior Man was the ideal human, filial piety was the virtue of virtues, and in general human relationships were to be regulated by the Golden Rule. Accompanying this lofty morality is a kind of ancestor worship. Under the emperor, sacrifices were offered to heaven and earth, the heavenly bodies, the imperial ancestors, various nature gods, and Confucius himself. These were abolished at the Revolution in 1912, but ancestor worship (better expressed as reverence and remembrance) remained a regular practice in the home. Under Communism Confucianism continued, Lin Piao being associated with the cult, but Mao Zedong undertook an anti-Confucius campaign 1974–76, which was not pursued by the succeeding regime.

Hinduism religion of the Hindus, which has a triad of three chief gods (the Trimurti): *Brahma* the Supreme Spirit, or *Atman*, who works creatively, as one of the triad, and brought into being the cosmos which is both real and an illusion (*'maya'*), since its reality is not lasting; the cosmos is itself personified as the goddess Maya.

Vishnu the preserver, who is thought to have taken various human forms including *Krishna* (hero of the epic *Mahabharata*, the guise in which he receives most popular adoration) and *Rama*. As *Jagganath* 'Lord of the World' he has a famous temple at Puri.

Shiva, the destroyer and re-creator, who represents the force for change in the universe and is depicted both as the supreme ascetic and as the supreme lover.

There are numerous lesser divinities, for example Ganesa, Hanuman, and Lakshmi, demons, ghosts, and spirits, who are also reverenced. Important ideas in Hinduism include the transmigration of souls and karma. The practice of Hinduism is a complex of rites and ceremonies performed within the framework of the caste system under the supervision of the Brahman priests and teachers. Temple worship is almost universally performed, and there are many festivals. In India and the rest of Asia there are over 475 million Hindus.

karma (Sanskrit 'fate'). In Hinduism the sum of a human being's actions, carried forward from one life to the next to result in an improved or worsened fate. Buddhism has a similar belief, except that no permanent personality is envisaged, the karma relating only to the physical and mental elements carried on from birth to birth, until the power holding them together disperses in the attainment of Nirvana.

caste a term generally used to denote the component groups of Indian or more particularly Hindu society. In India the caste system is derived traditionally from the four classes of early Hindu society – Brahmans (priests),. Kshatriyas (nobles and warriors), Vaisyas (traders and cultivators), and Sudras (servants), which were said to have originated from the head, arms, thighs, and feet respectively of Brahma, the Creator. A fifth class, the Untouchables, seen as polluting in its origin, its occupations, or its mode of life, remained and still largely remains outside the pale of Hindu society, for although the Indian Constituent Assembly of 1947 abolished 'untouchability', and made discrimination against the Scheduled

Castes or Depressed Classes illegal, and attempts have been made to enforce this, strong prejudice continues. The existing castes, which number probably some 3,000, exclusive of sub-castes, are regarded as having come into being by the interbreeding of these original groups.

International Society for Krishna Consciousness (ISKON) a Hindu sect introduced to the West by Swami Prabhupada (1896–1977), based on the demonstration of intense love for Krishna, especially by chanting the mantra 'Hare Krishna'. Members believe that by chanting the mantra and meditating on it, they may achieve enlightenment and so remove themselves from the cycle of reincarnation. They wear distinctive yellow robes and men often have most of their head shaven. Members of the movement are expected to live ascetic lives, avoiding meat and eggs, alcohol, tea, coffee and other drugs and gambling; sexual relationships should only take place within marriage and solely for procreation. Their holy books are the Hindu scriptures and particularly the *Bhagavad Gita*, which they study daily.

Islam religion (Arabic 'submission' to the will of Allah, the Muslim name for God), of which the creed declares: there is no God but Allah, and Muhammad is the Prophet or Messenger of Allah. Beliefs include Creation, Fall of Adam, Angels and the Jinn, Heaven and Hell, Day of Judgment, God's predestination of good and evil, and the succession of scriptures revealed to the prophets, including Moses and Jesus, but of which the perfect, final form is the *Koran* or *Quran* divided into 114 *suras* or chapters, said to have been divinely revealed to Muhammad, the original being preserved beside the throne of Allah in heaven. *sects* there are two main Muslim sects: *Sunni* whose members hold that the first three caliphs were all Muhammad's legitimate successors, and are in the majority. The name derives from the *Sunna* Arabic 'rule', the body of traditional law evolved from the teaching and acts of Muhammad. *Shi'ite* or *Shia* whose members believe that Ali was Muhammad's

first true successor; they number c 85 million, and are found in Iran, Iraq, Lebanon, and Bahrain. Holy men have greater authority in the Shi'ite sect. Breakaway sub-sects include the *Alawite* sect to which the ruling party in Syria belongs; and the *Ismaili* sect with the *Aga Khan* IV 1936– as its spiritual head. There is an Ismaili Centre (1985) in Kensington, London. Later schools include *Sufism*, a mystical movement in 17th century Iran. Generally speaking, Islam has not been a missionary religion, but after World War II a missionary movement, backing the militant organizations for the 'true Islamic state', developed. *Islamic law* Islam differs from Christianity in embodying a secular Islamic Law (the Shari'a or 'Highway'), which is clarified for Shi'ites by reference to their own version of the *sunna*, 'practice' of the Prophet as transmitted by his companions; the Sunni sect also take into account *ijma'*, the endorsement by universal consent of practices and beliefs among the faithful. A *mufti* is a legal expert who guides the courts in their interpretation, and in Turkey (until the establishment of the republic in 1924) had supreme spiritual authority. *organization* there is no organized church or priesthood, though Muhammad's descendants (the Hashim family) and popularly recognized holy men, mullahs and ayatollahs are accorded respect. *observances* the 'Five Pillars of the Faith' are: recitation of the creed, worship five times a day (facing the holy city of Mecca; the call to prayer is given by a muezzin, usually from the minaret or tower of a mosque), almsgiving, fasting sunrise to sunset through Ramadan (ninth month of the year, which varies with the calendar), and the pilgrimage to Mecca at least once in a lifetime.

Jainism a religion professed by about two and a half million Hindus, and sometimes regarded as an offshoot from Hinduism. Its sacred books record the teachings of Mahavira 599–527 BC, the latest of a long series of Tirthankaras, or omniscient saints and seers. Born in Vessali, now Bessarh, he became an ascetic at the age of 30, became omniscient (all-knowing) at 42, and preached for 30 years.

133

Jains believe that non-injury to living beings is the highest religion and their code of ethics is based on sympathy and compassion. They also believe in 'karma'. In Jainism there is no deity, and like Buddhism it is a monastic religion. There are two main sects: the *Digambaras*, who originally went about completely nude, and the *Swetambaras*.

Jehovah's Witnesses religious organization originated in the USA in 1872 by Charles Taze Russell 1852–1916. They attach great importance to Christ's second coming, which Russell predicted would occur in 1914, and which Witnesses still believe is imminent. The ensuing Armageddon and Last Judgment, which entail the destruction of all except the faithful, is to give way to the Theocratic Kingdom. Earth will continue to exist as the home of mankind, apart from 144,000 chosen believers who will reign with Christ in heaven. When Russell died in 1916, he was succeeded by Joseph Rutherford (d. 1942). Witnesses believe that they should not become involved in the affairs of this world, and their tenets, involving rejection of obligations such as military service, have often brought them into conflict with authority. Because of Biblical injunction against eating blood, Witnesses will not give or receive blood transfusions. Adults are baptized by total immersion. All Witnesses are expected to take part in house to house preaching; there are no clergy. The Watch Tower Bible and Tract Society and the Watch Tower Students' Association form part of the movement. Membership c. 1,000,000.

Judaism the religion of the Jews, founded on the Torah ('direction for living'), combining the Mosaic code and its oral interpretation. It was retained when the Jews were in exile in Babylon from 586 BC, and was reconstituted by Ezra on the return to Jerusalem. The ultimate destruction of the Temple at Jerusalem was countered by greater stress on the synagogue (in continental and US usage 'temple'), the local building for worship (originally simply the place where the Torah was read and expounded; its characteristic feature is still the Ark, or cupboard, where the Torah scrolls are

kept) and home observance. The work of lay rabbis (teachers), skilled in the Jewish law and ritual, also grew in importance, and in modern times they either act as spiritual leaders and pastors of their communities, or devote themselves to study. The *Talmud* compiled c. 200 AD combines the *Mishnah,* rabbinical commentary on the law handed down orally from 70 AD, and the *Gemara*, legal discussions in the schools of Palestine and Babylon. The *Haggadah* is that part of the Talmud which deals with stories of heroes. The *Midrash* is the collection of commentaries on the scriptures written 400–1200 AD, mainly in Palestine. The *creed* rests on the concept of one God, whose will is revealed in the Torah, and who has a special relationship with the Jewish people. Observances include: circumcision, daily services in Hebrew, and observance of the *Sabbath* (sunset on Friday to sunset Saturday), as a day of rest. Observed with more solemnity are *Rosh Hashanah* Jewish New Year (first new moon after the autumn equinox, announced by blowing a ram's horn) and, a week later, the religious fast *Yom Kippur*.

Mormon or 'Church of Jesus Christ of Latter-Day Saints'. Religious organization founded by Joseph Smith 1805–44. Born in Vermont, he received his first call in 1820, and in 1827 claimed to have been granted the revelation of the *Book of Mormon* (an ancient prophet), inscribed on gold plates and concealed a thousand years before in a hill near Palmyra, New York state. Christ is said to have appeared to an early American people after His ascension to establish His church in the New World, and the Mormon Church is a re-establishment of this by divine intervention. The Church was founded at Fayette, New York in 1830 and accepted the book as supplementing the Christian scriptures. Further settlements were rapidly established despite persecution, and Brigham Young and the Twelve Apostles undertook the first foreign Mormon mission in England, the earliest European converts reaching the USA in 1840. Their doctrines met with persecution, and Smith was killed in Illinois. To escape further persecution, Brigham Young led an emigration to the Valley of the Great Salt Lake in 1847 and in 1850 Utah was created a territory with Young as governor 1851–58. Most of the Mormons who remained in the Middle West (headquarters Independence, Missouri) accepted the founder's son Joseph Smith 1832–1914 as leader, adopted the name Reorganized Church of Jesus Christ of Latter-Day Saints, and claim to be the true successor of the original church. They do not accept the non-Christian doctrines later proclaimed by Young in 1852, notably that of polygamy, which Young attributed to the original founder in 1843 on no verifiable evidence: Smith is on record as condemning plural wives. The doctrine was formally repudiated by the Utah Mormons in 1890, and Utah was recognized as a State of the Union in 1896. Mormons believe that marriage is eternal and a necessary step to godhood, and that parenthood is both an obligation and a blessing. Entrance into the church is through baptism by total immersion; children are baptized at about eight years of age. Mormons believe that it is possible for the dead to be baptized vicariously and so enter heaven; because of this they make every effort to trace their ancestors for baptism. Members of the church are known as Saints, and are expected to donate one tenth of their income to the church; they must abstain from alcohol, tobacco, tea and coffee. Women cannot become priests; they are expected to be modest in dress and obedient to their husbands. The Mormons number c. 3,250,000; the Re-organized Church c. 205,000; both have branches in Britain.

Parseeism the religion of the followers of Zoroaster who fled from Persia after its conquest by the Arabs, and settled in India in the eighth century AD. They now live mainly in Bombay state, maintaining their rituals of the sacred fire and the exposure of their dead. They are noted for their success in business and philanthropy. They number about 100,000.

Rajneesh Meditation a form of meditation based on the teachings of Bhagwan Shree Rajneesh, who established an ashram or religious community in Poona, NW India, in the early 1970s. He gained many followers, both Indian and Western, but his teachings also created considerable opposition, and in 1981 the Bhagwan moved his ashram to Oregon, USA. Followers of the Bhagwan regard themselves as *Sannyas*, a term used for Hindu ascetics: they wear orange robes and carry a string of prayer beads. The Bhagwan teaches that there is a basic energy in the world, bioenergy, and that individuals can release this by Dynamic Meditation, which involves breathing exercises and explosive physical activity. Followers of Rajneesh, who now number about 500,000, are not expected to observe any specific prohibitions, but to be guided by their instincts. They are encouraged to live in large groups, so their children may grow up in contact with a variety of people.

Rastafarianism West Indian religion based on the ideas of Marcus Garvey, who preached that the only way for black people to escape their poverty and oppression was to return to Africa. When Haile Selassie (Ras Tafari, the Lion of Judah) was crowned Emperor of Ethiopia in 1930, this was seen as a fulfilment of prophecy, and Rastafarians acknowledged him as the Messiah, the incarnation of God (Jah). Rastafarians identify themselves with the Chosen People, the Israelites, of the Bible: Ethiopia is seen as the promised land, while all countries outisde Africa, and their cultures and institutions, are 'Babylon', the place of exile. Rastafarians use a distinct language, in particular using the term 'I and I' for 'we' to stress unity. Many Rastafarians do not cut their hair, because of Biblical injunctions against this, but wear their hair in long dreadlocks, often covered in woollen hats in the Rastafarian colours of red, green and gold. Food laws are very strict: for example, no pork or shellfish, no salt, milk or coffee. The term I-tal is used for food as close as possible to its natural state. Medicines should be made from natural herbs, and the use of ganja (marijuana) is seen as a sacrament. There are no churches, but meetings are held regularly for prayer, discussion and celebration, and at intervals there is a very large meeting or Nyabingi. There are currently about one million Rastafarians.

Scientology an 'applied religious philosophy', its name derived from Latin *scire* 'to know' and Greek *logos* 'branch of learning', founded in California in 1954 by Lafayette Ronald Hubbard 1911– as the Church of Scientology, its headquarters from 1959 being at Saint Hill Manor, East Grinstead, Sussex. It claims to 'increase man's spiritual awareness', but the movement has met with criticism.

Dianetics a form of psychotherapy developed by L Ron Hubbard in the USA, which formed the basis for Scientology. Hubbard believed that all mental illness and certain forms of physical illness are caused by engrams or incompletely assimilated traumatic experiences, both pre- and post-natal. These engrams can be confronted during therapy with an auditor and thus exorcised. An individual free from engrams would be a 'Clear' and perfectly healthy. Hubbard later developed this theory: behind each mind is a non-physical and immortal being, the Thetan, which has forgotten its true nature and is therefore trapped in a cycle of reincarnation, accumulating engrams with each lifetime. If these engrams are cleared, the individual will become an Operating Thetan, with quasi-miraculous powers.

Shinto the Chinese transliteration of the Japanese for Kami-no-Michi, the Way or Doctrine of the Gods, the indigenous religion of Japan. This is a mixture of nature-worship and loyalty to the reigning dynasty as descendants of the Sun-goddess, Amaterasu-Omikami. State Shinto was the national faith of Japan; its holiest shrine is at Ise, where in the temple of the Sun-goddess is preserved the mirror that she is supposed to have given to Jimmu, the first emperor, in the seventh century BC. *Sects* Shinto consists of 130 sects, each founded by an historical character; the sects are officially recognized, but are not State-supported, as was State Shinto until its disestablishment by General MacArthur's decree after World War II. Unquestioning obedience and devotion to the emperor is inculcated, but there is also an exemplary ethic.

Sikhism the religion professed by some ten million Indians living for the most part in the Punjab. It was founded by Nanak 1469–c. 1539. Its basis is the Unity of God and the Brotherhood of Man: Sikhism is strongly opposed to caste divisions. On Nanak's death he was followed as Guru – teacher – by a succession of leaders who converted the Sikhs – the word means disciple – into a military confraternity which established itself as a political power. Guru Gobind Singh instituted the Khanda-di-Pahul, the Baptism of the Sword, and established the Khalsa ('the pure'), the Brotherhood of the faithful, the Singhs. The Singhs wear the five Ks: *kes*, long hair; *kangha*, a comb; *kirpan*, a sword; *kachh*, short trousers; and *kara*, a steel bracelet. The last of the Gurus, Gobind Singh, was assassinated by a Muslim in 1708, and since then the Granth Sahib, the holy book of the Sikhs, has taken the place of a leader. On the partition of India many Sikhs migrated from W to E Punjab, and in 1966 the efforts of Sant Fateh Singh c. 1911–72 led to the creation of a separate Sikh state by partition of Punjab. However, the Alkali separatist movement agitates for a completely independent Sikh state, Khalistan, and a revival of fundamentalist belief was headed from 1978 by Sant Jarnail Singh Bhindranwale 1947–84, killed in the siege of the Golden Temple, Amritsar. In retaliation for this, the Indian Prime Minister, Indira Gandhi, was assassinated in October of the same year by her Sikh bodyguard. Heavy rioting followed, in which 1,000 Sikhs were killed. Mrs Gandhi's successor, Rajiv Ghandi, reached an agreement for the election of a popular government in the Punjab and for state representatives to the Indian Parliament with the moderate Sikh leader Sant Harchand Singh Longowal, who was himself killed in 1985 by Sikh extremists. The agreement did not mean an end to conflict, which still continues.

Taoism Chinese philosophical system, traditionally founded by Lao-zi in the sixth century BC, though the scriptures, *Tao Te Ching* were apparently compiled in the third century BC. The 'tao' or 'way' denotes the hidden

Principle of the Universe, and less stress is laid on good deeds than on harmonious interaction with the environment, which automatically ensures right behaviour. The second important work is that of Zhuangzi c. 389–286 BC, *The Way of Zhuangzi*. The later magical side of Taoism is illustrated by the *I Ching* or *Book of Changes*, a book of divination.

Transcendental Meditation (TM) a technique of focusing the mind based in part on Hindu meditation, introduced to Britain by the Maharishi Mahesh Yogi and popularized by the Beatles in the late 1960s. Such meditation is believed to bring benefit to the practitioner in the form of release from stress; devotees claim that if even as few as one per cent of the population meditated in this way, it would create peace in the world. Meditators are given a mantra (a special word or phrase) to chant. This mantra is never written down or divulged to anyone else. The Maharishi believes that through the practice of meditation special powers such as levitation, precognition and control over bodily functions can be developed.

Unification Church (Moonies) Church founded in Korea in 1954 by the Reverend Sun Myung Moon. World membership is about 200,000. The theology unites Christian and Taoist ideas, and is based on the book *Divine Principle* which teaches that the original purpose of creation was to set up a perfect family, in a perfect relationship with God; this was thwarted by the Fall of Man. Throughout history there have been attempts to renew this plan, which is now said to have found its fulfilment in Reverend and Mrs Moon. The Unification Church believes that marriage is essential for spiritual fulfilment, and marriage partners are chosen for members by Reverend Moon, though individuals are free to reject a chosen partner. Marriage, which takes the form of mass blessings by Reverend and Mrs Moon, is the most important ritual of the church; it is preceded by the wine or engagement ceremony. There are few other rituals, though there is a weekly pledge, which is a ceremony of rededication. The role of women

in the church is to some extent still influenced by its Korean origins, but this, like the church's extreme anti-Marxist stance, is undergoing change.

Zen abbreviation of Japanese *zenna*, 'quiet mind concentration', a variant of Buddhism introduced from India to Japan via China in the 12th century. *Zazen* or 'sitting meditation' involves periods in the cross-legged lotus position, during which all worldly concerns are banished and a state of selflessness reached which ultimately leads to 'enlightenment'.

Zoroastrianism the religion founded by Zoroaster, represented today by the Parsees. Its theology is dualistic, the Good God Ahura Mazda or Ormuzd being opposed by the Evil God, Angra Mainyu or Ahriman. These are represented in the Avesta as being perpetually in conflict, but ultimately the victory will be Ormuzd's. A ceremonial was devised for purifying and keeping clean both soul and body. Worship was at altars on which burnt the sacred fire. A priestly caste was instituted. The dead were exposed to vultures.

Rites of Passage

Most religions mark certain important stages in a person's life, such as birth, initiation, marriage, and death, by special ceremonies or rites of passage. These rituals provide a way of publicly recognizing a change of status; they are also a time for the whole community to reaffirm its faith.

Birth rites
Birth is often a time of rejoicing, but it is also a time of new responsibility and, especially in communities with a high infant mortality rate, a time of worry and danger. This ambivalence is reflected in some of the rituals associated with birth.

Hindu birth rites begin with the choice of a

suitable day for conception, and continue through pregnancy; the mother-to-be must avoid certain foods and recite verses from the Hindu holy books. When the baby is born, there are a number of further ceremonies including naming the child, the last of which, the shaving of the child's hair, may take place up to two years after the birth. Hindus believe that these ceremonies will help the child towards a better rebirth.

Sikh birth rites Sikhs believe that the first words a child should hear are those of the Mool Mantra, the beginning of the Sikh holy book, and so, as soon as the baby is born, it is washed and the words of the Mool Mantra whispered into its ear. A few weeks later the child is taken to the Gurdwara, the Sikh place of worship, to be named. The initial of the name is chosen by opening the Guru Granth Sahib at random.

Muslim birth rites the first words which a Muslim baby will hear are those of the call to prayer, which is used to call Muslims to the mosque or place of worship each day; these words, which contain the basic beliefs of Islam, are whispered into its ears. Seven days later, the child is named. This ceremony involves the shaving of the baby's head. If the child is a boy, he will also be circumcised (see below) at this time.

Jewish birth rites the surgical operation of *circumcision* consists of the removal of a small part of the foreskin. All Jewish boys must be circumcised on the eighth day after birth, as long as health permits. This is a reminder of the covenant or agreement which God made with Abraham. If the child is a girl, her name is announced in the synagogue (the Jewish place of worship) by the father on the week of her birth.

Christian birth rites universal in the Christian Church from its beginning has been the religious initiation rite of *baptism* (Greek 'to dip'), involving immersion in or sprinkling with water. In the baptismal ceremony, sponsors or godparents make vows on behalf of the child which are renewed by the child at confirmation. Baptism was originally administered to adults by immersion, and infant baptism has

been common only since the 6th century. In some of the Protestant churches, adults are still baptized by immersion in a pool of water. The immersion symbolizes death and new life.

Chinese birth rites Chinese babies are not named for the first month after birth; then the Full Month ceremony is held, with special foods, including red eggs which are symbols of luck and new life. The name given to the baby is a nickname designed to convince any malevolent spirits that the child is not worth stealing.

Initiation Rites

Initiation is a passage into full membersip of a group, whether religious or social. It gives the individual both rights and responsibilities.

Sikh initiation rites the tenth guru of Sikhism, Guru Gobind Singh, set up a group of dedicated Sikhs, the Khalsa; any sufficiently mature Sikh may apply to join the Khalsa. The ceremony is conducted by five members of the Khalsa in the presence of the Guru Granth Sahib, the Sikh holy book; it involves the drinking and sprinkling of amrit (sugar and water). Those initiated in the Khalsa must always wear five things known as the Five K's: uncut hair; a steel bracelet; a short sword; a comb and kachh, a type of shorts.

Jewish initiation is marked by the *bar mitzvah* (Hebrew 'son of the commandment'), initiation of a boy at the age of 13 into the adult Jewish community; less common is the bat mitzvah for girls. The boy reads a passage from the Torah in the synagogue on the Sabbath. After this, he is regarded as a full member of the congregation.

Christian initation is marked by *confirmation*, a rite by which a previously baptized person is admitted to full membership of the Christian Church. It consists in the laying on of hands by a bishop, in order that the confirmed person may receive the gift of the Holy Spirit.

Among Anglicans, the rite is deferred until the child is able to learn a catechism or series of questions and answers, containing the fundamentals of Christian doctrine, and an unconfirmed person is not usually allowed to receive Holy Communion. A child's first Holy Communion is also an initiation rite.

Marriage Rites

Marriage involves not only a change in status for the two people concerned, but also a new set of relationships for their families and the probability of children. In many cultures the choice of marriage partner is made by the parents.

Hindu marriage rites Hindu weddings may take place at the bride's home, or in a temple. The bride usually wears a red sari, and her hands and feet are painted with patterns in henna, an orange dye. The most important part of the ceremony is the seven steps which the bride and groom take round a sacred fire, which symbolize food, strength, wealth, good fortune, the seasons, and everlasting friendship.

Sikh marriage rites a Sikh wedding may be held anywhere, as long as the Guru Granth Sahib is present. During the ceremony, the couple show their assent to the marriage by bowing to the holy book. The couple walk together round the Guru Granth Sahib as a hymn written by the fourth Guru is sung: this hymn contains all the basic teachings of Sikhism.

Jewish marriage rites marriage is important in Judaism, since the Torah, the Jewish holy book, says that humanity should 'be fruitful and multiply'. The ceremony usually takes place in the synagogue, the place of worship. The bride and groom, with their parents, stand under a canopy or chupah. Blessings are recited by the rabbi, the religious leader, and the groom gives the bride a ring. At the end of the ceremony the groom steps on and shatters a glass as a reminder, amidst the happiness, of the destruction of the Temple at Jerusalem.

Christian marriage rites Christian marriages are usually celebrated at the place of worship (church or chapel). The groom is accompanied by a helper, or best man, while the bride is escorted by her father, who officially 'gives' her to her new husband, and by attendants (bridesmaids). The couple make promises to love, honour and care for each other and exchange rings.

Muslim marriage rites Muslim weddings may take place in the bride's home or in the place of worship, the mosque. The bride and groom are normally in separate rooms throughout the short ceremony. There is often a reading from the Koran, and a talk on the duties of marriage. The couple must consent to the marriage three times, and rings are exchanged.

Chinese marriage rites in Chinese weddings, the concept of yin and yang, the two complementary forces which make up the universe, plays a prominent part; among their other attributes yin is seen as female and yang as male. There is a series of rituals leading up to the wedding, including the giving of gifts, an exchange of horoscopes (a prediction of a person's fortune) and a payment to the bride's family. The ceremony itself involves offerings and prayers to the bridegroom's ancestors and the household gods.

Death Rites

Death rites fulfil three main purposes: to comfort and strengthen the dying person, to comfort those left behind, and to ensure the best possible outcome for the deceased person in the next world or next birth. In several religions, such as Sikhism, Judaism, and Islam, people are encouraged to speak a declaration of faith before death, and Sikhs and Muslims read from their holy books to the dying person. Some religions discourage mourning, because they feel that death should not be regarded as a tragedy for the individual, especially after a long life, while others, such as Judaism, set time aside for the family to grieve. There are many ways in which religions try to help the deceased in the afterlife. The Chinese offer practical help: since the afterlife may have resemblances to this life, replicas of useful goods, cars, washing machines, and money, are burnt at the funeral for the use of the deceased who will, with the other ancestors, now watch over the family.

Holy Books

Many religions have a book or books which are regarded as holy or as providing especial wisdom. These books are treated with great reverence and copies may be kept in a place particularly set aside or have specific ceremonies associated with them. Such books are sometimes referred to as scriptures.

Buddhist
Buddhism has a vast number of books which are revered because they contain the teachings of the Buddha. Since Buddhism was transmitted by word of mouth for about 500 years after the death of the Buddha, it is impossible to say which of these writings contain the original words of the Buddha and which are later additions. The main group of texts is known as the *Tipitaka* or *Tripitaka* (literally 'three baskets'), which are divided into three sections; however, the contents of these sections vary among the different schools of Buddhism.

Chinese
Since Chinese religion is a mixture of Buddhism, Confucianism and Taoism, the Chinese generally respect the writings of all three. The main text of Taoism is the *Tao Te Ching*, attributed to the traditional founder of Taoism, Lao-zi. Confucianism's main writings are those of Confucius himself, especially the Analects or 'selected sayings'.

Christian
Bible the authorized documentation (Greek *ta biblia* 'the books') of the Christian and Jewish religions. It comprises the *Old Testament* books recognized by both Jews and Christians (the first five are traditionally ascribed to Moses and known as the Pentateuch); *Apocryrypha* books not included in the final Hebrew canon, but recognized by Roman Catholics, though segregated or omitted in Protestant bibles, and the *New Testament* books recognized by the Christian Church from the fourth century as canonical. The latter include the Gospels, which tell of the life and teachings of Jesus, the history of the early church, teachings of St Paul, and mystical writings.

Hindu
Veda (Sanskrit, 'divine knowledge'). The most sacred of the Hindu scriptures, hymns written in an old form of Sanskrit; the oldest may date from 1500 or 2000 BC. The four main collections are: the Rigveda (hymns and praises); Yajurveda (prayers and sacrificial formulae); Sâmaveda (tunes and chants); and Atharvaveda, or Veda of the Atharvans, the officiating priests at the sacrifices.

Bhagavad-gita religious and philosophical poem (The Song of the Blessed) which is the supreme religious work of Hinduism.

Ramayana Sanskrit epic c. 300 BC, in which Rama, an incarnation of the god Vishnu, and his friend Hanuman (the monkey chieftain) strive to recover Rama's wife, Sita, abducted by demon king Ravana.

Jewish
The *Torah*, the Jewish holy book, is made up of five books attributed to Moses. They contain a traditional account of history from the creation of the world up to the death of Moses, as well as the laws by which Jews believe they should live. Other books which are important are the *Talmud*, compiled by rabbis or religious teachers between the first and fifth centuries AD, which interprets and expands on the Torah; and the books containing the Psalms (sacred songs) and the messages of prophets (people who speak on behalf of God).

Muslim
Koran more properly, *Quran*, though both are transliterations; the sacred book of Islam. Written in the purest Arabic, it contains 114 suras or chapters, and is stated to have been divinely revealed to the prophet Muhammad; the original is supposed to be preserved beside the throne of Allah in heaven.

Sikh
The Sikh holy book is the *Guru Granth Sahib*, also known as the Adi Granth or 'first book'. It is a collection of hymns by the Sikh gurus or

teachers, as well as by Muslim and Hindu writers, which was compiled largely by the fifth guru, Guru Arjan, and completed by the tenth guru, Guru Gobind Singh. On the death of the tenth guru, the Guru Granth Sahib took over the role of teacher and leader of the Sikhs. Guidance is sought by opening the holy book at random and reading verses. Any copy of the Guru Granth Sahib must have a special room to itself; people entering the room must cover their heads and remove their shoes. All copies of the holy book are idential, having 1,430 pages, and written in Gurmukhi, the written form of Punjabi.

Religious Figures

Abraham founder of the Jewish nation. Born at Ur, Abram was the son of Terah, and migrated to Haran, N Mesopotamia, with his father, his wife Sarah, and his nephew Lot. Proceeding to Canaan, he received Jehovah's promise of the land to his descendants, and after sojourning in Egypt during a famine, separated from Lot at Bethel before settling in Hebron. On re-naming him Abraham, 'father of many nations', Jehovah promised him a legitimate heir, and then tested him by a command to slay the boy Isaac in sacrifice. By his second wife, Keturah, Abraham had six sons. He was buried in Machpelah cave, Hebron.

Abu Bakr c. 573–634 AD. A close friend of Muhammad and caliph (teacher and leader of the Muslim community) 632–634 AD. Traditionally, it was Abu Bakr who encouraged those who had been companions of the prophet to memorize his teachings, which were later written down to form the Koran.

Al-Ghazzali 1058–1111 AD. Muslim philosopher and one of the most famous Sufis (Muslim mystics). Initially, he believed that God's exis-

tence could be proved by reason, but later he became a wandering Sufi, seeking God through mystical experience; he did not, however, turn his back on scholarly work, and his best-known book, *The Alchemy of Happiness* , was written on his travels. He was also responsible for easing the conflict between the Sufi and the Ulema, a body of Muslim religious and legal scholars.

Ali born 600 AD. Cousin and son-in-law of Muhammad, and elected fourth caliph of Islam in 656. Ali was opposed by Muhammad's wife Aisha, who accused him of plotting the death of his predecessor. This led to civil war, and Ali was finally assassinated in 661. Shi'ite Muslims believe that the caliphate passed to the descendants of Ali.

Asoka reigned 264–228 BC. Indian emperor, who was a Buddhist convert, he had edicts enjoining the adoption of his new faith carved on pillars and rock faces throughout his dominions, and many survive. In Patna, there are the remains of a hall built by him.

Augustine 354-430 AD. Christian saint, theologian, and a Father of the Church. Born at Tagaste, Numidia, of Roman descent, he studied rhetoric in Carthage where he became the father of a natural son, Adeodatus. He lectured at Tagaste and Carthage and for ten years was attached to the Manichaean heresy. In 383 he went to Rome, and on moving to Milan came under the influence of Ambrose. After prolonged study of Neo-Platonism Augustine was converted to Christianity and was baptized by Ambrose together with his son. Resigning his chair in rhetoric, he returned to Africa, his mother St Monica dying at Ostia on the journey, and settled at Tagaste. His son died at 17. In 391, while visiting Hippo, Augustine was ordained priest. In 395 he was given the right of succession to the bishopric of Hippo, and in 396 succeeded to the office. He died at Hippo during its siege by the Vandals.

Many of Augustine's books resulted from his share in three great controversies: he refuted Manichaeism; attacked and did much to eliminate Donatism (conference of Carthage, 411); and devoted the last 20 years of his life to the Pelagian controversy, in which he maintained the doctrine of original sin and the necessity of divine grace. He estimated the number of his works at 230, and also wrote many sermons, as well as pastoral letters. Augustine's most famous productions are his 'Confessions', his spiritual autobiography, and the influential *De Civitate Dei/The City of God* vindicating the Christian Church and Divine Providence in 22 books.

Bodhidharma 6th century BC Indian Buddhist. He entered China from S India c. 520, and was the founder of Zen ('religious meditation', Japanese word derived from Chinese *cha'an*), the school of Mahayana Buddhism in which intuitive meditation, prompted by contemplation of the beautiful, leads to enlightenment. It passed to Japan in the 12th century, where it is the best-known school.

Buddha title of prince Gautama Siddhartha c. 563–483 BC born at Lumbini in Nepal. At the age of 29, he left his wife and son to seek a way of escape from the burdens of existence, and after six years of austerity became enlightened (Buddha means 'enlightened one') under a Banyan or bo tree near Buddh Gaya. He acquired the Four Truths: the fact of pain or ill; that pain has a cause; that pain can be ended; and that it can be ended by following the Eightfold Way of right views, right intention, right speech, right action, right livelihood, right effort, right mindfulness, and right concentration, and so arriving at Nirvana, the extinction of all craving for things of the senses. He began teaching at Varanasi, and founded the Sangha, or order of monks, eventually dying at Kusinagara in Uttar Pradesh.

Confucius Latinized name (meaning 'Kong the Master') of Chinese sage Kong Zi 550–478 BC. Born in Lu, a small state in what is now the province of Shandong, at Qufu, he became a minor official. Taking to teaching, he gathered disciples, and was for a time so excellent a governor of a small town that he became prime minister of Lu. However, he went into exile when his advice was ignored, returning only in the last years of his life under a new ruler. He was buried at Qufu.

Jesus Christ c. 4 BC–c. 30 AD. Jesus (Hebrew *Messiah*, Greek *the Christ*) was the founder of Christianity, based on the account of his life in the four Gospels, (which form part of the Bible, the Christian holy book). Born in Bethlehem (a town in Israel), son of the Virgin Mary (of the peoples of Judah and the family of David), he was brought up as a carpenter by Mary's husband Joseph at Nazareth. In 26/27 AD his cousin John the Baptist began a preparatory mission, and baptized Jesus, whose Galilean ministry included two missionary journeys through the district, and the calling of 12 apostles or followers. His teaching, summarized in the Sermon on the Mount, aroused both religious opposition from the Pharisees, Jewish leaders, and secular opposition from the government of the day, the Herodian party. When he returned to Jerusalem a week before the Passover, he was greeted by the people as the Messiah or coming saviour, and the Jewish authorities (aided by one of his followers, Judas) had him arrested and condemned to death (after a hurried trial) by the religious court of Sanhedrin. The sentence was confirmed by the Roman procurator, Pontius Pilate, but three days after the Crucifixion (death by hanging on a cross), came reports of his resurrection, and later ascension to heaven.

Luther Martin 1483–1546. German Protestant reformer. Originally a monk, he became convinced of the primacy of grace (the freely given gift of God) over merit, 'justification by faith'. In 1517 he nailed on the church door at Wittenberg his 'Ninety-five Theses against Indulgences' (an abuse of power common in the church at the time), following this in 1519 with opposition to the infallibility and primacy of the Pope, and becoming an outlaw before the Empire and an apostate before the Church. In 1525 he married an ex-nun, and in 1530 formulated the Augsburg Confession, the basis of Lutheranism. His translation of the scriptures marks the emergence of modern German. Formerly condemned by Communism, he had by the 1980s been rehabilitated as a revolutionary socialist hero, and was claimed as patron saint by both East and West

Germany.

Maimonides 1135–1204 AD. Jewish rabbi (teacher) and philosopher influenced by the ideas of the Greek philosopher Aristotle. He drew up the *Thirteen Principles,* a summary of the basic beliefs of Judaism. His approach to reasoning aroused hostility in his lifetime, but he is now thought of as one of the great teachers of Judaism.

Mencius 371–289 BC. Confucian philosopher who developed and elaborated on the teachings of Confucius. He put great emphasis on the idea that human nature was basically good, and that failure to act in a virtuous way was a result of wrong environment. He believed that rulers should act in accordance with the will of heaven, and was outspoken in his condemnation of those who failed to live up to this ideal.

Moses Jewish lawgiver and judge who led the Israelites out of Egypt to the promised land of Canaan. According to the Torah, Moses was hidden among the bulrushes on the banks of the Nile when the Pharaoh commanded that all new-born male Hebrew children should be destroyed. He was found by a daughter of Pharaoh, who reared him. Eventually he became the leader of the Israelites in the Exodus, and the 40 years' wandering in the wilderness. On Mt Sinai he received from Jehovah the Ten Commandments engraved on tablets of stone, and died at the age of 120, after having been allowed a glimpse of the Promised Land from Mount Pisgah.

Muhammad or Mohammed, Mahomet, Mahound (Arabic 'praised') c. 570–632 AD. Founder of Islam, born in Mecca. Originally a shepherd and caravan conductor, he found leisure for meditation by his marriage with a wealthy widow in 595, and received his first revelation in 610. After some years of secret teaching, he openly declared himself the prophet of God in about 616, the Koran (revealed to him by God and later written down by his followers) being the basis of his teaching. Persecuted as the number of his followers increased, he fled to the town now known as Medina in 622 (the flight, *Hegira,*

which marks the beginning of the Islamic era). After the battle of Badr in 623, he was continuously victorious, entering Mecca as the recognized prophet of Arabia 630. The succession was troubled.

Nanak 1469–c. 1539. Indian guru, strongly opposed to caste divisions, founder of Sikhism on the basis of the Unity of God and the Brotherhood of Man.

Paul St c. 3–64 or 68 AD. One of the Apostles (the Jewish form of his name being Saul), he was born in Tarsus, son of well-to-do Pharisees, and had Roman citizenship. Opposed to Christianity, he took part in the stoning of the first Christian martyr Stephen, but was converted by a vision on the road to Damascus. He made great missionary journeys, for example to Philippi, Ephesus, hence becoming known as the 'Apostle of the Gentiles' (non-Jews). On his return to Jerusalem, he was arrested, appealed to Caesar, and (as a citizen) was sent to Rome for trial c. 57 or 59. After two years in prison, he may have been released before his final arrest and execution under Nero. Thirteen epistles in the New Testament are attributed to him. His theology was rigorous on such questions as sin and atonement, and his views on the role of women became those of the Church generally.

Ramakrishna 1834–86 AD. A teacher and mystic (one dedicated to achieving oneness with or a direct experience of God or some force beyond the normal world). Ramakrishna claimed that mystical experience was the ultimate aim of religions, and that all religions which led to this goal were equally valid.

Ranjit Singh Maharaja 1780–1839 AD. A military leader of the Sikhs who became ruler of the Punjab at the age of 20, and preserved it from capture by the British until his death.

Shankara 799–833 AD. Hindu philosopher who wrote commentaries on some of the major Hindu scriptures, as well as hymns and essays on religous ideas. Shankara was responsible for the final form of the Advaita Vedanta school of Hindu philosophy, which teaches that Brahman, the supreme being, is all that exists in the universe; everything else is illu-

143

sion. Shankara was fiercely opposed to Buddhism, and may have been largely responsible for its decline in India.

Zoroaster or Zarathustra c. 628–c. 551 BC. Persian founder of Zoroastrianism, who was assassinated by rival prophets.

Holy Places

The concept of *pilgrimage*, a journey to sacred places inspired by religious devotion, is common to many religions. For Hindus the holy places include Benares and the purifying Ganges; for Buddhists the places connected with the crises of Buddha's career; for the ancient Greeks the shrines at Delphi, Ephesus, among others; for the Jews, the sanctuary at Jerusalem; and for Muslims, Mecca. Among Christians, pilgrimages were common by the second century, and as a direct result of the established necessity of making pilgrimages there arose the numerous hospices catering for pilgrims, the religious orders of knighthood, and the Crusades. The great centres of Christian pilgrimages have been, or are, Jerusalem, Rome, the tomb of St James of Compostella in Spain, the shrine of Becket at Canterbury, and the holy places at La Salette and Lourdes in France.

Amritsar city in the Punjab, India, founded 1577. It is the religious centre of the Sikhs and contains the *Golden Temple* and Guru Nanak University 1969, named after the first Sikh Guru.

Jerusalem ancient city of Palestine, which is a holy place for Jews, Christians and Muslims. It was divided in 1948 between the new republic of Israel and Jordan. In 1950 the western New City was proclaimed as the Israeli capital, and following the Israeli capture of the eastern Old City in 1967 from the Jordanians, it was affirmed in 1980 that the united city was the

country's capital, but the United Nations does not recognize the claim.

history by 1400 BC Jerusalem was ruled by a king subject to Egypt, but c. 1000 BC David, the second king of Israel, made it the capital of a united Jewish kingdom. It was captured by Nebuchadnezzar 586 BC, who deported its population. Later conquerors include Alexander the Great and Pompey (63 BC), and it was under Roman rule that Jesus Christ was executed. In 70 AD a Jewish revolt led to its complete destruction by Titus. It was first conquered by Islam in 637; was captured by Crusaders, Christians who were fighting the Muslims in Israel, 1099, and recaptured by Saladin 1187, to remain under almost unbroken Islamic rule until the British occupation of Palestine in 1917.

Notable buildings include the *Church of the Holy Sepulchre* (built 335), and the mosque of the *Dome of the Rock*. The latter was built on the site of Solomon's Temple, and the *Western* ('wailing') *Wall*, held sacred by Jews, is part of the walled platform on which the Temple once stood.

Temple the centre of Jewish national worship at Jerusalem. Three temples occupied the site: *Solomon's Temple*, which was destroyed by Nebuchadnezzar; *Zerubbabel's Temple*, built after the return from Babylon; and *Herod's Temple*, which was destroyed by the Romans in 70 AD. The Mosque of Omar occupies the site. The *Wailing Wall* is the surviving part of the western wall of the platform of the enclosure of the Temple of Herod, so-called by tourists because of the oriental chanting style of the Jews in their prayers there. Under Jordanian rule Jews had no access to the place, but took this part of the city in the 1967 campaign.

Kyoto a city in S Honshu, Japan, which was the capital of Japan 794–1868, and has famous temples; to the south east is Ise, site of the most sacred Shinto shrine, rebuilt every 20 years in the form of a thatched seventh-century house, and containing the octagonal mirror of the sun-goddess Amaterasu.

Mecca city of Saudi Arabia, the holiest city of the Muslim world, where the Prophet was born. It stands in the desert, in a valley about 72 km/45 mi east of Jidda, its port on the Red Sea, with which it is linked by an asphalted road, and long before the time of Muhammad was a commercial centre, caravan junction, and place of pilgrimage. In the centre of Mecca is the *Great Mosque*, in whose courtyard is the *Kaaba*; it also contains the well *Zam-Zam*, associated by tradition with Ishmael, the son of Abraham, and his mother Hagar, and the *Maqām Ibrāhīm*, a holy stone supposed to bear the imprint of Abraham's foot.

kaaba the oblong building in the quadrangle of the Great Mosque at Mecca into the north-east corner of which is built the black stone declared by Muhammad to have been given to Abraham by Gabriel, and devoutly revered by Muslim pilgrims. The name means chamber.

Medina city in Saudi Arabia, about 355 km/220 mi north of Mecca. To Muslims it is a holy city second only to Mecca, since Muhammad lived here for many years after he fled from Mecca, and died here. The *Mosque of the Prophet* contains his reputed tomb, and those of the caliphs or Muslim leaders Abu Bakr, Omar, and Fatima, Muhammad's daughter.

Varanesi Indian city on the sacred Ganges river in Uttar Pradesh, more familiar in the West under the form Benares. It is holy to Hindus with a 5 km/3 mi frontage of stairways (ghats), leading up from the river to innumerable streets, temples, and the 1,500 golden shrines. The ritual of purification is daily practised by thousands of devout Hindus, who bathe from the ghats in the sacred river. At the burning ghats, the ashes, following cremation, are scattered on the river, a ritual supposed to ensure a favourable reincarnation.

Festivals

Buddhist festivals
Wesak the day of the Buddha's birth, enlightenment and death. A large act of worship is held and gifts given to monks; captive animals may be freed.
Dhammacakka celebrates the preaching of the Buddha's first sermon. Visits are made to monasteries and gifts are given to the monks.
Bodhi Day Mahayana Buddhist celebration of the Buddha's enlightenment.

Chinese festivals
New Year time when the Kitchen God, whose picture is in every home, returns to heaven to report on the family's behaviour during the year. There are elaborate lion dances and fireworks, and vegetarian feasts are eaten.
Chin Ming a time for visiting ancestral tombs, making offerings and remembering the dead.
Dragon Boat Festival celebrates the story of a brave official who persuaded a harsh emperor to relent over his crippling taxation of the people by drowning himself. Races are held between boats carved to resemble dragons, in memory of the boat chase to save the official's body from being eaten by dragons and demons.
Moon Festival commemorates the story of a brave woman who defied her husband, a wicked king, to stop him obtaining immortality, and was carried off by the gods to live on the moon. The festival is held at full moon and the moon is greeted with incense, lanterns and feasting.
Winter Festival time of feasting to build up strength for the winter ahead.

Christian festivals
Epiphany annual festival (6 Jan) of the Christian Church, celebrating the coming of the Magi or wise men to Bethlehem with gifts for the infant Christ, and symbolizing the man-

ifestation of Christ to the world. It is the twelfth day after Christmas, and marks the end of the Christmas festivities. In many countries the night before, called *Twelfth Night*, is marked by the giving of gifts.

Shrove Tuesday the day before Ash Wednesday. The name comes from the Anglo-Saxon *scrifan,* to shrive, and in former times it was the time for confession before Lent. Another name for it is Pancake Tuesday; the pancakes are a survival of merrymaking in anticipation of Lenten abstinence.

Ash Wednesday first day of Lent, the period in the Christian calendar leading up to Easter; in the Catholic Church the foreheads of the congregation are marked with a cross in ash, as a sign of penitence.

Lent in the Christian Church, the forty days' period of fasting which precedes Easter, beginning on Ash Wednesday, but omitting Sundays.

Palm Sunday the Sunday before Easter, and first day of Holy Week; so-called to commemorate Christ's entry into Jerusalem, when the crowd strewed palm leaves in his path.

Good Friday (probably a corruption of God's Friday). In the Christian Church, the Friday before Easter, which is kept in memory of the Crucifixion (the death of Jesus).

Easter feast of the Christian Church, commemorating the Resurrection of Christ. It developed from the Jewish Passover, but the English name derives from Eostre, Anglo-Saxon goddess of spring, who was honoured in Apr. Eggs are given at this time as a symbol of new life.

Whitsun celebrates the filling of the followers of Jesus with the Holy Spirit, which Christians believe to be the third aspect of God, after Jesus had returned to heaven. As the disciples went out and told everyone about Jesus, so at Whitsun Christians go on processions around the parish boundaries.

Advent the time leading up to Christmas; a time of preparation for Christians.

Christmas day on which the birth of Christ is celebrated by Christians. Although the actual birth date is unknown, the choice of a date near the winter solstice owed much to missionary desire to facilitate conversion of pagans, for example in Britain 25 Dec had been kept as a festival long before the introduction of Christianity. Many of its customs also have a non-Christian origin.

Hindu festivals

Mahashivaratri Festival of Siva, who is celebrated as lord of the dance, dancing on the demon of ignorance.

Holi a harvest time festival in honour of Krishna, when bonfires are lit; people throw coloured water at each other and play games and tricks as a reminder of Krishna's mischievous behaviour.

Rama Naumi celebration of the Birth of Rama. An eight-day fast during which the Ramayana is recited; the fast is broken on the ninth day with fruit and nuts, and offerings are made to Rama.

Raksha Bandhan a family festival in which sisters present their brothers with a bracelet of thread to protect them from harm, in return for which the brothers promise to look after their sisters.

Janmashtami celebration of the birthday of Krishna. Children act out stories of Krishna, and a statue of the young Krishna is used in the celebrations.

Dusshera a festival (also known as Durga Puja) which lasts ten days; the great goddess Devi is worshipped in her many forms.

Divali a new year festival which honours Lakshmi, goddess of fortune. Lights are lit in every window.

Jewish festivals

Purim celebrates the story of Esther, a Jewish woman who risked her life to save her people from treacherous slaughter. The story is read from a scroll in the synagogue, and the congregation boo and hiss when the villain's name is read out. It is a time for noisy parties and merriment.

Passover (*Pesach*) an ancient Jewish spring festival which commemorates the escape from slavery in Egypt. A special meal, the seder meal, is eaten and the story of how the Jews were saved by God from this bondage is told.

Shavuot or Pentecost commemorates the giving of the ten commandments to Moses.

Rosh Hashana the two-day holiday at the start of the Jewish New Year (first new moon after the autumn equinox).

Yom Kippur (Day of Atonement) day of Jewish religious fast held on the tenth day of Tishri (Sept-Oct), the seventh month of the Jewish year.

Succot the feast of Tabernacles (tents), a reminder of the time the Israelites spent wandering in the wilderness. Temporary homes of branches are built at the synagogue and sometimes at home.

Hanukkah celebrates the recapture and rededication of the Temple of Jerusalem by Judas Maccabeus in 164 BC. The festival lasts eight days; each day, a new candle is lit on a special candlestick or menorah.

Muslim festivals

The Muslim calendar is lunar, and correspondences with the Western calendar cannot be given; festivals fall 11–12 days earlier each year.

Lailat ul-Isra Wal Mi'raj celebrates Muhammad's night journey by horse to Jerusalem and up to heaven.

Lailat ul-Barah the night of forgiveness; a time to prepare for Ramadan.

Ramadan the ninth month of the Muslim year, throughout which a strict fast is observed during the hours of daylight.

Lailat ul-Qadr commemorates the night the Quran was first revealed to Muhammad.

Eid ul-Fitr the end of the fast of Ramadan. Gifts are given to charity, new clothes are worn and sweets are given.

Eid ul-Adha celebrates the faith of the prophet Abraham, who was prepared to sacrifice his son Ismail when Allah asked him to. Lamb is eaten and shared with the poor, as a reminder of the sheep which Allah provided as a sacrifice instead of Ismail.

Day of Hijra commemorates the journey of Muhammad from Mecca to Medina.

Sikh festivals

Hola Mohalla a three-day festival held at the time of the Hindu festival Holi. Sporting competitions and other tests of skill take place.

Baisakhi originally a harvest festival, it now celebrates the founding of the Khalsa, the Sikh brotherhood, and commemorates those Sikhs killed by British troops in Amritsar on Baisakhi, 1919.

Martyrdom of Guru Arjan commemorates the death of the fifth guru, Guru Arjan, who built the Golden Temple at Amritsar and compiled the main part of the Sikh holy book.

Divali celebrates the release from prison of the sixth guru, Guru Hargobind, who also managed to secure the release of 51 Hindu princes who were imprisoned with him.

Guru Nanak's birthday celebrates the birth of the founder of the first guru of Sikhism.

Martyrdom of Guru Tegh Bahadur commemorates the birth of the ninth guru, martyred for the faith.

Birthday of Guru Gobind Singh celebrates the birth of the tenth and last human guru of Sikhism, and the founder of the Khalsa.

month	festival	religion	commemorating
Jan			
6th	Epiphany	Western Christian	coming of the Magi
6th-7th	Christmas	Orthodox Christian	birth of Christ
18th-19th	Epiphany	Orthodox Christian	coming of the Magi
Jan-Feb	New Year	Chinese	Return of Kitchen God to heaven
Feb-Mar	Shrove Tuesday	Christian	day before Lent
	Ash Wednesday	Christian	first day of Lent
	Purim	Jewish	story of Esther
	Mahashivaratri	Hindu	Siva
Mar-Apr	Palm Sunday	Western Christian	first day of Holy Week
	Good Friday	Western Christian	Crucifixion of Christ
	Easter	Western Christian	Resurrection of Christ
	Passover	Jewish	escape from slavery in Egypt
	Holi	Hindu	Krishna
	Holi Mohalla	Sikh	(coincides with Holi)
	Rama Naumi	Hindu	birth of Rama
	Ching Ming	Chinese	remembrance of dead
Apr			
13th	Baisakhi	Sikh	founding of the Khalsa
Apr-May	Easter	Orthodox Christian	Resurrection of Christ
May-Jun	Shavuot	Jewish	giving of Ten Commandments to Moses
	Whitsun	Western Christian	filling of Jesus's followers with Holy Spirit
	Wesak	Buddhist	day of Buddha's birth, enlightenment and death
	Martyrdom of Guru Arjan	Sikh	death of fifth guru of Sikhism
Jun	Dragon Boat Festival	Chinese	Chinese martyr
	Whitsun Orthodox Christian		
Jul	Dhammacakka	Buddhist	preaching of Buddha's first sermon
Aug	Raksha Bandhan	Hindu	family
Aug-Sept	Janmashtami	Hindu	birthday of Krishna
Sept	Moon Festival	Chinese	Chinese hero
Sept-Oct	Rosh Hashana	Jewish	start of Jewish New Year
	Yom Kippur	Jewish	day of fasting
	Succot	Jewish	Israelites' time in the wilderness

month	festival	religion	commemorating
Oct	Dusshera	Hindu	goddess Devi
Oct-Nov	Divali	Hindu	goddess Lakshmi
	Divali	Sikh	release of Guru Hargobind from prison
Nov	Guru Nanak's Birthday	Sikh	founder of Sikhism
	Advent	Western Christian	preparation for Christmas
Nov-Dec	Bodhi Day	Buddhist (Mahayana)	Buddha's enlightenment
Dec	Hanukkah	Jewish	recapture of Temple of Jerusalem
	Winter Festival	Chinese	time of feasting
25th	Christmas	Western Christian	birth of Christ
Dec-Jan	Birthday of Guru Gobind Singh	Sikh	last (tenth) human guru of Sikhism
	Martyrdom of Guru Tegh Bahadur	Sikh	ninth guru of Sikhism

Mythological Figures

Achilles Greek hero of Homer's *Iliad*, the son of the sea nymph Thetis. She rendered him invulnerable, except for the heel by which she held him, by dipping him in the River Styx. He killed Hector in the Trojan War, and was himself killed by Paris with a poisoned arrow in the heel.

Actaeon in Greek mythology, a hunter who surprised Artemis bathing; she changed him to a stag and he was torn to pieces by his own hounds.

Adonis in Greek mythology, a youth beloved by Aphrodite. He was killed while boar-hunting, but was allowed to return from the lower world for six months every year to rejoin her. Worshipped as a god of vegetation, he was known as *Tammuz* in Babylonia, Assyria, and Phoenicia (where it was his sister, Ishtar, who brought him from the lower world). He seems also to have been identified with Osiris.

Aegir in Scandinavian mythology, the god of the sea.

Aeolus in Greek mythology, the god of the winds, who kept them imprisoned in a cave on the Lipari Islands.

Aesculapius in Greek and Roman mythology, the god of medicine; his emblem was a staff with a snake coiled round it, since snakes were believed to renew life by sloughing their skin. Sacred snakes were kept in the sanctuaries of Aesculapius at Epidaurus and elsewhere. The customary offering to Aesculapius was a cock.

Agamemnon in Greek mythology, a Greek hero, son of Atreus, King of Mycenae. He married Clytemnestra, and their children included Electra, Iphigenia, and Orestes. Setting out from Aulis to the Trojan War, he would have sacrificed Iphigenia to Artemis to secure fair winds (she was saved by the goddess and made a priestess). He led the capture of Troy, received Priam's daughter Cassandra as a prize, and was murdered by Clytemnestra and her lover, Aegisthus, on his return home. Orestes and Electra later killed the guilty couple. Aeschylus, Euripides, T S Eliot, O'Neill and Sartre all based plays on the theme.

Agni in Hindu mythology, the god of fire, the protector of humans against the powers of darkness, and the guardian of their homes.

Amaterasu in Japanese mythology, the sun-goddess, grandmother of Jimmu Tenno, first ruler of Japan, from whom the emperors claimed to be descended.

Amazon in Greek mythology, a member of a group of legendary female warriors living near the Black Sea, who cut off their right breasts to use the bow more easily; their queen, Penthesilea, was killed by Achilles at the siege of Troy.

Ammon in Egyptian mythology, the king of the gods, the equivalent of Zeus/Jupiter; the name is also spelt Amen/Amun, as in the name of the pharaoh Tutankh*amen*. In art, he is represented as a ram, as a man with a ram's head. or as a man crowned with feathers. He had famous temples at Siwa oasis, Libya and Thebes, Greece.

Andromeda in Greek mythology, a princess chained to a rock as a sacrifice to a sea monster. She was rescued by Perseus.

Anubis in Egyptian mythology, the jackal-headed god of the dead.

Aphrodite in Greek mythology, the goddess of love (Roman Venus, Phoenician Astarte, Babylonian Ishtar); said to be either a daughter of Zeus or sprung from the foam of the sea. She was the unfaithful wife of Hephaestus, the mother of Eros, and was awarded the prize for beauty by Paris; centres of her worship were Cyprus (Paphos) and Cythera.

Apollo in Greek mythology, the god of sun, music, poetry, and prophecy, agriculture and pastoral life, and leader of the Muses. He was the twin child (with Artemis), of Zeus and Leto. His chief cult centres were his supposed birthplace on the island of Delos, and Delphi. Ancient statues show Apollo as the embodiment of the Greek ideal of male beauty.

Arachne in Greek mythology, a girl weaver who beat Athena in a contest, and was transformed by her into a spider (Greek *arachne*).

Ares in Greek mythology, the god of war (Roman Mars). The son of Zeus and Hera, he was worshipped chiefly in Thrace.

Argus in Greek mythology, a giant with a hundred eyes, which Hera eventually transplanted to the tail of her favourite bird, the peacock.

Ariadne in Greek mythology, the daughter of Minos, king of Crete. When Theseus came from Athens as one of the victims offered to the Minotaur, she fell in love with him and gave him the ball of thread which enabled him to find his way out of the labyrinth.

Artemis in Greek mythology, the goddess (Roman Diana) of chastity, childbirth, and the young; she was envisaged as a virgin huntress; her cult centre was at Ephesus. She was later also identified with Selene, goddess of the moon.

Atalanta in Greek mythology, a huntress who challenged all her suitors to a foot race; if they lost they were killed. Milanion was given three golden apples to drop by Aphrodite; this ensured that when Atalanta stopped to pick them up, she lost the race.

Athena in Greek mythology, the goddess (Roman Minerva) of war, wisdom, and the arts and crafts, who was supposed to have sprung fully-armed from the head of Zeus. Her chief cult centre was Athens, where the Parthenon was dedicated to her. In Rome a statue of her (the 'Palladium'), allegedly brought by Aeneas from Troy, was kept in the temple of Vesta.

Atlas in Greek mythology, a N African king, transformed for his sins to a peak of the Atlas mountains, which were envisaged by the Greeks as supporting the heavens.

Aurora in Roman mythology, the goddess of dawn (Greek Eos).

Avalon in Celtic legend, the island of the blest or paradise, and in the Arthurian legend the land of heroes, to which the dead king was conveyed. It has been associated with Glastonbury.

Avatar in Hindu mythology, the descent of a deity to earth in a visible form. Most famous are the ten Avatars of Vishnu.

Bacchus in Greek and Roman mythology, the god of fertility (identified with Dionysus) and of wine; his rites were orgiastic.

Balder in Norse mythology, the son of Odin and Frigga and husband of Nanna, and the best, wisest, and most loved of all the gods. He was killed, at Loki's instigation, by a twig of mistletoe shot by the blind god Hodur.

Bes in Egyptian mythology, the god of music and dance, usually shown as a grotesque dwarf.

Calliope in Greek mythology, the Muse of epic poetry, and chief of the Muses.

Callisto in Greek mythology, the nymph beloved by Zeus (Jupiter).

Calypso in Greek mythology, a sea nymph who waylaid the homeward-bound Odysseus for seven years.

Cassandra in Greek mythology, the daughter of Priam, whose prophecies (for example of the fall of Troy) were never believed, because she had rejected the love of Apollo. She was murdered with Agamemnon.

Cassiopeia in Greek mythology, the mother of Andromeda.

Castor and Pollux/Polydeuces in Greek mythology, twin sons of Leda (by Zeus), brothers of Helen and Clytemnestra. Protectors of seamen, they were transformed at death to the constellation Gemini.

centaur in Greek mythology, a creature half human and half horse. They were supposed to live in Thessaly, and be wild and lawless: the mentor of Hercules, Chiron, was an exception.

Cerberus in Greek mythology, the three-headed dog guarding the entrance to Hades.

Ceres in Roman mythology, the corn goddess, identified with the Greek goddess Demeter.

Charon in Greek mythology, the boatman who ferried the dead over the river Styx.

Chiron in Greek mythology, the son of Kronos by a sea nymph. A centaur, he was the wise tutor of Jason and Achilles among others.

Circe in Greek mythology, an enchantress. In the *Odyssey* of Homer she turned the followers of Odysseus into pigs when she held their leader captive.

Clio in Greek mythology, one of the muses, the inventor of epic poetry and history.

Clytemnestra in Greek mythology, the wife of Agamemnon.

Cupid in Roman mythology, the god of love, identified with the Greek god Eros.

Cybele in Phrygian mythology, an earth goddess, identified by the Greeks with Rhea and honoured in Rome. The Corybantes (eunuch priests) celebrated her worship with orgiastic dances.

cyclopes in Greek mythology, giants who lived in Sicily, had a single eye, and lived as shepherds; Odysseus encountered them.

Daedalus in Greek mythology, an Athenian craftsman supposed to have constructed for King Minos the labyrinth in which the Minotaur was imprisoned. He fled from Crete with his son Icarus using wings made from feathers fastened with wax; Icarus flew too near the sun, and fell into the Aegean and was drowned.

Daphne in Greek mythology, a nymph, changed into a laurel tree to escape from Apollo's amorous pursuit.

Deirdre in Celtic mythology, beautiful intended bride of Conchobar.

Demeter in Greek mythology, goddess of agriculture (identified with Roman Ceres), daughter of Kronos and Rhea, and by Zeus mother of Persephone. She is identified with the Egyptian goddess Isis and had a temple dedicated to her at Eleusis where mystery religions were celebrated.

Diana in Roman mythology, goddess of hunting and the moon (Greek Artemis), daughter of Jupiter and twin-sister of Apollo.

Dionysus in Greek mythology, god of wine (son of Semele and Zeus), and also of orgiastic excess (an animal, or on occasion a child, being torn to pieces alive and eaten). He was identified with Bacchus, whose rites were less savage. His festivals, the *Dionysia*, were particularly associated with Athens; see theatre. Attendant on him were wild women (*maenads*) and goatlike men (*satyrs*) with pointed ears, horns and a tail.

Dis in Roman mythology, god of the underworld (Greek Pluto); ruler of Hades.

Erebus in Greek mythology, the god of darkness and the intermediate region between upper earth and Hades.

Eros in Greek mythology, boy-god of love (Roman *Cupid*), son of Aphrodite, and armed with bow and arrows; he fell in love with Psyche.

Europa in Greek mythology, princess of Tyre, carried off by Zeus (in the form of a bull); she personifies the continent of Europe.

Fates in Greek mythology, the three female figures, Atropos, Clotho and Lachesis, envisaged as elderly spinners, who decided the length of human life, and analogous to the Roman Parcae and Norse Norns.

Faunus in Roman mythology, god of fertility and prophecy, with goat's ears, horns, tail and hind legs, identified with the Greek Pan; in 1979 archaeological evidence showed that he was also worshipped in Britain.

Flora in Roman mythology, goddess of flowers, youth, and of spring.

Fortuna in Roman mythology, goddess of chance and good fortune. (Greek *Tyche*).

Frigga or *Freya* in Scandinavian mythology, wife of Odin and mother of Thor, goddess of married love and the hearth. Friday is named after her.

Furies in Greek mythology, the Erinyes, winged women with snake-like hair, spirits of vengeance, sometimes referred to appeasingly as the 'Kindly ones' (Eumenides).

Gaia or *Ge*. In Greek mythology, the goddess of the Earth. She sprang from primordial Chaos and herself produced Uranus, by whom she was the mother of the Cyclopes and Titans.

Galatea in Greek mythology, a Nereid. In legend, Pygmalion made a statue (later named Galatea) which was brought to life by Aphrodite.

Ge in Greek mythology, an alternative name for Gaia, goddess of the earth.

Gorgon in Greek mythology, any of three sisters, Stheno, Euryale and Medusa, who had wings, claws, enormous teeth, and snakes for hair. Medusa, the only one who was mortal,

152

was killed by Perseus, but her head was still so frightful, it turned the onlooker to stone. The winged horse Pegasus was supposed to have sprung from her blood.

Graces in Greek mythology, three goddesses (Aglaia, Euphrosyne, and Thalia), daughters of Zeus and Hera, the personification of grace and beauty and the inspirers of the arts and the sciences.

Hades in Greek mythology, the underworld where the spirits of the departed went after death, usually depicted as a cavern or pit underneath the earth. It was presided over by the god Hades or Pluto (Roman Dis). He was the brother of Zeus, and married Persephone, daughter of Demeter and Zeus. She was allowed to return to the upper world for part of the year, bringing spring with her. The entrance to Hades was guarded by the three-headed dog Cerberus. *Tartarus* was the section where the wicked were punished, for example Tantalus.

Harpies in early Greek mythology, wind spirits; in later legend they have horrific women's faces and the bodies of vultures.

Hathor in ancient Egyptian mythology, the sky-goddess, identified with Isis.

Hebe in Greek mythology, the goddess of youth, daughter of Zeus and Hera, and hand-maiden of the gods.

Hecate in Greek mythology, the goddess of witchcraft and magic, sometimes identified with Artemis and the moon.

Hector in Greek mythology, a Trojan prince, son of Priam, who, in the siege of Troy, was the foremost warrior on the Trojan side until he was killed by Achilles.

Hecuba in Greek mythology, the wife of Priam, and mother of Hector and Paris, captured by the Greeks after the fall of Troy.

Hel or *Hela* in Norse mythology, the goddess of the underworld.

Helen in Greek mythology, the daughter of Zeus and Leda, the most beautiful of women. Married to Menelaus, king of Sparta, she eloped with Paris in his absence, which precipitated the Trojan War. Afterwards she returned home with her husband.

Helios in Greek mythology, the sun-god and father of Phaethon, thought to make his daily journey across the sky in a chariot.

Hephaestus in Greek mythology, the god of fire and metalcraft (Roman Vulcan), son of Zeus and Hera; he was lame, and married Aphrodite.

Hera in Greek mythology, a goddess, sister-consort of Zeus, mother of Hephaestus, Hebe, and Ares; protector of women and marriage, and identified with Roman Juno.

Heracles in Greek mythology, a hero (Roman *Hercules*), son of Zeus and Alcmene, famed for strength. While serving Eurystheus, king of Argos, he performed 12 Labours, including the cleansing of the Augean stables.

Hermaphroditus in Greek mythology, the son of Hermes and Aphrodite. He was loved by a nymph who prayed for eternal union with him, so that they became one body with dual sexual characteristics, hence the term hermaphrodite.

Hermes in Greek mythology, a god, son of Zeus and Maia, and messenger of the gods; he has winged sandals and a staff around which serpents coil. Identified with the Roman Mercury and ancient Egyptian Thoth, he protected thieves, travellers, and merchants.

Hero and Leander in Greek mythology, a pair of lovers. Hero was a priestess of Aphrodite at Sestos on the Hellespont, in love with Leander on the opposite shore at Abydos. When he was drowned while swimming across during a storm, she threw herself into the sea out of grief.

Hesperides in Greek mythology, the mythical Greek maidens who guarded a tree bearing golden apples in the Islands of the Blessed.

Hestia in Greek mythology, the goddess (Roman Vesta) of the hearth, daughter of Chronos (Roman Saturn) and Rhea.

Hippolytus in Greek mythology, the son of Theseus, who cursed him for his supposed dishonourable advances to his stepmother Phaedra. Killed by Poseidon as he rode near the sea in his chariot, he was restored to life when his innocence was proved.

Horus in ancient Egyptian mythology, the

hawkheaded sun god, son of Isis and Osiris, of whom the pharaohs were thought the incarnation.

Hydra in Greek mythology, a monster with nine heads. Whenever a head was cut off, two new ones grew in its place. It was finally killed by Heracles.

Hygieia in Greek mythology, the goddess of health (Roman Salus), daughter of Aesculapius.

Hymen in Greek mythology, the god of marriage, shown as a youth with a bridal torch.

Io in Greek mythology, a princess loved by Zeus, who transformed her to a heifer to hide her from the jealousy of Hera.

Iphigenia in Greek mythology, the daughter of Agamemnon.

Irene in Greek mythology, goddess of peace (Roman Pax).

Janus in Roman mythology, god of doorways and passageways, the patron of the beginning of the day, month, and year, after whom January is named; he is represented as two-faced, looking in opposite directions.

Jason in Greek mythology, leader of the *Argonauts* who sailed in the Argo to Colchis in search of the Golden Fleece.

Jinn in Muslim mythology, a spirit able to assume human or animal shape.

Juno in Roman mythology, queen of the gods. Greek equivalent: Hera.

Jupiter in Roman mythology, king of the gods (Greek Zeus), son of Saturn. A sky god, he was associated with lightning and thunder bolts, and victory in war; he married his sister Juno.

Kali in Hindu mythology, the wife of Siva. She is the goddess of destruction and death.

Kronos or *Cronus* in Greek mythology, one of the Titans, ruler of the world, and father of Zeus, who overthrew him.

Lares and Penates in Roman mythology, spirits of the farm and of the store cupboard, often identified with the family ancestors, whose shrine was the centre of family worship in Roman homes.

Leda in Greek mythology, wife of Tyndareus, by whom she was the mother of Clytemnestra.

By Zeus, who came to her as a swan, she was the mother of Helen of Troy, Castor and Pollux.

Lethe in Greek mythology, a river of the underworld. To drink its waters was to forget the past.

Loki in Norse mythology, the god of evil, the slayer of Baldur, whose children were the Midgard serpent Jörmungander which girdles the Earth, the wolf Fenris, and Hela, goddess of the underworld.

Manu in Hindu mythology, the founder of the human race, who was saved by Brahma from a deluge.

Marduk in Babylonian mythology, the sun-god, creator of earth and man.

Mars in Roman mythology, the god of war, after whom the month of March is named.

Medea in Greek mythology, the sorceress daughter of the king of Colchis. When Jason reached the court, she fell in love with him, helped him acquire the Golden Fleece, and fled with him. When Jason married Creusa, Medea killed his bride with the gift of a poisoned garment, and also killed her own two children by Jason.

Medusa in Greek mythology, a mortal woman who was transformed into a Gorgon.

Melpomene in Greek mythology, the Muse of tragedy.

Mercury in Roman mythology, the messenger of the gods, identified with Greek Hermes.

Minerva in Roman mythology, the goddess of wisdom. Greek counterpart: Athena.

Minos in Greek mythology, a King of Crete (son of Zeus and Europa).

Minotaur in Greek mythology, a monster, half man-half bull, offspring of Pasiphaë, wife of King Minos of Crete and a bull. It lived in the labyrinth at Knossos and its victims were seven girls and seven youths, sent in annual tribute by Athens, until Theseus slew it, with the aid of Ariadne, the daughter of Minos.

Mithras in Persian mythology, the god of light.

Morpheus in Greek mythology, the god of dreams, son of Somnus, god of sleep.

Muses in Greek mythology, the nine daughters of Zeus and Mnemosyne (goddess of memory) and inspirers of creative arts: *Calliope* epic poetry; *Clio* history; *Erato* love poetry; *Euterpe* lyric poetry; *Melpomene* tragedy; *Polyhymnia* hymns; *Terpsichore* dance; *Thalia* comedy; *Urania* astronomy.

Naiad in classical mythology, a water-nymph.

Narcissus in Greek mythology, a beautiful youth who rejected the love of the nymph Echo. Condemned to fall in love with his own reflection, he pined away.

Nemesis in Greek mythology, the goddess of retribution, especially punishing hubris (Greek *hybris*), arrogant self-confidence.

Neptune in Roman mythology god of the sea, the equivalent of the Greek Poseidon.

Nereid in Greek mythology, a minor sea goddess who sometimes mated with mortals.

Nike in Greek mythology, goddess of victory, represented as 'winged', as in the statue from Samothrace in the Louvre. One of the most beautiful architectural monuments of Athens was the temple of Nike Apteros.

Niobe in Greek mythology, the daughter of Tantalus and wife of Amphion, the king of Thebes. Contemptuous of the mere two children of the goddess Leto, Apollo and Artemis, she died of grief, and was changed to stone by Zeus, when her own twelve offspring were killed by them in revenge.

nymph in Greek mythology, a guardian spirit of nature; *hamadryads* or *dryads* guarded trees; *naiads*, springs and pools; *oreads*, hills and rocks; *nereids*, the sea.

Oceanus in Greek mythology, the god (one of the Titans) of a river supposed to encircle the earth, and progenitor of other river gods, and the nymphs of the seas and rivers.

Odin chief god of Scandinavian mythology, the Woden or Wotan of the Germanic peoples. A sky god, he is resident in Asgard, at the top of the world-tree, and receives the souls of heroic slain warriors from the Valkyries, the 'divine maidens', feasting with them in his great hall, Valhalla. At Ragnarök (doomsday) the warriors were envisaged as fighting a final battle in support of Odin against the evil giants, a new order arising from the ensuing general destruction. The wife of Odin is Frigga or Freya, and

Thor is their son. Wednesday is named after him.

Orestes in Greek mythology, one of the children of Agamemnon and Clytemnestra.

Orion in Greek mythology, a giant of Boeotia, famed as a hunter.

Pan in Greek mythology, god (Roman Sylvanus) of flocks and herds, shown as a man with the horns, ears and hooves of a goat, and playing a shepherd's pipe.

Pandora in Greek mythology, the first woman. Zeus sent her to earth with a box of evils (to counteract the blessings brought to mortals by Prometheus's gift of fire); she opened it, and they all flew out. Only hope was left inside as a consolation.

peri in Persian myth, beautiful, harmless beings, ranking between angels and evil spirits, and ruled by Eblis, greatest of the latter.

Perseus in Greek mythology, son of Zeus and Danae. He slew Medusa, the Gorgon; rescued Andromeda; and became king of Tiryns.

Pleiades in Greek mythology, seven daughters of Atlas, who asked to be changed to a cluster of stars to escape the pursuit of Orion.

Polyhymnia in Greek mythology, the Muse of singing, mime and sacred dance.

Procrustes (Greek 'the stretcher') in Greek mythology, a robber who tied his victims to a bed; if they were too tall for it, he cut off the ends of their legs, and if they were too short stretched them.

Prometheus in Greek mythology, a Titan who stole fire from heaven for the human race. In revenge, Zeus had him chained to a rock with an eagle preying on his liver, until he was rescued by Hercules.

Romulus in Roman mythology, the legendary founder and first king of Rome, the son of Mars by Rhea Silvia. He and his twin brother Remus were exposed by their great-uncle Amulius, but were suckled by a she-wolf and rescued by a shepherd. On reaching manhood they killed Amulius and founded Rome. Having murdered Remus, Romulus reigned alone until he disappeared in a storm, and thereafter was worshipped as a god under the name of Quirinus.

Saturn in Roman mythology, an ancient god (possibly the god of agriculture, also identified with the Greek god Kronos). He was dethroned by his sons Jupiter, Neptune, and Pluto. At his festival in Dec gifts were exchanged, and slaves were briefly treated as their masters' equals.

satyr in Greek mythology, a cross between a man and a goat.

Selene in Greek mythology, the goddess of the moon; in later times identified with Artemis.

Semele in Greek mythology, mother of Dionysus by Zeus. She was consumed by lightning when jealous Hera suggested she ask her lover to appear in his full glory.

Sibyl in Roman mythology, a priestess of Apollo, especially the Cumaean Sibyl living in a cave near Naples, Italy. She offered to sell Tarquinius nine collections of prophecies, the *Sibylline Books*, but the price was too high. When she had destroyed all but three, he bought those for the identical price, and these were kept for consultation in emergency at Rome.

Siren in Greek mythology, a sea nymph who lured sailors on to rocks by her singing. Odysseus, in order to hear the Sirens safely, tied himself to the mast and stuffed his crews' ears with wax; the Argonauts escaped them because the singing of Orpheus surpassed that of the sirens.

Sisyphus in Greek mythology, king of Corinth who, after his evil life, was condemned to roll a huge stone uphill, which always fell back before reaching the top.

Styx in Greek mythology, the river surrounding the underworld.

Surya in Hindu mythology, the personification of the Sun.

Tantalus in Greek mythology, a king whose crimes were punished in Tartarus by food and drink he could not reach.

Tartarus in Greek mythology, the part of Hades where the wicked were punished.

Thalia in Greek mythology, the Muse of comedy and pastoral poetry.

Thor in Norse mythology, son of Odin and Frigga, god of thunder (his hammer), and represented as a man of enormous strength defending humans against demons. Thursday is named after him.

Thoth in Egyptian mythology, god of wisdom and learning, scribe of the gods.

Titan in Greek mythology, any of the giant children of Uranus and Gaia, who included Kronos, Rhea, Themis (mother of Prometheus and personification of law and order) and Oceanus. Kronos and Rhea were in turn the parents of Zeus, who ousted Kronos as the ruler of the world.

Triton in Greek mythology, a merman sea-god, the son of Poseidon and the sea-goddess Amphitrite. He is shown blowing on a conch.

Tyr in Norse mythology, the god of battles, whom the Anglo-Saxons called Týw, hence 'Tuesday'.

Uranus in Greek mythology, the sky-god, responsible both for the sun and rain. He was the son and husband of Gaia, by whom he fathered the Titans.

Valhalla in Norse mythology, the hall in Odin's palace where he feasts with the souls of the dead heroes of mortal battles.

Venus in Roman mythology, the goddess of love (Greek Aphrodite).

Vesta in Roman mythology, the goddess of the hearth (Greek *Hestia*). The sacred flame in her shrine in the Forum was kept constantly lit by the six *Vestal Virgins*.

Vulcan in Roman mythology, the god of fire and destruction, later identified with the Greek god Hephaestus.

Zeus in Greek mythology, chief of the gods (Roman Jupiter). He was the son of Kronos, whom he overthrew: his brothers and sisters included Demeter, Hades, Hera, and Poseidon. His offspring, either gods and goddesses, or godlike humans, included Apollo, Athena, Artemis, Castor and Polydeuces/Pollux, Dionysus, Hebe, Heracles, Hermes, Minos, Perseus, Persephone. As the supreme god he dispersed good and evil and was the father and ruler of all mankind. His emblems are the thunderbolt and aegis (shield), representing the thunder cloud.

Resources

Resources are things that can be used to provide the means to satisfy wants – in other words, they are not resources until people are able to use them. Because human wants are very diverse and extend from basic physical requirements such as food and shelter, through to ill-defined aesthetic needs, resources encompass a vast range of items. It is the intellectual resources of a society – its ideas and technologies – that determine which aspects of the environment meet that society's needs, and therefore become resources. In the 19th century uranium was simply a curiosity used only in the manufacture of coloured glass. Today, with the advent of nuclear technology, it is a vital energy resource. Though minerals such as coal and iron ores tend to dominate the perception of resources, the concept also embraces less tangible things such as beautiful landscapes and pleasant climates.

This section contains an overview of *Types of Resources,* and information on particular resources – *Minerals, Crops,* and *Commodities.*

Types of Resources

resources are often categorized into *human resources,* such as labour supplies and skills, and *natural resources*, such as climate, fossil fuels, and water. Natural resources are divided into those which are non-renewable and others which can be replenished (renewable). *Non-renewable resources* are things like coal, copper ores, and diamonds, which exist in strictly limited quantities. Once consumed they will not be replenished within the time-span of human history. In contrast, water supplies, timber, food crops, and solar power and similar resources can, if managed properly, provide a steady yield virtually for ever. These are termed replenishable or *renewable resources,* which may, in turn, be continuous (where supply is largely independent of people's actions) or flow (where supply is dependent on people's actions). However, inappropriate use of renewable resources can lead to their destruction, as for example when a fishery or forest is over-utilized and totally consumed.

demands for resources made by present-day societies are causing concern among many people, who consider that the present and future demands of industrial societies cannot be sustained for more than a century or two, and that once a resource base fails to meet a society's needs that society will collapse. However this view is not universally held, and other authorities contend that such analyses misunderstand the nature of resources.

resources for future generations will, they believe, be determined by the level of knowledge of future societies, and cannot be properly assessed by our current perceptions. As knowledge increases, new technologies will emerge, enabling materials which are currently of little importance to become valuable resources. The resource base can therefore expand as societies become better able to harness their environment to meet their needs.

Minerals

minerals are substances with a regular atomic structure and a composition which lies within defined limits. The term is also used loosely to mean any material which is extracted from the earth. Minerals are the materials which form rocks. They provide the oil, coal, metals, fertilizers, and building materials on which industrial societies depend. Many industrial nations are dependent on imports of

Resources
NATURAL RESOURCES

Renewable		Non-Renewable
Continuous Resources Supply is largely independent of people's actions:	*Flow Resources* Supply is very dependent upon people's actions:	Supply is permanently depleted if they are worked. They are mostly minerals:
solar power climates tidal power	timber wildlife attractive landscape water resources	coal copper ores oil phosphates

minerals from primary producer countries. The EEC imports over 95% of its chrome, copper and manganese. Many Third World countries are dependent on mineral exports to finance their economies. Conflict between the interests of exporting nations was highlighted in the 1970s by the restriction of oil exports by producers. Attention has been focussed on the adequacy of mineral resources to meet future needs, but the issue is complex; availability depends on the interaction of technology, price, and political factors as well as on the disposition of minerals within the earth's crust. *mineral ores* are concentrations of minerals which can be profitably worked. Concentration arises from specific geological processes, and consequently particular minerals are commonly associated with certain types of geological formation.

mineral reserves and mineral resources in casual conversation the terms reserves and resources are often interchanged. However, when discussing mineral resources the two refer to quite different things. *Mineral reserves* are the deposits which are known to exist, which are accessible and are of such quality

that under prevailing economic and technical conditions it is likely that they can be profitably extracted. *Mineral resources* include reserves plus deposits that are known but cannot currently be economically worked and deposits that have yet to be found. An increase in the price of a mineral or a change in technology or other conditions which lower the cost of extraction will make some marginally economic resources into reserves.

Mineral reserves may be increased by either the discovery of new deposits which can be economically worked, or by a favourable change in the economics associated with working deposits which were previously sub-economic. Such favourable changes may result from new lower cost extraction technologies or from a rise in the price of the mineral.

Reserves can also be reduced by events which make it unprofitable to work them (an example is the way tin deposits in Cornwall became uneconomic to mine after a collapse in tin prices in 1986). Because of this, mineral reserves constantly fluctuate in quantity and published figures should be interpreted with great caution.

MAJOR ECONOMIC MINERALS

Minerals and their sources

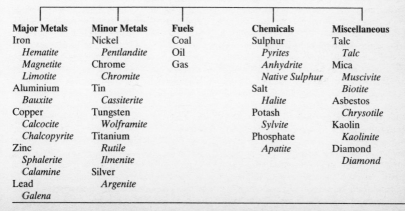

Major Metals	Minor Metals	Fuels	Chemicals	Miscellaneous
Iron	Nickel	Coal	Sulphur	Talc
Hematite	*Pentlandite*	Oil	*Pyrites*	*Talc*
Magnetite	Chrome	Gas	*Anhydrite*	Mica
Limotite	*Chromite*		*Native Sulphur*	*Muscivite*
Aluminium	Tin		Salt	*Biotite*
Bauxite	*Cassiterite*		*Halite*	Asbestos
Copper	Tungsten		Potash	*Chrysotile*
Calcocite	*Wolframite*		*Sylvite*	Kaolin
Chalcopyrite	Titanium		Phosphate	*Kaolinite*
Zinc	*Rutile*		*Apatite*	Diamond
Sphalerite	*Ilmenite*			*Diamond*
Calamine	Silver			
Lead	*Argenite*			
Galena				

Crops

crops are plants grown for human use. Over 80 crops are grown worldwide, providing people with the majority of their food, and supplying fibres, rubber, pharmaceuticals, dyes and other materials. Four main groups of crops are readily identifiable: food crops, forage crops, fibre crops, and miscellaneous crops.

food crops are grown specifically to feed people, and provide the bulk of people's food worldwide. The major types are cereals, roots, pulses, vegetables, fruits, oil crops, tree nuts, sugar, beverages, and spices. Cereals make the most important contribution to human nutrition. Though most food crops are carefully cultivated, crop production techniques and yields vary enormously from one part of the world to another.

cereal crops are grasses which are grown for their edible starch seeds. All major civilizations have depended upon them for food, and in 1985 world production exceeded 1.8 billion tonnes. Cereals are an attractive foodstuff as they are easy to store and contain about 75% carbohydrate and 10% protein. In recent years research has led to dramatic increases in cereal yields; in the decade 1975–85 cereal yields in Britain almost doubled and now commonly exceed six tonnes per hectare. If all the world's cereal crop was consumed directly by humans everybody could obtain an adequate dietary intake of protein and carbohydrate. However a large proportion of cereal production, particularly in affluent nations, is used as animal feeds to boost the production of meat, milk, butter, and eggs.

root crops in agriculture the term refers to turnips, swedes, and beets which are actually enlarged hypocotyls and contain little root, whilst in trade statistics it refers essentially to the tubers of potatoes, cassava, and yams.

These three crops are second in importance to cereals as human food and in the mid-1980s world production was just under 600 million tonnes. Food production per hectare from roots is higher than for cereals. Roots have a high carbohydrate content, but their protein content rarely exceeds 2%. Consequently communities relying too heavily upon roots may suffer from protein deficiency. *Potatoes* are the major temperate food crop. The major tropical root crops are cassava – a shrub which produces starchy tubers, yams, and sweet potatoes. Root crops are also widely used as animal feeds and may be processed to produce starch, glues, and alcohol.

pulses are crops such as peas and beans. They are grown primarily for their seeds which provide a concentrated source of vegetable protein and make a vital contribution to human diets, especially in poor countries where meat is scarce. In the mid-1980s world production was about 50 million tonnes a year. *Soyabeans* are the major temperate protein crop. Most are used for oil production or for animal feeds, though some are processed into 'meat substitutes'. Peanuts dominate pulse production in the tropical world, and are mostly consumed directly as human food. Pulses play a useful role in crop rotations as they help to raise soil nitrogen levels as well as acting as break crops.

vegetable crops are a diverse group of plants eaten for their leaves, stems, flower clusters, and buds. Some fruits such as pumpkins and tomatoes are also considered as vegetables because of the manner in which they are consumed. Most vegetables are annuals, that is plants that live for one year or less. Though vegetables are not major sources of protein or energy, they add variety to human diets and are an important source of vitamins A and C, as well as providing dietary fibre and minerals. Vegetables are succulent, easily damaged, and rapidly decompose. Consequently until recent years there was little international trade in them, and even today the bulk of production will be consumed close to where it is grown. As a high proportion never enters the commercial market, statistics probably underestimate the

CROPS USAGE

Group	Types	Major Plants
Food Crops	Cereals	Wheat, Rice, Maize, Sorghum
	Roots	Potatoes, Cassava, Yams, Sweet Potatoes
	Pulses	Soyabeans, Groundnuts, Lentils, Peas
	Vegetables	Cabbage, Carrots, Okra, Lettuce
	Fruits	Apples, Citrus, Plums, Mangoes
	Oil Crops	Olives, Sunflower, Rapeseed, Oil Palm
	Tree Nuts	Brazil nuts, Hazlenuts, Cashew nuts, Almonds
	Sugar	Sugar Cane, Sugar Beet, Sorghum
	Beverages and Spices	Tea, Coffee, Cocoa, Ginger, Mace
Forage Crops	Pure Stands	Kale, Rape, Mustard
	Mixed Crops	Grasses, Vetches, Lucerne, Clover
Fibre Crops	Coarse Fibres	Jute, Sisal, Hemp, Coir
	Fine Fibres	Cotton, Flax, Kapok, Ramie
Miscellaneous Crops	Rubber	Rubber Trees
	Tobacco	Tobacco
	Pharmaceuticals	Foxglove, Evening Primrose, Poppy
	Ornamentals and Fragrants	Orchids, Carnations, Roses, Lavender

amount grown. In the mid-1980s world production certainly exceeded 380 million tonnes.

fruits the seeds of plants together with the tissues which enclose them. These fleshy tissues have evolved to aid seed dispersal and are often colourful, sweet, juicy, and very palatable. The word fruit comes from the Latin *frui* meaning 'to enjoy'. Most fruits are borne by perennial plants. Like vegetables, they provide vitamins and minerals but little protein, and are often regarded as a semi-luxury. Recorded world production in the mid-1980s was approximately 300 million tonnes per year. Broadly fruits are divided into three types: *temperate fruits*, which require a cold season for satisfactory growth; *sub-tropical fruits*, which require warm conditions but can survive light frosts; and *tropical fruits*, which succumb if temperatures drop close to freezing point. In order of abundance the principal temperate fruits are apples, pears, plums, peaches and

apricots, cherries, and soft fruits like raspberries and strawberries. Sub-tropical fruits include oranges and other citrus fruits, dates, pomegranates, and avocados, while bananas, mangoes, pineapples, papaya, and litchis are typical tropical fruits. In recent decades technical advances have improved the storage and transportability of fruits and increasingly new trade routes are being established. Consequently 'exotic' tropical fruits are now available to consumers in temperate areas, and fresh temperate fruits are also available all year round.

oil crops vegetable oils are pressed from the seeds of many crops. All arable agricultural regions have their characteristic oil crops. Cool temperate areas grow rapeseed and linseed; warm temperate regions produce sunflowers, olives and soyabeans; tropical areas produce groundnuts, oil palm and coconuts. Some of the major vegetable oils such as soyabean oil,

MINERAL RESERVES AND RESOURCES

Reserves	Identified Deposits		Undiscovered Deposits
	Measured	Indicated	
Economics	Reserves		
Marginally Economic			
Submarginally Economic			Resources

groundnut oil, and cottonseed oil are derived from crops grown primarily for other purposes. Most vegetable oils are used as both edible oils and ingredients in industrial products such as soaps and varnishes, printing inks, and paints.

tree nuts nut is the common name for seeds which are enclosed in 'woody' shells. The kernels of most nuts provide a concentrated food with about 50% fat and a protein content of 10% to 20%, though a few, such as chestnuts, are high in carbohydrates and have only a moderate (5%) protein content. Most nuts are produced by perennial trees and bushes. Whilst the majority are obtained from plantations, considerable quantities of Brazil and pecan nuts are still collected from the wild. Records of production are incomplete but current estimates suggest that world production in the mid-1980s was only about four million tonnes per year. Besides being a useful food for people, nuts also provide edible and industrial oils.

sugar in the mid-1980s world production of refined sugar averaged approximately 100 million tonnes per year. The major sources are tropical cane sugar which accounts for about two-thirds of production, and temperate sugar beet. Sugar cane, which is a tropical grass, commonly yields over 20 tonnes of sugar per hectare per year, whereas sugar beet rarely exceeds seven tonnes per hectare per year. Beet sugar is more expensive to produce and its cultivation is often subsidised by governments which wish to support the agricultural sector and avoid over-dependence on the volatile world sugar market. Minor quantities of sugar are produced from maple trees (maple syrup) and from sorghum and date palms.

beverages and spices tea, coffee, cocoa, cola nuts, and hops are plant products which are

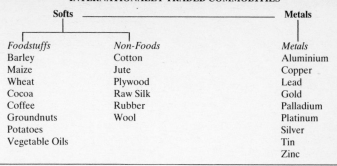

INTERNATIONALLY TRADED COMMODITIES

Softs		Metals

Foodstuffs	*Non-Foods*	*Metals*
Barley	Cotton	Aluminium
Maize	Jute	Copper
Wheat	Plywood	Lead
Cocoa	Raw Silk	Gold
Coffee	Rubber	Palladium
Groundnuts	Wool	Platinum
Potatoes		Silver
Vegetable Oils		Tin
		Zinc

widely used to impart pleasant flavours and stimulants to people's fluid intake. The juice of grapes and other fruits is fermented to produce wines, whilst fermented cereals form the basis of most beers. The alcoholic content of beers and wines can provide a useful addition to some people's energy intake. Spices are used to impart flavours and aromas to food. They have little food value, but increase the appetite and may facilitate digestion.

forage crops are crops like grass, clover and kale which are grown to feed livestock. Forage crops cover a greater area of the world than food crops, and grass, which dominates this group, is the world's most abundant crop, though much of it is still in an unimproved state. In areas where intense agriculture occurs forage crops often form break crops in a predominantly arable rotation.

fibre crops produce vegetable fibres. Temperate areas produce flax and hemp, but the most important fibre crops are cotton, jute, and sisal which are grown mostly in the tropical world. Cotton dominates fibre crop production.

miscellaneous crops are a diverse group of crops including tobacco, rubber, ornamental flowers, and perfume, pharmaceutical and dye-producing plants.

Commodities

commodities are essentially things produced for sale. They may be *consumer goods* like radios, or *producer goods* such as copper bars. *Commodity markets* deal in raw or semi-raw materials which are amenable to grading and which can be stored for considerable periods without deterioration. They developed to their present form in the 19th century, when industrial growth facilitated trading in large, standardized quantities of raw materials. Most markets encompass trading in 'commodity futures', that is trading for delivery several months ahead. Major commodity markets exist in Chicago, Tokyo, London, and elsewhere. Though specialized markets exist, such as silkworm cocoons in Tokyo, most trade relates to cereals and metals. 'Softs' is a term used for most materials other than metals.

Sociology

Sociology is the study of society, in particular of social order and social change, social conflict, and social problems. It studies social institutions, such as the family, law, and the church, as well as social concepts such as norm, role, and culture. What distinguishes sociology from other disciplines studying human behaviour is its emphasis on social factors, its attempt to study people in their social environment according to certain underlying moral, philosophical, and political codes of behaviour. Auguste Comte, who coined the term in 1830, is generally seen as the founder of modern sociology as a distinct and systematic discipline. He attempted to use the same philosophy (positivism) and research methods as the natural sciences to try to discover the underlying laws of social evolution and to make social knowledge more reliable, precise and systematic, capable of predicting social change and solving social problems.

Sociology today reflects a variety of perspectives and traditions. Its focus tends to be on contemporary industrial society, sometimes comparing it with pre-industrial society, and occasionally drawing on such related disciplines as history, geography, politics, economics, psychology, and anthropology. It concerns range from theories of social order and change to detailed analyses of small groups, individuals, and the routines of daily life. The relation between theory and method is one part of the current debate about whether sociology is or should be a science, and whether it can or should be free of ideology.

This section contains an overview of key *Perspectives* in sociology, definitions of *Terms and Concepts*, and biographical notes on *Key Thinkers* whose work has influenced the development of modern sociology.

Perspectives

ethnomethodology the study of social order and routines used by people in their daily lives, to explain how everyday reality is created and perceived. Ethnomethodologists tend to use small-scale studies and experiments to examine the details of social life and structure (such as conversations) that people normally take for granted, rather than construct large-scale theories about society.

functionalism the view of society as a system comprising a number of interrelated parts, all functioning on the basis of a common value system or consensus about basic values and common goals. Every social custom and institution is seen as having a function in ensuring that society works efficiently; deviance and crime are seen as a form of social sickness. Functionalists often describe society as an organism with a life of its own, above and beyond the sum of its members. Comte, Durkheim, and Parsons have taken functionalist approaches.

Marxism the social, economic, and political theory, also known as dialectical or historical materialism, developed by Marx and Engels, which sees social and political institutions progressively changing their nature as economic developments transform material conditions. The evolution from feudalism, through capitalism, to socialism as modes of production is seen as inevitable, and resistance of an existing system to change requires its overthrow in the class struggle. Marxism has proved one of the most powerful and controversial theories in modern history, and a key focussing point in the social sciences, inspiring both dedicated exponents and bitter opponents.

phenomenology the philosophical perspective, founded by Husserl, which in the social sciences concentrates on phenomena as objects of perception (rather than as facts or occurrences which exist independently) in attempting to examine the ways people think about and interpret the world around them. In contrast to positivism or 'scientific' philosophy, phenomenology sees reality as essentially relative and subjective, and uses such tools as ethnomethodology and symbolic interactionism to focus on the structure of everyday life.

positivism the philosophical perspective, founded by Comte, which argues that only that which can be seen really exists and that the only valid form of knowledge is that gathered by empirical scientific method. Also called *scientific philosophy*, it assumes that there is a fixed and objective reality whose underlying laws of cause and effect can be discovered and then used to predict and control natural phenomena. Positivism sees phenomena as facts or occurrences which exist independently, rather than as objects of perception.

symbolic interactionism sociological method, founded by G H Mead, that studies the behaviour of individuals and small groups through observation and description, viewing people's appearance, gestures, and language as symbols they use to interact with others in social situations. In contrast to theories such as Marxism or functionalism, which attempt to analyse society as a whole through economic or political systems, it takes a perspective of society from within, as created by people themselves.

Terms and Concepts

alienation a sense of frustration, isolation, and powerlessness; a feeling of loss of control over one's life; a sense of estrangement either from society or from oneself. As a sociological concept it was developed by Hegel and Marx, who used it as a description and criticism of the condition of workers in capitalist society. The term has also been used by non-Marxist writers to explain, for example, industrial unrest in modern factories.

anomie a state created by the breakdown of commonly agreed standards of behaviour and morality; the term is often used to refer to situations where the social order appears to have collapsed. It was developed as a sociological concept by Durkheim to describe societies in transition, particularly during industrialization.

bureaucracy an organization whose structure and operations are governed to a high degree by written rules and a hierarchy of offices: in its broadest sense, all forms of administration; in its narrowest, rule by officials. Contemporary writers have highlighted the problems of bureaucracy, such as its inflexibility and rigid adherence to rules, and the term today is often used critically rather than in its original neutral sense.

class the main form of social stratification in industrial societies, based primarily on economic and occupational factors, but also referring to people's style of living or sense of group identity. Within the social sciences, class has been used both as a descriptive category and as the basis of theories about industrial society. The most widely used descriptive classification in the UK, that of the Registrar-General, divides the population into five main classes (see next page). The main division is that between the manual and non-manual occupations being made. Such classifications have been widely criticized, however, on several grounds: that they reflect a middle-class bias that brain is superior to brawn; that they classify women according to their husband's occupation rather than their own; that they ignore the upper class, the owners of land and industry. Theories of class may see such social divisions either as a source of social stability (Durkheim) or social conflict (Marx).

community the sense of identity, purpose, and companionship that comes from belonging to a particular place, organization, or social group. The concept dominated sociological thinking in the first half of the 20th century, and inspired the academic discipline of *community studies*.

culture the way of life of a particular society or group of people, including patterns of thought, beliefs, behaviour, customs, traditions and rituals, dress, language, as well as art, music, and literature. Sociologists and anthropologists see culture as a key concept in describing and analysing human societies.

demography the study of the size, structure, and development of human populations to establish reliable statistics on such factors as birth and death rates, marriages and divorces, life expectancy, and migration. Demography is important in the social sciences as the basis for government planning in such areas as education, housing, welfare, transport, and taxation.

development in the social sciences, the term generally refers to economic development, the acquisition by a society of industrial techniques and technology; hence the common classification of the 'developed' nations of the First World and the poorer 'developing' or 'underdeveloped' nations of the Third World. The assumption that development in the sense of industrialization is inherently good has been increasingly questioned since the 1960s. Many universities today have academic departments of *development studies* which address the theoretical questions involved in proposing practical solutions to the problems of development in the Third World.

deviance abnormal behaviour; that is, behaviour that deviates from the norms or laws of a particular society or group, and so invokes social sanctions, controls, or stigma. The term may refer to minor abnormalities (such as nail-biting) as well as to criminal acts. Deviance is a relative concept: what is considered deviant in some societies is normal in others; and in a particular society the same act (killing someone, for example) may be either normal or deviant depending on the circumstances (in wartime or for money, for example). Some sociologists argue that the reaction of others, rather than the act itself, is what determines

167

SOCIAL CLASSES IN BRITAIN

	Middle Class
I	professional occupations: accountant, lawyer
II	intermediate occupations: managers, senior administrators
IIIN	skilled occupations (non-manual): policeman, nurse
	Working Class
IIIM	skilled occupations (manual): plumber, electrician
IV	semi-skilled occupations: machinist, mechanic
V	unskilled occupations: dustman, cleaner
	Other
	residual groups: students, armed forces

Social Classes in Britain as classified by the Registrar-General

whether an act is deviant.

elite a small group in a society with power, privileges, and status above others. An elite may be cultural, educational, religious, political, or social. Sociological interest has centred on how such minorities get, use, and hold on to power, and on what distinguishes elites from ordinary members of society.

ethnicity from Greek *ethnos*, 'a people', a term that overlaps with such social concepts as race, nation, class, and religion. Social scientists use the term ethnic group to refer to groups or societies who feel a common sense of identity, often based on a similar culture, language, religion, and customs. It may or may not include common territory, skin colour, or common descent. Whereas the concept of race was used from the outside to label people according to perceived biological features, ethnicity refers to people's own sense of cultural identity. The US, for example, is often described as a *multi-ethnic society* because many members would describe themselves as members of an ethnic group (Jewish, black, or Irish, for example) as well as their national one (American).

feudalism the main form of social stratification in medieval Europe. A system based primarily on land, it involved a hierarchy of authority, rights, and power that extended from the king downwards. An intricate network of duties and obligations linked royalty, nobility, lesser gentry, free tenants, villeins, and serfs. Feudalism was reinforced by a complex legal system and supported by the Christian church. With the growth of commerce, trade and industry in the 13th century, feudalism gradually gave way to class as the dominant form of social ranking.

Gemeinschaft and **Gesellschaft** German terms (roughly, 'community' and 'association') used by Ferdinand Tönnies (1855–1936) to contrast social relationships in traditional rural societies with those in modern industrial societies. He saw Gemeinschaft as intimate and positive, and Gesellschaft as impersonal and negative. In small-scale societies, where everyone knows everyone else, the social order is stable and the culture homogeneous. In large urban areas life is faster and more competitive, and relationships are more superficial, transitory, and anonymous.

ideology a set of ideas, beliefs, and opinions about the nature of people and society providing a framework for a theory about how society is or should be organized. The term is used by philosophers and social scientists in an analytical and neutral way, but it has more popularly been used to describe beliefs based on fanatical faith rather than rational argument.

kinship human relationship based on blood or marriage, and sanctified by law and custom. Kinship forms the basis for most human societies and for such social groupings as the family, clan, or tribe. Kinship is universal, although its social significance varies from society to society. Most human societies have evolved strict social rules, customs, and taboos regarding kinship, particularly to do with sexual behaviour (such as the prohibition of incest).

labelling defining or describing a person in terms of his or her behaviour; for example, describing someone who has broken a law as a criminal. In sociology, labelling theory deals with human interaction, behaviour, and control, particularly in the field of deviance. Social labelling has been seen as a form of social control in that labels affect both a person's self-image and other people's reactions. Crucial factors include who labels a person, and whether the label sticks.

marriage the legally or culturally sanctioned union of one man and one woman (monogamy); one man and two or more women (polygyny); one woman and two or more men (polyandry). The basis of marriage varies considerably in different societies (romantic love in the West; arranged marriages in some other societies), but most marriage ceremonies, contracts, or customs involve a set of rights and duties such as care and protection, and there is generally an expectation that children will be born of the union to continue the family line.

norms informal guidelines about what is, or is not, considered normal social behaviour (as opposed to rules and laws, which are formal guidelines). Such shared values and expectations vary from one society to another and from one situation to another, and range from crucial taboos such as incest or cannibalism to trivial customs and traditions, such as the correct way to hold a fork. Norms are an integral part of any society's culture and of any group or organization's subculture, and a key part of social control and social order.

peer group in the social sciences, a term used to refer to groups or collections of people who have a common identity based on such characteristics as similar social status, interests, age, or ethnic group. The concept has

proved useful in analysing the power and influence of workmates, schoolfriends, and ethnic and religious groups in socialization and social behaviour. In particular the term has become associated with the study of children and adolescents.

role in the social sciences, a term used to mean the part a person plays in society, either in helping the social system to work or in fulfilling social responsibilities towards others. Sociologists distinguish between formal roles, such as those of a doctor or politician, and informal roles, such as those of mother or husband, which are based on personal relationships. Social roles involve mutual expectations: a doctor can fulfil that role only if the patients play their part; a father requires the support of his children. *Role play* refers to the way children learn adult roles by acting them out in play (mothers and fathers; cops and robbers). Everyone has a number of roles to play in a society: a woman may be a mother, a wife, and a doctor at the same time, for example. *Role conflict* arises where two or more of a person's roles are seen as incompatible.

sect a small, voluntary, ideological group, usually religious in nature, aspiring to personal perfection and claiming a monopoly of access to truth or salvation. Sects are usually highly exclusive. They demand strict conformity, total commitment to their code of behaviour, and complete personal involvement, sometimes to the point of rejecting mainstream society altogether in terms of attachments, names, possessions and family. Most sects are short-lived, either because their appeal dies out and their members return to mainstream society, or because their appeal spreads and they become part of mainstream society (for example, Christianity). Sects are sociologically important as indicators of social change.

secularization the process through which religious thinking, practice, and institutions lose their social significance. The concept is based on the theory, held by some sociologists, that as societies become industrialized their religious morals, values, and institutions give way to secular ones.

socialization the process, beginning in childhood, by which a person learns how to become a member of a particular society, learning its norms, customs, laws, and ways of living. The main agents of socialization are the family, school, peer groups, work, religion, and the mass media. The main methods of socialization are direct instruction, rewards and punishment, imitation, experimentation, role play, and interaction. Some agents of socialization, such as the family and the peer group, may conflict with each other, offering alternative goals, values, and styles of behaviour.

social mobility the movement of groups and individuals up and down the social scale. The extent or range of social mobility varies in different societies. The caste system of India and the feudalism of medieval Europe are often cited as examples of closed societies, where little social mobility was possible; the class system of Western industrial societies is considered relatively open and flexible. Individual social mobility may occur through education, marriage, talent, and so on; group mobility usually occurs through change in the occupational structure caused by new technological or economic developments.

status an individual's social position, or the esteem in which he or she is held by others in society. These two forms of social prestige may be separate or interlinked. Formal social status is attached to a particular social position, occupation, role, or office. Informal social status is based on an individual's own personal talents, skills, or personality. Both within and between most occupations or social positions there is a status hierarchy. Accompanying high status are usually *status symbols*, such as insignia of office or an expensive car. Sociologists distinguish between *ascribed status*, which is bestowed by birth, and *achieved status*, the result of one's own efforts. Status is seen as a key influence on human behaviour, on the way people evaluate themselves and others.

stereotype (Greek 'fixed impression') a one-sided, irrational, and preconceived idea about a particular group or society. It is based on prejudice rather than fact, but by repetition stereotypes become fixed in people's minds, resistant to change or to factual evidence to the contrary. Stereotypes can prove dangerous when used to justify persecution and discrimination. Some sociologists believe that stereotyping reflects a power structure in which one group in society uses labelling to keep another group 'in its place'.

trade union an organized association of workers in a particular trade, formed to protect their interests and improve their conditions of work and wages. Sociological interest in trade unions has concentrated on the extent to which they have contributed to the stability of modern industrial societies or to social and industrial conflict.

urbanization the process by which the proportion of a population living in or around towns and cities increases. The growth of urban concentrations is a relatively recent phenomenon, dating back only about 150 years, although the world's first cities date back more than 5,000 years. Urbanization has had a major effect on the social structures of industrial societies, affecting not only where people live but how they live, and *urban sociology* has emerged as a distinct area of study.

Key Thinkers

Althusser Louis 1918– . French Marxist philosopher. Arguing against a view that the economic system determines the way we live, he divided each mode of production into four interacting elements – the economic, political, ideological and theoretical. He attempted to show how the ruling class ideology of a particular era is a crucial form of class control. Works include *For Marx* 1965 and *Lenin and Philosophy* 1969.

Chicago School of Sociology the first university department of sociology was founded in Chicago, Illinois, USA, in 1892. In the 1920s and 1930s, under Robert E Park, with W I Thomas, Ernest Burgess, Louis Wirth, and R McKenzie, it became an important centre for social science, studying modern urban life including crime and deviance in Chicago.

Comte Auguste 1798–1857. French philosopher and founder of sociology, a term he coined in 1830. He sought to establish sociology as a 'scientific' discipline, using positivism as the basis of a new science of social order and social development. In his six-volume *Cours de philosophie positive* 1830–42 he argued that human thought and social development evolve through three stages: the theological, the metaphysical and finally the positive or scientific. His early radical ideas were increasingly tempered by the political and social upheavals of his time.

Durkheim Emile 1858–1917. French sociologist. He analysed the bases of social order and the effects of industrialization on traditional social and moral order, and attempted to establish sociology as an academic discipline. Key works are *The Division of Labour in Society* 1893, comparing small-scale societies with industrial ones; *The Rules of Sociological Method* 1895, proclaiming positivism as the way forward for sociology as a science; and *Suicide* 1897, showing social causes of this apparently individual act.

Engels Friedrich 1820–95. German social and political philosopher. He wrote *The Condition of the Working Class in England* 1845, and collaborated with Marx on *The Communist Manifesto* 1848. His later works, such as *Origins of the Family, Private Property, and the State* 1884, helped popularize Marxism as well as using Darwinian ideas to give Marxism a scientific and deterministic flavour which was to influence later Soviet thinking.

Frankfurt School term for the Institute of Social Research, set up at Frankfurt University in Germany in 1923 as the first Marxist research centre. In the 1930s, under Max Horkheimer, a group which included Erich Fromm, Herbert Marcuse and T W Adorno tried to integrate the ideas of Marx and Freud in a synthesis known as *critical theory*. With the rise of Hitler, many of its members went to the USA and set up the Institute at Columbia University, New York.

Gramsci Antonio 1891–1937. Italian Marxist theorist who helped to found the Italian Communist Party in 1921, but was imprisoned by Mussolini in 1926 and spent virtually the rest of his life in prison. His *Prison Notebooks* include his famous concept of *hegemony*, a belief that real class control in capitalist societies is ideological and cultural rather than physical, and that bourgeois propaganda can only be revealed by radical education of the working class. His approach influenced European Marxists in their attempt to distance themselves from orthodox Soviet communism.

Husserl Edmund 1859–1938. German philosopher, whose theory of *phenomenology* concentrating on what is consciously experienced (phenomena), was influential in the development of sociology. His main works are *Logical Investigations* 1900, 1901, and *Phenomenological Philosophy* 1913.

Illich Ivan 1926– . Viennese-born social critic, who believes that modern technology and bureaucratic institutions are destroying individual skills and self-sufficiency, particularly in the Third World, and creating a new form of dependency, on experts and professionals. His solution is to abolish the institutions on which authority rests. Works include *Deschooling Society* 1971 and *Towards a History of Need* 1978.

Kuhn Thomas S 1922– . American historian of science, whose *The Structure of Scientific Revolutions* 1962 argued that all knowledge, even scientific knowledge, is relative, dependent on the paradigm (theoretical framework) that dominates a particular subject at a particular point in time. Such paradigms (such as Darwinism or Newtonian theory) are uncritically accepted as true, until a 'scientific revolution' creates a new orthodoxy.

Mannheim Karl 1893–1947. Hungarian sociologist, who settled in the UK in 1933. In *Ideology and Utopia* 1929 he argued that all

171

knowledge except mathematics and physics is ideological, a reflection of class interests and values. He distinguished between ruling class ideologies and those of utopian or revolutionary groups, arguing that knowledge is thus created by a continual power struggle between rival groups and ideas.

Marx Karl (Heinrich) 1818–83. German philosopher, economist and social theorist. His large body of work, much of it in collaboration with Engels, including *The Communist Manifesto* 1848 and *Capital* 1867–94, helped give birth to communist revolutions in Russia, China, and the Third World. His materialist conception of history and his analysis of capitalist society have made him possibly the single most influential thinker over the whole range of the social sciences in the 20th century.

Mead George Herbert 1863–1931. American philosopher and social psychologist, who helped to found the philosophy of pragmatism. His work on group interaction stimulated the development of role theory, phenomenology, and ethnomethodology.

Michels Robert 1876–1936. German social and political theorist. Originally a radical, he became a severe critic of socialism and Marxism, and in his last years was a supporter of Hitler and Mussolini. In *Political Parties* 1911 he propounded the 'Iron Law of Oligarchy', arguing that in any society there is a tendency towards rule by the few in the interests of the few, and that ideologies such as socialism and communism were merely propaganda to control the masses.

Mills C Wright 1916–62. American sociologist, whose concern for humanity, ethical values, and individual freedom led him to criticize the US establishment as well as analyse it. Originally in the liberal tradition, he later adopted a more radical standpoint. Works include *White Collar* 1951 and *The Power Elite* 1956.

Parsons Talcott 1902–79. American sociologist, professor of sociology at Harvard University from 1931 until his death. He was the author of over 150 books and articles, and

put forward the influential theory of structural functionalism. Works include *The Structure of Social Action* 1939 and *The Social System* 1951.

Popper Karl (Raimund) 1902– . Austrian philosopher of science, and social theorist critic of Marxism. He views scientific discovery as a process of falsification rather than verification – that ideas and theories can only be proved false, not correct. There is no such thing as objective knowledge, and good science involves a process of conjecture and refutation (trial and error) whereby ideas are tested, and in most cases rejected. A good theory is one that is falsifiable; a bad one (such as Marxism, in his view) is one that is not logically testable. Works include *The Logic of Scientific Discovery* 1934, *Conjectures and Refutations* 1963, and *Objective Knowledge* 1972.

Taylor Frederick Winslow 1856–1915. American management consultant, the founder of scientific management, which aims at improving working efficiency and industrial discipline. His ideas, published in *Principles of Scientific Management* 1911, were based on the breakdown of work to the simplest tasks, and the introduction of time and motion studies. His methods were most clearly expressed in 'assembly line' factories, but his ideas have been criticized for alienating workers.

Tönnies Ferdinand 1855–1936. German social theorist and philosopher. His main work *Gemeinschaft-Gesellschaft* 1887 contrasted traditional societies and small organizations with modern industrial societies and large organizations. He saw industrialization as a threat to traditional society's sense of community.

Weber Max 1864–1920. German sociologist, who emphasized cultural and political factors as key influences on economic development and individual behaviour. He undertook comparative analyses of ancient and modern civilizations and religions and he argued for the possibility of a scientific and value-free approach to research. Key works include *The Protestant Ethic and the Spirit of Capitalism* 1902 and *The Sociology of Religion* 1920.

Sport

Many sports can be traced to ancient Egyptian or Greek times. Coursing, for example, was believed to have taken place in Egypt in 3000 BC, using Saluki dogs. Wrestling certainly took place in Egypt more than 4,000 years ago, and the Greeks participated in boxing around 1500 BC.

The real development of the majority of today's sport as competitions, rather than pastimes, was in the 18th and 19th centuries, when sports such as cricket, football, rugby, golf, tennis, and many more became increasingly popular.

The traditional sports have changed very little over the years but the advent of television has led to more and more competitions within each sport. Television has also helped the growth and development of some sports; darts, snooker and bowls are three prime examples.

Thanks to large sums of money through sponsorship, most sports can look forward to a healthy future, and their superstars can continue to be among the highest-paid people in the world. But, when one sees the delicate skills of champions such as Steve Davis, Jack Nicklaus, Martina Navratilova, and John Lowe, there is no denying them such rewards for years of dedication to their sport.

This section begins with *Events and Records*, a brief history and description of many sports, with lists of recent champions and winners in each. It concludes with *Biographies* of a selection of the many sporting greats that have made the headlines and broken records over the years.

Events and Records

American football formally originated in a Princeton University/Rutgers University game in 1869. The goals and ball are those of English rugby, but the players are kitted out in protective suits against rough tackling, and the two teams of 11 men play on a field marked out in 'gridiron intervals', much closer together than those of the rugby pitch. The scoring rules are complex. It is strenuous and games are divided into four 15-minute periods.

Super Bowl first held 1967, it is an annual meeting between the winners of the National and American Football Conferences

1977 Oakland Raiders
1978 Dallas Cowboys
1979 Pittsburgh Steelers
1980 Pittsburgh Steelers
1981 Oakland Raiders
1982 San Francisco 49ers
1983 Washington Redskins
1984 Los Angeles Raiders
1985 San Francisco 49ers
1986 Chicago Bears
1987 New York Giants

angling fishing with rod and line; the most popular participant sport in the UK.

Freshwater coarse fishing includes members of the carp family and pike (not usually eaten and thrown back); freshwater game fish are salmon and trout.

seafishing the catch includes flatfish, bass, mackerel; big-game fish (again usually not eaten) include shark, tuna or tunny, marlin, and swordfish, usually caught from specially equipped motor-boats.

Competition angling is very popular and world championships exist for most branches of the sport. The oldest is the World Freshwater Championship, inaugurated in 1957, four years after the staging of the first European championship.

World Freshwater Championship
individual
1982 Kevin Ashurst *(England)*
1983 Rudiger Kremkus *(West Germany)*
1984 Bobby Smithers *(England)*
1985 Dave Roper *(England)*
1986 Lud Wever *(Holland)*
team
1982 Holland
1983 Belgium
1984 Luxembourg
1985 England
1986 Italy

archery the use of the bow and arrow, originally in war and the chase, later as a sport. Until the introduction of gunpowder in the 14th century, bands of archers were to be found in every European army, and up to the time of Charles II the practice of archery was fostered and encouraged by English rulers. By the mid-17th century archery was no longer important in warfare and interest waned until the 1780s, although in the north of England shooting for the Scorton Arrow has been carried on, with few breaks, from 1673. Organizations include the world governing body, the Fédération Internationale du Tir à l'Arc 1931; the British Grand National Archery Society 1861; and in the USA the National Archery Association 1879 and, for actual hunting with the bow, the National Field Archery Association 1940. In competitions, results are based on double FITA rounds, that is 72 arrows at each of four targets at 90, 70, 50, and 30 metres (70, 60, 50, and 30 for women). The best possible score is 2,880.

World Championships first held 1931 and formerly an annual event, now biennial
men – individual
1979 Darrell Pace *(United States)*
1981 Kyosti Laasonen *(Finland)*
1983 Richard McKinney *(United States)*
1985 Richard McKinney *(United States)*
1987 Vlademir Asheyev *(USSR)*
men – team
1979 United States
1981 United States

1983 United States
1985 South Korea
1987 South Korea
women – individual
1979 Jin-Ho Kim *(South Korea)*
1981 Natalia Butuzova *(USSR)*
1983 Jin-Ho Kim *(South Korea)*
1985 Irina Soldatova *(USSR)*
1987 Ma Xiagjuan (China)
women – team
1979 South Korea
1981 USSR
1983 South Korea
1985 USSR
1987 China

   association football or soccer, the earliest form of the game of football, originating in rural football in the UK. It is now played worldwide, under rules of the Football Association 1863. There are two teams of 11, with a large round ball and a low netted goal; only the goalkeeper may touch the ball with his hands.
World Cup first contested 1930, held every four years
1950 Uruguay
1954 West Germany
1958 Brazil
1962 Brazil
1966 England
1970 Brazil
1974 West Germany
1978 Argentina
1982 Italy
1986 Argentina
European Championship instituted 1958, first final 1960; held every four years
1960 USSR
1964 Spain
1968 Italy
1972 West Germany
1976 Czechoslovakia
1980 West Germany
1984 France
European Champions Cup first held 1955
1978 Liverpool *(England)*
1979 Nottingham Forest *(England)*
1980 Nottingham Forest *(England)*
1981 Liverpool *(England)*

1982 Aston Villa *(England)*
1983 SV Hamburg *(West Germany)*
1984 Liverpool *(England)*
1985 Juventus *(Italy)*
1986 Steau Bucharest *(Romania)*
1987 FC Porto *(Portugal)*
European Cup Winners Cup first held 1960
1978 Anderlecht *(Belgium)*
1979 Barcelona *(Spain)*
1980 Valencia *(Spain)*
1981 Dinamo Tbilisi *(USSR)*
1982 Barcelona *(Spain)*
1983 Aberdeen *(Scotland)*
1984 Juventus *(Italy)*
1985 Everton *(England)*
1986 Dinamo Kiev *(USSR)*
1987 Ajax *(Holland)*
UEFA Cup (formerly the Inter Cities Fairs Cup) first held 1955
1978 PSV Eindhoven *(Holland)*
1979 Borussia Moenchengladbach *(West Germany)*
1980 Eintracht Frankfurt *(West Germany)*
1981 Ipswich Town *(England)*
1982 IFK Gothenburg *(Sweden)*
1983 Anderlecht *(Belgium)*
1984 Tottenham Hotspur *(England)*
1985 Real Madrid *(Spain)*
1986 Real Madrid *(Spain)*
1987 IFK Gothenburg *(Sweden)*
FA Cup the world's premier knockout club competition, first held 1872; held annually in the UK
1978 Ipswich Town
1979 Arsenal
1980 West Ham United
1981 Tottenham Hotspur
1982 Tottenham Hotspur
1983 Manchester United
1984 Everton
1985 Manchester United
1986 Liverpool
1987 Coventry City
Football League Cup (currently known as the Littlewoods Cup, formerly known as the Milk Cup) first final 1961 in two stages, now a single game
1977 Aston Villa

1978 Nottingham Forest
1979 Nottingham Forest
1980 Wolverhampton Wanderers
1981 Liverpool
1982 Liverpool
1983 Liverpool
1984 Liverpool
1985 Norwich City
1986 Oxford United
1987 Arsenal
Division One Champions Football League
founded 1888–89
1976–77 Liverpool
1977–78 Nottingham Forest
1978–79 Liverpool
1979–80 Liverpool
1980–81 Aston Villa
1981–82 Liverpool
1982–83 Liverpool
1983–84 Liverpool
1984–85 Everton
1985–86 Liverpool
1986–87 Everton
Scottish Premier Division Champions
Scottish League formed 1890–91, reformed
into three divisions in 1975–76
1977–78 Rangers
1978–79 Celtic
1979–80 Aberdeen
1980–81 Celtic
1981–82 Celtic
1982–83 Dundee United
1983–84 Aberdeen
1984–85 Aberdeen
1985–86 Celtic
1986–87 Rangers
Scottish FA Cup first final held 1874
1978 Rangers
1979 Rangers
1980 Celtic
1981 Rangers
1982 Aberdeen
1983 Aberdeen
1984 Aberdeen
1985 Celtic
1986 Aberdeen
1987 St Mirren
   athletics competitive track and field events,

especially forms of running, jumping, walking,
throwing. Among the Greeks, vase paintings
show that competitive athletics were established at least by 1600 BC (Olympic Games).
However, the concept of the unpaid amateur is
a recent British innovation, ancient athletes
having been well paid and sponsored. Aristotle
paid the expenses of a boxer contestant at
Olympia, and chariot races were sponsored by
the Greek city states. Athletics have recently
been dominated by the 'world record';
development of computer selection of the best
potential competitors and analysis of motion
for greatest speed, and so on; specialization of
equipment for maximum performance (for
example, glass fibre vaulting poles, foam landing pads, aerodynamically designed javelins,
composition running tracks), and the unlawful
use of drugs, such as anabolic steroids and
growth hormones.

Olympic Champions The 23rd Olympics were
held in Los Angeles 1984, from 28 Jul to 12
Aug. Track and field champions:
men/women
100 metres Carl Lewis *(United States)*/Evelyn
Ashford *(United States)*
200 metres Carl Lewis *(United States)*/Valerie
Brisco-Hooks *(United States)*
400 metres Alonzo Babers *(United States)*/
Valerie Brisco-Hooks *(United States)*
800 metres Joachim Cruz *(Brazil)*/Doina
Melinte *(Romania)*
1,500 metres Sebastian Coe *(Great Britain)*/
Gabriella Dorio *(Italy)*
3,000 metres –/Maricica Puica *(Romania)*
5,000 metres Said Aouita *(Morocco)*/–
10,000 metres Alberto Cova *(Italy)*/–
marathon Carlos Lopes *(Portugal)*/Joan
Benoit *(United States)*
100 metres hurdles –/Benita Fitzgerald-Brown
(United States)
110 metres hurdles Roger Kingdom *(United
States)*/–
400 metres hurdles Edwin Moses *(United
States)*/Nawal El Moutawakel *(Morocco)*
3,000 metres steeplechase Julius Korir
(Kenya)/–
4 × 100 metres relay United States/United

States

4 × 400 metres relay United States/United States

20,000 metres walk Ernesto Canto *(Mexico)*/–

50,000 metres walk Raul Gonzalez *(Mexico)*/–

high jump Dietmar Moegenburg *(West Germany)*/Ulrike Meyfarth *(West Germany)*

pole vault Pierre Quinon *(France)*/–

long jump Carl Lewis *(United States)*/Anisoara Cusmir-Stanciu *(Romania)*

triple jump Al Joyner *(United States)*/–

shot put Alessandro Andrei *(Italy)*/Claudia Losch *(West Germany)*

discus Rolf Danneberg *(West Germany)*/Ria Stalman *(Holland)*

hammer Juha Tiainen *(Finland)*/–

javelin Arto Haerkoenen *(Finland)*/Tessa Sanderson *(Great Britain)*

decathlon Daley Thompson *(Great Britain)*/–

heptathlon –/Glynnis Nunn *(Australia)*

World Cross Country Championship first held in 1903 as the International Championships, it came under the auspices of the International Amateur Athletic Federation in 1973

men - individual/women - individual

1977 Leon Schotts *(Belgium)*/Carmen Valero *(Spain)*

1978 John Treacy *(Ireland)*/Grete Waitz *(Norway)*

1979 John Treacy *(Ireland)*/Grete Waitz *(Norway)*

1980 Craig Virgin *(United States)*/Grete Waitz *(Norway)*

1981 Craig Virgin *(United States)*/Grete Waitz *(Norway)*

1982 Mohamad Kedir *(Ethiopia)*/Maricica Puica *(Romania)*

1983 Bekele Debele *(Ethiopia)*/Grete Waitz *(Norway)*

1984 Carlos Lopes *(Portugal)*/Maricica Puica *(Romania)*

1985 Carlos Lopes *(Portugal)*/Zola Budd *(England)*

1986 John Ngugi *(Kenya)*/Zola Budd *(England)*

1987 John Ngugi *(Kenya)*/Annette Sergent *(France)*

men – team/women – team

1977 Belgium/USSR

1978 France/Romania

1979 England/United States

1980 England/USSR

1981 Ethiopia/USSR

1982 Ethiopia/USSR

1983 Ethiopia/United States

1984 Ethiopia/United States

1985 Ethiopia/United States

1986 Kenya/England

1987 Kenya/United States

World Records some of the principal world records as at 1 Jun 1987:

men

100 metres 9.93 seconds Calvin Smith *(United States)*

200 metres 19.72 Pietro Mennea *(Italy)*

400 metres 43.86 Lee Evans *(United States)*

800 metres 1:41.73 Sebastian Coe *(Great Britain)*

1,500 metres 3:29.46 Said Aouita *(Morocco)*

one mile 3:46.32 Steve Cram *(Great Britain)*

5,000 metres 13:00.40 Said Aouita *(Morocco)*

10,000 metres 27:13.81 Fernando Mamede *(Portugal)*

110 metres hurdles 12.93 Renaldo Nehemiah *(United States)*

400 metres hurdles 47.02 Edwin Moses *(United States)*

high jump 2.41 metres Igor Paklin *(USSR)*

long jump 8.90 Bob Beamon *(United States)*

triple jump 17.97 Willie Banks *(United States)*

pole vault 6.01 Sergei Bubka *(USSR)*

decathlon 8847 points Daley Thompson *(Great Britain)*

women

100 metres 10.76 seconds Evelyn Ashford *(United States)*

200 metres 21.71 Marita Koch *(East Germany)*

400 metres 47.60 Marita Koch *(East Germany)*

800 metres 1:53.28 Jarmila Kratochvilova *(Czechoslovakia)*

1,500 metres 3:52.47 Tatyana Kazankina *(USSR)*

one mile 4:16.71 Mary Decker *(United States)*

3,000 metres 8:22.62 Tatyana Kazankina *(USSR)*

10,000 metres 30:13.74 Ingrid Kristiansen

(Norway)
100 metres hurdles 12.26 Yordanka Donkova *(Bulgaria)*
400 metres hurdles 52.94 Marina Stepanova *(USSR)*
high jump 2.08 Stefka Kostadinova *(Bulgaria)*
long jump 7.45 Heike Dreschler *(East Germany)*
javelin 77.44 Fatima Whitbread *(Great Britain)*
heptathlon 7,161 points Jackie Joyner *(United States)*

badminton game played by two or four players with rackets and shuttlecocks, usually indoors. The object is to hit the shuttlecock over the net and to either ground the shuttle in the opponent's court, or force him/her to fail to return it over the net. Points can only be won if a person is serving and, normally, the first to 15 points is the winner (11 in women's singles). The name is derived from Badminton House, the Gloucestershire seat of the Duke of Beaufort, where badminton originated in the 1860s. The first rules were drawn up in 1876, and the Badminton Association was formed in 1893.

All England Championships instituted in 1899
men's singles/women's singles
1977 Flemming Delfs *(Denmark)*/Hiroe Yuki *(Japan)*
1978 Liem Swie King *(Indonesia)*/Gillian Gilks *(England)*
1979 Liem Swie King *(Indonesia)*/Lene Koppen *(Denmark)*
1980 Prakash Padukone *(Indonesia)*/Lene Koppen *(Denmark)*
1981 Liem Swie King *(Indonesia)*/Sun Ai Hwang *(South Korea)*
1982 Morten Frost *(Denmark)*/Zang Ailing *(China)*
1983 Luan Jin *(China)*/Zang Ailing *(China)*
1984 Morten Frost *(Denmark)*/Li Lingwei *(China)*
1985 Zhao Jianhua *(China)*/Han Aiping *(China)*
1986 Morten Frost *(Denmark)*/Kim Yun-Ja *(South Korea)*
1987 Morten Frost *(Denmark)*/Kirsten Larsen *(Denmark)*

Thomas Cup a men's team competition, first held 1948–49, then held triennially until 1984 when it became a biennial event
1979 Indonesia
1982 China
1984 Indonesia
1986 China

Uber Cup the women's equivalent of the Thomas Cup, first held 1957, then held triennially until 1984 when it became a biennial event
1978 Japan
1981 Japan
1984 China
1986 China

baseball the US national summer game, which traditionally originated in New York in 1839. Two teams of nine men play on a pitch marked out in the form of a 'diamond', which has a base at each corner. The ball is struck with a cylindrical bat, and the players try to make a run by circuiting the bases round the diamond before the ball can be retrieved. A 'home run' is a circuit on one hit. *World Series* first held as end of season match between the winners of the National and American leagues in 1903 and established as World Series of seven games in 1905
1977 New York Yankees *(American League)*
1978 New York Yankees *(American League)*
1979 Pittsburgh Pirates *(National League)*
1980 Philadelphia Phillies *(National League)*
1981 Los Angeles Dodgers *(National League)*
1982 St Louis Cardinals *(National League)*
1983 Baltimore Orioles *(American League)*
1984 Detroit Tigers *(American League)*
1985 Kansas City Royals *(American League)*
1986 New York Mets *(National League)*

basketball ball game invented by YMCA instructor, James Naismith, Springfield, Massachusetts, USA in 1891. There are two teams of five, plus seven substitutes, and a large inflated ball is thrown through a circular net goal 3.05 m/10 ft above the ground at each end of a rectangular court
World Championship first held 1950 for men, 1953 for women; held every four years
men
1950 Argentina

1954 United States
1959 Brazil
1963 Brazil
1967 USSR
1970 Yugoslavia
1974 USSR
1978 Yugoslavia
1982 USSR
1986 United States
women
1953 United States
1957 United States
1959 USSR
1964 USSR
1967 USSR
1971 USSR
1975 USSR
1979 United States
1983 USSR

billiards game played with cues and composition balls (one red, two white) on a rectangular table covered with a green cloth, and with six pockets, one at each corner and in each of the long sides at the middle. The world's greatest player was Walter Lindrum, whose phenomenal skill helped to kill the game in favour of pool, in which there is a greater element of chance; the most popular form of the latter is snooker.

World Professional Championship instituted in 1870, organized on a challenge basis; restored as an annual tournament in 1980

1980 Fred Davis *(England)*
1981 not held
1982 Rex Williams *(England)*
1983 Rex Williams *(England)*
1984 Mark Wildman *(England)*
1985 Ray Edmonds *(England)*
1986 Robert Foldvari *(Australia)*
1987 Norman Dagley *(England)*

bobsledding the sport of racing steel-bodied, steerable toboggans down a mountain ice-chute, manned by two or four people at speeds up to 130 kmph/80 mph. World championships have been held every year since 1931.

Olympic Champions four-man event introduced at the 1924 Winter Olympics, two-man in 1932
two-man/four-man

1948 Switzerland/United States
1952 West Germany/West Germany
1956 Italy/Switzerland
1960 not held
1964 Great Britain/Canada
1968 Italy/Italy
1972 West Germany/Switzerland
1976 East Germany/East Germany
1980 Switzerland/East Germany
1984 East Germany/East Germany

World Championship four-man championship introduced 1924, two-man 1931; in Olympic years winners automatically become world champions
two-man/four-man

1978 Switzerland/East Germany
1979 Switzerland/West Germany
1980 Switzerland/East Germany
1981 East Germany/East Germany
1982 Switzerland/Switzerland
1983 Switzerland/Switzerland
1984 East Germany/East Germany
1985 East Germany/East Germany
1986 East Germany/Switzerland
1987 Switzerland/Switzerland

bowls outdoor game played in England at least since the 13th century. It is played on *flat* or *crown greens* with biased bowls of lignum vitae (about 13 cm/5 in in diameter), and the object of the game is to draw each bowl as near as possible to the small white jack. The game can be played as singles, pairs, triples, or rinks (four players a side). The indoor game is becoming increasingly popular.

World Championship first held 1966 for men, 1969 for women
men: singles/pairs

1966 David Bryant *(England)*/Australia
1972 Malwyn Evans *(Wales)*/Hong Kong
1976 Doug Watson *(South Africa)*/South Africa
1980 David Bryant *(England)*/Australia
1984 Peter Bellis *(New Zealand)*/United States
triples/fours
1966 Australia/New Zealand
1972 United States/England
1976 South Africa/South Africa
1980 England/Hong Kong

1984 Ireland/England
women: singles/pairs
1969 Gladys Doyle *(Papua New Guinea)*/South Africa
1973 Elsie Wilke *(New Zealand)*/Australia
1977 Elsie Wilke *(New Zealand)*/Hong Kong
1981 Norma Shaw *(England)*/Ireland
1985 Merle Richardson *(Australia)*/Australia
triples/fours
1969 South Africa/South Africa
1973 New Zealand/New Zealand
1977 Wales/Australia
1981 Hong Kong/England
1985 Australia/Scotland

Waterloo Handicap first held 1907 at The Waterloo Hotel, Blackpool, it is Crown Green bowling's principal tournament
1977 Len Barrett
1978 Arthur Murray
1979 Brian Duncan
1980 Vernon Lee
1981 Roy Nicholson
1982 Dennis Mercer
1983 Stan Frith
1984 Steve Ellis
1985 Tommy Johnstone
1986 Brian Duncan

boxing fighting with the fists. The modern sport dates from the 18th century when fights were bare-knuckle and without timed rounds; Jack Broughton 1704–89, who was champion 1729–50, laid down the first 'rules' in 1743, and introduced gloves for his pupils; Queensberry Rules (drawn up by the 8th Marquess in 1866) still prevail in modified form; the ring is 6.10 m/20 ft square maximum and 4.3 m/14 ft square minimum. In professional boxing, a round lasts three minutes, with a one-minute interval between rounds. A world championship bout recognized by the World Boxing Association (WBA) and International Boxing Federation (IBF) lasts 15 rounds whereas those recognized by the World Boxing Council (WBC) last only 12, as do European and British title fights. Amateur contests last only three rounds. Professional boxers are classified from light-flyweight 49.5 kg/108 lb to heavyweight 88 kg/195 lb, with no upward limit. Amateurs do,

however, go up to super-heavyweights.
World Champions
heavyweight - since 1978
1978 Leon Spinks *(United States)*(Undisputed)
1978 Ken Norton *(United States) (WBC)*
1978 Muhammad Ali *(United States) (WBA)*
1978 Larry Holmes *(United States) (WBC)*
1979 John Tate *(United States) (WBA)*
1980 Mike Weaver *(United States) (WBA)*
1982 Mike Dokes *(United States) (WBA)*
1983 Gerry Coetzee *(South Africrica) (WBA)*
1984 Larry Holmes *(United States) (IBF)*
1984 Tim Witherspoon *(United States) (WBC)*
1984 Pinklon Thomas *(United States) (WBC)*
1984 Greg Page *(United States) (WBA)*
1985 Michael Spinks *(United States) (IBF)*
1985 Tony Tubbs *(United States) (WBA)*
1986 Tim Witherspoon *(United States) (WBA)*
1986 Trevor Berbick *(Canada) (WBC)*
1986 Mike Tyson *(United States) (WBC)*
1986 James Smith *(United States) (WBA)*
1987 Mike Tyson *(United States) (WBC/WBA)*
1987 Tony Tucker *(United States)* (IBF)
World champions at three different weights:
Bob Fitzsimmons *(Great Britain)* middleweight 1891, heavyweight 1897, light-heavyweight 1903

Tony Canzoneri *(United States)* featherweight 1928, lightweight 1930, junior-welterweight 1931

Barney Ross *(United States)* lightweight 1933, junior-welterweight 1933, welterweight 1934

Henry Armstrong *(United States)* featherweight 1937, welterweight 1938, lightweight 1938

Wilfred Benitez *(United States)* junior-welterweight 1976, welterweight 1979, WBC junior-middleweight 1981

Alexis Arguello *(Nicaragua)* WBA featherweight 1974, WBC junior-lightweight 1978, WBC lightweight 1981

Roberto Duran *(Panama)* lightweight 1972, welterweight 1980, WBA junior-middleweight 1983

Wilfredo Gomez *(Puerto Rico)* WBC junior-featherweight 1977, WBC featherweight 1984, WBA junior-lightweight 1985

Sugar Ray Leonard *(United States)* WBC

welterweight 1979, WBA junior-middleweight 1981, WBC middleweight 1987

Thomas Hearns *(United States)* WBA welterweight 1980, WBC junior-middleweight 1982, WBC light-heavyweight 1987

Great heavyweights include: John L Sullivan (bare-knuckle champion) 1882–92; Jim Corbett (first Marquess of Queensberry champion) 1892–97; Jack Dempsey 1919–26; Joe Louis 1937–49; Floyd Patterson 1956–59, 1960–62, Muhammad Ali 1964–67, 1974–78, 1978–79, and Larry Holmes 1978–85.

canoeing sport of propelling a lightweight, shallow boat, pointed at both ends, by paddles or sails. The construction of early canoes varied from the hollowed tree-trunk of African tribes to the framework covered with bark or skin used by the American Indians, the latter being the basis of modern plastic and fibreglass versions. Canoeing became a sport in the 19th century and the Royal Canoe Club in Britain was founded 1866. Two types of canoe are used: the *kayak*, which has a keel and is derived from the Eskimo model, in which the canoeist sits, and the *Canadian style canoe*, which has no keel and the canoeist kneels. In addition to straightforward racing, there are slalom courses, with up to 30 'gates' to be negotiated through rapids and round artificial rock formations. Penalty seconds are added to course time for touching suspended gate poles or missing a gate. One to four canoeists are carried.

Olympic Games introduced into the Olympics in 1936

men: Kayak singles
500 metres
1976 Vasile Diba *(Romania)*
1980 Vladimir Parfenovich *(USSR)*
1984 Ian Ferguson *(New Zealand)*
1000 metres
1976 Rudiger Helm *(East Germany)*
1980 Rudiger Helm *(East Germany)*
1984 Alan Thompson *(New Zealand)*
Kayak pairs
500 metres
1976 East Germany
1980 USSR

1984 New Zealand
1000 metres
1976 USSR
1980 USSR
1984 Canada
Kayak fours
1000 metres
1976 USSR
1980 East Germany
1984 New Zealand
Canadian singles
500 metres
1976 Aleksandr Rogov *(USSR)*
1980 Sergey Postrekhin *(USSR)*
1984 Larry Cain *(Canada)*
1000 metres
1976 Matija Ljubek *(Yugoslavia)*
1980 Lubomir Lubenov *(Bulgaria)*
1984 Ulrich Eicke *(West Germany)*
Canadian pairs
500 metres
1976 USSR
1980 Hungary
1984 Yugoslavia
1000 metres
1976 USSR
1980 Romania
1984 Romania
women: Kayak singles
500 metres
1976 Carola Zirzow *(East Germany)*
1980 Birgit Fischer *(East Germany)*
1984 Agneta Anderson *(Sweden)*
Kayak pairs
500 metres
1976 USSR
1980 East Germany
1984 Sweden

chess board game originating at least as early as the 2nd century AD. Two players use 16 pieces each, on a board of 64 squares of alternating colour, to try and force their opponent into a position where the chief piece cannot be moved or allowed to remain in the same position without its being taken. There are said to be more variations than there are atoms in the universe. The Fédération Internationale des Echecs (FIDE) was established in

1924. Leading players are rated according to the Elo System and Bobby Fischer (United States) is reckoned to be the greatest grand master of all time with a rating of 2,785. A world championship was established in 1851. Players of the rank of grand master can now be defeated by a computer.

World Champions first official world champion recognized 1886

men

1948 Mikhail Botvinnik *(USSR)*
1957 Vassiliy Smyslov *(USSR)*
1958 Mikhail Botvinnik *(USSR)*
1960 Mikhail Tal *(USSR)*
1961 Mikhail Botvinnik *(USSR)*
1963 Tigran Petrosian *(USSR)*
1969 Boris Spassky *(USSR)*
1972 Bobby Fischer *(United States)*
1975 Anatoliy Karpov *(USSR)*
1985 Gary Kasparov *(USSR)*

women

1927 Vera Menchik *(Great Britain)*
1950 Lyudmila Rudenko *(USSR)*
1953 Elizaveta Bykova *(USSR)*
1955 Olga Runtsova *(USSR)*
1958 Elizaveta Bykova *(USSR)*
1962 Nona Gaprindashvili *(USSR)*
1978 Maya Chiburdanidze *(USSR)*

cricket game played with bat and hard leather-covered ball. Its origin is obscure, but some form of bat and ball game has been played since the 13th century. In 1711 Kent played All England, and in 1735 a match was played between teams chosen by the Prince of Wales and the Earl of Middlesex. The Hambledon Club at Broad-Halfpenny Down in Hampshire was the first to be formed, in 1750. The Marylebone Cricket Club (MCC) was established in Thomas Lord's ground in Dorset Square in 1787, and in 1814 it moved to St John's Wood. Since then it has been the controlling authority and its ground the acknowledged headquarters of the game.

The first rules of cricket were drawn up in 1774. The game is played between two sides of 11 players each. Wickets are pitched at 20 m (22 yds) apart. A batsman stands at each wicket and the object of the game is to score more runs than the opponents. The bowler bowls to the batsman a stipulated number of balls (usually six), after which another bowler bowls from the other wicket. A run is normally scored by the batsman after striking the ball and exchanging ends with his partner, or by hitting the ball to the boundary line for an automatic four runs or six runs if the ball is hit directly over it without first hitting the ground. A batsman is usually got out by being (1) bowled; (2) caught; (3) run out; (4) stumped; (5) l.b.w. – when the ball hits his leg which is placed before the wicket. Games comprise either one or two innings – or turns – per team.

Every year series of Test Matches are played among member countries of the Commonwealth, where the game has its greatest popularity: Australia, India, New Zealand, Pakistan, the UK, Sri Lanka and the West Indies. Great cricketers have included W G Grace, Sir Jack Hobbs, W R Hammond, and Sir Len Hutton; the Australian Sir Don Bradman; the Indian K S Ranjitsinhji; the South African A D Nourse; and the West Indians Sir Leary Constantine, Sir Frank Worrell, and Sir Gary Sobers. Test matches take several days, but otherwise the majority of matches last one or three days.

County Championship first officially held 1890

1977 Middlesex and Kent *(shared)*
1978 Kent
1979 Essex
1980 Middlesex
1981 Nottinghamshire
1982 Middlesex
1983 Essex
1984 Essex
1985 Middlesex
1986 Essex

Refuge Assurance League (formerly John Player League) first held 1969

1977 Leicestershire
1978 Hampshire
1979 Somerset
1980 Warwickshire
1981 Essex
1982 Sussex
1983 Yorkshire

1984 Essex
1985 Essex
1986 Hampshire
NatWest Cup (formerly called the Gillette Cup)
first held 1963
1977 Middlesex
1978 Sussex
1979 Somerset
1980 Middlesex
1981 Derbyshire
1982 Surrey
1983 Somerset
1984 Middlesex
1985 Essex
1986 Sussex
Benson and Hedges Cup first held 1972
1977 Gloucestershire
1978 Kent
1979 Essex
1980 Northamptonshire
1981 Somerset
1982 Somerset
1983 Middlesex
1984 Lancashire
1985 Leicestershire
1986 Middlesex
World Cup first held 1975, contested every four years
1975 West Indies
1979 West Indies
1983 India

cycling cycle racing takes place on oval artificial tracks; or on the road, for example, the French Tour de France or the British Milk Race; or across country (cyclo-cross). There are several main types of races. *Stage races* are run over gruelling terrain and can last anything from three to five days up to three-and-a-half weeks, like the Tour de France, Tour of Italy, and Tour of Spain. *Criteriums* are fast, action-packed races around the closed streets of town or city centres. Each race lasts about an hour. *Road races* are run over a prescribed circuit, which the riders will lap several times. Such a race will normally cover a distance of approximately 100 miles. *Track racing* takes place on either a concrete or wooden banked circuit, either indoors or outdoors. In *time trialing* each

rider races against the clock, with all the competitors starting at different intervals.
Tour de France first held 1903
1977 Bernard Thevenet *(France)*
1978 Bernard Hinault *(France)*
1979 Bernard Hinault *(France)*
1980 Joop Zoetemelk *(Holland)*
1981 Bernard Hinault *(France)*
1982 Bernard Hinault *(France)*
1983 Laurent Fignon *(France)*
1984 Laurent Fignon *(France)*
1985 Bernard Hinault *(France)*
1986 Greg LeMond *(United States)*
Tour of Britain (Milk Race) first held 1951
1978 Jan Brzezny *(Poland)*
1979 Yuri Kashirin *(USSR)*
1980 Ivan Mitchtenko *(USSR)*
1981 Sergei Krivocheyev *(USSR)*
1982 Yuri Kashirin *(USSR)*
1983 Matt Eaton *(United States)*
1984 Oleg Czougeda *(USSR)*
1985 Erik van Lancker *(Belgium)*
1986 Joey McLoughlin *(Great Britain)*
1987 Malcolm Elliot *(Great Britain)*
World Professional Road Race Champions first held at the Nuburgring, West Germany 1927
1977 Francesco Moser *(Italy)*
1978 Gerrie Knetemann *(Holland)*
1979 Jan Raas *(Holland)*
1980 Bernard Hinault *(France)*
1981 Freddie Maertens *(Belgium)*
1982 Giuseppe Saroni *(Italy)*
1983 Greg LeMond *(United States)*
1984 Claude Criquielon *(Belgium)*
1985 Joop Zoetemelk *(Holland)*
1986 Moreno Argentin *(Italy)*

darts English game possibly first played with broken arrow-shafts, and reaching approximately its present form with a segmented round target by the 17th century. More than seven million people play darts worldwide. Television has helped popularize the sport in recent years and more big tournaments like the World Cup, Nations Cup, World Masters, and World Pairs have been inaugurated, all of which receive wide television coverage.
World Professional Championship first held in

Nottingham 1978
1978 Leighton Rees *(Wales)*
1979 John Lowe *(England)*
1980 Eric Bristow *(England)*
1981 Eric Bristow *(England)*
1982 Jocky Wilson *(Scotland)*
1983 Keith Deller *(England)*
1984 Eric Bristow *(England)*
1985 Eric Bristow *(England)*
1986 Eric Bristow *(England)*
1987 John Lowe *(England)*
News of the World Championship first held as a
national tournament 1947–48
1977 Mick Norris *(England)*
1978 Stefan Lord *(Sweden)*
1979 Bobby George *(England)*
1980 Stefan Lord *(Sweden)*
1981 John Lowe *(England)*
1982 Roy Morgan *(England)*
1983 Eric Bristow *(England)*
1984 Eric Bristow *(England)*
1985 Dave Lee *(England)*
1986 Bobby George *(England)*

equestrianism skill in horse riding,
especially as practised under International
Equestrian Federation rules when it is an
Olympic sport.
Showjumping competitive horse jumping over
a course of fences. The winner is usually the
competitor with fewest 'faults' (penalty marks
given for knocking down or refusing fences),
but in time competitions it is the competitor
completing the course most quickly, additional
seconds being added for mistakes.
World Championship first held 1953 for men,
1965 for women; since 1978 for both
men
1953 Francisco Goyoago *(Spain)*
1954 Hans-Gunter Winkler *(West Germany)*
1955 Hans-Gunter Winkler *(West Germany)*
1956 Raimondo D'Inzeo *(Italy)*
1960 Raimondo D'Inzeo *(Italy)*
1966 Pierre d'Oriola *(France)*
1970 David Broome *(Great Britain)*
1974 Hartwig Steenken *(West Germany)*
women
1965 Marion Coakes *(Great Britain)*
1970 Janou Lefebvre *(France)*

1974 Janou Tissot (born Lefebvre) *(France)*
mixed
1978 Gerd Wiltfang *(West Germany)*
1982 Norbert Koof *(West Germany)*
1986 Gail Greenough *(Canada)*
European Championship first held 1957 as separate competition for men and women; since
1975 they have competed together
1975 Alwin Schockemohle *(West Germany)*
1977 Johan Heins *(Holland)*
1979 Gerd Wiltfang *(West Germany)*
1981 Paul Schockemohle *(West Germany)*
1983 Paul Schockemohle *(West Germany)*
1985 Paul Schockemohle *(West Germany)*
British Showjumping Derby first held 1961 and
staged annually at Hickstead, Sussex
1977 Eddie Macken *(Ireland)*
1978 Eddie Macken *(Ireland)*
1979 Eddie Macken *(Ireland)*
1980 Michael Whitaker *(Great Britain)*
1981 Harvey Smith *(Great Britain)*
1982 Paul Schockemohle *(West Germany)*
1983 John Whitaker *(Great Britain)*
1984 John Ledingham *(Ireland)*
1985 Paul Schockemohle *(West Germany)*
1986 Paul Schockemohle *(West Germany)*
Three-Day Eventing horse trials testing the all-
round abilities of a horse and rider in: *dressage*
testing a horse's response to control; *cross-
country*, testing speed and endurance; and
showjumping in a final modified contest.
World Championship first held 1966
1966 Carlos Moratorio *(Argentina)*
1970 Mary Gordon-Watson *(Great Britain)*
1974 Bruce Davidson *(United States)*
1978 Bruce Davidson *(United States)*
1982 Lucinda Green (born Prior-Palmer)
(Great Britain)
1986 Virginia Leng (born Holgate) *(Great
Britain)*
Badminton Horse Trials first held 1949
1977 Lucinda Prior-Palmer *(Great Britain)*
1978 Jane Holderness-Roddam *(Great Britain)*
1979 Lucinda Prior-Palmer *(Great Britain)*
1980 Mark Todd *(New Zealand)*
1981 Captain Mark Phillips *(Great Britain)*
1982 Richard Meade *(Great Britain)*
1983 Lucinda Green *(Great Britain)*

1984 Lucinda Green *(Great Britain)*
1985 Virginia Holgate *(Great Britain)*
1986 Ian Stark *(Great Britain)*
1987 cancelled

fencing sport using the *foil,* derived from the light weapon used in practice duels; *épée,* a heavier weapon derived from the duelling sword proper; and *sabre,* in which cuts (it has two cutting edges) count as well as thrusts. Masks and protective jackets are worn, and hits are registered electronically in competitions.

Olympic Games men's fencing has been part of every Olympic programme since 1896 (women first competed in 1924, but only contest the foil). Recent winners:

foil – men
1960 Viktor Zhdanovich *(USSR)*
1964 Egon Franke *(Poland)*
1968 Ion Drimba *(Romania)*
1972 Witold Woyda *(Poland)*
1976 Fabio Dal Zotto *(Italy)*
1980 Vladimir Smirnov *(USSR)*
1984 Mauro Numa *(Italy)*
foil – women
1960 Heidi Schmid *(West Germany)*
1964 Ildiko Ujlaki-Rejto *(Hungary)*
1968 Elena Novikova *(USSR)*
1972 Antonella Ragno-Lonzi *(Italy)*
1976 Ildiko Schwarczenberger *(Hungary)*
1980 Pascale Trinquet *(France)*
1984 Jujie Luan *(China)*
épée
1960 Giuseppe Delfino *(Italy)*
1964 Grigoriy Kriss *(USSR)*
1968 Gyozo Kulcsar *(Hungary)*
1972 Csaba Fenyvesi *(Hungary)*
1976 Alexander Pusch *(West Germany)*
1980 Johan Harmenberg *(Sweden)*
1984 Phillipe Boisse *(France)*
sabre
1960 Rudolf Karpati *(Hungary)*
1964 Tibor Pezsa *(Hungary)*
1968 Jerzy Pawlowski *(Poland)*
1972 Viktor Sidiak *(USSR)*
1976 Viktor Krovopouskov *(USSR)*
1980 Viktor Krovopouskov *(USSR)*
1984 Jean-Francois Lamour *(France)*

golf game in which a small rubber-cored ball is hit with any of 14 clubs (woods or irons, according to the clubhead) from a platform tee into a series of 18 holes, usually about 275 m/300 yd distant, round a landscaped course. In *medal-play* the object is to take fewer strokes than an opponent, but in *match-play* the result depends on the winner of individual holes. The main fairway has short grass, and the green surrounding the hole is almost manicured, but sand bunkers or water at strategic points provide obstacles to progress, and the ball is also more difficult to extricate from the long bordering grass and shrubs, the 'rough'. A course measures some 5500 m/6000 yd, for which a good player will have a score of under 70 strokes; handicaps match unequal opponents. Golf originated in the 15th century in Scotland, where the Royal and Ancient Club at St Andrews dates from 1754.

British Open first held 1860
1977 Tom Watson *(United States)*
1978 Jack Nicklaus *(United States)*
1979 Severiano Ballesteros *(Spain)*
1980 Tom Watson *(United States)*
1981 Bill Rogers *(United States)*
1982 Tom Watson *(United States)*
1983 Tom Watson *(United States)*
1984 Severiano Ballesteros *(Spain)*
1985 Sandy Lyle *(Great Britain)*
1986 Greg Norman *(Australia)*
United States Open first held 1895
1977 Hubert Green *(United States)*
1978 Andy North *(United States)*
1979 Hale Irwin *(United States)*
1980 Jack Nicklaus *(United States)*
1981 David Graham *(Australia)*
1982 Tom Watson *(United States)*
1983 Larry Nelson *(United States)*
1984 Fuzzy Zoeller *(United States)*
1985 Andy North *(United States)*
1986 Ray Floyd *(United States)*
US Masters first held 1934
1977 Tom Watson *(United States)*
1978 Gary Player *(South Africa)*
1979 Fuzzy Zoeller *(United States)*
1980 Severiano Ballesteros *(Spain)*
1981 Tom Watson *(United States)*

1982 Craig Stadler *(United States)*
1983 Severiano Ballesteros *(Spain)*
1984 Ben Crenshaw *(United States)*
1985 Bernhard Langer *(West Germany)*
1986 Jack Nicklaus *(United States)*
1987 Larry Mize *(United States)*
United States PGA first held 1916
1977 Lanny Wadkins *(United States)*
1978 John Mahaffey *(United States)*
1979 David Graham *(Australia)*
1980 Jack Nicklaus *(United States)*
1981 Larry Nelson *(United States)*
1982 Ray Floyd *(United States)*
1983 Hal Sutton *(United States)*
1984 Lee Trevino *(United States)*
1985 Hubert Green *(United States)*
1986 Bob Tway *(United States)*

horse racing the sport of racing mounted or driven horses:

Flat racing is for thoroughbreds only. It was first popularized by the Stuarts; the Classic races are the Derby, first run 1780, the Oaks 1779 (both at Epsom), St Leger 1776 (at Doncaster), 2000 Guineas 1809, and 1000 Guineas 1814 (both at Newmarket). The Jockey Club (established in 1751) is the governing body. Major races abroad are the French Prix de l'Arc de Triomphe 1920 (at Longchamp), the Australian Melbourne Cup 1861 (at Flemington Park, Victoria), and the US Triple Crown Kentucky Derby 1875 (at Churchill Downs, Louisville), Preakness Stakes 1873 (at Pimlico, Baltimore), Belmont Stakes 1867 (at New York), and Washington DC International 1952 (at Laurel Park, Maryland).

Steeplechasing is a development of foxhunting, of which the *point-to-point* is the amateur version, and *hurdling* a version with only modest obstacles. The outstanding race is the Grand National 1836 (at Aintree, Liverpool) with 30 formidable jumps. The governing body is the National Hunt Committee.

Harness racing is for standard-bred horses pulling a two-wheeled 'sulky' on which the driver sits.

The Derby
horse/jockey

1978 Shirley Heights/Greville Starkey
1979 Troy/Willie Carson
1980 Henbit/Willie Carson
1981 Shergar/Walter Swinburn
1982 Golden Fleece/Pat Eddery
1983 Teenoso/Lester Piggott
1984 Secreto/Christy Roche
1985 Slip Anchor/Steve Cauthen
1986 Shahrastani/Walter Swinburn
1987 Reference Point/Steve Cauthen
The Oaks
horse/jockey
1977 Dunfermline/Willie Carson
1978 Fair Salinia/Greville Starkey
1979 Scintillate/Pat Eddery
1980 Bireme/Willie Carson
1981 Blue Wind/Lester Piggott
1982 Time Charter/Billy Newnes
1983 Sun Princess/Willie Carson
1984 Circus Plume/Lester Piggott
1985 Oh So Sharp/Steve Cauthen
1986 Midway Lady/Ray Cochrane
1000 Guineas
horse/jockey
1978 Enstone Spark/Ernie Johnson
1979 One in a Million/Joe Mercer
1980 Quick As Lightning/Brian Rouse
1981 Fairy Footsteps/Lester Piggott
1982 On The House/John Reid
1983 Ma Biche/Freddy Head
1984 Pebbles/Philip Robinson
1985 Oh So Sharp/Steve Cauthen
1986 Midway Lady/Ray Cochrane
1987 Miesque/Freddy Head
2000 Guineas
horse/jockey
1978 Roland Gardens/Frankie Durr
1979 Tap On Wood/Steve Cauthen
1980 Known Fact/Willie Carson
1981 To-Agori-Mou/Greville Starkey
1982 Zino/Freddy Head
1983 Lomond/Pat Eddery
1984 El Gran Senor/Pat Eddery
1985 Shadeed/Lester Piggott
1986 Dancing Brave/Greville Starkey
1987 Don't Forget Me/Willie Carson
St Leger
horse/jockey

1977 Dunfermline/Willie Carson
1978 Julio Mariner/Eddie Hide
1979 Son of Love/Alain Lequeux
1980 Light Cavalry/Joe Mercer
1981 Cut Above/Joe Mercer
1982 Touching Wood/Paul Cook
1983 Sun Princess/Willie Carson
1984 Commanche Run/Lester Piggott
1985 Oh So Sharp/Steve Cauthen
1986 Moon Madness/Pat Eddery

Grand National
horse/jockey (amateurs are shown as Mr)
1977 Red Rum/Tommy Stack
1978 Lucius/Bob Davies
1979 Rubstic/Maurice Barnes
1980 Ben Nevis/Mr Charles Fenwick
1981 Aldaniti/Bob Champion
1982 Grittar/Mr Dick Saunders
1983 Corbiere/Ben De Haan
1984 Hallo Dandy/Neale Doughty
1985 Last Suspect/Hywel Davies
1986 West Tip/Richard Dunwoody
1987 Maori Venture/Steve Knight

Prix de L'Arc de Triomphe
horse/jockey
1977 Alleged/Lester Piggott
1978 Alleged/Lester Piggott
1979 Three Troikas/Freddy Head
1980 Detriot/Pat Eddery
1981 Gold River/Gary Moore
1982 Akiyda/Yves Saint-Martin
1983 All Along/Walter Swinburn
1984 Sagace/Yves Saint-Martin
1985 Rainbow Quest/Pat Eddery
1986 Dancing Brave/Pat Eddery

Washington DC International
horse/jockey
1977 Johnny D/Steve Cauthen
1978 Mac Diarmida/Jean Cruguet
1979 Bowl Game/Jorge Velasquez
1980 Argument/Lester Piggott
1981 Providential II/Alain Lequeux
1982 April Run/Cash Asmussen
1983 All Along/Walter Swinburn
1984 Seattle Song/Cash Asmussen
1985 Vanlandingham/Don MacBeth
1986 Lieutenant's Lark/Robbie Davis
judo synthesis of the most valuable methods

– judo meaning 'gentle way' – from the many forms of jujitsu, 'the soft art', the traditional Japanese skill of self-defence and offence without weapons, which was originally practised as a secret art by the feudal Samurai. In modern times judo has been adopted throughout the world as a compulsory subject in the armed forces, the police, and in many schools. When it is practised as a sport the two combatants wear special loose-fitting, belted jackets and trousers to facilitate holds, and the falls are broken by a special square mat: when one has established a painful hold that the other cannot break, the latter signifies his surrender by slapping the ground with a free hand. Degrees of proficiency are indicated by the colour of the belt: for novices white; after examination, brown (three degrees); and finally, black (nine degrees).

World Championships first held 1956, now contested biennially
open class
1969 Masatoshi Shinomaki *(Japan)*
1971 Masatoshi Shinomaki *(Japan)*
1973 Kazuhiro Ninomiya *(Japan)*
1975 Haruki Uemura *(Japan)*
1979 Sumio Endo *(Japan)*
1981 Yasuhiro Yamashita *(Japan)*
1983 Angelo Parisi *(France)*
1985 Yoshimi Masaki *(Japan)*
over 95 kg
1969 Shuja Suma *(Japan)*
1971 Wim Ruska *(Holland)*
1973 Chonufuhe Tagaki *(Japan)*
1975 Sumio Endo *(Japan)*
1979 Yasuhiro Yamashita *(Japan)*
1981 Yasuhiro Yamashita *(Japan)*
1983 Yasuhiro Yamashita *(Japan)*
1985 Yong-Chul Cho *(South Korea)*
under 95 kg
1969 Fumio Sasahara *(Japan)*
1971 Fumio Sasahara *(Japan)*
1973 Nobuyaki Sato *(Japan)*
1975 Jean-Luc Rouge *(France)*
1979 Tengiz Khubuluri *(USSR)*
1981 Tenzig Khubuluri *(USSR)*
1983 Valeriy Divisenko *(USSR)*
1985 Hitoshi Sugai *(Japan)*

under 86 kg
1969 Isamau Sonoda *(Japan)*
1971 Shozo Fujii *(Japan)*
1973 Shozo Fujii *(Japan)*
1975 Shozo Fujii *(Japan)*
1979 Detlef Ultsch *(East Germany)*
1981 Bernard Tchoullouyan *(France)*
1983 Deltef Ultsch *(East Germany)*
1985 Peter Seisenbacher *(Austria)*
under 78 kg
1979 Shozo Fujii *(Japan)*
1981 Neil Adams *(Great Britain)*
1983 Nobutoshi Hikage *(Japan)*
1985 Nobutoshi Hikage *(Japan)*
under 70 kg
1969 Hiroshi Minatoya *(Japan)*
1971 Hizashi Tsuzawa *(Japan)*
1973 Kazutoyo Nomura *(Japan)*
1975 Vladimir Nevzorov *(USSR)*
1979 Kyoto Katsuki *(Japan)*
1981 Chon Hak Park *(South Korea)*
1983 Hidetoshi Nakanichi *(Japan)*
1985 Ahn Byeong-Keun *(South Korea)*
under 65 kg
1979 Nikolai Soludkhin *(USSR)*
1981 Katsuhiko Kashiwazaki *(Japan)*
1983 Nikolai Soludkhin *(USSR)*
1985 Yuri Sokolov *(USSR)*
under 60 kg
1969 Yoshio Sonoda *(Japan)*
1971 Takao Kawaguchi *(Japan)*
1973 Yoshiharu Minamo *(Japan)*
1975 Yoshiharu Minamo *(Japan)*
1979 Thierry Ray *(France)*
1981 Yasuhiko Mariwaki *(Japan)*
1983 Khazret Tletseri *(USSR)*
1985 Shinji Hosokawa *(Japan)*

lacrosse Canadian ball game, adopted from the American Indians, and named from a fancied resemblance of the lacrosse stick to a bishop's crozier. Thongs across its curved end form a pocket to carry the small rubber ball, and the pitch is approximately 100 m/110 yd long and a minimum 55 m/60 yd wide in the men's game, which is played ten a side; the women's pitch is larger, and they play 12 a side. The goals are just under 2 m/6 ft square, with loose nets.

188

World Championship first held in 1967 for men, 1969 for women
men
1967 United States
1974 United States
1978 Canada
1982 United States
1986 United States
women
1969 Great Britain
1974 United States
1978 Canada
1982 United States
1986 Australia

motor racing competitive events, beginning with a timed trial from Paris to Rouen in 1894, which enjoy great popularity for spectator excitement and for manufacturers' and drivers' prestige. Great **road races** have included the mountainous Targa Florio (Sicily), and Mille Miglia (Italy). The Le Mans 24–Hour Race 1923 is the foremost proving ground for sports cars. Other famous circuits include Brands Hatch, Brooklands (to 1939) and Silverstone, UK; Nurburgring, Germany; and Indianapolis, USA. In **Grand Prix** motor racing (1906) individual events in numerous different countries, notably the Monaco Grand Prix, count towards the world championship, introduced 1950. For the driver of the production car, **motor rallies**, often time-checked across a continent, are popular, the toughest being the East African Safari 1953 run every Easter. The first six drivers in each race score points. The one with the most points at the end of the season is declared champion.

World Driver's Championship first held 1950
1978 Mario Andretti *(United States)*
1979 Jody Scheckter *(South Africa)*
1980 Alan Jones *(Australia)*
1981 Nelson Piquet *(Brazil)*
1982 Keke Rosberg *(Finland)*
1983 Nelson Piquet *(Brazil)*
1984 Niki Lauda *(Austria)*
1985 Alain Prost *(France)*
1986 Alain Prost *(France)*
Le Mans Grand Prix d'Endurance
1977 Jacky Ickx *(Belgium)*/Jurgen Barth *(West*

(United States)
1978 Didier Pironi *(France)*/Jean-Pierre Jassaud *(France)*
1979 Klaus Ludwig *(West Germany)*/Bill Whittington *(United States)*/Don Whittington *(United States)*
1980 Jean-Pierre Jassuad *(France)*/Jean Rondeau *(France)*
1981 Jacky Ickx *(Belgium)*/Derek Bell *(Great Britain)*
1982 Jacky Ickx *(Belgium)*/Derek Bell *(Great Britain)*
1983 Vern Schuppan *(Austria)*/Al Holbert *(United States)*/Hurley Haywood *(United States)*
1984 Klaus Ludwig *(West Germany)*/Henri Pescarolo *(France)*
1985 Klaus Ludwig *(West Germany)*/'John Winter'*(West Germany)*/Paolo Barilla *(Italy)*
1986 Hans Stuck *(West Germany)*/Derek Bell *(Great Britain)*/Al Holbert *(United States)*
Indianapolis 500 first held 1911
1978 Al Unser *(United States)*
1979 Rick Mears *(United States)*
1980 Johnny Rutherford *(United States)*
1981 Bobby Unser *(United States)*
1982 Gordon Johncock *(United States)*
1983 Tom Sneva *(United States)*
1984 Rick Mears *(United States)*
1985 Danny Sullivan *(United States)*
1986 Bobby Rahal *(United States)*
1987 Al Unser *(United States)*
orienteering sport of pedestrian route-finding invented in Sweden 1918. Competitors start at minute intervals, and have their control cards stamped at points (approximately 0.8 km/0.5 mi apart) marked on a map.
World Championships first held 1966
individual (men/women)
1970 Stig Berge *(Norway)*/Ingrid Hadler *(Norway)*
1972 Aage Hadler *(Norway)*/Sarolta Monspart *(Finland)*
1974 Bernt Frilen *(Sweden)*/Mona Norgaard *(Denmark)*
1976 Egil Johansen *(Norway)*/Liisa Veijalainen *(Finland)*
1978 Egil Johansen *(Norway)*/Anne Berit Eid

(Norway)
1979 Oyvin Thon *(Norway)*/Outi Bergonstrom *(Finland)*
1981 Oyvin Thon *(Norway)*/Annichen Kringstad *(Norway)*
1983 Morten Berglia *(Norway)*/Annichen Kringstad *(Norway)*
1985 Kari Sallinen *(Finland)*/Annichen Kringstad *(Norway)*
relay (men/women)
1970 Norway/Sweden
1972 Sweden/Finland
1974 Sweden/Sweden
1976 Sweden/Sweden
1978 Norway/Finland
1979 Sweden/Finland
1981 Norway/Sweden
1983 Norway/Sweden
1985 Norway/Sweden
rowing propulsion of a boat by oars, either by one rower with two oars (sculling) or by crews (two, four, or eight persons) with one oar each, often with a coxswain (steersman). *Doggett's Coat and Badge* 1715, begun for Thames watermen, and the first English race, still survives; rowing as a sport began with the English Leander Club, 1817, followed by the Castle Garden boat club, USA, 1834. Chief annual races in the UK are the Boat Race; Thames head of the river race; and the events of Henley royal regatta, also a major international event; in the USA the Harvard-Yale boat race is held on the Thames at New London, and the Poughkeepsie regatta is a premier event.
World Championship first held 1962 for men, 1974 for women
men – single sculls
1977 Joachim Dreifke *(East Germany)*
1978 Peter-Michael Kolbe *(West Germany)*
1979 Perrti Karppinen *(Finland)*
1981 Peter-Michael Kolbe *(West Germany)*
1982 Rudiger Reiche *(East Germany)*
1983 Peter-Michael Kolbe *(West Germany)*
1985 Perrti Karppinen *(Finland)*
1986 Peter-Michael Kolbe *(West Germany)*
women – single sculls
1977 Christine Scheiblich *(East Germany)*

189

1978 Christine Scheiblich-Hann *(East Germany)*
1979 Sanda Toma *(Romania)*
1981 Sanda Toma *(Romania)*
1982 Irina Fetisova *(USSR)*
1983 Jutta Hampe *(East Germany)*
1985 Cornelia Linse *(East Germany)*
1986 Jutta Hampe *(East Germany)*
The Boat Race first held 1829, rowed annually between Putney and Mortlake by crews from the Oxford and Cambridge University rowing clubs
1977–85 Oxford
1986 Cambridge
1987 Oxford
wins Cambridge 69 Oxford 63
Doggett's Coat and Badge first held 1715, the oldest continuous sporting trophy still regularly contested
1977 J C Dwan
1978 A McPherson
1979 F K Bearwood
1980 W R Woodward-Fisher
1981 W Hickman
1982 G Anness
1983 P Hickman
1984 S McCarthy
1985 R B Spencer
1986 C Woodward-Fisher

Rugby football originated at Rugby 'public school' in 1823, when a boy ran with the ball for the first time. There are 15 players a side, an oval ball, and the goal is high (above a crossbar). 'Tries' may also be scored, by 'touching down' the ball beyond the goal-line. Its most characteristic feature is the 'scrum-(mage)', a kind of heads-down free-for-all which restarts the game after some infringements of the rules. The Rugby Union was founded in 1871.

Rugby Union
International Championship instituted 1884, it is now a a five-nations tournament involving the four Home Countries, and France
1977 France
1978 Wales
1979 Wales
1980 England

1981 France
1982 Ireland
1983 France and Ireland
1984 Scotland
1985 Ireland
1986 France
1987 France
County Championship inaugurated 1889
1977 Lancashire
1978 East Midlands
1980 Lancashire
1981 Northumberland
1982 Lancashire
1983 Gloucestershire
1984 Gloucestershire
1985 Middlesex
1986 Warwickshire
1987 Yorkshire
John Player Special Cup the English club knockout tournament, first held 1971–72
1977 Gosforth
1978 Gloucester
1979 Leicester
1980 Leicester
1981 Leicester
1982 Gloucester and Moseley
1983 Bristol
1984 Bath
1985 Bath
1986 Bath
1987 Bath
Rugby League the Rugby League was founded in 1895 as the Northern Union, when northern clubs broke away from the Rugby Football Union who refused players 'broken time' payments for loss of earnings when playing Saturdays. Twenty-one clubs from Lancashire and Yorkshire were present at the first meeting at the George Hotel, Huddersfield. The number of players was reduced from 15 (as in Rugby Union) to 13 in 1906. Unlike Rugby Union, the use of the scrum plays a less important role as rule changes over the years have tended to make it a more open and fast-moving game.
Challenge Cup final first held 1897, and at Wembley Stadium since 1929
1978 Leeds
1979 Widnes

1980 Hull Kingston Rovers
1981 Widnes
1982 Hull
1983 Featherstone Rovers
1984 Widnes
1985 Wigan
1986 Castleford
1987 Halifax
Premiership Trophy introduced at the end of the 1974–75 season, it is a knockout competition involving the top eight clubs in the league
1977 St Helens
1978 Bradford Northern
1979 Leeds
1980 Widnes
1881 Hull Kingston Rovers
1982 Hull
1983 Widnes
1984 Hull Kingston Rovers
1985 St Helens
1986 Warrington
1987 Wigan

skating self-propulsion on ice by means of bladed skates, or on other surfaces by skates with four small rollers. Ice-skating became possible as a world sport from the opening of the first artificial ice-rink in London in 1876, and the chief competitive events are *figure skating*, for singles or pairs, which includes both compulsory figures and freestyle combinations to music; *ice dancing*, which is increasingly a choreographed combination of ballet and popular dance movements welded to an artistic whole, exemplified by John Curry, and Jayne Torvill and Christopher Dean; and simple *speed skating*. The modern roller skate was the invention of James L Plympton, who opened the first rink at Newport, Rhode Island, USA, in 1866; events are as for ice-skating.
World Championships first world figure skating championships held 1896
men
1977 Vladimir Kovalyev *(USSR)*
1978 Charles Tickner *(United States)*
1979 Vladimir Kovalyev *(USSR)*
1980 Jan Hoffman *(East Germany)*
1981 Scott Hamilton *(United States)*

1982 Scott Hamilton *(United States)*
1983 Scott Hamilton *(United States)*
1984 Scott Hamilton *(United States)*
1985 Alexsander Fadeev *(USSR)*
1986 Brian Boitano *(United States)*
1987 Brian Orser *(Canada)*
women
1977 Linda Fratianne *(United States)*
1978 Annett Potzsch *(East Germany)*
1979 Linda Fratianne *(United States)*
1980 Annett Potzsch *(East Germany)*
1981 Denise Beillmann *(Switzerland)*
1982 Elaine Zayak *(United States)*
1983 Rosalynn Sumners *(United States)*
1984 Katerina Witt *(East Germany)*
1985 Katerina Witt *(East Germany)*
1986 Debi Thomas *(United States)*
1987 Katerina Witt *(East Germany)*
pairs
1977 Aleksandr Zaitsev and Irina Rodnina *(USSR)*
1978 Aleksandr Zaitsev and Irina Rodnina *(USSR)*
1979 Randy Gardner and Tai Babilonia *(United States)*
1980 Sergei Shakrai and Marina Tcherkasova *(USSR)*
1981 Igor Lisovsky and Irina Vorobyeva *(USSR)*
1982 Tassilo Thierbach and Sabine Baess *(East Germany)*
1983 Oleg Vasiliev and Yelena Valova *(USSR)*
1984 Paul Martini and Barbara Underhill *(Canada)*
1985 Oleg Vasiliev and Yelena Valova *(USSR)*
1986 Sergei Grinkov and Ekaterina Gordeeva *(USSR)*
1987 Sergei Grinkov and Ekaterina Gordeeva *(USSR)*
ice dance
1977 Andrei Minenkov and Irina Moiseyeva *(USSR)*
1978 Gennadi Karponosov and Natalia Linichuk *(USSR)*
1979 Gennadi Karponosov and Natalia Linichuk *(USSR)*
1980 Andras Sallay and Krisztine Regoczy *(Hungary)*

1981 Christopher Dean and Jayne Torvill *(Great Britain)*

1982 Christopher Dean and Jayne Torvill *(Great Britain)*

1983 Christopher Dean and Jayne Torvill *(Great Britain)*

1984 Christopher Dean and Jayne Torvill *(Great Britain)*

1985 Andrei Bukin and Natalia Bestemianova *(USSR)*

1986 Andrei Bukin and Natalia Bestemianova *(USSR)*

1987 Andrei Bukin and Natalia Bestemianova *(USSR)*

skiing self-propulsion on snow by means of elongated runners for the feet, slightly bent upward at the tip, known from c. 3000 BC, but developed for the modern sport only from 1896 when it became possible to manoeuvre more accurately. Events include *downhill* (with speeds up to 80 km/50 mi an hour); *slalom*, in which a series of turns between flags have to be negotiated; *cross-country racing*; and *ski jumping*, when over 150 m/400 ft is achieved from ramps up to 90 m/295 ft high.

Alpine World Cup first held 1967

men – overall

1977 Ingemar Stenmark *(Sweden)*
1978 Ingemar Stenmark *(Sweden)*
1979 Peter Luescher *(Switzerland)*
1980 Andreas Wenzel *(Liechtenstein)*
1981 Phil Mahre *(United States)*
1982 Phil Mahre *(United States)*
1983 Phil Mahre *(United States)*
1984 Pirmin Zurbriggen *(Switzerland)*
1985 Marc Girardelli *(Luxembourg)*
1986 Marc Girardelli *(Luxembourg)*
1987 Pirmin Zurbriggen *(Switzerland)*

women

1977 Lisa-Marie Morerod *(Switzerland)*
1978 Hanni Wenzel *(Liechtenstein)*
1979 Annemarie Moser-Proell *(Austria)*
1980 Hanni Wenzel *(Liechtenstein)*
1981 Marie-Therese Nadig *(Switzerland)*
1982 Erika Hess *(Switzerland)*
1983 Tamara McKinney *(United States)*
1984 Erika Hess *(Switzerland)*
1985 Michela Figini *(Switzerland)*

1986 Maria Walliser *(Switzerland)*
1987 Maria Walliser *(Switzerland)*

snooker derivative (via pool) of billiards, played with 22 balls: 15 reds (value 1 point); the single 'pool' balls, black (value 7 points), pink (6), blue (5), brown (4), green (3), yellow (2), and the white 'cue ball'. The object is to pocket a red ball and a 'pool' ball alternately, each time returning the 'pool' ball (but not the red) to the table until all the reds are pocketed, when the 'pool' balls are then potted in order of numerical value. The maximum possible 'break' (score at one turn) is 147. The advent of television, enabling large audiences to view the game has increased its popularity.

World Professional Championship first held 1927

1978 Ray Reardon *(Wales)*
1979 Terry Griffiths *(Wales)*
1980 Cliff Thorburn *(Canada)*
1981 Steve Davis *(England)*
1982 Alex Higgins *(Northern Ireland)*
1983 Steve Davis *(England)*
1984 Steve Davis *(England)*
1985 Dennis Taylor *(Northern Ireland)*
1986 Joe Johnson *(England)*
1987 Steve Davis (England)

World Amateur Championship instituted 1963

1963 Gary Owen *(England)*
1966 Gary Owen *(England)*
1968 David Taylor *(England)*
1970 Jonathan Barron *(England)*
1972 Ray Edmonds *(England)*
1974 Ray Edmonds *(England)*
1976 Doug Mountjoy *(Wales)*
1978 Cliff Wilson *(Wales)*
1980 Jimmy White *(England)*
1982 Terry Parsons *(Wales)*
1984 O B Agrawal *(India)*
1985 Paul Mifsud *(Malta)*
1986 Paul Mifsud *(Malta)*

speedway the sport of motorcycle racing on a dirt track. The first organized races were in Australia in 1923 and the first track in Britain opened at Droylsden, near Manchester, in 1927. Four riders compete in each heat over four laps. A series of heats make up a match or competition. In Britain there are two leagues, the British League and the National League. World championships exist for individuals, pairs, four-man teams, long-track racing, and ice speedway.

World Championships **first held 1936**
individual
1977 Ivan Mauger *(New Zealand)*
1978 Ole Olsen *(Denmark)*
1979 Ivan Mauger *(New Zealand)*
1980 Mike Lee *(England)*
1981 Bruce Penhall *(United States)*
1982 Bruce Penhall *(United States)*
1983 Egon Muller *(West Germany)*
1984 Erik Gundersen *(Denmark)*
1985 Erik Gundersen *(Denmark)*
1986 Hans Nielsen *(Denmark)*
pairs first held 1970.
1977 Malcolm Simmons and Peter Collins *(England)*
1978 Malcolm Simmons and Gordon Kennett *(England)*
1979 Ole Olsen and Hans Nielsen *(Denmark)*
1980 Dave Jessup and Peter Collins *(England)*
1981 Bruce Penhall and Bobby Schwartz *(United States)*
1982 Dennis Sigalos and Bobby Schwartz *(United States)*
1983 Kenny Carter and Peter Collins *(England)*
1984 Peter Collins and Chris Morton *(England)*
1985 Erik Gundersen and Tommy Knudsen *(Denmark)*
1986 Erik Gundersen and Hans Nielsen *(Denmark)*
team first held 1960
1977 England
1978 Denmark
1979 New Zealand
1980 England
1981 Denmark
1982 United States
1983 Denmark
1984 Denmark
1985 Denmark
1986 Denmark

squash game played in an enclosed court 9.75 m/32 ft long and 6.40m/21 ft wide, usually by two persons, with rackets and a small 'squashy' synthetic rubber ball. The ball must hit the far (front) wall of the court (away from both players) above the 1.83m/6 ft line when served, and on rebounding may be played almost anywhere within the boundary of the court in order to prevent the other player being able to return it. Owing to the small size of the court, it did not become a spectator sport until television popularized it in the 1970s and 1980s.

World Open Championship **first held 1975**
men
1976 Geoff Hunt *(Australia)*
1977 Geoff Hunt *(Australia)*
1979 Geoff Hunt *(Australia)*
1980 Geoff Hunt *(Australia)*
1981 Jahangir Khan *(Pakistan)*
1982 Jahangir Khan *(Pakistan)*
1983 Jahangir Khan *(Pakistan)*
1984 Jahangir Khan *(Pakistan)*
1985 Jahangir Khan *(Pakistan)*
1986 Ross Norman *(New Zealand)*
women
1976 Heather McKay *(Australia)*
1979 Heather McKay *(Australia)*
1981 Rhonda Thorne *(Australia)*
1983 Vicky Cardwell *(Australia)*
1985 Sue Devoy *(New Zealand)*

World Amateur ISRF Championships **first held 1967**
1977 Maqsood Ahmed *(Pakistan)*
1979 Jahangir Khan *(Pakistan)*
1981 Steve Bowditch *(Australia)*
1983 Jahangir Khan *(Pakistan)*
1985 Jahangir Khan *(Pakistan)*

swimming self-propulsion of the body through water. The competition strokes are: *breaststroke* (developed from the 16th century); the *front crawl* (developed by the Australians from a South Sea Island method in the early 20th century, and still the fastest stroke); the *backstroke* (developed in the 1920s, it enables the swimmer to breathe very freely); and the *butterfly* (developed from the breaststroke in the USA in the 1930s, and the second fastest of the strokes). In competition the swimmer enters the water with a 'racing plunge' except in the backstroke when they start in the water, or dive. Diving events are divided into *spring-*

193

board and the **higher firm-board** events. Underwater swimming, developed with the invention of frogman equipment (foot flippers, breathing apparatus, and individual motor propulsion), has techniques of its own. Solo and duet synchronized swimming has become popular in recent years.

World Championships first held 1973
1986 champions
men
50 metres freestyle Tom Jaeger *(United States)*
100 metres freestyle Matt Biondi *(United States)*
200 metres freestyle Michael Gross *(West Germany)*
400 metres freestyle Rainer Henkel *(West Germany)*
1500 metres freestyle Rainer Henkel *(West Germany)*
100 metres backstroke Igor Poliansky *(USSR)*
200 metres backstroke Igor Poliansky *(USSR)*
100 metres breaststroke Victor Davis *(Canada)*
200 metres breaststroke Jozsef Szabo *(Hungary)*
100 metres butterfly Pablo Morales *(United States)*
200 metres butbutterfly Michael Gross *(West Germany)*
200 metres individual medley Tamas Darnyi *(Hungary)*
400 metres individual medley Tamas Darnyi *(Hungary)*
4 × 100 metres freestyle medley United States
4 × 200 metres freestyle medley East Germany
4 × 100 metres medley relay United States
springboard diving Greg Louganis *(United States)*
highboard diving Greg Louganis *(United States)*
women
50 metres freestyle Tamara Costache *(Romania)*
100 metres freestyle Kristin Otto *(East Germany)*
200 metres freestyle Heike Friedrich *(East Germany)*
400 metres freestyle Heike Friedrich *(East Germany)*
800 metres freestyle Astrid Strauss *(East Germany)*
100 metres backstroke Betsy Mitchell *(United States)*
200 metres backstroke Cornelia Sirch *(East Germany)*
100 metres breaststroke Sylvia Gerasch *(East Germany)*
200 metres breaststroke Silke Hoerner *(East Germany)*
100 metres butterfly Kornelia Gresler *(East Germany)*
200 metres butterfly Mary Meagher *(United States)*
200 metres individual medley Kristin Otto *(East Germany)*
400 metres individual medley Kathleen Nord *(East Germany)*
4 × 100 metres freestyle relay East Germany
4 × 200 metres freestyle relay East Germany
4 × 100 metres medley relay East Germany
springboard diving Gao Min *(China)*
highboard diving Chen Lin *(China)*
synchronized swimming
solo Carolyn Waldo *(Canada)*
duet Canada
team Canada

table tennis a development in Britain c. 1880 from real tennis, known until 1926 as (and still informally) 'ping pong'. The two or four players use solid-headed bats and plastic balls on a rectangular table 2.74 m/9 ft by 1.52 m/5 ft, over a net 15.25 cm/6 in high. Points are scored if the opponent makes a fault (fails to return a ball, strikes into the net, and so on), and 21 points make a game, a match normally being two out of three games.

World Championships first held 1926
Swaythling Cup (men's team)
1969 Japan
1971 China
1973 Sweden
1975 China
1977 China
1979 Hungary
1981 China
1983 China
1985 China
1987 China

Corbillon Cup (women's team)
1967 Japan
1969 USSR
1971 Japan
1973 South Korea
1975 China
1977 China
1979 China
1981 China
1983 China
1985 China
1987 China
men's singles
1967 Nobuhiko Hasegawa *(Japan)*
1969 Shigeo Ito *(Japan)*
1971 Stellan Bengtsson *(Sweden)*
1973 Hsi En-Ting *(China)*
1975 Istvan Jonyer *(Hungary)*
1977 Mitsuru Kohno *(Japan)*
1979 Seiji Ono *(Japan)*
1981 Guo Yue-Hua *(China)*
1983 Guo Yue-Hua *(China)*
1985 Jiang Jialiang *(China)*
1987 Jiang Jialiang *(China)*
women's singles
1967 Sachiko Morisawa *(Japan)*
1969 Toshiko Kowada *(Japan)*
1971 Lin Hui-Ching *(China)*
1973 Hu Yu-Lan *(China)*
1975 Pak Yung-Sun *(North Korea)*
1977 Pak Yung-Sun *(North Korea)*
1979 Ke Hsin-Ai *(China)*
1981 Ting Ling *(China)*
1983 Cao Yan-Hua *(China)*
1985 Cao Yan-Hua *(China)*
1987 He Zhili *(China)*

tennis a racket and ball game invented in England in the late 19th century, and referred to as 'lawn tennis' whether played on a grass or composition court; some features (the hitting of a cloth ball over a central net) derive from real tennis, which originated in France in the 12th century, as does the method of scoring. The aim of the two or four players is to strike the ball into the prescribed area of the court, with oval-headed rackets (strung with gut or nylon), in such a way that it cannot be returned. The game is won by those first winning four points (called 15, 30, 40, game), unless both sides reach 40 (deuce) when two consecutive points are needed to win. A set is won by winning six games with a margin of two over opponents, though a tie-break system operates, at six games to each side (or in some cases eight) except in the final set. Major events include the Davis Cup 1900 for international men's competition, and Wightman Cup 1923 for US and UK women's teams, and the annual All England Tennis Club Championships, for international professionals of both sexes at Wimbledon. Women winners of five successive titles are Martina Navratilova 1982–86, Suzanne Lenglen 1919–23; of the men Bjorn Borg has won five successive titles 1976–80 and William Renshaw won six between 1881–86; the youngest male winner was 17-year-old West German Boris Becker, 1985.

Wimbledon Championships first held 1877
men's singles
1977 Bjorn Borg *(Sweden)*
1978 Bjorn Borg *(Sweden)*
1979 Bjorn Borg *(Sweden)*
1980 Bjorn Borg *(Sweden)*
1981 John McEnroe *(United States)*
1982 Jimmy Connors *(United States)*
1983 John McEnroe *(United States)*
1984 John McEnroe *(United States)*
1985 Boris Becker *(West Germany)*
1986 Boris Becker *(West Germany)*
women's singles
1977 Virginia Wade *(Great Britain)*
1978 Martina Navratilova *(Czechoslovakia)*
1979 Martina Navratilova *(Czechoslovakia)*
1980 Evonne Goolagong-Cawley *(Australia)*
1981 Chris Evert-Lloyd *(United States)*
1982 Martina Navratilova *(United States)*
1983 Martina Navratilova *(United States)*
1984 Martina Navratilova *(United States)*
1985 Martina Navratilova *(United States)*
1986 Martina Navratilova *(United States)*
United States Open first held 1881 as the United States Championship, and became the United States Open in 1968
men's singles
1977 Guillermo Vilas *(Argentina)*
1978 Jimmy Connors *(United States)*

1979 John McEnroe *(United States)*
1980 John McEnroe *(United States)*
1981 John McEnroe *(United States)*
1982 Jimmy Connors *(United States)*
1983 Jimmy Connors *(United States)*
1984 John McEnroe *(United States)*
1985 Ivan Lendl *(Czechoslovakia)*
1986 Ivan Lendl *(Czechoslovakia)*
women's singles
1977 Chris Evert *(United States)*
1978 Chris Evert *(United States)*
1979 Tracy Austin *(United States)*
1980 Chris Evert-Lloyd *(United States)*
1981 Tracy Austin *(United States)*
1982 Chris Evert-Lloyd *(United States)*
1983 Martina Navratilova *(United States)*
1984 Martina Navratilova *(United States)*
1985 Hana Mandlikova *(Czechoslovakia)*
1986 Martina Navratilova *(United States)*
Davis Cup
1977 Australia
1978 United States
1979 United States
1980 Czechoslovakia
1981 United States
1982 United States
1983 Australia
1984 Sweden
1985 Sweden
1986 Australia

trampolining originally used as a circus or show business act, trampolining dates to the early part of the 20th century. It developed as a sport in 1936 when the American George Nissen developed a prototype model 'T' trampoline. It is basically gymnastics performed on a sprung canvas sheet which allows the performer to reach great heights before landing again. Marks are gained for carrying out difficult manoeuvres. Synchronized trampolining and tumbling are also popular forms of the sport.

World Championships first held 1964
men
1968 Dave Jacobs *(United States)*
1970 Wayne Miller *(United States)*
1972 Paul Luxon *(Great Britain)*
1974 Richard Tisson *(France)*

1976 Richard Tisson *(France)* and Evgeni Janes *(USSR)*
1978 Evgeni Janes *(USSR)*
1980 Stewart Matthews *(Great Britain)*
1982 Carl Furrer *(Great Britain)*
1984 Leon Pioline *(France)*
1986 Leon Pioline *(France)*
women
1968 Judy Wills *(United States)*
1970 Renee Ransom *(United States)*
1972 Alexandra Nicholson *(United States)*
1974 Alexandra Nicholson *(United States)*
1976 Svetlana Levina *(USSR)*
1978 Tatyana Anisimova *(USSR)*
1980 Ruth Keller *(Switzerland)*
1982 Ruth Keller *(Switzerland)*
1984 Sue Shotton *(Great Britian)*
1986 Tatyana Lushina *(USSR)*

volleyball team game invented in the USA in 1895, played on a court 18 m (59 ft) long by 9 m (29 ft 6 in), divided into two by a net 1 m (3 ft 3 in) deep suspended above the court. The six players of each team rotate in position through the six sub-sections into which each half of the court is divided behind the attack line. The ball, slightly smaller than a basketball, is hit with palm or fist, the aim being to ground it in the opponents' court.

World Championships first held 1949 for men, 1952 for women
men
1968 USSR
1970 East Germany
1972 Japan
1974 Poland
1976 Poland
1978 USSR
1980 USSR
1982 USSR
1984 United States
1986 United States
women
1968 USSR
1970 USSR
1972 USSR
1974 Japan
1976 Japan
1978 Cuba

1980 USSR
1982 China
1984 China
1986 United States

water polo developed in England in 1869, it was originally called 'Soccer-in-Water'. The Swimming Association of Great Britain recognized the game in 1885. The idea is to score goals, as in soccer, at each end of a swimming pool. An inflated ball is passed among the players, who must swim around the pool without the aid of the bottom of the pool. A goal is scored when the ball is thrown past the goalkeeper and into the net.

World Championships first held 1973, they are held during the world swimming championships
1973 Hungary
1975 USSR
1978 Italy
1982 USSR
1986 Yugoslavia

water skiing propulsion across water on a ski, or skis, wider than those used for skiiing on snow, by means of a rope (23 m/75 ft long) attached to a speedboat. The first person known to have 'danced on water' on a wooden plank was Eliseo of Tarentum in the 14th century. Ralph Samuelson (USA) pioneered the sport as it is known today in 1922. The governing body, the United Internationale de Ski Nautique, was founded in 1946. In competitive water skiing, competitions are for overall performances, slalom, tricks, and jumping, in which distances of 200 feet can be reached. The skis vary in design according to the type of event.

World Championships first held 1949
men – overall
1969 Mike Suyderhoud (United States)
1971 George Athans *(Canada)*
1973 George Athans *(Canada)*
1975 Carlos Suarez *(Venezuela)*
1977 Mike Hazelwood *(Great Britain)*
1979 Joel McClintock *(Canada)*
1981 Sammy Duvall *(United States)*
1983 Sammy Duvall *(United States)*
1985 Sammy Duvall *(United States)*

women – overall
1969 Liz Allan *(United States)*
1971 Christy Weir *(United States)*
1973 Lisa StJohn *(United States)*
1975 Liz Allan-Shetter *(United States)*
1977 Cindy Todd *(United States)*
1979 Cindy Todd *(United States)*
1981 Karin Roberge *(United States)*
1983 Ana-Maria Carrasco *(Venezuela)*
1985 Karen Neville *(Australia)*

weightlifting feats of strength by lifting weights were performed at the Ancient Olympics, but the first championships in similar form to those of today were held at the Café Monico, Piccadilly, London in 1891. The International Weightlifting Federation was formed in 1920. The object is to lift the heaviest possible weight above one's head to the satisfaction of the judges. There are two lifts, the *snatch*, and the *clean and jerk*. The aggregate weight lifted at both is taken into consideration. The snatch is when the barbell is lifted from the floor to an outstretched arm position above the head in one continuous movement and the bar must be held in position for two seconds. In the clean and jerk the bar is lifted to the chest in the first movement and then above the head in the second.

World and Olympic Champions the first recognized world championships were in 1898, and weightlifting was included in the Olympics for the first time in 1896. The Olympic champion is automatically that year's world champion.

Weight/1984 Olympic Champions/1986 World Champions
52 kg/Zeng Guoqiang (*China*)/Sevdalim Harinov (*Bulgaria*)
56 kg/Wu Shude (*China*)/Mitko Grablev (*Bulgaria*)
60 kg/Weiqiang Chen (*China*)/Naum Shalamnov (*Bulgaria*)
67.5 kg/Jingyuan Pao (*China*)/Mikhail Petrov (*Bulgaria*)
75 kg/Karl-Heinz Radschinsky/(*West Germany*)/Alexander Varbanov (*Bulgaria*)
82.5 kg/Petre Becheru (*Romania*)/Ansen Zlatev (*Bulgaria*)
90 kg/Nicu Vlad (*Romania*)/Anatoliy Khrapati

197

(*USSR*)

100 kg/Rolf Milser (*West Germany*)/Nicu Vlad (*Romania*)

110 kg/Norberto Oberburger (*Italy*)/Yuriy Zakharovich (*USSR*)

110 kg/Dinko Lukin (*Australia*)/Antonio Krastev (*Bulgaria*)

yachting the sport of racing a small and light vessel on water. Most prominent of English yacht clubs is the Royal Yacht Squadron, established at Cowes in 1812, and the Yacht Racing Association was founded in 1875 to regulate the sport. The Observer Singlehanded Transatlantic Race 1960 is held every four years: the record is held by Yvon Fauconnier (France) 16 days 6 hrs 25 mins, 1984. At the Olympic Games, seven categories exist. They are: *Soling*, *Flying Dutchman*, *Star*, *Finn*, *Tornado*, *470*, and *Windglider* (*Boardsailing*), which was introduced at the 1984 Los Angeles games. The Finn and Windglider are solo events, the Soling Class is for three-man crews, while all other classes are for crews of two.

America's Cup first contested 1870

1903 Reliance
1920 Resolute
1930 Enterprise
1934 Rainbow
1937 Ranger
1958 Columbia
1962 Weatherly
1964 Constellation
1967 Intrepid
1970 Intrepid
1974 Courageous
1977 Courageous
1980 Freedom
1983 Australia II
1987 Stars and Stripes

Admiral's Cup first organized 1957

1971 Great Britain
1973 West Germany
1975 Great Britain
1977 Great Britain
1979 Australia
1981 Great Britain
1983 West Germany
1985 West Germany

Sporting Greats

Adams Neil 1958– . English judo champion. The most successful British international judo competitor of modern times, he won two junior and five senior European titles 1974–85, eight senior national titles, and two Olympic silver medals 1980, 1984. In 1981 he was world champion in the 78 kg class.

Agostini Giacomo 1943– . Italian motor cycle road race rider. He made his reputation during the 1960s and went on to win a record 15 world titles 1966–75. He was 500cc champion seven times in succession 1966–72 and won a record 122 world championship races.

Alexeev Vasily 1942– . Russian weightlifter. Reputedly the strongest man in the world, he was world champion 1970–77, and broke 80 world records, a new record in itself in any sport. He was Olympic super-heavyweight champion 1972 and 1976 and European champion 1970–78. At one time the most decorated man in the Soviet Union, he carried the flag at the opening ceremony for the 1980 Moscow Olympics, but he performed disappointingly in the competition and retired soon afterwards.

Botham Ian Terence 1955– . English all-round cricketer. He made his debut for Somerset 1974 and his first test match opportunity came against Australia in 1977. He has since broken the record for the most wickets in a test career (357 wickets, 96 catches and 4636 runs by the end of the 1986 English season). Generally acknowledged to be a brilliant cricketer, he is a controversial figure and has been disciplined by the Cricket Council. He started playing for Worcestershire in 1987. He has also played Football League soccer for Scunthorpe United.

Bristow Eric 1957– . English darts player, nicknamed 'the Crafty Cockney'. He was world professional champion 1980–81, 1983–86, and has also won World Masters, World Cup, British Open, Nations' Cup and News of the World titles.

Bryant David 1931– . English flat green bowls player, who has won every major honour in the game: three world titles (two singles, one triples), three world indoor titles and a record five Commonwealth Games titles. He is known as a great sportsman who is generous in defeat, and his trademark is a pipe held between his teeth, often unlit.

Caslavska Vera 1943– . Czech gymnast. The first of the great post-war female gymnasts, she won a record 21 Olympic, world, and European titles, beginning with the one she gained on the beam at the 1959 European championship. She ended her international career at the 1968 Olympics where she won four gold medals which she then gave away, one to each of the four leaders of her country, at the time of the Soviet invasion.

Charlton Robert (Bobby) 1937– . English footballer, who played for England and Manchester United. He scored a record 49 goals for England in 106 appearances. He won three League championship medals, one FA Cup and one European Cup Winner's medal. He was Footballer of the Year 1966 and European Player of the Year 1967. On retiring from play, he went into football club management.

Clark Jim 1936–68. Scottish motor racing driver. He was world champion 1963 and 1965, and spent all his Formula One career with Colin Chapman's Lotus team. He won 25 grand prix races during his career, then a record. He was killed at Hockenheim, West Germany, during a Formula Two race.

Coe Sebastian 1956– . English middle distance runner. He was Olympic 1500 metres champion 1980 and 1984. During 1979–81 he broke seven world records at 800, 1000 and 1500 metres and one mile. In the 1980s he has suffered from a series of injuries and illness.

Connolly Maureen 1934–69. American lawn tennis player. Nicknamed 'Little Mo' because she was 5'2" tall, she was the first woman to perform the Grand Slam by winning all four major titles in one year (1953). Three times Wimbledon champion 1952–54, French champion 1953–54, Australian champion 1953 and US champion 1951–53, she was forced to retire in 1954 after a riding accident and later died of cancer.

Davis Steve 1957– . English snooker player. He won his first major professional title in 1980 (Coral UK Championship), and has since won over 30 major events including the world professional title 1981, 1983–84, 1987.

Fraser Dawn 1937– . Australian swimmer. The only person, male or female, to win the same event at three consecutive Olympic Games. She won 100 metres freestyle 1956, 1960, 1964, broke 27 world records and was the first woman to break the one-minute barrier for the 100 metres. She won six Commonwealth Games gold medals 1958, 1962. Controversial at times, she was banned by the Australian swimming authority for ten years, although the ban was lifted after four.

Khan Jahangir 1963– . Pakistani squash player. After losing to Geoff Hunt (Australia) in the final of the 1981 British Open, he did not lose again until Nov 1986 when Ross Norman (New Zealand) beat him in the World Open championship final, breaking his run of five times world champion. He was world amateur champion 1979, 1983, 1985 and British Open champion 1982–86. His father, Roshan Khan, won the British Open in 1956.

Killy Jean-Claude 1943– . French skiier. He won all three gold medals (slalom, giant slalom and downhill) at the 1968 winter Olympics in Grenoble. The first World Cup winner 1967, he retained the title 1968 and also won six world titles.

King Billie Jean 1943– . American tennis player, born Moffitt. She won her first Wimbledon title 1961 (doubles with Karen Hantze), and broke Elizabeth Ryan's record when she won her 20th title in 1979 (doubles with Martina Navratilova). She won the singles title six times, and the singles titles at the other Grand Slam tournaments, the French, Australian and US Opens.

Lewis Carl 1956– . American athlete. At

the 1984 Olympics, he won four gold medals, in the 100 metres, 200 metres, sprint relay and long jump. He won three gold medals at the inaugural world championships in 1983. His sister, Carol Lewis, is also a world class long jumper.

Matthews Sir Stanley 1915– . English footballer. He played soccer for Blackpool, Stoke City and England and was the first footballer to be knighted. He won the FA Cup Winner's medal in 1953 at 38. An outstanding right winger known as the 'wizard of the dribble', he made 701 league and 54 international appearances. The first Footballer of the Year, in 1948, he again won the title in 1963. He was also the first European Player of the Year in 1956.

McBride Willie John 1940– . Irish Rugby Union player. He was capped 63 times by Ireland, and won a record 17 British Lions caps. He went on five Lions tours, 1962, 1966, 1968, 1971 and in 1974 as captain, when they returned from South Africa undefeated.

Merckx Eddie 1945– . Belgian cyclist, known as the 'Cannibal'. Turned professional 1966, and won his first classic, the Milan-San Remo. He won the Tour de France five times 1969–72 and 1974, and wore a record 96 leader's yellow jerseys. He won 54 races in the 1971 season. He was three times world road race champion.

Monti Eugenio 1928– . Italian sportsman, the most successful bobsleigh driver of all time. Between 1957–68 he won a record 11 world titles at two- and four-man bob. In 1968 he won Olympic gold medals in both events. On his retirement that year, he was appointed Italian team manager. He shared many of his successes with Sergio Siorpaes.

Navratilova Martina 1956– . Lawn tennis player. Born in Prague, Czechoslovakia, she was naturalized American 1981. A dominant figure in women's tennis since 1978, she won the Wimbledon singles title seven times including five in succession 1982–86, and has won over US$10 million in prize money. Her total of

43 Grand Slam event titles is second only to Margaret Court's record of 66.

Nicklaus Jack William 1940– . American golfer. Nicknamed 'The Golden Bear', he has won a record 20 major titles: US Amateur 1959, 1961; US Masters 1963, 1965–66, 1972, 1975, 1986; US Open 1962, 1967, 1972, 1980; US PGA 1963, 1971, 1973, 1975, 1980; British Open 1966, 1970, 1978. He was the oldest winner of the Masters in 1986. His son, Jack (Jnr), also plays professional golf.

Sobers Sir Garfield St Aubrun (Gary) 1936– . West Indian all round cricketer, born Barbados. He scored 8032 test runs and took 235 wickets in his career. He holds the record for the highest individual test innings, 365 not out against Pakistan 1957–58. He hit a record six sixes off one over for Nottinghamshire CCC against Glamorgan at Swansea 1968 (the unfortunate bowler was Malcolm Nash). He was knighted 1975.

Spitz Mark Andrew 1950– . American swimmer. At the 1968 Olympics he won two golds, silver and bronze medals and at the 1972 Olympics a record seven gold medals (all in world record-breaking times) making a total of 11 medals. He set 26 world records 1967–72 before turning professional 1972.

Sullivan Jim 1903–77. Welsh Rugby League player. Born in Cardiff, he played Rugby Union for his home town team. He joined Wigan RLFC 1921. Between the wars he established himself as the sport's greatest goalkicker, achieving 2859 goals in his 25–year career. He retired from playing in 1946 but continued as a coach.

Wightman Hazel 1886–1974. American lawn tennis player (born Hotchkiss). She won singles, doubles and mixed doubles at US championships 1909, 1910 and 1911. She donated a silver cup (Wightman Cup) in 1920, to be contested by international teams. Great Britain and the US played for the Cup in 1923 and since then they have been the only two competing nations.

Women in Society

Over the past decade people have begun to realize that the world is often viewed and subsequently analysed through male eyes, and that this ignores the lives of half the world's population. The examination of women's position in society is now considered worthy of serious academic study, and many institutions of higher education run courses which cover this area. Indeed, in a period of financial restraint in educational spending in the UK, Women's Studies has been one of the few areas of growth in recent years in the humanities and social sciences. There is no fixed curriculum in Women's Studies, but it aims to develop alternative perspectives and methodologies grounded in women's own experiences.

This section contains *Biographies* of some notable women, and a *Chronology* of women's rights in the UK. Many of the women included in the biographical section have been referred to as feminists. Some would not have chosen to describe themselves in this way, and might even have been repelled by the label. However, they all recognized women's subordination and, in one sphere or another, sought to end it. Progress is at last being made, but contradictions still exist between the formal equality of the sexes which is now enshrined in the Equal Pay and the Sex Discrimination Acts and the inequalities between the sexes which remain, both in many state policies and in everyday life.

Biographies

Addams Jane 1860–1935. American sociologist and feminist. She founded and led one of the earliest community centres at Hull House, Chicago, in 1889 and was Vice-President of the National American Woman Suffrage Association from 1911 to 1914. In 1915 she led the Women's Peace Party and the first Women's Peace Congress. Her publications include *Newer Ideals of Peace* 1907 and *Twenty Years at Hull House* 1910. She was a co-winner of the Nobel Peace Prize 1931.

Anderson Elizabeth Garrett 1836–1917. First English woman doctor, born Garrett. She qualified in 1865 as a medical practitioner, despite prejudiced opposition, and established a dispensary for women in 1866, which survives as the Elizabeth Garrett Anderson Hospital (diagnostic). She was the sister of Millicent Fawcett and the first (and only) female member of the British Medical Association (1873–92). In 1908 she became mayor of her native Aldeburgh in Suffolk, England's first woman mayor.

Anthony Susan B 1820–1906. American pioneering feminist, who also worked for the anti-slavery and temperance movements. Her campaigns included demands for equality of pay for female teachers, the Married Women's Property Act and women's suffrage. In 1869 with Elizabeth Cady Stanton she founded the National Woman Suffrage Association. From 1868 to 1870 she edited and published a radical women's newspaper *The Revolution* and from 1881 to 1886 she worked on the *History of Woman Suffrage*. She was instrumental in setting up the International Council of Women and founded the International Woman Suffrage Alliance in 1904 in Berlin.

Beauvoir Simone de 1908–86. French socialist, feminist, and author, who taught philosophy at the Sorbonne 1931–43. Her book *The Second Sex* 1949 is a classic text which became a seminal work for many feminists. Her novel of post-war Paris, *Les Mandarins* 1954, has characters resembling Camus, Koestler, and Sartre (she was long associated with the last-named); and she also published autobiographical volumes.

Becker Lydia 1827–90. English botanist and campaigner for women's rights. Born in Manchester, she developed an interest in botany, gave lectures to girls' schools and corresponded with Darwin. Her first publication was *Botany for Novices* 1864. In 1865 she established the Manchester Ladies Literary Society as a forum for women to study scientific subjects. She campaigned for women's suffrage and in 1867 she co-founded and became secretary of the National Society for Women's Suffrage. In April 1868 she was the first woman to speak in public on women's rights when she addressed the British Association Congress with a paper entitled 'Some supposed differences in the minds of men and women in regard to educational necessities'. In 1870 she founded a monthly newsletter *The Women's Suffrage Journal* and edited it over the next 20 years. She organized a women-only demonstration in support of female suffrage in the Free Trade Hall in Manchester, and became secretary of the London Central Committee for Women's Suffrage and eventually a parliamentary candidate.

Behn Aphra 1640–89. English novelist and playwright, the first English woman to earn her living as a writer. Although celebrated in her day, she was often criticized for her sexual explicitness. She was also unusual in often presenting her novels and plays from a woman's point of view. She had the patronage of James I and was employed as a government spy in Holland in 1666. In 1688 her novel *Oronooko* the first attack on slavery in English literature was published. From 1670–1687 fifteen of her plays were produced to great acclaim. Her best play was *The Rover* which attacked forced and mercenary marriages.

Besant Annie 1847–1933. British socialist,

feminist, and activist. Separated from her clerical husband in 1873 because of her free-thinking views, she was associated with the radical atheist Charles Bradlaugh and the Fabians, and became a disciple of the mystic Madame Blavatsky in 1889. She thereafter preached theosophy and, as a supporter of Indian independence, became president of the Hindu National Congress in 1917.

Butler Josephine Elizabeth 1828–1906. British social reformer who agitated for the admission of women to higher education, helped to secure the Married Women's Property Act, and campaigned against Victorian attitudes towards single women and for the improvement of the lot of prostitutes. She carried on a campaign against the Contagious Diseases Acts of 1862–70, which made women in garrison towns liable to compulsory examination for venereal disease. As a result of Butler's campaigns, the acts were repealed in 1883.

Cady Stanton Elizabeth 1815–1902. American feminist who founded and led the first women's movement in the US and who worked for the abolition of slavery. She was the friend and political collaborator of Susan B Anthony, and together they founded the National Woman Suffrage Association in 1869, with Stanton as its first president. Also with Anthony she wrote and compiled the *History of Woman Suffrage* from 1881–86 and organized the International Council of Women in Washington DC. Her publications include: *Degradation of Disenfranchisement* and *Solitude of Self* 1892 both of which had enormous influence, and in 1885 and 1898 she published (in two parts) a feminist critique of the Bible: *The Woman's Bible*.

Davison Emily 1872–1913. English militant suffragette, who died while trying to stop the King's horse at the Derby at Epsom and was trampled by the horse. A teacher with degrees from Oxford and London universities, she joined the Women's Social and Political Union in 1906 and served several prison sentences for militant action such as stone throwing, setting fire to pillar boxes, and bombing Lloyd George's country house. Her coffin was carried through London draped in the colours of the suffragette movement – purple, white, and green – and escorted by 2,000 uniformed suffragettes.

Fawcett Millicent 1847–1929. English suffragette, younger sister of Elizabeth Garrett Anderson. A non-militant, she rejected the violent acts of some of her contemporaries in the suffrage movement. She joined the first Women's Suffrage Committee in 1867 and emerged as the leader of the women's suffrage movement in 1890. She was president of the National Union of Women's Suffrage Societies from 1897-1918. She was also active in property reform and campaigned for the right of married women to own their own property. Her publications include *Political Economy for Beginners* 1870, *Women's Suffrage* 1912 and *Women's Victory and After*.

Firestone Shulamith 1945– . Canadian feminist writer, a founder member of Redstockings (a radical feminist organization) and also the New York Radical Feminists. Her book *The Dialectic of Sex* 1970, had a great influence on the thinking of feminists in the early 1970s. She was also one of the most influential early organizers of the Women's Liberation Movement in the US.

Friedan Betty 1921– . American liberal feminist, influential in the women's movement in the 1970s. Her book *The Feminine Mystique* 1963 was one of the earliest and most influential books for the women's movement both in the USA and in Britain. She founded the National Organization for Women (NOW) in 1966 and was its first president. She also founded the National Women's Political Caucus in 1971, and the first women's bank in 1973, and called the First International Feminist Congress in 1973. She was popularly nicknamed 'the mother of the new feminist movement'. Her later book *The Second Stage* 1981 seems to move towards a position of more freedom of choice for individual women rather than a concern for restrictions imposed upon women generally by society.

Greer Germaine 1939– . Australian feminist who gained overnight fame and notoriety with the publication of *The Female Eunuch* 1970. She became a familiar figure in the British media and as a *Sunday Times* columnist. Later works include *The Obstacle Race* 1979 - a study of contemporary women artists - and *Sex and Destiny: The Politics of Human Fertility* 1984. The most recent book appears to contradict the earlier ideas of sexual freedom which are expressed in *The Female Eunuch*.

Holtby Winifred 1898–1935. British novelist, poet, and journalist. An ardent advocate of women's freedom and racial equality, she is best known for her novel *South Riding* 1936, set in her native Yorkshire. Her other works include an analysis of women's position in contemporary society *Women and a Changing Civilization* 1934.

Kollontai Alexandra 1872–1952. Russian revolutionary, politician, diplomat, and writer. Enraged at the appalling conditions of factory workers in Russia, she devoted herself to improving conditions for the working class and, later, for working women. She studied economics in Zurich from 1898 and in 1905 published *On the Question of Class Struggle*. She was harassed by the police for her views and in 1914 she went into exile in Germany. On her return to Russia she joined the Bolsheviks and toured the US. She was the only female member of the first Bolshevik government as Commissar for Public Welfare. In 1918 she organized the first all-Russian Congress of Working and Peasant Women. A controversial figure in the government, she was sent abroad by Stalin, first as Trade Minister, then as ambassador to Sweden in 1943. She took part in the armistice negotiations ending the Soviet-Finnish War in 1944. She also campaigned for domestic reforms such as acceptance of free love, simplification of divorce laws and collective childcare. Her book *The Love of Worker Bees* 1923 aroused great controversy.

Millett Kate 1934– . American radical feminist lecturer, writer and sculptor, whose book *Sexual Politics* 1970 was a landmark in feminist thinking. She was one of the earliest and most influential theorists of the Women's Movement and was a founding member of the

National Organization of Women (NOW). Later books include *Flying* 1974, *The Prostitution Papers* 1976 and *Sita* 1976.

Mitchell Juliet 1940– . British psychoanalyst and writer. She first came to public notice with an article in New Left Review (1966) entitled *The Longest Revolution*. It was one of the first attempts to combine socialism and feminism using Marxist theory to try to explain the reasons behind women's oppression. Of her more recent publications, *Women's Estate* 1971 and *Psychoanalysis and Feminism* 1974 have had great influence on feminist thinking.

Pankhurst Emmeline 1858–1928. British suffragette, born Goulden. Founder of the Women's Social and Political Union in 1903, she launched in 1906 the militant suffragette campaign, and was several times imprisoned and then released after hunger-strikes. In 1926 she turned her attention to politics and joined the Conservative Party. She became the prospective parliamentary candidate for the Whitechapel district of London. She was the mother of two prominent feminists, *Dame Christabel Pankhurst* (1880–1958), the political leader of the suffragette movement, and *Sylvia Pankhurst* (1882–1960), who suffered nine times under the 'Cat and Mouse Act', was a pacifist in World War I, and a staunch supporter of the Ethiopian cause against Italy.

Perkins Gilman Charlotte 1860–1935. American feminist socialist lecturer, poet, novelist and historian. She described herself as a humanist. *The Yellow Wallpaper* 1892 is a fictional account of her own breakdown. She is best known as the author of *Women and Economics*, which became a feminist classic, proposing the ending of the division between 'men's work' and 'women's work' by abolishing housework. She wrote many books over the period 1900 to 1923 and from 1909 to 1916 wrote and published a magazine *The Forerunner* in which her feminist Utopian novel *Herland* 1915 was serialized. She committed suicide on discovering that she was dying of breast cancer.

Rich Adrienne 1929– . American radical feminist poet and writer. In the 1960s her poetry was closely involved with the student and anti-war movements in the USA but since then she has concerned herself with women's issues. In 1974, when given the National Book Award, she declined to accept it as an individual but with Alice Walker and Audrey Rich accepted it on behalf of all women. In 1976 she published *Of Woman Born*, on motherhood as a personal experience rather than as a institution, and *On Lies, Secrets and Silence*.

Rowbotham Sheila 1943– . British socialist feminist, historian, lecturer and writer. She first taught in schools and then became involved with the Workers Educational Association. An active socialist since the early 1960s, she has contributed to several left-wing journals. Her pamphlet *Women's Liberation and the New Politics* 1970 laid down the fundamental approaches and demands of the emerging British women's movement. Other publications include: *Hidden from History* 1973; *Women's Consciousness, Man's World* 1973 and *Beyond the Fragments* 1979.

Steinem Gloria 1934– . American journalist and liberal feminist who emerged as a leading figure in the American new women's movement in the late 1960s. She was also involved in other radical protest campaigns against racism and the Vietnam War. She co-founded the *Women's Action Alliance* in 1970 and also *Ms* magazine. In 1983 a collection of her best-known articles was published as *Outrageous Acts and Everyday Rebellions*.

Walker Alice 1944– . American poet, novelist, critic, and essay writer. She was active in the civil rights movement in the US in the 1960s and as a black woman has written about the double burden for women of racist and sexist oppression. She is consulting editor of *Ms* magazine and has taught both Women's and Black Studies. She has published three volumes of poetry, two collections of short stories, and three novels; *The Color Purple* 1983 won a Pulitzer Prize and has been made into a film.

Wollstonecraft Mary 1759–97. British feminist whose controversial book *Vindication of the Rights of Women* 1792 demanded equal educational opportunities for women. She joined a group of radical intellectuals called the English Jacobins. She married William Godwin and died in giving birth to a daughter, Mary, who was later to become Mary Shelley, the author of *Frankenstein*.

Woolf Virginia 1882–1941. British novelist, philosopher and critic, born Stephen. Her first novel *The Voyage Out* 1915 explores the tensions experienced by women who want marriage and a career. In *Mrs Dalloway* 1922, she perfected her 'stream of consciousness' technique. Among her later books are *To the Lighthouse* 1927, *Orlando* 1928, and *The Years* 1928, which considers the importance of economic independence for women. With her husband, Leonard Sidney Woolf, she founded the Hogarth Press in 1917. She committed suicide by drowning herself.

1562   Statute of Artificers made it illegal to employ men or women in a trade before they had served seven years' apprenticeship. (It was never strictly enforced for women, as many guilds still allowed members to employ their wives and daughters in workshops.)

1753   Lord Hardwick's Marriage Act brought marriage under state control and created a firmer distinction between the married and unmarried.

1803   Abortion was made illegal.

1836   Marriage Act reform permitted civil weddings and enforced the official registration of births, deaths and marriages.

1839   Custody of Infants Act allowed mothers to have custody of their children under seven years old.

1840s   A series of factory acts limited the working day and occupations of women and children. Bastardy amendment put all the responsibility for the maintenance of an illegitimate child on to its mother.

1857   Marriage and Divorce Act enabled a man to obtain divorce if his wife had committed adultery. (Women were only eligible for divorce if their husband's adultery was combined with incest, sodomy, cruelty, etc.)

1857–82 Married Women's Property Acts allowed them to own possessions of various kinds in their own right for the first time.

1861   Abortion became a criminal offence even if performed as a life saving act or done by the woman herself.

1862–70 Contagious Diseases Acts introduced compulsory examination of suspected prostitutes for venereal disease.

1860s   Fathers could be named and required to pay maintenance for illegitimate children.

1864   Schools Enquiry Commission recommendations led to the establishment of high schools for girls.

1867   Second Reform Act enfranchised the majority of male householders. First women's suffrage committee was formed in Manchester.

1869   Women ratepayers were allowed to vote in municipal (local) elections.

1871   Newham College, Cambridge, was founded for women.

1872   Elizabeth Garrett Anderson Hospital for women opened in London.

1874   London School of Medicine for women was founded.

1878   Judicial separation of married couples became possible. Maintenance orders could be enforced in court.

1880   TUC adopted principle of equal pay for women.

1882   Married Women's Property Act meant that wives were given legal control over their own earned income.

1883   Contagious Diseases Acts were repealed.

1885   Age of consent was raised to 16.

1887	National Union of Women's Suffrage Societies became a nationwide group under Millicent Fawcett.
1903	Women's Social and Political Union was founded by Emmeline and Christabel Pankhurst.
1905–10	Militant campaigns split WSPU. Sylvia Pankhurst formed East London Women's Federation.
1918	Parliament (Qualification of Women) Act gave the vote to women householders over 30.
1923	Wives were given equal rights to sue for divorce on the grounds of adultery.
1925	Guardianship of Infants Act gave women equal rights to the guardianship of their children.
1928	The 'Flapper' Vote: all women over 21 were given the vote.
1937	Matrimonial Causes Act gave new grounds for divorce including desertion for three years and cruelty.
1946	Royal Commission on equal pay was formed.
1944	Butler Education Act introduced free secondary education for all.
1948	Cambridge University allowed women candidates to be awarded degrees.
1960	Legal aid became available for divorce cases.
1967	Abortion Law Reform Act made abortion legal under medical supervision and within certain criteria.
1969	Divorce reform was introduced which reduced the time a petitioner needed to wait before applying for a divorce.
1973	Matrimonial Causes Act provided legislation to enable financial provision to be granted on divorce.
1975	Sex Discrimination and Equal Pay Acts. National and Scottish Women's Aid Federations were formed.
1976	Domestic Violence and Matrimonial Proceedings Act. Sexual Offences (Amendment) Act attempted to limit a man's defence of consent in rape cases.
1977	Employed married women's option to stay partially out of the National Insurance system was phased out. Women qualified for their own pensions.
1980	Social Security Act allowed a married woman to claim Supplementary Benefit and Family Income Supplement if she was the main breadwinner.
1983	Government forced to amend the 1975 Equal Pay Act to conform to EEC directives.
1984	Matrimonial and Family Proceedings Act made it less likely for a woman to be granted maintenance on divorce. It also reduced the number of years a petitioner must wait before applying for a divorce to one year.
1986	Granting of invalid care allowance was successfully challenged in European Court of Justice. Sex Discrimination Act (Amendment) allowed women to retire at the same age as men, and lifted legal restrictions preventing women from working night shifts in manufacturing industries. Firms with less than five employees were no longer exempt from the Act.

The Arts

The earliest art, whether painting or drama, literature or music, probably had magical and religious functions. The development of Western art, however, unlike the art of many other cultures, has been accompanied by a growing body of philosophy and criticism. Aesthetic criteria introduced by the ancient Greeks still influence our perceptions and judgements of art, notably the belief that art should represent or reflect reality, and that it should give pleasure and exaltation.

Two currents of thought run through our ideas about art. In one, derived from Aristotle, art is concerned with *mimesis* ('imitation'), the representation of appearances, and gives pleasure through the accuracy and skill with which it depicts the real world. The other view, derived from Plato, holds that the artist is inspired by the Muses (or by God, the inner impulses, or the collective unconscious) to express that which is beyond appearances – inner feelings, eternal truths, or the essence of the age.

Theorists have answered the question 'what is art?' in a number of different ways, and critics have talked about 'good art' and 'bad art'. The term art has been used at various times to refer to all the processes and products of human skill, imagination, or invention – the art of government, or the art of logic, for example, as well as the art of poetry. For in a broad sense, all art is the opposite of nature: this meaning is embodied in the contrast between 'artificial' – that is, created by people – and 'natural'.

This part of the Pocket Encyclopedia contains sections on the Visual Arts, Architecture, Cinema, Photography, Literature, Theatre, and Music and Dance. Each section focusses on a particular art, but also forms part of an overview of the arts in general. The art of theatre, for example, may combine elements of literature, music, and dance. The work of an individual artist, however outstanding, also needs to be set in the context of his or her society: an artist's theme and style, or mode of depicting, relate both to an inner vision and to the world outside.

Visual Arts

In the visual arts of Western civilizations, painting and sculpture have been the dominant forms for many centuries. This has not always been the case in other cultures. Islamic art, for example, is one of ornament, for under the Muslim religion artists were forbidden to usurp the divine right of creation by portraying living creatures. In some cultures masks, tattoos, pottery, and metalwork have been the main forms of visual art. In the recent past technology has made new art forms possible, such as photography and cinema, and today electronic media have led to entirely new ways of creating and presenting visual images.

This section first gives an overview of the main styles and movements in Western art, in a historical sequence: *Ancient Art* looks at prehistoric art, the art of early civilizations, the art of ancient Egypt, and the art of early Aegean civilizations. Then *Classical Art* looks at the art of ancient Greece and Rome. Next, *Medieval Art* looks at early Christian and Byzantine art, the art of the Dark Ages, and the art of the Middle Ages. This is followed by *The Italian Renaissance*, the art of *The 15th and 16th Centuries* in Northern Europe, England, and Spain, *The 17th Century* in Europe, *The 18th Century* in Europe, *The 19th Century* in Europe, and *The 20th Century*. Finally, *Eastern Art* looks briefly at the arts of Islamic civilizations, of China, of India, and of Japan. Within the historical sections, outstanding individual artists and their works have been selected to represent their period or movement: a table of *Great Artists* provides a biographical summary. Architecture, and the modern arts of Cinema and Photography, are treated in separate sections.

Ancient Art

prehistoric art 25,000–1000 BC. The history of the fine arts, painting and sculpture, begins about 21,000 BC in the Paleolithic, or Old Stone Age. Vivid, lifelike images of animals and humans have been found incised, painted or sculptured on the walls deep inside the caves where our ancestors sheltered, mostly in Spain and in south western France, but also in Portugal, Sicily, and Russia. The images of reindeer, mammoth, horses and bison are most common, varying from very small to almost lifesize. It is thought that they served as part of a 'magic' ritual to ensure a successful hunt. Paintings such as those at the cave of Lascaux in France show great skill in draughtsmanship, with vigorous and sweepingly graceful outlines. Stone Age people also used flint tools to carve small figurines in bone, horn, or stone. The most famous of these is the so-called Venus of Willendorf, a limestone statuette 4.5 in high, found in lower Austria and dating from about 21,000 BC. Her exaggeratedly bulbous form makes clear her magic significance as a fertility figure.

art of early civilizations 14,000–300 BC. Architecture became the new art form when people began to settle in communities as farmers rather than as hunters. They decorated their buildings with sculpture, imposing a sense of pattern and order on them, although Stonehenge in Britain 1800–1400 BC had not achieved this sophistication. In Europe, *Celtic art* ornamented tombs, crosses, metalwork and pottery with stylized animal and plant forms in swirling curvilinear patterns. Pottery had reached Europe from the Near East where it began as early as 5500 BC in Mesopotamia, where sign pictures also grew into cuneiform (wedge-shaped) writing. The Near and Middle East produced many highly developed urban civiliz-

ations, including the *Sumerian* 4000 BC, and the *Persian* 550 BC. In these cultures, sculptures and reliefs of people, gods, and animals decorated palaces, temples, and tombs telling stories or praising their gods and rulers. A fine example is the grand stairway of the *Persian royal palace*, Persepolis, from 518–516 BC. Outstanding examples of precious metalwork, glassware, and pottery also survive, of which there are splendid collections in the British Museum and the Louvre.

Egyptian art 3000–200 BC. The Great Sphinx at Giza 2680–2565 BC, a gigantic human-headed lion carved from an outcropping of natural rock, is the supreme example of Egyptian sculpture. 185 ft long and 63 ft high, it was meant to guard for eternity the god-king's pyramid tomb nearby. Most Egyptian art is funerary, largely consisting of sculptured relief panels painted in bright, lifelike colours covering the walls of tombs and temples. They depend on strong, simple outlines, the main aim being clarity: to picture in their idealized prime the dead, their servants and families, and the objects, animals, foods and activities they enjoyed so that they could be magically transported into the afterworld to be enjoyed forever. Human forms are recomposed almost diagrammatically to show the whole of a person, face and legs in profile, upper torso in front view, hips three-quarters and with the eye magnified. If anything needed further description a hieroglyphic label would be added. Statues, whether of wood or stone, were also generally painted. They retain a strong cubic sense of the block from which they were hewn, with the figures facing straight ahead, the arms in a single unit with the body. The serene vision of eternity found in all Egyptian art is epitomized in the beautiful portrait head of Queen Nefertiti in the Staatlich Museum, Berlin, dating from about 1360 BC.

art of Aegean civilizations 2800–100 BC. The *Minoan* and *Mycenean* civilizations flourished in the area of the Aegean Sea from about 2800 BC. Based on Crete, Minoan society was pleasure-loving and open, and its major monument, the new palace at Knossos 1700 BC, was decorated with cheerful frescoes of scenes from daily life, plants, birds and leaping fish and dolphins. Their pottery was painted in the same fresh, spontaneous style with plant and animal motifs curving to suit the form of the vases. In 1400 they were conquered by the Myceneans from the Peloponnese, whose art reflected its more warlike society. Instead of airy palaces, they constructed fortified citadels such as Mycenae itself, which was entered through the Lion Gate 1330, named for the remarkable monumental sculpture that adorns it. In the nearby Cyclades Islands a unique art form emerged about 2800: the small marble Cycladic figures much admired today, which represent the Great Mother Goddess in such streamlined simplicity that her face is simply an elongated oval with a triangular nose. Many of the ideas and art forms of these early sea-faring civilizations were to be adapted by the Greeks who came from Central Asia between 2000–1000 BC to establish their own splendid culture that was to dominate Western taste and thought for many centuries.

Classical Art

Greek art 1000–27 BC. Greek temples are almost sculptures in themselves, designed not to be entered but to be looked at. The sculptured reliefs which decorated them, such as the Elgin Marbles in the British Museum, which came from the Parthenon in Athens, show perfectly the Greek artistic ideal: the human form at its most beautiful.

The major periods of Greek art can be divided into the Archaic (late 8th century–480 BC), Classical (480–323 BC), and Hellenistic (323 –27 BC). No large-scale painting survives, although colour was very important, and even the white marble sculptures we admire today

were originally brightly painted.

In the **Archaic** period the statues of naked standing men *kouroi* and draped females *korai* show an Egyptian influence in their rigid frontality. By about 500 BC the figure was allowed to relax its weight on to one leg and immediately seemed to come alive. The archaic smile which gave these early figures a certain cheerful sameness vanished in the **Classical** period when expressions assumed a dignified serenity. Further movement was introduced in new poses such as in Myron's bronze *Diskobolus/The Discus Thrower* 460–50 BC, and in the rhythmic Parthenon reliefs of men and horses supervised by Pheidias. Artists were no longer anonymous and among sculptors whose work is known are **Praxiteles**, **Scopas**, **Lysippus**, and **Polykleitos**, whose *Doryphoros/The Spear Carrier* 450–440 BC was of such harmony and poise that it set a standard for beautiful proportions which is still in use today. Praxiteles introduced the female nude into the sculptural repertory with the graceful *Aphrodite of Knidos* c. 350 BC. It was easier to express movement in bronze, hollow-cast by the lost wax method, but few bronze sculptures survive and many are known only through Roman copies in marble. The **Hellenistic** period, when the Greek Empire under Alexander the Great spread to Egypt and beyond Iraq, produced such sculptures as the *Winged Victory of Samothrace* with its dramatic drapery, the expressive *Dying Gaul* and the tortured *Laocoon*, which explored the effects of movement and of deeply-felt emotion.

Vase painting is the one form of Greek painting which has survived the centuries. Good, even great, artists worked as both potters and painters until the 5th century BC and the works they signed were exported throughout the Empire. Made in several standard shapes and sizes, the pottery served as functional containers for wine, water, and oil. The first decoration took the form of simple lines and circles, from which the *Geometric style* emerged near Athens in the 10th century BC. It consisted of precisely drawn patterns, the most characteristic being the key meander. Gradually the bands of decoration multiplied and the human figure, geometrically stylized, was added.

About 700 BC the potters of Corinth invented the *Black Figure* technique in which the unglazed red clay was painted in black with mythological scenes, gods and battles in a narrative frieze. About 530 BC Athenian potters reversed the process and developed the more sophisticated *Red Figure* pottery, which allowed for more detailed and elaborate painting of the figures in red against a black background. This grew increasingly naturalistic, with lively scenes of daily life. The finest examples date from the mid-6th century to mid-5th century BC at Athens. Later painters tried to follow major art trends and represent spatial depth, thus dissipating the unique quality of their fine linear technique.

The ancient Greeks excelled in carving gems and cameos, and in jewellery and metalwork. They also invented the pictorial mosaic and from the 5th century BC onwards floors were paved with coloured pebbles depicting mythological subjects. Later, specially cut cubes of stone and glass called *tesserae* were used, and Greek craftsmen working for the Romans reproduced famous paintings such as that of *Alexander at the Battle of Issus* from Pompeii, giving us some idea of these lost masterpieces.

Roman art 753 BC–410 AD. During the 8th century BC the Etruscans appeared as the first native Italian civilization, north and west of the river Tiber. Their art shows influences of archaic Greece and the Near East. Their coffins (*sarcophagi*), carved with reliefs and topped with portraits of the dead, reclining on one elbow as if at an eternal banquet, were to influence the later Romans and early Christians.

Under Julius Caesar's successor Augustus 27 BC–14 AD the Roman Empire was established. Art and architecture played an important role in unifying the European nations under Roman rule. The Romans greatly admired Greek art and became the first collectors, importing vast quantities of marbles and bronzes, and even Greek craftsmen to make copies. Realistic portrait sculpture was an important original development by the Romans. A cult of heroes began and in public places official statues of generals, rulers and philosophers were erected. The portrait bust developed as a new art form from about 75 BC; these were serious, factual portraits of a rugged race of patriarchs to whose wisdom and authority their subject nations should reasonably submit.

Narrative relief sculpture also flourished in Rome, again linked to the need to commemorate publicly the glorious victories of their heroes. These appeared on monumental altars, triumphal arches and giant columns such as *Trajan's Column* 106–113 AD which records his historic battles like a strip cartoon, winding its way around the column for 656 ft. Strict realism in portraiture gave way to some Greek-style idealization in the propaganda statues of the emperors, befitting their semi-divine status. Gods and allegorical figures feature with Rome's heroes on such narrative relief sculptures as those on Augustus's giant altar to peace, the *Ara Pacis* 13–9 BC.

Very little *Roman painting* has survived, and much of what has is the volcanic eruption of Mount Vesuvius in 79 AD which buried the southern Italian seaside towns of Pompeii and Herculaneum under ash, thus preserving the lively and impressionistic wall paintings which decorated the holiday villas of an art-loving elite. Favourite motifs were illusionistic and still-life. A type of interior decoration known as *Grotesque*, rediscovered in Rome during the Renaissance, combined swirling plant motifs, strange animals and tiny fanciful scenes. Grotesque was much used in later decorative schemes whenever it was fashionable to quote the Classical period.

The art of *mosaic* was universally popular throughout the Roman Empire. It was introduced from Greece and used for floors as well as walls and vaults, in *trompe l'oeil* effects, geometric patterns and scenes from daily life and mythology.

Medieval Art

early Christian and Byzantine art 330–
1453 AD. In 313 the Emperor Constantine was
converted to Christianity and made it one of
the official religions of the Roman state.
Churches were built, and artistic traditions
adapted to the portrayal of the new Christian
saints and symbols. Roman burial chests *(sarcophagi)* were adopted by the Christians and
their imagery of pagan myths gradually
changed into biblical themes.

Byzantine style developed in the East in
Constantinople which in 330 became the headquarters of the Roman Empire. An Eastern
Christian tradition was maintained there until
1453 when Constantinople was conquered by
the Turks. The use of mosaic came to be
associated with both Byzantine art and early
Christian church decoration in the West. As
Ravenna became the Western imperial capital
in the 5th century, the ecclesiastical buildings
there, built in the 5th and 6th centuries, are a
glorious tribute to the art of mosaic, presenting
powerful religious images on walls and vaults
in brilliant, glittering colour. Byzantine art
moved away from the natural portrayal of
people and froze into stylization symbolizing
the divine. Ornament flattened into intricate
lacework patterns. Oriental, highly decorative
and unchanging, the Byzantine style can be
seen in the icons, often thought to be miracle-
working, which have remained for centuries
the main religious art of Greece and Russia.

art of the Dark Ages 252–900 AD. The 500
years between the fall of the Roman Empire
and the establishment of Charlemagne's new
Holy Roman Empire in 800 are known as the
Dark Ages, and its art that of the *Migration
Period*. Through a time of turmoil and invasion, with the northern 'barbarians' overrunning the old Mediterranean civilizations, the
Christian church maintained its stability and
the interchange of artistic traditions fostered
creativity.

The art of the migrant peoples consisted
mainly of portable objects, articles of personal
use or adornment. They excelled in metalwork
and jewellery, often in gold with garnet or
enamel inlays and ornamented with highly
stylized, animal-based interlace patterns. This
type of ornament was translated into manuscript illumination such as the decorated
pages of the *Lindisfarne Gospel* in the British
Museum which dates from the 7th century, or
the 8th-century *Book of Kells* in Trinity College, Dublin. With Charlemagne's Christian
Empire modelled on that of ancient Rome, a
cultural renaissance ensued, drawing its
inspiration from the late Classical artistic traditions of the early Christians. At Charlemagne's
capital, Aachen, the human figure was reintroduced into art and continuous narrative
was rediscovered in the *Tours Bibles* produced
there. They in turn influenced the sculptured
reliefs on the bronze doors at St Michael's
Church, Hildesheim in Germany, dating from
1015, the first doors cast in one piece in the
West since Roman times.

art of the Middle Ages 900–1400 AD.
Under the unifying force of the Latin Church, a
new civilization spread across Europe which
during the 10th century produced a style in art
called *Romanesque*, and in England, *Norman*.
Chiefly evident in relief sculpture surrounding
church portals, on capitals and corbels, it
translated manuscript illuminations into stone,
combining naturalistic elements from the
antique Roman style with the fantastic, poeti-
cal, and pattern-loving Celtic and Germanic
tradition. Imaginary beasts, monsters, saints
and sinners mingle with humour and innocence
in an enchanted world of biblical themes. Fine
examples remain in Burgundy and south west
France, extending down into Spain on the
pilgrimage route to Santiago de Compostela.

Gothic during the late 12th and 13th centuries
European cities began to raise great cathedrals, and the sculptural decoration became
more monumental. The cathedrals of Chartres

and Reims in France had such extensive sculptural programmes that many artists came from far afield to work and learn there. A new interest in the natural world is shown in such examples as the strikingly life-like founder figures of Naumberg Cathedral, East Germany, c. 1245, or in the naturalistic foliage on the capitals at Southwell in Nottinghamshire, England.

With the increased height of the cathedrals, stained glass windows became their new glory. Chartres, where an entire set of stained glass is preserved, awesomely illustrates the magical effect of coloured light seemingly suspended within its dark interior. Both windows and sculpture, by depicting the lives of the saints and texts from the bible, gave the faithful an encyclopedic view of the Christian history of the world.

Art patronage, although still mainly concerned with religious imagery, now burgeoned in the many small courts of Europe and under this influence art became more stylized, delicate and refined. Even the Virgin Mary was portrayed as an elegant young queen. In her most characteristic pose, holding the Christ child in her arms, her weight shifts gracefully on to one hip causing her body to form an S-curve and her drapery to fall into elegant folds. This figure stance, the 'Gothic sway', became a hallmark of the period. Court patronage produced exquisite small ivories, precious goldsmith's work, devotional books illustrated with miniatures, and tapestries which warmed cold castle walls, depicting romantic tales or the joys of springtime.

In Italy, the monumentality of the antique Roman past subdued the spread of northern Gothic ideas. A type of *Gothic Classicism* was developed by the sculptors Nicola and Giovanni **Pisano** (working 1258–1314), whose four great pulpits carved in relief (Siena, Pisa, Pistoia) show the influence of antique sarcophagi but also that of French Gothic in the dramatic expressiveness of their figures.

An innovative group of painters brought the art of *fresco painting*, always important in Italy, to a new height.

Giotto's cycle of the lives of Mary and Christ in the Arena Chapel, Padua c.1300 set a new standard for figural naturalism, seen as proto-Renaissance, and in the Town Hall of Siena Ambrogio **Lorenzetti** illustrated the effects of *Good and Bad Government* (1337) in panoramic townscapes and landscapes.

Panel painting, in jewel-like colours on a gold background, developed from Byzantine models, and the Sienese painter **Duccio**'s *Maestá* for the High Altar of Siena Cathedral (1308–11) achieved a peak of expressive power of line and colour. Simone **Martini** developed this into courtly refinement in both frescoes (for example Assisi, Siena) and panel paintings, and became a major influence on the *International Gothic* style which in the years around 1400 achieved the perfect mix of French courtliness and the Italian command of form, together with a delight in the observed details of nature. A magnificent example of this moment in art can be seen in the miniatures painted for the devotional book, the *Très Riches Heures du Duc de Berry*, by the Flemish **Limbourg** brothers in about 1415.

The Italian Renaissance

Florence the rebirth or 'Renaissance' of Classical art and learning began in Florence in the early 15th century. The self-made men of Florence, merchants and bankers, saw themselves as direct descendants of the great men of ancient Rome and, led by the Medici family, vied with each other in patronage of all the arts, building palaces and churches filled with sculptured and painted monuments to themselves. People, and the delightful world they lived in, were suddenly important.

The most far-reaching innovation of the period, which was one of continual discovery and rediscovery, was the invention of scientific *perspective* by Filippo **Brunelleschi** 1377–1446, the architect who later built the dome of Florence Cathedral. Perspective allowed artists to create an authentic three-dimensional space, correctly sized to the figures within their paintings. Pictorial illusionism was the game and anyone could play. **Masaccio** 1401–28 immediately seized on it for his frescoes in the Brancacci Chapel, Santa Maria del Carmine, in which the apostles look like Roman gods. The sculptor **Donatello** c.1386–1466 used perspective in his relief sculptures. His bronze statues like the youthful *David* 1430–32, the first free-standing nude since antiquity, or his equestrian statue of the mercenary General Gattamelata (Padua, 1443) look back to Classical prototypes but have the alert liveliness of all early Renaissance art. In his later work, such as his wood-carving of the aged Mary Magdalene 1445, he sought dramatic expression through distortion, even ugliness. His only real rival was the goldsmith and bronze sculptor Lorenzo **Ghiberti** 1378–1455, who only gradually adapted his graceful International Gothic style to Renaissance ideals in such works as the gilt-bronze Baptistery doors which Michelangelo called 'The Gates of Paradise'.

Paolo **Uccello**'s 1397–1475 decorative paintings reflect an obsessive interest in mathematical perspective.

Fra Angelico c.1400–55 used sweet colours and a delicately simple style to express his religious feeling. Andrea Del **Castagno**'s style was fiercely linear. The antithesis of his violent suffering figures are **Piero** della Francesca's strangely silent ones. Solidly rounded in pale light, immobile within perfect perspective spaces, they express an enigmatic timelessness. His mastery of geometry, proportion, form and colour is breathtakingly evident in his frescoes of *The Legend of the True Cross* in San Francesco in Arezzo 1452–66.

Many skilful sculptors produced public statues, grandiose tombs, Roman-style portrait busts and innumerable versions of the Madonna and Child. The Florentines enjoyed seeing themselves in religious paintings and they appear in crowd scenes in many magnifi-

cent frescoes in the churches of their city, such as those by Domenico del **Ghirlandaio**. He was the most popular painter in Florence in the latter part of the century, respected for his 'warts and all' honesty which is epitomized in his portrait of *An Old Man with a Child* c.1480 in the Louvre. His contemporaries included **Pollaiuolo**, whose interest centres on the nude in action, **Verrocchio**, famous for the equestrian statue of Bartolomeo Colleoni in Venice 1481–96, and **Botticelli** 1445–1510 whose poetic, gracefully linear paintings of Madonnas and mythological subjects such as *The Birth of Venus* 1482 show the Florentine ideal of female beauty. Almost every art work produced included some reference to antiquity, either in form or content.

Leonardo da Vinci 1452–1519. Through his genius, the art of the early 16th century became the *High Renaissance*, attaining a grandeur that appealed particularly to the popes, who now became the leading art patrons in their attempt to build the 'New Rome'. Leonardo's enquiring scientific mind led him to investigate every aspect of the natural world from anatomy to aerodynamics. His notebooks and drawings remain his finest legacy, but his experiments also revolutionized painting style. Instead of a white background, he used a dark one to allow the overlying colour a more three-dimensional existence. He invented 'aerial perspective' whereby the misty atmosphere (*sfumato*) blurs and changes the colours of the landscape as it dissolves into the distance. His principle of grouping figures within an imaginary pyramid, linked by their gestures and emotions, became a High Renaissance compositional rule. His *Madonna on the Rocks* (Louvre, Paris) exemplifies all these ideas.

Michelangelo Buonarroti 1475–1564. His giant talent dominated the High Renaissance, with no other artist able to escape his influence. He said of his stone carvings, such as the monumental *David* in Florence 1501–4 that he was simply revealing the figure hidden within the block. His massive figure style was translated into paint in the Sistine Chapel frescoes (Vatican, Rome) covering the ceiling with human figures, mostly nude, all grandly Classical, telling the Old Testament story from Genesis to the Deluge 1508–11 and finishing on the altar wall with a titanic *Last Judgement* 1541.

Raphael Santi 1483–1520. He quickly mastered the innovations of Leonardo and Michelangelo and in 1509 was commissioned to fresco the *Stanza della Segnature* in the Vatican, where his classicist *School of Athens* is his masterpiece. Immensely prolific and popular, he combined both sweetness and grandeur in his work.

Mannerism the next major art movement was heralded by Raphael's princial follower, Giulio **Romano**, who exaggerated Raphael's style into an individual one of his own. This flouted the 'rules' of Renaissance order and harmony by striving for idiosyncratic, sometimes alarming, effects. The Florentine **Andrea** del Sarto 1486–1531 and his assistants **Pontormo** and **Rosso** Fiorentino each pursued self-consciously mannered styles, as did Giorgio **Vasari**, who is chiefly remembered for his book *The Lives of the Most Excellent Architects, Painters and Sculptors* 1550 in which he himself coined the term 'Mannerist' and laid down the chronology of the history of art which is still in use today. Mannerism appealed particularly to courtly patrons and it became increasingly effete. The Medici, now Grand Dukes, employed such artists as the sculptor Benvenuto **Cellini**, as famous for his racy autobiography as for the gilt salt cellar he made for the King of France, Agnolo **Bronzino**, whose patrician portraits display a stony hauteur, and **Giovanni** da Bologna whose elegant small bronze statuettes were widely reproduced.

Venice the Venetian Renaissance was slow in coming because of the city's traditional links with the East. Two non-Venetians were influential: **Antonello** da Messina c. 1430–79, who in 1475 brought to Venice the new Flemish technique of oil painting, and Andrea **Mantegna** c. 1431–1506, an archaeologically-minded painter whose figures looked like antique sculptures. Giovanni **Bellini** c. 1430–

1516 specialized in devotional pictures of the Madonna, but his sensitive appreciation of light and colour introduced that sensual Venetian talent which later made **Titian** (Tiziano Vecelli) 1487–1576 the preferred painter of the Emperor Charles V and his son Philip II of Spain. His fellow-painter **Giorgione** died young, leaving only a few mysteriously poetic works. **Veronese** (c. 1528–88) and Jacopo **Tintoretto** 1518–94 worked on a much larger scale, Veronese excelling in sumptuous *trompe l'oeil* interior decorations and Tintoretto in dramatic religious paintings, spectacularly lit and composed with daring foreshortening. His paintings for the Venetian Scuola di San Rocco 1566–88 in their exciting exuberance foreshadow the next major movement, the *Baroque*.

The 15th and 16th Centuries

Northern Europe took its artistic inspiration from Gothic sources, always more precious and less monumental than the Italians, but shared their insatiable interest in realistic portrayals of themselves and their world.

Netherlands one of the first examples of the new *humanism* is in the work of Claus **Sluter** c. 1380–1406. His mourning figures on the tomb of Philip the Bold, Duke of Burgundy, their faces hidden by the hoods of their robes, are poignantly mute but solidly real people.

In Flanders, where the patrons were wealthy merchants, Robert **Campin** 1378–1444 put his *Madonna and Child before a Firescreen* 1420–30 (National Gallery, London) into an ordinary living room and through its open window showed a Flemish town. Mary's halo is replaced by the circular firescreen behind her, an example of disguised symbolism, making the supernatural seem real.

Among Campin's followers, all marvellous

draughtsmen, was Jan **van Eyck** d.1441 whose strength lay in his detailed analysis of the beauty of the world around him. His personal recipe for oil painting, a stunning innovation, makes his colours glow like precious jewels. In his *Arnolfini Wedding* 1434 (National Gallery, London) the bride and groom appear in a domestic interior crammed with disguised symbols, in a kind of pictorial marriage certificate. Flemish realism reached Italy with the Portinari Altarpiece, an *Adoration of the Shepherds* by Hugo van der **Goes** d. 1481. Commissioned by the Medici agent in Bruges, it was sent to Florence where it had a considerable effect on Italian artists. The quietly contemplative portraits of Hans **Memlinc** d. 1481 sum up the achievement of 15th-century Netherlands painters.

Individual styles proliferated in the 16th century. Hieronymous **Bosch** c. 1450–1516 painted nightmare pictures filled with tiny human figures caught in a surrealist demonic world. Pieter **Bruegel** the Elder 1525/30–69 treated biblical subjects as contemporary events, sympathetically viewing a miserable humanity. In his paintings of the seasons 1565 he brilliantly evokes both winter's icy silence and the golden warmth of summer.

Germany the giant among German artists was Albrecht **Dürer** 1471–1528. His intellectual powers put him in line with the great Italian masters and their influence introduced a new solidity of form into his basically Gothic style. Particularly important as a graphic artist, he was widely influential through woodcuts and engravings. Mathias **Grünewald** c. 1460–1528, a tragic visionary, used colour symbolically in the Isenheim Altar in Colmar 1512–15, painted for hospital patients to see his Crucified Christ, covered with festering wounds, sharing their suffering. Lucas **Cranach** the Elder 1473–1538 painted self-conscious courtly nudes, and Albrecht **Altdorfer** c. 1489–1538 painted landscapes in which tiny human figures are dwarfed by nature's immensity.

Spain Philip II did not care for the work of **El Greco** 1541–1614, the painter who really established Spain as an artistic centre. Trained in Venice, and particularly influenced by Tintoretto, he developed his hallucinatory style in Toledo, where his patrons were ecclesiastics and the intelligentsia. In his *Burial of Count Orgaz* 1586 the flame-like figures and unearthly colours typically blend mystic vision and reality.

England Renaissance ideas arrived with the German Hans **Holbein** the Younger 1497–1543, by 1536 court painter to Henry VIII. His piercing portraits of the king and his wives, and his delicate portrait drawings, give a superb pictorial record of the Tudor court. The court of Elizabeth I comes to life for us through the art of the miniature. Nicholas **Hilliard** c. 1547–1619 developed an unparalleled technique, delicate, refined and often lyrically poetic as in his *Young Man Amid Roses* c. 1590, (Victoria and Albert Museum, London).

France Jean **Fouquet** c. 1420–81 painted miniatures as well as altarpieces in which Italian influences take tangible shape. Jean **Clouet** d. 1541 and his son François d. 1572 were court painters to King Francis I. Jean Clouet's portrait of the king splendidly expresses his concern with elegance and decoration, and François' half-nude portrait of Diane de Poitiers, *The Lady in Her Bath*, is a piece of refined eroticism. His style reflects Italian Mannerist ideas as developed by the so-called *School of Fontainebleau* founded by **Rosso** Fiorentino and **Primataccio** who came to decorate the royal hunting lodge in the 1530s. They devised a unique type of stucco decoration combining figures in high relief with decorative swags, cartouches and strapwork. These Mannerist motifs were copied all over northern Europe, where they were called 'Renaissance'.

The 17th Century

Italy in Rome, the Counter Reformation of the Catholic church against Protestantism launched an exciting, emotionally appealing new style, the *Baroque*. The sculptor-architect Gianlorenzo **Bernini** 1598–1680 was its principal exponent, revitalizing Rome with his exuberantly dramatic masterpieces. His *Ecstasy of St Teresa* at Santa Maria della Vittoria is a theatrical set-piece in which supernatural light pours from a hidden window to illuminate the rapturous saint whose body seems to shudder as an angel prepares to pierce her heart with the arrow of divine love.

Large-scale illusionistic fresco painting transformed ceilings into heavens, thronged with flying saints and angels. A spectacular example is **Pietro** da Cortona's colossal *Allegory of Divine Providence* 1629–37 in the Barberini Palace, glorifying the pope and his family. Hundreds of figures are drawn upwards towards God's golden light in which swarm bees, the Barberini family emblem.

Balancing this flamboyant artistic stream were the *Classicists*, who even in religious commissions looked back to the concepts of harmony and order of antiquity. Annibale **Carracci** 1560–1609 in the years around 1600 decorated Cardinal Farnese's gallery of antique sculpture in the Farnese Palace, turning the walls and ceiling into a *trompe l'oeil* classical picture gallery. He also initiated the landscape as a new category of art with his *Flight into Egypt* 1603, which has as its real subject an idealized vision of the classical Roman countryside, harmonious and calm.

Among Annibale's assistants who became famous in their own right were the consistently classicizing **Domenichino** 1581–1641 and Guido **Reni** 1575–1642 who often succumbed to popular taste with emotional paintings of

repentant sinners rolling tearful eyes towards heaven.

The work of Michelangelo Merisi da **Caravaggio** 1573–1619 introduced something totally different and unique, a harsh realism in which ordinary folk with dirty feet appear as saints and apostles lit by a raking spotlight, as if God's piercing eye had picked them out from the surrounding blackness of sin. One of his most striking followers was Georges de **La Tour** 1593–1652, a French artist whose simplified figures assume a spiritual purity, modelled by God's light in the form of a single candle shining in the darkness.

France art was used to establish the splendour of Louis XIV's centralized authority and divine kingship. Although grandiose in the extreme, the decorative schemes, portraits and history paintings produced by the members of the new artists' Academy (formed 1648) were based on Classical rules, rigidly controlled by Charles **Lebrun** 1619–90, who was appointed First Painter to the King in 1662. He was the first director of the Academy and of the Gobelins Manufactory, which employed its members to produce the art, tapestries and furnishings for Louis's new Palace of Versailles.

The two major French artists of the century lived in Rome, escaping the constricting grip of the Academy. **Claude** Lorrain 1600–82 was the first painter to specialize entirely in landscapes, reducing the story-telling elements to small foreground figures. The romantic suggestiveness of the Classical past appealed to him, and he created an enchanting idyllic world, luminous and poetic. The intellectual Nicolas **Poussin** 1594–1665 composed his classical landscapes with mathematical precision, but his people remained important, noble and heroic. Not even his religious works escape the pervasive influence of antiquity. In his *Last Supper* 1647 (Edinburgh) Christ and the disciples lounge on couches as if at a Roman banquet.

Spain as in Rome, art in Spain aimed to excite Counter-Reformation zeal. José **Ribera** 1591–1652 carried a Caravaggesque style to brutal extremes to shock people into identifying with the sufferings inherent in Christian history. Francisco **Zurbarán** 1598–1664 expressed religious feeling in the opposite way, with solemn, silent monks and saints lost in a private world of meditation. Bartolomé Estebán **Murillo** 1617–82 painted sentimental Holy Families and sugar-sweet Madonnas fluently, cheerfully, and with a graceful feather touch and lovely colours.

Diego Rodriguez de Silva **Velazquez** 1599–1660 was the giant of Spanish painting, reflecting many aspects of the 17th-century Spanish world. By 1623 he was court painter to Philip IV in Madrid, where he was influenced by Philip's collection of 16th-century Venetian paintings. The most fascinating of his lifelike portraits of the Spanish court is *Las Meninas/The Ladies-in-Waiting* 1655, a complex group portrait which includes Velazquez himself at his easel, and the king and queen as pale reflections in a mirror.

Netherlands Peter Paul **Rubens** 1577–1640 brought the sensual exuberance of the Italian Baroque to the Netherlands. A many-sided genius, artist, scholar and diplomat, he used his powerful pictorial imagination to create, with an army of assistants, innumerable religious and allegorical paintings for the churches and palaces of Catholic Europe. His largest commission was the cycle of 21 enormous canvases allegorizing the life of Marie de Medici, Queen of France (Louvre, Paris). His sheer delight in life can be seen in his magnificent colours, opulent nudes and expansive landscapes.

Rubens's Grand Baroque style did not suit the Protestant merchants of the new Dutch Republic, who wanted small paintings reflecting their own lives and interests. Among the artists who responded to this demand, the towering genius was **Rembrandt** van Rijn 1606–69, all of whose paintings hint at some inner drama. In his portraits and biblical scenes he saw light as a spiritual mystery which momentarily allows his characters to loom out of the surrounding shadows. His self-portraits (nearly 100 in number) touchingly trace the drama of his own passage through life and even the large group portrait, *The Night Watch* 1642 becomes a suspense story. A master draughtsman and printmaker, over 1,000 drawings survive.

The greatest of the straightforward portraitists was Frans **Hals** 1581/5–1666 whose free brush strokes caught fleeting moments brilliantly in such paintings as the so-called *Laughing Cavalier* 1624.

Genre pictures, scenes of daily life, merrymakers and peasants, often uncouth, comic or satirical, were the speciality of such painters as Jan **Steen** 1626–79 in whose anecdotal scenes of traditional festivals or slovenly households the pleasures of drink, gluttony and wantonness hold sway.

During the 1650s genre painters took a different view of their society. Instead of depicting boisterous low-life, painters like Pieter de **Hooch** 1629–84 chose scenes of domestic virtue, well-ordered households where families live in harmony in quiet sunlit rooms. Jan **Vermeer** 1632–75 was the greatest master of these scenes of peaceful prosperity, arranging domestic interiors as if they were abstract forms and enclosing his characters within an enamelled world of pearly light. *A Young Woman Standing at a Virginal* (National Gallery, London) is a superb example of the small group of paintings he produced, each one a masterpiece.

The Dutch specialities of seascape and landscape changed dramatically during the century, with the emphasis on low horizons and a great expanse of sky. Experts in this were Aelbert **Cuyp** 1620–91 who bathed his views in a golden light, and Jacob van **Ruisdael** 1638/9–1709, who painted in many moods, responding to the shifting patterns of light and shade in nature.

Still-life painting also burgeoned: fruit, flowers, fish, banquets, breakfasts, groaning boards of every kind, in which the artist displayed skill in painting inanimate objects, often with a hidden religious significance.

England Charles I had employed Rubens to paint the ceiling of the Banqueting House in

221

Whitehall 1629–30. Rubens's assistant Anthony **van Dyck** became court painter in 1632 and created magnificent portraits of the aristocracy, cool and elegant in shimmering silks. The German Peter **Lely** succeeded him under the Restoration to depict a society that exudes an air of well-fed decadence. By contrast, the English-born Samuel **Cooper** 1609–72, painter to the Parliamentarians and most famous for his portraits of Oliver Cromwell ('warts and all'), was a miniaturist whose serious, objective portraits raised the status of his art to that of oil painting.

The 18th Century

France the beginning of the 18th century saw the start of a frivolous new style in art, the *Rococo*. Jean-Antoine **Watteau** 1684–1721 devised for his aristocratic patrons the *Fête Gallante*, a type of painting in which amorous couples in poetic landscapes contemplate the transience of life and love.

The more overtly sensual work of François **Boucher** 1703–70, First Painter to Louis XV, included voluptuous scenes of naked gods and goddesses. Painting at the same time, but completely against the mainstream, was Jean-Baptiste-Siméon **Chardin** 1699–1779, whose still-lifes and genre scenes have a masterful dignity. Jean-Honoré **Fragonard** 1732–1806 continued with the Rococo theme under Louis XVI, light-heartedly reflecting the licentiousness of courtly life, but all this changed with the Revolution and in 1789 Neo-Classicism became the dominant style under the Republic. Its artistic dictator, Jacques-Louis **David** 1748–1825 in his *Death of Marat* turned a political murder into a classical tragedy. Later, under Napoleon's Empire, David painted heroic portraits and scenes celebrating its glory.

Italy Antonio **Canova** 1757–1822, the sculptor, also exalted Napoleon and his family in classicizing portraits, and the vogue for this style dominated most English and European sculpture right through the Victorian era. Rococo illusionistic fresco painting in Italy was the special province of Giovanni-Battista **Tiepolo** 1696–1770, a Venetian who decorated palaces and churches there and elsewhere in Europe. His painted ceilings became vast, airy regions whose delicate colour shadings made the sky seem endless.

The *vedutisti* (view-painters) produced souvenir views for the English gentlemen on the Grand Tour to complete their education with a first-hand sight of Renaissance and Classical art. In Venice, Francesco **Guardi** 1712–93 painted atmospheric visions of the floating city, pulsating with life. The views of (Giovanni) Antonio **Canaletto** 1697–1768, though faithfully observed, are static in comparison.

In Rome, Giovanni Battista **Piranesi** 1720–78 produced etchings inspired by his feeling for the poetry of ruins. His most original work, however, was a series which turned the ruins into images of terrifying imaginary prisons, fantasies of architectural madness.

Spain produced one artist of enormous talent and versatility at this time, Francisco de **Goya** y Lucientes 1746–1828, whose work expresses a wide range of feeling and emotion and explores a variety of themes. Court painter to Charles IV and later to Joseph Bonaparte under the French occupation of Spain, his portraits were acutely perceptive, his war scenes savagely dramatic, his religious paintings believable and his strange late fantasies powerfully imaginative. He is often seen as the source of 20th-century art.

England produced a memorable group of fine artists, each expressing the varied interests of the age. Joseph **Wright** of Derby 1734–97, scientifically-minded, painted such scenes as *Experiment with an Air Pump* 1768. George **Stubbs** 1724–1806 specialized in horse paintings, based on painstaking scientific investigation. Sir Joshua **Reynolds** 1723–92, first president of the Royal Academy (founded

1768) wanted to introduce the *European Grand Manner* into English painting with history paintings on exalted themes of heroism, but the demand was for portraits and his were confident but lacking in spontaneity, based more on theory than on inspiration.

Thomas **Gainsborough** 1727–88 was also a popular portraitist, although he would have preferred to paint landscapes and made much of them in the backgrounds of his pictures. William **Hogarth** 1697–1764 is best known through engravings of his satirical series of paintings such as *The Rake's Progress*.

Reacting against the academic theorizing of Reynolds, the poet William **Blake** 1757–1827 illustrated his writings with mystical visions and the imaginative Henry **Fuseli** 1741–1825 plundered the depths of his subconscious for grotesque and fantastic dream images in such paintings as *The Nightmare* 1782.

The 19th Century

The 19th century was the age of industrialization, when the newly powerful middle classes became patrons of art.

France vast historical, religious and mythological pictures were no longer greatly in demand and after the fall of Napoleon in 1814 French artists trained in the *Academic Grand Manner* had to seek new dramatic themes. They looked to the world around them, and Theodore **Géricault** 1791–1824 found his subject in the gruesome sufferings of the survivors of a recent shipwreck which he portrayed in his huge *Raft of the Medusa* 1816 (Louvre, Paris). His desire to express and evoke emotion put Géricault among the *Romantics* whose art sought to speak passionately to the heart, in contrast to the *Classicists* who appealed to the intellect. These two opposing approaches dominated much of the art of the century.

Eugène **Delacroix** 1798–1863 became the best-known Romantic painter. His *Massacre of Chios* 1824 (Louvre) shows Greeks enslaved by wild Turkish horsemen, a contemporary atrocity. Admired as a colourist, he used a technique of divided brushwork – adjacent brush marks of contrasting colour which the eye mixes as it scans – which anticipates the Impressionists. He learned this from seeing Constable's *Hay Wain* when it was exhibited in Paris in 1824.

By contrast, the brushwork is invisible in the enamelled paintings of Jean-Auguste-Dominique **Ingres** 1780–1867, the leading exponent of French Neo-Classicism. Drawing was the foundation of his style, emphasizing line and control at the expense of colour and expression.

Gustave **Courbet** 1819–77, reacting against both Classicists and Romantics, set out to establish a new *Realism*, based solely on direct observation of the things around him. His *Burial at Ornans* 1850 showed ordinary working people gathered round a village grave and shocked the Establishment art world with its 'vulgarity' and 'coarseness'. Another Realist was Honoré **Daumier** 1808–79 whose lithographs of the 1830s dissected Parisian society with a surgeon's scalpel.

Throughout Europe, 19th-century artists found their ideal subject matter in the landscape. In France, Jean-Baptiste-Camille **Corot** 1796–1875 made it acceptable by recomposing his open-air studies into a harmonious, classical whole, although a romantic mood pervades his later misty confections. Theodore **Rousseau** 1812–67 led a group of artists who in 1844 sought refuge from the Industrial Revolution in the woods of Barbizon near Paris. Their close observation of nature produced a new awareness of its changing moods. Jean-François **Millet** 1814–75 also settled at Barbizon but his romantic landscapes, such as *The Angelus* 1857–59 (Louvre), introduce idealized peasants who manage to commune with nature while toiling to wrest from it their daily bread.

Germany a different, more melancholy Romantic sensibility invaded the landscapes of a small group of painters working in Germany.

Seeking to express the mystery of God in nature and people's oneness with it, the evocative paintings of Caspar David **Friedrich** 1774–1840 usually include a small poetic figure contemplating distant mountain peaks or moonlit seashores.

England the two greatest artists of the century were landscapists: Joseph Mallord William **Turner** 1775–1851 and John **Constable** 1776–1837, both finding inspiration in the thriving English watercolour school. Turner was the master painter of English Romanticism. Not concerned with the human figure, it was always through nature itself that he could express human feeling, as in the poignant last voyage of the ship *The Fighting Temeraire* 1839 (Tate Gallery, London). His increasing obsession with light and its deep emotional significance turned his late pictures into misty abstract visions. Reputedly his dying words were 'The sun is God'.

Constable was also fascinated with the effects of light. He made innumerable painted sketches of the changing windy sky and in his *Hay Wain* 1821 used white marks like snowflakes to express the way light gives the landscape its freshness and sparkle. His technique of broken brush strokes gave great vibrancy and life to his colours and portended the developments of Impressionism.

Although primarily interested in romantic literary or biblical themes, the *Pre-Raphaelite* movement led by Dante Gabriel **Rossetti** in the 1840s and 1850s, took a detailed look at nature in their claim to a realistic vision, from which the medievalist designer-artist William **Morris** 1834–96 developed his stylized patterns of leaves and flowers for fabrics and wallpapers.

The opposition to the Pre-Raphaelites was led by two Establishment artists, Frederic, Lord **Leighton** 1830–96 and Sir Lawrence **Alma-Tadema** 1836–1912, whose equally romantic view pretended to Classicism by centring on pseudo genre scenes of daily life in ancient Greece and Rome. This pleased their educated patrons enough to earn knighthoods for them both.

Impressionism in the second half of the century in France took an innovative look at nature. A direct precursor was Edouard **Manet** 1832–83, who carried on Courbet's scientific spirit of realism, making the eye the sole judge of reality. Stylistically, he gave up modelling forms in volume to suggest them by juxtaposed colours and gradations of tones, and like Courbet the subject matter of his pictures was always modern life. His *Déjeuner sur l'herbe/Luncheon on the Grass* (Louvre) updated a Renaissance prototype to 1862.

The Impressionists delighted in depicting real life but the scenes and objects they painted became increasingly less important than the way they were affected by the ever-changing play of light. Evolving in the 1860s, the Impressionist group painted out of doors, capturing the immediacy and freshness of light on rippling water or on moving leaves. To catch these fleeting moments they broke up the forms they painted into fragments of pure colour laid side by side directly on the canvas, rather than mixing them on a palette. The members of the group were Alfred **Sisley** 1839–99, Camille **Pissarro** 1831–1903, Claude **Monet** 1840–1926 whose *Impression, Sunrise* of 1872 gave the movement its name, Pierre-Auguste **Renoir** 1841–1919, and Edgar **Degas** 1834–1917.

By the late 1870s they had each gone on to pursue individual interests, and the acceptance of a common purpose had had its day. Sisley and Pissarro continued painting landscapes, but Renoir was more interested in the female nude and Degas in 'snapshot' studies of dancers and jockeys. Monet remained obsessed with the optical effects of light on colour and carried his original fragmented technique to the final extreme in series of paintings such as those of the façade of Rouen Cathedral 1894 or his famous water lilies, showing the changing colour effects at different times of day. With these variations on a theme the actual subject did not matter at all, and in this he anticipated the abstract art of the 20th century.

Post-Impressionism other artists of the same generation who used the innovations of the Impressionists as a basis for developing their own styles are called the Post-Impressionists. They include Paul **Cézanne** 1839–1906 ,who infused something more permanent into their spontaneous vision by using geometrical shapes to form a solid scaffolding for his pictorial compositions, and Georges **Seurat** 1859–91, who achieved greater structure in his landscapes through the technique of *Pointillism* (also known as *Neo-Impressionism*) which turns the Impressionist's separate brush-strokes into minute points of pure colour. The eye then mixes these for itself. Green grass, for instance, is made up of closely packed points of blue and yellow. In this painstaking method any idea of spontaneity vanishes, and the effect is stable and serene.

Henri de **Toulouse-Lautrec** 1864–1901 portrayed the low-life of Parisian bars and music halls without sentiment or judgement. Like Degas, he recorded contemporary life in informal poses from odd angles and his bold, colourful posters show the influence of Japanese colour prints.

The great Dutch individualist Vincent **van Gogh** 1853–90 longed to give visible form to every emotion and used violent rhythmic brushwork and brilliant unnatural colours to express his inner passions, even in something as simple as a pot of sunflowers. Paul **Gauguin** 1848–1903 also went beyond the Impressionists' notion of reality, seeking a more direct experience of life in the magical rites of so-called primitive peoples in his colourful works from the South Seas.

Symbolism was a movement initiated by poets as a reaction to materialist values, and their 1886 Manifesto sought to re-establish the imagination in art. Their most admired painter was Gustave **Moreau** 1826–98 whose paintings of biblical and mythological subjects contain psychological overtones expressed through exotic settings, strange colours and eerie light. Odilon **Redon** 1840–1916 translated dreams into bizarre and striking visual images.

The Nabis (Hebrew 'prophet') were followers of Gauguin who used simple forms and flat colours as he did for emotional effect, in a new style called *synthetisme*. Among the Nabis, Pierre **Bonnard** 1867–1947 and Edouard **Vuillard** 1868–1940 were less concerned with mystical ideas and found that with contemporary domestic interiors they could develop their interest in sumptuously coloured and patterned surfaces. Their work was dubbed *intimisme*.

sculpture the work of the Parisian Auguste **Rodin** 1840–1917 shows an extraordinary technical facility and a deep understanding of the human form. A romantic realist who infused his forms with passion, such famous sculptures as *The Thinker* and *The Kiss* were originally designed for a never completed giant set of bronze doors, *The Gates of Hell*, a theme taken from Dante's *Divine Comedy*. The Musée Rodin in Paris houses many examples of his work and their preparatory drawings.

The 20th Century

The 20th century has been an age of '-isms' in art. Using their newly-won freedom, artists created such a bewildering variety of art that categorization became necessary. During the century the theory behind a work of art gradually became more important. The Post-Impressionist and Symbolist ideas of delving within the self to express the invisible were developed by Matisse, Picasso, and many other artists. Each successive movement in art shocked the public but, at the same time, many artists were producing individual works quite separate from these movements.

Pablo **Picasso** 1881–1973, the Spanish painter, was the artistic giant of the 20th century. His masterly draughtsmanship, visual intelligence, and immense originality made him the source of many revolutionary changes. His *Les Demoiselles d'Avignon* 1907 was inspired by Cézanne and by African art in its simplified forms and distortions of shape and colour. In addition to producing the first Cubist painting, Picasso was also regarded as a founder of Surrealism, but in the 1930s his work took on a more serious foreboding and anguished aspect, culminating in *Guernica* 1936, where all his expressive innovations are used to show the universal horror felt in the civilized world by Franco's bombing of a Basque town in the Spanish Civil War. He continued to paint into his 80s, having also become an original sculptor and potter. Picasso's overwhelming creativity has impressed his genius and original vision on the world.

Fauvism was a movement which began in France about 1905. The *Fauves* (French 'wild beasts') exaggerated reality, contorted shapes and heightened colours to show they were painting more than what they saw in nature. Henri **Matisse** 1869–1954, the leader of the movement, spent his life working on the basic expressionism of colour and form, greatly influencing 20th-century art and art theory. André **Derain** 1880–1954 developed further Gauguin's style of *cloisonnisme*, using large areas of solid colour. Maurice **de Vlaminck** 1876–1958 exaggerated Van Gogh's heavy outlines, and Georges **Rouault** 1871–1958 used heavy dark colours for his moral themes of sad Messiah-like clowns, prostitutes, and evil lawyers. Although the Fauve movement only lasted until 1908, it was the foundation of French *Expressionism*.

Cubism Together with Georges **Braque** 1882–1963 Picasso developed *Cubism* and introduced such techniques as collage, with cut-up photographs, printed texts, and objects included in the painting. Cubism avoided emotional and narrative expression to depict almost colourless shapes split up into a series of semi-geometric facets overlapping, interlocking and semi-transparent as though seen from different viewpoints. The aim was to show objects as they are known to be rather than as they happen to look at a particular moment. Cubism announced that a work of art exists in its own right rather than as a representation of the real world, and it attracted such artists as

226

Juan Gris, Albert Gleizes, Fernand Leger, Jean Metzinger, and Robert Delauney.

Futurism the Italian poet Filippo **Marinetti** 1876–1944 published the *Futurist Manifesto* in 1909 urging Italian artists to join him in Futurism. They eulogized the modern world and the 'beauty of speed and energy' in their works, trying to capture the dynamism of a speeding motor car or train by combining the shifting geometric planes of Cubism with vibrant colours. Gino Severini painted a topsy-turvy landscape as if seen from the moving window of a *Suburban Train Arriving at Paris* 1915 (Tate Gallery) and Giacomo **Balla** represented the abstract idea of speed by the moving object in such pictures as *Abstract Speed-wake of a Speeding Car* 1919 (Tate Gallery). Umberto **Boccioni**, a sculptor, froze his figures as if they were several frames of a film moving at once.

Vorticism was a similar movement in Britain, led by Percy **Wyndham Lewis** 1884–1957. It uses angular abstract shapes to excite the eye into the sensation of movement.

Expressionism Germany was the scene of two successive Expressionist groups. In 1905 a group of artists in Dresden started *Die Brücke* ('The Bridge'), developing Fauve ideas. Led by Ernst Ludwig **Kirchner** 1880–1938, they sought to charge everything with spiritual significance, using raw colours to express different emotions. The group broke up in 1913. In Munich *Der Blaue Reiter* ('The Blue Rider') group was set up in 1911 by Wassily *Kandinsky* 1866–1944 who painted the first *abstract* or *non-objective* painting. The English artist Roger *Fry* called Kandinsky's work 'pure visual music' when it was shown in London in 1913.

Suprematism Kasimir **Malevich** 1878–1935, working in Russia with Futurist ideas of dynamism and Cubist ideas of expressing more than the physical, juxtaposed simple geometrical shapes of solid colour to describe the supremacy of feeling in creative art, calling it Suprematism. From the first of these works in 1913, each one became simpler until there was only a white square on a black background and finally a white square on a white background, the ultimate in spiritual enlightenment. With the square indiscernable from the background, this is the first work where the idea is more important than the result.

Constructivism was a contemporary movement in Moscow which rejected the past and invented images for the new age. Naum **Gabo** 1890–1977 made scaffolding-like giant heads showing that what is beneath the surface of anything is more important than the surface. He and Vladimir **Tatlin** 1885–1953 described intangible time through three-dimensional progressions of stretched string, forcing the eye to travel along them and so 'through time'. They aimed to create art for the Revolution which, however, rejected them.

De Stijl Piet **Mondrian** 1872–1944, the Dutch painter, like Malevich, tried to express the 'truths of the Universe' through pure aesthetics. Using primary colours, black, white, and mid-grey, he painted parallel horizontal lines which intersected vertical ones. The perfection described by the parallel lines, the right-angle intersections, and the rectangles of pure colour mirrored the ultimate perfection of the universe. In 1917 he headed a group called De Stijl ('The Style') which included Theo **van Doesburg** 1883–1931. They believed in the concept of the 'designer', that all life, work, and leisure should be surrounded by art. Everything functional should be aesthetic as well.

Dada, so called for its infantile associations, was a movement born around 1915 out of the desire to shock, and to question established artistic rules and values. Much of it was impermanent, performance art which lasts only as long as it is performed, or made from the ephemeral waste products of society. In Germany Kurt **Schwitters** 1887–1948 and Max **Ernst** 1891–1976 created collages of disposable rubbish such as bus tickets and advertisements. Marcel **Duchamp** 1887–1968, who produced humorous pastiches of other artists, reduced the creative act to one of choice by putting everyday items like a bicycle wheel mounted on a kitchen stool on display and calling them 'ready-mades'.

Surrealism Dada was short-lived yet many aspects survived into Surrealism. Max Ernst and Jean (Hans) **Arp** 1887–1966, both Dadaists, developed paintings which juxtaposed everyday objects and themes in bizarre, dream-like ways, as did the Italian Giorgio **de Chirico** 1887–1978. The writer André Breton (1896–1966) published the first *Surrealist Manifesto* in 1924, which based itself on Freud's new discovery of the subconscious and the importance of dreams in psychoanalysis. René **Magritte** 1898–1967 painted dream-world scenes filled with Jungian symbolism and humorous couplings of illusion and reality. Salvador **Dali** 1904– used photographic clarity to depict contorted landscapes and figures which seem both familiar and disconcerting.

The 1930s produced some remarkable individual talents, with France becoming less and less the centre of the art world. In Britain Paul **Nash** 1889–1946 and Graham **Sutherland** 1903–80 turned their landscape paintings into mysterious or poetically haunting scenes. Stanley **Spencer** 1891–1959 depicted religious and dream-like scenes under the disguise of everyday life. The Swiss Paul **Klee** 1879–1940 painted humorous semi-abstract pictures to call forth reactions from the subconscious. Marc **Chagall** 1881–1955 also delved into this realm using Russian Jewish images from his youth.

Abstract Expressionism many European artists moved to the USA in the years around World War II. New York became the centre of world art and Abstract Expressionism its first major movement. Influenced by Mondrian and other Europeans who settled there, American artists diverged into two groups: the *Gesture*, or *Action Painters*, and the *Colour Field Painters*. Jackson **Pollock** 1912–56 led the Gesture Painters. By putting his canvas on the floor and swirling paint on it he created a complex web of multicoloured trails which the spectator could retrace with his eyes, thereby reliving the artist's dynamic act of creation. The Colour Field Painter Mark **Rothko** 1903–70 filled large canvases with patches of solid colour, the contemplation of which offered the spectator a transcendental experience.

Pop Art because abstract art was not instantly understandable by all, it was thought to be only for the elite, and a group of younger artists launched Pop Art in 1956. Using popular imagery such as soup tins, comic-strips, or movie-star faces, it was a mischievous, cheerful art called by one of its British initiators, Richard Hamilton, 'low-cost, mass-produced, young and Big Business'. Allen Jones, Peter Blake, and David **Hockney** took part in the movement. In the USA artists including Andy **Warhol** 1930–87 with his repetitive images and Roy **Lichtenstein** 1923– with his re-arranged comic-strips seemed more interested in commenting on the materialistic values inherent in their borrowed imagery.

Op Art used abstraction to create optical illusions, confusing the spectator's eye with coloured lines and dots that apear to jump, blend, and waver. Bridget **Riley** 1931– has made these optical investigations a central part of her work.

three-dimensional art the desire to create movement in art also inspired sculptors like Jean **Tinguely** 1925– whose machine constructions are run by electricity, and Alexander **Calder** 1898–1976 who invented *mobiles*, flat shapes attached in interesting patterns to rods that hang from the ceiling and move gently in the air. Among the sculptors in more traditional materials, Constantin **Brancusi** 1876–1957 created smooth, reflective egg-like shapes suggesting aspects of birth and life; Henry **Moore** 1898–1986 made gradually more abstract and monumental forms by refining the shapes of his *Reclining Woman*; Jacob **Epstein** 1880–1959 emphasized expressive meaning through exaggerated human features and Alberto **Giacometti**'s 1901–66 distinctive stick men were an attempt to describe human mental and spiritual isolation.

contemporary trends there have been several movements since the 1960s, all of which resemble Dada in their antagonistic attitude to artistic ideas of the past.

Super Realism, successor to Pop Art, sought to imitate reality so precisely as to be uncanny, as in the sculptures of Duane Hanson, or paintings of Richard Estes.

Minimalism strove to express a narrow purity of vision through its concern for the physical materials used.

Conceptualism saw the idea as so important that the actual art object was no longer necessary.

Performance Art involved 'events', ephemeral in the extreme.

At the same time, some artists evolved new individual styles. The painter Francis **Bacon** 1910– contorts and mutilates his human figures to express the unpleasant emotions imposed on them by modern life. In the 1980s there was a swing back to figurative art, and the '-isms' gave way to the 'neo-' with such movements as *Neo-Expressionism* and *Neo-Geo(metric)* which acknowledge the art of the past and use freely visual images from the present, by dipping into the worldwide data bank of images created by modern communications. By adapting, combining, and revitalizing our vast store of images, today's artists can express the fragmentation which is characteristic of the present age.

Eastern Art

Islamic art is one of ornament, for under the Muslim religion artists could not usurp the divine right of creation by portraying living creatures. Intricate, interlacing patterns based on geometry, Arabic calligraphy, and stylized plant motifs (including the swirling 'Arabesque') swarm over surfaces, structured by a rigid sense of symmetry. Lustreware pottery, ceramic tiles, and carpets were primary art forms. In Islamic Persia miniature painting illustrating literary or historical scenes, often in a lovingly detailed Paradise Garden setting, flourished during the Safavid period 1502–1736 and after 1526 under the Moghul Empire in India.

Chinese art manifested itself in pottery as early as 4000 BC, and its porcelains, and jade and ivory carvings, are major art forms. Painting was influenced by calligraphy; the ideographic script, which used the same brush, ink, and paper, called for the same dexterity, and produced the same spontaneous impression. Whether as hanging scrolls or handscrolls that unrolled to provide a continuous picture, paintings on silk and paper included calligraphy, often a poem. Traditional subjects were a bamboo branch, sprig of blossom, or snowy mountain landscape. Seen from a bird's-eye view, the space within a landscape was as meaningful as the subject.

Indian art influenced all of South-East Asia. From Buddha's death (48 BC) it centred on the religion which revered him as 'The Incarnation of the Truth'. Images of the Buddha followed a symbolic pattern: his plumpness signified well-being, his posture relaxation, his expression tranquillity. Hinduism also flourished and both Buddhist and Hindu temples were covered in high-relief sculpture. By the 13th century Hinduism became the major religion. The figures of its many exotic deities are rounded and sensuous, their poses based on religious dance movements. Eroticism enters with exuberantly amorous couples symbolizing the unity of the divine. Miniature painting, beginning in the 11th century, reached its peak under the Moghuls (16th–17th centuries).

Japanese art mastered all the Chinese and Buddhist traditions, adding its own interest in surface texture, bright colours, and dramatic compositions. Their most original contribution to world art was the *Ukiyo-e* colour print. Originating in genre paintings of 16th– to 17th century theatre scenes, actors, and bathhouse girls, it developed into the woodcut, and after 1740 the true colour print, while its subject matter expanded beyond the amusements of daily life to include flowers, birds, animals, and landscapes. Their brilliant combination of flat decorative colour and expressive pattern influenced 19th-century European art. Masters included **Utamaro** 1753–1806 and **Hokusai** 1760–1849. Distinguished artists also worked in miniature sculpture, producing tiny carved *netsuke* figures, widely collected in the West.

GREAT ARTISTS

Period	Artist
Classical	Myron 4th century BC Phidias c.500 BC Praxiteles 4th century BC Lysippus 4th century BC
Medieval	Pisano 1245–1314 Giotto c.1266–1337 Lorenzetti 1306?–45 Duccio c.1255/60–c.1318
Italian Renaissance	Masaccio 1401–28 Donatello c.1386–1466 Piero della Francesca 1410/20–92 Botticelli 1445–1510 Leonardo da Vinci 1452–1519 Michelangelo 1475–1564 Raphael 1483–1520
Mannerism	Vasari 1511–74 Bellini c.1430–1516 Mantegna c.1431–1506 Titian 1487–1576
15th and 16th centuries outside Italy	Van Eyck d.1441 Bosch c.1450–1516 Bruegel the Elder 1525/30–69 Dürer 1471–1528 El Greco 1541–1614 Holbein 1497–1543
17th century	Bernini 1598–1680 Carracci 1560–1609 Caravaggio 1573–1619 Claude Lorrain 1600–82 Poussin 1594–1665 Rubens 1577–1640 Rembrandt 1606–69 Steen 1626–79 Vermeer 1632–75 Van Dyck 1599–1641
18th century	Watteau 1684–1721 David 1748–1825 Canova 1757–1822 Tiepolo 1696–1770 Goya 1746–1828 Reynolds 1723–92 Gainsborough 1727–88 Hogarth 1697–1764
19th century	Delacroix 1798–1863 Ingres 1780–1867 Friedrich 1774–1840 Turner 1775–1851 Constable 1776–1837 Monet 1840–1926 Renoir 1841–1919 Cezanne 1839–1906 Van Gogh 1853–90 Rodin 1840–1917
20th century	Picasso 1881–1973 Matisse 1869–1954 Kandinsky 1866–1944 Mondrian 1872–1944 Duchamp 1887–1968 Magritte 1898–1967 Dali 1904– Klee 1879–1940 Pollock 1912–56 Rothko 1903–70 Hockney 1937– Moore 1898–1986 Brancusi 1876–1957 Epstein 1880–1959 Bacon 1910–

Architecture

Architecture is the art of building structures. The term covers the design of any structure for living or working in: houses, churches, temples, palaces, castles; and, as such, the style of building of any particular country at any period of history. Some theorists include under the term architecture only structures designed by a particular architect. Here, however, it includes so-called vernacular architecture: traditional buildings such as the cottages and farms of particular areas that have evolved slowly through the centuries but can claim no particular designer.

This section contains an overview of the *History* of Western architecture with a look at important styles in their historical context; *Biographies* of a selection of people who have made significant contributions to architecture, town planning, and landscape design; and definitions of *Terms* used in architecture.

History

Ancient the earliest buildings were shelter structures, more or less permanent, which began to appear during the Bronze Age: circular bases constructed of dry-stone walling, with thatched roofs. All over Europe, the same societies began to erect megaliths for religious reasons we can only guess at; Stonehenge (c. 2000 BC) is a fairly late example. But it was in the Middle East, between 3000 and 1200 BC, that the first civilization arose, the Babylonian, and with it the first examples of what we should call architecture. Ur was a walled city dominated by a *ziggurat*, a huge structure topped by a temple. The civilization of ancient Egypt provided the *pyramids*, massive monuments of exact symmetry with decorative sculptures and wall painting and the first use of the decorated column and lintel to form colonnades. Examples include Karnak, Akhenaton, Abu Simbel, tombs of the Valley of the Kings, and the temple of Isis at Philea.

Classical with the Greeks, between about the 16th and the 2nd century BC, architecture as an art form really came into being. Their codification and use of the Classical orders – Doric, Ionic and Corinthian – provided a legacy which, refined and modified by the Romans, has influenced all subsequent Western architecture. The great example of Greek architecture is the Parthenon. The Romans were the first to use bricks and cement to produce the vault, arch and dome; they added the Tuscan and Composite orders to the Greek system. The emphasis in Roman architecture was on impressive public buildings (Colosseum), basilicas (Pantheon), triumphal arches and monuments (Trajan's Column) and aqueducts (Nîmes).

Byzantine in Byzantium a wholly Christian architecture was developing, from the 4th century onwards, with churches based on the Greek cross plan (Hagia Sophia, Istanbul; St Mark's, Venice); they used formalized, symbolic painted and mosaic decoration.

Romanesque the architecture of the Christianity of the West developed first as Romanesque, 8th to 12th century, marked by rounded arches, solid volumes and emphasis on perpendicular elements. In England, this was the period of Norman architecture (Durham Cathedral). Experiments in vaulting led towards the Gothic.

Gothic this architectural style developed in France in the 12th century and lasted until the 16th. It is marked out by the use of the rib vault, pointed arch and flying buttress, particularly in religious buildings; there is an emphasis on the vertical, with galleries and arcades replacing internal walls. It is divided into *Early Gothic* (Sens Cathedral), *High Gothic* (Chartres Cathedral) and *Late Gothic* or *Flamboyant*. In England the corresponding divisions are *Early English* (Salisbury Cathedral), *Decorated* (Wells Cathedral) and *Perpendicular* (King's College Chapel, Cambridge).

Islamic in Spain, from the 7th century onwards, the Moorish occupation was also having a profound influence on Christian architecture, introducing the dome and the pointed arch (later incorporated into Gothic). Examples of influential Islamic buildings are the Great Mosque, *Cordova*, and the Alhambra, Granada.

Renaissance the 15th and 16th centuries saw the rebirth of Classical architecture in the *Neo-Classical movement*, largely through the work of Vitruvius. Major Italian architects were Alberti, Brunelleschi, Bramante, Michelangelo, Raphael and Palladio; in England *Palladianism* was represented by Inigo Jones. A 16th-century offshoot was *Mannerism*, in which motifs were used in deliberate opposition to their original significance, that is, for their manner rather than their meaning.

Baroque the architecture of the 17th and 18th centuries was exuberantly extravagant, and seen at its best in large-scale public buildings in the work of Bernini, Borromini,

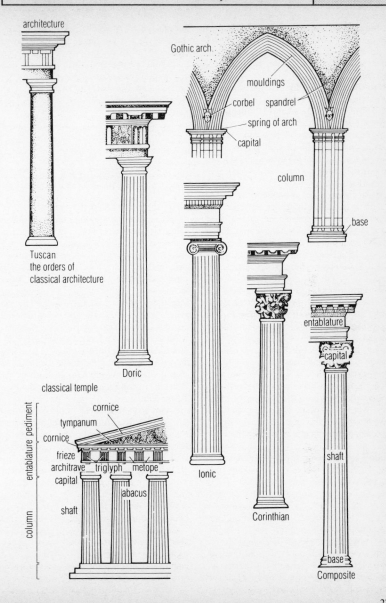

architecture

Gothic arch

mouldings

corbel   spandrel

spring of arch

capital

column

base

Tuscan
the orders of
classical architecture

Doric

entablature

capital

shaft

base
Composite

Ionic

Corinthian

classical temple

pediment
entablature
cornice
tympanum
cornice
frieze
architrave   triglyph   metope
capital
abacus
column
shaft

Vanbrugh, Hawksmoor, and Wren. Its last stage is the *Rococo*, characterized by still greater extravagance, a new lightness in style, and the use of naturalistic motifs such as shells, flowers and trees.

Neo-Classical the 18th and 19th centuries saw a return to classical principles, for example in the large-scale rebuilding of London and Paris by Adam, Nash and Haussman.

Neo-Gothic the later 19th century saw a renewed enthusiasm for the Gothic style in the *Gothic revival*, particularly evident in churches and public buildings (*Houses of Parliament* by Sir Charles Barry).

Art Nouveau a new movement surfaced at the end of the 19th century, characterized by sinuous, flowing shapes, informal room plans and attention not only to architectural design but to every last detail of the interior. The style is best seen in England in the work of Charles Rennie Mackintosh (Glasgow Art School) and in Spain by that of Antonio Gaudi.

Modernism an increasing emphasis on rationalism and rejection of ornament led to Modernism, also known as *Functionalism* or *International Style*, which sought to exclude everything that did not have a purpose, and used the latest technological advances in glass, steel and concrete to full advantage. Major architects include Frank Lloyd Wright, Mies van der Rohe, Le Corbusier, and Alvar Aalto.

town planning with the planning of whole new cities such as in the 1950s Le Corbusier's Chandigarh in India and Brasilia in Brazil, town planning emerged as a discipline in its own right.

neo-vernacular by the 1970s a reversion from the modern movement's box-like structure and synthetic materials began to be felt in a renewed enthusiasm for *vernacular* architecture (traditional local styles), to be seen in the work of, for instance, the British firm Darbourne and Darke.

Post-Modernism in the 1980s a post-modernist movement has emerged, split into two camps: *high tech*, represented in Britain by architects such as Norman Foster, Richard Rogers and James Stirling (Hong Kong and

Shanghai Bank, Lloyd's, Staatsgalerie Stuttgart respectively), and architects using elements from the architecture of previous times, whether consciously obeying the tenets of the Classical orders – *Neo-Classicism* yet again – like Quinlan Terry, or using such elements at whim, like Michael Graves.

Biographies

Aalto Alvar 1898–1976. Finnish architect and designer. One of Finland's first modernists, he evolved an architectural style entirely his own, characterized by asymmetry, curved walls and contrast of natural materials. His work included the Hall of Residence, Massachusetts Institute of Technology, Cambridge, Massachusetts 1947–49; Finlandia Hall, Helsinki 1972. He also invented bent plywood furniture in 1932.

Abercrombie Sir Leslie Patrick 1879–1957. Pioneer of British town planning. He is best known for his work of replanning British cities after damage in World War II (such as the Greater London Plan, 1944) and for the New Towns policy.

Adam Robert 1728–92. Scottish architect and interior decorator, leader of the British Neo-Classical revival. In the interiors of Harewood House, Luton Hoo, Syon House, Osterley Park and others, he employed delicate stucco decoration with Neo-Classical motifs. With his brother, *James Adam* (1732–94), also an architect, he speculatively developed the Adelphi near Charing Cross, London, largely rebuilt in 1936.

Alberti Leon Battista 1404–72. Italian Renaissance architect and theorist, noted for his recognition of the principles of Classical architecture and their modification for Renaissance practice in *On Architecture* 1452/1485.

Barry Sir Charles 1795–1860. British architect of the Neo-Gothic Houses of Parliament at Westminster 1840–60.

Borromini Francesco 1599–1667. Italian Baroque architect. He worked under Bernini, later his rival, on St Peter's, Rome, and created the oval-shaped San Carlo alle Quatro Fontane, Rome.

Bramante Donato c. 1444–1514. Italian Renaissance architect and artist. Inspired by Classical designs, he was employed by Pope Julius II in rebuilding part of the Vatican and St Peter's.

Breuer Marcel 1902– . Hungarian-born architect and designer, who studied and taught at the Bauhaus. He is best known for his tubular steel chair, 1925, the first of its kind. He moved to England, then to the USA, where he was in partnership with Gropius 1937–40. His buildings show an affinity with natural materials; best known among them is the Bijenkorf, Rotterdam (with Elzas) 1953.

Brown Lancelot 1716–83. English gardener and architect, known as 'Capability Brown' because he said sites had 'capability'; his works include Blenheim Palace, Oxfordshire, with mounds, curved paths, and lakes, Highclere Hampshire; and Bowood Wiltshire.

Brunel Isambard Kingdom 1806–1959. British engineer and inventor (son of Sir Marc Brunel), who made major contributions in ship-building and bridge-construction. His work includes the Clifton Suspension Bridge over the river Severn at Bristol, and the Saltash Bridge over the river Tamar near Plymouth, and the ships *Great Western* 1838, the *Great Britain* 1845 and the *Great Eastern* 1858.

Brunelleschi Filippo 1377–1446. Italian Renaissance architect. One of the earliest and greatest Renaissance architects, a pioneer in the scientific use of perspective. He was responsible for the construction of the dome of Florence Cathedral (completed 1438), a feat deemed impossible by many of his comtemporaries.

Burlington Richard Boyle, 3rd Earl of, 1694–1753. British architect and architectural patron; one of the premier exponents of Palladianism in Britain. His buildings – best known

among them is Chiswick House in London 1725–29 – are characterized by absolute adherence to the Classical rules and are consequently somewhat dry and fastidious.

Casson Sir Hugh 1910– . British architect, director of architecture for the Festival of Britain 1948–51 and president of the Royal Academy of Arts from 1976.

Chambers Sir William 1726–96. British architect, popularizer of Chinese influence (Kew Gardens pagoda) and designer of Somerset House, London.

Cockerell Charles 1788–1863. British architect who built mainly in a Neo-Classical style derived from antiquity and from Wren. His best known surviving buildings are the Ashmolean Museum and Taylorian Institute in Oxford 1841–45.

Foster Norman 1935– . British architect of the high-tech school. His best known buildings are the Willis Faber office, Ipswich 1975, the Sainsbury Centre for the Visual Arts, Norwich 1978, and the Hong Kong and Shanghai Bank, Hong Kong 1986.

Fuller Richard Buckminster 1895–1983. American architect, inventor in 1947 of the lightweight geodesic dome, a half-sphere of triangular components independent of any buttress or vault.

Gaudí Antonio 1852–1926. Spanish architect, noted for his flamboyant style. He was influenced by Moorish and medieval architecture. His Church of the Holy Family, Barcelona, begun 1883, was still under construction when he died.

Geddes Sir Patrick 1854–1932. A pioneering British town planner, who established the current theory of town planning, in particular the importance of surveys and research work. His major work is *City Development* 1904.

Gibbs James 1682–1754. English Neo-Classical architect whose works include St Martin's-in-the-Fields, London 1722–26, Radcliffe Camera, Oxford 1737–49.

Gropius Walter Adolf 1883–1969. German-born American architect, founder-director of the Bauhaus school in Weimar 1919–28, and an advocate of team architecture and artistic standards in industrial production. From 1937 he lived in the USA, becoming professor of architecture at Harvard and designing the Harvard Graduate Centre 1949–50.

Haussmann Georges Eugène, Baron Haussmann 1809–91. French administrator, who replanned medieval Paris 1853–70, with wide boulevards and parks.

Hawksmoor Nicholas 1661–1736. English architect, assistant to Wren in London churches and St Paul's; joint architect with Vanbrugh of Castle Howard and Blenheim Palace. The original west towers of Westminster Abbey, long attributed to Wren, are his.

Howard Sir Ebenezer 1850–1928. British planner and founder of the ideal of the Garden City. His major work is *Tomorrow* 1898 (republished as *Garden Cities of Tomorrow* in 1902).

Jekyll Gertrude 1843–1932. British landscape gardener, who collaborated with Edwin Lutyens. She used natural construction materials, was sensitive to colour, as shown in her 'grey garden' of silver-leaved plants, and abandoned Victorian 'bedding-out' to draw on the tradition of the cottage garden.

Jencks Charles 1939– . American architectural theorist and furniture designer. He coined the term 'post-modern architecture' and wrote the influential book *The Language of Post-Modern Architecture*.

Johnson Philip Cortelyou 1906– . American architect, who invented the term international style. He began designing in the style of Mies van der Rohe (house at New Canaan, 1949) but became one of the early, and spectacular, exponents of Post-Modernism. His best known building is the giant AT&T building in New York, a pink skyscraper with a Chippendale cabinet top 1978.

Jones Inigo 1573–c. 1652. The first true English Renaissance architect, influenced by Palladio. His two visits to Italy gave him an unrivalled knowledge of Renaissance architecture in Italy. He designed the Queen's House, Greenwich 1616, and the Banqueting Hall, Whitehall 1619 and scenery for Jonson's masques.

Kahn Louis 1901–74. American architect, noted for his unusual 'service' towers surrounding the main working spaces of buildings such as Salk Laboratories, La Jolla, California.

Lasdun Sir Denys 1914– . British architect, whose works include the National Theatre on the South Bank. He was knighted in 1976.

Le Corbusier. Pseudonym of Charles Edouard Jeanneret 1887–1965. Swiss-born French architect, for whom the house was a habitable machine to be designed to functional criteria. His works include the Palace of the Nations, Geneva, Cité Radieuse, Marseille, and the town plan for Chandigarh, India.

Lethaby William Richard 1857–1931. English architect, and assistant to Richard Norman Shaw. He embraced the principles of William Morris and Philip Webb and had a great influence in the Arts and Crafts Movement, especially as first director of the Central School of Arts and Crafts (which he helped to found) from 1894.

Le Vau Louis 1612–70. French architect, who drafted the plan of Versailles, and built the Louvre and Tuileries.

Loos Adolf 1870–1933. Viennese architect. He rejected the ornamentation and curved lines of the Viennese Art Nouveau. His main importance is as a polemicist; his most famous and influential article was *Ornament and Crime*, published in 1908.

Lutyens Sir Edwin Landseer 1869–1944. British architect, whose works include the government buildings in New Delhi, Hampstead Garden Suburb, the Whitehall Cenotaph, London YWCA, and the British Embassy in Washington.

Mackintosh Charles Rennie 1868–1928. Scottish Art Nouveau architect, designer and painter, whose work includes the Glasgow School of Art 1896.

Mackmurdo Arthur H 1851–1942. English designer and architect. He founded the Century Guild in 1882, a group of architects, artists, and designers inspired by William Morris and John Ruskin. His book and textile designs are forerunners of Art Nouveau.

Mansart Jules-Hardouin 1646–1708. French

architect of the Palace of Versailles and the Grand Trianon, and designer of the Place de Vendôme and the Place des Victoires, Paris.

Michelangelo 1475–1564. Italian sculptor, painter, architect, and poet, Michelangelo di Lodovico Buonarroti Simoni. In addition to his work as an artist, Michelangelo was one of the greatest architects. His most important works are the façade for Brunelleschi's church of San Lorenzo in Rome 1514; the Biblioteca Laurenziana 1525–26; his designs for the Capitol 1539; and the completion of St Peter's in Rome 1546–64 (begun by Bramante).

Mies van der Rohe Ludwig 1886–1969. German-born American architect, director of the Bauhaus 1929–33. His works include the new Illinois Institute of Technology 1941, where he taught 1938–58, and the bronze and glass Seagram Building, New York 1956-59.

Morris William 1834–96. British poet, craftsman, and socialist. Although known principally for his furniture, wallpaper, church decorations and beautifully decorated books, he also had a considerable influence on a generation of architects, including William Lethaby and Philip Webb.

Nash John 1752–1835. British architect, who designed Regent's Park and its terraces, Regent Street (later rebuilt), and Marble Arch, intended as the entrance gate to Buckingham Palace.

Nervi Pier Luigi 1891–1979. Italian architect, who used soft steel mesh within concrete to give it flowing form. His best known works include the Turin exhibition hall 1949, and the UNESCO building in Paris 1952.

Niemeyer Oscar 1907– . Brazilian architect, joint designer of the United Nations headquarters in New York, and of many buildings in Brasilia.

Olbrich Joseph Maria 1867–1908. Viennese architect who worked under Otto Wagner and was opposed to the lush over-ornamentation of Art Nouveau. His most important buildings, however, remain Art Nouveau in spirit: the Vienna Secession 1897–78, the Hochzeitsturm 1907 and the Tietz department store, both in Dsseldorf.

Palladio Andrea 1508–80. Italian architect, who from 1540 designed country houses, such as the Villa Rotonda near Vicenza, for patrician families of the Venetian Republic and whose work had a profound influence on generations of Neo-Classical architects.

Paxton Sir Joseph 1801–65. British architect, garden superintendent to the Duke of Devonshire from 1826, and designer of the Great Exhibition building of 1851 (Crystal Palace), revolutionary in its structural use of glass and iron.

Pei I M 1917– . Chinese-born American modernist/high tech architect. His best known buildings include the John Hancock tower, Boston, the National Airlines terminal at Kennedy Airport, New York, and the extension to the National Gallery, Washington DC. Projects during the 1980s include renovations to the Louvre Museum, Paris, and new work for Canary Wharf, London dockland.

Piranesi Giovanni Battista 1720–78. Italian architect, most influential for his powerful etchings of Roman antiquities and as a theorist of architecture, advocating imaginative use of Roman models.

Repton Sir Humphrey 1752–1818. English landscape gardener, who coined the term 'landscape gardening'. He was a leading landscape gardener of the generation after Lancelot Brown, and worked for some years in partnership with John Nash. Repton was responsible for the landscaping of some 200 gardens and parks.

Richardson Harry Hobson 1838–86. American architect, who built a great deal in a Romanesque style derived from that of northern Spain. He had a strong influence on Louis Sullivan.

Rogers Richard 1933– . British architect whose works include the Pompidou Centre in Paris 1977 and the Lloyd's building in London 1986.

Ruskin John 1819–1900. British art and social critic, whose writings had a profound influence on architecture. His enthusiasm for medieval architecture helped establish the Neo-Gothic style, and his belief in the importance of the work of craftsmen helped pave the way for the Arts and Crafts Movement.

Saarinen Eero 1910–61. American architect, son of Eliel Saarinen; he was born in Finland, but taken to the USA in 1923 by his father. His works include the American Embassy in London, and Dulles Airport, Washington.

Saarinen Eliel 1873–1950. Finnish-American architect, founder of the Finnish Romantic school, of which Helsinki railway station is an example. He contributed to US skyscraper design by his work in Chicago.

Sant'Elia Antonio 1888–1916. Italian architect. Although he died (in World War I) too early to achieve much in the way of building, his drawings, conveying a Futurist vision of a metropolis with skyscrapers, traffic lanes and streamlined factories, were influential.

Schinkel Karl Friedrich 1781–1841. Prussian architect of the Neo-Classical style, recognized as the greatest German architect of the 19th century. Major works include the Old Museum, Berlin 1823–30, and the Charlottenhof and the Roman Bath 1826 and 1833 in the park of Potsdam.

Scott Sir George Gilbert 1811–78. British architect, largely responsible for the mid-19th-century Gothic revival in England; his restoration work in Ely Cathedral and Westminster Abbey had debatable results, but his Albert Memorial, Foreign Office, and St Pancras Station won contemporary and more recent praise.

Scott Sir Giles Gilbert 1880–1960. British architect, grandson of Sir George Scott, and designer of Liverpool Anglican Cathedral, Cambridge University Library, and Waterloo Bridge 1945.

Serlio Sebastiano 1475–1554. Italian painter, architect and architectural theorist. He was most important as the author of *L'Architettura* 1537–51, practical rules for the use of the Classical orders and spread the Neo-Classical style throughout Europe.

Shaw Richard Norman 1831–1912. British architect. His style was eclectic, using elements from vernacular and Georgian architecture rather than the Gothic and Tudor then popular. Major buildings include New Zealand Chambers, London 1872, Lowther Lodge, Kensington 1873 (now the Royal Geographical Society), Shaw's house, Hampstead 1875.

Smirke Robert 1780–1867. Leading Greek Revival architect in Britain; designer of the British Museum.

Soane Sir John 1753–1837. British architect, whose individual Neo-Classical style resulted in works curiously presaging modern taste. Little of his major work, the Bank of England, London, remains. Other buildings include his own house in Lincoln's Inn Fields, London, now the Soane Museum.

Spence Sir Basil 1907–76. British architect. He was professor of architecture at the Royal Academy 1961–68, and his controversial works include Coventry Cathedral, Sussex University, the British Embassy in Rome, the Home Office and Knightsbridge Barracks. He was knighted in 1960 and awarded an OM in 1962.

Stirling James 1926– . British architect. He designed the engineering building at Leicester University, and the Clore Gallery (the extension to house the Turner collection of the Tate Gallery), opened 1987.

Sullivan Louis Henry 1856–1924. American architect, influenced by Harry Richardson. He worked in Chicago and designed early skyscrapers such as the Wainwright Building, St Louis 1890 and the Guaranty Building, Buffalo 1894. He was influential in the anti-ornament movement. Frank Lloyd Wright was his pupil.

Summerson Sir John 1904– . English architectural scholar and critic, and curator of Sir John Soane's museum 1945–84. Influential books include *Georgian London* 1945, and *The Classical Language of Architecture* 1964.

Tange Kenzo 1913– . Japanese architect, whose works include the National Gymnasium, Tokyo, for the 1964 Olympics, and the city plan of Abuja, Nigeria (completed 1986).

Terry Quinlan 1937– . British Neo-Classical architect whose work includes many country houses, for example Merks Hall, Great Dunmow, Essex 1982, and the Richmond riverside project commissioned 1984.

Unwin Sir Raymond 1863–1940. Leading English town planner of the time, who put the Garden City ideals of Sir Ebenezer Howard into practice, overseeing Letchworth (begun 1903), Hampstead Garden Suburb (begun 1907) and Wythenshawe outside Manchester (begun 1927).

Venturi Robert 1925– . American architect and pioneer of Post-Modernism. His best known books are *Complexity and Contradiction in Architecture* 1967 and *Learning from Las Vegas* 1972. He was commissioned for London's National Gallery extension in 1986.

Vitruvius (Marcus Vitruvius Pollio) 1st century BC Roman architect, whose ten-volume interpretation of Roman architecture *De architectura* influenced Alberti, Palladio, and many others.

Voysey Charles Francis Annesley 1857–1941. British architect and designer. His fame as an architect rests on his country houses, which are characteristically asymmetrical with massive buttresses, long sloping roofs and rough-cast walls; he designed all furniture and interior details with a cosy sentimentality.

Wagner Otto 1841–1918. Viennese architect who at first designed in the Art Nouveau style, for example Vienna Stadtbahn 1894–97, but later rejected ornament in favour of rationalism, as in his Post Office Savings Bank, Vienna 1904–6. He influenced younger Viennese architects.

Waterhouse Alfred 1830–1905. English architect. He was a leading exponent of Victorian Neo-Gothic using, typically, multi-coloured tiles and bricks. His best known work is the Natural History Museum in London 1868.

Webb Philip 1831–1915. English architect. He designed almost exclusively houses, including the Red House for William Morris, and was one of the leading figures, with Richard Norman Shaw and C F A Voysey, in the revival of domestic English architecture in 19th century. Houses include Joldwyns, Surrey 1873, Clouds, East Knoyle, Wiltshire 1880, and Standen, East Grinstead 1891–94.

Wilkins William 1778–1839. English architect who pioneered the Greek Revival in England with his design for Downing College, Cambridge. He is best known for the unsuccessful National Gallery, which ruined his reputation.

Wren Sir Christopher 1632–1723. English architect. Professor of astronomy at Oxford from 1660, he was asked to plan the rebuilding of the city after the Great Fire of London of 1666. His plan was not adopted but his individual buildings include St Paul's Cathedral (1675–1710), and other City churches (St Michael's, Cornhill, St Bride's, Fleet Street, St Mary-le-Bow, Cheapside), the Sheldonian Theatre and Ashmolean Museum at Oxford, and part of Hampton Court Palace.

Wright Frank Lloyd 1869–1959. American architect whose freedom from convention and rule was influential worldwide, for example his own home Taliesin West, Wisconsin 1938, and the Guggenheim Museum, New York 1959.

Wyatt James 1747–1813. English architect, contemporary of the Adam brothers, who designed in the Neo-Gothic style. His over-enthusiastic 'restorations' of medieval cathedrals earned him the nickname 'Wyatt the Destroyer'.

Terms

arch a curved structure consisting of several wedge-shaped stones or other hard blocks which are supported by their mutual pressure. The term is also applied to any curved structure which is an arch in form only.

Art Deco a style, in art and architecture, originating in France in 1925, and continuing through the 1930s, using rather heavy, geometric simplification of form, for example Radio City Music Hall, New York.

Arts and Crafts a social movement based in design and architecture, founded by William

Morris in the latter half of the 19th century and supported by Pugin and Ruskin, stressing the importance of manual processes and largely anti-machine in spirit.

atrium an inner, open courtyard.

Baroque term used to describe the ornate European art and architecture of the 17th and 18th centuries, and used broadly to characterize the historical period.

basilica a type of Roman public building, consisting of a hall with side aisles divided off by rows of columns, which was adopted by Christians for early churches.

Bauhaus a school founded in 1919 by the architect Walter Gropius at Weimar in an attempt to fuse all the arts and crafts in a unified whole. Moved to Dessau under political pressure in 1925, it was closed by the Nazis in 1933. Associated with the Bauhaus were Klee, Kandinsky and Ludwig Mies van der Rohe. The tradition never died, and in 1972 the Bauhaus Archive was installed in new premises in W Berlin.

buttress a reinforcement, in brick or masonry, built against a wall to give it strength. A *flying buttress* is an arc transmitting the force of the wall to be supported to an outer buttress, common in Gothic architecture.

Byzantine term used to describe the style of religious art and architecture of Byzantium and the Eastern Orthodox Christian church from the 4th century, characterized by the use of formalized, symbolic painted and mosaic decorations.

cantilever a horizontal beam fixed at one end to a rigid support and free to move at the other end. This type of structure is used widely in building; in cantilever bridges, where the projecting arms are built inwards from the piers to meet in the centre of the span, and in cantilever cranes where a straight steel truss rests on a central support.

caryatid a building support or pillar, in the shape of a woman; a male figure is a *telamon* or *atlas*.

church a Christian place of worship. A typical Latin cross plan church is illustrated but the main elements are found in all churches.

Chicago school a style of unornamented skyscrapers developed in Chicago in the late 19th century by, among others, Louis Sullivan.

cladding a thin layer of external covering, for example, tiles, wood, stone, concrete.

Classical architecture the architecture of ancient Greece and Rome. This provided a legacy which has influenced all subsequent Western architecture.

cloister a convent or monastery, and more particularly a covered walk within these, often opening on to a courtyard.

colonnade a row of columns supporting arches or an entablature.

De Stijl name of Dutch avant-garde art periodical founded by Theo van Doesburg and Piet Mondrian, which gave its name to a group of abstractionist artists and architects, including Gerrit Rietveld.

dome (cupola) a roof or vault built on a circular base, or on a pendentive if the base is of any other shape. A dome can be round or pointed, in a variety of forms.

garden city a self-sufficient community, designed to combine the advantages of town and country living, proposed in 1899 by Sir Ebenezer Howard 1850–1928, founder of the association which established Letchworth in Hertfordshire.

gargoyle a spout projecting from the roof gutter of a building with the purpose of directing water away from the wall. The term is usually applied to the ornamental forms found in Gothic architecture; these were carved in stone and took the shape of fantastic animals, angels, or human heads.

golden section a proportion, possibly derived from Euclid, in which the third term is the sum of the first and second; that is $A:B = B:(A+B)$, believed since the ancient Greeks to be particularly pleasing.

Gothic term used to describe 12th- to 16th-century European architecture, characterized by the use of the rib vault, pointed arch, and flying buttress.

ha-ha a sunken boundary wall permitting an unobstructed view beyond a garden; a device much used by Capability Brown.

types of masonry

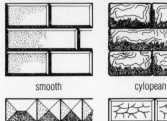

smooth   cylopean

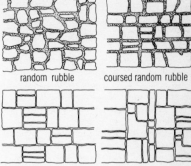

random rubble   coursed random rubble

diamond-pointed   vermiculated

squared coursed rubble   square-snecked rubble

masonry the art of building with stone.

mezzanine an architectural term derived from the diminutive of the Italian word for middle; it is a storey with a lower ceiling placed between two higher storeys, usually between the ground and first floors of a building.

minaret a slender turret or tower attached to an Islamic mosque. It has one or more balconies, from which the *muezzin* calls the people to prayer five times a day.

module in construction, a part which governs the form of the rest; for example Japanese room sizes are traditionally governed by multiples of standard tatami floor mats; modern prefabricated buildings are mass-produced in a similar way.

obelisk a tall, tapering column of stone; much used in ancient Egyptian as well as Roman architecture.

pantheon originally a temple for worshipping all the gods, such as that in ancient Rome, rebuilt by Hadrian and still used as a church; now, as the Panthéon, Paris, a building where famous people are buried.

peristyle a range of columns surrounding a building or open courtyard.

piano nobile the main floor of a house, containing the main reception rooms.

portico a porch with pediment and columns.

Renaissance in architecture, term used to describe the period from about 1420 to 1550 in Italy, characterized by a renewed interest in Classical (particularly Roman) principles of design. In the other arts the term is also used more broadly to refer to this historical period throughout Europe.

Rococo term used to describe an 18th-century European style of art and architecture, characterized by elaborate ornamentation and the use of naturalistic motifs.

Romanesque term used to describe Western Christian architecture of the 8th to 12th centuries, marked by rounded arches, solid volumes, and emphasis on perpendicular elements. In England the style was called *Norman*.

skyscraper a type of tall building first developed in 1868 in New York, USA, where land prices were high and the geology adapted to such methods of construction; today techniques have been evolved which also make them possible on London's clay and in earthquake areas. The world's highest is in Chicago.

town planning the design of buildings or groups of buildings in a physical and social context, concentrating on the relationship between various buildings and their environment, as well as on their uses.

vault an arched ceiling or roof built mainly of stone or bricks.

241

vernacular the domestic or peasant building tradition of different localities, not designed by trained architects; for example thatched cottages in England, stone in Scotland, adobe huts in Mexico, wooden buildings in the Nordic countries.

Wiener Werkstätte a group of Viennese craftsmen and designers established in 1903 by Joseph Hoffman and Moser under the influence of William Morris's Arts and Crafts Movement.

Cinema

Cinema is a modern art. It borrows from the other arts, such as music, drama, and literature, but, unlike them, is entirely dependent for its origins on technological developments. Since the earliest picture shows by the Lumière brothers in 1895, cinema has changed enormously. Indeed, considering its relatively short life, it has developed at a rate unparalleled in any other art form. The last few decades in particular have seen a fundamental change in the style of films, reflected in a shift away from the idea of studio control and star supremacy prevalent in the days of silent films and the Hollywood of the 1930s and 1940s to the idea of film as a form of artistic expression, the creation of an individual director (or, more rarely, producer). But whatever its form, cinema has, throughout its history, reflected and recorded contemporary social attitudes and changes in taste and lifestyle. It has also – in its ability to amuse, excite, anger, move and disturb – often sought to influence these attitudes and changes. Whether providing a reflection of reality, or an escape from it, a pure entertainment, or a unique and personal artistic creation, the appeal of cinema is universal.

This section provides an overview of the wide-ranging appeal and varied nature of cinema. It contains *Biographies* of a selection of some of the many people who, in different ways, have made a significant and unique contribution to cinema; a list of *Academy Award Winners* in the principal categories of best film, director, actor and actress; and a *Chronology* of film, marking important dates and events that are generally considered to be landmarks in the development of film as a technique as well as an art.

Biographies

Allen Woody. Pseudonym of American comedian, writer, film director, and clarinettist Allen Stewart Konisberg 1935– . A versatile comedian-philosopher, Allen is best known for his cynical, witty, often self-deprecating parody and special brand of off-beat humour. His films include *Play It Again Sam* 1972, *Annie Hall* 1977 – (for which he won three Academy Awards), and *Hannah and Her Sisters* 1986 – all of which he also directed.

Antonioni Michelangelo 1912– . Italian film director, famous for his subtle analysis of neuroses and personal relationships of the leisured classes. His work includes *L'Avventura* 1960, *Blow Up* 1967 and *The Passenger* 1975.

Attenborough Sir Richard 1923– . British actor, film producer, and director. An influential figure in the British cinema, he was outstanding in the film roles of Pinkie in *Brighton Rock* 1947 and the murder suspect Christie in *10 Rillington Place* 1970; films directed include *Oh! What a Lovely War* 1968, *A Bridge Too Far* 1976, dealing with Arnhem, and *Gandhi* 1982, which won six Academy Awards. He was knighted in 1976.

Balcon Sir Michael 1896–1977. British film producer, responsible for the 'Ealing Comedies' of the 1940s and early 1950s, *Kind Hearts and Coronets* 1949, and *The Lavender Hill Mob* 1951.

Bardot Brigitte 1934– . French film actress, whose appeal as a 'sex kitten' did much to popularize French cinema internationally. Her films include *And God Created Woman* 1950.

Barrault Jean-Louis 1910– . French actor and director of the Théâtre de France/Odéon 1959–68. He showed his gifts as a mime artist in the films *Les Enfants du Paradis* 1944, and *La*

Ronde 1950, both now classics.

Bergman Ingmar 1918– . Swedish film producer and director. Regarded by many as one of the greatest film artists, his work deals with complex moral, psychological and metaphysical problems and is often heavily tinged with pessimism. His work include *Wild Strawberries* 1957, *The Seventh Seal* 1957, *Persona* 1966, *Cries and Whispers* 1972, *The Serpent's Egg* 1978, *Autumn Sonata* 1978, and *Fanny and Alexander* 1982.

Bergman Ingrid 1917–82. Swedish actress, whose films include *Casablanca* 1943 and *For Whom the Bell Tolls* 1943. By leaving her husband for film producer Roberto Rossellini, whom she married in 1950, she broke an unofficial moral code of Hollywood 'star' behaviour and was ostracized for many years. She was re-admitted to make *Anastasia* 1956, for which she won an Academy Award. Her later films include *Murder on the Orient Express* 1974.

Berkeley Busby 1895–1976. American film director, who used female dancers to create large-scale pattern effects in ingeniously extravagant sets, for example *Gold Diggers of 1933* in 1933.

Bertolucci Bernardo 1940– . Italian director, regarded as one of the most talented of the younger generation of Italian film directors. His work combines political and historical satire with an elegant visual appeal. His films include *The Spider's Stratagem* 1970, *The Conformist* 1970, *Novecento/1900* 1976, but he is probably best known for his controversial *Last Tango in Paris* 1972.

Bogarde Dirk. Stage name of Dutch-born British actor Derek van den Bogaerde 1921– . After initial success in popular British films, he has gone on to acquire an international reputation for more complex roles in films such as *Death in Venice* 1971.

Boulting John 1913–85 and Roy 1913– . British twin-brother director-producer team that was particularly influential in the years following World War II. Their films include *Brighton Rock* 1947. *Lucky Jim* 1957, and *I'm All Right Jack* 1959.

Bow Clara 1905–65. American silent film actress, known as the 'It' girl from the sex appeal of her appearance in *It* 1927.

Boyer Charles 1899–1977. French film actor, who made his name in Hollywood in the 1930s as the 'great lover' in films such as *Mayerling* 1937 and *The Garden of Allah* 1936.

Brando Marlon 1931– . American actor whose naturalistic style of acting and casual mumbling speech earned him a place as one of the most distinctive actors of all time. His films include *A Streetcar Named Desire* 1951, *Julius Caesar* 1953, *On the Waterfront* 1954, *The Godfather* 1972.

Buñuel Luis 1900–83. Spanish surrealist film director, famous for his controversial and often anti-clerical films, for example *L'Age d'Or The Golden Age* 1930 and *The Discreet Charm of the Bourgeoisie* 1972.

Caine Michael. Stage name of British actor Maurice Micklewhite 1933- . Noted for his dry, laconic Cockney style. His films include *The Ipcress File* 1965, *Alfie* 1966, *The Eagle Has Landed* 1976, and *Mona Lisa* 1986.

Capra Frank 1897– . American film director. His films, which often have sentimental, idealistic heroes, include *It Happened One Night* 1934, *Mr Deeds Goes to Town* 1936, and *You Can't Take It With You* 1938.

Carné Marcel 1909– . French film director, his work is noted for its atmosphere and subtle characterization. His films include *Le Jour se léve* Daybreak 1939 and *Les Enfants du Paradis* 1944.

Cassavetes John 1929– . American actor and film director, who appeared in many films, including *The Dirty Dozen* 1967 and *Rosemary's Baby* 1968. He has also directed experimental, apparently improvised films, including *Shadows* 1960 and *The Killing of a Chinese Bookie* 1980.

Chaplin Sir Charles Spencer ('Charlie') 1889–1977. British actor and film director. One of the outstanding figures of the early cinema, he began his career in silent films such as *The Tramp* 1915, *The Gold Rush* 1925, *Modern Times* 1936, then progressed to films with sound, *The Great Dictator* 1940. Despite his

many other films, he is probably still best remembered as a comical bowler-hatted figure with baggy trousers and moustache. He was knighted in 1975.

Cimino Michael 1943– . American film director, who established his reputation with *The Deer Hunter* 1978 (which won five Academy Awards). His other films include *Heaven's Gate* 1980 and *The Year of The Dragon* 1986.

Clair René. Pseudonym of French film director René Lucien Chomette 1898–1981. His *Sous les Toits de Paris* Under the Roofs of Paris 1930 was one of the first French sound films.

Colman Ronald 1891–1958. British actor who specialized in the role of the romantic hero in Hollywood during the 1920s and 1930s. His films include *A Tale of Two Cities* 1936, *Lost Horizon*, *The Prisoner of Zenda* 1937, and *A Double Life* 1948 (for which he received an Academy Award).

Cooper Gary 1901–62. American actor who came to epitomize the sincere Yankee in films such as *Mr Deeds Goes to Town* 1936 and *Sergeant York* (for which he won an Academy Award in 1941).

Coppola Francis Ford 1939– . Director and screenwriter, in 1972 he directed *The Godfather*, one of the biggest money-makers of all time. Other successes include *The Godfather Part II* (which, like the original, won several Academy Awards) and *Apocalypse Now* 1979.

Crawford Joan 1908–77. American film actress, noted for her strongly dramatic roles, as in *Mildred Pierce* 1945 (for which she won an Academy Award).

Crosby Harry Lillis (Bing) 1904–77. American dance-band singer of the 1920s, who went on to popularize the image of the relaxed crooner in the 1930s and 1940s, with songs such as 'Pennies from Heaven' and 'White Christmas' (featured in films with those titles). He also made a series of 'road' film comedies with Dorothy Lamour and Bob Hope, for example *Road to Singapore* 1940.

Davis Bette 1908– . American actress, who made her name playing strong-willed, independent women in the 1930s and 1940s.

Later films included *Dangerous* 1935 and *Jezebel* 1938 (both winning her Academy Awards), and *Whatever Happened to Baby Jane?* 1962.

De Mille Cecil B(lount) 1884–1959. American film director, who specialized in biblical epics, for example *The Ten Commandments* 1956.

De Niro Robert 1943– . American actor, best known for his sensitive portrayal of strong and often complex characters. His films include *Mean Streets* 1973, *Taxi Driver* 1976, *The Deer Hunter* 1978, also *The Godfather Part II* 1974, and *Raging Bull* 1979 for both of which he won Academy Awards.

De Sica Vittorio 1902–74. Italian actor and director. His film *Bicycle Thieves* remains a classic example of post-war Italian Neo-Realism (a movement characterized by a 'naturalistic' style of film-making).

Dean James. Stage name of American actor James Byron 1931–55. Killed in a road accident when only his first film *East of Eden* 1955, had been shown, he posthumously became a cult figure with *Rebel Without a Cause* 1955 and *Giant* 1956.

Dietrich Marlene. Stage name of the German-American actress Magdalene von Losch 1904– . She first won fame by her appearance with Emil Jannings in *The Blue Angel* 1930, and went on to Hollywood where her husky voice and 'smouldering' image made her a superstar for 30 years.

Disney 'Walt' (Walter Elias) 1901–66. American film-maker whose name has become almost a by-word for family entertainment. He is best remembered as the inventor of the famous children's cartoon characters Mickey Mouse, Donald Duck, Bambi, and so on.

Eastwood Clint 1930– . American film actor, who started the vogue for 'spaghetti westerns' in films such as *A Fistful of Dollars* 1964.

Eisenstein Sergei Mikhailovich 1898–1948. Soviet film director who pioneered the use of montage (a technique of deliberately juxtaposing shots in such a way as to create a particular meaning) as a means of propaganda, as in *Battleship Potemkin* 1925.

Fairbanks Douglas 1883–1939. American actor, famous for his swashbuckling style, whose silent films include *The Three Musketeers* 1915. He and Mary Pickford, whom he married in 1920, were idolized as 'the world's sweethearts'.

Fairbanks Douglas, Junior 1909– . American actor, son of Douglas Fairbanks, who excelled in similar roles, for example *The Prisoner of Zenda* 1937.

Fassbinder Rainer Werner 1946–82. German film director, noted for his enormous productivity (over 30 films) and stylized films about love, hate, and prejudice, such as *Fear Eats the Soul* 1974.

Fellini Federico 1920– . Italian film director, noted for his strongly subjective poetic imagery. His films include *La Strada* 1954, *La Dolce Vita* 1960, and *8 1/2* 1963.

Fields W(illiam) C(laude) 1879–1946. American actor and screenwriter. One of the most original comedians to appear in films, his distinctive speech and professed anti-establishment attitudes gained him enormous popularity in films such as *The Bank Dick* 1940 and *Never Give a Sucker an Even Break* 1941. He has remained a cult figure over 40 years after his death.

Flaherty Robert 1884–1951. American pioneer documentary film director. His most famous film is *Nanook of the North* 1920.

Flynn Errol 1909–59. Australian actor, noted for his dashing, swashbuckling roles. His films include *Captain Blood* 1935 and *The Master of Ballantrae* 1953.

Fonda Henry 1905–82. American film actor whose engaging sincerity made him ideal in the role of the American pioneer and honourable man. His films include *Grapes of Wrath* 1940.

Fonda Jane 1937– . American actress, daughter of Henry Fonda, and active in left-wing politics; she won Academy Awards for her performances in *Klute* 1971 and *Coming Home* 1979.

Ford John 1895–1973. Irish-American film director. Active from the silent days, he was one of the original creators of the 'western'.

His *Stagecoach* 1939 is generally regarded as a masterpiece of the genre.

Gable Clark 1901–60. American actor celebrated for his romantic roles, and nicknamed the 'king of Hollywood'. His most famous role was as Rhett Butler in *Gone With the Wind* 1939.

Gance Abel 1889– . French director, whose *Napoléon* 1927, recently re-released to wide critical acclaim, is generally regarded as a masterpiece.

Garbo Greta. Stage name of Swedish actress Greta Lovisa Gustafsson 1905– . One of the first silent Hollywood stars, she went on to become a legend. Her films include *Anna Christie* 1930, *Mata Hari* 1931, *Anna Karenina* 1935, and *Ninotchka* 1939.

Garland Judy. Stage name of American singer and actress Frances Gumm 1922–69. She is best remembered for her childhood role of Dorothy in *The Wizard of Oz* 1939, featuring the song 'Over the Rainbow'.

Godard Jean-Luc 1930– . French film director, known for his highly innovative use of cutting and visual juxtapositions. His films include *A Bout du Souffle* 1959.

Goldwyn Samuel 1882–1974. American film producer. One of the leading figures in the Hollywood power struggles of the 1920s and 1930s, he was famed for his 'Goldwynisms', such as 'Anyone who visits a psychiatrist should have his head examined.'

Grant Cary. Stage name of Anglo-American actor Archibald Leach 1904–86. His screen personality as the witty, casual, debonair man made him a favourite for more than three decades. His films include *The Philadelphia Story* 1940 and *Notorious* 1946.

Grierson John 1898–1972. Scottish film producer who pioneered the documentary film in Britain. His films include *Drifters* 1929 and *Night Mail* 1936.

Griffith D(avid) W(ark) 1875–1948. American film director and one of the most influential figures in the development of the cinema as an art. Pioneer of the techniques of flashback, close-up and longshot, his masterpiece as director was *Birth of a Nation* 1915.

Guinness Sir Alec 1914– . Celebrated British character actor who has excelled in dramatic portrayals. His performance in *Bridge on the River Kwai* 1957 earned him an Academy Award. He was knighted in 1959.

Harlow Jean. Stage name of American film actress Harlean Carpentier 1911–37. A toughly frank sex symbol of the 1930s, she was the first 'platinum blonde'. Her films include *Hell's Angels* 1930 and *Saratoga* 1937.

Hawks Howard 1896–1977. American director and producer of a wide range of films with popular appeal, including *The Big Sleep* 1946.

Head Edith 1900–81. American costume designer for a thousand films, who won eight Academy Awards, for films including *The Heiress* 1949 and *The Sting* 1973.

Hepburn Katharine 1909– . American actress whose gangly grace and husky voice brought stardom in films from *Morning Glory* 1933, to *Guess Who's Coming to Dinner* 1967, and *The Lion in Winter* 1968, for all of which she received Academy Awards.

Hitchcock Sir Alfred 1899–1980. British-American film director. Noted for creating suspense in his mystery films, his camera-work, and his hallmark of making 'walk-on' appearances in his own films, which include *The Thirty-Nine Steps* 1935, *Strangers on a Train* 1951, *Psycho* 1960, and *The Birds* 1963.

Hoffman Dustin 1937– . American actor who popularized the role of the anti-hero in the 1960s and 1970s. His films include *The Graduate* 1967, *Midnight Cowboy* 1969, and *Kramer vs Kramer* 1979, for which he won an Academy Award.

Howard Leslie. Stage name of British film actor Leslie Stainer 1893–1943. He specialized in the romantically idealistic, sensitive hero. His films include *The Scarlet Pimpernel* 1935, and *Gone With the Wind* 1939.

Howard Trevor Wallace 1916– . British film actor best known for his role in *Brief Encounter* 1945.

Ivory James 1928– . American director best known for his collaboration with Indian producer Ismael Merchant. Merchant-Ivory productions include *Shakespeare Wallah* 1965,

The Europeans 1979, *Heat and Dust* and *Room with a View* 1986.

Jolson Al. Stage name of Russian-born American singer Asa Yoelson 1886–1950. He was a star of early sound films, for example *The Jazz Singer* 1927.

Karloff Boris. Stage name of British actor William Henry Pratt 1887–1969, Best known for his appearances in horror films such as *The Mummy* 1932, his portrayals of the Frankenstein monster have become classics.

Kaye Danny. Stage name of American film comedian Daniel Kominski 1913–87. His films include *The Secret Life of Walter Mitty* 1946. In 1954 he was given a special Academy Award for his 'unique talents, his service to the industry and the American people'.

Keaton Buster. Stage name of American comedian Joseph Frank Keaton 1896–1966. One of the great silent-film comedians, his films include *The General* 1926.

Korda Sir Alexander 1893–1956. Hungarian-born British film producer and director, a dominant figure during the 1930s and 1940s. His films include *The Private Life of Henry VIII* 1933, *The Third Man* 1950, and *Richard III* 1956.

Kubrick Stanley 1928– . American-born British film director, producer, and screenwriter. After initial success in Hollywood, he moved to Britain in 1961 where he made films such as *Dr Strangelove* 1964. His *2001: A Space Odyssey* 1968 has acquired the status of a classic among science fiction films.

Kurosawa Akira 1910– . Japanese director whose films, including *Throne of Blood* 1957, *Kagemusha*, and *Ran* are characterized by their magnificent epic quality and visual splendour. He is one of the few Japanese directors to gain international acclaim.

Lang Fritz 1890–1976. Austrian film director with a distinctive style of film-making. His works are heavily tinged with pessimism and include *Metropolis* 1925 and *The Big Heat* 1953.

Laughton Charles 1899–1962. Anglo-American character actor, who specialized in larger-than-life roles such as the king in *The Private Life of Henry VIII* 1933 (for which he won an Academy Award).

Laurel and Hardy Stan Laurel 1890-1965 and Oliver Hardy 1892-1957. American film comedians (Laurel was English-born). The most successful comedy team in the history of the screen, their unique partnership survived the transition from silent films to sound, and delighted audiences for decades. Their films were revived as a worldwide cult in the 1970s and include *Way Out West* 1937 and *A Chump at Oxford* 1940.

Lean Sir David 1908– . British film director who specializes in atmospheric films. His work includes *The Bridge on the River Kwai* 1957, *Lawrence of Arabia* 1962 (for which he won Academy Awards) and *A Passage to India* 1985.

Losey Joseph 1909–84. Influential American director, who also worked in the UK, and whose films include *The Servant* 1963 and *The Go-Between* 1971.

Lubitsch Ernst 1892–1947. German-American film director, known for his stylish comedies, for example *Ninotchka* 1939, starring Greta Garbo.

Lucas George 1944– . American director and producer. He is best known for his collaboration with Steven Spielberg on *Star Wars* 1977, *The Empire Strikes Back* 1980, and *Return of the Jedi* 1983.

Lumière Auguste 1862–1954 and Louis 1864–1948. French brothers, pioneers of the colour photograph and the commercial cinema.

Merchant Ismael 1936. Indian producer, who collaborated with James Ivory on films including *Shakespeare Wallah* 1965, *The Europeans* 1979, *Heat and Dust* 1983, and *Room with a View* 1986.

Mills Sir John 1908– . British actor-director, who established his reputation in stiff-upper-lip wartime roles, as in *In Which We Serve* 1942. Later films include *Ryan's Daughter* 1971 (for which he received an Academy Award). He was Knighted in 1976.

Monroe Marilyn. Stage name of American actress Norma Jean Mortenson 1926–62, who has become a screen legend since her death.

Her films include *The Seven Year Itch* 1955 and *Some Like It Hot* 1959.

Murnau Pseudonym of the German film director Friedrich Wilhelm Plumpe 1889–1931, one of the greatest directors of the classic period of silent films. His films include *Nosferatu* 1922.

Newman Paul 1925– . American actor and director. Hollywood's leading male star of the 1960s and 1970s, he has a series of creditable performances to his name in films such as *The Hustler* 1962 and *The Color of Money* 1986 (for which he won an Academy Award).

Olivier Laurence Kerr, Baron Oliver 1907– . English actor and director. Although predominantly a stage actor, his acting and direction of filmed versions of Shakespeare's plays have received outstanding critical acclaim, for example *Henry V* 1944, *Hamlet* 1948 (both of which earned him Academy Awards), and *Richard III* 1955.

Ozu Yasujiro 1903–63. Japanese film director who has gained popularity in the West in recent years. His films include *Tokyo Story* 1953.

Pasolini Pier Paolo 1922–75. Italian film director, one of the most influential figures of the post-war years. His films include *The Gospel According to St Matthew* 1904 and *The Decameron* 1970.

Polanski Roman 1933– . French-born director. He suffered a traumatic childhood in Nazi-occupied Poland and later, his wife, actress Sharon Tate, was the victim of a particularly brutal murder. His tragic personal life is reflected in a fascination with horror and violence in his work. His films include *Repulsion* 1965, *Cul de Sac* 1966, *Rosemary's Baby* 1968, and *Tess* 1979.

Powell Michael 1905– . English director, best known for his collaboration with screenwriter Emeric Pressburger. Their work, often criticized for over-extravagance, shows an extraordinary imagination and originality. Films include *Black Narcissus* 1947 and *A Matter of Life and Death* 1946.

Puttnam David Terence 1941– . British film producer largely influential in reviving the British film industry internationally. Notable successes include *Chariots of Fire* 1981 and *The Killing Fields* 1984.

Ray Satyajit 1921– . Indian film director, noted for his trilogy of life in his native Bengal: *Pather Panchali/Unvanquished* and *The World of Apu* 1955–59.

Reed Sir Carol 1906–76. British film producer and director, an influential figure in the British film industry of the 1940s. His work includes *The Third Man* 1950.

Renoir Jean 1894–1979. French film director, noted for his sensitive and subtle portrayal of social realism and his use of powerful visual imagery. His films include *La Grande Illusion/Grand Illusion* 1937 and *Regle du Jour/The Rules of the Game* 1939. In 1975 he received an honorary Academy Award for his life's work.

Resnais Alain 1922– . French director whose work is characterized by a preoccupation with memory and non-conventional concepts of time. His distinctive techniques are much admired, and his *L'Année Dernière à Marienbad/Last Year at Marienbad* 1961 is generally regarded as a masterpiece.

Roeg Nicolas 1928– . British film director. His work is noted for its stylish visual appeal and imaginative, often off-beat, treatment of subjects. His films include *Walkabout* 1971, *Don't Look Now* 1973, and *Castaway* 1986.

Russell Ken 1927– . British director. A flamboyant film-maker, he is often criticized for self-indulgence in his work, which is full of vitality, imagination and extravagance. His films include *Women in Love* 1969, *The Music Lovers* 1971, *Altered States* 1979, and *Gothic* 1986.

Scorsese Martin 1942– . American director whose films concentrate heavily on complex characterization and the theme of alienation. His work includes *Mean Streets* 1973, *Taxi Driver* 1976, *Raging Bull* 1979, and *The Color of Money* 1986.

Selznick David O(liver) 1902–65. American film producer. His independent company Selznick International was responsible for many influential films of the 1930s and 1940s, including *Gone With the Wind* 1939.

Spielberg Steven 1947– . American director, whose hugely successful films, including *Close Encounters of the Third Kind* 1977, *Raiders of the Lost Ark* 1983, and *ET* 1985 have given popular cinema a new 'respectable' appeal.

Stewart James 1908– . American actor who specialized in the role of the gangly, stubbornly honest, ordinary American, for example *Mr Smith Goes to Washington* 1939.

Streep Meryl 1951– . American actress noted for her strong character roles. Her films include *The Deer Hunter* 1978, *Kramer vs Kramer* 1979, and *Out of Africa* 1986.

Tarkovsky Andrei 1932–86. Russian film director whose work is characterized by unorthodox cinematic techniques and visual beauty. His films include the science fiction epic *Solaris* 1972, *Mirror* 1975, and *The Sacrifice* 1986.

Tati Jacques. Stage name of French actor and film director Jacques Tatischeff 1908–82. A brilliant comic mime artist, he is best remembered for *Monsieur Hulot's Holiday* 1953.

Taylor Elizabeth 1932– . English-born American actress, one of the most popular screen personalities of all time. Her films include *Butterfield 8* 1960 (for which she won an Academy Award) and *Cleopatra* 1963.

Temple Shirley 1928– . American actress, most successful child star of the 1930s. Her films include *Bright Eyes* 1934, in which she sang 'Good Ship Lollipop' and for which she received an Academy Award.

Truffaut Francois 1932–84. French director who won international acclaim with *Jules et Jim* 1961 and *Day for Night* 1973 (for which he won an Academy Award). His work was largely influenced by Hitchcock.

Valentino Rudolf 1895–1926. Italian film actor, the archetypal romantic lover of the Hollywood silent films, for example *The Sheik* 1922 and *Blood and Sand* 1922.

Visconti Luchino 1906–76. Italian film director who pioneered the naturalistic style of film-making, that was later to be associated with De Sica. His films include *Ossessione/Obsession* 1942, *Il gattopardo/The Leopard* 1963, and *Death in Venice* 1971.

Wajda Andrzej 1926– . Polish director. One of the major figures in post-war European cinema, his work includes the cult film *Ashes and Diamonds* 1953 and *Man of Marble* 1977.

Warhol Andy 1927–87. American filmmaker and pop artist, whose plotless experimental avant-garde films, though ridiculed by some, were an important part of the cultural scene of the 1960s and 1970s. His work includes *Sleep* 1963, *Flesh* 1968, and *Trash* 1980.

Wayne John. Stage name of American actor Marion Morrison 1907–79, nicknamed 'duke', from the name of a dog he once owned, Wayne was the archetypal 'western' star. His films include *Stagecoach* 1939 and *True Grit* 1969 (for which he won an Academy Award).

Weir Peter 1938– . Australian director. His works are characterized by their atmospheric quality and often contains a strong spiritual element. They include *Picture at Hanging Rock* 1975, *Witnesss 1985, and Mosquito Coast* 1986.

Welles Orson 1915–86. American writer, actor, director. Experimentalist and controversial life-force of the cinema whose first Hollywood film *Citizen Kane* 1941 is still regarded by many critics as the best film ever made.

Wilder Billy 1906– . Austrian-American film director, noted for such sophisticated comedies as *Some Like it Hot* 1959 and *The Apartment* 1960.

ACADEMY AWARD WINNERS ('OSCARS')

Annual cinema awards have been given from 1927 onwards by the American Academy of Motion Pictures, nicknamed 'Oscars' (1931), allegedly because a new secretary exclaimed (of the bronze statuette presented to winners) 'That's like my uncle Oscar!'

Year	Award	
1970	*Best Picture:*	*Patton*
	Best Director:	Franklin J Schaffner *Patton*
	Best Actor:	George C Scott *Patton*
	Best Actress:	Glenda Jackson *Women in Love*
1971	*Best Picture:*	*The French Connection*
	Best Director:	William Friedkin *The French Connection*
	Best Actor:	Gene Hackman *The French Connection*
	Best Actress:	Jane Fonda *Klute*
1972	*Best Picture:*	*The Godfather*
	Best Director:	Bob Fosse *Cabaret*
	Best Actor:	Marlon Brando *The Godfather*
	Best Actress:	Liza Minnelli *Cabaret*
1973	*Best Picture:*	*The Sting*
	Best Director:	George Roy Hill *The Sting*
	Best Actor:	Jack Lemmon *Save The Tiger*
	Best Actress:	Glenda Jackson *A Touch of Class*
1974	*Best Picture:*	*The Godfather II*
	Best Director:	Francis Ford Coppola *The Godfather II*
	Best Actor:	Art Carney *Harry and Tonto*
	Best Actress:	Ellen Burstyn *Alice Doesn't Live Here Anymore*
1975	*Best Picture:*	*One Flew Over the Cuckoo's Nest*
	Best Director:	Milos Forman *One Flew Over the Cuckoo's Nest*
	Best Actor:	Jack Nicholson *One Flew Over the Cuckoo's Nest*
1976	*Best Picture:*	*Rocky*
	Best Director:	John G Avildsen *Rocky*
	Best Actor:	Peter Finch *Network*
	Best Actress:	Faye Dunaway *Network*
1977	*Best Picture:*	*Annie Hall*
	Best Director:	Woody Allen *Annie Hall*
	Best Actor:	Richard Dreyfuss *The Goodbye Girl*
	Best Actress:	Diane Keaton *Annie Hall*

1978	*Best Picture:*	The Deer Hunter
	Best Director:	Michael Cimino *The Deer Hunter*
	Best Actor:	Jon Voight *Coming Home*
	Best Actress:	Jane Fonda *Coming Home*
1979	*Best Picture:*	*Kramer vs Kramer*
	Best Director:	Robert Beaton *Kramer vs Kramer*
	Best Actor:	Dustin Hoffman *Kramer vs Kramer*
	Best Actress:	Sally Field *Norma Rae*
1980	*Best Picture:*	*Ordinary People*
	Best Director:	Robert Redford *Ordinary People*
	Best Actor:	Robert de Niro *Raging Bull*
	Best Actress:	Sissy Spacek *Coalminer's Daughter*
1981	*Best Picture:*	*Chariots of Fire*
	Best Director:	Warren Beatty *Reds*
	Best Actor:	Henry Fonda *On Golden Pond*
	Best Actress:	Katharine Hepburn *On Golden Pond*
1982	*Best Picture:*	*Gandhi*
	Best Director:	Richard Attenborough *Gandhi*
	Best Actor:	Ben Kingsley *Gandhi*
	Best Actress:	Meryl Streep *Sophie's Choice*
1983	*Best Picture:*	*Terms of Endearment*
	Best Director:	James L Brooks *Terms of Endearment*
	Best Actor:	Robert Duvall *Tender Mercies*
	Best Actress:	Shirley MacLaine *Terms of Endearment*
1984	*Best Picture:*	*Amadeus*
	Best Director:	Milos Forman *Amadeus*
	Best Actor:	F Murray Abraham *Amadeus*
	Best Actress:	Sally Field *Places in the Heart*
1985	*Best Picture:*	*Out of Africa*
	Best Director:	Sidney Pollack *Out of Africa*
	Best Actor:	William Hurt *Kiss of the Spider Woman*
	Best Actress:	Geraldine Page *The Trip to Bountiful*
1986	*Best Picture:*	*Platoon*
	Best Director:	Oliver Stone *Platoon*
	Best Actor:	Paul Newman *The Color of Money*
	Best Actress:	Marlee Matlin *Children of A Lesser God*

1826–34	Various machines invented to show moving images: the stroboscope, zoetrope, and thaumatrope.
1872	Eadweard Muybridge demonstrated movement of horses' legs using 24 cameras.
1877	Invention of Praxinoscope; developed as a projector of successive images on screen in 1879 in France.
1878–95	Marey, a French physiologist, developed various forms of camera for recording human and animal movements.
1887	Augustin le Prince produced the first series of images on a perforated film; Thomas Edison, having developed the phonograph, took the first steps in developing a motion-picture recording and reproducing device to accompany recorded sound.
1888	William Friese-Green showed the first celluloid film and patented a movie camera.
1889	Edison invented 35mm film.
1890–94	Edison, using perforated film, perfected his Kinetograph camera and Kinetoscope individual viewer; developed commercially in New York, London and Paris.
1895	The Lumière brothers, Auguste (1862–1954) and Louis (1864–1948) projected, to a paying audience, a film of a train arriving at a station. Some of the audience fled in terror.
1896	Pathe introduced the Berliner gramophone, using discs in synchronization with film. Lack of amplification, however, made the performances ineffective.
1899	Edison tried to improve amplification by using banks of phonographs.
1900	Attempts to synchronize film and disc were made by Gaumont in France and Goldschmidt in Germany, leading later to the American Vitaphone system.
1902	Georges Méliès (1861–1938) made *Le Voyage dans la Lune/A Trip to the Moon*.
1903	The first 'western' was made in the USA: *The Great Train Robbery* by Edwin S Porter.
1906	The earliest colour film (Kinemacolor) was patented in Britain by George Albert Smith.
1908–11	In France, Emile Cohl experimented with film animation.
1910	With the dominating influence of the Hollywood Studios, film actors and actresses began to be recognized as international stars.
1912	In Britain, Eugene Lauste designed experimental 'sound on film' systems.
1914–18	Full newsreel coverage of World War I.
1915	*The Birth of a Nation*, D W Griffith's epic on the American civil war, was released in the USA.
1918–19	A sound system called Tri-Ergon was developed in Germany which led to sound being recorded on film photographically. The photography of sound was also developed by Lee De Forest in his Phonofilm system.
1923	First sound film (as Phonofilm) demonstrated.
1927	Release of the first major sound film, *The Jazz Singer*, Warners in New York. The first Academy Awards (Oscars) were given.

1928	Walt Disney released his first Mickey Mouse cartoon, *Steamboat Willie*.
1932	Technicolor (three-colour) process was used for a Walt Disney cartoon film.
1952	Cinerama (wide-screen presentation) was introduced in New York.
1953	Commercial 3–D (three-dimensional cinema) and wide screen Cinemascope were launched in the USA.
1976–77	Major films became widely available on video for viewing at home.

Photography

Photography is a process for producing images on sensitized materials by various forms of radiant energy: for example, visible light, ultra-violet, infra-red, or X-rays; radioactive radiation; or an electron beam. Alhazen (965–1038), Arab scientist and mathematician, described the principles of the lens and camera obscura (a tiny hole in the wall of a darkened room which can produce an inverted image of the scene outside) and the theory of human vision in the early 11th century, but modern photography began in the 19th century.

This section contains *Biographies* of a selection of people who have made important contributions to the technical and artistic development of photography, definitions of technical *Terms*, and a *Chronology* of the history of photography.

Biographies

Adams Ansel 1902–84. American photographer, particularly known for his superbly-printed images of dramatic landscapes and organic forms of the American West. He was associated with the Zone System of exposure estimation.

Atget Eugene 1857–1927. French photographer. He took up photography at the age of 40, and for 30 years documented urban Paris, leaving a huge body of work.

Avedon Richard 1923– . American photographer. A successful fashion photographer with *Harper's Bazaar* magazine in New York in the mid 1940s, he has become one of the highest-paid commercial photographers.

Beaton Cecil 1904–80. British portrait and fashion photographer, designer, illustrator, diarist and noted conversationalist.

Brandt Bill 1905–83. British photographer, who produced a large body of richly-printed and romantic black and white studies of people, London and nudes. He also published many photographic books.

Brassäi. Pseudonym of Gyula Halesz 1899–1986. French photographer of Hungarian origin. From the early 1930s on he documented, mainly by flash, the nightlife of Paris, before turning to more abstract work.

Cameron Julia Margaret 1815–79. British photographer. She made lively, portraits of the Victorian intelligentsia using a large camera, five-minute exposures and wet plates.

Cartier-Bresson Henri 1908– . French photographer. Considered the greatest of photographic artists. His documentary work was achieved using a small format camera. He was noted for his ability to structure the image and to capture the decisive moment.

Daguerre Louis Jacques Mande 1787–1851. French pioneer of photography. Together with

Niépce, he is credited with the invention of photography (though others were reaching the same point simultaneously). His method of producing daguerreotypes 1835, a one-off image process, was patented in 1839, to be superseded ten years later by Fox Talbot's negative/positive process.

Evans Walker 1903–75. American photographer, best known for his documentary photographs of changing America during the 1930s and 1940s.

Fenton Roger 1819–69. British photographer. The world's first war photographer, he went to the Crimea in 1855; he also founded the Royal Photographic Society in London.

Herschel Sir John 1792–1871. English scientist and astronomer who discovered and used hypo (sodium thiosulphate) as a print fixer, the word 'photography' from Greek *photos* ('light') and *graphos* ('drawing') and the terms 'negative' and 'positive'.

Hill and Adamson David Octavius Hill 1802–70 and Robert R Adamson 1821–48. Scots photographers who, working together, turned out 2,500 calotypes (mostly portraits) in five years from 1843.

Hine Lewis 1874–1940. American sociologist. He recorded in photographs child labour conditions in US factories at the beginning of this century, his work leading to a change in the law.

Kertesz Andre 1894–1986. American photographer. A master of the 35mm format camera, he recorded his immediate environment in places such as Paris and New York with wit and style.

Lartigue Jacques-Henri 1894–1986. French photographer. He began taking extraordinary and humorous photographs of his family at the age of seven, and went on to make autochrome colour prints of beautiful women.

Moholy-Nagy Laszlo 1895–1946. American photographer. Through his illuminating theories and practical experiments he had enormous influence on the photography of this century.

Muybridge Eadweard 1830–1904. British photographer. He made a series of animal locomotion photographs in the US in the 1870s which proved that, at speed, animals often do not touch the ground. He then explored motion in birds and humans.

Penn Irving 1917– . American fashion, advertising, portrait, editorial and fine art photographer. He has been associated with *Vogue* magazine in the US throughout his long career.

Steichen Edward 1897–1973. American photographer, best known for his innovative fashion, portrait and documentary work.

Steiglitz Alfred 1864–1946. American photographer. After forming the Photo Secession group in 1903, he began the magazine *Camera Work*. Through exhibitions at his gallery '291' in New York he established photography as an art form.

Strand Paul 1890–1976. American photographer, who used large format cameras for his strong, clear, close-up photographs of natural objects.

Talbot William Henry Fox 1800–77. British pioneer of photography. He made photograms several years before Daguerre's invention was announced and invented the Calotype process, the first negative/positive method. *The Pencil of Nature* 1844 by Fox Talbot was the first book of photographs published.

Uelsmann Jerry 1934– . American photographer, noted for his dream-like images, which he creates by synthesizing many elements into one with great technical skill.

Weston Edward 1886–1958. American photographer. A founder-member of the F64 group, he is noted for technical mastery in his Californian landscapes and nude studies.

Terms

aperture an opening through which light passing through the lens to strike the film can be controlled by shutter speed and iris diaphragm, set mechanically or electronically at various diameters.

ASA a numbering system for rating the speed of films, devised by the American Standards Association. It has now been superseded by **ISO**, the International Standards Organisation.

autochrome a single-plate additive colour process devised by the Lumière brothers in 1903. It was the first commercially available process, in use from 1907 to 1935.

calotype a paper-based photograph using a wax paper negative, the first example of the negative/positive process invented by Fox Talbot around 1834.

camera obscura a darkened box with a tiny hole for projecting the inverted image of the scene outside on a screen inside.

Cibachrome a process of printing directly from transparencies introduced in 1963, now marketed by Ilford UK Ltd. Distinguished by rich, saturated colours, it can be home-processed and is one of the most permanent processes.

daguerreotype a one-off photographic image taken by using mercury vapour and iodine sensitized silvered plates; discovered by Daguerre in 1835.

exposure meter a device for measuring light to indicate correct duration of exposure. Reflected light meters average readings reflected from the subject; incident meters measure light falling on the subject.

'f' stops a series of numbers on the lens barrel designating the size of the variable aperture; altering them also changes the appearance of the image.

hypo a term for sodium thiosulphate, discovered in 1819 by Sir John Herschel and used as a fixative for photographic images from 1837.

negative/positive a reverse image, which when printed is again reversed, restoring the original scene. Invented by Fox Talbot around 1834.

orthochromatic film or paper of decreased sensitivity, which can be processed with a red

257

safe-light. Blue objects appear lighter and red ones darker because of increased blue sensitivity.

panchromatic highly sensitive black and white film made to render all visible spectral colours in correct grey tones. It is always developed in total darkness.

Polaroid an American corporation set up by Dr Edwin Land in 1947 when he invented film which yields instant finished prints. Colour Polaroid cameras were introduced in 1963.

SLR camera a single lens reflex camera, in which the image is seen in the taking lens. This type of camera is the most widely used today, and usually comes in 35 mm format.

telephoto lens a lens of longer focal length than normal, taking a very narrow view, and giving a large image through a combination of telescopic and ordinary photographic lenses.

thaumatrope a disc with two different pictures at opposite ends of its surface which combine into one when rapidly rotated because of the persistence of visual impressions.

35 mm a width of film, the most popular format for the modern camera. The 35 mm camera falls into two categories, the SLR and the rangefinder.

TLR camera a twin lens reflex camera, which has a viewing lens mounted above and parallel to the taking lens, of the same angle of view and focal length.

wide-angle lens a lens of shorter focal length than normal, increasing spatial depth between objects taking in a wider angle of view.

zoetrope an optical toy with a series of pictures on the inner surface of a cylinder. When rotated and viewed through a slit, it gives the impression of continuous motion.

zoom lens a lens which by variation of focal length allows speedy transition from long-shots to close-ups.

Zone System a system of exposure estimation which groups infinite tonal gradations into ten zones, zone 0 being black and zone 10 white. An 'f' stop change in exposure is required from zone to zone.

1515   Leonardo da Vinci described the camera obscura.

1750   The painter Canaletto used a camera obscura as an aid to his painting in Venice.

1790   Thomas Wedgewood in England made photograms – placing objects on leather, sensitized using silver nitrate.

1826   Nicephore Niépce 1765–1833, a French doctor, produced the world's first photograph from nature on pewter plates with a camera obscura and an eight-hour exposure.

1835   Niépce and L J M Daguerre produced the first daguerreotype camera photograph.

1839   Daguerre was awarded an annuity by the French government and his process given to the world.

1841   Fox Talbot's calotype process was patented – the first multi-copy method of photography using a negative/positive process, sensitized with silver iodide.

1843   Hill and Adamson began to use calotypes for portraits in Edinburgh.

1844   Fox Talbot published the first photographic book, *The Pencil of Nature.*

1851   Fox Talbot used a one-thousandth of a second exposure to demonstrate high-speed photography.

1855   Roger Fenton made documentary photographs of the Crimean War from a specially constructed caravan with portable darkroom.

1859   Under the pseudonym Nadar, Gaspard-Felix Tournachan 1820–1910, French writer, caricature amd photographer, made photographs underground in Paris using battery-powered arc lights.

1860   Queen Victoria was photographed by Mayall. Abraham Lincoln was photographed by Matthew Brady for political campaigning.

1861   The single lens reflex plate camera was patented by Thomas Sutton.

1862   Nadar took aerial photographs over Paris.

1870   Julia Margaret Cameron used long lenses for her distinctive portraits.

1878   In the US Eadweard Muybridge analysed the movements of animals through sequential photographs, using a series of cameras.

1880   A silver bromide emulsion was fixed with hypo. Photographs were first reproduced in newspapers in New York using the half-tone engraving process. The first twin-lens reflex camera was produced in London.

1889   Eastman Company in the US produced the Kodak No. 1 camera and roll film, facilitating universal, hand-held snapshots.

1902   In Germany Deckel invented a prototype leaf shutter and Zeiss introduced the Tessar lens.

1904   The autochrome colour process was patented by the Lumière brothers.

1905   Alfred Steiglitz opened the gallery '291' in New York promoting photography. Lewis Hine used photography to expose the exploitation of children in American factories, causing protective laws to be passed.

1907   The autochrome process began to be factory-produced.

1914   Oskar Barnack designed a prototype Leica camera for Leitz in Germany.

1924   Leitz launched the first 35 mm camera, the Leica, delayed because of World War I. It became very popular with photo-journalists because it was quiet, small, dependable and had a range of lenses and accessories.

1929   Rolleiflex produced a twin-lens reflex camera in Germany.

1935   In the US, Mannes and Godowsky invented Kodachrome transparency film, which has great sharpness and rich colour quality. Electronic flash was invented in the US. Social documentary photography received wide attention through the photographs of Dorothea Lange, Margaret Bourke-White, Arthur Rothstein, Walker Evans, and others taken for the US government's Farm Security Administration of the plight of the poor tenant farmers in the mid-West.

1936   *Life* magazine, noted for photo-journalism, was first published in the US.

1938   *Picture Post* magazine was introduced in the UK.

1940   Multigrade enlarging paper by Ilford was made available in the UK.

1945   The Zone System of exposure estimation was explained in the book *Exposure Record* by Ansel Adams.

1947   Polaroid black and white instant process film was invented by Dr Edwin Land, who set up the Polaroid corporation in Boston, Massachusetts. The principles of holography were demonstrated in England by Dennis Gabor.

1955   Kodak introduced Tri-X, a black and white 200 ASA film.

1959   The zoom lens was invented in Germany by Voigtlander.

1960   Laser was invented in the US, making holography possible. Polacolor, a self-processing colour film, was introduced by Polaroid, using a 60–second colour film and dye diffusion technique.

1963   Cibachrome, paper and chemicals for printing directly from transparencies, was made available by Ciba-Geigy of Switzerland. One of the most permanent processes, it is marketed by Ilford in the UK.

1969   Photographs were taken on the moon by US astronauts.

1972   SX70 system, a single lens reflex camera with instant prints, was produced by Polaroid.

1980   Ansel Adams sold an original print *Moonrise:Hernandez* for $45,000, a record price, in the US. Voyager 1 sent photographs of Saturn back to earth across space.

1985   Minolta Corporation in Japan introduced the world's first body-integral autofocus single lens reflex camera.

Literature

The great body of world literature consists of words set apart in some way from ordinary everyday communication. In the ancient oral traditions, before stories and poems were written down, literature had a mainly public function – mythic and religious. As literary works came to be preserved in writing, and then, eventually, printed, their role tended to become more private, as a vehicle for the exploration and expression of emotion and of the human situation. Aesthetic criteria came increasingly to the fore; the English poet and critic Coleridge defined prose as words in their best order, and poetry as the 'best' words in the best order. The distinction between verse and prose is not always clear cut, but in practice poetry tends to be metrically formal (making it easier to memorize), whereas prose corresponds more closely to the patterns of ordinary speech. Poetry therefore had an early advantage over prose in the days before printing, which it has not relinquished until comparatively recently. Over the centuries poetry has taken on a wide range of forms, from the lengthy narrative such as the epic to the lyric, expressing personal emotion in songlike form; from the ballad, and the 14-line sonnet, to the extreme conciseness of the 17-syllable Japanese haiku. Prose came into its own in the West as a vehicle for imaginative literature with the rise of the modern novel in the 18th century.

This section consists of an overview of various *Literary Genres* and types of literature; biographical notes on a selection of the world's *Great Writers*; lists of recent winners of *Literary Prizes*; and a *Chronology* highlighting major developments and leading writers in world literature from ancient to modern times. Throughout this section the emphasis is on non-dramatic literature; plays and playwrights are treated separately in the Theatre section. Language, and the languages of the world, the material of literature – including grammar and usage – are covered in a separate section.

Literary Genres

allegory the description or illustration of one thing in terms of another; a work of poetry or prose in the form of an extended metaphor or parable which makes use of symbolic fictional characters, as in the allegorical romantic epic *The Faerie Queene* 1590–96 by Edmund Spenser in homage to Queen Elizabeth I. Allegory is often used for moral purposes, as in John Bunyan's *Pilgrim's Progress* 1678. Medieval allegory often used animals as characters; this tradition survives today in such works as *Animal Farm* 1945 by George Orwell.

biography an account of a person's life. When it is written by that person, it is an *autobiography*. Biography can be simply a factual narrative, but it was also firmly established as a literary form in the 18th century in England with *Lives of the English Poets* 1779–81 by Samuel Johnson and Samuel Boswell's biography of Johnson 1791.

children's literature in the sense of works specifically written for children is relatively recent; the earliest known illustrated children's book in English is *Goody Two Shoes* 1765, possibly written by Oliver Goldsmith. *Fairy tales* were originally part of a vast range of oral literature, credited only to the writer who first recorded them, such as Charles Perrault. During the 19th century several writers including Hans Christian Andersen wrote original stories in the fairytale genre; others, such as the Grimm brothers, collected (and sometimes adapted) existing stories. Early children's stories were always written with a moral purpose; this was particularly true in the 19th century, apart from the unique case of Lewis Carroll's *Alice* books. The late 19th century was the great era of children's literature in the UK, with Lewis Carroll, Beatrix Potter, Charles Kingsley, and J M Barrie. It was also the golden age of illustrated children's books, with such artists as Kate Greenaway. Among the great 20th-century children's writers in English have been Kenneth Grahame (*The Wind in the Willows* 1908) and A A Milne (*Winnie the Pooh* 1926). *Adventure stories* have often appealed to children even when written for adults – examples include *Robinson Crusoe* by Daniel Defoe, and the satirical *Gulliver's Travels* by Jonathan Swift. *Books about animals* today occupy a position which seems to be both for adults and children – *Watership Down* by Richard Adams is an example.

detective fiction novels or short stories in which a mystery is solved mainly by the action of a professional or amateur dective. Where the mystery to be solved concerns the commission of a crime, the work is called *crime fiction*. The earliest work of detective fiction as understood today was *Murders in The Rue Morgue* 1841 by Edgar Allen Poe, and his detective Dupin became the model for those who detected by deduction from a series of clues. The most popular deductive sleuth was Sherlock Holmes in the stories by Sir Arthur Conan Doyle. The height of the genre was the 'golden age': the period from the 1920s to the 1940s, when the most famous writers were women – Agatha Christie, Margery Allingham, Dorothy L Sayers. Types of detective fiction include the *police procedural*, where the mystery is solved by detailed police work, as in the work of Swedish writers Maj Sjowall and Per Wahloo; the *inverted novel*, where the identity of the criminal is known from the beginning, only the method or the motive remaining to be discovered, as in *Malice Aforethought* by Francis Iles; the *hard-boiled school* of private investigators begun by Raymond Chandler and Dashiell Hammett, which became known for its social realism and explicit violence. More recently, the form and traditions of the genre are used as a framework within which to explore other concerns, as in *Innocent Blood* and *A Taste For Death* by P D James, *The Name of the Rose* by Umberto Eco, and the works of many women writers who explore feminist ideas, for example Barbara Wilson with *Murder in the Collective* . As with most genres, crime fiction has produced its oddities: *Murder in Pastiche* by Marion Mainwaring is written in the styles of nine famous writers; Agatha Christie, Georgette Heyer and Ellis Peters have all written detective novels with historical settings; *Murder Off Miami* by Dennis Wheatley was a dossier containing real clues such as photographs, ticket stubs, and hairpins for the reader to solve the mystery. The solution was in a closed envelope at the back of the book.

epic a narrative poem or cycle of poems dealing with some great action, often the founding of a nation or the forging of national unity, and often using religious or cosmological themes. In the Western tradition, the crucial works are the *Iliad* and *Odyssey* attributed to Homer, works probably intended to be chanted in sections at feasts. Greek and later criticism, which considered the Homeric epic the highest form of poetry, produced a genre of *secondary epic*, notably the *Aeneid* of Virgil, Tasso's *Jerusalem Delivered* and Milton's *Paradise Lost*, which attempt to emulate Homer, often for a patron or a political cause. The term epic is also applied to narrative poems of other traditions in Europe: the Anglo-Saxon *Beowulf* and the Finnish *Kalevala*; in India the *Ramayana* and *Mahabharata*; the Babylonian *Gilgamesh*; all of these had evolved in different societies to suit similar social needs and used similar literary techniques.

essay a short prose work which deals in a personal and often meditative way with a particular subject. The term was first used in French, for Montaigne's *Essais* 1580–95, and the form became popular in the 18th century with the development of periodicals such as the *Tatler* and *Spectator* in England. In the 19th century the essay was often used as a vehicle for literary criticism. The term essay is less used today, although its form and approach survive, particularly in newspapers and magazines as 'opinion pieces'.

fantasy non-realistic fiction. Much of the world's fictional literature could be called fantasy, but as a contemporary genre fantasy started to thrive in the late 1960s after the success of Tolkien's *Lord of the Rings* 1954–55. Earlier works by such writers as Lord Dunsany, Hope Mirrlees and E R Eddison which are not classifiable in fantasy subgenres such as science fiction, horror, or the ghost story could be called fantasy. Dominant themes, drawn from the stock of world literature, used by Tolkien and his imitators, are those of the quest for a cure for evil and the reconciliation of the demands of the fantasy world and the more domestic claims of the ordinary world. Much fantasy is pseudo-medieval in subject matter and tone, following the spirit rather than the substance of Tolkien; but another strong influence has been the work of Mervyn Peake – *Titus Groan* 1946, *Gormenghast* 1950, and *Titus Alone* 1959 – in its grotesquerie and passion. Important works since Tolkien are Ursula Le Guin's *Earthsea Trilogy* and Stephen Donaldson's *Thomas Covenant*. Important works in the more urban tradition of Peake are John Crowley's *Little Big*, Michael Moorcock's *Gloriana* and Gene Wolfe's *Free, Life Free*. Much of the matter of such books overlaps with that of *magic realist* writers like Gabriel Garcìa Márquez and Angela Carter.

fiction a general term for any work or type of work whose content is completely or largely invented; the opposite of fact. In the 20th century the term is usually used to refer to imaginative works of narrative prose (such as the novel or the short story), and contrasted with *non-fiction* such as history, biography, or works on practical subjects, and with *poetry*. This usage reflects the dominance in contemporary Western literature of the novel as a vehicle for imaginative literature: strictly speaking, poems can also be fictional (as opposed to factual). Genres such as the *historical novel* often combine a fictional plot with real events; *biography* may also be 'fictionalized' through the use of imagined conversations or events.

free verse poetry without metrical form. At the beginning of the 20th century, under the very different influences of Whitman and Mallarmé, many poets became convinced that the

19th century had done most of what could be done with regular metrical forms and rejected regular metre in much the same spirit as Milton had rhyme, preferring irregular metres which made it possible to express thought clearly and without distortion. This was true of T S Eliot and the Imagists; it was also true of poets who, like the Russians Essnin and Mayakovsky, placed emphasis on public performance. Poets including Robert Graves and the later Auden have criticized free verse on the ground that it lacks the difficulty of true accomplishment, but their own metrics would have been considered loose much of the time by earlier critics. The freeness of free verse is largely relative.

historical novel a fictional prose narrative set in the past. Literature set in the historic past has always abounded, but Sir Walter Scott began the modern tradition by setting imaginative romances of love, impersonation, and betrayal in a past based on known fact; his use of historical accuracy, and that of European imitators such as Manzoni, gave rise to the genre. Some historical novels of the 19th century were overtly nationalistic, but most were merely novels set in the past to heighten melodrama while providing an informative framework; the genre was used by Victor Hugo and Charles Dickens, among many others. In the 20th century the historical novel also became concerned with exploring psychological states and the question of the difference in the mentality of the past. Successful examples of this are Robert Graves' novels about the Roman Emperor Claudius *I, Claudius* and *Claudius the God* and Margaret Yourcenar's *Memoirs of Hadrian*. The less serious possibilities of the historical novel were exploited by writers including Jeffery Farnol, Stanley Weyman, and Rafael Sabatini in the early 20th century as *historical romance*; Dorothy Dunnett and George MacDonald Fraser revived the historical romance with some success in the late 1960s. The historical novel acquired sub-genres – the stylized *Regency novel* of Georgette Heyer and her imitators; the *Napoleonic War sea story*, notably those of C S Forester and Patrick O'Brien. These forms

have developed their own conventions, particularly when imitating a massively popular ancestor – this has happened in large degree to the *western*, many of which use gestures from Owen Wister's classic *The Virginian*, and to the *novel of the American South* in the period of the Civil War in the wake of Margaret Mitchell's *Gone With the Wind*. Perhaps the most popular sub-genre of the historical novel in the late 20th century has been sequences of *novels about families*, often industrialists of the early 19th century.

horror a modern genre of fiction, devoted primarily to scaring the reader, but often also aiming at a catharsis of common fears through their exaggeration into the bizarre and grotesque. Horror is derived from the Gothic novel, which dealt in shock effects, as well as from folk tales and ghost stories throughout the ages. Dominant figures in the horror tradition are Mary Shelley (*Frankenstein* 1818), Bram Stoker, and H P Lovecraft and, among contemporary writers, Stephen King and Clive Barker. Horror writing tends to use motifs such as vampirism, the eruption of ancient evil, and monstrous transformation, which often derive from folk traditions, as well as more modern concerns such as psychopathology.

literary criticism the establishment of principles governing literary composition, and the assessment of literary works. The earliest systematic literary criticism was the *Poetics* of Aristotle; a later Greek critic was the author of the treatise *On the Sublime*, usually attributed to Longinus. Horace and Quintilian were influential Latin critics. The Italian Renaissance introduced humanist criticism, and the revival of classical scholarship exalted the authority of Aristotle and Horace. Like literature itself, European criticism then applied Neo-Classical, Romantic, and modern approaches. Contemporary criticism often applies insights to literary works from structuralism, semiotics, feminism, Marxism, and psychoanalysis, whereas earlier criticism tended to deal with moral or political ideas, or with a literary work as a formal object independent of its creator.

novel an extended fictional prose narrative,

often including some sense of the psychological development of the central characters and of their relationship with a broader world. There were works that could be called novels in ancient Greece and Rome, and a similar tradition existed in Japan as early as the 11th century, but the modern novel took its name and inspiration from the Italian *novella*, a kind of short tale which became popular in the 13th century. Boccaccio and other 14th- and 15th-century Italian writers were widely translated and influenced the development of the European novel; Cervantes in Spain (*Don Quixote* 1605) was also influential through translations into French and English. By the 18th century the works of Fielding (*Tom Jones* 1749), Richardson, Sterne, and Smollett had firmly established the tradition of the novel in England. By the 19th century the novel had become the main form of narrative fiction in Europe and the USA, for both writers and readers, and had begun to be divided into sub-genres such as the *novel of manners* or domestic novel, the *historical novel*, and the *Gothic romance*.

oral literature stories which are or have been transmitted in spoken form, such as public recitation, rather than through writing or printing. Most preliterate societies seem to have had a tradition of oral literature, including short 'folk tales', legends, proverbs, and riddles as well as longer narrative works; and most of the ancient epics – such as the Greek *Odyssey* and the Mesopotamian *Gilgamesh* – seem to have been composed and added to over many centuries before they were committed to writing. Some ancient stories from oral traditions have only been written down as literary works relatively recently, such as the Finnish *Kalevala* (1822); many *fairy tales*, such as those collected in Germany in the early 19th century by the Grimm brothers, also come into this category. The extent to which this sort of *folk literature* has been consciously embellished and altered, particularly in Europe in the 19th century for nationalistic purposes, is controversial.

poetry the imaginative expression of emotion or thought, often in metrical form, and often in figurative language. Poetry has traditionally been distinguished from *prose* (ordinary written language), especially with the term *verse* or rhythmical arrangement of words, although the distinction is not always clear cut. Poetry is often divided into *lyric*, or song-like poetry (sonnet, ode, elegy, pastoral), and *narrative*, or story-telling poetry (ballad, lay, epic). Poetic form has also been used as a vehicle for satire (by Pope, for example), parody, and expositions of philosophical, religious, and practical subjects.

romance in medieval times the term was used for tales of love and adventure, in verse or prose, which became popular in France about 1200 and spread throughout Europe. There were *Arthurian romances* about the legendary King Arthur and his knights, and romances based on the adventures of Charlemagne and on classical themes. The term gradually came to mean any fiction remote from the conditions and concerns of everyday life. In this sense, romance is a broad term which can include or overlap with such genres as the *historical novel* or *fantasy*. In the 20th century the term *romantic novel* is often used disparagingly, to imply a contrast with a realistic novel.

satire a work, in poetry or prose, which uses wit, humour, or irony, often through allegory or extended metaphor, to ridicule human pretensions or expose social evils. The Roman poets Juvenal and Horace wrote *Satires*, and the form became particularly popular in Europe in the 17th and 18th centuries, used by Voltaire in France and by Pope and Swift in England. Satire is related to *parody* in its intention to mock, but satire tends to be more subtle and to mock an attitude or a belief, whereas parody mocks a particular work such as a poem by imitating its style, often with purely comic intent rather than to make a moral point. Both satire and parody, to be effective, require a knowledge of the original attitude, person, or work that is being mocked (although much satire, such as *Gulliver's Travels* by Swift, can also be enjoyed simply on a literal level, as an adventure story).

science fiction is sometimes known as *SF*, allowing the alternative versions *science fantasy* and *speculative fiction*. The genre often takes its ideas and concerns from current ideas in science and social science (or at second or later hands from earlier works in the genre) and aims to shake up standard perceptions of reality. SF works are often set in the near or far future and deal with such matters as travel through space or time, robots, aliens, utopias and dystopias (often satiric), and psychic powers. The genre is sometimes held to have had its roots in the works of Mary Shelley, notably *Frankenstein* 1818; important early practitioners were Jules Verne and H G Wells. In the 20th century the American pulp magazine tradition of SF produced writers such as Arthur C Clarke, Isaac Asimov, Robert Heinlein and Frank Herbert; a consensus of 'pure storytelling' and traditional values was disrupted by writers associated with the British magazine *New Worlds* – Brian W Aldiss, Michael Moorcock, J G Ballard – and by younger American writers – Joanna Russ, Ursula le Guin, Thomas Disch, Gene Wolfe – who used the form for serious literary purposes and for political and sexual radicalism. Thriving SF traditions, only partly influenced by, and not influencing, the Anglo-American one, exist in France, Germany, and Eastern Europe.

short story a short work of prose fiction, which in general either sets up and resolves a single narrative point or sets up and leaves hanging a mood or an atmosphere. Various lengths of short narrative fiction were used before, and as alternatives to, the novel, and many writers of the 19th century wrote occasional short stories, but the form achieved real significance in the hands of Chekhov, Kipling, de Maupassant and Katherine Mansfield. In the 20th century the short story is also often used for genre pieces such as detective fiction and science fiction.

Great Writers

Abu Nuwās Hasan ibn Hāni 762–c. 815. Arab poet. His work was based on old forms, but the new freedom with which he used them, his eroticism, and his ironic humour, have contributed to his reputation as perhaps the greatest of Arab poets.

Austen Jane 1775–1817. English novelist, noted for her domestic novels of manners. All her novels are set within the confines of middle-class English provincial society, and show her skill at drawing characters and situations with delicate irony. Her first attempt was the burlesque *Love and Friendship* written in 1790; her mature works are *Sense and Sensibility* 1811 (like its successors, published anonymously), *Pride and Prejudice* 1813, *Mansfield Park* 1814, *Emma* 1816, *Persuasion* 1818, and *Northanger Abbey* 1818, a skit on the Gothic novel. The same spirit pervades her *Letters*, especially to her sister Cassandra.

Balzac Honoré de 1799–1850. French novelist. His first success, *Les Chouans* 1829, was inspired by Sir Walter Scott, but his major work was the monumental series *La Comédie humaine* (planned as 143 volumes, of which only 80 were completed), which portrayed vice and folly in contemporary French society. It includes *Eugénie Grandet* 1833, dealing with avarice; *Le Père Goriot* 1834, doting fatherly love; *Cousine Bette* 1846, jealousy; and *Cousin Pons* 1847, greed.

Bashō. Pseudonym of Japanese poet Matsuo Munefusa 1644–94. The master of the haiku, a 17–syllable poetic form with lines of 5, 7, and 5 syllables, which he infused with subtle allusiveness and made the accepted form of poetic expression in Japan. His most famous work is *Oku-no-hosomichi/The Narrow Road to the Deep North* 1694, an account of a visit to northern Japan, which consists of haikus interspersed with prose passages.

Baudelaire Charles Pierre 1821–67. French poet, whose work combined rhythmical and musical perfection with a morbid romanticism and eroticism, often using oriental imagery (he had been sent to India as a young man because of his dissipation), and finding beauty in decadence and evil. His first book of verse, *Les Fleurs du mal/Flowers of Evil* 1857, caused a scandal, and was condemned by the censor as endangering public morals, but was enormously influential, paving the way for Rimbaud, Verlaine, and the symbolist school.

Blake William 1757–1827. British mystical poet and artist. His works, for which he engraved both text and illustrations himself, embody his own mystic mythology, and include *Songs of Innocence* 1789, *The Marriage of Heaven and Hell* 1793, *Songs of Experience* 1794, and *Milton* 1804 (his most famous lines, set to music as 'Jerusalem', are taken from the preface). He also produced illustrations for *Paradise Lost*, *The Book of Job*, and Dante's *Divine Comedy*.

Boccaccio Giovanni 1313–75. Italian writer, best remembered for his *Decameron* 1348–53, containing 100 tales as told by ten young people seeking refuge from the plague in the country. Its bawdiness and exuberance as well as narrative skill and characterization made the work enormously popular and influential, inspiring Chaucer, Shakespeare, Dryden, and Keats among many others.

Brontë family of English writers, including the three sisters *Charlotte* 1816–55, *Emily Jane* 1818–48 and *Anne* 1820–49, and their brother *Patrick Branwell* 1817–48, who were brought up in isolation at Haworth rectory (now a museum) in Yorkshire. In 1846 the sisters published a volume of poems under the pseudonyms Currer (Charlotte), Ellis (Emily) and Acton (Anne) Bell. In 1847 (using the same names), they published the novels *Jane Eyre* (by Charlotte), *Wuthering Heights* (by Emily), and *Agnes Grey*, Anne's much weaker work. During 1848–49 Branwell, Emily, and Anne all died of tuberculosis. Charlotte subsequently published *Shirley* 1849, in which the

heroine resembles Emily, and *Villette* 1853.

Burns Robert 1759–96. Scottish poet, born at Alloway near Ayr, notable for his use of the Scots dialect at a time when it was not considered 'suitable' for literature. His fame rests equally on his poems, published in *Poems, Chiefly in the Scottish Dialect* 1786, including 'Holy Willie's Prayer', 'Tam o'Shanter', 'The Jolly Beggars', and 'To a Mouse', and his songs, of which he contributed some 300 to Johnson's *Scots Musical Museum* 1787–1803, and Thomson's *Scottish Airs with Poetry* 1793–1811, sometimes wholly original, sometimes adaptations of traditional works.

Byron George Gordon, 6th Baron Byron 1788–1824. English poet, who became the symbol of Romanticism and political liberalism throughout Europe in the 19th century. He published his first volume *Hours of Idleness* 1807, and attacked its harsh critics in *English Bards and Scotch Reviewers* 1809. He gained fame with the first two cantos of *Childe Harold* 1812, romantically describing his tours in Portugal, Spain and the Balkans (third canto 1816, fourth 1818). This was followed by *The Prisoner of Chillon 1816*, showing the influence of Shelley, *Beppo* 1818, *Mazeppa* 1819, and his masterpiece *Don Juan* 1819–24. He dabbled in Italian revolutionary politics, and sailed for Greece in 1823 to further the Greek struggle for independence, but died of fever at Missolonghi.

Camoëns or **Camões,** Luís Vaz de 1524–80. Portuguese poet. A soldier and adventurer, he was shipwrecked in 1558, but the manuscript of his poem, the *Lusiads*, was saved with him. It was published in 1572, telling of the voyages of the Portuguese explorer Vasco da Gama and incorporating much Portuguese history, and is considered the country's national epic. His posthumously published lyric poetry is also now valued.

Cervantes *(Saavedra)* Miguel de 1547–1616. Spanish novelist, playwright, and poet. He wrote several plays, and his pastoral romance *Galatea* was published in 1585. His masterpiece *Don Quixote*, telling of a knight errant out of his time, and of his servant Sancho Panza, appeared in 1605 and immediately achieved great success; within a few years it had been translated into English and French, and it was an important influence on the development of the European novel. He also wrote *Novelas Exemplares* 1613, a collection of short poems, the *Viage del Parnaso* 1614, a burlesque poem, and a sequel to *Don Quixote* 1615, considered even better than the first in construction and characterization.

Chaucer Geoffrey c. 1340–1400. The greatest and most influential English poet of the Middle Ages. He held various official appointments, such as controller of London customs, and was sent on missions to Italy (where he may have met Boccaccio and Petrarch), France, and Flanders. His early work showed formal French influence, as in his adaptation of the French allegorical poem on courtly love the *Romaunt of the Rose*; more mature works reflected the influence of Italian realism, as in his long narrative poem *Troilus and Criseyde*, adapted from Boccaccio. In his masterpiece, *The Canterbury Tales* c. 1387, a collection of tales told by a group of pilgrims on their way to the shrine of Thomas Becket, he showed his own genius for metre and characterization. The popularity of his work assured the dominance of the southern English dialect in literature.

Dante Alighieri 1265–1321. Italian poet, soldier and politician. A Florentine, he fell in love with Beatrice (Portinari) in 1274, a love which survived her marriage to another and her death in 1290, which Dante described in *La Vita Nuova* c. 1295. His *Divina Commedia* c. 1307–21, an imaginary journey through Hell, Purgatory and Paradise, under the guidance of Virgil, representing Reason, and Beatrice, representing Faith, is generally considered the greatest poem of the Middle Ages.

Defoe Daniel c. 1660–1731. English novelist and journalist, best remembered for his adventure novel *Robinson Crusoe* 1719. A master of realistic narrative, he was also the author of the pirate story *Captain Singleton* 1720, the picaresque novel *Moll Flanders* 1722, and much political satire.

Dickens Charles 1812–70. English novelist, noted for his memorable characters (such as Mr Micawber and Uriah Heep), and for his portrayals of the social evils of Victorian England. As a child of 12 he worked briefly in a blacking factory (as did the hero of *David Copperfield* 1849). He wrote *Sketches by Boz* for the *Morning Chronicle*. The publication of the first number of the *Pickwick Papers* 1836 made him famous. This was followed by *Oliver Twist* 1838, *Nicholas Nickleby* 1839, *Barnaby Rudge* 1840, and *The Old Curiosity Shop* 1841, all in weekly parts. A visit to the USA in 1842 was reflected in *American Notes* and *Martin Chuzzlewit* 1843. *A Christmas Carol*, also 1843, was the first of his Christmas books. Later novels were *Dombey and Son* 1848, *Bleak House* 1853, *Hard Times* 1854, *Little Dorrit* 1857, *A Tale of Two Cities* 1859, a historical novel indebted to Carlyle's *French Revolution*; *Great Expectations* 1861, *Our Mutual Friend* 1864, and *Edwin Drood*, influenced by Wilkie Collins's mystery stories but left unfinished at his death.

Donne John 1572–1631. British metaphysical poet, so called because of his use of subtle imagery and figurative language. His appointment as private secretary to Sir Thomas Egerton was ended by his secret marriage to Ann More (died 1617), niece of Egerton's wife, the subject of many of his love poems. Originally a Roman Catholic, he took orders in the Anglican Church in 1615, and as Dean of St Paul's 1621–31 was noted for his sermons. His poetry was not collected for publication until after his death, and was long out of favour, but he is now recognized as one of the greatest English poets. Many of his sonnets are popularly known by their first lines, such as 'No man is an island' and 'Death, be not proud'.

Dostoevsky Fyodor Mihailovich 1821–81. Russian novelist. His first novel, *Poor Folk*, appeared in 1846. In 1849 he was arrested as a socialist revolutionary, and was sent to the penal settlement at Omsk for four years. Pardoned in 1859, he published the humorous *Village of Stepanchikovo*, *The House of the Dead* 1861, recalling his prison experiences, and *The Insulted and the Injured* 1862. He lived abroad for a period, but returned to Russia in 1871. *Crime and Punishment* 1866, *The Idiot* 1868, and the great work of his last years, *The Brothers Karamazov* 1880, all show his genius for psychological analysis of character and creating narrative tension.

Eliot George. Pseudonym of English novelist Mary Ann Evans 1819–80. From 1851 she worked in London on the *Westminster Review*, and from 1854 she lived with philosopher and critic George Henry Lewes (1817–78). She published *Amos Barton*, the first of the *Scenes of Clerical Life*, in 1857 under the name of George Eliot. She portrayed rural Victorian society, particularly its intellectual hypocrisy, with realism and irony in *The Mill on the Floss* 1860, *Silas Marner* 1861, and *Middlemarch* 1872, her masterpiece.

Eliot T(homas) S(tearns) 1888–1965. American-born poet, critic, and dramatist, British subject 1927. Settling in London in 1915, he expressed the disillusionment of the generation affected by World War I in his first volume, *Prufrock and other Observations* 1917. He established his central position in modern poetry with his bleak vision *The Waste Land* 1922. *Ash Wednesday* 1930 reflected his emergence in 1927 as an Anglo-Catholic, as did the poetic drama *Murder in the Cathedral* 1935, dealing with Becket. *The Cocktail Party* 1949 attempted a revival of contemporary verse drama. His collection *Old Possum's Book of Practical Cats* 1939 was used for the musical *Cats* 1981. He was also an influential literary critic, helping, for example, to re-assess the importance of Donne.

Fielding Henry 1707–54. English novelist, whose individual genius at narrative influenced the form and technique of the novel and helped to make it the most popular form of literature in England. *Joseph Andrews* 1742 began as a parody of Samuel Richardson's sentimental *Pamela*, but became a success in its own right. His masterpiece is *Tom Jones* 1749, which he described as a 'comic epic in prose'.

Firdawsî Mansûr Abu'l-Qâsim c. 935–c. 1020. Persian poet, generally considered the greatest epic poet of Persia. His *Shahnama/ The Book of Kings* relates the history of Persia in 60,000 verses, and includes the legend of Sohrab and Rustum, in which the father unknowingly kills his son in battle.

Flaubert Gustave 1821–80. French novelist, one of the greatest of the 19th century. His masterpiece, noted for its psychological realism, is *Madame Bovary* 1857, the story of a country doctor's wife who commits suicide after a series of unhappy love affairs. Other works include *Sentimental Education* 1869, *Three Tales* 1877, and *Dictionary of Trite Ideas*, a collection of clichés and stock phrases amassed throughout his life.

Goethe Johann Wolfgang von 1749–1832. German poet, novelist, dramatist, philosopher and statesman, generally considered the founder of modern German literature. At first inspired by the works of Shakespeare, he wrote the play *Götz von Berlichingen* 1773. He became the leader of the romantic and emotional *Sturm und Drang* ('storm and stress') movement with the autobiographical novel *The Sorrows of the Young Werther* 1774. His masterpiece is the poetic play *Faust* 1808, completed in a second part in 1831. A visit to Italy 1786–88 inspired the classical dramas *Iphigenie auf Tauris* 1787 and *Tasso* 1790. Also memorable are the *Wilhelm Meister* novels 1796–1829, and his lyrics, many of which were set to music.

Hâfiz Shams al-Din Muhammad c. 1326–90. Persian poet, generally considered the greatest lyric poet of Persia. Born in Shiraz, he taught in a Dervish college there. His *Diwan*, a collection of short odes, contains some extolling the pleasures of life and others satirizing his fellow Dervishes.

Hardy Thomas 1840–1928. English poet and novelist. In his novels, set in the imaginary county of 'Wessex' in SW England, human loves and hates are played out against a harshly indifferent force of nature which he believed to govern the world. His novels include *Far from the Madding Crowd* 1874, *The Return of the Native* 1878, *The Mayor of Casterbridge* 1886, *The Woodlanders* 1887, and *Tess of the*

D'Urbervilles 1891, which caused an outcry because the heroine was a woman seduced. Even greater antagonism was roused by *Jude the Obscure* 1895, which reinforced his decision to confine himself to verse. He also wrote remarkable love lyrics, especially those linked with his dead first wife Emma Gifford, and a blank verse panorama of the Napoleonic Wars, *The Dynasts* 1904–8.

Heine Heinrich 1797–1856. German revolutionary and romantic poet. His *Reisebilder*, which announced his revolutionary sympathies, appeared in 1826, and the *Buch der Lieder/Book of Songs* in 1827. From 1831 he lived mainly in Paris, as a correspondent for German newspapers. Schubert and Schumann set many of his songs to music.

Homer c. 800 BC. Legendary Greek epic poet, according to tradition a blind minstrel and the author of the *Iliad* and the *Odyssey*. The *Iliad* tells of the siege of Troy, and the *Odyssey* of the adventures of Ulysses returning from it. Although there is controversy about the origin of the poems (they are now generally believed to stem from a number of bards of ancient oral tradition), they are landmarks which had an enormous influence on all of subsequent Western literature.

Horace (Quintus Horatius Flaccus) 65–8BC. Roman poet. Son of a freedman, he fought under Brutus at Philippi and lost his estate, but was introduced by Virgil to Maecenas in c. 38, who gave him a small property in the Sabine hills, and recommended him to the patronage of Augustus. He published in 35–30 *Satires* on contemporary society, and in his *Odes* and *Epistles* dealt with both political and personal themes with unrivalled economy and grace of language. He also wrote an influential critical work, *Ars poetica*.

Iqbāl Sir Muhammad 1873–1938. Islamic poet and thinker, generally considered the greatest modern Islamic poet. His literary works, in Urdu and Persian, were mostly verse in the classical style, suitable for public recitation. His most celebrated work is the Persian *Asrā-e khūdī/Secrets of the Self* 1915, in which he put forward a theory of the self which was

the opposite of the traditional abnegation of Islam. He sought through his writings to arouse Muslims to take their place in the modern world, and was an influence on the movement which led to the creation of Pakistan.

James Henry 1843–1916. Anglo-American novelist, whose main theme is the impact of European culture upon the American soul. Novels include *Roderick Hudson* 1876, *The American* 1877, *The Portrait of a Lady* 1881, *Washington Square* 1881, *The Bostonians* 1886, *The Wings of a Dove* 1902, *The Ambassadors* 1903, and *The Golden Bowl* 1904. The supernatural tale *The Turn of the Screw* 1898 was used for an opera by Benjamin Britten. After 1875 he lived in Europe, becoming a naturalized British subject in 1915. His style, always subtle, became increasingly complex.

Joyce James Augustin Aloysius 1882–1941. Irish writer, born in Dublin, who revolutionized the form of the English novel with his 'stream of consciousness' technique. His works include *Dubliners* 1914 (short stories), *Portrait of the Artist as a Young Man* 1916 (semi-autobiographical), and *Ulysses* 1922, which records the events of a single Dublin day, mingling direct narrative with the unspoken and unconscious reactions of the characters. The book, banned at first for obscenity in England and the USA, was enormously influential. *Finnegan's Wake* 1939 continued Joyce's experiments with language, attempting a synthesis of all existence.

Kālidāsa ?c. 5th century AD. Indian epic poet and dramatist, who according to tradition served at the court of King Vikramaditya at Ujjain. His works, in Sanskrit, include the classic drama *Sakuntala*, the love story of King Dushyanta for the nymph Sakuntala.

Keats John 1795–1821. English poet, a leading figure in the Romantic movement. He published *Poems* 1817, and *Endymion* 1818. In 1819 he wrote the richly imaginative *The Eve of St Agnes*, the *Odes* (including odes *To Autumn*, *On a Grecian Urn*, and *To a Nightingale*), and in this year he fell hopelessly in love with Fanny Brawne. In 1820 he published his last volume of poetry; stricken with tuberculosis, he went to Italy hoping for a cure, but died in Rome. Valuable insight into his own feelings is provided by his *Letters*, published in 1848.

Lawrence D(avid) H(erbert) 1885–1930. British novelist and poet, who in his work expressed his belief in emotion and the sexual impulse as creative and true to human nature. Son of a Nottinghamshire miner, he achieved fame with the semi-autobiographical *Sons and Lovers* 1913. In 1914 he married Frieda von Richthofen, with whom he had run away in 1912, and who was the model for Ursula Brangwen in *The Rainbow* 1915, and its sequel *Women in Love* 1921. His travels in search of health (he suffered from tuberculosis, from which he eventually died near Nice) prompted books such as *Mornings in Mexico* 1927. Most famous of his novels is *Lady Chatterley's Lover* 1928, banned as obscene in the UK until 1960. He also excelled in the short story, such as 'The Woman Who Rode Away'.

Li Bo 701–762. Chinese poet. He wrote in traditional forms, but his exuberance, the boldness of his imagination, and the intensity of his feeling have won him recognition as perhaps the greatest of all Chinese poets. Although he was mostly concerned with higher themes, he is also noted for his celebration of the joys of drinking.

Mann Thomas 1875–1955. German novelist, particularly concerned with the theme of the artist's relation to society. His first novel, *Buddenbrooks* 1900, dealt with an old Hanseatic family in his native Lübeck, and *The Magic Mountain* 1924 led to a Nobel prize in 1929. Forced abroad by the Nazi regime, he became a US citizen in 1940. Later works were *Dr Faustus* 1947 and *Confessions of Felix Krull* 1954. Most famous of his short stories was 'Death in Venice' 1913.

Milton John 1608–74. English Puritan poet. His early poems include the pastoral *L'Allegro* and *Il Penseroso* of 1632, the masque *Comus* 1633, and the elegy for a dead friend *Lycidas* 1637. His middle years were devoted to the Puritan cause, writing pamphlets, including one advocating divorce, and another

(*Areopagitica*) freedom of the press. From 1649 he was (Latin) secretary to the Council of State, his assistants (as his sight failed) including Marvell. The masterpieces of his old age are his epic poems on biblical themes, *Paradise Lost* 1667, *Paradise Regained* 1677, and the classic drama *Samson Agonistes*, also 1677. His majestic use of language has been compared with that of Virgil.

Montaigne Michel Eyquem de 1533–92. French writer, noted for his creation of the essay form. A lawyer, he became mayor of Bordeaux 1581–85, publishing his *Essais* from 1580. They deal with all aspects of life from an urbanely sceptical viewpoint, and through the translation of John Florio in 1603 influenced Shakespeare and other English writers.

Murasaki Shikibu 978–c. 1015 pseudonym of an unknown Japanese woman writer. Her masterpiece of romantic prose fiction, the *Tale of Genji*, written about 1015, is one of the great works of Japanese literature, and has been described as the world's first novel.

Petrarch (Italian *Petrarca*), Francesco 1304–74. Italian poet, a friend of Boccaccio, and a devotee of the classical tradition, who has been called the father of modern poetry. His *Il Canzoniere* were sonnets in praise of his idealized love 'Laura', whom he first saw in 1327 (a married woman, she refused to become his mistress) and who died of plague 1348. His 14-line sonnets, in a form which was given the name Petrarchan, were influential for centuries.

Pope Alexander 1688–1744. English poet and satirist, noted for his biting wit, which he expressed in the form of heroic couplets. His *Essay on Criticism* 1711 pilloried literary figures of the age, and his mock-heroic poem *Rape of the Lock* 1712 established his reputation. He translated the *Iliad* 1715–20 and the *Odyssey* 1725–26, and also wrote the much-quoted philosophical *Essay on Man* 1733–34 and *Moral Essays* 1731–35. Many of his lines have attained almost the status of proverbs, such as 'A little knowledge is a dangerous thing'.

Proust Marcel 1871–1922. French novelist. An invalid from childhood, he retired after the death of his father (1904) and mother (1905) to the quiet of a cork-lined room in his Paris flat to write his mammoth autobiographical series of novels *À la Recherche du Temps Perdu/ Remembrance of Things Past* 1913–27.

Rabelais François c. 1494–1553. French Renaissance humanist and satirist, best remembered for *Pantagruel* 1532–33 and *Gargantua* 1534, satiric allegories laced with coarse humour which tell of the adventures of the giant Gargantua and his son Pantagruel.

Shakespeare William 1564–1616. English dramatist and poet, generally considered the greatest English playwright. His works are central to English literature as well as theatre. Early plays, written c. 1589–93, were the tragedy *Titus Andronicus*; the comedies *The Comedy of Errors, The Taming of the Shrew,* and *Two Gentlemen of Verona*; the three parts of *Henry VI*; and *Richard III*. About 1593 he came under the patronage of the Earl of Southampton, to whom he dedicated his long poems *Venus and Adonis* 1593 and *Lucrece* 1594; he also wrote for him the comedy *Love's Labour's Lost*, satirizing Raleigh's circle, and seems to have dedicated to him his sonnets written c. 1593–96, in which the mysterious 'Dark Lady' appears. From 1594 Shakespeare was a member of the chamberlain's (later the king's) company of players, and had no rival as a dramatist, with the lyric plays *Romeo and Juliet, Midsummer Night's Dream,* and *Richard II* 1594–95, followed by *King John* and *The Merchant of Venice* in 1596. The Falstaff plays of 1597–99: *Henry IV* (parts I and II), *Henry V,* and *The Merry Wives of Windsor* (said to have been written at the request of Elizabeth I), brought his fame to its height. About the same time he wrote *Julius Caesar* 1599. The period ended with the lyrically witty *Much Ado about Nothing, As You Like It,* and *Twelfth Night* c. 1598–1601. With *Hamlet* 1601, a 'darker' period seems to begin, reflected also in the comedies *Troilus and Cressida, All's Well that Ends Well,* and *Measure for Measure* c. 1601–4. *Othello, Macbeth,* and *King Lear* followed 1604–6, together with *Timon of Athens* in which pessimism reaches its depths.

Antony and Cleopatra and *Coriolanus* 1607–8 have a more balanced acceptance of life. Shakespeare was only part author of *Pericles*, but like the other plays of c. 1608–11, *Cymbeline, The Winter's Tale,* and *The Tempest,* it has a sunset glow about it. During 1613 he collaborated with Fletcher in *Henry VIII* and probably in *Two Noble Kinsmen.* The collected edition of his plays (the First Folio) was published in 1623 by his fellow-actors, Heminge and Condell.

Shelley Percy Bysshe 1792–1822. English poet, a leading figure in the Romantic movement. His collaboration in the pamphlet *The Necessity of Atheism* in 1811 caused his expulsion from Oxford. In London he fell in love with 16–year-old Harriet Westbrook, whom he married in 1811, but they were soon estranged. Political freedom was the theme of his revolutionary poem *Queen Mab* 1813. In 1814 he left England with Mary Wollstonecraft Godwin, whom he married in 1816 and who became known as the writer Mary Shelley, author of *Frankenstein* 1818. By 1818 they were living in Italy, where he produced the tragedy *The Cenci* 1819, the lyric drama *Prometheus Unbound* 1820, and *Adonais* 1821, on the death of Keats, as well as his most famous short lyrics, 'Ode to the West Wind', 'The Cloud', and 'To a Skylark'. He was drowned while sailing near Spezia.

Soyinka Wole 1934– . Nigerian writer, who was a political prisoner in Nigeria 1967–69 (prison memoirs *The Man Died* 1972). His works include the play *The Lion and the Jewel* 1963, and *Aké, The Years of Childhood,* an autobiography.

Spenser Edmund 1552–99. English poet, best remembered for his allegorical poem *The Faerie Queene* 1590–96, in homage to Queen Elizabeth, of which only six of the planned 12 books were published. His other works include *The Shepheard's Calendar* 1579, the *Epithalamion* 1595, and love sonnets. He has been called the 'poet's poet' for his versification, richness of language, and fertile imagery.

Sterne Laurence 1713–68. Irish writer, best remembered for his unique comic masterpiece

The Life and Opinions of Tristram Shandy, Gent. 1760–67, an eccentrically whimsical and bawdy work which foreshadowed many of the techniques and literary devices of 20th-century novelists, including Joyce. He also wrote the popular *Sentimental Journey through France and Italy* 1768.

Swift Jonathan 1667–1745. Irish poet and satirist, best known for his *Gulliver's Travels* 1726, a satire on people and political institutions which has also appealed to generations of children and adults as an adventure story. He also wrote *A Tale of a Tub* 1697, and many poems and political pamphlets.

Tagore (Sir) Rabindranath 1861–1941. Indian writer in Bengali. One of the most influential Indian authors of the 20th century, he translated into English his own verse *Gitanjali* ('song offerings') 1912 and his verse play *Chitra*, which brought him world fame.

Tolstoy Leo Nikolaievich 1828–1910. Russian novelist. His masterpieces are *War and Peace* 1864, an epic novel dealing with the Napoleonic Wars, and *Anna Karenina* 1877. He preached his own version of ascetic Christianity in his didactic later books *What is Religion?* and *The Kreutzer Sonata* and his novel *Resurrection* 1900, which influenced Gandhi.

Turgenev Ivan Sergeievich 1818–83. Russian writer, noted for his poetic realism, his pessimism, and his skill at characterization, particularly of women. Major works include the play *A Month in the Country* 1849, and the novels *A Nest of Gentlefolk* 1858, *Fathers and Sons* 1862, and *Virgin Soil* 1877. His series of *A Sportsman's Sketches* 1852 strongly criticized serfdom. He lived abroad from 1856.

Villon François 1431–85. French poet, noted for his satiric humour, pathos, and lyric power in works which used the *argot* (slang) of the time. Very little of his work survives, but his best known poem is the *Ballade des dames du temps jadis* containing the line 'Ou sont les nièges d'antan?'('Where are the snows of yesteryear?').

Virgil (Publius Vergilius Maro) 70–19 BC. Roman poet. Born near Mantua, he was of the small farmer class whose life he celebrated in his pastoral *Eclogues* 37 BC, and *Georgics* or 'Art of Husbandry' 30 BC. His epic poem, the *Aeneid*, in 12 books, glorified the dynasty of his patron Augustus. By the 3rd century his works were used for divination, and he was popularly thought a magician. He was one of the most influential Roman writers, partly because his apparent forecast of the birth of Christ in the fourth eclogue led to his acceptance as an 'honorary Christian' by the medieval church.

Wordsworth William 1770–1850. English poet, a leading figure in the Romantic movement. In 1797 he settled with his sister Dorothy in Somerset to be near Coleridge, collaborating with him in *Lyrical Ballads* 1798 (which included 'Tintern Abbey') and attempting to avoid poetic diction and 'give the charm of novelty to things of every day'. From 1799 he lived in the Lake District. Outstanding among later works were the *Poems* 1807 (including 'Intimations of Immortality'), and *The Prelude* (written by 1805, published 1850), which was written to form part of the great autobiographical work *The Recluse*, never completed.

Yeats William Butler 1865–1939. Irish poet and playwright, a leader of the Celtic revival, and a founder of the Abbey Theatre in Dublin . His early poetry was romantically lyrical, as in 'The Lake Isle of Innisfree', and he drew on Irish legend for his poetic plays *The Countess Cathleen* 1892 and *The Land of Heart's Desire* 1894. His later works were sharper and had a mystical aspect; his mystical beliefs were expressed in his prose work *A Vision* 1925 and 1937. His later books of poetry include *The Wild Swans at Coole* 1919 and *The Winding Stair* 1933.

Booker Prize for fiction (British)

1969	P H Newby *Something to Answer For*
1970	Bernice Rubens *The Elected Member*
1971	V S Naipaul *In a Free State*
1972	John Berger *G*
1973	J G Farrell *The Siege of Krishnapur*
1974	Nadine Gordimer *The Conservationist*; Stanley Middleton *Holiday*
1975	Ruth Prawer Jhabvala *Heat and Dust*
1976	David Storey *Saville*
1977	Paul Scott *Staying On*
1978	Iris Murdoch *The Sea, The Sea*
1979	Penelope Fitzgerald *Offshore*
1980	William Golding *Rites of Passage*
1981	Salman Rushdie *Midnight's Children*
1982	Thomas Keneally *Schindler's Ark*
1983	J M Coetzee *Life and Times of Michael K*
1984	Anita Brookner *Hotel du Lac*
1985	Keri Hulme *The Bone People*
1986	Kingsley Amis *The Old Devils*

Nobel Prize for Literature (International)

1970	Alexander Solzhenitsyn (Russian)
1971	Pablo Neruda (Chilean)
1972	Heinrich Böll (West German)
1973	Patrick White (Australian)
1974	Eyvind Johnson, Harry Edmund Martinson (both Swedish)
1975	Eugenio Montale (Italian)
1976	Saul Bellow (American)
1977	Vincente Aleixandra (Spanish)
1978	Isaac Bashevis Singer (American)
1979	Odysseus Elytis (Greek)
1980	Czeslaw Milosz (Polish-American)
1981	Elias Canetti (Bulgarian-British)
1982	Gabriel García Márquez (Colombian-Mexican)
1983	William Golding (British)
1984	Jaroslav Seifert (Czechoslovakian)
1985	Claude Simon (French)
1986	Wole Soyinka (Nigerian)

Prix Goncourt for fiction (French)

1970	Michel Tournier *Le Roi des aulnes*
1971	Jacques Laurent *Les Bêtises*
1972	Jean Carrière *L'Épervier de Maheux*
1973	Jacques Chessex *L'Ogre*
1974	Pascal Lainé *La Dentellière*
1975	Emile Ajar *La Vie devant soi*
1976	Patrick Grainville *Les Flamboyants*
1977	Didier Decoin *John L'Enfer*
1978	Patrick Modiano *Rue des boutiques obscures*
1979	Antonine Maillet *Pelagie-la-Charrette*
1980	Yves Navarre *Le Jardin d'acclimation*
1981	Lucien Bodard *Anne Marie*
1982	Dominique Fernandez *Dans la Main de l'ange*
1983	Frederick Tristan *Les Égares*
1984	Marguerite Duras *L'Amant*
1985	Yann Queffelec *Les Noces barbares*
1986	Michel Host *Valet de Nuit*

Pulitzer Prize for fiction (American)

1970	Jean Stafford *Collected Stories*
1972	Wallace Stegner *Angle of Repose*
1973	Eudora Welty *The Optimist's Daughter*
1975	Michael Shaara *The Killer Angels*
1976	Saul Bellow *Humboldt's Gift*
1978	James Alan McPherson *Elbow Room*
1979	John Cheever *The Stories of John Cheever*
1980	Norman Mailer *The Executioner's Song*
1981	John Kennedy Toole *A Confederacy of Dunces*
1982	John Updike *Rabbit is Rich*
1983	Alice Walker *The Color Purple*
1984	William Kennedy *Ironweed*
1985	Alison Lurie *Foreign Affairs*
1986	Larry McMurtry *Lonesome Dove*
1987	Peter Taylor *A Summons to Memphis*

c. 1500 BC *Vedas*, Hindu scriptures, written in Sanskrit.

12th century *I Ching/Book of Changes*, Chinese work on divination, attributed to Wen Wang.

8th century Homer, Greek epic poet, reputed to be the author of the *Iliad* and *Odyssey* .

c. 650 *Epic of Gilgamesh* written down, Mesopotamian epic poem (the story itself is at least 1,500 years older).

c. 612 Sappho, Greek lyric woman poet, was born.

518 Pindar, Greek writer of odes, was born.

5th century The *Pentateuch* (five books of Moses) of the Jewish *Bible* (Old Testament) reached its final form. Other parts of the Bible (Psalms and Proverbs) were much older.

c. 400 the *Upanishads*, prose and verse commentaries on the *Vedas* (Hindu scriptures).

c. 310 Theocritus, Greek pastoral poet, was born.

c. 300 The *Mahabharata* and *Ramayana*, Hindu epic poems.

106 Cicero, Roman orator and prose writer, was born.

70 Virgil, Roman poet, author of the *Aeneid*, was born.

65 Horace, Roman poet, was born.

43 Ovid, Roman poet, was born.

60 AD Juvenal, Roman satirist, was born.

1st century The Gospels of the Christian New Testament were written.

5th century Kālidāsa, Indian poet, regarded as the greatest writer in classical Sanskrit, was writing.

c. 450 Germanic invasion of England, from which the development of English as an independent language is dated.

7th century The *Quran* or *Koran*, the Islamic scriptures, was written.

618–906 Tang Dynasty in China, the great period of Chinese poetry. Book printing was invented in China.

c. 670–80 Caedmon, the earliest English Christian poet, was composing.

699 Li Bo, Chinese poet, was born.

713 Du Fu, Chinese poet, was born.

750–1050 'Golden Age' of classical Arabic literature.

c. 750 *Beowulf*, the only surviving Old English heroic epic; *Wanderer* and *Seafarer*, Old English elegaic poems; 'Golden Age' of Chinese poetry.

762 Abu Nuwās, Arab poet, was born.

c. 800 *Meng Shu*, a collection of edifying Chinese anecdotes for children, was introduced into Japan. One of the earliest known examples of children's literature, it was influential until the 19th century.

890 *Anglo-Saxon Chronicle* recording historic events until 1140 was begun.

c. 890 *Cantilène de Ste Eulalie*, earliest known French poem.

c. 900   *Arabian Nights* begun.

c. 955   Firdawsî, Persian poet, was writing.

c. 1015   *The Tale of Genji* by Murasaki Shikibu, romantic novel, one of the greatest Japanese prose works.

c. 1066   Omar Khayyam, Persian poet and scientist, was writing.

1066   Norman Conquest of England. Over the next 100 years Old English developed into Middle English. The French of the ruling classes had an increasing effect on the language and literature.

c. 1110   Rise of Troubadour poetry in France and Provence.

1140   Chrétien of Troyes, French court poet, author of Arthurian romances, was born.

c. 1150   Rise of Middle English lyric poetry; rise and development of Icelandic sagas.

c. 1200   *Niebelungenlied* , German epic poem; *Ancrene Riwle/Rule for Anchoresses*, Middle English devotional prose.

c. 1225   *Roman de la Rose/Romance of the Rose* by Guillaume de Lorris, influential French allegorical poem on courtly love, later adapted by Chaucer.

1304   Petrarch, Italian poet, was born.

1307–21   Dante Alighieri, greatest Italian poet, wrote his *Divina Commedia/Divine Comedy*.

1340   Geoffrey Chaucer, greatest late medieval English poet, was born. Works include *The Canterbury Tales* 1387 and *Troilus and Criseyde* c. 1388.

1348–53   Boccaccio, Italian poet, wrote his *Decameron*.

c. 1362   Hâfiz, Persian poet, was born.

c. 1362–98 William Langland wrote his *Piers Plowman*, didactic allegorical poem.

c. 1400   *Gawain and the Green Knight* , anonymous English Arthurian romance, was written.

1431   François Villon, French poet, was born.

1470   Sir Thomas Malory wrote his *Le Morte d'Arthur*, a cycle of Arthurian legends.

1477   William Caxton established the first printing press in England.

1494   François Rabelais, French satirist, was born.

1524   Luis Vaz de Camoëns, Portuguese epic poet, was born.

1532   Ludovico Ariosto, Italian poet, wrote his romantic epic *Orlando Furioso*.

c. 1560   Hsu Wei wrote his *Ching P'ing Mei*, the first Chinese classic novel.

1572   John Donne, first of the major English 'metaphysical' poets, was born.

1575   Torquato Tasso, Italian poet, wrote his romantic epic *Gerusalemme Liberata/ Jerusalem Liberated*.

1590–96   Edmund Spenser, English poet, wrote his allegorical romantic epic *Faerie Queene*.

1590–1600 William Shakespeare wrote his sonnets.

1605	Miguel de Cervantes, Spanish novelist, published the first part of his novel *Don Quixote*.
1611	Authorized Version of the Bible was published in English.
1631	John Dryden, English poet and dramatist, was born.
1667	John Milton, English poet, wrote his *Paradise Lost*, an epic on the Fall of Man.
1668	*Oroonoko* by English woman novelist Aphra Behn.
1670	Andrew Marvell, English poet, was writing.
c. 1675	Poems by Bashō (pen-name of Matsuo Munefusa) brought the Japanese haiku form into popularity.
1648	*The Pilgrim's Progress* by John Bunyan, English writer.
1688	Alexander Pope, English poet and satirist, was born.
1719	*Robinson Crusoe* by Daniel Defoe, English novelist.
1720	Novels were first serialized in English newspapers.
1728	*Gulliver's Travels* by Jonathan Swift, Irish author and satirist.
1741	*Pamela* by Samuel Richardson, English novelist, one of the founders of the modern novel.
1748	John Cleland, English writer, published *Memoirs of a Woman of Pleasure*, better known as *Fanny Hill*.
1749	Johann Wolfgang von Goethe, German poet, dramatist, novelist, and philosopher, was born; *Tom Jones* by Henry Fielding, English novelist.
1750	Thomas Gray, English poet, wrote 'Elegy in a Country Churchyard'.
1755	*Dictionary of the English Language* by Samuel Johnson, English author and lexicographer.
1757	William Blake, English poet and artist, was born.
1759	Robert Burns, Scottish poet, was born; Voltaire, French author and satirist, wrote *Candide*.
1760	Cao Xuequin's *The Dream of the Red Chamber*, the most famous Chinese novel; volumes 1–2 of *Tristram Shandy*, comic novel by Laurence Sterne, English novelist.
1765	*Goody Two-Shoes*, one of the earliest illustrated children's books in England, possibly by the poet Oliver Goldsmith.
1775	*Sturm und Drang* ('storm and stress') movement, the beginning of Romanticism, expanded in Germany .
1776	Edward Gibbon, English historian, began to publish his *The Decline and Fall of the Roman Empire*.
1778	William Hazlitt, English essayist, was born.
1788	Lord Byron, English Romantic poet, was born.
1791	*Life of Samuel Johnson* by James Boswell.
1792	Percy Bysshe Shelley, English Romantic poet, was born.

1795 John Keats, English Romantic poet, and Thomas Carlyle, Scottish writer and historian, were born.

1797 Heinrich Heine, German Romantic poet, was born.

1798 William Wordsworth and Samuel Taylor Coleridge published their *Lyrical Ballads*, the first major work of the Romantic period in England; Adam Mickiewicz, Polish poet, was born.

1799 Alexander Pushkin, Russian poet, was born.

1803 Ralph Waldo Emerson, American poet, was born.

1809 Alfred Tennyson, English poet, Edgar Allan Poe, American writer of horror fantasy, and Nikolai Gogol, Russian novelist and short story writer, were all born.

1810 Alfred de Musset, French poet, was born.

1813 *Pride and Prejudice* by Jane Austen, English novelist.

1815 Mikhail Lermontov, Russian poet, was born.

1818 Ivan Turgenev, Russian novelist, was born; *Frankenstein*, philosophical horror novel, by Mary Shelley, English novelist.

1819 *Ivanhoe*, historical novel, by Walter Scott, Scottish novelist.

1822 *Kalevala*, Finnish legends collected from oral tradition, was published.

1827 Honoré de Balzac began his *Comédie humaine/Human Comedy*, a series of novels and stories.

1830 *Le Rouge et le noir/The Red and the Black* by Stendhal, French novelist .

1842 Stéphane Mallarmé, French symbolist poet, was born.

1844 Gerard Manley Hopkins, English poet, and Paul Verlaine, French poet, were born.

1847 Charlotte Brontë, English novelist, published *Jane Eyre*, her sister Emily Brontë published *Wuthering Heights*, and William Thackeray, English novelist, published *Vanity Fair*.

1850 *David Copperfield* by Charles Dickens, English novelist. *The Scarlet Letter*, by Nathaniel Hawthorne, American novelist.

1851 *Moby Dick* by Herman Melville, American novelist.

1854 Arthur Rimbaud, French symbolist poet, was born.

1855 *Leaves of Grass*, by Walt Whitman, American poet.

1856 *Madame Bovary* by Gustave Flaubert, French novelist.

1857 *Les Fleurs du mal/Flowers of Evil* by Charles Baudelaire, French poet; *Barchester Towers* by Anthony Trollope, English novelist.

1858 *The Song of Hiawatha* by Henry Wadsworth Longfellow, American poet .

1861 Rabindranath Tagore, Indian philosopher and poet, was born.

1862 *Les Misérables* by Victor Hugo, French writer.

1864 *War and Peace* by Leo Tolstoy, Russian novelist.

1865	William Butler Yeats, Irish poet, was born; *Alice's Adventures in Wonderland* by Lewis Carroll, English mathematician and author.
1866	*Crime and Punishment* by Fyodor Dostoevsky, Russian novelist.
1868	Maxim Gorky, Russian author, was born; *The Moonstone*, first English detective novel, by Wilkie Collins, English novelist.
1869	*The Ring and the Book* by Robert Browning, English poet.
1871	*Middlemarch* by George Eliot, English novelist.
1873	Muhammad Iqbal, Urdu poet, was born.
1875	Thomas Mann, German novelist, and Rainer Maria Rilke, German poet, were born.
1876	*Tom Sawyer* by Mark Twain, American novelist.
1881	*The Portrait of a Lady* and *Washington Square* by Henry James, American novelist.
1885	*Germinal* by Émile Zola, French novelist.
1887	*A Study in Scarlet*, the first Sherlock Holmes story, by Arthur Conan Doyle, English detective story writer.
1891	*Tess of the D'Urbervilles* by Thomas Hardy, English novelist and poet; Osip Mandelshtam, Russian poet, was born.
1895	*The Time Machine* by H G Wells, English novelist and science fiction writer.
1899	Jorge Luis Borges, Argentinian short story writer, was born.
1900	*Lord Jim* by Joseph Conrad, Polish-born English novelist.
1901	*Kim* by Rudyard Kipling, English novelist, short story writer, and poet.
1908	*The Wind in the Willows* by Kenneth Grahame, English author.
1910	Arnold Bennett, English novelist, published the first of his Clayhanger series of novels.
1913	*Sons and Lovers* by D H Lawrence, English novelist; Marcel Proust, French novelist, published the first part of his *À la récherche du temps perdu/ Remembrance of Things Past*.
1917	English writer P G Wodehouse published *The Man with Two Left Feet*, his first work featuring Jeeves and Bertie Wooster.
1917–18	Wilfred Owen, English poet, wrote his war poetry.
1918	Aleksandr Blok, Russian symbolist poet, wrote 'The Twelve', a poem greeting the Russian revolution.
1920	*Bliss* by Katherine Mansfield, New Zealand short story writer.
1922	*The Waste Land* by T S Eliot, Anglo-American poet; *Ulysses* by James Joyce, Irish novelist; Andrei Bely, Russian symbolist novelist and poet, published the definitive version of his novel *Petersburg*.
1924	*A Passage to India* by E M Forster, English novelist.
1925	Posthumous publication of *The Trial*, by Franz Kafka, Czech novelist.

1926   *The Murder of Roger Ackroyd* by Agatha Christie, English detective story writer.

1927   *Steppenwolf* by Herman Hesse, German writer; *To the Lighthouse* by Virginia Woolf, English writer.

1928   *Mariana Pinada* by Federico García Lorca, Spanish poet and playwright.

1929   *A Farewell to Arms* by Ernest Hemingway, American novelist .

1932   *Brave New World* by Aldous Huxley, English novelist.

1934   *Tender is the Night* by F Scott Fitzgerald, American novelist; *Tropic of Cancer* by Henry Miller, American novelist; Wole Soyinka, Nigerian author, was born.

1937   *La Nausée/Nausea* by Jean-Paul Sartre, French novelist and philosopher.

1938   *Brighton Rock* by Graham Greene, English novelist.

1939   *The Grapes of Wrath* by John Steinbeck, American novelist.

1942   *L'Étranger/The Outsider* by Albert Camus, French novelist.

1945   *Animal Farm* by George Orwell, English author; *Brideshead Revisited* by Evelyn Waugh, English novelist.

1948   *The Age of Anxiety* by W H Auden, English poet; *The Naked and the Dead* by Norman Mailer, American novelist.

1950   The *70 Cantos* by Ezra Pound, American poet.

1951   *The Catcher in the Rye* by J D Salinger, American novelist.

1953   Ian Fleming, English novelist, published *Casino Royale*, first 'James Bond' novel; *Dans le labyrinthe/In the Labyrinth* by Alain Robbe-Grillet.

1954   *Lord of the Flies* by William Golding, English novelist, *Lord of the Rings* by J R R Tolkien, English writer and scholar; *Lucky Jim* by Kingsley Amis, English novelist; *Bonjour Tristesse/Hello Sadness* by Françoise Sagan, French novelist; posthumous publication of *Under Milk Wood* by Dylan Thomas, Welsh poet.

1955   *Lolita* by Vladimir Nabokov, Russian-American novelist.

1956   *The Outsider* by Colin Wilson, English novelist; *Anglo Saxon Attitudes* by Angus Wilson, English novelist.

1957   *Voss* by Patrick White, Australian novelist; *On the Road* by Jack Kerouac, American novelist.

1958   *Doctor Zhivago* by Boris Pasternak, Russian poet and novelist; *Breakfast at Tiffany's* by Truman Capote, American novelist .

1959   *Die Blechtrommel/The Tin Drum* by Günter Grass, German novelist.

1960   *The Loneliness of the Long Distance Runner* by Alan Sillitoe, English novelist.

1961   *A Severed Head* by Iris Murdoch, English novelist.

1962   *One Day in the Life of Ivan Denisovich* by Alexander Solzhenitsyn, Russian novelist.

1963   *The Collector* by John Fowles, English novelist; *The Spy Who Came In From the Cold* by John Le Carré, English novelist .

1964   *Herzog* by Saul Bellow, American novelist; *The Whitsun Weddings* by Philip Larkin, English poet.

1965   *For The Union Dead* by Robert Lowell, American poet.

1966   Paul Scott, English novelist, began his 'Raj Quartet' series of novels.

1967   *Cíen años de soledad/A Hundred Years of Solitude* by Gabriel García Márquez, Colombian novelist.

1968   *Couples* by John Updike, American novelist.

1969   *Portnoy's Complaint* by Philip Roth, American novelist; *Slaughterhouse Five* by Kurt Vonnegut, American novelist.

1973   Roland Barthes, influential French critic, published *Le Plaisir du texte/The Pleasure of the Text*.

1975   *The History Man* by Malcolm Bradbury, British novelist.

1979   Doris Lessing, British novelist, began the *Canopus in Argus* series of novels.

1980   *Earthly Powers* by Anthony Burgess, British novelist.

1982   *Monsignor Quixote* by Graham Greene, British Novelist.

1983   *The Color Purple* by Alice Walker, American novelist; *Name of the Rose* by Umberto Eco, Italian novelist and critic.

1984   *The Unbearable Lightness of Being* by Milan Kundera, Czech novelist.

1985   Mario Vargas Llosa, Peruvian novelist, published *Historia de Mayta/The Real Life of Alejandro Mayta*.

1987   *The Wrench* by Primo Levi, Italian writer.

Theatre

Theatre, as distinct from literature, is a living art. Shakespeare's *Hamlet*, for example, taken as a work of literature, has been the subject of a huge body of literary criticism. As a piece of drama, however, it is open to infinite interpretation, for no two performances – even by the same actor – can ever be the same. Furthermore, *Hamlet* is generally regarded as 'good' literature, but a performance with poor direction and poor acting can turn it into 'bad' theatre. As a result theatre, perhaps even more than literature, is subject to the tastes and fashions of its day – both in content and presentation. This section is therefore intended to provide an introduction to the theatre today, to the events and people that have formed it and, in considering dramatic works, to those which are still most frequently performed. For the term 'theatre' encompasses three separate and yet interdependent areas: in its most literal sense, it is the place where the drama unfolds, whether it is the mobile carts of medieval times or highly mechanized theatre complexes such as the Barbican Centre in London; it is also the world of actors, directors, designers and indeed theatre-goers themselves; and, finally, it is the drama or 'piece of theatre', whether *Hamlet* or a pantomime. Theatre in this context covers any live entertainment performed by actors, with the exception of opera and dance, which are treated in separate sections.

This section contains an introduction to various *Theatrical Genres*, types of drama and important movements, giving a brief definition and history for each; *Biographies* of important figures in the theatre; and a *Chronology* of theatrical events which puts theatrical developments since ancient times in their historical perspective. Since it is impossible to measure the achievement of Ibsen, for example, as a playwright, against the skills of Gielgud as an actor, or indeed to compare Gielgud's performance as Macbeth with that of Kean a hundred years earlier, the biographical section should not be regarded as a 'top 50'. Rather, it is a selection of some people of the theatre who, in their different ways, have all played a major role in its development.

Theatrical Genres

Absurd, Theatre of the term applied to the works of a group of playwrights in the 1950s, including Beckett, Ionesco, Genet and Pinter. They expressed through drama the belief that in a godless universe human existence has no meaning or purpose and therefore all communication breaks down. This concern was shown in the form as well as the content of their plays, so that logical construction and argument gives way to irrational and illogical speech and to its ultimate conclusion, silence, as in Beckett's play *Breath* 1970.

burlesque in the 17th and 18th centuries, a form of satirical comedy parodying a particular play or dramatic genre. For example, Gay's *The Beggar's Opera* 1728 is a burlesque of 18th-century opera, and Sheridan's *The Critic* 1777 satirizes the sentimentality in the drama of this time. In the US the term burlesque was used for a sex and comedy show invented by Michael Bennett Leavitt in 1866 consisting of a variety of acts including acrobats, chorus and comedy numbers. During the 1920s the strip-tease was introduced to counteract the growing popularity of the cinema, and Gypsy Rose Lee became its most famous artiste. Burlesque was banned in New York in 1942.

circus (Latin 'circle') originally, in Roman times, an arena for chariot races and gladiatorial combats. In modern times, it is an entertainment, often held in a large tent or 'big top', involving performing animals, acrobats and clowns. In 1897 the American Phineas Taylor Barnum created the 'Greatest Show on Earth' which included a circus, menagerie and 'freaks', all transported in 100 rail cars.

comedy in the simplest terms, a drama with a happy ending, as opposed to tragedy. Since much comedy relies on topical allusion and taste many comedies, successful during their time, have subsequently been forgotten. The comic tradition was established by Aristophanes, Menander, and the Roman writers Terence and Plautus. In medieval times, the Vices and Devil of the Morality plays developed into the stock comic characters of the Renaissance *Comedy of Humours* with such notable villains as Jonson's Mosca in *Volpone*. The timeless comedies of Shakespeare and Molière were followed in England during the 17th century by the witty *Comedy of Manners* of Restoration writers such as Etherege, Wycherley and Congreve. Their often coarse but always vital comedies became toned down in the later Restoration dramas of Sheridan and Goldsmith. A fashion for sentimental comedies dominated most of the 19th century and left little that is remembered today until its close brought the realistic tradition of Shaw and the elegant social comedies of Wilde. The polished comedies of Coward and Rattigan from the 1920s to 1940s were eclipsed during the late 1950s and 1960s by a trend towards satire and a more cynical humour as seen in the works of Joe Orton and Peter Nichols. From the 1970s the 'black comedies' of Alan Ayckbourn have dominated the English stage.

commedia dell'arte popular form of Italian improvised drama in the 16th and 17th centuries. It was performed by specially trained troupes of actors with their own stock characters and situations. It exerted considerable influence on writers such as Molière and on the English genres Pantomime, Harlequinade, and the Punch and Judy show. It laid the foundation for a tradition of mime, particularly in France, which has continued with the contemporary mime of Jean-Louis Barrault and Marcel Marceau.

Cruelty, Theatre of a theory advanced by Antonin Artaud in his book *Le Théâtre et son double* 1938 and adopted by a number of writers and directors including Peter Brook. It aims to shock the audience into an awareness of basic, primitive human nature, through the release of feelings usually repressed by conventional behaviour.

farce a broad form of comedy involving

stereotyped characters in complex, often improbable situations frequently revolving around extra-marital relationships, hence the term 'bedroom farce'. Originating from the physical knockabout comedy of Greek satyr plays and the broad humour developed from medieval religious drama, the farce was developed and perfected during the 19th century by Labiche and Feydeau in France, and Pinero in England. In modern times two notable English series have been the Aldwych farces of Ben Travers in the 1920s and 1930s and the Whitehall farces produced by Brian Rix during the 1950s and 1960s.

Kabuki popular form of Japanese drama incorporating music, dance and acting, developed during the 17th century from the more aristocratic 'No' tradition. Plays are long, episodic, and based mainly on legendary themes, although content is secondary to the display of elaborate costumes, staging and virtuoso ability of the actors, who are all male.

masque a spectacular and essentially aristocratic entertainment with a fairy or mythological theme in which music, dance, and extravagant costumes and scenic design were more important than plot. It reached its height of popularity at the English court between 1600 and 1640, with the collaboration of Ben Jonson as writer and Inigo Jones as stage designer. The masque had great influence on the development of ballet and opera, and the elaborate frame in which it was performed developed into the proscenium arch.

melodrama although today often used as a derogatory term, it was first applied to plays accompanied by music, which became popular throughout Europe during the 19th century. The early melodramas used extravagant theatrical effects for artificially heightening the violent emotions and actions, and were frequently played against a Gothic background of mountains or ruined castles. Beginning with the early work of Goethe and Schiller, it was popularized in France by Pixérécourt and first introduced to England in an unauthorized translation by Thomas Holcroft as *A Tale of Mystery* in 1802.

mime in modern usage, a term for acting in which gestures, movements and facial expression replace dialogue. In ancient Greece mime was a crude, realistic comedy with speech and exaggerated gesture. It is essential to the stage actor's repertory of expression, and plays an important role in ballet. It has also developed as a form of theatre in its own right, particularly in France, where Marcel Marceau and Jean-Louis Barrault have continued the traditions established in the 19th century by Deburau and back to the practices of the commedia dell'arte in Italy.

Morality plays late medieval drama, derived from the Mystery plays, which aimed to instruct. The dramas were allegories of human life in which the Virtues and Vices were personified, the latter often to comic effect. *Everyman* is the most famous example which survives today. The Morality plays had an important influence on the course of Elizabethan drama and the Jonsonian Comedy of Humours.

music hall light entertainment consisting of a 'variety' of songs and comic turns which reached its heyday during the early 20th century. It arose from tavern entertainment; special music halls were built and soon Empires and Hippodromes were established in most English towns. Famous music hall performers have included Albert Chevalier, Marie Lloyd, Harry Lauder and George Formby. Many had their special character 'trademark' such as Vesta Tilley's immaculate masculine outfit as Burlington Bertie. With the onset of radio and television, music hall declined but has had something of a revival in the informal entertainment of the pub – the place of its origin. The American equivalent is known as 'Vaudeville'.

musical comedy a popular form of theatre combining a story with elements of song and dance often performed by a chorus. Derived from light opera, the first examples were staged by George Edwardes at the Gaiety Theatre in London from 1892. Typical of the 1920s were *The Student Prince* 1924 and *The Desert Song* 1926 by Sigmund Romberg, but

285

the genre reached a more sophisticated expression in America during the 1930s and 40s with the work of George Gershwin, Cole Porter, Irving Berlin and Jerome Kern, and in England with Noel Coward and the more romantic Ivor Novello. The word 'comedy' was dropped and the era of the 'musical' arrived with Rodgers and Hammerstein's *Oklahoma!* in 1943, bringing with it a more integrated combination of plot and music, as in Lerner and Loewe's *My Fair Lady* 1956 and Bernstein's *West Side Story* 1957. Sandy Wilson's *The Boy Friend* 1953 revived the British musical, and was followed by hits such as Bart's *Oliver* 1960, *Oh What a Lovely War!* 1963 produced by Joan Littlewood and Charles Chiltern, and finally the hugely successful Lloyd Webber musicals including *Jesus Christ Superstar* 1970, *Cats* 1981, and *The Phantom of the Opera* 1986.

Mystery (or Miracle) plays medieval religious dramas based on stories from the Old and New Testaments which were performed around the time of church festivals, reaching their height in Europe during the 15th and 16th centuries. A whole cycle running from the Creation to the Last Judgement was performed in separate scenes on mobile wagons by various town guilds. Four English cycles survive, Coventry, Wakefield (or Townley), Chester, and York. Versions are still performed, notably the York cycle at York. The German equivalent, the *Mysterienspiel* , survives today as the *Passion Play*. It is essentially concerned with the Crucifixion of Christ and the most famous takes place every ten years at Oberammergau.

No (or Noh) stylized, classical drama of Japan; an aristocratic form as opposed to the popular Kabuki, developed from the 14th century by Kwanami and his son. The plays are based on mythical themes which are expressed through music, chant and dance. There is no scenery but costumes and masks are elaborate.

pageant originally the wagon on which medieval plays were performed; the term was later applied to the moving, spectacular procession of songs, dances and tableaux which became fashionable during the 1920s and which

exists today in forms such as the Lord Mayor's Show in London. Related to the pageant is the open-air entertainment *Son et Lumière*, in which the history of a place is performed in a series of episodes accompanied by sound, and lighting effects projected on to the site of a castle, for example.

pantomime in the English theatre, a traditional Christmas entertainment descended from the harlequin spectacles of the 18th century and burlesque of the 19th century, which gave rise to the tradition of the principal boy being played by an actress and the dame by an actor. The role of the harlequin diminished altogether as themes developed on folktales such as *The Sleeping Beauty* and *Cinderella*, and with the introduction of additional material such as popular songs, topical comedy and audience participation. The term 'pantomime' was also applied to Roman dumbshow performed by a masked actor, to 18th-century ballets with mythical themes, and, in 19th-century France, to the wordless Pierrot plays from which modern 'mime' developed.

puppet theatre a form of drama acted by puppets usually manipulated by unseen operators. There are many types of puppet; probably the best known in England are finger or glove puppets, of which the most famous is Punch, who has developed from the Pulcinella of the commedia dell'arte. By the 16th and 17th centuries refined versions of the travelling puppet shows became popular with the aristocracy and puppets were extensively used as vehicles for caricature and satire until the 19th century. There has been a revival of interest in the 20th century, partly stimulated by the influence of the Joruri tradition in Japan with its large, intricate puppets and by leading exponents such as Obraztsov and his Moscow Puppet Theatre, and most recently by Fluck and Law, whose satirical 'Spitting Image' puppets, caricaturing famous people, have appeared on television.

revue a stage presentation involving short satirical and topical items in the form of song, sketches and monologues. The first revue seems to have been *Under the Clock* 1893 by

Hicks and Brookfield. Until the 1920s revues were spectacular entertainments, but the 'intimate revue' (such as *Sweet and Low* 1943) became increasingly popular under Cochran, who employed writers such as Noel Coward. During the 1960s the satirical revue took off with the Cambridge Footlights' production *Beyond the Fringe*, firmly establishing the revue tradition among the young and at 'fringe' theatrical events. Another offshoot is the 'continuous revue' blending comedy and nudity, started at the Windmill Theatre in London and running 'continuously' (hence its name) from the 1930s until 1964.

tragedy very generally, a play dealing with a serious theme, usually one in which a character falls to disaster either as a result of personal failings or circumstances beyond his or her control. The Greek view of tragedy, as defined by Aristotle and expressed by the great tragedians Aeschylus, Euripides, and Sophocles, provided the subject matter for later tragic dramas, but it was the Roman Seneca (whose works were intended to be read rather than acted) who influenced the Elizabethan tragedy of Marlowe and Shakespeare. French classical tragedy developed under the influence of both Seneca and an interpretation of Aristotle which gave rise to the theory of unities of time, place and action, as observed by Racine, one of its greatest exponents. In Germany the tragedies of Goethe and Schiller led to the exaggerated melodrama, which replaced pure tragedy. In the 18th century unsuccessful attempts were made to 'domesticate' tragedy. In the 20th century tragedies in the narrow Greek sense of dealing with exalted personages in an elevated manner have virtually died out. Tragedy has been replaced by dramas with 'tragic' implications or overtones, as in the work of Ibsen, Pinter and Osborne, for example, or by the hybrid tragi-comedy.

tragi-comedy a drama which contains elements of tragedy and comedy; for example, Shakespeare's 'reconciliation' plays such as *The Winter's Tale*, which reaches a tragic climax but then lightens to a happy conclusion. A tragi-comedy is the usual form for plays in

the tradition of the Theatre of the Absurd, such as *En attendant Godot/Waiting for Godot* 1953 by Beckett and *Rosencrantz and Guildenstern are Dead* 1967 by Stoppard.

Biographies

Aeschylus c 525–456 BC. Greek dramatist. He wrote some 90 plays, of which seven survive, including *The Suppliant Women* c 490 BC and the trilogy *Oresteia* 458 BC, dealing with the curse on the house of Agamemnon. He is widely regarded as the founder of European tragedy.

Anouilh Jean 1910– . French playwright, whose plays dramatize his concerns with the contrasts between innocence and experience, poverty in a world of riches, and the role of memory. His plays include *Antigone* 1942 *L'Invitation au château/Ring Round the Moon*, 1947, *Colombe* 1950, and *Becket* 1959, about Thomas à Becket and Henry II.

Aristophanes c 448–380 BC. Greek comic dramatist, who satirized contemporary issues such as the new learning of Socrates in *The Clouds* 423 BC and the power of women in *Lysistrata* 411 BC. The chorus plays a prominent role, frequently giving the play its title, as in *The Birds* 414 BC, *The Wasps* 422 BC, and *The Frogs* 405 BC.

Ayckbourn Alan 1939– . British dramatist, and director of the Theatre-in-the-Round, Scarborough, from 1959. His prolific output, characterized by his acute ear for comic dialogue, includes the trilogy *The Norman Conquests* 1974, *Woman in Mind* 1986 and *A Small Family Business* 1987.

Beaumarchais Pierre Augustin Caron de 1732–99. French dramatist. His two best known comedies, *The Barber of Seville* 1775 and *The Marriage of Figaro* 1784, ridiculing the aristocracy, inspired operas of those titles by

287

Rossini and Mozart.

Beckett Samuel 1906– . Irish novelist and dramatist, who wrote in French and English. His most famous play, *En attendant Godot/ Waiting for Godot* 1952, in which two tramps wait endlessly for the enigmatic 'Godot', is possibly the best known example of Theatre of the Absurd, portraying the 'absurdity' of the human condition in an irrational universe. This predicament is explored to further extremes in *Fin de Partie/End game* 1957 and *Happy Days* 1961.

Bernhardt Sarah. Stage name of French actress Rosine Bernard 1845–1923. Particularly noted for her golden voice, she dominated the stage of her day, frequently performing at the Comédie-Française. Her most famous roles were as Cordelia in *King Lear*, Racine's *Phèdre*, Doña Sol in Hugo's *Hernani* and in the male roles of *Hamlet* and of Napoleon's son in Rostand's *L'Aiglon*.

Brecht Bertolt 1898–1956. German, Marxist writer, whose 'alienation' theory, requiring the audience and actors to adopt a critical detachment from the drama, is the antithesis of the nomal 'suspension of disbelief' in the theatre. His work includes *The Threepenny Opera* 1928 (an adaptation of Gay's *The Beggar's Opera*) with music by Kurt Weill, *Galileo* 1938, *Mother Courage* 1941 and *The Caucasian Chalk Circle* 1949. From 1949 he established in East Germany the Berliner Ensemble, a theatre group.

Chekhov Anton Pavlovich 1860–1904. Russian dramatist. His play *The Seagull* 1896 was a failure at first, but succeeded when revived by Stanislavsky for the Moscow Arts Theatre in 1898, for which Chekhov also wrote *Uncle Vanya* 1899, and his two masterpieces *The Three Sisters* 1901 and *The Cherry Orchard* 1904. The latter illustrate Chekhov's sense of atmosphere and internal development of character.

Congreve William 1670–1729. English dramatist, the greatest exponent of Restoration Comedy, whose plays are noted for the elegance of their construction and prose style. He had immediate success with *The Old Bachelor* 1693, followed by *The Double Dealer* 1694, and

Love for Love 1695. His most famous play, *The Way of the World* 1700, with its delightful heroine Millamant, was not well received at the time.

Corneille Pierre 1606–84. French dramatist, regarded as the founder of French classical drama. His most famous play *Le Cid* 1637, a tragi-comedy and landmark in French drama, was attacked by critics for its form, but it enjoyed huge public success. A series of classical tragedies followed, *Horace* 1639, *Cinna* 1640, *Polyeucte* 1643, and a comedy, *Le Menteur* 1643. After the failure of *Pertharite* 1652, his fame began to diminish in favour of Racine.

Coward Sir Noël 1899–1973. English actor, director, dramatist and composer. He is best remembered for his sophisticated comedies, *The Vortex* 1924, *Hay Fever* 1925, *Private Lives* 1930, with Gertrude Lawrence, and *Blithe Spirit* 1941. He appeared in a number of first productions of his plays.

Craig Edward Gordon 1872–1966. British director and designer, the son of actress Ellen Terry. His first stage production was Purcell's *Dido and Aeneas* 1900, and he subsequently staged productions throughout Europe including Ibsen's *The Vikings* 1903, in which his mother appeared. His innovations and theories on stage design and lighting effects, expounded in *On the Art of the Theatre* 1911, have had a huge influence on stage production in Europe and the USA.

Eliot T(homas) S(tearns) 1888–1965. Poet and dramatist, born in the USA and a British subject from 1927. He initiated a revival of poetic drama with *Murder in the Cathedral* 1935, about the murder of Thomas à Becket, which was followed by *The Family Reunion* 1939 with its classical overtones. In his later plays, *The Cocktail Party* 1949 and *The Confidential Clerk* 1953, he assumed the form of a drawing-room comedy and turned to a plainer verse style. The Lloyd Webber musical *Cats* 1981 used his verse.

Euripides c 484–407 BC. Greek dramatist. His influence on later drama was probably more important than that of either of the other two great tragedians, Aeschylus and Sophocles. A realist, concerned with individual passions and social issues rather than higher principles, he wrote the tragedies *Bacchae* 405, *Electra* 413, *Trojan Women* 415 and *Medea* 431, and the tragi-comedies *Iphigenia in Tauris* 413 and *Alcestis* 438.

Farquhar George 1678–1707. Late Restoration dramatist, born in Ireland. His most famous plays, *The Recruiting Officer* 1706 and *The Beaux' Stratagem* 1707, are in the tradition of the Restoration Comedy of Manners.

Garrick David 1717–79. British actor and theatre manager. He was responsible for changing the acting style of his time by replacing the traditional declamatory delivery with a naturalness of manner. He is noted for his performances as Richard III, Hamlet and Lear. In 1747 he became manager of the Drury Lane Theatre in London, and was responsible for a number of significant theatrical conventions, including concealed stage lighting and banishing spectators from the stage.

Goethe Johann Wolfgang von 1749–1832. German poet, dramatist, and man-of-letters. His first play, *Götz von Berlichingen* 1773, inspired by the work of Shakespeare, became the cornerstone of the romantic 'Sturm und Drang' movement. A stay in Italy, 1786–88, inspired the classical dramas *Iphigenie auf Tauris* 1787 and *Torquato Tasso* 1789. His masterpiece, the poetic play *Faust*, was published in two parts 1808 and 1832. Its length and sheer scale present enormous staging difficulties, producers have often resorted to using *Urfaust*, an earlier draft.

Gielgud Sir John 1904– . British actor and producer. A great-nephew of the actress Ellen Terry, he made his début at the Old Vic in 1921, attracted notice as Romeo in 1924, and created his most famous role as Hamlet in 1929. Although he is probably best known as a Shakespearean actor, his numerous stage appearances include performances in plays by Chekhov and Sheridan, and in works by the modern playwrights Alan Bennett, Peter Shaffer, and David Storey.

Granville-Barker Harley 1877–1946. British theatre director and author. Although he

wrote plays including *The Madras House* 1910 and *Waste* 1907, his major contribution to the development of British theatre was as director-manager with J. E. Vedrenne at the Royal Court Theatre from 1904–18, directing plays by Shaw, Yeats, Ibsen, Galsworthy, and Masefield. From 1927–47 he wrote the scholarly series *Prefaces to Shakespeare*, which long influenced the staging of Shakespeare.

Hall Sir Peter (Reginald Frederick) 1930– . British theatre director. From 1960–68 he directed the Royal Shakespeare Theatre at Stratford, and developed the Royal Shakespeare Company at the time when the Aldwych became its London base. He was director of the National Theatre from 1973 and also artistic director at Glyndebourne from 1984.

Ibsen Henrik 1828–1906. Norwegian dramatist whose work, characterized by its poetic realism, revolutionized the course of European drama. The two verse-dramas, *Love's Comedy* 1862 and *Peer Gynt* 1867, were followed by his masterly series of realistic social dramas: *Pillars of Society* 1877, *A Doll's House* 1879, *Ghosts* 1881, *An Enemy of the People* 1882, *The Wild Duck* 1884, *Rosmersholm* 1886, *The Lady from the Sea* 1888 and *Hedda Gabler* 1890. His later plays include *Little Eyolf* 1894 and *When We Dead Awaken* 1899.

Ionesco Eugène 1912– . Romanian-born French dramatist, a leading exponent of the Theatre of the Absurd movement. Most of his plays are in one act and express his concern with the futility of language as a means of communication, as in *La Cantatrice chauve/ The Bald Prima Donna* 1950, *La Leçon/The Lesson* 1951 and *Les Chaises/The Chairs* 1951. His full-length plays include *Rhinocéros* 1958 and *Le Roi se meurt/Exit the King* 1961.

Irving Sir Henry. Stage name of English actor-manager John Brodribb 1838–1905. From 1871 he established himself as the leading actor of the late 19th century, chiefly at the Lyceum Theatre in London, where he became manager from 1878. He staged a series of successful Shakespearean productions there, including *Romeo and Juliet* 1882, with himself and Ellen Terry playing the leading roles. In

1895 he was the first actor to be knighted.

Jonson Ben 1572–1637. English dramatist. His first success, *Every Man in His Humour* 1598, established the English Comedy of Humours in which each character embodies a 'humour' or vice such as greed, lust or avarice. His first tragedy *Sejanus* 1603 included Burbage and Shakespeare in the cast, but it is for his classic comedies that he is most famous: *Volpone, or The Fox* 1606, *The Alchemist* 1610, and *Bartholomew Fair* 1614. He collaborated with Inigo Jones on numerous court masques between 1605 and 1612.

Lessing Gotthold Ephraim 1729–81. German dramatist and critic. His play *Miss Sara Sampson* 1755 was the first tragedy of ordinary German life and his next play *Minna von Barnhelm* 1767, the first bourgeois comedy.

Lorca Frederico García 1898–1936. Spanish poet and dramatist, whose works are now receiving a considerable revival 50 years after his death in the Spanish Civil War. His best works are the three powerful and intense tragedies: *Bodas de sangre/Blood Wedding* 1933, a savage story of feuding families, *Yerma* 1934, and possibly his finest, *La Casa de Bernarda Alba/The House of Bernarda Alba* 1936, first produced professionally in London in 1986 with Glenda Jackson as the tyrannical mother heading a household of sisters.

Marlowe Christopher 1564–93. English poet and dramatist, a powerful influence on Shakespeare and the course of Elizabethan drama. In 1587–88 he wrote the flamboyant verse drama *Tamburlaine the Great*, which was followed by *The Tragical History of Doctor Faustus* c 1589, *The Jew of Malta* c 1590, a grim comedy standing mid-way between the medieval Morality play and Jonson's Comedy of Humours, and the historical drama *Edward II* c 1591–2. He was murdered, allegedly in a pub brawl, but probably for political reasons.

Miller Arthur 1915– . American playwright. His plays, deeply concerned with family relationships and contemporary American values, include *All My Sons* 1947, a condemnation of war profiteering, *Death of a Salesman* 1949, *The Crucible* 1953, about witch-hunting

in Salem in the 17th century, and *After the Fall* 1964, in which the character of Maggie is allegedly based on the actress Marilyn Monroe, to whom he was married 1956–61.

Molière pseudonym of Jean-Baptiste Poquelin 1622–73. Actor and greatest French comic dramatist, who founded and acted in the Illustre-Théâtre in Paris from 1643. He established his reputation with *Les Précieuses ridicules* 1658. This was followed by his great satiric masterpieces, which include *L'Ecole des femmes* 1662, *Le Tartuffe* 1664, banned until 1667 for attacking the hypocrisy of the clergy, *Le Misanthrope* 1666, *Le Médecin malgré lui* 1666, *L'Avare* 1668, *Le Bourgeois gentilhomme* 1670, and *Le Malade imaginaire* 1673.

Olivier Laurence Kerr, Baron Olivier 1907– . British actor and producer. He established his reputation at the Old Vic, particularly in *Hamlet* 1937. His other major stage roles include Henry V, Richard III and Archie Rice in Osborne's *The Entertainer*, which were all filmed. He was director of the Chichester Festival Theatre 1961–65 and first director of the National Theatre Company 1962–73.

O'Neill Eugene Gladstone 1888–1953. American dramatist. His first full-length play, *Beyond the Horizon* 1920, won a Pulitzer Prize. His best plays are characterized by a down-to-earth quality even when he is experimenting with expressionism, symbolism, or stream of consciousness, and include *The Emperor Jones* 1921, *Desire under the Elms* 1924, *Mourning Becomes Electra* 1931 (a version of Aeschylus' *Oresteia*) and *The Iceman Cometh* 1939. He was awarded a Nobel Prize in 1936.

Pinero Sir Arthur Wing 1855–1934. British dramatist, a leading exponent of the 'well-made' play, enjoying a huge success in his time with his farces *The Magistrate* 1885, *Dandy Dick* 1887, and *The Cabinet Minister* 1890. A departure to more substantial social drama came with *The Second Mrs Tanqueray* 1893, a 'problem play', and the comedies *Trelawny of the 'Wells'* 1898 and *The Gay Lord Quex* 1899.

Pinter Harold 1930– . English dramatist. Many of his plays are tragi-comedies on the theme of the breakdown of communication, broadly in the tradition of the Theatre of the Absurd. His notable stage plays include *The Birthday Party* 1958, *The Caretaker* 1960, *The Homecoming* 1965 and a series of one act plays, *The Lover* 1963, *Silence* and *Landscape* 1969 and *No Man's Land* 1975.

Pirandello Luigi 1867–1936. Italian novelist and dramatist. His early plays were adaptations of his short stories showing the futility of human endeavour and the impossibility of defining reality. Central to these concerns are his best known play, *Sei personaggi in cerca d'autore/Six Characters in Search of an Author* 1921, and *Enrico Quarto/Henry IV* 1922.

Racine Jean 1639–99. French dramatist, and greatest exponent of the classical tragedy. Most of his plays have a woman in the title role, as in *Andromaque* 1667, *Iphigénie* 1674, and *Phèdre* 1677. After the failure of *Phèdre*, he gave up writing for the theatre, but was persuaded by Mme de Maintenon to write two religious dramas, *Esther* 1689 and *Athalie* 1691, which achieved posthumous success.

Reinhardt Max. Stage name of American-Austrian theatrical producer Max Goldmann 1873–1943. He excelled in lavish spectacles, such as *Oedipus Rex* in Berlin 1910 and *The Miracle* with Lady Diana Cooper at Olympia, London, in 1911, which are remembered for his control of huge crowds on stage, and use of new techniques of lighting and stage devices. He also directed small-scale intimate dramas in Berlin theatres and founded the Salzburg Festival in 1920. From 1933 he worked in the USA.

Sartre Jean-Paul 1905–80. French writer and philosopher. A founder of Existentialism, he expressed its tenets in his dramas *Les Mouches/The Flies* 1942, a retelling of the Orestes myth, and *Huis-clos/In Camera* (also called *No Exit*) 1944, in which three characters are confined in a hell of their own making. In 1951 his most ambitious, but less theatrically successful, play *Le Diable et le Bon Dieu* was written followed by *Les Séquestrés d'Altona/ The Condemned of Altona* 1959.

Schiller Johann Christoph Friedrich von 1759–1805. German Romantic poet and playwright. He was a friend of Goethe and a leading exponent of the 'Sturm und Drang' movement. His first play *Die Räuber/The Robbers* 1781 was an immediate success, particularly with the young. His later works include the historical trilogy *Wallenstein* 1798–99, and *Maria Stuart* 1800, *Die Jungfrau von Orleans/The Maid of Orleans* 1801, and *Wilhelm Tell* 1804.

Shaffer Peter (Levin) 1926– . English dramatist, whose first play *Five Finger Exercise* 1958 was successfully produced in London and New York. His other plays include the epic *The Royal Hunt of the Sun* 1964, about the Spanish conquest of the Incas, *Black Comedy* 1965, the powerful psychological drama *Equus* 1973, and *Amadeus* 1979 about Salieri and Mozart.

Shakespeare William 1564–1616. English playwright and poet, the greatest English dramatist. By 1589 he was an established actor and playwright in London and from 1594 was a member of the Chamberlain's (later the King's) company of players. His work first appeared as a collected body in the First Folio, published in 1623 by Heninge and Condell, but it is difficult to date individual plays with precision. Very roughly, they divide into the following periods: c 1590–1600 the history plays and comedies, including *Henry IV* (parts I and II), *Henry V*, *Richard III*, *A Midsummer Night's Dream* and *As You Like It*, c 1601–1607 the great tragedies and darker comedies, including *Hamlet*, *Othello*, *Macbeth*, *King Lear*, *Measure for Measure* and *Troilus and Cressida*, c 1608–1612 the mature 'romance' or 'reconciliation' plays, including *The Tempest* and *The Winter's Tale*. For the first 200 years after his death, Shakespeare's plays were frequently performed in cut or revised form (Nahum Tate's *King Lear* was given a happy ending), and it was not until the 19th century, with the critical assessments of Coleridge and Hazlitt, that the original texts were restored. Since then the plays have been consistently performed throughout the world, and have exerted an immeasurable influence on the history of the theatre.

Shaw George Bernard 1856–1950. Irish dramatist and critic. A prolific writer, he allied himself with a new and essentially political and polemical movement in the theatre, aiming in his work to engage the intellect rather than the emotions of his audience. His plays include *Mrs Warren's Profession* (1893, but banned until 1902 because it dealt with prostitution), *Arms and the Man* 1894 (about war), *Candida* 1903, the epic *Man and Superman* 1903, *Major Barbara* 1905, *Pygmalion* 1913 (adapted as the musical *My Fair Lady*), *Heartbreak House* 1917, and *St Joan* 1924.

Sheridan Richard Brinsley 1751–1816. Anglo-Irish dramatist and theatre manager. He was manager of the Drury Lane Theatre from 1776, rebuilt it in 1794, and continued until 1809 when it was destroyed by fire. He is best remembered for his two social dramas, *The Rivals* 1775, with the comic Mrs Malaprop, and *The School for Scandal* 1777 – masterpieces of the Comedy of Manners.

Sophocles 496–406 BC. Greek dramatist. He wrote over 100 plays, of which seven tragedies and a satyr play survive, including *Ajax* c 450 BC, *Antigone* c 441, *Oedipus Rex* c 425, *Electra* 409 and *Oedipus at Colonus* 406. His dramas are subtle studies of the interaction between character and circumstance or fate. He introduced a third actor to the stage and reduced the chorus to a lyrical device emphasising changes of mood rather than directly affecting the action.

Stanislavsky Konstantin Sergeivich 1863–1938. Russian actor, director and teacher of acting. He founded the Moscow Art Theatre in 1918 and achieved his greatest success as a director with his productions of Chekhov and Gorky. He was the originator of 'method' acting, which he described in *My Life in Art* 1924 and other works, and which had great influence on acting techniques in Europe and the USA. He rejected the declamatory style of acting in favour of an approach concentrating on the psychological development of character.

Strindberg August 1849–1912. Swedish dramatist and novelist, who wrote over 50 plays in a variety of styles including historical plays, symbolic dramas (the two-part *The Dance of Death* 1901) and 'chamber plays' such as *The Ghost (or Spook) Sonata* 1907. His two best known plays, *The Father* 1887 and *Miss Julie* 1888, are both powerful studies of human frailty and hostility between the sexes.

Synge J(ohn) M(illington) 1871–1909. Irish playwright, a leading figure in the Irish dramatic revival of the early 20th century. His six plays show a poetic ear for the speech patterns of the Aran Islands and West Ireland where they are set, and are classics of Irish drama. They include *In Shadow of the Glen* 1903, *Riders to the Sea* 1904, and his masterpiece, *The Playboy of the Western World* 1907, which caused riots at the Abbey Theatre, Dublin, when first performed.

Vega Carpio Lope Felix de 1562–1635. Spanish Renaissance playwright, enormously influential on the course of Spanish drama and writers such as Molière. He wrote over 1,500 plays, most of which are tragi-comedies. He set out his views on drama in *Arte nuevo de hacer comedias/The New Art of Writing Plays* c 1609, while reaffirming the classical form. Possibly his best known play is *Fuenteovejuna* 1614, acclaimed in this century as the first proletarian drama.

Webster John 1580–1634. English dramatist, who ranks after Shakespeare as the greatest tragedian of his time and the one whose plays are most frequently revived today. His two great plays *The White Devil* c 1612 and *The Duchess of Malfi* 1614 are dark, violent tragedies obsessed with death and decay, and infused with poetic brilliance.

Wilde Oscar 1854–1900. Irish writer. In the theatre he is best known for his elegant, stylish comedies with witty dialogue, such as *Lady Windermere's Fan* 1892, *A Woman of No Importance* 1893, *An Ideal Husband* 1895, and his most consistently successful play, *The Importance of Being Earnest* 1895.

Williams Tennessee 1914–83. Pseudonym of American playwright Thomas Lanier Williams. He excelled in creating the atmosphere of life in the Deep South in *The Glass Menagerie* 1945, *A Streetcar Named Desire* 1947, and *Cat on a Hot Tin Roof* 1955.

c 3200 BC	Beginnings of Egyptian religious drama, essentially ritualistic.
c 600	Choral performances (dithyrambs) in honour of Dionysus formed beginnings of Greek tragedy, according to Aristotle.
c 534	First festival of tragedy held at Athens and won by Thespis.
500–300	Great age of Greek drama which included tragedy, comedy and satyr plays (grotesque farce).
468	Sophocles' first victory at Athens festival. His use of a third actor altered the course of the tragic form.
458	Aeschylus' *Oresteia* first performed.
c 425–388	Comedies of Aristophanes including *The Birds* 414, *Lysistrata* 411 and *The Frogs* 405. In tragedy the importance of the chorus diminished under Euripides, author of *The Bacchae* 405.
c 350	Menander's 'New Comedy' of social manners developed.
c 330	The *Poetics* of Aristotle analysed the nature of tragedy. Theatre of Dionysus built in Athens.
c 240 BC *AD 200*	Emergence of Roman drama, adapted from Greek originals under Plautus, Terence and Seneca. All were to have great influence on Elizabethan writers.
c AD 375	Kālidāsa's *Sakuntalā* marked the height of Sanskrit drama in India.
c 970	Earliest Christian liturgical drama, written by Ethelwold, Bishop of Winchester.
1210	Priests were forbidden to appear on public stage. This led to secularization of drama in the vernacular.
c 1250–1500	European Mystery (or Miracle) plays flourished, first in the churches, later in market places, and performed in England by town guilds.
c 1375	No (or Noh) drama developed in Japan.
c 1495	*Everyman*, the best known of all the Morality plays, first performed.
1500–1600	Italian commedia dell'arte troupes performed popular, improvised comedies; they were to have a large influence on Molière and on English Harlequinade and Pantomime.
c 1551	Nicholas Udall's *Ralph Roister Doister* written, the first English comedy.
c 1576	First English playhouse, 'The Theatre', built by James Burbage in Shoreditch, London.
1587	Marlowe's *Tamburlaine the Great* marked an important advance in the use of blank verse and the beginning of the great age of Elizabethan and Jacobean drama in England.
c 1589	Kyd's *Spanish Tragedy* - the first of the 'revenge' tragedies.
1594	Lord Chamberlain's Men formed; a theatre company to which Shakespeare was attached as actor/writer from 1595.
1599	The Globe Theatre built on Bankside, Southwark, London.
c 1590–1612	Shakespeare's greatest plays, including *Hamlet* and *King Lear*, were written.

293

1604   Inigo Jones designed *The Masque of Blackness* for James I, written by Ben Jonson. Masques were the height of fashion at the English court around this time.

1613   The Globe Theatre burned down (rebuilt 1614; demolished 1644).

1614   Lope de Vega's *Fuenteovejuna* marked Spanish renaissance in drama.

1637   Corneille's *Le Cid* established classical tragedy in France.

1642   Act of Parliament closed all English theatres.

1660   With the restoration of Charles II to the English throne, dramatic performances recommenced. The first professional actress appeared as Desdemona in Shakespeare's *Othello* .

1664   Molière's *Tartuffe* was banned for three years by religious factions.

1667   Racine's first success, *Andromaque*.

1680   Comédie-Française formed by Louis XIV.

1700   Congreve, the greatest exponent of Restoration Comedy, wrote *The Way of the World* .

1716   First known American theatre built at Williamsburg.

1728   Gay's *The Beggar's Opera* first performed.

1737   Stage Licensing Act in England required all plays to be licensed and approved by the Lord Chamberlain before performance.

1747   Garrick became manager of Drury Lane Theatre, London.

1767–8   In Germany, Lessing's *Minna von Barnhelm* and publication of *Hamburgische Dramaturgie*.

1773   In England, Goldsmith's *She Stoops to Conquer* and Sheridan's *The Rivals* 1775 established the Comedy of Manners. Goethe's *Götz von Berlichingen* was the first 'Sturm und Drang' play (literally storm and stress); this German Romantic movement, depicting extravagant emotions, was influential throughout Europe at this time and led to the rise of English melodrama.

1775   Sarah Siddons, English tragedy actress, made her début at the Drury Lane Theatre.

1781   Schiller's *Die Räuber/The Robbers*.

1784   Beaumarchais' *Le Mariage de Figaro/The Marriage of Figaro* (written 1778) finally performed after difficulties with censorship because of its alleged revolutionary tendencies.

1802   Holcroft's *A Tale of Mystery* marked the rise of melodrama in England.

1814   Edmund Kean's London début as Shylock in Shakespeare's *The Merchant of Venice*.

1815   Gas lighting installed at Covent Garden.

1830   Hugo's *Hernani* caused riots in Paris. His work marked the beginning of a new Romantic drama, changing the course of French theatre.

1838   The début of the French tragic actress, Rachel, at the Comédie-Française

1843   The Theatres Act further strengthened the powers of the Lord Chamberlain to censor plays.

1869   Sarah Bernhardt's first success, in *Le Passant* in Paris.

1878   Henry Irving became actor-manager of the Lyceum with Ellen Terry as leading lady.

1879   Ibsen's *A Doll's House* – an example of Ibsen's hugely influential plays, which marked the beginning of realism in European theatre.

1888   Strindberg's *Miss Julie*.

1893   Shaw wrote *Mrs Warren's Profession* (banned until 1902 because it deals with prostitution). Shaw's works brought the new realistic drama to Britain and introduce a social and political issues as subjects for the theatre.

1895   Wilde's *The Importance of Being Earnest*.

1896   The first performance of Chekhov's *The Seagull* failed.

1899   Abbey Theatre, Dublin, founded by WB Yeats and Lady Gregory, marked the beginning of an Irish dramatic revival.

1904   Chekhov's *The Cherry Orchard* . Founding of Royal Academy of Dramatic Art (RADA) by Beerbohm Tree in London, to train young actors.

1904–7   Granville Barker and JE Vedrenne were managers of the Royal Court Theatre and directed works by Shaw, Yeats, Ibsen, Galsworthy.

1919   Theatre Guild founded in US to perform less commercial new plays.

1923   Shaw's *St Joan* . O'Casey's first play, *The Shadow of a Gunman* .

1925   Coward's *Hay Fever* . Travers' *A Cuckoo in the Nest* , the first of the Aldwych farces.

1928   Brecht's *Die Dreigroschenoper/The Threepenny Opera* with score by Kurt Weill. In US Jerome Kern's *Show Boat* with Paul Robeson, one example of the success of musical comedies. Others by Cole Porter, Irving Berlin, George Gershwin became popular.

1930   Gielgud's first performance as Hamlet.

1935   T.S. Eliot's *Murder in the Cathedral*.

1943   The first of the 'musicals', *Oklahoma!* opened.

1947   First Edinburgh Festival with fringe theatre events. Tennessee Williams's *A Streetcar Named Desire* .

1953   Arthur Miller's *The Crucible* opened during the period of 'witch-hunting' of communists in US under McCarthy. *En attendant Godot/Waiting for Godot* by Beckett exemplified the Theatre of the Absurd.

1956   English Stage Company formed at the Royal Court Theatre to provide a platform for new dramatists. Osborne's *Look Back in Anger* included in its first season.

1957   Bernstein's *West Side Story* opened in New York.

1960   Pinter's *The Caretaker*.

1961   Royal Shakespeare Company formed under directorship of Peter Hall, based at Stratford and the Aldwych, London.

1963–4   National Theatre Company formed at the Old Vic under the directorship of Sir Laurence Olivier.

1965   Edward Bond's *Saved* initially banned by the Lord Chamberlain.

1967   Stoppard's *Rosencrantz and Guildenstern are Dead* . Success in US of *Hair* – first of the 'rock' musicals.

1968   Abolition of theatre censorship in UK.

1970   Peter Brook's production of *A Midsummer Night's Dream*.

1976   National Theatre opened a new theatre complex on the South Bank, London.

1980   Howard Brenton's *The Romans in Britain* led to a private prosecution of the director for obscenity.

1982   Royal Shakespeare Company moved to the Barbican Centre, London.

1982–3   Trevor Nunn's production *Nicholas Nickleby* won Tony award, marking its success in UK and US.

1987   Agatha Christie's *The Mousetrap* entered its 35th year, the longest running play in the world. The Museum of Theatre opened in Covent Garden, London. Planning permission was granted for the building of a replica of Shakespeare's Globe Theatre by Sam Wanamaker on the original site.

Music and Dance

This section looks at the forms, styles, terms and people important in Western music and dance. The music of other cultures is often based on scale divisions different from ours and could not be discussed here without using complex terminology. Despite its long history and substantial artistic achievements, the significance of non-western music was not properly recognized in the West until Debussy listened to a Japanese gamelan orchestra at the Paris Exposition of 1889. The sounds he heard affected his own music, which in turn influenced the ideas of younger composers. Messiaen was similarly stimulated by hearing a Balinese gamelan orchestra at another Paris exposition, in 1931. Contemporary composers have not waited for the unfamiliar to arrive in the West, but have travelled to find it. Messiaen's pupils Boulez and Stockhausen made extensive trips to Indonesia and Japan; Benjamin Britten also went to Bali. David Fanshawe has spent time in Africa and Tonga. Philip Glass studied with the Indian sitarist Ravi Shankar, while a fellow graduate of the Juilliard School, Steve Reich, visited Ghana to study African drumming. This is a time of exciting cross-fertilization between cultures. Zubin Mehta, born in India, is now conductor of the New York Philharmonic, and a Japanese conductor, Seiji Ozawa, is music director in Boston; the compositions of a New Yorker, John Cage, arouse great enthusiasm in Tokyo. Music is moving, perhaps, towards a universal language.

This section contains biographies and a table of *Great Composers* in the classical tradition, a table of major *Operas* and their first performances, sections on *Jazz* and *Popular Music*, definitions of important *Musical Terms*, and a chronology of *Milestones in Musical History*. This is followed by a table of major works in *The Ballet Repertory* and a *Chronology* of milestones in the history of dance.

GREAT COMPOSERS

Giovanni Palestrina	c.1525–1594	Italian	motets, masses
Claudio Monteverdi	1567–1643	Italian	operas, vocal music
Henry Purcell	1659–1695	English	vocal music, operas
Antonio Vivaldi	1678–1741	Italian	concertos, chamber music
Georg Frideric Handel	1685–1759	German	oratorios, operas, orchestral music
Johann Sebastian Bach	1685–1750	German	keyboard, choral music, concertos
Joseph Haydn	1732–1809	Austrian	symphonies, oratorios, chamber music
Wolfgang Amadeus Mozart	1756–1791	Austrian	symphonies, operas, chamber music
Ludwig van Beethoven	1770–1827	German	symphonies, chamber music, opera
Carl Maria von Weber	1786–1826	German	operas, concertos
Gioacchino Rossini	1792–1868	Italian	operas
Franz Schubert	1797–1828	Austrian	songs, symphonies,chamber music
Hector Berlioz	1803–1869	French	operas, symphonies
Felix Mendelssohn	1809–1847	German	symphonies, concertos
Frederik Chopin	1810–1849	Polish	piano music
Robert Schumann	1810–1856	German	piano, vocal music, concertos
Franz Liszt	1811–1886	Hungarian	piano, orchestral music
Richard Wagner	1813–1883	German	operas
Giuseppe Verdi	1813–1901	Italian	operas
César Franck	1822–1890	Belgian	symphony, organ works
Bedrich Smetana	1824–1884	Czech	symphonies, operas
Anton Bruckner	1824–1896	Austrian	symphonies
Johann Strauss II	1825–1899	Austrian	waltzes, operettas
Johannes Brahms	1833–1897	German	symphonies, concertos
Camille Saint-Saëns	1835–1921	French	symphonies, concertos operas
Modest Mussorgsky	1839–1881	Russian	operas, orchestral music
Peter Ilyich Tchaikovsky	1840–1893	Russian	ballet music, symphonies
Antonin Dvořák	1841–1904	Czech	symphonies, operas
Edvard Grieg	1843–1907	Norwegian	concertos, orchestra music
Nikolai Rimsky-Korsakov	1844–1908	Russian	operas, orchestral music
Leos Janáček	1854–1928	Czech	operas, chamber music
Edward Elgar	1857–1934	English	orchestral music
Giacomo Puccini	1858–1924	Italian	operas
Gustav Mahler	1860–1911	Czech	symphonies
Claude Debussy	1862–1918	French	operas, orchestral music
Richard Strauss	1864–1949	German	operas, orchestral music
Carl Nielsen	1865–1931	Danish	symphonies
Jean Sibelius	1865–1957	Finnish	symphonies, orchestral music
Sergei Rachmaninov	1873–1943	Russian	symphonies, concertos
Arnold Schoenberg	1874–1951	Austrian	operas, orchestral and chamber music
Maurice Ravel	1875–1937	French	piano, chamber music
Béla Bartók	1881–1945	Hungarian	operas, concertos
Igor Stravinsky	1882–1971	Russian	ballets, operas
Anton Webern	1883–1945	Austrian	chamber, vocal music
Alban Berg	1885–1935	Austrian	operas, chamber music
Sergei Prokofiev	1891–1953	Russian	symphonies, ballets
George Gershwin	1898–1937	American	musicals, operas
Dmitri Shostakovich	1906–1975	Russian	piano music
Olivier Messiaen	1908–	French	piano, organ, orchestral music
Benjamin Britten	1913–1976	English	vocal music, opera
Karlheinz Stockhausen	1928–	German	electronic, vocal music

Great Composers

Bach Johann Sebastian 1685–1750. Born in Eisenach, Germany, he worked in Weimar and Leipzig. A master of contrapuntal technique, his music marks the culmination of the Baroque polyphonic style. His huge output includes orchestral works such as the six *Brandenburg Concertos* 1721, organ works, more than 200 cantatas and large-scale choral works such as the *St Matthew Passion* 1729 and the Mass in B Minor 1733.

Bartók Béla 1881–1945. Born in Sinnicolaul Mare, Hungary. With Zoltan Kodaly, he made an extensive study of the folk music of Hungary, Slovakia and Rumania, which led him to develop a new musical language making tonal use of the 12 notes of the chromatic scale. His works include six string quartets 1908–39, the opera *Bluebeard's Castle* 1911 and the *Concerto for Orchestra* 1943. He spent the last five years of his life in the USA.

Beethoven Ludwig van 1770–1827. Born in Bonn, he settled in Vienna in 1792. From the age of 30 he was troubled with increasing deafness. In a career which spanned the decline of Classicism and the growth of Romanticism, his mastery of musical expression in every genre made him the dominant influence in 19th-century music. His orchestral works, which include nine symphonies, five piano concertos and one violin concerto, are probably the most frequently performed in the repertoire. His 32 piano sonatas, 16 string quartets and other chamber music also remain popular.

Berg Alban 1885–1935. Born and lived in Vienna. Like Webern, he studied with Schoenberg and used the latter's serial technique, though there are tonal and Romantic elements in his music. His best-known works are the operas *Wozzeck* 1925 and *Lulu* 1937 and violin concerto 1935.

Berlioz Hector 1803–69. Born in Côte-St André, near Grenoble. He was the only great French Romantic composer. Much of his music has a theatrical quality and was inspired by contemporary drama and literature. His mastery of thematic development, and in particular the idea of using a recurring 'fixed idea' (*idée fixe*), is evident in works such as the *Symphonie Fantastique* 1830 and *Harold in Italy* 1834. Ahead of his time in his innovative use of orchestral colouring and contrasts, he was barely acknowledged in France during his life, though he did receive the Légion d'Honneur for his *Grand Messe des Morts* 1837.

Brahms Johannes 1833–97. Born in Hamburg, he moved to Vienna in 1863. Using traditional classical forms, he expanded their scope, thus bridging the gap between Classicism and Romanticism in German music. His four symphonies, two piano concertos and violin concerto, all written after he had reached his forties, are part of the Romantic repertoire. He also wrote piano and chamber works, songs and the non-liturgical *German Requiem* 1857–68.

Britten Benjamin 1913–76. Born in Lowestoft, Suffolk. After a short period in the USA 1939–42, he spent the rest of his life in Aldeburgh where, with the tenor Peter Pears, he founded the annual music festival. He wrote some instrumental works but his main achievement lies in his vocal and, in particular, his operatic works. His first opera *Peter Grimes* 1945 was followed by chamber operas such as *Albert Herring* 1947 and several other large-scale operas such as *Billy Budd* 1951. He wrote the *War Requiem* for the consecration of Coventry Cathedral in 1962.

Bruckner Anton 1824–96. Born in Ansfelden, Austria, he settled in Vienna in his forties. A Classic-Romantic in his use of form, he shows Wagnerian influence in the solemnity and expansiveness of his work. His nine symphonies, in particular the Fourth 1881 and Seventh 1884, have now won universal acclaim. A deeply religious man, he also wrote three masses and a *Te Deum* 1881–84.

Chopin Frédéric 1810–49. Born in Selazowa Wola, Poland, of half French, half Polish parentage, he lived in Paris from 1831. A virtuoso performer, he composed almost entirely for the piano, producing a new repertory for the instrument including 27 études, 25 preludes, three sonatas and two concertos. Influenced by the Italian opera composer Bellini, and the by Irish composer Field, his music displays and innovative keyboard technique an rhythm (especially his use of rubato) and strong nationalistic flavour in its passion and use of folk music. The year before his death, from consumption, he gave concerts in England and Scotland.

Debussy Claude 1862–1918. Born in St Germain-en-Laye, France, he spent most of his life in Paris. Influenced by both Impressionist painters and Symbolist poets, his work moved from the naturalistic (his early tone poem *Prélude à l'Aprè-midi d'un Faune* 1894) to the more purely abstract *La Mer* 1905 and the ballet *Jeux* 1912). He developed an original, delicate language using a scale of whole tones and innovative harmonies and achieved a new range of timbres and rhythms for both piano and orchestra. He completed one opera, *Pelléas et Mélisande* 1902, based on a play by Maeterlinck.

Dvořák Antonin 1841–1904. Born in Nelahozeves, Czechoslovakia. He spent much of his life in Prague, but visited England eight times and was head of the National Conservatory in New York 1892–95. He was an important nationalist composer, and his direct, fresh style is best exemplified in his orchestral and chamber works, including nine symphonies, the two *Slavonic Dances* 1878–86, the cello concerto and some notable string quartets.

Elgar Edward 1857–1934. Born in Broadheath, near Worcester, England, he lived in Malvern and then Hereford. Working in obscurity for many years, he first gained national recognition with the *Enigma Variations* 1899, followed by the oratorio *The Dream of Gerontius* 1900, the *Cockaigne* overture 1901 and the *Pomp and Circumstance Marches* 1901–07. Later came the two symphonies 1908 and

1911, and the cello concerto 1919. The combination of tenderness and nobility in his music makes him widely admired in Britain, but he is still little appreciated worldwide.

Franck César 1822–90. Born in Liège, he left Belgium in 1844 and spent the rest of his life in Paris. Influential as an organist, teacher and composer. There are elements of the Romantic and mystical in his work. His organ works, particularly the *Pièce heroique* 1878 and *Three Chorales* 1890, are widely admired, as are the *Symphonic Variations* 1885 and the symphony of 1889.

Gershwin George 1898–1937. Born in New York. A jazz pianist and composer of popular songs, mostly with lyrics by his brother Ira, his *Rhapsody in Blue* 1924 brought notice from more intellectual audiences. His other principal works include a piano concerto, the tone poem *An American in Paris* 1928, and the opera *Porgy and Bess* 1935.

Grieg Edvard 1843–1907. Born in Bergen, Norway, he was determinedly Norwegian in his musical inspiration. Much of his best music is small scale, namely his songs, dances and piano works. Among orchestral works are the Piano Concerto 1869, one of the most popular in the concert repertoire, and the incidental music for Ibsen's *Peer Gynt* 1876.

Handel George Frideric 1685–1759. Born in Halle, Germany, he spent most of his life in England. He came to dominate English musical life with his efforts to convert audiences to Italian opera and his subsequent elecation of the oratorio to a more important musical form, culminating in the *Messiah* 1742, written in three weeks. He also wrote several instrumental works, including the orchestral suites *The Water Music* 1715 and *Music for the Royal Fireworks* 1749.

Haydn Joseph 1732–1809. Born in Rohrau, near Bratislava, he spent much of his life as kapellmeister to the Austrian Esterházy family, but visited London twice. A teacher of both Mozart and Beethoven, he was a major exponent of the classical sonata form in his numerous chamber and orchestral works (he wrote over 100 symphonies). He also wrote much choral music, the best-known including the oratorios *The Creation* 1798 and *The Seasons* 1801.

Janáček Leŏs 1854–1928. Born in Hukvaldy, Czechoslovakia, he lived much of his life in Brno. Essentially a theatrical composer, he had his first success with the opera *Jenufa*. His other operas, including *Katya Kabanova* 1921 and *The Cunning Little Vixen* 1924, and his choral music, especially the *Glagolitic Mass* 1927, all show his individual use of rhythm, tonality and form.

Liszt Franz 1811–86. Born in Raiding, Hungary, he lived for periods in Paris, Weimar and then Rome, where he turned to a religious life and became known as the Abbé Liszt. Highly regarded as a brilliant pianist, he produced some 400 original compositions and 900 transcriptions for piano, as well as inventing a new orchestral form in his *Symphonic Poem*. A champion of his contemporaries, especially Wagner, he promoted 'The Music of the Future', breaking new ground with his use of chromaticism.

Mahler Gustav 1860–1911. Born in Kaliště, Czechoslovakis, he worked as a conductor throughout his life, notably with the Vienna Opera and the New York Philharmonic. His massive, richly textured symphonies, the moving *Das Lied Von der Erde/Song of the Earth* and his song cycles display a synthesis of Romanticism and new uses of chromatic harmonies and musical forms. His work has gained in popularity with modern audiences after several decades of neglect.

Mendelssohn Felix 1809–47. Born in Hamburg, he travelled extensively, often to Britain, before settling in Düsseldorf and then Leipzig. Using Classical forms he was nevertheless an early Romantic in the subjective quality he brought to his work. The overture and incidental music to *A Midsummer Night's Dream* 1827/43, the *Fingal's Cave* overture 1832, the violin concerto 1845 and the *Italian* 1833 and *Scottish* 1842 Symphonies have always been popular works in the concert repertoire.

Messiaen Oliver 1908– . Born in Avignon, France, he has spent most of his life in Paris, where he was appointed organist at La Trinité church in 1931. A devout christian, he considers that his music has two predominant elements: religious faith and colour. An innovator both with tone and rhythm, his teaching influenced contemporary composers including Boulez and Stockhausen. Among his better-known works are the *Quatuor pour la fin du temps* 1941, the large-scale *Turangalila Symphony* 1949, and several organ pieces.

Monteverdi Claudio 1567–1643. Born in Cremona, Italy, he lived in Mantua and Venice, where he was director of music at St Mark's. The greatest 17th-century Italian composer and an exponent of monody and recitative as opposed to polyphony, he holds an important place in European music. His operas *Orfeo* 1607 and *The Coronation of Poppea* 1642 are two early masterpieces in the form. He also wrote many madrigals, motets and much sacred music, notably the *Vespers* 1610, a six-part mass.

Mozart Wolfgang Amadeus 1756–91. Born in Salzburg, Austria. A child prodigy, he travelled extensively in his early youth, settling in Vienna from the age of 25, where he died a pauper. Strongly influenced by Haydn, his music marks the height of the Classical age in its purity of melody and form. His large output includes operas such as *The Marriage of Figaro* 1786, *Don Giovanni* 1787, *The Magic Flute* 1791, nearly 50 symphonies, chamber and keyboard music. His last work was his *Requiem*.

Mussorgsky Modest 1839–81. Born in Karevo in Pskov, Russia. After an early career in the army, he became a civil servant, but his life was cut short by alcoholism. A member of the nationalist group, The Five, he was influenced by both folk music and literature, and was largely self-taught. His best-known compositions include *A Night on the Bare Mountain* 1867, *Pictures at an Exhibition* 1874 and the opera *Boris Godunov* 1874, one version of which was 'revised' by Rimsky-Korsakov.

Nielsen Carl 1865–1931. Born in Norre-Lyndelse, Denmark's greatest composer. His works show an openness to new musical ideas and a reaction against Romanticism. He is best known for his six symphonies, but his compositions also include the Clarinet Concerto 1928, chamber and piano works, and two operas *Saul and David* 1902 and *Maskarade* 1906.

Palestrina Giovanni Pierluigi da c. 1525–94. Born in Palestrina, near Rome, he worked for most of his life in Rome in the service of the church. He wrote much secular and sacred choral music, his religious work gaining him a reputation as the master of polyphonic vocal music. Apart from motets and madrigals, his greatest achievement is considered to be his 105 masses, which include the outstanding *Missa Papae Marcelli.*

Prokofiev Sergei 1891–1953. Born in Sontsovka, Russia, he travelled widely as a pianist and lived in Paris for a while, before returning to Russia in 1932. He was essentially a classicist in his use of form, but his extensive and varied output demonstrates great lyricism, humour and craftsmanship. The range of his work is displayed in compositions such as the *Classical Symphony* 1918, the operas *Love for Three Oranges* 1921 and *War and Peace* 1946, the ballets *Romeo and Juliet* 1938 and *Cinderella* 1945, and the children's classic *Peter and the Wolf* 1936.

Puccini Giacomo 1858–1924. Born in Lucca, Italy, one of the most popular opera composers. His reputation was firmly established with *Manon Lescaut* 1893. This, and other favourites such as *La Bohème* 1896, *Tosca* 1900, *Madame Butterfly* 1904, and the unfinished *Turandot* 1926, all show his strong gift for melody and dramatic effect.

Purcell Henry 1659–95 born in London, he was composer to the Chapel Royal and, from 1679, organist at Westminster Abbey. His versatility, creative genius and ability to express extremes of joy and sadness, have given him a reputation as the greatest English composer. Some of the best-known of his 500 compositions are *Dido and Aeneas* 1689, *King Arthur* 1691, *The Fairy Queen* 1692, *The Indian Queen* 1692, and *Ode on St Cecilia's Day* 1692.

Rachmaninov Sergei 1873–1943. Born in Semyonovo, he left Russia in 1917 to travel as a concert pianist in the West, and later settled in

California. A great advocate of melodic invention, he wrote some fine music for piano, including the Second and Third 1901 and 1909 concertos and *Rhapsody on a Theme of Paganini* 1934. His 79 songs make him the creator of the Russian Lied; also popular are the Second Symphony 1908 and *The Bells* 1913.

Ravel Maurice 1875–1937. Born in Ciboure, near St Jean de Luz, France. He was a pupil of Fauré, and his compositions show a personal synthesis of influences from Classicism to Impressionism. Particularly admired for his brilliant piano works and his use of orchestral colour, well-known examples include the *Rhapsodie espagnole 1908, Daphnis et Chloë 1912, La Valse* 1920, *Bolero* 1928, and the two piano concertos 1931/32.

Rimsky-Korsakov Nikolai 1844–1908. Born in Tikhvin, Russian. Initially a naval officer, he wrote part of his First Symphony 1865 at sea. The most prolific of the nationalist group The Five, he is most admired for his colourful orchestration as in *Capriccio espagnol* 1887 and *Scheherezade* 1888. His 15 operas include the posthumously performed *The Golden Cockerel* 1909.

Rossini Gioacchino 1792–1868. Born in Pesaro, Italy. Influenced by Mozart, Rossini quickly emerged as an opera composer, popular for his sense of melody and humour. He wrote 36 operas betwen 1810 and 1829, including *The Barber of Seville* 1816 (which took him just 13 days), and *La Cenerentola* 1817. After *William Tell* 1829, he wrote nothing until the *Stabat Mater* 1842, *Petite Messe solonelle* 1864 and pieces later assembled by Respighi as the ballet *La boutique fantasque* 1919.

Saint-Saëns Camille 1835–1921. Born in Paris. A prolific composer in all genres, much influenced by Liszt, he is best remembered for the symphonic poem *Danse macabre* 1874, the succesful opera *Samson and Delilah* 1877, the Third Symphony 1886, and concertos for piano, violin and cello. He is also noted for his musical joke, the *Carnival of the Animals* 1886.

Schoenberg Arnold 1874–1951. Born in Vienna, he settled in the USA in 1934. An influential and revolutionary composer in his use of the 12–note system, his experimentation with atonality and the serial technique of composition continued throughout his life. Notable works are the string sextet *Verklärte Nacht* 1899, the music drama *Die Gluckliche Hand* 1908–1913, the song cycle *Pierrot Lunaire* 1912, in which *Sprechgesange* (German 'speech-song') is used, and his incomplete opera *Moses and Aaron* 1930.

Schubert Franz 1797–1828 born in Vienna. Heir to Haydn and Mozart, he was an early Romantic whose greatest contribution was his many songs or *Lieder*, which combine the expression of strong emotions with pure melody. The huge output of his brief life also includes nine symphonies, piano and chamber music, such as the *Trout Quintet* 1819, and seven masses.

Schumann Robert 1810–1856 born in Zwickau, near Dresden, Germany. Important to the Romantic movement, both as a prolific composer and able critic, he suffered increasingly from depression, finally attempting suicide and dying in an asylum two years later. His many *Lieder*, four song cycles, and piano works best display his talent for creativity and expression, but he also wrote chamber, choral, and orchestral music, including the four symphonies 1841–53, the Piano Concerto 1845, and the Cello Concerto 1860.

Shostakovich Dmitri 1906–75 born in St Petersburg, Russia. Often considered the 'composer-laureate of the Soviet state', he nevertheless had a turbulent relationship with officialdom, which is reflected in his music. Retaining tonality, he wrote 15 symphonies, several of which are programmatic in their depiction of political events. His other works include string quartets, operas and piano works.

Sibelius Jean 1865–1957 born in Hämeenlinna, Finland. From the age of 32 he was supported as a composer by the state, though he stopped composing in his sixties. Mainly respected as a major symphonist in Scandinavia, Britain and the USA, he displayed a strong personal style from the outset. His works include strongly nationalistic symphonic poems such as *En Saga* 1893, *Finlandia* 1900, *Tapiola* 1926, and the popular Violin Concerto 1904.

Smetana Bedřich 1824–84 born in Litomyšl, Czechoslovakia. An important national figure, he founded a school of music in Prague and became director of the national theatre in 1866, the year that his hugely successful comic opera *The Bartered Bride* was premiered. Despite becoming deaf in 1874, he continued to compose, producing works such as the cycle of six symbolic poems *My Country* 1874–79, but eventually ended his life in an asylum.

Stockhausen Karlheinz 1928– born in Mödrach, near Cologne, Germany. The most influential avant-garde composer of the second half of the 20th century, he has continued to explore new musical sounds and compositional techniques since the 1950s, using electronic music in particular. His major works include *Klavierstücke* 1952–85, *Momente* 1961–64, revised 1972, *Mikrophonie I* 1964 and *Mikrophonie II* 1965. In recent years he has concentrated on a cycle of seven musical ceremonies, starting with *Donnerstag aus Licht* 1977–80.

Strauss Johann II 1825–99. Born in Vienna, he is the member of the famous music-making family whose works are still most performed. These include *The Blue Danube* 1867, *Tales from the Vienna Woods* 1868, *Wine, Women and Song* 1869, *Vienna Blood* 1973, *Roses from the South* 1880, *Voices of Spring* 1883, and the operetta *Die Fledermaus* 1874.

Strauss Richard 1864–1949. Born in Munich, Germany. A prominent conductor, he was influenced by the German heritage but had a strongly personal style, particularly in his use of bold, colourful orchestration. He first established his reputation with tone poems such as *Don Juan* 1889, *Till Eulenspiegel's Merry Pranks* 1895, and *Also sprach Zarathustra* 1896. He then moved on to operatic success with *Salome* 1905, and *Elektra* 1909, both of which have elements of polytonality, followed by a reversion to a more traditional style with *Der Rosenkavalier* 1911.

Stravinsky Igor 1882–1971. Born at Ora- nienbaum, near St Petersburg, Russia, he lived in Paris from 1920 before moving to the USA and becoming naturalized in 1945. He was a major 20th-century figure. He first reached prominence with the ballets *The Firebird* 1910 and *Petrushka* 1911, but his early masterpiece was the controversial *The Rite of Spring* 1913 with its unconventional use of rhythms and harmonies. His versatility is evident in the varied nature of his works: the Neo-Classicism of his ballet *Pulcinella* 1920, the choral- orchestral *Symphony of Psalms* 1930, and his later use of serial techniques in works such as the *Canticum Sacrum* 1955 and the ballet *Agon* 1953–57.

Tchaikovsky Peter Ilyich 1840–93. Born in Votkinsk, he was the first Russian composer to establish a reputation with Western audiences. His strong sense of melody, personal expres- sion and brilliant orchestration are clear throughout his large output; this includes six symphonies, three piano concertos, a violin concerto, symphonic poems, the ballets *Swan Lake* 1877, *The Sleeping Beauty* 1890, and *Nutcracker* 1892, and the opera *Eugene Onegin* 1879.

Verdi Giuseppe 1813–1901. Born in Le Ron- cole, Parma. The great Italian opera composer of the Romantic period, he brought his native operatic style to new heights of dramatic expression, working to perfect and develop his technique throughout his life. His operas range from his early success with *Nabucco* 1842 to *Falstaff* 1893, and include *Rigoletto* 1851, *Il Trovatore* 1853, *La Traviata* 1853 and *Aida* 1871. He also wrote a magnificent *Requiem* in 1884.

Vivaldi Antonio 1678–1741. Born in Venice, Italy, he spent much of his life there as a teacher but died in poverty in Vienna. A prolific composer, he is noted for instrumental works works – over 400 concertos, 23 sym- phonies and 75 sonatas – and his development of the solo concerto is especially significant. His music, which also includes over 40 operas and much sacred music, was largely neglected until the 1930s.

Wagner Richard 1813–83. Born in Leipzig, Germany, he led a turbulent life in Europe, falling in and out of favour with the German authorities, until he settled there to work on his national theatre at Bayreuth, eventually com- pleted in 1876. His vision of opera as a 'music drama', or total art form, caused wide contro- versy, as did his development of new operatic forms and his use of recurring Leitmotivs. He worked ceaselessly to achieve his aims, pro- ducing operas such as *Lohengrin* 1846–48, *Tristan and Isolde* 1865 and the massive four- opera work *The Ring of the Nibelung* 1876. His last work was *Parsifal* 1882.

Weber Carl Maria von 1786–1826. Born in Eutin, Germany. Often considered the first Romantic composer, he was also the founder of German national opera with *Der Freischütz* 1821. Of his several operas, only *Euryanthe* 1823 is entirely sung. He also wrote piano music such as *Invitation to the Dance* 1819, and *Konzertstück* 1821. He died in London after launching his opera *Oberon* 1826.

Webern Anton 1883–1945. Born in Vienna, Austria. He studied with Schoenberg, adop- ting atonality and then 12–note composition, but used it more rigorously in delicate, highly crafted short forms. Works such as his Sym- phony 1928 have been very influential.

MAJOR OPERAS AND THEIR FIRST PERFORMANCES

Date	Opera	Composer	Librettist	Place
1607	Orfeo	Monteverdi	Striggio	Mantua
1642	The Coronation of Poppea	Monteverdi	Busenello	Venice
1689	Dido and Aeneas	Purcell	Tate	London
1724	Julius Caesar in Egypt	Handel	Haym	London
1762	Orpheus and Eurydice	Gluck	Calzabigi	Vienna
1786	The Marriage of Figaro	Mozart	Da Ponte	Vienna
1787	Don Giovanni	Mozart	Da Ponte	Prague
1790	Così fan tutte	Mozart	Da Ponte	Vienna
1791	The Magic Flute	Mozart	Schikaneder	Vienna
1805	Fidelio	Beethoven	Sonnleithner	Vienna
1816	The Barber of Seville	Rossini	Sterbini	Rome
1821	Der Freischütz	Weber	Kind	Berlin
1831	Norma	Bellini	Romani	Milan
1835	Lucia di Lammermoor	Donizetti	Cammarano	Naples
1836	Les Huguenots	Meyerbeer	Scribe	Paris
1842	Russlan and Ludmilla	Glinka	Shirkov/Bakhturin	St Petersburg
1850	Lohengrin	Wagner	Wagner	Weimar
1851	Rigoletto	Verdi	Piave	Venice
1853	Il Trovatore	Verdi	Cammarano	Rome
1853	La Traviata	Verdi	Piave	Venice
1859	Faust	Gounod	Barbier/Carré	Paris
1865	Tristan and Isolde	Wagner	Wagner	Munich
1866	The Bartered Bride	Smetana	Sabina	Prague
1868	Die Meistersinger von Nürnberg	Wagner	Wagner	Munich
1871	Aida	Verdi	Ghislanzoni	Cairo
1874	Boris Godunov	Mussorgsky	Mussorgsky	St Petersburg
1874	Die Fledermaus	Johann Strauss II	Haffner/Genée	Vienna
1875	Carmen	Bizet	Meilhac/Halévy	Paris
1876	The Ring of the Nibelung	Wagner	Wagner	Bayreuth
1879	Eugene Onegin	Tchaikovsky	Tchaikovsky/Shilovsky	Moscow
1881	The Tales of Hoffman	Offenbach	Barbier	Paris
1882	Parsifal	Wagner	Wagner	Bayreuth
1885	The Mikado	Sullivan	Gilbert	London
1887	Otello	Verdi	Boito	Milan
1890	Cavalleria Rusticana	Mascagni	Menasci/Targioni-Tozzetti	Rome
1890	Prince Igor	Borodin	Borodin	St Petersburg
1892	Pagliacci	Leoncavallo	Leoncavallo	Milan
1892	Werther	Massenet	Blau/Milliet/Hartmann	Vienna
1896	La Bohème	Puccini	Giacosa/Illica	Turin
1900	Tosca	Puccini	Giacosa/Illica	Rome
1902	Pelléas et Mélisande	Debussy	Maeterlinck	Paris
1904	Jenůfa	Janáček	Janáček	Brno
1904	Madame Butterfly	Puccini	Giacosa/Illica	Milan
1905	Salome	Richard Strauss	Wilde/Lachmann	Dresden
1909	The Golden Cockerel	Rimsky-Korsakov	Byelsky	Moscow
1911	Der Rosenkavalier	Richard Strauss	Hofmannsthal	Dresden
1918	Duke Bluebeard's Castle	Bartók	Balázs	Budapest
1925	Wozzeck	Berg	Berg	Berlin
1935	Porgy and Bess	Gershwin	Ira Gershwin/Heyward	Boston
1937	Lulu	Berg	Berg	Zürich
1945	Peter Grimes	Britten	Slater	London
1946	War and Peace	Prokofiev	Prokofiev/Mendelson	Leningrad
1951	The Rake's Progress	Stravinsky	Auden/Kallman	Venice
1978	Paradise Lost	Penderecki	Fry	Chicago
1986	The Mask of Orpheus	Birtwistle	Zinovieff	London

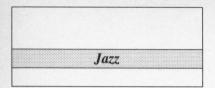

Jazz

Jazz syncopated music characterized by improvisation, which developed in the USA at the turn of this century out of black American popular music.

1880-1900 originated mainly in New Orleans
1917 centre of jazz moved to Chicago (Louis Armstrong) and St Louis
1920s growth of 'swing' music
1930s New York jazz and swing orchestras: Paul Whiteman, Fletcher Henderson, Glenn Miller, Dorsey brothers
1940s the 'big bands': Duke Ellington, Woody Herman, Benny Goodman, Stan Kenton, Count Basie
1950s increasing diversity of styles: Charlie Parker, Dizzy Gillespie, Miles Davies, Stan Getz, Thelonius Monk, Modern Jazz Quartet
1960s 'free form' jazz: Ornette Coleman, John Coltrane
1970s jazz rock: Weather Report
1980s diversity of styles and traditions; e.g. jazz funk, Grover Washington jr; traditional, Wynton Marsalis; Caribbean, Courtney Pine; anarchic, Loose Tubes.

Jazz Greats

Armstrong 'Satchmo' (Louis) 1900–71. American jazz trumpet player and singer, who first came to prominence in the 1920s with the Creole Jazz Band and his own Hot Five and Hot Seven. He was legendary for his trumpet technique and improvisation, and for his gravelly voice.

Basie 'Count' (William) 1904–84. American band leader, pianist, and organist, who won great popularity for his simplified swinging style of music. He developed the big band sound and led impressive groups of musicians in a career spanning more than 50 years.

Bechet Sidney Joseph 1897–1959. American virtuoso soprano saxophonist, the first jazz artist to achieve fame with this instrument. He joined Noble Sissle's band in Paris in 1928 and later became a major entertainer in France.

Beiderbecke 'Bix' (Leon Bismarcke) 1903–31. American jazz cornettist and pianist. He was greatly inspired by the classical composers Debussy, Ravel and Stravinsky. A romantic soloist with Paul Whiteman's orchestra, he became legendary after his early death.

Blakey Art 1919– . (Muslim name: Abdullah Ibn Buhaina). Dynamic American jazz drummer, famous for his rolls and explosions. He formed and led The Jazz Messengers from 1955 onwards, and widely explored and expanded percussion possibilities, including the assimilation of African rhythms.

Brand 'Dollar' (Adolf Johannes) 1934– . (Muslim name: Abdullah Ibrahim). South African pianist and composer. He first performed in the US in 1965, and has had a great influence on the fusion of African rhythms with American jazz. His compositions range from songs to large works for orchestra.

Coleman Ornette 1930– . American alto saxophonist and composer. He has created controversial new jazz sounds for the symphony orchestra. In a classical manner, he accords priority to the composition and restrains improvisation in performance.

Coltrane 'Trane' (John William) 1926–67. American jazz saxophonist who rose to fame in 1955 with the Mile Davis' quintet. He was a powerful and highly individual artist whose performances were noted for experimentation.

Davis Miles Dewey Jr. 1926– . American jazz trumpeter and band leader. He heralded a new era of 'cool' jazz in the 1950s and introduced a lighter, more lyrical sound in solo performances with his own Miles Davis Orchestra, formed in 1948.

Dodds Johnny 1892–1940. American clarinettist, generally ranked among the top New Orleans jazz clarinettists. He was most successful with The New Orleans Wanderers and noted for his warmth of tone and improvisation.

Ellington 'Duke' (Edward Kennedy) 1899–1974. American pianist who had an outstanding career as a composer and orchestrator of jazz. He wrote numerous pieces for his own jazz orchestra, with which he achieved great success, and became one of the most important figures in jazz over 55 years.

Fitzgerald Ella 1918– . American jazz singer, recognized as one of the greatest voices of jazz, capturing the essence of this musical idiom, although she has sometimes been criticized for lack of emotional depth.

Getz 'Stan' (Stanley) 1927– . American tenor saxophonist of the 1950s 'cool school'. He was also the first American musician to be closely identified with the Latin American influenced 'bossa nova' sound.

Goodman 'Benny' (Benjamin David) 1909–1986. American clarinettist, nicknamed 'the King of Swing' for the new jazz idiom he introduced. He is also significant for leading racially integrated bands, thus breaking down racial barriers in the world of jazz musicians.

Hawkins 'Bean' (Coleman Randolph) 1904–69. American virtuoso tenor saxophonist. He became a soloist with Fletcher Henderson's Orchestra, and was the most influential figure in bringing the jazz saxophone to prominence as a solo instrument.

Holiday 'Billie', 'Lady Day' (Eleanora) 1915–59. American singer who became a legendary soloist in the 1940s and 1950s. She was famous for the depth of feeling she conveyed with the 'swing' style. Although not a blues singer as such, she brought an individual blues sound to everything she sang.

Joplin Scott 1868–1917. American ragtime pianist and composer in Chicago. His 'Maple Leaf Rag' 1899 was the first instrumental sheet music to sell a million, and 'The Entertainer' was the theme tune of the film *The Sting* 1973, and revived his popularity. He was an influence

on Jelly Roll Morton and other early jazz musicians.

Mingus Charles 1922–79. American bassist and composer. He was influential for his experimentation with atonality and dissonant effects, opening the way for the new style of free collective improvisation of the 1960s.

Modern Jazz Quartet American jazz group specializing in group improvisation, formed 1952, led by pianist John Lewis (1920–), with Milt Jackson (1923–) on vibraphone, bass player Percy Heath (1923–), and drummer first Kenny Clarke and later Connie Kay; disbanded 1974 although reunited in the 1980s for touring. Noted for elegance and mastery of form, they were sometimes criticized for being too 'classical'.

Monk Thelonious 1917–82. American jazz pianist and composer. He became popular in the 1950s and was significant as a major composer and pioneer of the 'be-bop' style.

Morton 'Jelly Roll' (Ferdinand Joseph) 1885–1941. Pioneer American jazz pianist, singer and composer, who achieved fame with the Red Hot Peppers. Influenced by Scott Joplin, he played a major part in the development of jazz from ragtime to swing by means of improvisation and imposing his own personality upon the music.

Parker 'Charlie', 'Bird', 'Yardbird', (Charles Christopher) 1920–55. American alto saxophonist and composer, closely associated with trumpeter Dizzy Gillespie in developing the 'be-bop' style. His mastery of the art of improvisation influenced performers on all jazz instruments.

Reinhardt 'Django' (Jean Baptiste) 1910–53. Gypsy guitarist of German origin, born in Belgium. He was most famous for his haunting, melodic improvisation at a slow tempo, and was the first European jazz artist to influence American jazz musicians.

Rollins 'Sonny' Theodore Walter 1930– . American tenor saxophonist and jazz composer. A leader of the 'hard bop' school, he is known for the intensity and bravado of his music, and for his skillful improvisation.

Smith Bessie 1894–1937. American jazz and

blues singer, born in Mississippi, USA, known as 'Empress of the Blues' in the 1920s.

Tatum 'Art' (Arthur) 1910–56. American virtuoso jazz pianist who first achieved fame in the 1930s. He improvised superlatively with guitarist Tiny Grimes in a trio from 1943, and maintained his superb artistry in concert solo performances.

Tristano 'Lennie' (Lennard Joseph) 1919–78. American jazz pianist and composer. A radically austere musician, he gave an academic foundation the 'cool school' of jazz in the 1940s and 1950s, at odds with the 'be-bop' tradition, and was active as a teacher.

Young 'Pres' (Lester Willis) 1909–59. American tenor saxophonist and jazz composer. He was a major figure in the development of his instrument for jazz music from the 1930s, and in the emergence of 'cool' jazz as a new style. He was also noted as an accompanist to Billie Holiday in the late 1930s.

Popular Music

pop music modern popular music began after World War II, with the growth of the 'teenager' and the electronic media, and was symbolized by the new electronic instrument, the guitar:

rock and roll had its roots in jazz, blues, country music, and gospel music, noted exponents being Chuck Berry, and Bill Haley and the Comets. Elvis Presley was the giant of this era. It led to *rock* in various forms - folk rock, hard rock, acid rock - and has continued to splinter and variegate, e.g. the New Romanticism of Boy George in female dress in the 1980s.

the Liverpool sound, partly inspired by rock and roll and partly by English and Irish folk tradition, is symbolized by the Beatles. It later also became associated with 'dropping out', seeking religion in the East rather than the West,

and drug-taking.

folk music became important in the early 1960s with singers such as Bob Dylan, Joan Baez and Joni Mitchell; it was associated with the early student protest movement, and the lyrics were often sophisticated.

country and western became popular especially in Nashville, Tennessee in the 1940s and 1950s. Famous singers include Hank Williams and Johnny Cash.

rhythm and blues and *hard rock* brought a more earthy rebellion than the wholesome Beatles in the 1960s and 1970s, pioneered by the Rolling Stones.

soul derived largely from the blues, e.g. Ray Charles, Aretha Franklin, Sam Cooke.

the Motown sound (from Detroit, the 'motor city') from the early 1960s combined pop with soul: Marvin Gaye; the Supremes.

psychedelic rock, with a flowering of advanced electronic equipment for both light and sound, began about 1967 with the Doors, leading by 1980 to the spectacular stage performance of Pink Floyd in *The Wall* with a story line and modern rock.

reggae was linked with black Africa (and Rastafarianism) in its musical themes, heavy rhythms, and overwhelming sound; it spread from the Caribbean, becoming a cult in the USA and the UK in the 1970s. Bob Marley was the leading exponent.

punk American 'rotten' rock of the mid-1970s, which returned to its unsophisticated origins, and in Britain was associated with unnaturally coloured hair in spiky styles, torn clothes and safety-pins, e.g. the Sex Pistols.

Pop Musicians

Baez Joan 1941– . American folk singer who came to prominence in the early 1960s with her versions of traditional English and American folk songs such as 'Silver Dagger'. She introduced Bob Dylan to a wide audience and later became a leading pacifist and anti-war campaigner.

Beatles The. English pop group, formed 1960, the first UK group to achieve international stardom and challenge the dominance of American rock and roll in the early 1960s. The members, all born in Liverpool, were *George Harrison* 1943– ; *John Winston Lennon* 1940–80; *James Paul McCartney* 1942– ; and *Richard Starkey* stage name 'Ringo Starr' 1940– . They made their name in the Cavern Club in Liverpool (later razed, but restored in 1982). Using songs written by Lennon and McCartney, they took the pop world by storm 1963–5 with the Liverpool sound; they influenced the dress, life-style and thought of young people, even beyond the break-up of the group in 1971, when they developed as individual performers, especially John Lennon (with his wife, Yoko Ono, until he was shot dead in 1980), and Paul McCartney with the group Wings. Numbers of the original 'group' period included 'She Loves You' 1963, 'A Hard Day's Night' 1964, 'Can't Buy Me Love' 1964, 'Yesterday' 1965, 'Yellow Submarine' 1966, 'Eleanor Rigby' 1966, and also the complex electronic syntheses of their album *Sergeant Pepper's Lonely Hearts Club Band* 1967.

Berry Chuck (Charles Edward) 1931– . American rock and roll singer and guitarist. Influenced by rhythm and blues, he was one of the pioneers of rock and roll from the mid-1950s with a string of hits including 'Maybellene' 1955 and 'Roll Over Beethoven' 1956.

Bowie David 1947– . Stage name of British pop star David Jones. Born in Brixton, London, and inspiration in the 1970s of 'glitter rock' and 'European' electronic music; his albums include *Ziggy Stardust* 1972.

Byrds The. American pioneering folk-rock group, formed 1964, described at the time as America's answer to the Beatles. Original group included Roger McGuinn, David Crosby, Gene Clark, Chris Hillman, and Michael Clarke. Best remembered for their early hits 'Mr Tambourine Man' 1965 (a version of

Bob Dylan's song) and 'Eight Miles High' 1966, they moved towards jazz rock and country rock in the late 1960s.

Cash Johnny 1932– . American country singer and guitarist, the first to bring country music to a wide audience with his million-selling song 'I Walk the Line' 1956. He has also sung gospel, rockabilly, and blues, and his songs have become classics.

Charles Ray 1930– . American blues and soul singer and pianist, blind from childhood, who also became a rock and roll star from 1959 with his first big hit, 'What'd I Say'. Perhaps best known for his recording of Hoagy Carmichael's ballad 'Georgia on My Mind' 1960, he influenced rock and soul in the 1960s and had become a legend by the 1980s.

Clapton Eric 1945– . English blues and rock guitarist, singer and composer, member of groups Yardbirds and Cream in the 1960s. One of the pioneers of heavy rock and an influence on younger musicians, he later adopted a more subdued style.

Cooke Sam 1931–64. American soul singer and songwriter, who began his career as a gospel singer and turned to pop music in the late 1950s. His hits, which have become classics, include 'You Send Me' 1957 and 'Wonderful World' 1960 (re-released 1986).

Doors The. American psychedelic and hard rock group, formed 1965. Original members were *Jim Morrison* 1943–71, Ray Manzarek, Robby Krieger, and John Densmore. Their first hit was 'Light My Fire' from their first album *Doors* 1967. Noted for their raw energy, and controversial for Morrison's arrests (for obscene language in 1967 and indecent exposure on stage in 1969), they came to symbolize the violent aspects of the youth revolution of the late 1960s.

Dylan Bob. Stage name of American singer and songwriter Robert Zimmerman 1941– . His early songs, in his albums *Freewheelin'* 1963 and *The Times They Are A-Changin'* 1964, were in the 1960s folk music tradition, associated with the US civil rights movement and anti-war protest, and the lyrics were more imaginative than in most pop music of the time.

He turned towards rock in *Another Side of Bob Dylan* 1964 and was accused by his early fans of 'selling out'. He later became a Christian.

Gaye Marvin 1939–84. American soul singer and songwriter, whose songs were classic examples of the Detroit Motown sound in the 1960s. A leading solo vocalist (hits include 'How Sweet It Is' 1964 and 'I Heard it Through the Grapevine' 1968), he was also notable in duets with the female Motown singers Mary Wells, Tammi Terrell, and Diana Ross.

Haley Bill 1927–81. American pioneer of rock and roll. His songs 'Rock Around the Clock' 1954 (recorded with his group The Comets and featured in the 1955 film *Blackboard Jungle*) and 'Shake, Rattle and Roll' 1955 came to symbolize the beginnings of the rock and roll era.

Hendrix Jimi (James Marshall) 1942–70. American rock guitarist and singer, who influenced a generation of musicians in the US and the UK with his showmanship (he burned his guitar at the 1967 Monterey Pop Festival) as well as his legendary technique.

Holly Buddy 1936–59. American rock and roll singer, guitarist, and composer, born Charles Hardin Holley in Lubbock, Texas. His hallmark was dark horn-rimmed glasses, and his songs include 'That'll be the Day' 1957, 'Peggy Sue' 1957, and 'Maybe Baby' 1958. After his death in a plane crash his great influence on rock music, particularly in the UK, was recognized, and his songs have become classics.

John Elton 1947– . Stage name of English rock singer, pianist and composer, Reginald Dwight, probably the most famous solo rock performer of the 1970s. His elaborate costumes and stage manner made his image as well known as his music, and he remained popular in the 1980s, although a throat problem forced him to stop touring in 1986 and threatened his career.

Joplin Janis 1943–70. American blues and acid rock singer, born in Texas, who became a symbol and a victim of the 1960s drug culture. She was lead singer with the San Francisco group Big Brother and the Holding Company

from 1966, and started a solo career in 1969 with the album *Kozmic Blues*. Her biggest hit, Kris Kristofferson's 'Me and Bobby McGee', was released in 1971 after her death.

Lewis Jerry Lee 1935– . American country and rock and roll singer and pianist. His trademark was the 'pumping piano' style in hits which included 'Great Balls of Fire' 1957 and 'What'd I Say' 1961.

Marley 'Bob' (Robert Nesta) 1945–80. Jamaican reggae singer, a Rastafarian whose songs, many of which were topical and political, popularized reggae in the UK and the US in the late 1970s. His best known song is 'No Woman No Cry', and classic albums include *Natty Dread* 1975 and *Exodus* 1977.

Mitchell Joni 1943– . Canadian singer and songwriter. Like Bob Dylan and Joan Baez, she began in the 1960s folk style, and first came to wide attention when her songs were recorded by Judy Collins, achieving popularity herself as a singer with 'Big Yellow Taxi' 1970. Her vocal style has incorporated elements of rock and jazz, and her lyrics are original and full of sophisticated and striking imagery.

Pink Floyd. British psychedelic rock group, formed 1966, the most successful group to emerge from London's hippie scene in the late 1960s. Original members were Syd Barrett, Roger Waters, Richard Wright, and Nick Mason. Pink Floyd is perhaps best remembered for the albums *The Dark Side of the Moon* 1973 and *The Wall* 1979, with its spinoff film starring Bob Geldof.

Presley Elvis 1935–1977. American singer and guitarist, born in Tupelo, Mississippi, probably the greatest and most influential performer of the rock and roll era. With his early hits 'Heartbreak Hotel' 1956, 'Hound Dog' 1956, and 'Love Me Tender' 1956, he created an individual vocal and guitar style, influenced by southern blues and gospel music, country music, and early rock and roll. He later became more subdued and appealed to a broader audience.

Redding Otis 1941–67. American soul singer and songwriter. He combined classic rock and roll with soul in hits like 'My Girl' 1965, but was perhaps at his best and most exciting in live performance (as in 'Respect', recorded at the Monterey Pop Festival in 1967). His biggest hit, 'Dock of the Bay' 1968, was released after his death in a plane crash.

Rolling Stones. English band formed 1963, notorious as the 'bad boys' of rock. Original members were Mick Jagger, Keith Richard, Brian Jones, Bill Wyman, Ian Stewart, and Charlie Watts. Their earthy sound was influenced by rhythm and blues, and their rebel image was contrasted with the wholesomeness of the early Beatles, whom they rivalled in popularity by the end of the 1960s. By the 1980s they had become a rock and roll institution. Classic early hits included 'Satisfaction' 1965, 'Paint it Black,' 1966, 'Let's Spend the Night Together' 1967, 'Honky Tonk Woman' 1969.

Supremes, The. American female vocal group, pioneers of the Motown sound, formed 1959 in Detroit, originally as a quartet and from 1962 as a trio with Diana Ross, Mary Wilson, and Florence Ballard. The most successful female group of the 1960s, they combined pop with soul in a string of hits on the Tamla Motown label, beginning with '*Where Did Our Love Go*' 1964 and '*Baby Love*' 1964. In 1969 Diana Ross left the group and became a star as a soloist.

Musical Terms

acoustics the science of sound; the term is often used to refer to the sonic characteristics of a concert hall.

aleatory music term for music produced by chance procedures, such as by throwing dice (Latin *alea*) or using computers. Pioneered by the American composer John Cage in the 1950s.

alto (Italian 'high') 1) low-register female voice also called *contralto*; 2) an unusually high adult male voice, also known as a counter tenor; 3) (French) viola.

anthem a short, usually elaborate, religious choral composition, sometimes accompanied by the organ.

aria (Italian 'air') solo vocal piece in opera or oratorio, often in three sections, the third repeating the first, after a contrasting central section.

atonality music which avoids the use of a key centre or tonic and in which the 12 notes of the octave are used impartially. It was foreshadowed in the 19th century in the later works of Liszt but not widely adopted until the music of Schoenberg and his followers in the 20th century.

avant-garde (French 'vanguard') in music, compositions ahead of their time; the term usually refers to the work of Boulez, Stockhausen and others produced after World War II.

bagatelle (French 'trifle') a short character piece, often for piano.

ballade a term used by Chopin, Brahms, Liszt and Grieg, among others, for a dramatic instrumental piece, possibly inspired by the literary equivalent.

baritone lower-range male voice midway between bass and tenor.

Baroque term used to describe the period in music between 1600 and 1750 and the style associated with its major composers, e.g. Vivaldi, Bach and Handel.

bass 1) lowest range of male voice; 2) lower regions of musical pitch.

bel canto (Italian 'beautiful song') term which usually refers to the 18th-century Italian style of singing with great emphasis on perfect technique and beautiful tone which reached its peak in the operas of Rossini, Donizetti and Bellini.

big band description of jazz sound created in the late 1930s and 1940s by bands of 15 or more players, such as those of Duke Ellington, Benny Goodman, when there is more than one instrument to some of the parts.

blues vocal tradition inherited from Amercian black spirituals which has influenced jazz and rock. Epitomized by the St Louis Blues 1913, it consists typically of a 12–bar phrase and use of flattened notes in the melody.

cadenza usually a bravura passage for the soloist in a concerto.

canon a form for a number of 'voices' or parts in which each enters successively, at fixed time intervals, in exact imitation of each other. The parts may then end together or continue their repetition as in a round.

cantata an extended sacred or secular choral work, sometimes with solo voices, and usually with orchestral accompaniment.

capriccio (Italian 'caprice') a short, lively instrumental piece, often humorous or whimsical in character.

chamber music music written for a small instrumental group, such as a string quartet, in which each part is played by a single instrument.

chorale a traditional hymn tune of the German Protestant Church.

chromatic a scale proceeding by semitones. All 12 notes in the octave are used rather than the seven notes of the diatonic scale.

Classical term generally used to refer to the period when emphasis was on form and balanced proportions of music rather than the expression of emotion. The Classical age reached its height in the 18th century, for example, in the music of Haydn and Mozart. The term is also used broadly to mean 'serious' as opposed to popular music.

clef the symbol used to indicate the pitch of the lines of the staff in musical notation.

coda (Italian 'tail') a concluding section of a movement added to indicate finality.

coloratura a rapid ornamental vocal passage with runs, trills, etc. A *coloratura soprano* has a light, high voice suited to such music.

concerto a composition, usually in three movements, for solo instrument (or instruments) and orchestra.

concrete music term used for music created by reworking natural sounds on record or tape, in particular that of Pierre Schaeffer in 1948.

continuo short for *basso continuo,* the bass line on which a keyboard player, often accompanied by a bass stringed instrument, built up a harmonic accompaniment in much 17th-century music.

contralto another name for the female alto voice.

counterpoint the simultaneous combination of two or more independent melodic lines to form a harmonious whole.

country and western music derived from Anglo-American folk song, a 'hillbilly' style which became popular from about 1925, originating in Nashville, Tennessee. Singers such as Johnny Cash also influenced much pop music.

diatonic a diatonic scale consists of the seven notes of any major or minor key.

dodecaphonic a term applied to the 12–note system of composition.

Dixieland jazz name given to early jazz style which originated in New Orleans in the early 20th century.

dominant the fifth degree of the scale, for example G in C major.

electronic music music produced since the 1950s in which composers such as Stockhausen and Boulez work with electronically assembled or arranged sounds.

étude (French 'study') a musical exercise designed to develop technique.

film score music specially written to accompany films, either live, as with early silent films, or for the soundtrack.

form the shape or structure of a piece of music.

fugue (Latin 'flight') a complicated contrapuntal form for a number of parts or 'voices' which enter successively in imitation of each other.

gamelan a type of Indonesian orchestra, mainly using tuned metal percussion instruments, the music of which has influenced Western composers.

glissando a rapid uninterrupted scale produced by sliding the finger across the keys or strings.

Gregorian chant plainsong choral chants associated with Pope Gregory the Great 590–

604, which became standard in the Roman Catholic Church.

harmony any simultaneous combination of sounds, but particularly the succession and relationship of chords.

harmonics the series of sounds of different pitches generated naturally by the vibration of a pipe or string when a note is played. This gives tone colour or timbre to an instrument.

impromptu a short piano piece that suggests spontaneity.

intermezzo a short orchestral interlude often used between the acts of an opera to denote the passage of time.

interval the pitch difference between two notes, usually measured in terms of the diatonic scale.

jazz music derived from an amalgam of Afro-American styles in the southern states of the USA early this century, mainly characterized by rhythmic syncopation and improvised harmonies. Since then several different strands of jazz have developed, for example 'modern' jazz since the 1940s.

key 1) the diatonic scale around which a piece of music is written, that is, a passage in C major will mainly use the notes of the C major scale; 2) the lever activated by a keyboard player.

leitmotiv (German 'leading motive') a recurring theme or motive used to indicate a character or idea – a technique used especially by Wagner in his operas.

libretto (Italian 'little book') the text of an opera or other dramatic vocal work, or the scenario of a ballet.

lied (German 'song') a genre particularly associated with the Romantic songs of Schubert, Schumann, Brahms and Wolf.

madrigal a secular composition for several voices, which reached its height in Italy in the 16th century and became popular in Elizabethan England.

Mass in music, the setting of the invariable parts of the Mass, that is *Kyrie, Gloria, Credo, Sanctus* with *Benedictus,* and *Agnus Dei,* such as Bach's Mass in B Minor.

meistersinger amateur musician in Germany who organized themselves into guilds.

mezzo-soprano female voice halfway between soprano and contralto.

melody a sequence of notes forming a theme or tune.

minimalism term used to refer to the music contemporary American composers such as Steve Reich, Philip Glass, and Terry Riley in which the repetition of short figures is used extensively.

minnesingers German poet-musicians of courtly love in the 12th and 13th centuries.

minuet European courtly dance of the 17th century, later used with the trio as the third movement in a classical symphony.

modulation movement from one key to another in harmony.

monody declamation by accompanied solo voice, used particularly at the turn of the 16th and 17th centuries.

motet a form of sacred, polyphonic music for unaccompanied voices which originated in the 13th century.

movement a section of a large work, such as a symphony, which is often complete in itself.

nationalism in music, a movement which became evident in the 19th century when composers (such as Smetana and Grieg) showed particular concern for the folk material of their country, the local instruments and, above all, the national spirit and its expression in music.

nocturne a lyrical, dreamy piano piece introduced by John Field and adopted by Chopin.

opera an extended, dramatic work where all, or most, of the text is sung, with instrumental accompaniment.

operetta a light opera, which may use spoken dialogue.

opus (Latin 'work') a term, used with a figure, to indicate the numbering of a composer's works, usually in chronological order.

oratorio a setting for solo voices, chorus and orchestra of a religious or contemplative text, performed in a church or concert hall.

orchestration the scoring of a composition

313

for orchestra.

overture an orchestral introduction to an opera or ballet. A *concert overture*, such as Mendelssohn's *Fingal's Cave,* is a piece designed purely for the concert hall.

pizzicato (Italian 'pinched') strings of an instrument (such as a violin) plucked, not bowed.

plainsong ancient chant of the Christian Church first fixed by Ambrose, Bishop of Milan, and then by Pope Gregory in the 6th century.

polyphony music combining two or more 'voices', each with an individual melody.

polytonality the simultaneous use of more than one key. A combination of two keys is bitonality.

pop music general term for modern popular music, often using electronic instruments, which has developed since World War II.

prelude a composition intended as the preface to further music, or as a mood-setting introduction to a stage work, as in Wagner's *Lohengrin*; as used by Chopin, a short piano work.

programme music term for music that tells a story, depicts a scene or painting, or illustrates a literary or philosophical idea, such as Beethoven's *Pastoral Symphony*.

punk a style of rock music popular in the late 1970s, as in the music of the Sex Pistols.

ragtime piano style particularly popular at the turn of the century, as in Scott Joplin's *Maple Leaf Rag* 1899, which became absorbed into jazz.

recitative speech-like declamation of narrative episodes in opera.

reggae music of Caribbean Rastafarian origin, based on local folk and rock, widely popular since the 1970s, as in the songs of Bob Marley.

requiem the Mass for the Dead in the Roman Catholic Church. Notable settings include those by Mozart and Berlioz.

rhapsody an instrumental fantasia, often based on folk melodies, such as Lizst's *Hungarian Rhapsodies*.

rock and roll the first main movement in

pop music, which became popular in the 1950s, as in the songs of Chuck Berry, Bill Haley and the Comets, and Elvis Presley.

rock opera popular form of modern opera using rock and jazz elements, as in *Jesus Christ Superstar*.

Romanticism in music, a term which generally refers to a preoccupation with the expression of emotion and with nature and history as a source of inspiration. Often linked with nationalistic feelings, the Romantic movement reached its height in the 19th century, as in the works of Schumann, Wagner.

rondo a form of instrumental music where the principal subject is repeated several times. Rondo form is often used for the last movement of a sonata or concerto.

rubato from *tempo rubato* (Italian 'robbed time') a slight flexibility in the tempo for extra expressive effect, usually in keyboard music.

scale progression of notes which varies according to the musical system being used, for example, the seven notes of the diatonic scale, the 12 notes of the chromatic scale. Major and minor scales derive from the Ionian and Aeolian modes respectively, two of the 12 modes or scales of ancient music.

scherzo (Italian 'joke') a lively piece, usually in rapid triple time, often the third movement of a symphony or sonata.

serenade a piece for chamber orchestra or wind instruments in several movements, originally intended for evening entertainment, such as Mozart's *Eine Kleine Nachtmusik*.

serialism another name for the twelve-note system of composition.

sinfonietta an orchestral work which is of a shorter, lighter, nature than a symphony.

sonata a work, usually in three or four related movements, for solo piano, or an instrument with piano accompaniment.

sonata form or first movement form, used extensively in the Classical period in chamber and symphonic music, consisted of the exposition, development and recapitulation of two main themes.

soprano the highest range of female voice.

suite formerly a grouping of old dance

314

forms, the term has more recently been used to describe a set of instrumental pieces, sometimes assembled from a stage work, such as Tchaikovsky's *Nutcracker Suite*.

symphonic poem a term originated by Liszt for his 13 one-movement orchestral works which interpret a story from literature or history, and used by many other composers. Richard Strauss preferred the title *tone poem*.

symphony an extended orchestral work usually in four related movements, though the term has come to be used more loosely.

syncopation the deliberate upsetting of rhythm by shifting the accent to a beat that is normally unaccented.

tempo (Italian 'time') the speed at which a piece of music is played.

theme the basic melody or musical figure from which a piece of music is developed.

tenor the highest range of adult male voice.

timbre the tone colour of an instrument.

toccata a display piece for keyboard instrument, particularly the organ.

tonality music which is centred on a single key, in contrast to *atonality* and *polytonality*.

tone poem another name for *symphonic poem* as used by Richard Strauss.

tonic the first degree or key note of the scale, for example C in C major.

twelve-note system a system of composition in which the 12 notes of the chromatic scale are arranged in a particular order, called 'series' or 'note-row'. The entire work consists of restatements of the series in any of its formations. Schoenberg and Webern were the most important and influential composers to use this technique.

variations a series of different developments of one self-contained theme, such as *Variations on the St Anthony Chorale* by Brahms.

vibrato a slight but rapid fluctuation of pitch, in voice or instrument.

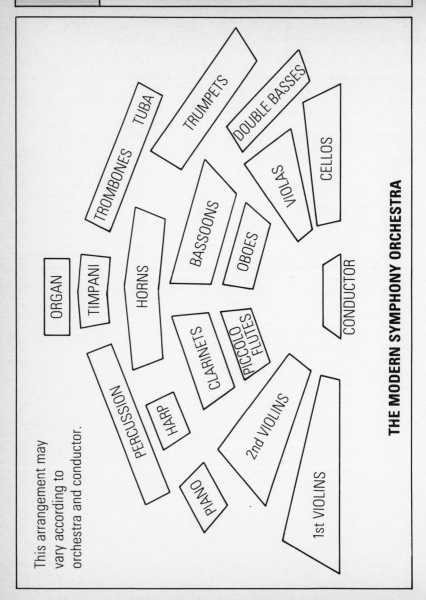

THE MODERN SYMPHONY ORCHESTRA

This arrangement may vary according to orchestra and conductor.

PITCH AND COMPASS OF VOICE AND INSTRUMENT

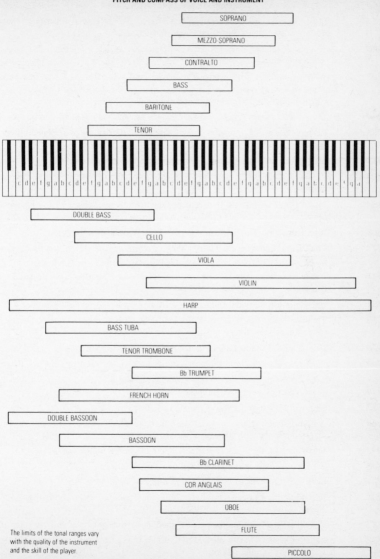

The limits of the tonal ranges vary
with the quality of the instrument
and the skill of the player.

317

Milestones in Musical History

590AD   St Gregory the Great was elected pope. His enlightened leadership inspired church music to new heights, initiating Gregorian Chant.

1026   The Italian monk Guido d'Arezzo completed his treatise *Micrologus*. He founded modern notation and tonic sol-fa.

1207   Walther von der Vogelweide, Tannhauser and Wolfram von Eschenbach competed in a song contest at Wartburg Castle, as the age of the minnesingers or German poet-musicians approached its height.

1240   The earliest known canon, *Sumer is Icumen In,* was composed around this year.

1280   *Carmina burana,* a collection of students' songs, was compiled in Benediktbuern, Bavaria.

1288   France's greatest troubadour, Adam de la Halle, died in Naples.

1320   *Ars nova,* a tract by Philippe de Vitry, gave its name to a new, more graceful era in music.

1364   Music's first large-scale masterpiece, the *Notre Dame Mass* of Guillaume de Machaut, was performed in Rheims at the coronation of Charles V of France.

1453   John Dunstable, England's first important composer, died in London.

1473   The earliest known printed music, the *Collectorium super Magnificat* by Johannes Gerson, was published in Esslingen, near Stuttgart.

1521   Josquin des Prez, the leading musician of his time, died in Condé-sur-Escaut, Burgundy.

1564   The violin was designed and manufactured by Andrea Amati in Cremona.

1575   Thomas Tallis and William Byrd jointly published their *Cantiones sacrae,* a collection of 34 motets.

1576   Hans Sachs, the most famous of mastersingers, died in Nuremberg.

1597   The first opera, *La Dafne* by Jacopo Peri, was staged privately at the Corsi Palazzo in Florence.

1610   Monteverdi's *Vespers* was published in Venice.

1637   The world's first opera house opened in Venice.

1644   Antonio Stradivarius was born. More than 600 of his violins, made in Cremona, survived into the 20th century.

1672   The violinist John Banister pioneered public concerts in London.

1709   Bartolomeo Cristofori built the first piano in Florence.

1721   Bach completed his six *Brandenburg Concertos*.

1722   Jean-Philippe Rameau's book *Traité de l'harmonie* founded modern harmonic theory.

1725   Vivaldi's *The Four Seasons* was published in Amsterdam.

1732   Covent Garden Theatre opened in London. It was later destroyed twice, in 1808 and 1856, by fire, but rebuilt.

1742   Handel's *Messiah* received its world première in Dublin.

1757 Johann Stamitz died in Mannheim, where he had founded the world's first virtuoso orchestra.

1761 Haydn took up liveried service as vice kapellmeister with the aristocratic Esterházy family, to whom he was connected until his death in 1809.

1788 Mozart completed his last three symphonies, nos 39–41, in six weeks.

1795 The composer and inventor Thomas Wright introduced metronome markings.

1798 The *Allgemeine Musikalische Zeitung,* which became an influential journal of music criticism, was first published in Leipzig.

1805 Beethoven's *Eroica* Symphony vastly expanded the horizons of orchestral music.

1815 Schubert's output for this year included two symphonies, two masses, 20 waltzes and 145 songs.

1821 Weber's opera *Der Freischütz* heralded the start of the Romantic era.

1828 The limits of instrumental virtuosity were redefined by Paganini's Vienna debut.

1830 Berlioz's dazzlingly avant-garde and programmatic *Symphonie Fantastique* startled Paris concertgoers. The work did not reach Britain or the USA for 36 years.

1831 Grand opera was inaugurated with *Robert le Diable* by Meyerbeer.

1851 Jenny Lind, the singer managed by P T Barnum, earned $176,675 from nine months' concerts in the USA.

1842 The Vienna Philharmonic Orchestra gave its first concerts.

1854 In Weimar, Liszt conducted the premières of his first symphonic poems.

1855 Like most orchestras around this date, the New York Philharmonic for the first time sat down while playing (cellists were already seated).

1865 Wagner's opera *Tristan and Isolde* scaled new heights of expressiveness using unprecedented chromaticism. Schubert's *Unfinished Symphony* (1822) was premièred in Vienna.

1875 The first of a series of collaborations between Arthur Sullivan and the librettist W S Gilbert, *Trial by Jury,* was given its première.

1876 Wagner's *The Ring of the Nibelung* was produced in Bayreuth. Brahms's First Symphony was performed in Karlsruhe.

1877 Edison invented the cylindrical tin-foil phonograph, but few showed interest.

1883 The Metropolitan Opera House opened in New York with a production of Gounod's *Faust.*

1885 Liszt composed *Bagatelle without Tonality* (his *Faust Symphony* of 1857 opened with a twelve-note row).

1894 Debussy's *Prélude à l'Après-midi d'un Faune* anticipated 20th-century composition with its use of the whole-tone scale.

1895 Henry Wood conducted the first Promenade Concert at the Queen's Hall in London. The 'Proms' moved to the Royal Albert Hall in 1941.

1899 Scott Joplin's *Maple Leaf Rag* was published in Sedalia, Missouri.

1902   Enrico Caruso recorded ten arias in a hotel room in Milan, the success of which established the popularity of the phonograph. By the time of his death in 1921 he had earned $2,000,000 from sales of his recordings.

1908   Saint-Saëns became the first leading composer to write a film score, for *L'Assassinat du Duc de Guise.*

1911   Irving Berlin revolutionized songwriting with *Alexander's Ragtime Band.*

1912   Schoenberg's atonal *Pierrot Lunaire,* for reciter and chamber ensemble, foreshadowed many similar small-scale quasi-theatrical works.

1913   Stravinsky's ballet *The Rite of Spring* precipitated a riot at its première in Paris.

1919   Schoenberg, who was experimenting with serial technique, set up the Society for Private Musical Performances in Vienna, which lasted until 1921.

1922   Alessandro Moreschi, last of the castrati, died in Rome.

1925   Louis Armstrong made his first records with the Hot Five. Duke Ellington's Washingtonians also started recording.

1927   Jerome Kern's *Showboat,* with libretto by Oscar Hammerstein II, laid the foundations of the modern American musical.

1937   The NBC Symphony Orchestra began its 17–year association with Arturo Toscanini, one of the greatest conductors in the history of music.

1938   Prokofiev's score for Eisenstein's *Alexander Nevsky* raised film music to new levels.

1939   Elisabeth Lutyens was one of the first English composers to use twelve–note composition in her Chamber Concerto no. 1 for nine instruments.

1940   Walt Disney's *Fantasia* introduced classical music, conducted by Leopold Stokowski, to a worldwide audience of filmgoers.

1942   In Chicago, John Cage conducted the premiere of his *Imaginary Landscape no 3*, scored for marimbula, gongs, tin cans, buzzers, plucked coil, electric oscillator, and generator.

1951   The first opera commissioned for television, Menotti's *Amahl and the Night Visitors,* was shown on American television on Christmas Eve.

1952   John Cage's piano piece 4' 33", consisting of 4 minutes and 33 seconds of silence, was presented in Woodstock, New York. The BBC Symphony Orchestra was founded in London under Sir Adrian Boult.

1954   Stockhausen's *Electronic Studies* for magnetic tape were broadcast in Cologne. Edgard Varèse's *Déserts*, the first work to combine instruments and pre-recorded magnetic tape, was performed in Paris. Bill Haley and the Comets recorded 'Rock Around the Clock' and 'Shake, Rattle and Roll' heralding Rock and Roll.

1955   Boulez's *Le Marteau sans Maître,* for contralto and chamber ensemble, was performed in Baden-Baden. Its formidable serial technique and exotic orchestration was acclaimed by the avant-garde.

1956   The first annual Warsaw Autumn festival of contemporary music was held. This became particularly important for the promotion of Polish composers such as Lutoslawksi and Penderecki. Elvis Presley recorded 'Heartbreak Hotel', 'Hound Dog' and 'Love me Tender'.

1957   Leonard Bernstein's *West Side Story* was premiered in New York. A computer, programmed at the University of Illinois by Lejaren Hiller and Leonard Isaacson, composed the *Illiac Suite* for string quartet.

1959   Ronnie Scott's Club opened in Soho, London, later to become a jazz centre of worldwide importance

1963   Shostakovich's opera *Lady Macbeth of Mezensk*, earlier banned and condemned in *Pravda* 1936, was produced in a revised version as *Katerina Ismailova.*

1965   Robert Moog invented a synthesizer that considerably widened the scope of electronic music.

1965   The film soundtrack of *The Sound of Music*, with music by Rodgers and lyrics by Hammerstein, was released and went on the dominate the popular music charts for the next two years.

1967   The Beatles' album *Sgt Pepper's Lonely Hearts Club Band*, which took over 500 hours to record, was released.

1968   The pop oratorio, *Joseph and his Amazing Technicolour Dreamcoat* – the first collaboration between composer Andrew Lloyd Webber and lyricist Tim Rice – was given its first perfomance at a London school.

1969   Peter Maxwell Davies' theatre piece *Eight Songs for a Mad King* for vocalist and six instruments, was premiered in London by the Pierrot Players, later to become the Fires of London ensemble under Davies' direction.

1973   The London Philharmonic Orchestra visited China, the first Western orchestra to do so since the Cultural Revolution. The Sydney Opera House was officially opened. Mike Oldfield's *Tubular Bells*, which was to sell eight million copies worldwide, was released.

1976   Philip Glass' opera *Einstein on the Beach*, using the repetitive techniques of minimalism, was given its first performance in Paris.

1977   The Institute for Research and Coordination of Acoustics and Music (IRCAM) was founded in Paris under the direction of Pierre Boulez, for visiting composers to make use of advanced electronic equipment.

1978   Philips announced the invention of the compact disc, the first fully digital audio system for domestic use. The first discs, 12cm in diameter and capable of playing over an hour of continuous music, were launched in the West in March 1983.

1983   Messiaen's only opera, *Saint François d'Assise*, was given its first performance in Paris. Lutoslawski's Third Symphony was premièred to worldwide acclaim by the Chicago Symphony Orchestra under Sir George Solti.

1986   Glyndebourne Opera performed *Don Giovanni* and *A Midsummer Night's Dream* at the official opening of the Hong Kong Academy for the Performing Arts, whose first students had enrolled two years earlier.

DATE	BALLET	COMPOSER	CHOREOGRAPHER	PLACE
1670	Le Bourgeois Gentilhomme	Lully	Beauchamp	Chambord
1735	Les Indes Galantes	Rameau	Blondy	Paris
1761	Don Juan	Gluck	Angiolini	Vienna
1778	Les Petits Riens	Mozart	Noverre	Paris
1801	The Creatures of Prommetheus	Beethoven	Viganò	Vienna
1828	La Fille Mal Gardée	Hérold	Aumer	Paris
1832	La Sylphide	Schneitzhoeffer	F. Taglioni	Paris
1841	Giselle	Adam	Coralli/Perrot	Paris
1842	Napoli	Gade/Paulli/Helsted/Lumbye	Bournonville	Copenhagen
1844	La Esmeralda	Pugni	Perrot	London
1869	Don Quixote	Minkus	M Petipa	Moscow
1870	Coppélia	Delibes	Saint-Léon	Paris
1876	Sylvia	Delibes	Mérante	Paris
1877	La Bayadère	Minkus	M Petipa	St Petersburg
1877	Swan Lake	Tchaikovsky	Reisinger	Moscow
1882	Namouna	Lalo	L Petipa	Paris
1890	The Sleeping Beauty	Tchaikovsky	M Petipa	St Petersburg
1892	Nutcracker	Tchaikovsky	M Petipa/Ivanov	St Petersburg
1898	Raymonda	Glazunov	M Petipa	St Petersburg
1905	The Dying Swan	Saint-Saëns	Fokine	St Petersburg
1907	Les Sylphides	Chopin	Fokine	St Petersburg
1910	Carnival	Schumann	Fokine	St Petersburg
1910	The Firebird	Stravinsky	Fokine	Paris
1911	Petrushka	Stravinsky	Fokine	Paris
1911	Le Spectre de la Rose	Weber	Fokine	Monte Carlo
1912	L'Après-midi d'un Faune	Debussy	Nijinsky	Paris
1912	Daphnis et Chloë	Ravel	Fokine	Paris
1913	Jeux	Debussy	Nijinsky	Paris
1913	Le Sacre du Printemps	Stravinsky	Nijinsky	Paris
1915	El Amor Brujo	Falla	Imperio	Madrid
1917	Parade	Satie	Massine	Paris
1919	La Boutique Fantasque	Rossini/Respighi	Massine	London
1919	The Three-Cornered Hat	Falla	Massini	London
1923	La Creation du Monde	Milhaud	Börlin	Paris
1923	Les Noces	Stravinsky	Nijinska	Paris
1924	Les Biches	Poulenc	Nijinska	Monte Carlo
1927	The Red Poppy	Glière	Lashchilin/Tikhomirov	Moscow
1928	Apollon Musagète	Stravinsky	Balanchine	Paris
1928	Le Baiser de la Fée	Tchaikovsky	Nijinska	Paris
1928	Bolero	Ravel	Nijinska	Paris
1929	The Prodigal Son	Prokofiev	Balanchine	Paris
1929	La Valse	Ravel	Nijinska	Monte Carlo
1931	Bacchus and Ariane	Roussel	Lifar	Paris
1931	Façade	Walton	Ashton	London
1931	Job	Vaughan Williams	de Valois	London
1937	Checkmate	Bliss	de Valois	Paris
1937	Les Patineurs	Meyerbeer/Lambert	Ashton	London
1938	Billy the Kid	Copland	Loring	Chicago
1938	Gaîté Parisienne	Offenbach/Rosenthal	Massine	Monte Carlo
1938	Romeo and Juliet	Prokofiev	Psota	Brno, Moravia

DATE	BALLET	COMPOSER	CHOEOGRAPHER	PLACE
1942	Gayaneh	Khachaturian	Anisimova	Molotov-Perm
1942	The Miraculous Mandarin	Bartók	Milloss	Milan
1942	Rodeo	Copland	de Mille	New York
1944	Appalachian Spring	Copland	Graham	Washington
1944	Fancy Free	Bernstein	Robbins	New York
1945	Cinderella	Prokofiev	Zakharov	Moscow
1949	Carmen	Bizet	Petit	London
1951	Pineapple Poll	Sullivan/Mackerras	Cranko	London
1956	Spartacus	Khachaturian	Jacobson	Leningrad
1957	Agon	Stravinsky	Balanchine	New York
1959	Episodes	Webern	Balanchine	New York
1962	A Midsummer Night's Dream	Mendelssohn	Balanchine	New York
1962	Pierrot Lunaire	Schoenberg	Tetley	New York
1964	The Dream	Mendelssohn/Lanchbery	Ashton	London
1965	Lied von der Erde	Mahler	MacMillan	Stuttgart
1967	Anastasia	Martinu	MacMillan	New York
1968	Enigma Variations	Elgar	Ashton	London
1969	The Taming of the Shrew	Stolze/Scarlatti	Cranko	Stuttgart
1972	Duo Concertante	Stravinsky	Balanchine	New York
1974	Elite Syncopations	Joplin, etc	MacMillan	London
1976	A Month in the Country	Chopin/Lanchbery	Ashton	London
1978	Mayerling	Liszt/Lamchbery	MacMillan	London
1978	Symphony of Psalms	Stravinsky	Kylian	Scheveningen, The Netherlands
1980	Gloria	Poulenc	MacMillan	London
1980	Rhapsody	Rachmaninov	Ashton	London

1000 BC King David danced 'with all his might' before the ark of the covenant in Jerusalem – one of the earliest instances of ritual dance.

405 BC *Bacchae* by Euripides was staged in Athens. The play demanded a considerable amount of dancing.

142 BC Consul Scipio Aemilianus Africanus closed the burgeoning dance schools of Rome in a drive against hedonism.

774 AD Pope Zacharias forbade dancing.

1050 The *Ruodlieb* , a poem written by a monk at Tegernsee, Bavaria, contained the first European reference to dancing in couples.

1313 Rabbi Hacén ben Salomo of Zaragoza, in Aragon, like many other Jews in medieval times, was the local dancing master.

1489 A rudimentary allegorical ballet was performed in honour of the marriage of the Duke of Milan, at Tortona, Italy.

1581 In Paris, the first modern-style unified ballet, the *Ballet Comique de la Reine*, was staged at the court of Catherine de Medici.

1588 Dance and ballet's first basic text, *L'Orchésographie*, by the priest Jehan Tabouret, was printed in Langres, near Dijon.

1651 In London, John Playford published *The English Dancing Master*. The 18th edition (1728) described 900 country dances.

1661 Louis XIV founded L'Académie Royale de Danse in Paris.

1670 The first classic ballet, *Le Bourgeois Gentilhomme*, was produced in Chambord, France.

1681 In Paris, women appeared in ballet for the first time in the opera-ballet *Le Triomphe de l'amour* .

1734 The dancer Marie Sallé streamlined the traditional costume, and Marie Camargo shortened her skirts.

1760 The great dancer and choreographer Jean-Georges Noverre published in Lyon *Lettres sur la danse et sur les ballets*, one of the most influential of all ballet books.

1778 Noverre and Mozart collaborated on *Les Petits Riens* in Paris. The cast included the celebrated Auguste Vestris.

1812 The waltz arrived in England. The couples, wrote Byron, were 'like two cockchafers spitted on the same bodkin'.

1820 Carlo Blasis, teacher and choreographer, published his *Traité élémentaire theoretique et pratique de l'arte de la danse* in Milan which, together with his later works of dance theory, codified techniques for future generations of dancers.

1821 The first known picture of a ballerina *sur les pointes*, the French Fanny Bias by F. Waldeck, dates from this year.

1832 The first performance of *La Sylphide* at the Paris Opéra opened the Romantic era of ballet and established the central significance of the ballerina. Marie Taglioni, the producer's daughter, who took the title role, wore the new-style diaphanous dress.

1841   Ballet's Romantic masterpiece *Giselle,* with Carolotta Grisi in the leading role, was produced in Paris.

1844   The polka reached London.

1866   *The Black Crook*, the ballet-extravaganza from which American vaudeville and musical comedy developed, began its run of 474 performances in New York.

1870   *Coppélia* , 19th-century ballet's comic masterpiece, was presented in Paris.

1877   *Swan Lake* was premiered in Moscow, but failed through poor production and choreography. The Petipa-Ivanov version, in which Pierina Legnani performed her famous 32 fouettés , established the work in 1895.

1897   Anna Pavlova made her debut in St Petersburg with the Imperial Russian Ballet.

1905   Isadora Duncan appeared in Russia, making an immense impression with her 'anti-ballet' innovations derived from Greek dance.

1906   Vaslav Nijinsky made his debut in St Petersburg.

1909   The first Paris season given by Diaghilev's troupe of Russian dancers, later to become known as the Ballets Russes, marked the beginning of one of the most exciting periods in Western ballet.

1913   The premiere of Stravinsky's *Le Sacre du Printemps/The Rite of Spring* provoked a scandal in Paris.

1914   The foxtrot was introduced in England.

1926   Martha Graham, one of the most innovative figures in modern ballet, gave her first recital in New York. In England, students from the Rambert School of Ballet, opened by Marie Rambert in 1920, gave their first public performance in *A Tragedy of Fashion* , the first ballet to be choreographed by Frederick Ashton.

1928   The first performance of George Balanchine's *Apollon Musagète* in Paris, by the Ballets Russes, marked the birth of Neoclassicism in ballet.

1931   Ninette de Valois' Vic-Wells ballet gave its first performance in London. In 1956 the company became the Royal Ballet.

1933   The Hollywood musical achieved artistic independence through Busby Berkeley's kaleidoscopic choreography in *Forty-Second Street* and Dave Gould's airborne finale in *Flying down to Rio*, in which Fred Astaire and Ginger Rogers appeared together for the first time.

1940   The Dance Notation Bureau was established in New York for recording ballets and dances.

1948   The New York City Ballet was founded with George Balanchine as principal choreographer. The immensely popular film *The Red Shoes* appeared, choreographed by Massine and Robert Helpman and starring Moira Shearer.

1950   The Festival Ballet, later to become the London Festival Ballet, was created by Alicia Markova and Anton Dolin, who had first danced together with the Ballets Russes in 1929.

1952   Gene Kelly starred and danced in the film *Singin' in the Rain* .

1953   The American experimental choreographer Merce Cunningham, who often worked with the composer John Cage, formed his own troupe.

1956   The Bolshoi Ballet opened its first season in the West at Covent Garden in London, with Galina Ulanova dancing in *Romeo and Juliet*, startling audiences with its dramatic style.

1957   Jerome Robbins choreographed Leonard Bernstein's *West Side Story*, demonstrating his outstanding ability to work in both popular and classical forms.

1960   The progressive French choreographer Maurice Béjart renamed his Brussels-based company *Ballet du XXième Siècle*.

1961   Rudolf Nureyev defected while dancing with the Kirov Ballet in Paris. He was to have a profound influence on male dancing in the West. The South African choreographer John Cranko became director of the Stuttgart Ballet for which he was to produce several major ballets.

1962   Glen Tetley's ballet *Pierrot Lunaire*, in which he was one of the three dancers, was premiered in New York. In the same year he joined the Nederlands Dans Theater.

1965   American choreographer Twyla Tharp produced her first works.

1966   The School of Contemporary Dance was founded in London, from which Robin Howard and the choreographer Robert Cohan created the London Contemporary Dance Theatre, later to become an internationally renowned company. The choreographer Norman Morrice joined the Ballet Rambert and the company began to concentrate on contemporary works.

1968   Arthur Mitchell, the first black dancer to join the New York City Ballet, founded the Dance Theatre of Harlem.

1974   Mikhail Baryshnikov defected while dancing with a Bolshoi Ballet group in Toronto.

1978   The release of Robert Stigwood's film *Saturday Night Fever* popularized disco dancing worldwide.

1980   Natalia Makarova, who had defected in 1979, staged the first full-length revival of Petipa's *La Bayadère* in the West with the American Ballet Theatre in New York.

1981   Wayne Sleep, previously principal dancer with the Royal Ballet, starred as lead dancer in Andrew Lloyd-Webber's musical *Cats*, choreographed by Gillian Lynne.

1983   The release of the film *Flashdance* reflected the current cult of break dancing.

1984   The avant-garde group Michael Clark and Company made its debut in London.

Science and Technology

Activities such as healing, star-watching, engineering, and warfare have been practised in many societies since ancient times, often with success. The European scientific revolution between about 1650 and 1800, however, propelled all these activities into an accelerating rate of progress, largely through its replacement of medieval speculative philosophy with a novel combination of observation, experimentation and rationality. The continued success of that revolution, and its economic value, is shown by the worldwide spread of applied science. It is clear also that the phenomenon is double-edged, as exemplified by the way the earth has armed itself with nuclear weapons while at the same time ridding itself of the smallpox virus.

The method of scientific research includes an interaction between tradition, experimentation and observation, and deduction. The subject area called Philosophy of Science investigates the nature of this complex interaction, in particular the extent of its ability to gain access to the truth about the material world. Traditionally, pure science and especially physics has been the main area of study for philosophers. Today, serious questions concerning the proper use of science and the role of science education are restructuring this field of study.

This part of the Pocket Encyclopedia contains sections on Astronomy, Computing, Earth Sciences, Life Sciences, Medicine, Physics, Chemistry, Mathematics, and Technology. Each section focusses on a particular topic, but also forms part of an overview of science and technology in general. Galileo, for example, was central not only to astronomy but also to mathematics and physics. Scientists tend to be remembered for their spectacular discoveries and technologists for inventions, but, in addition, the common theme running through all of the sciences is the aim to produce reliable explanations of, and laws about, the material world, and, through technology, to apply science for practical purposes.

Astronomy

Astronomy – 'the science of the stars' – deals with celestial bodies such as our earth, its moon, the sun, the other planets and members of our solar system, and stars and other bodies in all of space. It is concerned with their positions and motions; with their sizes, masses, temperatures and physical conditions; with their origins and fates; and, ultimately, with the origin, evolution and fate of the entire Universe.

Astronomy is the oldest science – there are observational records from Babylonia, China and Ancient Egypt. Through the Greeks and Ptolemy of Alexandria, to the flowering of European astronomy with Copernicus, Brahe, Kepler and Galileo, right to the powerful radio-telescopes and deep-space probes of today, astronomy deals with the ultimate questions in science. Its vast distances and time spans, and concepts such as bent space and black holes, defy the mind's grasp. How big is the Universe? When did it, and presumably time, begin? How do newer discoveries, such as pulsars, fit into our interpretations of the astronomical data?

An important new development is radio astronomy, the study of radio waves emitted naturally by objects in space. In 1931 Karl Jansky first detected radio waves from the centre of our galaxy. Since World War II astronomers have mapped the spiral structure of our galaxy from the radio waves given out by interstellar gas, and have detected many individual radio sources within our galaxy and beyond. Radio astronomers have also detected weak background radiation thought to be from the Big Bang explosion that marked the birth of the Universe.

This section contains a historical overview or *Chronology*, from the very first scientific observations of the sky to the most up-to-date 'close encounters' with comets; a *Journey to the Stars*, working outwards from our earth; a review of *Celestial Bodies*, from small to big; a digest of important *Places and Organizations* in astronomy; a list of key *Terms*; *Biographies* of great astronomers, and details of *Space Research*.

2300 BC	Chinese astronomers made their earliest observations.
2000 BC	Babylonian priests made their first observational records.
1900 BC	Stonehenge was constructed: first phase.
365 BC	The Chinese observed the satellites of Jupiter with the naked eye.
3rd century BC	Aristarchus argued that the sun is the centre of the solar system.
2nd century AD	Ptolemy's complicated earth-centred system was promulgated, which dominated the astronomy of the Middle Ages.
1543 AD	Copernicus revived the ideas of Aristarchus in *De Revolutionibus*.
1608	Lippershey invented the telescope, which was first used by Galileo in 1609.
1609	Kepler's first two laws of planetary motion were published (the third appeared in 1619).
1632	Leiden established the world's first official observatory.
1633	Galileo's theories were condemned by the Inquisition.
1675	The Royal Greenwich Observatory was founded in England.
1687	Newton's *Principia* was published, including his 'law of universal gravitation'.
1704	Halley predicted the return of the comet now named after him, which reappeared in 1758: it was last seen in 1985-86.
1781	Herschel discovered Uranus and recognized stellar systems beyond our galaxy.
1796	Laplace elaborated his theory of the origin of the solar system.
1801	Piazzi discovered the first asteroid, Ceres.
1814	Fraunhofer first studied absorption lines in the solar spectrum.
1846	Neptune was discovered by Galle and D'Arrest.
1859	Kirchhoff explained dark lines in the sun's spectrum.
1887	The earliest photographic star charts were produced.
1889	E E Barnard took the first photographs of the Milky Way.
1890	The first photograph of the spectrum was taken.
1908	The Tunguska comet fell in Siberia.
1920	Eddington began the study of interstellar matter.
1923	Hubble proved that the galaxies are systems independent of the Milky Way, and by 1930 had confirmed the concept of an expanding universe.
1930	The planet Pluto was discovered by Clyde Tombaugh at the Lowell Observatory, Arizona, USA.
1931	Jansky founded radioastronomy.
1945	Radar contact with the moon was established by Z Bay of Hungary and the US Army Signal Corps Laboratory.

1948	The 200–inch Hale reflector telescope was installed at Mount Palomar, California, USA.
1955	The Jodrell Bank radioastronomy 'dish' in England was completed.
1957	The first Sputnik satellite (USSR) opened the age of space observation.
1962	The first X-ray source was discovered in Scorpio.
1963	The first quasar was discovered by Mount Palomar observatory.
1967	The first pulsar was identified by Jocelyn Bell and Antony Hewish at Cambridge, England.
1969	The first manned moon landing was made by US astronauts.
1970	The black hole theory was confirmed for the first time.
1976	A 236–inch reflector telescope was installed at Mount Semirodniki (USSR).
1976	Viking probes (USA) soft-landed on Mars; experiments indicated no signs of life.
1977	Uranus was discovered to have rings.
1977	The spacecraft Voyager 1 and 2 were launched, the latter passing Jupiter and Saturn 1979—81, and Uranus 1986; due Neptune 1989.
1978	The spacecraft Pioneer Venus 1 and 2 reached Venus.
1978	A satellite of Pluto, Charon, was discovered by James Christie of the US Naval Observatory.
1978	Herculina was discovered to be the first asteroid with a satellite.
1979	The UK infra-red telescope (UKIRT) was established on Hawaii.
1985	Halley's comet returned.
1986	Voyager 2 discovered six new moons around Uranus.

Journey to the Stars

earth the planet on which we live: it is the third planet outward from the sun, lying with its satellite, the moon, between Venus and Mars. Its orbit round the sun is an ellipse of which one focus is formed by the sun. The mean distance of earth from the sun is c. 149,597,870 km/92,955,800 mi. The plane of its orbit is called the ecliptic, and it is inclined to the earth's equatorial plane at an angle of 23.4°; this inclination is responsible for the phenomena of the seasons. The earth, moving at an average speed of 30 km/18.5 mi a second, makes a complete circuit in the solar year, 365 days 5 h 49 min 46 s. It has also a daily movement, rotating about its own axis in 23 h 56 min 4.1 s, which is responsible for day and night. By using atomic clocks it has been possible to prove that the earth's rate of rotation is slowing down.

The earth is an oblate spheroid or, taking into account an 18–metre rise at the N Pole and a 26–metre depression at the S Pole, 'pear-shaped'. The equatorial diameter is 12,756 km/7926.5 mi and the polar diameter is 12,713 km/7900 mi; the earth's equatorial circumference is 40,076 km/24,902 mi and its polar circumference is 40,009 km/24,860 mi.

moon the natural satellite of the earth, 3,476 km/2,160 mi in diameter, with a mass 1/81 that of the earth. Its average distance from earth is 384,400 km/238,850 mi, and it orbits earth every 27.32 days (the *sidereal month*). The moon spins on its axis so that it keeps one side permanently turned towards the earth. The moon is illuminated by sunlight, and goes through a cycle of phases from New (invisible) via First Quarter (half moon) to Full and back again to New, every 29.53 days (the *synodic month*, also known as a *lunation*).

The moon has no air or water. On its sunlit side

temperatures reach 130° C, but during the two-week lunar night the surface temperature drops to −170° C. Its composition is rocky, with a surface heavily scarred by meteorite impacts that have formed craters up to 240 km/150 mi across. The youngest craters are surrounded by bright rays of ejected rock. The largest scars have been filled by dark lava to produce the lowland plains known as seas or *maria*. These dark patches form the familiar 'man-in-the-moon' pattern. Rocks brought back by Apollo astronauts show the moon is 4,600 million years old, the same age as the earth. Unlike the earth, most of the moon's surface features were formed within the first 1,000 million years of its history when it was subjected to heavy bombardment by meteorites.

The origin of the moon is open to debate. Theories suggest that it split from the earth; that it was a separate body captured by earth's gravity; or that it formed in orbit around the earth. The latest idea suggests that the moon was formed from debris thrown off when a body the size of Mars struck the earth early in the earth's history.

sun the star at the centre of the solar system, around which the earth and other planets orbit. Its diameter is 1,392,000 km/865,000 mi, and it lies 149,597,870 km/92,955,800 mi from earth. The sun is composed of about 70% hydrogen and 30% helium by mass, with other elements making up less than 1%. The temperature at its centre is probably 15 million °C. Like all stars, the sun generates energy by nuclear fusion reactions that turn hydrogen into helium at its centre. The sun is about 4,700 million years old, nearly halfway through its total predicted lifetime of 10,000 million years.

It spins on its axis every 25 days near its equator, but more slowly towards the poles. Its rotation can be followed by watching the passage of dark sunspots across its disk. Sometimes bright eruptions called flares occur near sunspots. Above the sun's photosphere lies a layer of thinner gas called the chromosphere, visible only in special instruments or at eclipses. Tongues of gas called prominences

MAJOR SPACE PROGRAMMES

Name	Launch Date	Number of flights	Main achievements
Ariane (European)	1979-	continues	Launch rocket for satellites based in Korou, French Guiana; operated commercially by Arianespace
Apollo (USA)	1968-72	7	Saturn rockets as launchers; Neil Armstrong first person on moon; collected rocks and dust; 6 moon landings in all
Gemini (USA)	1965-66	10	Edward White first US space walker; first space docking
Giotto (European)	1985-86	1	Flew within 600 km of Halley's comet nucleus
Mercury (USA)	1961-63	6	Alan Shepherd first US spaceman; John Glenn first American in orbit
Pioneer (USA)	1958-78	continues	Probed the outer planets; Pioneer 10 first to leave solar system
Salyut (USSR)	1971-82	7	Scientific research, observation aboard orbiting space station
Skylab (USA)	1973	4	Scientific research aboard converted Saturn V upper stage
Soyuz (USSR)	1967-	continues	Ferries cosmonauts to Salyut space stations
Space Shuttle (USA)	1981-	continues	First reusable manned spacecraft; research, observation and experimentation
Spacelab (European)	1985-	continues	Workspace and equipment module for Space Shuttle's cargo bay
Sputnik (USSR)	1957-61	10	Sputnik 1 first artificial satellite; Sputnik 2 took first creature (dog, Laika) into space
Voskhod (USSR)	1964-65	2	First multi-person crew (3 men); Alexi Leonov first space walker
Vostok (USSR)	1961-63	6	Yuri Gagarin first spaceman; Valentina Tereshkova first spacewoman
Voyager (USA)	1977-79	2	Deep-space probes, ultimately leaving solar system

extend from the chromosphere into the corona, a halo of hot gas surrounding the sun. Gas boiling from the corona streams outwards through the solar system, forming solar wind. Activity on the sun, including sunspots, flares and prominences, waxes and wanes during the *solar cycle* every 11 years or so.

solar system the sun and all the other bodies in orbit around it: the nine planets, their moons, asteroids and comets. The solar system is thought to have formed from a cloud of gas and dust in space 4,600 million years ago. The sun contains 99% of the mass of the solar system. The edge of the solar system is not clearly defined; it is marked only by the limit of the sun's gravitational influence, which extends about 1.5 light years, almost halfway to the nearest star.

Milky Way the faint band of light crossing the sky, consisting of countless stars in the plane of our galaxy, too distant to be seen individually by the naked eye. The name Milky Way is sometimes also used for our galaxy. The densest parts lie in the constellation Sagittarius, towards the centre. In places, the Milky Way is interrupted by lanes of dark dust which obscure light from the stars beyond, such as the Coalsack Nebula in Crux (the Southern Cross) and the Cygnus Rift.

Celestial Bodies

celestial body 'of the sky'; an object which is seen outside the earth and its atmosphere, ranging from tiny fragments of rock a few centimetres across to giant stars hundreds of times the size of our sun. The term is not usually used for artificial objects such as rockets and space probes.

meteor a flash of light in the sky, popularly known as a *shooting star*, caused by a particle of dust burning up in the atmosphere. Most

meteors are smaller than grains of sand. They enter the atmosphere at speeds up to 70 km/45 mi per sec and burn up by friction at a height of around 100 km/60 mi. On any clear night, several *sporadic* meteors can be seen each hour. But several times each year the earth encounters swarms of dust shed by comets, which give rise to a *meteor shower*. The meteors in a shower seem to radiate from one particular point in the sky, after which the shower is named, e.g. the Perseid meteor shower of August appears to radiate from the constellation Perseus. A particularly brilliant meteor is termed a *fireball*.

meteorite a piece of rock or metal from space that reaches the surface of the earth, moon or other body. Meteorites are thought to be fragments from asteroids, although some may be pieces from the heads of comets. Over 5,000 meteorites are estimated to hit the earth each year. Most fall in the sea or in remote areas and are never recovered. Most meteorites are stony in composition, although some are made of iron and a few have a mixed rock-iron composition. The largest known meteorite is iron, weighing 60 tonnes, which lies where it fell in prehistoric times at Grootfontein, Namibia. Meteorites are slowed down by the earth's atmosphere, but if they are moving fast enough they can form a crater on impact.

satellite any small body that orbits a larger one, either natural or artificial. Natural satellites are called moons. The first *artificial satellite,* Sputnik 1, was launched into orbit around the earth by the USSR in 1957. Artificial satellites are used for scientific purposes, communications, weather forecasting, and military purposes. At any time there are several thousand artificial satellites orbiting the earth, including active satellites, satellites that have ended their working lives, and discarded sections of rockets. The largest artificial satellites can be seen by the naked eye. Artificial satellites eventually re-enter the earth's atmosphere. Usually they burn up by friction, but sometimes debris falls to the earth's surface, as with Skylab.

asteroid any of many thousands of small

bodies, composed of rocks and iron, that orbit the sun. They are also known as minor planets. Most asteroids lie in a belt between the orbits of Mars and Jupiter, though some are on orbits that bring them close to the earth, and some, such as the Apollo asteroids, even cross the earth's orbit. Asteroids are thought to be fragments left over from the formation of the solar system. As many as 100,000 may exist, but their total mass is only a few hundredths the mass of the moon. The largest is Ceres, 1,000 km/621 mi in diameter. The brightest as seen from earth is Vesta, which has a light-coloured surface.

comet a small, icy body orbiting the sun on a highly elliptical path. A comet consists of a central nucleus a few kilometres across, often likened to a dirty snowball because it consists mostly of ice mixed with dust. As the comet approaches the sun the nucleus heats up, releasing gas and dust which form a tenuous *coma* up to 100,000 km/60,000 mi across, around the nucleus. Gas and dust stream away from the coma to form the comet's tail, which may extend for millions of kilometres.

Comets are believed to have been formed at the birth of the solar system. Billions of them now reside in the *Oort cloud* beyond the planets. The gravitational effect of passing stars pushes some towards the sun, when they become visible from earth. Most comets swing around the sun and return to distant space, not to be seen again for thousands or millions of years. But some have their orbits altered by the gravitational pull of the planets so that they reappear every 200 years or less. These are termed *periodic comets*. Of the 800 or so comets whose orbits have been calculated, about 1 in 5 is periodic; the only one visible to the naked eye is Halley's comet. That with the shortest known period is Encke's comet, which orbits the sun every 3.3 years. A dozen or more comets are discovered every year, some by amateur astronomers.

moon in astronomy, any small body that orbits a planet. That which orbits Earth is known as the Moon. Mercury and Venus are the only planets in our solar system that do not

have moons.

planet a body in orbit around a star. Planets do not give out light of their own, but reflect the light of the central star. Planets can be made of rock, metal or gas. There are nine planets in the solar system, orbiting the sun. The inner four, called the *terrestrial planets*, are small and rocky, and include our planet Earth. The outer planets are large balls of liquid and gas; the largest is Jupiter, which contains more than twice as much mass as all the other solar-system planets combined. There is no good evidence for any planets beyond Pluto. Other stars almost certainly have planets, but they would be too faint to see from earth.

nebula a cloud of gas and dust in space. Nebulae are the birthplaces of stars. One is the Orion nebula, visible to the naked eye below the 'belt' of Orion. It is an *emission nebula*, glowing brightly because its gas is energized by stars that have formed within it. In another type of bright nebula, a *reflection nebula*, light from stars is reflected off grains of dust in the nebula, as surrounds the stars of the Pleiades cluster. A *dark nebula* appears as a dark patch silhouetted on a lighter background, such as the Coalsack Nebula in Crux (the Southern Cross) and the Horsehead Nebula in Orion. Some nebulae are produced by gas thrown off from dying stars.

neutron star a very small, dense star composed mostly of atomic particles called neutrons. These stars are thought to form when massive stars explode as supernovae at the ends of their lives. In the explosion, the protons and electrons of the star's atoms merge to make neutrons. A neutron star may have the mass of our sun, or more, compressed into a globe only 20 km/12 mi in diameter. Being so small, neutron stars can spin very quickly. The rapidly 'flashing' radio stars called pulsars are believed to be neutron stars. A neutron star cannot have a mass of more than about three suns, or its gravity will be so strong that it shrinks even further to become a black hole.

pulsar a celestial source that emits pulses of energy at very regular intervals, ranging from a few seconds to small fractions of a second.

Pulsars were discovered in 1967 at the Mullard Radio Astronomy Observatory, Cambridge, England, by a team under Antony Hewish. Over 300 radio pulsars are now known in our galaxy, although a million may exist. They are thought to be rapidly rotating neutron stars, which flash at radio and other wavelengths like a lighthouse as they spin. Two pulsars, the one in Crab Nebula and one in the constellation Vela, give out flashes of visible light. Pulsars gradually slow down as they get older, and eventually the flashes fade. *X-ray pulsars* are a related class of object caused by hot gas falling on to a spinning neutron star in a binary system.

star a luminous globe of gas, producing its own heat and light by nuclear reactions. Our own sun is an average star. Stars consist mostly of hydrogen and helium gas. They are born from large clouds of gas in space. Surface temperatures range from above 30,000 °C down to 2,000 °C, and the corresponding colours from blue-white to red. The brightest stars have masses 100 times that of the sun, and emit as much light as millions of suns. They live for less than a million years before exploding as supernovae. An example is the peculiar star Eta Carinae, visible in the southern hemisphere. The faintest stars are the red dwarfs, less than one-thousandth the brightness of the sun. The smallest mass possible for a star is about 8% that of the sun (80 times the mass of the planet Jupiter), otherwise nuclear reactions do not take place. Objects with less than this critical mass shine only dimly, and are termed *brown dwarfs*. There is no clear distinction between a small brown dwarf and a large planet.

For most of a star's life, energy is produced by the fusion of hydrogen into helium at its centre. Towards the end of its life, a star like the sun swells up into a red giant, before losing its outer layers as a planetary nebula, and finally shrinking to become a white dwarf.

galaxy a congregation of millions or billions of stars, held together by gravity. There are two main shapes. *Spiral* galaxies are flattened in shape, with a central bulge of old stars surrounded by a disk of younger stars, arranged in spiral arms like a catherine wheel. Barred spirals are a class of spiral galaxies that have a straight bar of stars across their centre, from the ends of which the spiral arms emerge. The arms of spiral galaxies contain gas and dust from which new stars are still forming. *Elliptical* galaxies contain old stars and very little gas. They include the most massive galaxies known, containing a million million stars. Some elliptical galaxies are thought to be merged spiral galaxies. Most galaxies occur in clusters, containing anything from a few to thousands of members. Although the Universe is expanding, individual clusters do not expand: rather, the space between clusters expands.

Our own galaxy, the Milky Way, is a spiral type about 100,000 light years in diameter, containing at least 100,000 million stars. It is a member of a small cluster, the Local Group. Our sun lies in one of its spiral arms, about 25,000 light years from the centre.

radio galaxy a galaxy that is a strong source of radio waves. All galaxies, including our own, emit some radio waves, but radio galaxies are up to a million times more powerful. In many cases the strongest radio emission comes not from the visible galaxy but from two clouds, invisible in an optical telescope, that can extend for millions of light years either side of the galaxy. This double structure at radio wavelengths is also shown by some quasars, suggesting a close relationship between the two types of object. In both cases, the source of energy is thought to be a massive black hole at the centre. Some radio galaxies are thought to result from two galaxies in collision, or which have recently merged.

quasar an object that appears star-like but which lies far off in the Universe, named for its *quasi-stellar* appearance. Light from quasars shows large redshifts, which places them far off in the universe, the most distant lying 10,000 million light years or more away. Although quasars are small, with diameters of less than a light year, they give out as much energy as hundreds of galaxies. Quasars are thought to be the brilliant centres of distant galaxies, caused by stars and gas falling towards an immense black hole at the galaxy's centre. Some quasars emit radio waves, which is how they were first identified in 1963, but most are radio-quiet. About 3,000 are now known. They are important in studies of the early history of the Universe.

black hole a hypothetical object whose gravity would be so great that nothing could escape from it, not even light. Anything that fell into a black hole would not be seen again. Black holes are thought to form when massive stars, much heavier than our sun, shrink at the ends of their lives. A black hole can grow by sucking in more matter, including other stars, from the space around it. Matter that falls into a black hole is squeezed to infinite density at the centre of the hole. Black holes can be detected because gas falling towards them becomes so hot that it emits x-rays. Satellites above the earth's atmosphere have detected x-rays from a number of objects in our galaxy that might be black holes. Massive black holes containing the mass of millions of stars are thought to lie at the centres of quasars. Microscopic black holes may have been formed in the chaotic conditions of the Big Bang. The English physicist Stephen Hawking has shown that such tiny black holes could 'evaporate' and explode in a flash of energy.

Universe all of space and its contents. The Universe is mostly empty space, dotted with galaxies for as far as telescopes can see. The most distant detected galaxies and quasars lie 10,000 million light years or more away. The Universe is thought to be between 10,000 million and 20,000 million years old, and to have originated in a immense explosion called the Big Bang. The space between the galaxies is expanding. Whether or not the expansion will continue depends on the average density of matter in the Universe. If the density is above a critical value, then gravity will eventually slow the expansion and reverse it. However, observations suggest that there is not enough matter in the Universe to halt the expansion, which will continue forever.

Places and Organizations

Arecibo the site in Puerto Rico of the world's largest single radio-telescope dish, 305 m/1,000 ft in diameter. Suspended between towers in a hollow in the hills, it uses the rotation of the earth to scan the sky. It is operated by the US's Cornell University.

Baikonour The name given in the USSR to the rocket launching site at Tyuratam.

Cape Canaveral promontory on the Atlantic coast of Florida, USA, 367 km/228 mi N of Miami. It was known 1963–73 as Cape Kennedy. The John F. Kennedy Space Center, from which all US manned space flights have been launched, is here.

Edwards Air Force Base military USAF centre in California, situated on a dry lake bed, with extensive runways and advanced facilities. Often used as a landing site by the Space Shuttle.

European Space Agency (ESA) an organization of European nations to engage in space research and technology for peaceful purposes. ESA was founded in 1975 by Belgium, Denmark, France, West Germany, Ireland, Italy, Netherlands, Spain, Sweden, Switzerland and the United Kingdom, with headquarters in Paris. ESA has developed various scientific and communications satellites, the Giotto space probe, the Ariane rocket and has built Spacelab for the USA. ESA plans to build its own space station, Columbus, for attachment to the US space station, and is working on its own shuttle project, Hermes.

Intelsat International Telecommunications Satellite Organization, established in 1964 to operate a worldwide system of communications satellites. More than a hundred countries are members of Intelsat, with headquarters in Washington DC, USA. Intelsat satellites are stationed in geostationary orbit over the Atlantic, Pacific and Indian Oceans. The first Intelsat satellite was *Early Bird*, launched in 1965.

Jodrell Bank site in Cheshire, England, of the Nuffield Radio Astronomy Laboratories of the University of Manchester. Its largest instrument is the 76 m/250 ft radio dish, completed in 1957 and modified in 1970. A 38 m × 25 m/125 ft × 83 ft elliptical radio dish was introduced in 1964, capable of working at shorter wavelengths. These radio telescopes are used in conjunction with five smaller dishes to produce detailed maps of radio sources.

Kennedy Space Center the NASA installation at Cape Canaveral, Florida. Headquarters of the Center are on Merritt Island. Apollo spacecraft and the Space Shuttle have been launched from here. The Center is dominated by the Vehicle Assembly Building, 160 m/525 ft tall, used for assembly of Saturn rockets and Space Shuttles.

Kourou second-largest town of French Guiana, NW of Cayenne. It is the site of the Guiana Space Centre engaged in work for the European Space Agency. Situated near the equator, it is an ideal site for launches of satellites into geostationary orbit.

NASA National Aeronautics and Space Administration. The US government agency, founded in 1958, for non-military spaceflight and aeronautical research. Its headquarters are in Washington DC and its major installation is at Cape Canaveral.

observatory a site or facility for observation of natural phenomena, especially astronomical. The earliest recorded observatory was at Alexandria, built by Ptolemy Soter, c 300 BC. The erection of observatories was revived in W Asia c 1000 AD, and extended to Europe. That built on Hven Island, Denmark, in 1576, for Tycho Brahe, was elaborate, but survived only to 1597. It was followed by those at Paris 1667, Greenwich 1675, and Kew 1769. Among the most famous modern observatories are the Hale at Mount Palomar, California; Kitt Peak in Arizona; La Palma in the Canary Islands; and Mount Semirodniki in the Caucasus, which have the most powerful optical telescopes covering the sky from the northern

hemisphere. Famous radio astronomy observatories include Jodrell Bank, the Mullard at Cambridge, England, Arecibo in Puerto Rico, Effelsberg in W Germany, and Parkes in Australia. Until recently the skies of the southern hemisphere were comparatively neglected, but in the 1970s important optical telescopes were established at Cerro Tololo, Chile; La Silla, Chile; and Siding Spring, Australia. Observatories can now also be set up in orbit, above the earth's atmosphere, as satellites, in space stations, and in the Space Shuttle.

Palomar Mount the location of an observatory, 80 km/50 mi NE of San Diego, California, having a 5 m/200 in diameter reflector. When dedicated in 1948 it was the largest optical telescope in the world.

Parkes the site in New South Wales, Australia, of the Australian National Radio Astronomy Observatory, featuring a radio telescope of 64 m/210 ft aperture, run by the Commonwealth Scientific and Industrial Research Organization (CSIRO).

Plesetsk a rocket-launching site in the Soviet Union, 170 km/105 mi S of Archangel. From here the USSR has launched unmanned satellites since 1966, many of them for military purposes.

Royal Greenwich Observatory the national astronomical observatory of the UK, founded in 1675 at Greenwich, E London, by King Charles II to provide navigational information for seamen. The eminence of the Observatory's work meant that, in 1884, Greenwich Time and the Greenwich Meridian were adopted as international standards of reference. After World War II the Observatory was moved to Herstmonceux Castle in Sussex, and plans to move to Cambridge in 1990. The Observatory also operates telescopes on La Palma in the Canary Islands, including the 4.2 m/165 in William Herschel Telescope commissioned in 1987.

Tyuratam the main space launching site in the USSR, NE of the Aral Sea. It is the Soviet equivalent of the USA's Cape Canaveral, but much larger. The Soviets refer to it as Baikonour, which is a town some distance away. The first earth satellites were launched from here. All Soviet manned space flights, and all Soviet space probes, have been launched from Tyuratam.

Yerkes Observatory astronomical centre in Wisconsin, USA. Founded by George Hale in 1897, it houses the world's largest optical refracting optical telescope, with a lens of diameter 102 cm/40 in.

Terms

astronomical unit the average distance of the earth from the sun. 149,597,870 km/92,955,800 mi.

Big Bang the hypothetical event which marked the origin of the Universe as we know it. At the time of the Big Bang, the entire Universe and all space and matter were squeezed into a hot, super-dense state. The Big Bang explosion threw this material outwards, producing the expanding Universe. The cause of the Big Bang is unknown; observations of the current rate of expansion of the Universe suggest that it took place between 10,000 million and 20,000 million years ago.

constellation in astronomy, one of the 88 areas into which the sky is divided for the purposes of identifying and naming objects. The first constellations were simple star patterns in which early civilizations visualized gods, sacred beasts and mythical heroes. The constellations in general use today have been modified and extended from a list of 48 known to the ancient Greeks, who inherited some from the Babylonians. The modern list of 88 constellations was officially adopted by the International Astronomical Union in 1930.

eclipse the event when one astronomical body passes into the shadow of another. A *solar eclipse* occurs when the moon passes in front of the sun as seen from earth, and covers it partially or totally. A solar eclipse can happen only during a new moon. During a total elipse

planets

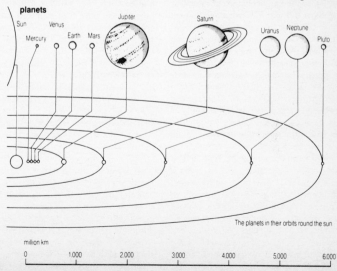

The planets in their orbits round the sun

the sun's corona can be seen. A total solar eclipse can last just over 7.5 minutes, although partial eclipse will be visible from Cornwall on 11 Aug 1999. When the moon is at its farthest from earth it does not completely cover the face of the sun, leaving a ring of sunlight visible. This is an *annular eclipse* (from the Latin word *annulus*, ring). Between two and five solar eclipses occur each year.

A *lunar eclipse* occurs when the moon passes into the shadow of the earth, so that the moon's surface becomes dim until emerging from the shadow. Lunar eclipses may be partial or full, and they can happen only at full moon. Total lunar eclipses last for up to 100 minutes; the maximum number each year is three.

light year a measure of distance (not time) – the distance travelled by a beam of light in one year, 9.461×10^{12} km/5.88 million million mi.

magnitude measure of the brightness of a star or other celestial object. Faint objects have larger magnitudes, sixth magnitude being the faintest visible to the naked eye under good conditions. The brightest objects have negative (minus) magnitudes, such as Sirius, the brightest star in the night sky, which is magnitude -1.46. A difference of five magnitudes is equal to a brightness difference of 100 times; each magnitude step is equal on this geometric scale to a brightness difference of 2.512 times. *Apparent magnitude* is the brightness that an object appears from earth. *Absolute magnitude* is measured at the standard distance of 10 parsecs (32.6 light years) from the star. The apparent magnitude of the sun is -26.8, but its absolute magnitude is only $+4.8$.

orbit the path of one body in space around another, such as the orbit of the earth around the sun, or the moon around the earth. When the two bodies are similar in mass, as in a double star, both bodies move around their common centre of mass. The movement of objects in orbit follows Kepler's laws, which apply to artificial satellites as well as to natural bodies. As stated by the laws, the orbit of one body around another is an ellipse. The ellipse can be highly elongated, as in the case of comet orbits around the sun, or it may be almost

circular, as in planets and some artificial satellites. The closest point of a planet's orbit to the sun is called *perihelion*; the most distant point is *aphelion*. (For a body orbiting the earth, the closest and furthest points of the orbit are called *perigee* and *apogee*.)

parsec in astronomy, a unit of distance measurement applied to stars and galaxies. One parsec is equal to 3.2616 light years. It is the distance at which a star would have a parallax of one second of arc using as base line the earth's orbital radius around the sun.

radio astronomy the study of radio waves emitted naturally by objects in space. Radio emission comes from hot gas (*thermal radiation*), electrons spiralling in magnetic fields (*synchroton radiation*), and specific wavelengths (*lines*) emitted by atoms and molecules in space, such as the 21cm line emitted by hydrogen gas. Among the radio sources in our galaxy are the remains of supernova explosions, such as the Crab Nebula, and pulsars. Strong sources beyond our galaxy include radio galaxies and quasars. Their existence far off in the Universe demonstrates how the Universe has been evolved with time. Radio astronomers have also detected weak *background radiation* thought to be from the Big Bang explosion that marked the birth of the Universe.

radio telescope an instrument for detecting radio waves from the Universe. Radio telescopes usually consist of a metal bowl, which collects and focuses radio waves like a concave mirror collects and focuses light waves. Other radio telescopes are shaped like long troughs, while some consist of simple rod-shaped aerials. Radio telescopes are much larger than optical telescopes, because the wavelengths they detect are much longer than the wavelength of light. Even a large dish such as that at Jodrell Bank can see the radio sky less clearly than a small optical telescope sees the visible sky. The largest single radio astronomy dish is 305 m/1,000 ft across, at Arecibo, Puerto Rico.

redshift in astronomy, the lengthening of the wavelengths of light from an object, as a result of the object's motion away from us. It is an example of the Doppler effect. Lengthening the wavelengths causes them to move or shift towards the red end of the spectrum, hence the name. The amount of redshift can be measured by the displacement of lines in an object's spectrum. By measuring the amount of redshift in light from stars and galaxies, astronomers can tell how quickly these objects are moving away from us. The redshift in light from galaxies is evidence for the expanding Universe. A strong gravitational field can also produce a redshift in light; this is termed *gravitational redshift*.

solar wind a stream of atomic particles, mostly protons and electrons, from the sun's corona flowing outwards through the solar system at speeds from 300 km/200 mi to 1,000 km/600 mi per second. The fastest streams come from 'holes' in the sun's corona that lie over areas where there is no surface activity. The solar wind pushes the gas of comets' tails away from the sun, and 'gusts' in the solar wind cause geomagnetic disturbances and aurorae on earth.

telescope a device for collecting and focusing light and other forms of electromagnetic radiation (see also radio telescope). A telescope produces a magnified image, which makes the object seem nearer, and it shows fainter objects than can be seen by the eye alone. A telescope with a large *aperture*, or opening, can see finer detail and fainter objects than one with a small aperture.

There are two main types of optical telescope: the *refracting telescope*, which uses lenses, and the *reflecting telescope*, which uses mirrors. A third type, the *catadioptric telescope*, with a combination of lenses and mirrors, is becoming increasingly popular. The largest refracting telescope in the world has an aperture of 102 cm/40 in at Yerkes Observatory, Wisconsin, USA.

The largest reflector, with a 6 m/236 in mirror, is at Zelenchukskaya, USSR. Telescopes with larger apertures are planned, but they will be composed of numerous smaller mirrors. The first such *multiple-mirror telescope* was installed on Mount Hopkins, Arizona, in 1979. It con-

sists of six mirrors of 1.8 m/72 in aperture, which perform like a single 4.5 m/176 in mirror. Large telescopes can now be placed in orbit, above the distorting effects of the earth's atmosphere. Telescopes in space have been used to study infrared, ultraviolet and X-rays that do not penetrate the atmosphere, but which carry much information about the births, lives and deaths of stars and galaxies. The 2.4 m/95 in Space Telescope, due for launch in 1988, will see the sky more clearly than any telescope on earth.

unidentified flying object (UFO) any light or object seen in the sky whose immediate identity is not apparent. The term *flying saucer* was coined after a 1947 sighting by Kenneth Arnold. On investigation, the vast majority of UFOs turn out to be natural or artificial objects, most notably bright stars and planets, meteors, aircraft and satellites. Despite unsubstantiated claims, there is no evidence that UFOs are alien spacecraft, and few scientists believe that UFOs represent anything genuinely unknown.

zodiac name given by the ancient Greeks to that zone of the heavens containing the paths of the sun, moon and the five planets then known. It was about 1° in width, and the stars contained in it were grouped into 12 signs each 3° in extent, viz. Aries, Taurus, Gemini, Cancer, Leo, Virgo, Libra, Scorpio, Sagittarius, Capricorn, Aquarius, Pisces. The modern constellations do not cover the same areas of sky as the zodiacal signs of the same name.

Biographies

Aristarchus of Samos 310-264 BC Greek astronomer, famed as being the first to maintain that the earth revolves round the sun.

Brahe Tycho 1546-1601. Danish astronomer who made the observations from which

Johannes Kepler proved that planets orbit the sun in ellipses. His observations of the comet of 1577 showed that it moved on an orbit among the planets, overthrowing the Greek view that comets were in the earth's atmosphere.

Copernicus Nicolaus 1473–1543. Polish astronomer. For 30 years he worked on the hypothesis that the motion of the earth was responsible for the apparent movements of the heavenly bodies, but his great work *De Revolutionibus Orbium Coelestium* was not published until the year of his death. In this work he postulated that the sun is the centre of our system, and he thus became a prime founder of modern astronomy.

Flamsteed John 1646–1719. First Astronomer Royal of England. Born near Derby, he was appointed astronomer to Charles II in 1675, and began systematic observations of the positions of the stars, moon and planets at Greenwich in the following year. His observations were posthumously published in 1725.

Galileo Galilei 1564–1642. Italian mathematician, astronomer, and physicist, born at Pisa. He developed the telescope and was the first to see the four main satellites of Jupiter, mountains and craters on the moon, and Venus's appearance going through 'phases' as would be expected if it were orbiting the sun. His observations and arguments were an unwelcome refutation of the ideas of Aristotle currently taught at the (church-run) universities, especially because they made plausible for the first time the sun-centred theory of Copernicus.

Hale George Ellery 1868–1938. US astronomer, who made pioneer studies of the sun and founded three major observatories. Born in Chicago, he invented the spectroheliograph in 1889, a device for photographing the sun at particular wavelengths. In 1897 he founded the Yerkes Observatory in Wisconsin, with a 102 cm/40 in refracting telescope, the largest refractor ever built. In 1904 he moved to Mount Wilson, California, where he discovered that sunspots are cooler areas on the sun, associated with strong magnetic fields. In 1917 he established a 2.5 m/100 in reflector on

Mount Wilson. This was the world's largest telescope until superseded in 1948 by the 5 m/200 in reflector on Mount Palomar, which was also planned by Hale before he died.

Halley Edmund 1656–1742. English astronomer. Born in London, he became friendly with Sir Isaac Newton, whose *Principia* he financed. He is remembered as having observed Halley's Comet in 1682 and for accurately predicting (in 1704) that it would reappear in 1758. He was Astronomer Royal from 1720.

Herschel Sir William 1738–1822. British astronomer. In 1781 he discovered Uranus, and later several of its satellites. During his appointment as astronomer to George III from 1782 he discovered the motion of the double stars round one another, and recorded it in his *Motion of the Solar System in Space* 1783. He constructed a 1.2 m/4 ft telescope, of 12 m/40 ft focal length, at Slough, in 1789, and discovered infra-red solar rays in 1800. He was helped in his observations by his sister *Caroline Lucretia Herschel* (1750–1848), who discovered eight comets. His son *Sir John Frederick William Herschel* (1792–1871) was also an astronomer and established an observatory near Capetown in 1834, where he discovered thousands of close double stars, clusters and nebulae, reported in 1847.

Hoyle Sir Fred 1915– . British astronomer, carried out pioneering work on the evolution of stars and the formation of the chemical elements. His work on the evolution of stars was published in *Frontiers of Astronomy* 1955. In 1957, with Geoffrey and Margaret Burbridge and William Fowler, he showed that chemical elements heavier than hydrogen and helium are built up by nuclear reactions inside stars. He has created controversy by suggesting, with Chandra Wickramasinghe, that life originates in the gas clouds of space and is delivered to the earth and planets by passing comets (*Lifecloud* 1978).

Hubble Edwin Powell 1889–1953. American astronomer, discovered the existence of other galaxies outside our own, classified them according to their shape, and discovered the expansion of the Universe. In 1925 he introduced the classification of galaxies as spirals, barred spiral and ellipticals. In 1929 he announced **Hubble's law**, i.e. that the galaxies are moving apart at a rate that increases with their distance, an observation that can be explained by the expanding Universe.

Kepler Johannes 1571–1630. German mathematician and astronomer, proved that the planets orbit the sun in ellipses, and discovered the three laws of planetary motion that bears his name. Born in Württemberg, he became assistant to Tycho Brahe in 1600 and succeeded him as Imperial Mathematician in 1601. His analysis of Tycho's observations of the planets led him to discover **Kepler's laws**, the first two of which he published in *Astronomia Nova* 1609 and the third in *Harmonices Mundi* 1619.

Lemaître Georges Edouard 1894–1966. Belgian cosmologist who put forward the Big Bang theory for the origin of the Universe. In 1927, Lemaître predicted that the entire Universe was expanding, which Hubble confirmed, and suggested that the expansion had been started by an initial explosion, the Big Bang, a theory that is now generally accepted.

Lovell Sir Bernard 1913– . British astronomer. During World War II he worked at the Telecommunications Research establishment (1939–45), and in 1951 became professor of radio astronomy at the University of Manchester and director of Jodrell Bank Experimental Station (now Nuffield Radio Astronomy Laboratories). His books include *Radio Astronomy* 1951 and *The Exploration of Outer Space* 1961.

Oort Jan Hendrik 1900– . Dutch astronomer, who in 1927 calculated the mass and size of our galaxy, and the sun's distance from its centre, from the observed movements of stars around the galaxy's centre. In 1944 Oort's student Hendrik van de Hulst calculated that hydrogen in space would emit radio waves at 21 cm wavelength, and in the 1950s Oort's team mapped the spiral structure of our galaxy from the radio waves given out by interstellar hydrogen. In 1950 Oort proposed that comets exist in a vast swarm, now called the **Oort Cloud**, at the edge of the solar system.

Ptolemy (Claudius Ptolemaeus) c 100–178 AD. Astronomer and geographer. A native of Egypt, he carried out observations in Alexandria, and published a Geography which was a standard source of information until the 16th century. His greatest work was known as the *Almagest*, in which he developed the theory of Aristotle that the earth is the centre of the Universe, with the sun, moon and stars revolving around it. Not until 1543 was the *Ptolemaic system* superseded by the theory of Copernicus.

Ryle Sir Martin 1918–84. British radio-astronomer, Astronomer-Royal 1972–82. At the Mullard Radio Astronomy Observatory, Cambridge, he developed the technique of sky-mapping using 'aperture synthesis', combining smaller 'dishes' to give the characteristics of one large one. His work on the distribution of radio sources in the Universe brought confirmation of the 'Big Bang theory'.

Whipple Fred Lawrence 1906– . US astronomer, director of the Smithsonian Astrophysical Observatory 1955–73, predicted in 1949 that the nucleus of a comet is like a dirty snowball, confirmed in 1986 by space probe studies of Halley's Comet.

1903   Tsiolkovsky published the first practical paper on astronautics.

1926   Goddard launched the first liquid fuel rocket.

1937–45   Werner von Braun developed the V2 rocket.

1957   Sputnik 1 (Russian 'fellow-traveller': USSR), the first space satellite, orbited earth at a height of 229–898 km/142–558 mi in 96.2 min on 4 Oct; Sputnik 2 (USSR), was launched 3 Nov carrying a live dog 'Laika' (died on board 10 Nov).

1958   Explorer 1 (USA), the first US satellite, 31 Jan discovered Van Allen radiation belts.

1960   Tiros 1 (USA), the first weather satellite, was launched 1 Apr.

1961   Vostok 1 (USSR), first manned spaceship (Yuri Gagarin), was recovered on 12 Apr after a single orbit at a height of 175–142 km/109–88 mi in 89.1 min.

1962   Friendship 7 (USA); John Glenn was the first American in orbit round the earth on 20 Feb; Telstar (USA), a communications satellite, sent the first live television transmission between USA and Europe.

1963   Vostok 6 (USSR); Valentina Tereshkova was the first woman in space 16–19 Jun.

1966   Venera 3 (USSR), space probe, launched Nov 1965, crash-landed on Venus 1 Mar, the first man-made object to reach another planet.

1967   Soyuz 1 (USSR); Vladimir Komarov was the first man to be killed in space research when his ship crash-landed on earth on 24 Apr.

1969   Apollo-Saturn 11 (USA) was launched 16–24 Jul; Neil Armstrong was the first man to walk on the moon.

1970   Luna 17 (USSR) was launched 10 Nov; its unmanned lunar vehicle, *Lunokhod*, took photos and made soil analyses on the moon.

1971   Salyut 1 (USSR), the first orbital space station, was established 19 Apr; it was visited by the Soyuz 11 manned spacecraft.

1971–2   Mariner 9 (USA) was the first space probe to orbit another planet, when it circled Mars.

1972   Pioneer 10 (USA), earth's first starship, was launched 3 Mar; it reached Jupiter 1973; in 1983 it made its first passage of the asteroid belt, reached Neptune, and passed on into the first voyage beyond the solar system. Apollo 17 (USA) was launched Dec.

1973   Skylab 2 (USA), the first US orbital space station, was established.

1975   Apollo 18 (USA), 15–24 Jul, made a joint flight with Soyuz 19 (USSR), in a link-up in space.

1976   Viking 1 (USA), unmanned spacecraft, was launched 20 Aug 1975; it reached Mars, the spacecraft lander touching down on 20 Jul 1976; Viking 2 (USA) was launched 9 Sept 1975, its lander touching down on Mars 3 Sept 1976.

1977   Voyager 1 (USA), launched 5 Sept 1977, and Voyager 2 (USA), launched 20 Aug, both unmanned spacecraft, reached Jupiter Jan/Jul 1979, Uranus 1986, and are expected to reach Neptune 1989.

344

1978	Pioneer Venus 1 (USA) was launched 20 May 1978 and Pioneer Venus 2 (USA) on 20 Aug 1978; both reached Venus Dec.
1979	Ariane (European Space Agency satellite launcher) was launched.
1981	Space Shuttle (USA), first re-usable manned spacecraft, was launched 12 Apr.
1982	Venera 13 and 14 (USSR) landed on Venus; soil samples indicated that the surface is similar to earth's volcanic rock.
1985	Two Vega probes (USSR) released balloons for the first time into the atmosphere of another planet (Venus).
1986	Space Shuttle (USA) exploded shortly after launch killing all seven crew members. The space probe *Giotto* showed Halley's comet to be one of the darkest objects ever detected in the solar system, with an irregular nucleus 14.5 km/9 mi × 3km/2 mi. Voyager 2 reached Uranus and found it to have six more moons than was previously thought, making 12 known moons in all.

Computing

Computing, or computer studies, is the science of the design and application of machines that can handle and manipulate data, which are generically known as computers. The term computer is derived from the verb 'compute', which means to reckon or calculate, and the first of these machines were built specifically to perform calculations for gun-firing and navigation tables. The early machines were all mechanically operated but modern computers are all electronic and are used mainly for commercial applications such as word processing, handling payrolls and bank balances, controlling industrial robots, and monitoring the functioning of cars, space vehicles and medical equipment. Current research is concerned with developing computers that can handle data faster and more 'intelligently' than before.

The five parts of this section comprise an overview of *How Computers Work,* describing the basic components and functioning of an electronic computer and highlighting the four main types of modern computer; a more detailed description of the *Main Parts of a Computer* as used with a typical business machine; a definition of some *Basic Computer Terms* that include various technical words relating to the electronics of computing; a *Table of Programming Languages* that compares the nature and uses of eight common types of coding used to instruct a computer what to do with the data supplied; and a *Chronology of Computing* that starts with the development of the first machines capable of handling complex mathematical calculations and leads to the creation of supercomputers.

How Computers Work

Background the earliest computing device was the abacus used by the ancient Greeks and Romans and still in use in the East today. There are mechanical devices using sliding scales, similar to the slide-rule, which date back almost two millennia, for performing various kinds of calculation, usually as an aid to navigation. In 1642, the French philosopher-mathematician Blaise Pascal built a mechanical adding machine, and in 1671, German philosopher-mathematician Gottfried Leibniz built a machine to perform multiplication. In 1835, British mathematician Charles Babbage designed the first mechanical computer, the analytical engine. The work of another British mathematician Alan Turing, in the 1930s, marked the next major milestone. He developed the mathematical theory of computation and, in particular, showed how a machine could be conceived which could perform any computation (the so-called Turing Machine). The digital computer is the direct descendant of these ideas. In the 1940s, American mathematician John von Neumann developed the basic design for today's electronic computers. Finally, with the development of the transistor in 1952 and the subsequent microelectronics revolution, the Computer Age was started.

Basic system a computer is a collection of various components. At the heart is the CPU (central processing unit), which performs all the computations. This is supported by memory which holds the current program and data, and 'logic arrays' which help move information around the system. A main power supply is needed and, in the case of a mini- or mainframe computer, a cooling system. The computer's 'device driver' circuits control the peripheral devices, or add-ons, which can be attached.

These will normally be keyboards and VDU (visual display unit) screens for user input and output, disc drive units for mass memory storage, and printers for printed output.

A computer can only carry out tasks as commanded by the programmer, who translates instructions written in everyday language into a program that is a coded form matching the electronic coding within the computer's internal machinery. The program and data to be manipulated – text, figures, images, or sounds - are input into the computer which then processes the data and outputs the results. The results can be printed out or displayed on a VDU, or stored in a memory unit for subsequent manipulation. Whatever the task, a computer can function in only one of four ways: input/output operations, arithmetical operations (addition, subtraction, multiplication, and division), logic and comparison operations (for example, is the value of A equal to, less than, or greater than B), and movement of data to, from, and within the central memory of the machine. The programmer's role is to devise a set of instructions, an *algorithm*, that utilizes these four functions in a combination appropriate to the job in question.

Types there are four 'sizes' corresponding roughly to their memory capacity and processing speed. *Microcomputers* are the smallest and the most common and are used in small businesses, at home and in schools. They are usually single-user machines and are often referred to as home computers. *Minicomputers*, also known as personal computers, are generally larger and will be found in medium-sized businesses and university departments. They may support from a dozen to 30 or so users at once. *Mainframes*, which can often service several hundreds of users all at once are found in large organizations such as national companies and government departments. *Supercomputers* are the most powerful of all. There are very few in the world and are mostly used for special highly complex scientific tasks, such as analysing the results of nuclear physics experiments and weather forecasting.

Main Parts of a Computer

CPU (central processing unit) is the part of the computer that reads the program, fetches data, performs operations on the data in accordance with the program, and outputs its results. It is composed of five main elements: the *ALU* (arithmetic and logic unit), which contains the basic operations (its 'instruction set') and applies them to data; a *program counter* to keep track of the program being executed; a number of *registers* for storing intermediate results and data awaiting processing; (normally) an *electronic clock* which emits regular pulses that co-ordinate the CPU's activities; a *control unit* for organizing the processing.

graphics tablet in computing, also known as a bit pad, this is an input device consisting of a pressure-sensitive tablet on which marks can be made with a stylus. The position of any mark is automatically identified and communicated to a computer for interpretation. A graphics tablet is often used with a form overlaid for users to tick boxes in positions that each relate to specific registers in the computer, but some recent development in handwriting recognition may increase its versatility in the future.

joystick in computing, an input device, similar to a joystick used to control the flight of an aircraft, which signals to a computer the direction and extent of displacement of a hand-held lever. Often used to control the movement of a *cursor* (marker) on a VDU (computer screen), joysticks are most popular for moving predetermined specific shapes, or icons (such as space invader characters) in computer games. They allow fast and direct input.

keyboard in computing, an input device resembling a typewriter keyboard, which sends signals to a computer indicating which keys have been depressed. There are many variations on the layout of keys and the labelling of keys for different purposes. Extra numeric keys may be added, as can special-purpose function keys, such as LOAD, SAVE, PRINT, whose effect can be defined by programs in the computer.

light pen in computing, an input device resembling an ordinary pen, used to indicate or mark locations on a computer screen. At its tip, the pen has a photoreceptor which emits signals as light from the screen passes beneath it. From the timing of this signal and a grid-like representation of the screen in the computer's memory, a computer program can calculate the position of the light pen. With certain computer aided design (CAD) programs, the light pen can be used to instruct the computer to change the shape, size, position and colours of sections of a screen image.

memory in computing, any device, collection of devices or components in a computer system used to store data and programs either permanently or temporarily. There are two main types: internal memory and external memory. *Internal memory* is either read-only (stored in ROM, PROM and EPROM chips) or it is read/write (stored in RAM chips). Read-only memory stores information that must be constantly available or accessed very quickly, and that is unlikely to need to be changed. It is non-volatile, that is, it is not lost when the computer is switched off. Read/write memory is volatile; it stores programs and data temporarily only while the computer is switched on. *External memory* is permanent, non-volatile memory employing storage devices which include magnetic discs (such as floppy discs, hard discs), magnetic tape (e.g. tape streamers, cassettes), laser discs including CD-ROM (compact discs) and bubble memories. By rapidly swapping blocks of information in and out of internal memory from external memory, the limited size of a computer's memory may artificially be increased. To the user, this virtual memory, as it is called, gives the impression of a very large internal

349

memory. All computer memory stores information in binary code (using the binary number system). Memory capacity is measured in K (kilobyte).

modem (*MO*dulator-*DEM*odulator) an electronic device for converting digital (discrete) signals from a computer into analogue (continuous) signals on a telecommunications network and vice versa.

mouse in computing, an input device, used to control a pointer on a computer screen. Moving the mouse across a desk-top produces corresponding movement in the pointer. A mouse normally has one or more controlling buttons on its 'head' to instruct the computer in a specific way when the pointer is superimposed on a menu option on the screen, and its connecting wire is its 'tail'.

plotter an output device that draws pictures under computer control. Flatbed plotters move a pen up and down across a flat drawing surface while roller plotters roll the drawing paper past the pen as it moves from side to side.

printed circuit board (*PCB*) an electrical circuit created by laying (printing) 'tracks' of a conductor such as copper onto one or both sides of an insulating board. Components such as integrated circuits (chips), resistors and capacitors can be soldered onto the surface of the board (surface-mounted) or, more commonly, attached by inserting their connecting pins or wires into holes drilled in the board.

printer in computing, an output device for producing printed copy of textual, numeric and graphical data. Types include the *daisywheel*, which produces good quality text but no graphics; the *dot matrix*, which creates character patterns from a matrix of small dots, producing text and graphics, but of indifferent quality; and the *laser printer*, which reproduces high quality text and graphics.

touch screen an input device allowing the user to communicate with the computer by pointing a finger at a display screen. Typically, the screen detects the finger either through a sensitive membrane or when the finger interrupts a grid of light beams crossing the screen surface. Software in the device then calculates

the centre-point of the finger and communicates the co-ordinates (grid reference) to the computer.

VDU (visual display unit) an electronic output device for displaying the data processed by a computer on a screen. The oldest and the most popular type is the *cathode ray tube* (*CRT*), which uses essentially the same technology as a television screen. Plasma display technology is similar to that of domestic fluorescent light tubes; points of luminous gas are created, under the computer's control, from which images can be constructed. *Liquid crystal display* (*LCD*) relies on a property of certain substances to change the polarity of light and to realign their molecules in the presence of an electric field. The electrodes that govern the process are shaped into segments of

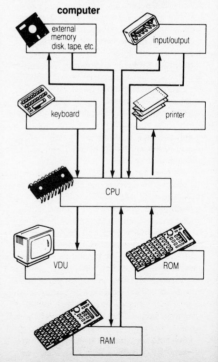

computer

characters and numbers from which a computer-controlled display is made up.

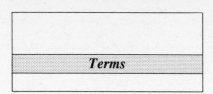

Terms

address in a computer memory, a number indicating a specific location. At each address, a single piece of data can be stored. For microcomputers, this normally amounts to one byte (enough to represent a single character such as a letter or number). The maximum capacity of a computer memory depends on how many memory addresses it can have. This is normally measured in units of 1,024 bytes (known as kilobytes, or Kb or K).

assembly code computer programming language closely related to the internal codes of the machine itself. It consists chiefly of a set of short mnemonics which are translated, by a program called an assembler, into machine code for the computer's CPU (central processing unit) to follow directly. In assembly language for example, JMP means 'jump' and LDA is 'load accumulator'. Used by programmers who need to write very fast or efficient programs.

binary number system or code a system of numbers to base two using combinations of the two digits 1 and 0. The value of any position in a binary number increases by powers of 2 (doubles) with each move from right to left (1, 2, 4, 8, 16, etc). For example, 1011 in the binary number system means $(1 \times 8) + (0 \times 4) + (1 \times 2) + (1 \times 1)$, which adds up to 11 in the everyday, decimal system (which uses successive powers of 10). Binary numbers play a key role in modern digital computers where they form the basis of the internal coding of information, the values of bits (short for 'binary digits') being represented as on/off (1 and 0) states of switches and high/low voltages in circuits.

BINARY NUMBER SYSTEM

binary (base 2)	octal (base 8)	decimal (base 10)	hexadecimal (base 16)
0	0	0	0
1	1	1	1
10	2	2	2
11	3	3	3
100	4	4	4
110	5	5	5
110	6	6	6
111	7	7	7
1000	10	8	8
1001	11	9	9
1010	12	10	A
1011	13	11	B
1100	14	12	C
1101	15	13	D
1110	16	14	E
1111	17	15	F
10000	20	16	10
1111111	377	255	FF
11111010001	3721	2001	7D1

bit a binary digit or place in a binary number.

byte in computing, a sequence or string of usually eight bits (binary digits) constituting a unit of memory or a character (a letter, number or symbol). Strictly it is a subdivision of a 'word' (the number of bits of information that a computer can process in a single operation, perhaps 32 bits in a minicomputer and 64 in a mainframe). A byte is a subdivision of this and is the number of bits needed to represent a single character (eight bits in extended ASCII, the American Standard Code for Information Interchange). Also now refers to a single memory location; computer memory size is measured in thousands of bytes (kilobytes or Kb) or millions of bytes (megabytes or Mb).

database in computing, a structured, centralized collection of data, organized to allow access by several or many different user programs. The data is held in files and arranged into hierarchies, networks, or relations – the three main types of database structure. For

351

example, a telephone directory stored as a database might allow all the people whose names start with the letter B to be selected by one program, and all those living in London by another. A database management system (DBMS) program ensures that the integrity of the data is maintained by controlling the degree of access of the application programs using the data. Databases are normally used by large organizations with mainframes or minicomputers. A collection of databases is known as a databank.

digital in electronics and computing, a term meaning 'coded as numbers'. A digital computer operates on symbols which are internally coded as binary numbers. A *digital display* shows discrete values as numbers (as opposed to an analogue signal such as the continuous sweep of a pointer on a dial). *Digital recording* is a technique whereby the pressure of sound waves is sampled more than 30000 times a second and the values recorded as numbers which, during playback, are re-converted to sound waves. This gives very high quality reproduction. *Digital data transmission* uses a similar technique, converting all signals (whether pictures, sounds or words) into numeric (normally binary) codes before transmission and then re-converting them on receipt. This virtually eliminates any distortion or degradation of the signal during transmission, storage or processing. *Digital electronics* is the technology which underlies the techniques described above.

fifth generation computer an anticipated new type of computer based on emerging microelectronic technologies. The basis will be very fast computing machinery, with many processors working in parallel. These will be possible because of very large-scale integration (VSLI) which can put many more circuits onto a silicon chip. Such computers will run advanced 'intelligent' programs. The other four generations are usually said to be:
First Generation (1943–1959): based on valves and wire circuits
Second Generation (1959–1964): based on transistors and printed circuits

Third Generation (1964–72): first machines to use integrated circuits
Fourth Generation (from 1972): based on large scale integration (LSI) of circuits.
The Fifth-generation Project is a 10–year research programme begun in Japan in 1982 to develop the new type of computer systems. It has been a spur for several other national and international programmes including *ESPRIT* in Europe and *Alvey* in the UK.

machine code in computing, a binary (two-state) code in which computer programs are expressed as a prerequisite to being executed by the computer. Once, all computer programs had to be written in machine code. Later, assembler (or assembly code) and, finally, high-level programming languages were developed which are easier for people to use and can automatically be translated into machine code prior to execution.

microprocessor a computer's central processing unit (CPU) contained on a single integrated circuit. The appearance of the first microprocessors in 1971 heralded the introduction of the microcomputer, a small, cheap computer built around a microprocessor. The pocket calculator is also a product of microprocessor technology.

operating system (*OS*) in computing, a program that controls the routine operations of a computer; it is sometimes called DOS (disc operating system) when the program is on disc. The operating system looks after the computer's filing system and handles the input and output of data and programs between the processor unit, external memory devices (such as disc drives) and input and output devices such as keyboard and visual display unit (VDU). Many makes of computer have their own operating system, but some are accepted standards. These include CP/M (by Digital Research) and MSDOS (by Microsoft) for microcomputers; and Unix (by Bell Laboratories) for minicomputers.

RISC acronym for Reduced Instruction Set Chip. A kind of computer processor on a single silicon chip offering speed and size improvements over current chips. Computers based on

RISC chips have just become commercially available and considerably outperform their predecessors.

robot any computer-controlled machine that can be taught or programmed to do work. Records of mechanical people and animals having been built go back more than 2000 years, bolstered by the fabulous creations of popular myth. However, it is only since the advent of the computer that the true robot has emerged. The most common types are mechanical 'arms'. Fixed to the floor or a workbench, they perform functions such as paint spraying or assembling parts in factories.

silicon chip popular term for an integrated circuit with microscopically small components on a piece of silicon crystal only a few millimetres square. This tiny circuit, often with upwards of a million components, is mounted in a rectangular plastic package with metal pins down the long sides so that they can be connected to printed circuit boards for inclusion in electronic devices such as computers, calculators, televisions, car dashboards and domestic appliances.

Programming Languages

programming language in computing, a special notation in which instructions for controlling a computer are written. Programming languages are designed to be easy for users to write and read but must be capable of being mechanically translated (by a compiler or interpreter) into the machine code that the computer can execute. The table overleaf shows eight different ways of instructing a computer to find the total of the numbers 1 to 10 each using a different language.

programming in computing, the activity of writing statements in a programming language for the control of a computer. Applications programming is for 'end user' programs, such as word-processing packages. Systems programming is for operating systems and the like, which are concerned more with the internal workings of the computer.

There are several programming styles. *Procedural programming*, in which programs are written as lists of instructions which the computer obeys in sequence, is by far the most popular. It is the 'natural' style, closely matching the computer's own sequential operation. Procedural programming languages, such as BASIC and COBOL, all support three basic constructs: sequence (executing statements in the list in strict order); iteration (looping through parts of the list); selection (jumping to different parts of the list when different conditions are met). *Declarative programming*, such as in the programming language Prolog, does not describe how to solve a problem, but rather describes the logical structure of the problem. Running such a program is more like proving an assertion than following a procedure. *Functional programming* is a style based largely on the definition of functions. There are very few functional programming languages, Hope and ML being the most widely used, though many more conventional languages (for example C) make extensive use of functions. *Object oriented programming*, the most recently developed style, involves viewing a program as a collection of objects which behave in certain ways when they are passed certain 'messages', for example an object might be defined to represent a table of figures which will be displayed on screen when a 'display' message is received.

Today most programming is done at a computer terminal using special-purpose program-editing software, rather like word processing. In the past, the process was more laborious, with programs having to be coded as holes punched into cards or paper tape.

PROGRAMMING LANGUAGES

Language	Main Uses	Description	Examples
assembler	Jobs needing speed and good control of the machine	fast and efficient but very hard to debug once written	LD B,AH SUB A SUMJ:ADD A,(B) DEC B JR NZ,SUMJ JP [display routine]
BASIC	in education and at home	easy to learn but lacks many of the features of other languages	10 SUM = 0 20 FOR J = 1 TO 10 30 SUM = SUM + J 40 NEXT J 50 PRINT SUM

C	systems programming	fast and efficient; has now largely replaced assembler for such jobs	sum = 0;
			for (j=1; j=10; j++)
			  sum = sum +j;
			printf("%d/n", sum);

COBOL	business programming	oriented strongly to commercial work; used almost exclusively for it	SET SUM TO 0.
			PERFORM SUM-J
			VARYING
			  J FROM 1 BY 1 UNTIL
			  J = 10.
			DISPLAY SUM.
			SUM=J. COMPUTE
			SUM=SUM+J.

Fortran	scientific programming	at first, lacking in features of other languages; since 1977 has been much improved	SUM = 0
			   DO 10 J = 1, 10
			    WRITE (1,100) SUM
			10 SUM = SUM + J
			100 FORMAT (1X, 16)

Lisp	artificial intelligence systems and research programming	a list processing language with many functional features. The code can look obscure	(SETQ SUM 0) (REPEAT ((UNTIL GREATERP J 10)) (PRINT SUM)) (SETQ SUM (PLUS SUM J)) (SETQ J (ADD1 J)))

Pascal	education, business, systems and scientific programming	a good all-rounder; easy to learn, with a set of features	sum : = 0;
			for j : = 1 to 10 do
			  sum : = sum + j;
			writeln(sum);

Prolog	artificial intelligence systems and research programming	the first logic programming language and the only one in common use	sum—j(11, SUM) :-
			  write (SUM),nl.
			sum—j(J, SUM) :-
			  SUM1 is SUM + J,
			  J1 is J + 1,
			  sum—j(J1, SUM1).
			[call using sum—j
			(1, 0).]

1614	Scottish mathematician John Napier invented logarithms.
1625	William Oughtred (1575–1660) invented the slide rule.
1623	Wilhelm Schickard (1592–1635) invented the first mechanical calculating machine.
1645	Blaise Pascal produced a calculator.
1672–74	Leibniz built his first calculator, the Stepped Reckoner.
1801	Joseph-Marie Jacquard developed an automatic loom controlled by punched cards.
1820	First mass-produced calculator (the Arithmometer, by Charles Thomas de Colmar 1785–1870).
1822	Charles Babbage's first model for the Difference Engine.
1830s	Babbage created the first design for the Analytical Engine.
1890	Herman Hollerith developed the punched card ruler for the USA census.
1936	Alan Turing published the mathematical theory of computing.
1938	Konrad Zuse constructed the first binary calculator, using Boolean algebra.
1943	'Colossus' electronic code-breaker developed at Bletchley Park, England; Harvard University Mark I or Automatic Sequence-Controlled Calculator (partly financed by IBM): the first program-controlled calculator.
1945	ENIAC (Electronic Numerator, Integrator, Analyser and Computer) completed at the University of Pennsylvania.
1948	Manchester University (England) Mark I, completed: first stored-program computer.
1951	Ferranti Mark I: the first commercially produced computer; 'Whirlwind', the first real-time computer, built for the USA air defence system; investigation of transistor.
1952	EDVAC (Electronic Discrete Variable Computer) completed at the Institute for Advanced Study, Princeton, USA (by von Neumann and others).
1953	Magnetic core memory developed.
1957	FORTRAN, the first high-level computer language, developed by IBM.
1958	The first integrated circuit.
1963	The first minicomputer built by Digital Equipment (DEC): the PDP-8; the first electronic calculator (Bell Punch Company).
1964	IBM System/360: the first compatible family of computers.
1965	The first supercomputer: the Control Data CD6600.
1970	The first microprocessor: the Intel 4004.
1974	CLIP-4, the first computer with a parallel architecture.
1975	The first personal computer: Altair 8800.
1981	The Xerox Start system, the first WIMP system (Windows, Icons, Menus and Pointing devices).
1985	The Inmos T414 Transputer, the first 'off the shelf' RISC microprocessor for building parallel computers.

Earth Sciences

Earth Sciences has emerged in recent years as an enlightened synthesis of several traditional disciplines such as geology, meteorology, oceanography, geophysics and geochemistry. Its importance is increasingly being recognized in that, like its biological counterpart ecology, the scientific study of our planet's structure and its past will hold the key to how we affect its future. Humans are in an ever-increasing position of power over global aspects of nature, and in order to ensure our future we must learn to preserve and conserve the earth and use its resources in a sustainable way. The mining and extraction of metals and minerals and gems, the prediction of weather and earthquakes, the pollution of the atmosphere and the 'greenhouse effect', and the gigantic forces that shaped the world we live in, all fall within the scope of Earth Sciences.

This section contains a look back at *Ice Ages*, and a digest of the exciting recently-developed concepts of continental drift and plate tectonics – *The Changing Earth*. There are explanations of *Geological Terms*, the workings of *Atmosphere and Weather*, and *Mapping Earth's Surface*. In addition there are definitions of *Geological Features*, plus a brief look at our planet's *Mineral Wealth*. Complementary material, from the viewpoint of human wants, can be found in the section on Resources under the general heading Society.

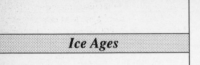

sheet spread over N Europe, reaching Ireland and the Atlantic, leaving its remains as far south as Switzerland. Formerly there were thought to have been only three or four such periods, but recent research has shown about 20 major incidences. For example, ocean-bed cores record the absence or presence in their various layers of such cold-loving small marine animals as radiolaria, which indicate a fall in

THE GEOLOGICAL TIME CHART

Millions of Years ago	Begins Period		Era	Eon
1.8	Quarternary		Cenezoic	Phanerozoic
5	Plicocene			
22.5	Miocene			
38	Oligocene	Tertiary		
54	Eocene			
65	Palaeocene			
141	Cretaceous		Mesozoic	
195	Jurassic			
230	Triassic			
280	Permian		Palaeozoic	
345	Carboniferous			
395	Devonian			
435	Silurian			
500	Ordovician			
570	Cambrian			
2500	Pre-Cambrian			Proterozoic
				Archaean

Ice Age any period of glaciation occurring in the earth's history but most commonly in the Pleistocene period, immediately preceding historic times. However, other ice ages have occurred throughout geological time. Between ice ages came interglacials, when temperatures rose, ice melted and sea levels rose. Europe and America underwent glacial conditions similar to those of the polar regions today. On the North American continent the glaciers reached as far south as the Great Lakes and the ice

ocean temperature at regular intervals.

The occurrence of an ice age is governed by a combination of factors (the Milankovitch hypothesis): (1) the earth's change of attitude in relation to the sun, that is, the way it tilts in a 41,000 year cycle and at the same time wobbles on its axis in a 22,000–year cycle, making the time of its closest approach to the sun come at different seasons; and (2) the 92,000–year cycle of eccentricity in its orbit round the sun, changing from an elliptical to a near circular orbit, the severest period of an ice age coinciding with the approach to circularity. According to calculations, the ice reached a maximum in the present cycle 6000 years ago. There is a possibility that the ice age is not yet over. It will probably reach another maximum in 60,000 years.

MAJOR ICE AGES

Name (European/US)	date (years ago)
Pleistocene:	
Riss and Wurm/Wisconsin	80,000–10,000
Mindel/Illinoian	550,000–400,000
Gunz/Kansan	900,000–700,000
Danube/Nebraskan	1.7–1.3 million
Permo-Carboniferous	330–250 million
Ordovician	440–430 million
Verangian	615–570 million
Sturtian	820–770 million
Gnejso	940–880 million
Huronian	2,700–1,800 million

The Changing Earth

crust the outermost part of the structure of the earth, consisting of two distinct parts. The *oceanic* crust is on average about 10 km/6.2 mi thick and is fairly even in composition. Beneath a surface sediment lies a layer of basalt, then a layer of gabbro. The composition of the whole oceanic crust shows a high proportion of *si*licon and *ma*gnesium and is given the name *sima* by geologists.

In contrast the *continental* crust is extremely complex. It varies in thickness between about 40 and 70 km/25 and 44 mi, being deeper beneath mountain ranges. It consists of a great many rock types, including a surface layer of sedimentary and volcanic rocks overlying a zone of metamorphic rocks built on a thick layer of granodiorite. *Si*licon and *al*uminium

dominate the composition and the term *sial* is given to continental crustal material. Because of the movements of plate tectonics, the ocean crust is nowhere older than about 200 million years. However parts of the continental crust are more than ten times that age.

mantle the section of the earth's structure between the crust and the core. It is separated from the former by the Mohorovičić discontinuity, and from the latter by the Gutenberg discontinuity. Mantle material is thought to consist of silicates such as olivine and spinel. The patterns of seismic waves passing through it show its lower layers to be solid. However from 75 km to 250 km/45 to 155 mi in depth is a zone through which seismic waves pass more slowly (the 'low velocity zone'). The inference is that materials in this zone are close to their melting points and they are partly molten. The low velocity zone is probably the asthenosphere, on which ride the solid mantle and the crust above it, constituting the rigid plates of the lithosphere.

core the innermost part of the structure of the earth. It is divided into an inner core, the upper boundary of which is 1600 km/940 mi from the centre, and an outer core, 1820 km/1060 mi thick. Both parts are thought to be made of nickel and iron, with the inner core being solid and the outer core being liquid. The temperature may be 3,000°C. These hypotheses are based on seismology (the observation of the paths of earthquake and other vibrational waves through the earth), and calculations of the earth's density.

plate tectonics the concept in earth sciences that attributes continental drift and sea-floor spreading to the continual formation and destruction of huge curved 'plates' making up the crust, the outermost layer of the earth. Convection currents within the earth's mantle produce upwellings of new material along lines at the earth's surface. These lines are the oceanic ridges. The new material forms plates at the surface and these move away from the oceanic ridges. When two plates meet, one rises over the other and the lower is absorbed back into the mantle. These 'subduction zones' occur in ocean trenches. The continents take little part in the generation and destruction of plate material, being made of a lighter substance, and they are carried passively here and there on the moving plates. The concept was first formulated in the mid-1960s, as a modification of Alfred Wegener's early ideas of continental drift, and has gained widespread acceptance amongst earth scientists.

seafloor spreading the growth of the ocean crust outwards (sideways) from oceanic ridges. It was first detected by British geophysicists Vine and Matthews in 1963, when they noted that the floor of the Atlantic ocean was made of rocks that were arranged in strips, each strip being magnetized either normally or reversely (due to changes in the earth's polarity when the North Pole becomes the South Pole and vice versa, termed magnetic reversal). These strips were parallel to one another and to the oceanic ridge. The inference was that each strip was formed at some stage in geological time when the magnetic field was polarized in a certain way. Confirmation came when sediments were discovered to be deeper further away from the oceanic ridge, because they had been in existence longer and had more time to accumulate. Nowadays the concept of seafloor spreading has been incorporated into plate tectonics.

ocean ridge the seabed topographic feature that indicates the presence of a constructive plate margin, where the giant curved plates that make up the earth's surface are formed. Such a ridge can rise many thousands of metres above the surrounding abyssal plain. Such ridges usually have rift valleys along their crests, indicating where the flanks are being pulled apart by the growth of the lithospheric plates beneath. The crests, being made of new rocks, are usually quite free of sediment, while increasing depths of sediment are found with increasing distances down the flanks.

ocean trench the seabed topographic feature that indicates the presence of a destructive plate margin, where the giant curved plates that make up the earth's surface are destroyed. The under-riding (subduction) of one plate beneath an adjacent one means that the bed of

the ocean is dragged downwards. Oceanic trenches are found around the edge of the Pacific Ocean and the north-east Indian Ocean, with minor ones in the Caribbean and near the Falkland Islands. They represent the deepest parts of the ocean floor, the deepest being the Marianas Trench with a depth of 11,022 m/36,160 ft.

rift valley a valley formed by the subsidence of a block of the earth's crust between two or more parallel faults. Rift valleys are usually steep-sided and form where the crust is being pulled apart, as at oceanic ridges, or in the Great Rift Valley that runs roughly north–south in East Africa.

continental drift theory in geology first **continental drift**

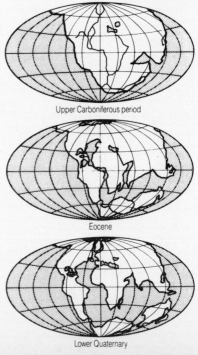

Upper Carboniferous period

Eocene

Lower Quaternary

proposed by Alfred Wegener (German meteorologist and geophysicist 1880–1930) that the earth consisted some 200 million years ago of a single large continent, which he called *Pangaea,* and which subsequently broke apart to form the continents as we know them today. The theory of plate tectonics has provided a convincing explanation of how such vast movement may have occurred.

seismology the study of earthquakes and how their shock waves travel through the earth. By examining the global pattern of waves produced by an earthquake, seismologists can deduce the nature of the materials through which they have passed. This leads to an understanding of the earth's internal structure. On a smaller scale artificial earthquake

waves, generated by explosions or mechanical vibrators, can be used to search for subsurface features in, for example, oil or mineral exploration.

tremor a small-intensity earthquake.

earthquake a shaking or convulsion of the earth's surface, the scientific study of which is called seismology. Earthquakes result from a build-up of stresses within rocks until strained to fracturing point. Most occur along faults (fractures or breaks) in the earth's strata. These tectonic earthquakes are the greatest and most wide-spread in their effects. The great majority are under the sea. The magnitude of an earthquake is measured on the Richter scale. The point at which an earth-

earthquake belts

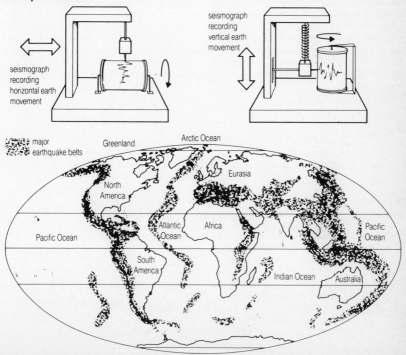

seismograph recording horizontal earth movement

seismograph recording vertical earth movement

major earthquake belts

Greenland | Arctic Ocean

North America

Eurasia

Atlantic Ocean | Africa

Pacific Ocean

South America

Indian Ocean | Australia

Pacific Ocean

quake originates is the *seismic focus*. The point on earth's surface directly above this is the *epicentre* . The possibility of prediction is being investigated by measurement of underground pressure waves and the study of such phenomena as the change of gases in the crust, the level of water in wells and the behaviour of animals. The possibility of earthquake prevention is remote.

epicentre the point on the earth's surface immediately above the focus of an earthquake. Most damage usually takes place at an earthquake's epicentre. It is also used to refer to a point directly above or below a nuclear explosion ('ground zero').

tidal wave a misleading name for a tsunami.

tsunami a giant wave generated by an undersea earthquake or other disturbance. In the open ocean it may take the form of several successive waves, travelling at tens of kilometres per hour but with an amplitude of only a metre or so, hence usually unnoticed by ships at sea. In the coastal shallows, however, the tsunami slows down and increases in height, producing a towering wave tens of metres high that can sweep far inland with great loss of life and property. Before each wave there may be a sudden unexpected withdrawal of water from the coast. Tsunami is a Japanese word meaning 'harbour wave'. A common term for the phenomenon is, misleadingly, a 'tidal wave'.

Mercalli scale the scale used to measure the *intensity* of an earthquake. (It differs from the Richter scale in that the latter measures *magnitude*.) Intensity is a subjective value, based on observed phenomena, and varies from place to place with the same earthquake. It was named after the Italian seismologist Giuseppe Mercalli (1850–1914).

Richter scale a scale of the *magnitude* of an earthquake. (Magnitude differs from the intensity which is measured by the Mercalli scale.) The magnitude is a function of the total amount of energy released, and each point on the Richter scale represents a ten-fold increase in energy over the previous point. The scale is named after its originator, the American seismologist Charles Richter (1900–85).

MERCALLI SCALE

Intensity value	Desription
I	only detected by instrument
II	felt by people resting
III	felt indoors; hanging objects swing; feels like passing traffic
IV	feels like passing heavy traffic; standing cars rock; windows, dishes and doors rattle; wooden frames creak
V	felt outdoors; sleepers woken; liquids spill; doors swing
VI	felt by everybody; people stagger; windows break; trees and bushes rustle; weak plaster cracks
VII	difficult to stand upright; noticed by vehicle drivers; plaster, loose bricks, tiles and chimneys fall; bells ring
VIII	car steering affected; some collapse of masonry; chimney stacks and towers fall; branches break from trees; cracks in wet ground
IX	general panic; serious damage to buildings; underground pipes break; cracks and subsidence in ground
X	most buildings destroyed; landslides; water thrown out of canals
XI	rails bent; underground pipes totally destroyed
XII	damage nearly total; rocks displaced; objects thrown into air

RICHTER SCALE

Magnitude value	Relative amount of energy released	Notable examples
1		
2		
3		
4	1	Carlisle, 1979 (a significant one for Britain)
5	30	San Francisco
6	100	San Fernando, 1971
7	30,000	Chimbote
8	1,000,000	Tangsham, 1976
		San Francisco, 1906
		Lisbon, 1755 Alaska, 1964

Geological Terms

geology the science of the earth, its origin, composition, structure, and history. It is divided into several branches: mineralogy deals with the minerals of the earth: petrology deals with rocks; stratigraphy deals with the deposition of successive beds of sedimentary rocks; palaeontology deals with fossils; and tectonics deals with the deformation and movement of the earth's crust.

THE MAJOR BRANCHES

'Hard rock' geology	petrology - igneous and metamorphic rocks
	mineralogy - minerals
	geochemistry - matter
	geophysics - energy
'Soft rock' geology	petrology - sedimentary rocks
	palaeontology - fossils
	stratigraphy - dating and sequence of beds (strata)
	sedimentology - deposition of sediments
Structural geology	the structures of rock
Geormorphology	landscapes, their formation and destruction

petrology the study of rocks, their mineral composition and their origins.

stratigraphy the sequence of formation of layers or beds (strata) in sedimentary rocks, and the conditions under which they formed. It involves the investigation of sedimentary structures to determine ancient geographies and environments, and the study of fossils for identifying and dating particular beds.

tectonics the study of the movements of the rocks. On a small scale, tectonics involves the formation of folds and faults. On the large scale it deals with the movements of vast regions of the earth's surface (plate tectonics).

uniformitarianism the principle that 'the present is the key to the past'. In other words, the processes that can be seen operating at the earth's surface today are the same as those that have operated throughout geological time. For example, desert sandstone rocks containing sand-dune formations formed in the past under conditions similar to those operating in pres-ent-day deserts. The principle was formulated by pioneer geologist James Hutton.

igneous rock a rock formed from cooling magma or lava, and solidifying from a molten state. Igneous rocks are classified according to

363

their feldspar character, grain size, texture and chemical composition.

IGNEOUS ROCKS

Particle size

Oxygen content	Coarse (plutonic)	Medium	Fine (volcanic)
less than 45% *(ultrabasic)*	peridotite kimberlite		
45-52% *(basic)*	gabbro	dolerite	basalt
52-66% *(intermediate)*	diorite seyenite		andesite trachyte
more than 66% *(acid)*	granite		chyolite

metamorphic rock a rock altered in structure and composition by pressure and heat although it does not melt (in which case it would be an igneous rock).

METAMORPHIC ROCKS

Main primary material (before metamorphisis)

typical depth and temperature of formation	shale with several minerals	sandstone with only quartz	limestone with only calcite
15 km 300°C	slate	quartzite	marble
20 km 400°C	schist		
25 km 500°C	gneiss		
30 km 600°C	hornfels	quartzite	marble

sedimentary rock a rock formed by the accumulation and cementation of particles, usually in water and under gravity.

bed in geology, the unitary 'building block' of sedimentary rock. A bed consists of a simple layer of rock, often separated above and below from other beds by well defined partings called bedding planes. It can be from a millimetre to many metres thick, and can extend over any area. Also used to indicate the floor beneath a body of water (lake bed) and a layer formed by a fall of particles (lava bed).

erosion the processes whereby the rocks and soil of the earth's surface are loosened, worn away and transported (the often confused term, weathering, does not involve trans-

portation). There are two forms - chemical and physical. Chemical erosion involves the altera tion of the mineral component of the rock, by means of rainwater or the substances dissolved in it, and its subsequent movement. The decay of granite by the conversion of its feldspar minerals into china clay by carbonic acid in rainwater, and the dissolving of limestone in caves and potholes, are examples. Physical erosion involves the breakdown and transportation of exposed rocks by physical forces. The shattering of cliff-faces in mountainous areas by the expansion of frost in the rock cracks, and the movement of boulders in an avalanche, are examples. In practice the two work together. Water, consisting of sea waves and currents, rivers and rain; ice, in the form of glaciers, frost and melting snow; and wind, hurling sand fragments against exposed rocks and moving dunes along, are the most potent forces of erosion.

intrusion a mass of igneous rock that has

formed by 'injection' of molten rock into existing cracks beneath the surface of the earth, as distinct from a volcanic rock mass which has erupted from the surface.

lava the molten material exuded from a volcano which cools to form extrusive igneous rock. Lava differs from its parent magma in that the fluid 'fractionates' on its way to the surface of the earth, that is, certain heavy or high-temperature minerals settle out and the constituent gases form bubbles and boil away into the atmosphere. A lava high in silica is very stiff and does not flow far, while low-silica lava can flow for long distances.

or sand, or consolidated into a hard mass as an igneous, sedimentary or metamorphic rock.

strata (singular: stratum) layers or beds of sediment or sedimentary rocks, usually well defined and separated from each other by bedding planes. Strata form horizontally under gravity, but large-scale crust movements may tilt, crack, twist or even invert them. After being buried beneath other rocks, erosion or earthquakes or the processes of mountain-building may expose them at the surface. Their study is termed stratigraphy.

weathering the process by which exposed rocks are broken down by the action of rain,

WEATHERING

Physical weathering	*temperature changes* - weaking rocks by expansion and contraction
	frost - wedging rocks apart by the expansion of water on freezing
	rain - making loose slopes unstable
	wind - wearing away rocks by sandblasting, and moving sand dunes along
	unloading - the loosening of rock layers by release of pressure after the erosion and removal of those layers above
Chemical weathering	*carbonation* - the breakdown of calcite by reaction with carbonic acid in rainwater
	hydrolysis - the breakdown of feldspar into china clay by reaction with carbonic acid in rainwater
	oxidation - the breakdown of iron-rich minerals due to rusting
	hydration - the expansion of certain minerals due to the uptake of water
Gravity	*soil creep* - the slow downslope movement of surface material
	landslide - the raid downward movement of solid material
	avalanche - scouring by ice, snow, and accumulated debris
Rivers	*abrasion* - wearing away stream beds and banks by trundling boulders along
	corrosion - the wear on the boulders themselves as they are carried along
Glaciers	deepening of valleys by the weight of ice
	scouring of rock surfaces by embedded rocky debris
Sea	*hydraulic effect* - expansion of air pockets in rocks and cliffs by constant hammering by waves
	abrasion and corrosion - see **Rivers**

magma molten material beneath the earth's surface from which igneous rocks are formed. This may not be the same as lava extruded at the surface, since as magma rises to form lava it may distill off some its gaseous components, and some of its solids may crystallize before eruption.

rock the constituent of the earth's crust, either in its unconsolidated form as clay, mud,

frost, wind and the other elements of the weather. Two types of weathering are recognized. The first is *physical* weathering. This involves such effects as frost wedging, in which water trapped in a rock crack expands on freezing and splits the rock. The second type is *chemical* weathering. The carbon dioxide in the atmosphere combines with the rain water to produce weak carbonic acid, which may

365

react with certain minerals in the rocks and break them down. The two types of weathering usually go hand-in-hand. Indeed, in some cases it is still not clear which type is involved. For example, 'onion-skin' weathering that produces rounded inselbergs in arid regions, such as Ayers Rock in central Australia, may be caused by the daily physical expansion and contraction of the surface rock layers in the heat of the sun. Or it may be caused by the chemical reaction of the minerals just beneath the surface with the infrequent rains.

Atmosphere and Weather

meteorology the scientific observation and study of the phenomena of weather and climate. At meteorological stations readings are taken of the more important factors determining weather conditions. Atmospheric pressure is measured by a mercury barometer, temperature by a screened thermometer, and humidity by a hydrometer, which expresses relative humidity as a percentage of the maximum. Winds are categorized by the Beaufort Scale, and the Beaufort weather code signifies every weather condition by suitable initials, with capitals denoting intensity. Cloud observations gauge how many tenths of sky are covered by each type, and rainfall is collected by a funnel and measured each 12 hours. Specially equipped weather ships maintained by several nations, including Britain, at a number of ocean stations, report on weather conditions and advise air traffic. They carry radar and twice daily make balloon soundings of wind, temperatures and humidity. Increasing costs have reduced their number, and there is growing reliance on reports from satellites which signal back a wide range of information, and on a broader basis, but offering some practical difficulties of interpretation. All these data are reported to, and collated by, central agencies, such as the Meteorological Office, London, and US Weather Bureau, Washington. They are then pooled on an international basis. Computers have enabled a promising start to be made in the stupendous task of using physical laws to calculate the future trend and to give long-range weather forecasts.

weather the day-to-day variations of meteorological and climatic conditions at a particular place.

climate weather conditions at a particular place over a period of time. Climate encompasses all the meteorological elements and the factors that influence them. The primary factors that determine the variations of climate over the surface of the earth are (a)the effect of latitude and the tilt of the earth's axis to the plane of the orbit about the sun (66.5°); (b)the difference between land and sea; (c) contours of the ground; and (d) location of the area in relation to ocean currents. Climate types were first classified by Vladimir Köppen in 1918. The complexity of the distribution of land and sea, and the consequent complexity of the general circulation of the atmosphere, makes the distribution of the climate extremely complicated. Centred on the equator is a belt of tropical rain-forest which may be either constantly wet or monsoonal, that is, seasonal with wet and dry seasons in each year. Bordering each side of this is a belt of savannah, with lighter rainfall and less dense vegetation. After this usually comes a transition through steppe (semi-arid) to desert (arid), with a further transition through steppe to Mediterranean climate with dry summer, followed by the moist temperate climate of middle latitudes. Next comes a zone of cold climate with moist winter, but where the desert extends into middle latitudes the zones of Mediterranean and moist temperate climates are missing, and the transition is from desert to a cold climate with moist winter. In the extreme E of Asia a cold climate with dry winters extends from about 7° N to 3° N. The polar caps have tundra and ice-cap climates, with little or no precipitation. Catastrophic variations to climate may be caused by the impact of another planetary body, or clouds resulting from volcanic activity.

isobar a line drawn on maps and weather charts linking all places with the same atmospheric pressure (usually measured in millibars) at a given time. When used in weather forecasting, the distance between the isobars is an indication of the barometric gradient. Where they are close together cyclonic weather is indicated, bringing strong winds and a depression, and where far apart anticyclonic bringing fine weather and lighter winds. The pressures indicated on the meteorological charts have generally been corrected to sea-level.

isotherm a line on a map linking all places having the same temperature at a given time.

cyclone an area of low atmospheric pressure. Cyclones are formed by the mixture of cold, dry polar air with warm, moist equatorial air. These masses of air meet in temperate latitudes; the warm air rises over the cold, resulting in rain. Winds blow in towards the centre in an anti-clockwise direction in the northern hemisphere, clockwise in the southern hemisphere; the systems are characterized by variable weather, and are common over the British Isles. They bring rain or snow, winds up to gale force, low cloud, and sometimes fog. Tropical cyclones are a great danger to shipping (the tornado is a rapidly moving cyclone). In middle high latitudes low-pressure systems are referred to as depressions or lows; the term cyclone is avoided.

anticyclone an area of high atmospheric pressure are caused by descending air, which becomes warm and dry. Winds radiate from a calm centre, taking a clockwise direction in the northern hemisphere, and an anticlockwise direction in the southern hemisphere. Anticyclones are associated with clear weather and distinguished by the absence of rain and violent winds. In summer they bring hot, sunny days and in winter they bring fine, frosty spells, although fog and low cloud are not uncommon.

depression in meteorology, a cyclonic area or 'low' – a region of low atmospheric pressure.

In the midlatitudes (such as the UK) they are usually associated with wet, windy, unsettled weather.

front in meteorology, the interface between two air masses of different temperature or humidity. Fronts are usually found when warm air from one region of the earth's surface meets cold air from another. Warm air, being lighter, tends to rise above the cold; its moisture is carried upwards and usually falls as rain or snow - hence the changeable weather conditions at fronts. Fronts are rarely stationary but move with the air masses. A warm front brings warm air into an area occupied by cold air; a cold front does the reverse.

current the flow of a body of water or air moving in a definite direction. Oceanic currents may be: *drift currents*, broad and slow-moving; *stream currents*, narrow and swift-moving, e.g. Gulf Stream and Kuroshio/Japan Current; *upwelling currents* which bring cold, nutrient-rich water from the ocean bottom to provide food for plankton, which in turn supports fish and sea birds, such as Gulf of Guinea Current and the Peru (Humboldt) Current. Once in ten years or so, the latter, which runs from the Antarctic up the W coast of South America, turns warm, with heavy rain and rough seas, and has disastrous results (as in 1982–3) for the Peruvian anchovy industry and wildlife.

Coriolis effect named after its discoverer, French mathematician Gaspard Coriolis 1792–1843, it results from the deflective force of the earth's W-to-E rotation. Winds and ocean currents are deflected to the right in the N and to the left in the S hemisphere. It has to be allowed for in launching guided missiles, but has negligible effect on the clockwise or anticlockwise direction of water running out of a bath.

weather areas divisions of the sea areas around Great Britain for the purpose of weather forecasting for shipping, particularly to indicate where strong and gale-force winds are expected.

atmosphere the mixture of gases which surrounds the earth, prevented from escaping

weather areas

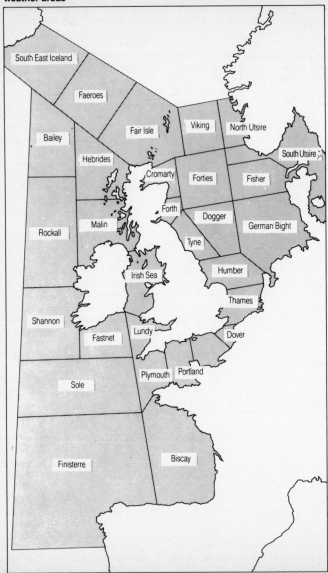

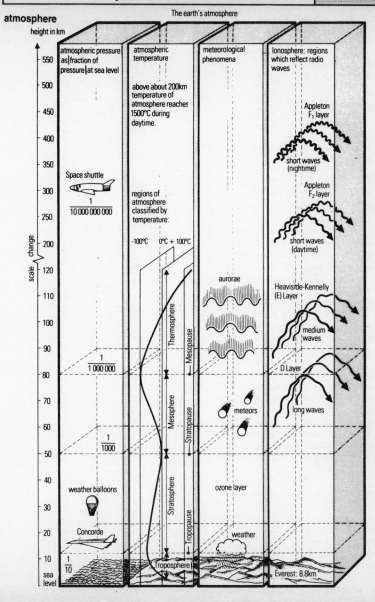

atmosphere

The earth's atmosphere

height in km

atmospheric pressure as fraction of pressure at sea level

atmospheric temperature

meteorological phenomena

Ionosphere: regions which reflect radio waves

above about 200km temperature of atmosphere reaches 1500°C during daytime.

Appleton F₁ layer

short waves (nighttime)

Space shuttle

$\dfrac{1}{10\ 000\ 000\ 000}$

Appleton F₂ layer

regions of atmosphere classified by temperature:

short waves (daytime)

-100°C   0°C +100°C

scale change

aurorae

Heaviside-Kennelly (E) Layer

Thermosphere

Mesopause

medium waves

$\dfrac{1}{1\ 000\ 000}$

D Layer

Mesosphere

Stratopause

long waves

meteors

$\dfrac{1}{1000}$

Stratosphere

weather balloons

ozone layer

Tropopause

Concorde

$\dfrac{1}{10}$

weather

Troposphere

sea level

Everest: 8.8km

369

by the pull of the earth's gravity. As we go higher in the atmosphere, a small and smaller fraction of it is 'resting' above us, so atmospheric pressure decreases. In its lowest layer, the *troposphere*, the atmospheric pressure consists of nitrogen (78%) and oxygen (21%), both in molecular form (two atoms bound together). The other 1% is largely argon, but there are very small quantities of other gases, as well as water vapour. The troposphere is heated by the earth, which is warmed by infra-red and visible radiation from the sun. Warm air rises in the troposphere, cooling as it does so. This is the primary cause of rain and most other weather phenomena.

cloud water vapour condensed into minute water particles which float in masses in the atmosphere. Like fogs or mists, from which clouds are distinguished by the height at which they occur above the ground, they are formed by the cooling of air charged with water vapour which condenses on tiny dust particles. Clouds are usually classified according to the height at which they occur and their shape.

fog cloud that collects at the surface of the earth, composed of water vapour which has condensed on particles of dust in the atmosphere. Cloud and fog are both caused by the air temperature falling below dew point. The thickness of fog is dependent on the number of water particles it contains. Usually, fog is formed by the meeting of two currents of air, one cooler than the other, or by warm air flowing over a cold surface. Sea fogs commonly occur where warm and cold currents meet, and the air above them mixes. Fog frequently forms on calm nights over the land, as the land surface cools more rapidly than the air immediately above it. Officially, fog refers to a condition when visibility is reduced to 1 km/0.62 mi or less, and mist or haze to that giving a visibility of 1–2 kilometres. A mist is produced by condensed water particles, and a haze by smoke or dust.

smog a natural fog containing impurities (unburned carbon and sulphur dioxide) from domestic fires, industrial furnaces and certain power stations, and internal combustion

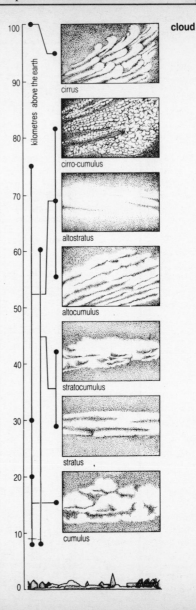

cloud

cirrus

cirro-cumulus

altostratus

altocumulus

stratocumulus

stratus

cumulus

kilometres above the earth

engines (petrol or diesel). The use of smoke-less fuels, the treatment of effluent and penalties for excessive smoke from poorly maintained and operated vehicles can be extremely effective in cutting down smog. It can cause substantial illness and loss of life, particularly among chronic bronchitics, and damage to wildlife.

precipitation the meteorological term for water that falls to earth from the atmosphere. As such it covers rain, snow, sleet, hail, dew and hoar frost.

rain precipitation in the form of separate drops of water that fall to the earth's surface from clouds. The drops are formed by the accumulation of droplets that condense from water vapour in the air. The condensation is

(with records of over 400 mm). It is caused by the circulation of moisture in strong convection currents, usually within cumulonimbus-type cloud. Water droplets freeze as they are carried upwards. Further layers of ice are deposited around this nucleus as the circulation continues, until they become too heavy to be supported by the currents and they fall as a hailstorm.

frost condition of the weather when the air temperature is below freezing 0°C/32°F. Water in the atmosphere then freezes and crystallizes on the ground or exposed objects. As cold air is heavier than warm, *ground frosts* are more common than *hoar frost*, which is formed by the condensation of water particles in the same way as dew collects.

BEAUFORT SCALE

Number	Description	Features	Air speed mi per hr	m per sec
0	calm	smoke rises vertically; water smooth	less than 1	less than 0.3
1	light air	smoke shows wind direction; water ruffled	1-3	0.3-1.5
2	slight breeze	leaves rustle; wind felt on face	4-7	1.6-3.3
3	gentle breeze	loose paper blows around	8-12	3.4-5.4
4	moderate breeze	branches sway	13-18	5.5-7.9
5	fresh breeze	small trees sway, leaves blown off	19-24	8.0-10.7
6	strong breeze	whistling in telephone wire; sea spray from waves	25-31	10.8-13.8
7	moderate gale	large trees sway	32-38	13.9-17.1
8	fresh gale	twigs break from trees	39-46	17.2-20.7
9	strong gale	branches break from trees	47-54	20.8-24.4
10	whole gale	trees uprooted, weak buildings collapse	55-63	14.5-28.4
11	storm	widesread damage	64-72	28.5-32.6
12	hurricane	widespread structural damage	Above 73	Above 32.7

usually brought about by cooling, either when the air rises over a mountain range or when, being a warm air mass, it rises above a cooler air mass.

hail precipitation in the form of pellets of ice, typically of a few millimetres' diameter

snow flaked particles caused by the condensation in air of excess water vapour below freezing point. Light reflecting in the crystals, which have a basic hexagonal (six-sided) geometry, gives snow a white appearance.

dew moisture that collects on the ground

during clear, calm nights, particularly after a warm day. As temperature falls during the night the air and the water vapour in it become chilled. Condensation takes place on the cooled surfaces of grass, leaves, etc. When the moisture begins to form, the surrounding air is said to have reached its dew-point. If the temperature falls below freezing point during the night, the dew will freeze, or if the temperature is low and the dew-point is below freezing point, the water vapour condenses directly into ice; in both cases hoar frost is formed.

wind a lateral movement of the earth's atmosphere. Although modified by features such as land and water, there is a basic worldwide system. A belt of low pressure (the doldrums) lies along the equator. The Trade Winds blow towards this from the Horse Latitudes (high pressure areas 3° N and 3° S of the equator), blowing from the NE in the northern hemisphere, and from the SE in the southern. The *Westerlies* (also from the Horse Latitudes) blow from the SW north of the equator and from the NW to the south. Cold winds blow outwards from high-pressure areas at the poles. More local effects result from the land heating and cooling faster than the adjacent sea, producing onshore winds in the daytime and offshore winds at night.

Beaufort scale system of recording wind velocity, devised in 1806 by Admiral Sir Francis Beaufort (1774–1857), who became hydrographer to the Royal Navy in 1829. It is a numerical scale ranging from 0 to 17, calm being indicated by 0 and a hurricane by 12; 13–17 indicate degrees of hurricane force. In 1874 it received international recognition; it was modified in 1926. Measurements are made at 10 m above ground level.

tornado an extremely violent revolving storm, caused by a rising column of warm air propelled by strong wind. The diameter of the tornado may be a few hundred metres or less, but it rises to a great height, and is marked by swirling funnel-shaped clouds. Tornadoes moving at speeds of up to 400 kph/250 mph are common in the Mississippi basin and cause

great destruction. The most severe tornadoes are always accompanied by thunderstorms.

tornado

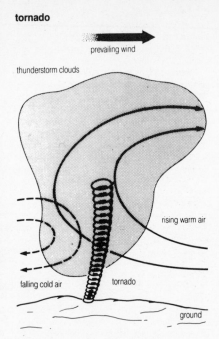

prevailing wind

thunderstorm clouds

rising warm air

falling cold air   tornado

ground

typhoon a violent revolving storm occurring chiefly in autumn along the eastern seaboard of Asia between the Philippines and Japan. Typhoon is the local term for hurricane.

hurricane a revolving storm in tropical regions. A hurricane begins between 1° and 2° N or S of the equator and moves westwards. A central calm area, called the eye, is surrounded by inwardly spiralling winds of up to 320 kph/200 mph. A hurricane is accompanied by lighting and torrential rain and can cause extensive damage and loss of life along the western shores of tropical oceans. In meteorology a hurricane is a wind of force 12 or more on the Beaufort scale.

Mapping Earth's Surface

map a diagrammatic representation, for example, of part of the earth's surface or the distribution of the stars. Modern maps are made using aerial photography; a series of overlapping stereoscopic photographs are taken which can then be used to prepare a three-dimensional image. Laser beams, microwaves, and infra-red equipment are also used for land surveying, and satellite pictures make a valuable contribution when large areas are under survey.

projection in cartography, the means of depicting the spherical surface of the earth on a flat piece of paper. The theory is that, if a light were placed at the centre of a transparent earth, the surface features could be thrown as shadows on a piece of paper placed close to the surface. This paper may be flat and placed on a pole (azimuthal or zenithal), or may be rolled cylindrically around the equator (cylindrical), or may be in the form of a tall cone resting on the equator (conical). The resulting maps differ from one another, distorting either area or direction, and each is suitable for a particular purpose. For example, projections distorting area the least are used for distribution maps, and those with least distortion of direction are used for navigation charts. The Flemish map-maker Gerhard Kremer 1512–94 devised *Mercator's projection* in which the parallels and meridians on maps are drawn uniformly at 9°. The true area of countries is increasingly distorted the farther N and S they are from the Equator.

poles The geographic N and S points of penetration of the earth's surface by the axis about which it rotates. The magnetic poles are the points towards which a freely suspended magnetic needle will point, and they vary continually; in 1985 the magnetic North Pole was some 350 km/218 mi NW of Resolute Bay in Canada's Northwest Territories. It moves northwards c.10 km/6 mi each year, although it can vary in a day by about 80 km/50 mi from its average position. It is relocated every decade in order to update navigational charts. Periodic changes within the earth's core cause a reversal of the magnetic poles (the last occasion was 700,000 years ago), and it is calculated that in about 1200 years' time the N magnetic pole will become the S magnetic pole. Many animals, including migrating birds and fish, are thought to orientate themselves partly using the earth's magnetic field.

latitude and longitude *latitude* is the angular distance of any point from the equator, measured N or S along the earth's curved surface, equalling the angle between the respective horizontal planes. It is measured in degrees, minutes, and seconds, each minute equalling one sea-mile (1.85 km) in length. *Longitude* is the angle between the terrestrial meridian drawn from the pole, through a place, and a standard meridian now taken at Greenwich, England. All determinations of longitude are based on the earth turning through 36° in 24 hours, or the sun reaching 1° W each hour. At the equator one degree of longitude measures about 112 km/70 mi.

nautical mile a unit of distance used in navigation. It equals the average length of one minute of arc on a great circle of the earth. In the United Kingdom it was formerly defined as 6080 feet. The International Nautical Mile is now defined as 1852 m.

Arctic Circle an arbitrary line drawn round the North Pole at 66°33' N. The region N of this line experiences at least one night during the northern summer when the sun never sets ('midnight sun'), and at least one day during the northern winter when the sun never rises. The Arctic Ocean, which occupies much of the Arctic Circle, is frozen to great depths in winter; there is no land beneath it, as there is under the South Pole's Antarctic ice cap.

Antarctic Circle an imaginary line that runs round the South Pole at latitude 66°33' S. The region south of this line experiences at least

map projection

conical

azimuthal

cylindrical: Mercator's projection

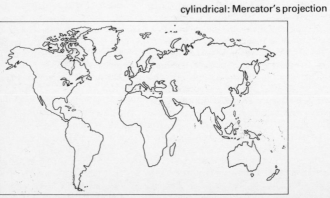

one night during the southern summer during which the sun never sets, and at least one day during the southern winter during which the sun never rises. The line encompasses the continent of Antarctica and the Antarctic Ocean.

equator the *terrestrial equator* is the great circle whose plane is perpendicular to the earth's axis (the line joining the poles). Its length is 40,076 km/24,901.8 mi, divided into 360° of longitude. The *celestial equator* or Equinoctial is the circle in which the plane of the terrestrial equator intersects the celestial sphere.

tropics the tropics of Cancer and Capricorn, defined by the parallels of latitude 23° 28' N and S of the equator, are the limits of the area of earth's surface in which the sun is directly overhead for at least one day each year.

great circle a plane cutting through a sphere, and passing through the centre point of the sphere, cuts the surface along a great circle. Thus, on the earth, all meridians of longitude are half great circles; of the parallels of latitude, only the equator is a great circle. The shortest route between two points on the earth's surface is along the arc of a great circle, and these are used extensively in air routes (although on maps, due to vagaries of their projection, they are not straight lines).

meridian a great circle drawn on the earth's surface passing through both poles, and thus through all places with the same longitude. Terrestrial longitudes are usually measured from the Greenwich Meridian.

International Date Line A modification of the 180th meridian which marks the difference in time between E and W. The date is put forward a day when crossing the line going W, and back a day when going E. Much of this line runs through the mid Pacific Ocean, with local deviations around land to avoid having two dates at the same time in an island or nation. The IDL was chosen at the International Meridian Conference in 1884.

Geological Features

archipelago a group of islands, or an area of sea containing a group of islands. The islands of an archipelago are often volcanic in origin, formed either when a hot spot within the earth's mantle produces a chain of volcanoes on the surface, such as the Hawaiian Archipelago, or at a destructive plate margin where the subduction (under-riding) of one plate beneath another produces an arc-shaped island group, such as the Aleutian Archipelago. Alternatively an archipelago may be caused by a rise in sea level flooding a hilly landscape, leaving hills as islands.

caldera in geology, a very large basin-shaped crater. Calderas are found at the tops of volcanoes, where the original peak has collapsed into an empty chamber beneath. The basin, many times larger than the original volcanic vent, may be flooded, producing a crater lake, or the flat floor may contain a number of small volcanic cones, showing where the volcanic activity continued after the collapse.

canyon a deep narrow hollow running through mountains.Canyons are cut by river action, usually in areas of low rainfall, where the river receives water from outside the area.

crater a bowl-shaped topographic feature, usually round and with steep sides. Craters are formed by explosive events such as the eruption of a volcano or by the impact of a meteorite. A caldera is a much larger feature.

delta a triangular tract of land at a river's mouth, formed by deposited silt or sediment. Familiar examples of large deltas are those of the Mississippi, Ganges and Brahmaputra, Rhône, Po, Danube, and Nile; the shape of the last-named is like the Greek letter Δ, and thus gave rise to the name.

desert area without sufficient vegetation to

support human life. Scientifically this term includes the ice areas of the polar regions, although a desert is generally thought of as restricted to the earth's warmer zones particularly at the latitudes of the tropics. The tropical desert belts are caused by the descent of dry air that has already risen and dropped its water at the equator.

Deserts constitute almost a third of the earth's land surface and may have existed from time immemorial, or be created by changes in climate, or by the human-aided process of desertification, including over-grazing, destruction of timber shelter belts, and the overpopulation which leads to exhaustion of the soil by too intensive cultivation without restoration of fertility.

dune a bank or hill of wind-drifted sand. Loose sand is blown and bounced along by the wind, up the windward side of a dune. The sand particles then fall to rest on the lee side, while more are blown up from the windward. In this way a dune moves gradually downwind. Dunes are seen in sandy deserts and along beaches.

fault in geology, a crack in a rock along which the two sides have evidently moved, due to differing strains in the adjacent rock bodies. Displacement of rock masses horizontally or vertically along a fault may be microscopic, or they may be massive causing major earthquakes.

glacier a mass of ice which originates in mountains in the snowfields above the snow-line, where the annual snowfall exceeds the annual melting and drainage. Under the weight of the layers above, the snow compacts to ice, and under pressure the ice can move plastically (glacier flow). It moves slowly down a valley or depression, and is constantly replenished from its source.

hot spot in geology, a hypothetical region of high thermal activity in the earth's mantle. It is believed to be the origin of many chains of ocean islands, such as Polynesia (including Hawaii) and the Galapagos. A volcano forms on the ocean crust immediately above the hot spot, is carried away by plate tectonic movement, and becomes extinct. A new volcano forms beside it, above the hot spot. The result is an active volcano and a chain of increasingly old and eroded volcanic stumps stretching away in the direction of plate movement.

lake body of still water lying in depressed ground without direct communication with the sea. Lakes are common in glaciated mountain regions, along the course of gently declining rivers, and in low land near the sea. The main classifications are by origin as follows: *glacial lakes* such as in the Alps; *barrier lakes* formed by landslides, valley glaciers, etc.; *crater lakes*; *tectonic lakes* occurring in natural features.

mesa a flat-topped mountain with steep cliff sides, particularly those found in the desert areas of the USA and Mexico.

mountain a large-scale topographic feature where the earth's surface rises to great heights with steep sides and a narrow top (summit). Height is either relative (in relation to the local surroundings) or absolute (usually taken as height above sea level). The distinction between high hills and low mountains is vague and depends on local topography, generally occurring at around 1000 m/3300 ft. The tallest land mountain is Mount Everest, in the Himalaya range, at 8848 m/29,028 ft above sea level.

peninsula a tongue of land surrounded on three sides by water but still attached to a larger landmass. The state of Florida, USA, is a classic example.

river a body of water, larger than a stream, that flows downwards along a particular course. It originates at a point called its source, and enters the sea or a lake at its mouth. Along its length it may be joined by smaller rivers called tributaries, all these together forming the river system.

Mineral Wealth

mineralogy the study of minerals. The classification of minerals is chiefly based on their chemical constitution, *viz.* metallic, ionic, and molecular. In addition, their crystallographic and physical characters, their mode of formation and occurrence form part of the study. In the case of minerals of economic importance a knowledge of mining and metallurgy is also needed.

Mohs scale a scale useful in mineral identification because any mineral will scratch any other mineral lower on the scale than itself, and similarly it will be scratched by any other mineral higher on the scale.

MOHS SCALE

Number	Defining mineral	Other substances compared
1	talc	
2	gypsum	2½ fingernail
3	calcite	3½ copper coin
4	fluorite	
5	apatite	5½ steel blade
6	orthoclase	5¾ glass
7	quartz	7 steel file
8	topaz	
9	corundum	
10	diamond	

The scale is not regular; diamond, at number 10, the hardest natural substance, is 90 times harder in absolute terms than corundum, number 9.

gem a mineral precious by virtue of its composition, hardness and rarity, cut and polished for ornamental use, or engraved. Of 120 minerals known to have been used as gemstones, only about 25 are in common use in jewellery; of these, the diamond, emerald, ruby, and sapphire are classified as precious, and the topaz, amethyst, opal, aquamarine, etc., as semi-precious.

diamond a precious gem stone, the hardest natural substance known (10 on Mohs scale). Composed of carbon and with a chemical formula C, it crystallizes in the cubic system; other common crystals are octahedra and dodecahedra. Rough diamonds are dull or greasy before being cut, and only some 20% are suitable as gems. Industrial diamonds are used for cutting (for example the tungsten carbide tools used in steel mills are themselves cut with diamond tools), grinding, polishing. Diamonds act as perfectly transparent windows, and do not absorb infrared radiation, hence their use aboard NASA space-probes to Venus in 1978.

emerald green variety of the mineral beryl, $Be_3Al_2Si_6O_{18}$.

ruby the red transparent gem variety of the mineral corundum, Al_2O_3, crystallizing in the hexagonal system; it is without true cleavage. They have been produced artificially and are widely used in lasers.

sapphire the blue transparent gem variety of the mineral corundum, Al_2O_3.

topaz a mineral, fluosilicate of aluminium, $Al_2SiO_4(FOH)_2$. It is usually yellow, or pink if it has been heated, and is used in making jewellery.

amethyst a variety of quartz, SiO_2, coloured violet by the presence of small quantities of manganese, and used as a semi-precious stone.

opal a non-crystalline form of silica, occurring in stalactites in volcanic rocks. The common opal is opaque, milk-white, yellow, red, blue, or green, and lustrous. The precious opal is colourless, having innumerable cracks from which emanate brilliant colours produced by minute crystals of cristobalite.

aquamarine a blue variety of the mineral beryl $Be_3Al_2Si_6O_{18}$.

377

Life Sciences

Life Sciences has emerged in recent years as an enlightened synthesis of several traditional disciplines including biology, zoology, and botany, and newer, more specialized areas of study such as biophysics and sociobiology. The scientific study of the living world as a whole has led to many new ideas and discoveries, as well as to an emphasis on ecology, the study of living organisms in their natural environment. This approach reflects our growing awareness that we, as humans, are one small part of the living world, and that we have ever-increasing power to conserve or destroy, or even create, life as we choose.

This section begins with an overview of the *Main Branches* of the life sciences, and then looks at different topics in turn: *Evolutionary Biology* deals with theories of the origins of life; *Reproduction and the Life Cycle* looks at the processes by which life continues on earth; *Ecology and Resources* looks at the relationships between life and the environment as a whole and at positive ways in which conservation can be practised; *Order in the Living World* deals with the classification of different forms of life; *The Microscopic World* looks at the smallest elements of life. These are followed by overviews of *Animals* and *Plants*, *Biographies* of people who have made important contributions to the life sciences, and a look at *The New Synthesis* of classical genetics and the new science of molecular biology, including key terms.

Main Branches

biology the science of life. The word was first used by the German physician Treviranus in 1802, and was popularized by Lamarck. Strictly speaking, biology includes all the life sciences, for example, anatomy and physiology, cytology, zoology and botany, ecology, genetics, biochemistry and biophysics, animal behaviour, embryology, and plant breeding. Although medical students such as Hippocrates, in the fifth century BC, made the first accurate biological observations, describing medicinally useful plants and their properties, attempts at a scientific physiology were bound to fail in the absence of scientific instruments, a tradition of experiment, and a body of organized knowledge with its own terminology. Only with the Renaissance did free enquiry come into its own. The 16th century saw the production of encyclopaedias of natural history, such as that of Gesner (1516–65), and the beginnings of modern anatomy, notably at Padua under Versalius (1514–64), who was succeeded by Fabricius. William Harvey, a student at the latter, laid the foundation of modern physiology by his work on the circulation of the blood – the first time any basic function of the body had been scientifically explained. Linnaeus introduced a binomial system of classification. During the 19th century, attempts to understand the origins of the great diversity of life forms gave rise to several theories of biological evolution, culminating in Darwin's theory of evolution by natural selection. The ensuing debates over the processes of evolution then stimulated an interest in the new fields of embryology and genetics towards the end of the century. More recently still, the application of the principles of chemistry to organic substances led to developments in biochemistry and molecular biology.

agriculture cultivation of land by humans, developed in Egypt at least 17,000 years ago. Its modernization began in 18th-century Britain, and its mechanization in 19th-century USA. Following World War II, there was an explosive growth in agricultural chemicals – herbicides, insecticides, fungicides, fertilizers; in the 1960s there was development of high-yielding species for special conditions, especially in the *green revolution* in the Third World, and in the industrialized countries cattle and poultry production on 'production lines' and battery systems; in the 1970s there was a movement towards more sophisticated natural methods and a reversion to *organic farming* without chemical sprays and fertilizers; in the 1980s hybridization by genetic engineering methods was developed, and pest control by the use of chemicals plus pheromones.

bioengineering the application of engineering to biology and medicine. Common applications include the design and use of artificial limbs, joints and organs, including hip joints and heart valves.

biophysics the application of physical laws to the properties of living organisms. Examples include using the principles of mechanics to calculate the strength of bones and muscles, and thermodynamics to study plant and animal energetics.

botany the study of plants. It is subdivided into a number of smaller studies, such as the identification and classification of plants (termed taxonomy), their external formation (plant morphology), their internal arrangement (plant anatomy), their microscopic examination (histology), their life history (plant physiology), and their distribution over the earth's surface in relation to their surroundings (plant ecology). Palaeobotany concerns the study of fossil plants, while economic botany deals with the utility of plants. Horticulture, agriculture, and forestry are specialized branches of botany. The most ancient botanical record is carved on the walls of the temple at Karnak, about 1500 BC. The first Greek Herbal was drawn up about 350 BC by

Diocles of Carystus. Botanical information was collected into the works of Theophrastus of Eresus (380–287 BC), a pupil of Aristotle, who founded the technical plant nomenclature. Cesalpino in the 16th century sketched out a system of classification based on flowers, fruits, and seeds, while Jung (1587–1658) used flowers only as his criterion. John Ray (1627–1705) arranged plants systematically, based on his findings on fruit, leaf and flower, and described about 18,600 plants. Swedish Carl von Linné or Linnaeus (1707–78), who founded systematics, included in his classification all known plants and animals, and giving each a binomial descriptive label. Banks, Solander, Brown, Bauer, and others travelled throughout the world studying plants, and found that all could be fitted into a systematic classification based on Linnaeus' work. Linnaeus was also the first to recognize the sexual nature of flowers, this work being followed up later by Sprengel, Amici, Robert Brown, and Charles Darwin. Later work revealed the detailed cellular structure of plant tissues, and the exact nature of photosynthesis. Sachs (1832–97) defined the function of chlorophyll, and the significance of plant stomata. In the period since World War II much has been achieved towards the clarification of cell function, repair and growth by the hybridization of plant cells: the combination of the nucleus of one cell with the protoplasm of another.

embryology the study of the changes undergone by living matter in its early life history, from fertilization to birth or hatching.

ethology the comparative study of animal behaviour in its natural setting, pioneered during the 1930s by K Lorenz and K von Frisch who, along with N Tinbergen, received the Nobel prize in 1973. Ethology is concerned with the causal mechanisms (both the stimuli that elicit behaviour and the physiological mechanisms controlling it), as well as the development of behaviour, its function and evolutionary history. Ethologists believe that the significance of an animal's behaviour can only be understood in its natural context, and emphasized the importance of field studies and an evolutionary perspective. A recent development within ethology is sociobiology.

histology study of the microscopic structure of the tissues of organisms.

horticulture the art of growing flowers, fruit and vegetables. Courses in horticulture usually include outdoor gardening, propagation, and hothouse care.

physiology that branch of biology that deals with the functioning of living animals.

sociobiology the application of population genetics to the evolution of behaviour. It builds on W D Hamilton's concept of inclusive fitness to emphasize that the evolutionary function of behaviour is to allow an organism to contribute as many of its own alleles as it can to future generations (an idea encapsulated in Dawkins' notion of the 'selfish gene'). Contrary to some popular interpretations, it does not assume that all behaviour is genetically determined. The use of game theory is an important aspect of sociobiology.

zoology the branch of biology concerned with the study of animals. It includes description of present-day animals, the evolution of animal forms, anatomy, physiology, embryology, and geographical distribution.

Evolutionary Biology

evolution a slow process of change from one form to another, as in the evolution of the universe from its formation in the Big Bang to its present state, or in the evolution of life on earth. With respect to the living world, the idea of continuous evolution can be traced as far back as Lucretius in the first century BC, but it did not gain wide acceptance until 19th century following the work of Sir Charles Lyell, J B Lamarck, Charles Darwin and T H Huxley. Darwin assigned the major role in evolutionary change to natural selection acting on genetic variation, which is ultimately produced by spontaneous changes (mutations) in the genetic material of organisms. *Natural selection* occurs because those individuals that are better adapted to their particular environments reproduce more effectively, thus contributing more genes to future generations. Darwin's theory was later combined with Mendel's discoveries in genetics, to give the modern theory of evolution, often called neo-Darwinism. Although neither the general concept of evolution nor the importance of natural selection is doubted by biologists, there remains dispute over other possible processes involved in evolutionary change. Besides natural selection and sexual selection, chance may play an important role in deciding which genes become characteristic of a population, a phenomenon sometimes referred to as 'genetic drift'. In addition, it is now clear that evolutionary change does not always occur at a constant rate, but that the process sometimes shows long periods of relative stability interspersed with periods of rapid change. This has led to new theories, such as punctuated equilibrium model.

extinction in biology, the complete disappearance of a species. In the past extinctions generally occurred because species were unable to adapt quickly enough to a changing environment. Today, most extinctions are due to human activity. Some species, such as the dodo of Mauritius, the moas of New Zealand and the passenger pigeon of North America have been exterminated by hunting. Others become extinct when their habitat is destroyed. Mass extinctions are episodes during which whole groups of species have become extinct, the best known being that of the dinosaurs, other large reptiles and various marine invertebrates some 65 million years ago. Another mass extinction occurred about 10,000 years ago when many giant species of mammals died out. This is known as the 'Pleistocene overkill' because their disappearance was probably hastened by the hunting activities of prehistoric humans.

homologous in biology, an organ or struc-

ture possessed by members of different taxonomic groups (species, genera, families, orders) which, although now different in form or usage, originally derived from the same structure in a common ancestor. The wing of a bat, the arm of a monkey and the flipper of a seal are homologous, because they all derive from the forelimb of an ancestral mammal. The wing of a bird and the wing of an insect are not homologous, even though they are both used for flying, because they are not derived from the same structure.

natural selection the process whereby gene frequencies in a population change due to certain organisms producing more descendants than others, because they are better able to survive and reproduce. Natural selection results in the genetic constitution of the population, and ultimately the species, being altered in favour of the particular genes that successful individuals bear. The accumulated effect of natural selection is to produce adaptations such as the thick coat of a polar bear or the spade-like forelimbs of a mole. It was recognized by Darwin as the main process driving evolution.

nature the living world, including plants, animals, fungi, and all microorganisms.

neo-Darwinism the modern theory of evolution, built up during the 1930s by integrating Darwin's theory of evolution through natural selection with the theory of genetic inheritance founded on the work of Gregor Mendel.

human species, origins of evolution of modern humans from ancestral primates. The African apes (gorilla and chimpanzees) are shown by anatomical and molecular comparisons to be our closest living relatives. The date of the split between the human and African ape lines is not known from fossil finds, but molecular clock studies put it at five million years ago or more. There are no ape or *hominid* (of the human group) fossils from this period. The oldest known hominid remains date from 3.5 million years ago, from Ethiopia and Tanzania. They show hominids were already walking upright at this time. There is disagreement over the status of these creatures, known as *Australopithecus afarensis*. Some believe they were our direct ancestors, other that they were an off-shoot of the line that led to modern humans. The first stone tools date from about a million years later, probably made by the hominid *Homo habilis*, who had a slightly larger body and brain than *A. afarensis*. Other *Australopithecus* hominids among them *A. robustus* and *A. gracilis*, lived in Africa at the same time as *H. habilis*, but these are not generally considered to be our ancestors. Over 1.5 million years ago a new hominid species, *H. erectus*, with a much larger brain, appeared in Africa. It is not clear if *H. Habilis* evolved from *A. afarensis*, but it is generally believed that *H. erectus* evolved from *H. habilis* The erectus people were probably the first to use fire, and the first to move out of Africa. Their remains are found as far afield as China, Spain, and southern Britain. Modern humans, *H. sapiens sapiens*, and the Neanderthals *H. sapiens neanderthalensis*, are probably descended from *H. erectus*. Neanderthals were large-brained but heavily-built, probably adapted to the cold conditions of the ice ages. They lived in Europe and the Middle East, and died out about 40,000 years ago, leaving *H. sapiens sapiens* as the only remaining species of the hominid group.

phylogeny the historical sequence of changes that occurs in a given species during the course of evolution.

punctuated equilibrium model an evolutionary theory which claims that periods of rapid change alternate with periods of relative stability (stasis), and that the appearance of new lineages is a separate process from the gradual evolution of adaptive changes within a species. The idea was developed in 1972 by Niles Eldridge and Steven J Gould to explain discontinuities in the fossil record. The pattern of stasis and more rapid change is now widely accepted, but the second part of the theory remains unsubstantiated.

saltation the idea that an abrupt genetic change can occur in an individual, which then gives rise to a new species. The idea has now been largely discredited.

speciation the emergence of a new species

during evolutionary history. One cause of speciation is the geographical separation of populations of the parent species, followed by their reproductive isolation, so that they no longer produce viable offspring if they interbreed. Other less common causes of speciation are assortative mating, and the appearance of polyploidy.

Reproduction and the Life Cycle

life the ability to grow, stay in 'working order', reproduce, and respond to such stimuli as light, heat and sound. It is thought that life began about 4,000 million years ago, the earliest fossil evidence being thread-like chains of cells discovered in 1980 in deposits in the northwest of Australia, that have been dated as 3,500 million years old.

It seems probable that the original atmosphere of earth consisted of carbon dioxide, nitrogen and water and that complex organic molecules such as amino acids were created when the atmosphere was bombarded by ultra-violet radiation or by atmospheric lightning. Experiments in the laboratory have attempted to replicate these conditions and have successfully shown that amino acids and purine and pyrimidine bases (which make up DNA) and other vital molecules can be created in this way. The earliest forms of cellular life were very probably bacteria-like and from these developed the network of plant and animal life of today.

life cycle in biology, the sequence of different stages through which members of a given species pass. Most vertebrates have a simple life cycle consisting of the production of sex cells or gametes, fertilization and a period of development as an embryo, followed by a period of juvenile growth after hatching or birth, with a concluding phase of sexual reproduction which terminates at death. Invertebrate life cycles are generally more complex and may involve major reconstitution of the individual's appearance (metamorphosis) and completely different styles of life. Thus, dragonflies live an aquatic life as larvae and an aerial life during the adult phase. In many other invertebrates and protozoa there are several different stages in the life cycle, and in parasites these often occur in different host organisms. Plants have a special type of life cycle with two distinct phases, known as an alternation of generations.

reproduction the process by which a living organism produces other organisms similar to itself. Reproduction may be asexual or sexual.

sexual reproduction a reproductive process which requires the union, or fertilization, of the gametes (except in fungi). These are generally produced by two different individuals, although self-fertilization can occur in hermaphrodites. Most organisms other than bacteria and cyanobacteria show some sort of sexual process. Except in some lower organisms, the gametes are of two distinct types, called eggs and sperm. The organisms producing the eggs are called females, and those producing the sperm, males.

asexual reproduction a biological term applied to reproductive processes which are not sexual and so which do not involve fusion of gametes. They include binary fission, in which the parent organism splits into two or more 'daughter' organisms, or budding, in which a new organism is formed initially as an outgrowth of the parent organism. The asexual production of spores, as in ferns and mosses, is another common process, and many plants reproduce asexually by means of runners, rhizomes, bulbs and corms.

alternation of generations the typical lifecycle of terrestrial plants and some seaweeds, in which there are two distinct forms occurring alternately. One is diploid and produces haploid spores by meiosis; this is called the sporophyte (spore-producer). The other is haploid and produces gametes (sex cells); this is called the gametophyte (gamete-producer).

The gametes fuse to form a diploid zygote which develops into a new sporophyte, and so the sporophyte and gametophyte alternate. In mosses, the familiar green moss plant is gametophyte, while the long-stalked spore capsules growing from it are sporophyte. In ferns the familiar plant is the sporophyte and the gametophyte, which grows separately from it, is very small and inconspicuous. All higher plants are sporophytes, and the gametophyte is not seen because it completes its life within the body of the sporophyte. The lifecycles of certain animals (for example, jellyfish) are sometimes said to show alternation of generations, but this is rarely as regular and clearly-defined as in plants.

sporophyte the diploid spore-producing generation in the life cycle of a plant that undergoes alternation of generations.

gametophyte the haploid generation in the lifecycle of a plant that produces gametes.

parthenogenesis the development of an ovum (egg) without any genetic contribution from a male. In most cases, there is no fertilization at all, but in a few the stimulus of being fertilized by a sperm is needed to initiate development, although the male's chromosomes are not absorbed into the nucleus of the ovum. Parthenogenesis is the normal means of reproduction in some plants (for example, dandelions) and animals (for example, certain fish and rotifers). Certain sexually reproducing species, such as aphids, show parthenogenesis at some stage in their life cycle, and it can be artificially induced in many animals (for example, rabbits) by cooling, pricking or applying acid to an egg.

gamete a cell generated for sexual reproduction. In most organisms, the gametes are haploid, that is they contain half the number of chromosomes of the parent, due to reduction division or meiosis. In higher organisms, gametes are of two distinct types, large immobile ones known as eggs or egg-cells and small ones known as sperm. In some lower organisms the gametes are all the same, or they may belong to different mating strains but have no obvious differences in size or appearance.

pollen the grains formed by seed plants that contain the male gametes. In angiosperms pollen is produced within anthers, and in most gymnosperms it is produced in male cones. A pollen grain is typically yellow and, when mature, has a hard outer wall. Since pollen grains are extremely resistant to decay, much important information on the vegetation of earlier times can be gained from the study of fossil pollen. The study of pollen grains is known as palynology.

sperm strictly speaking, the male gamete of animals, but the name is also sometimes applied to the motile male gametes, or antherozoids, of lower plants. In most animals, the sperm are motile, and are propelled by a long flagellum, but in some (for example, crabs and lobsters) they are non-motile. Each sperm cell looks rather like a tadpole, with a head capsule containing a nucleus, a middle portion containing mitochondria (which provide energy) and the long tail or flagellum behind.

ovum the female gamete (sex-cell) before fertilization. In animals, it is called an egg, and is produced in the ovaries. In plants, where it is also known as an egg-cell or oosphere, the ovum is produced in an ovule. The ovum is non-motile. It must be fertilized by a male gamete before it can develop further, except in cases of parthenogenesis.

fertilization in sexual reproduction, the union of two gametes (sex cells, often called egg and sperm) to produce a zygote, which combines the genetic material contributed by each parent. In terrestrial insects, mammals, reptiles and birds, fertilization occurs within the female's body; in the majority of fish and amphibians, and most aquatic invertebrates, it occurs externally, when both sexes release their gametes freely into the water. In most fungi, gametes are not released, but the hyphae of the two parents grow towards each other and fuse to achieve fertilization. In higher plants, pollination precedes fertilization. In self-fertilization the male and female gametes come from the same plant; in cross-fertilization they come from different plants. Self-fertilization occurs rarely in her-maphrodite animals.

zygote the name given to an ovum (egg) after fertilization, but before it undergoes cleavage at the start of its development.

egg in animals, the ovum, or female gamete (reproductive cell). After fertilization by a sperm cell, it begins to divide to form an embryo. Eggs may be deposited by the female (ovipary) or they may develop within her body (vivipary and ovovivipary). In the oviparous reptiles and birds, the egg is protected by a shell, and well supplied with nutrients in the form of yolk. In plants, the ovum is called an egg-cell.

seed the reproductive structure of higher plants (angiosperms and gymnosperms). It develops from a fertilized ovule and consists of an embryo and a food store, surrounded and protected by an outer seed coat, called the testa. The food store is contained either in a specialized nutritive tissue, the endosperm, or in the cotyledons of the embryo itself. In angiosperms the seed is enclosed within a fruit, whereas in gymnosperms it is usually naked and unprotected, once shed from the female cone. Following germination the seed develops into a new plant but there may be a delay in germination to ensure growth occurs under favourable conditions.

spore a small reproductive or resting body, usually consisting of just one cell. Unlike a gamete, it does not need to fuse with another cell in order to develop into a new organism. Spores are produced by the lower plants, most fungi, some bacteria, and certain protozoa. They are generally light and easily dispersed by wind movements. Plant spores are haploid and are produced by the sporophyte, following meiosis.

embryo early development stage of animals and plants following fertilization of an ovum (egg cell), or parthenogenetic activation of an ovum. In animals the embryo exists either within an egg (where it is nourished by food contained in the yolk), or in mammals, in the uterus of the mother.

metamorphosis a period during the life cycle of many invertebrates, most amphibians and some fish, during which the individual's body changes from one form to another through a major reconstitution of its tissues. Thus, adult frogs are produced by metamorphosis from tadpoles, while butterflies are produced from caterpillars following metamorphosis within a pupa.

larva the young of an animal, in species where the young has a different appearance and way of life from the adult. Larvae are typical of the invertebrates, and some (for example, shrimps) have two or more distinct larval stages. (However, some invertebrates hatch as tiny replicas of their parents, while in others the young differ only slightly, for example, the nymphs of certain insects.) Among vertebrates, it is only the amphibians and some fish that have a larval stage. The process whereby the larva changes into an adult is known as metamorphosis.

pupa the non-feeding, largely immobile stage of some insect life cycles, in which larval tissues are broken down and adult tissues and structures are formed. In most insects it is exarate, with the appendages (legs, antennae, wings) visible outside the pupal case, but in butterflies and moths it is obtect, with the appendages developing inside the pupal case.

ageing in common usage, the period of deterioration of the physical condition of a living organism that leads to death; but in biological terms, the entire life-process, beginning at the moment when as egg is fertilized and starts to develop into a new individual, and continuing to its eventual death. Three current theories attempt to account for ageing. The first suggests that the process is genetically determined, to remove individuals that can no longer reproduce by causing their death. The second suggests that it is due to the accumulation of mistakes during the replication of DNA at cell division. The third suggests that it is actively induced by pieces of DNA which move between cells, or cancer-causing viruses; these may become abundent in old cells and induce them to produce unwanted proteins or interfere with the control functions of their DNA.

Ecology and Resources

ecology the study of the relationship between an organism and the environment in which it lives, including other living organisms and the non-living surroundings. The term was first introduced by the biologist Ernst Haeckel in 1866. Ecology may be concerned with individual organisms (for example, behavioural ecology, foraging strategies), with populations or species (for example, population dynamics) or with entire communities (for example, competition between species for access to resources, or predator-prey relationships). Applied ecology is concerned with the management and conservation of habitats and the consequences and control of pollution.

conservation in the life sciences, care for, and protection of, the biosphere. Since the 1950s it has been increasingly realized that the earth, together with its atmosphere, animal and plant life, and mineral and agricultural resources, form an interdependent whole which is in danger of irreversible depletion and eventual destruction unless positive measures are taken to conserve a balance. Action by governments has been supplemented by private agencies, such as the World Wildlife Fund. In attempts to save particular species or habitats, a distinction is often made between *preservation*, that is maintaining the pristine state of nature exactly as it was or might have been, and *conservation*, the management of natural resources in such a way as to allow any of its excess production to be controlled, or to be used for commercial purposes, including integration of the requirements of the local human population with those of the animals, plants or the habitat being conserved.

endangered species a plant or animal species whose numbers are so few that it is at risk of becoming extinct. Thus, there are only about 50 Javan rhino alive today and, unless active steps are taken to promote this species' survival, it will probably be extinct within a few decades. Officially designated endangered species are listed by IUCN.

CITES *Convention on International Trade in Endangered Species.* An international agreement signed by 81 countries under the auspices of the IUCN to regulate the trade in endangered species of animals and plants. Because it was first signed in 1973 at Washington DC, it is sometimes known as the *Washington Convention.*

Organizations

Countryside Commission an official conservation body, created for England and Wales under the Countryside Act 1968.

International Union for the Conservation of Nature (IUCN) an organization established by the United Nations to promote the conservation of wildlife and habitats in the national policies of member states.

Nature Conservancy Council (NCC) a UK government agency established in 1973 to oversee nature conservation. It is responsible for designating and managing National Nature Reserves and other conservation areas (for example, Sites of Special Scientific Interest, SSSIs) and for the enforcement of legislation that protects wildlife and habitats.

World Wildlife Fund an international organization established in 1961 to raise funds for conservation by public appeal. Its headquarters are at Gland, Switzerland, but many countries have their own autonomous branches. Projects include conservation of particular species (for example, the tiger and giant panda) or special areas (for example, the Simen Mountains, Ethiopia).

Feeding relationships

trophic level in ecology, the position occupied by a species (or group of species) in a food chain. The main levels are primary producers (for example, plants), primary consumers (for example, herbivores), secondary consumers (for example, carnivores), and decomposers.

autotroph any living organism which synthesizes organic substances from inorganic molecules using light or chemical energy. All green plants and many planktonic organisms are autotrophs, using sunlight to convert carbon dioxide and water into sugars by photosynthesis. A few bacteria use chemical energy; for example, some bacteria use the chemical energy of sulphur compounds to synthesize organic substance. Materials synthesized and stored by autotrophs provide the energy sources of all other organisms: they are the *primary producers* in all food chains.

heterotroph any living organism that obtains its energy from organic substances which have been produced by other organisms. All animals and fungi are heterotrophs, and they include herbivores (which feed on autotrophs), carnivores (which feed on other heterotrophs), and saprotrophs (which feed on dead animal and plant material).

herbivore an animal which feeds on green plant material. In a broader sense, any animal that lives by eating plants or their products, including seeds, fruit and nectar, as well as photosynthetic organisms in the plankton. Herbivorous animals are more numerous than other types because their food is the most abundant. They form a vital link in the food chain between plants and carnivores.

carnivore an animal which eats other animals. Sometimes confined to animals that eat the flesh of vertebrate prey, but often used more broadly, to include animals that eat any other animals, even microscopic ones. Carrion eaters may or may not be included. Additionally, the name carnivore is sometimes used to refer to members of the mammalian group Carnivora, which includes cats, dogs, bears, badgers, and weasels.

omnivore an animal which feeds on both plant and animal material. Omnivores have digestive adaptations intermediate between those of herbivores and carnivores, with relatively unspecialized digestive systems and gut micro-organisms which can digest a variety of foodstuffs.

food chain or food web the sequence of organisms through which energy and other

387

nutrients are successively transferred in an ecological system. The main components of the sequence are the autotrophs or *primary producers*, principally plants and photosynthetic microorganisms, the herbivores that feed on them, the carnivores that feed on the herbivores, and the decomposers that break down the dead bodies and waste products of all three groups, ready for recycling. Many organisms, however, feed at several different levels (for example, omnivores such as bears and badgers, feed on both fruit and meat), so that the relationships often form a complex web rather than a simple chain.

parasite a creature depending on another for the necessities of life, for example, lice, fleas, the acarus that causes scabies, tapeworms, and the microscopic organisms that cause syphilis and malaria. Plants, too, may be parasitic.

host an organism that is parasitized by another. In commensalism, the partner that does not benefit may also be called the host.

epiphyte a plant which grows on another plant or object above the surface of the ground, and which has no roots in the soil. An epiphyte does not parasitize the plant it grows on, but merely uses it for support.

saprophyte an obsolete term for a saprotroph. It reflected the mistaken belief that fungi and bacteria, the principal saprotrophs, were plants, hence the ending *-phyte* (Greek: plant).

commensalism a relationship between two species whereby one (the commensal) benefits from the association, while the other neither benefits nor suffers. For example, certain species of millipede and silverfish inhabit the nests of army ants and live by scavenging on the refuse of their hosts, but without affecting the ants.

symbiosis closely interdependent relationship between two different species of animals or plants for their mutual benefit ('mutualism'). For example, trichonympha live in the stomach of wood termites digesting the wood (for its own food) and converting it to carbohydrate for the host who would otherwise be unable to digest wood. Another example is the lichen (a symbiotic relationship between a fungus and an alga). In a broader (less correct) sense, symbiosis may also refer to commensal relationships (whereby one species lives with a host without conferring either benefit or harm on the host: for example, house mice living in human habitations) and parasitism (whereby one species lives in or on a host species at the host's expense: for example, the flea).

Terms

biological control the control of pests such as insects and fungi through biological means, rather than the use of chemicals. This can include breeding resistant crop strains (for example, wheat varieties resistant to the fungi that cause 'rust'), inducing infertility in the pest (for example, by sterilizing male insects, or spraying with a juvenile hormone that prevents insect larvae maturing into adults), breeding viruses that attack the pest species, or introducing the pest's natural predator (for example, the release of a cactus-eating moth caterpillar to control the spread of prickly pear cactus in Australia). Biological control is preferable to chemical control of pests because it tends to be naturally self-regulating for example, the predators of a pest will die off when there are few pests left to eat), and it does not involve using pesticides that affect human health. However living systems are so complex that it is difficult to predict all the consequences of introducing a biological controlling agent.

biomass the gross weight of organisms present in a given area. It may be specified for one particular species (for example, earthworm biomass), for a category of species (for example, herbivore biomass) or for all species (total biomass).

biosphere or *ecosphere* that region of the earth's surface (land and water), and the atmosphere above it, which can be occupied by living organisms.

carbon cycle the sequence by which carbon circulates and is recycled through the natural world. The carbon element from carbon dioxide in the atmosphere is taken up, during the process of photosynthesis, the oxygen component being released back into the atmosphere. Photosynthesis is carried out by plants and by organisms such as diatoms and dinoflagellates in the oceanic plankton. The carbon they accumulate is later released back into circulation through the decomposition of decaying plant matter, the consumption of plant matter or plankton by herbivores, or the burning of fuels such as coal (fossilized plants). Today, the carbon cycle is being altered by the increased consumption of fossil fuels, and burning of large tracts of tropical forests, as a result of which levels of carbon dioxide are building up in the atmosphere and contributing to the greenhouse effect.

carrying capacity in ecology, the maximum number of animals of a given species that a particular area can support. When the carrying capacity is exceeded, there is insufficient food (or other resources) for all members of the population. The population may then be reduced by emigration, reproductive failure, or death through starvation.

environment in ecology, the sum of conditions affecting a particular organism, including physical surroundings, climate and influences of other living organisms. In common usage, 'the environment' often means the total global environment, without reference to any particular organism. In genetics, the external influences that affect an organism's development, and thus its phenotype.

eutrophication the over-enrichment of lake waters, primarily by nitrate fertilizers washed from soil by rain, and phosphates from detergents in municipal sewage. These encourage the growth of algae to the extent of eliminating oxygen, thereby making the water uninhabitable for fish and other animal life.

fertility an organism's ability to reproduce. Individuals become infertile (unable to reproduce) when they cannot generate gametes (eggs or sperm) or when their gametes cannot yield a viable embryo after fertilization.

greenhouse effect the atmosphere, like the glass of a greenhouse, lets much of the sun's visible and near ultraviolet radiation through it to warm the earth's surface. The warm earth

re-radiates electromagnetic radiation but of a far lower frequency (for infrared) to which the atmosphere, like glass, is not as transparent. This 'trapping' or 'greenhouse' effect contributes to raising the earth's temperature. Activities of people, such as burning fossil fuels, which increase the carbon dioxide (a good infrared absorber) in the atmosphere are tending to promote the greenhouse effect; conceivably the earth's temperature could rise enough for polar ice to melt, raising the sea level dangerously.

habitat in ecology, the localized environment in which an organism lives. Habitats are often described by the dominant plant type or physical feature, thus an oak-wood habitat or rocky seashore habitat.

indicator species a plant or animal whose presence or absence in an area indicates certain environmental conditions. For example, some lichens sensitive to sulpur dioxide in the air, and absence of these species indicates stmospheric pollution. Many plants show a preference for either alkaline or acid soil conditions, while certain plants, mostly trees, require aluminium, and are only found in soils where it is present.

nature reserve area set aside to preserve its original scenic formation or vegetation, and often to provide a sanctuary and breeding ground for rare birds or animals. The National Parks Act, 1949, gave powers to designate such areas in Britain, to be placed in the charge of the Nature Conservancy Council established 1973.

niche in ecology, the 'place' occupied by a species in its habitat, including its food requirements, the time of day at which it feeds, the parts of the habitat it uses (for example, trees or open grassland). Ecological theory holds that two species cannot occupy exactly the same niche and coexist; they will be in direct competition and one will eventually give way to the other.

nitrogen cycle in ecology, the process whereby nitrogen is passed through the ecosystem. Nitrogen in the form of inorganic compounds (such as nitrates) in the soil is absorbed by plants and turned into organic compounds (such as proteins) in plant tissue. A proportion of this nitrogen is consumed by herbivores and used for their own biological processes, with some of this in turn being passed on to the carnivores. The nitrogen is finally returned to the soil, either as excreta or when the organisms die, to be returned to inorganic form by bacterial decomposers. Although this atmosphere contains a great deal of free nitrogen, this cannot be used by most organisms. However, certain bacteria and cyanobacteria are capable of nitrogen fixation, that is they can extract nitrogen directly from the atmosphere and convert it to compounds such as nitrates which other organisms can use. Some nitrogen-fixing bacteria live in a mutualistic association with leguminous plants (peas and beans) or other plants (for example, alder) where they form characteristic nodules on the roots. The presence of such plants greatly increases the nitrate content, and hence the fertility of the soil.

nitrogen fixation the process in which nitrogen in the atmosphere is converted into nitrogenous compounds either by lightning, or by the action of microorganisms, such as cyanobacteria and bacteria.

pesticide a chemical such as DDT which is used to destroy pests (usually insects).

pollution the harmful effect on the environment of the by-products of any human activity, principally industrial and agricultural processes, for example, noise, smoke, gases, chemical effluents in seas and rivers, indestructible pesticides, sewage and household waste. Natural disasters such as volcanic eruptions may also cause pollution through ash ejected into the atmosphere and deposited on the land surface. Natural dispersal and breakdown counters pollution to a degree, but it rapidly escalates to danger level. Complete control would involve increases in production costs for the industries concerned, but failure to implement adequate controls results in damage to the environment, and an increase in the incidence of cancer, and other diseases. It could also eventually lead to areas that have become

heavily polluted being uninhabitable.

recycling the reclamation of potentially useful material from household and industrial waste, thus reducing pollution, saving expenditure on scarce raw materials, and slowing down the depletion of non-renewable resources.

sewage disposal the disposal of human excreta and other water-borne waste products from houses, factories, streets. It is conveyed through sewers and treated before being discharged into rivers or the sea. Sewage works are the responsibility of local authorities. The sludge may be spread over fields attached to the works, or it may be processed and sold as a fertilizer. In places near the coast, raw sewage may be dumped into the sea. The use of raw sewage as a fertilizer, (as long practised in China) has the drawback that disease-causing microorganisms may survive in the soil and be taken into the body by consumption of subsequent crops.

standing crop in ecology, the total number of individuals of a given species alive in a particular area at any moment. It is sometimes measured as the weight (or biomass) of a given species.

succession in ecology, the change that occurs in the structure and composition of the vegetation in a given area from the time it is first colonized, or after it has been disturbed (for example, by fire, flood, or clearance). If allowed to proceed undisturbed, succession leads naturally to a climax community (for example, oak forest or *savannah* grassland) that is determined by the climate and soil characteristics of the area.

sustained yield cropping in wildlife conservation the removal of surplus individuals from a population of organisms such that the population maintains a constant size. This usually requires selective removal of animals of all ages and both sexes to ensure a balanced population structure. Excessive cropping of young females, for example, may lead to fewer births in following years, and a fall in population size. The appropriate cropping frequencies can be determined from an analysis of a life table.

water cycle in ecology, the natural circulation of water through the biosphere. Water is lost from the earth's surface to the atmosphere either by evaporation from the surface of lakes, rivers and oceans or through the transpiration of plants. This atmospheric water forms clouds which, under the appropriate conditions, condense to deposit moisture on the land and sea as rain or snow.

Order in the Living World

taxonomy an alternative name for the science of biological classification.

classification the arrangement of organisms into a hierarchy of groups, on the basis of their similarities in biochemical, anatomical or physiological characters. Species are assumed to share characters because they acquire them from a common ancestor. (Care is taken to exclude shared characteristics known to be due to convergent evolution.) Such a classification is thus thought to mirror the evolutionary relationships between organisms. The basic grouping is a species, several of which may constitute a genus, which in turn are grouped into families, and so on up through orders, classes, phyla (or, in plants, divisions) to kingdoms.

binomial system of nomenclature the system in which all organisms are identified by a two-part Latinized name. Devised by the biologist Linnaeus, it is also known as the Linnean System. The first name identifies the genus, the second the species within that genus. Usually the names are descriptive. Thus, the name of the dog, *Canis familiaris, means the 'familiar species of the dog genus', Canis being Latin for 'dog'. Each species is defined by an officially designated type specimen* housed at a particular museum. The rules for naming organisms in this way are specified in a number of International Codes of Taxonomic Nomenclature administered by two International Commissions on Nomenclature, one zoological and one botanical.

phylum a division of animals or plants which contains several classes.

genus a set of species that share a large number of characteristics in common. Thus, all doglike species (including dogs, wolves and jackals) belong to the genus *Canis*. Species of the same genus are thought to be descended from a common ancestor species. Related genera are grouped into families.

species in biology, a distinguishable group of organisms, which resemble each other or consist of a few distinctive types (as in polymorphism), and which can all interbreed (actually or potentially) to produce fertile offspring. Species are the lowest level in the system of biological classification. Examples include lions, Douglas fir, cabbage white butterflies and sperm whales. All living human beings belong to the same species because they can all interbreed, even though they may differ considerably in such features as skin colour, height, head shape, and so on.
Related species are grouped together in a genus. Within a species there are usually two or more separate populations, which may become distinctive enough, in time, to be designated sub-species or varieties, and could eventually give rise to new species, through speciation.

The Microscopic World

cell in biology, a discrete, membrane-bound portion of living matter – the unit of physical life. Bacteria, amoebae, and certain other microorganisms consist of single cells. Plants and animals are composed entirely of cells of various kinds. The body of a mammal (including that of the human species) originates from an organism consisting of a single-cell – an ovum or egg-cell generated by the female and fertilized by fusion with a spermatozoon or seed-cell generated by the male. The fertilized ovum (embryo) is a microscopic body chiefly consisting of protoplasm, or clear jelly, the simplest form of living substance. The protoplasmic part of the cell is called the cytoplasm. It is enclosed in a membranous wall and contains a small spherical body called a nucleus – an essential part of most cells, without which they cannot reproduce. The only cells of the body which have no nucleus are the red blood cells. The nucleus of the embryo contains a denser spot called the nucleolus, but many kinds of cells do not.

The composition of the protoplasm varies, but its breakdown products when the cell dies are mostly proteins. It contains also carbohydrates, fats, and the lipoids lecithin and cholesterin, besides inorganic salts such as the phosphates and chlorides of potash, soda, and lime. The cell wall in most animal cells is not a definite membrane, but the shape of the cell is maintained by surface tension or chemical action.

Cells reproduce by division, a complicated process which starts in the nucleus. The function of the cell is to convert energy from one form into another, for example, food and oxygen into chemical energy. Sexual reproduction is performed by the union of two special kinds of cells. When the human ovum is fertilized by fusion with a spermatozoon, the new cell contains the chromosomes from both – 48. The sex of the new individual is determined by the distribution of the special sex chromosomes. The ordinary cells of the female body have two X chromosomes; the cells of the male body have an X and a Y chromosome – two different types. The mature ovum contains one X chromosome and the mature spermatozoon contains either an X or a Y chromosome.

If on fertilization two X chromosomes meet, the result is a female; if an X and a Y meet, the result is a male. All men thus inherit from their fathers one Y chromosome which gives their male characteristics: some (perhaps one in 300) inherit two, which give added height, greater emotional instability, inability to bear frustration, and great aggressiveness. These men are often criminally violent, and possession of the Y-factor, immediately detectable under the microscope, has (as in France and Australia 1968) been successfully pleaded in mitigation in murder cases.

Ionization arising from gamma or X-radiation can damage chromosomes, and in the case of reproduction chromosomes this may lead to disruption of the chromosomes and potential degradation of the offspring.

In 1976 the barrier between the plant and animal kingdoms was broken by the achievement in the laboratory (in UK, USA and Hungary), of the fusion of a plant and animal cell to form a hybrid, e.g. red blood cell from a hen and a yeast cell, using polyethylene glycol as a fusing agent. There has as yet been no development beyond a single cell.

cytology the study of cells, especially in relation to their functions. Major advances have been made possible in this field by the development of electron microscopes.

Terms

archaebacteria a name given to three groups of bacteria whose DNA differs significantly from that of other bacteria (called the 'eubacteria'). All are strict anaerobes, that is, they are killed by oxygen. This is a primitive condition, and shows that the archaebacteria are related to the earliest life forms, which appeared about 4,000 million years ago, when there was little oxygen in the earth's atmosphere. The methanogens represent one group of archaebacteria.

bacillus a group of rod-like bacteria that occur everywhere in the soil and air, and are responsible for diseases such as anthrax as well as causing food spoilage.

bacteria microscopic unicellular organisms with prokaryotic cells. They are now classified biochemically, but their varying shapes provide a rough classification, for example, *cocci* are round or oval, *rods* are cylindrical, and *spirillae* are spiral. They reproduce by binary fission, and since this may occur approximately every 20 minutes, a single bacterium is potentially capable of producing 16 million copies of itself in a day. Bacteria mutate readily, a characteristic which accounts both for the rapid emergence of strains which are resistant to antibiotics. Unlike viruses, bacteria do not necessarily need contact with a live cell to become active. Bacteria are generally thought of as harmful, and certain types do cause disease. However, many other types perform useful functions in the healthy human body, break down waste products or improve soil fertility. Bacteria are essential in many food and industrial processes, for example, making butter, cheese and yoghurt, as well as curing tobacco, tanning leather, and sewage disposal. Bacteria cannot normally survive temperatures above 10°C/21°F, but those in deep sea hot vents in the eastern Pacific are believed to withstand temperatures of 35°C/66°F.

bacteriophage a virus that attacks bacteria.

diatom class of microscopic unicellular algae (marine or freshwater), class Bacillariophyceae, which as fossils constitute diatomaceous earth (diatomite) used in the rubber and plastics industries, and as living creatures are a constituent of plankton.

eukaryote one of the two classes into which all living organisms (except viruses) are divided. The cells of eukaryotes possess a clearly defined nucleus, bounded by a membrane, within which DNA is formed into distinct chromosomes. Their cells contain mitochondria, chloroplasts and other organelles which are lacking in the cells of the alternative class, the prokaryotes. All organisms other than bacteria and cyanobacteria are eukaryotic.

microbe in biology, a microscopic organism, a germ, bacillus, micro-organism, or bacterium, which has life and the ability to multiply.

procaryote one of the two classes of living cell, that in which there is no definite nucleus, as in bacteria and blue-green algae.

protozoa a group of single-celled eukaryotic organisms without rigid cell walls. Some, such as amoeba, ingest other cells, but most are saprotrophs or parasites. A few of the euglenoids contain chlorophyll and are photosynthetic. The group is polyphyletic, that is, it contains organisms which have different evolutionary origins.

slime mould an extraordinary organism that shows some features of fungi and some of protozoa. Slime moulds are not closely related to any other group, although they are often classed, for convenience, with the fungi. They fall into two main types, the *cellular slime moulds* and the *plasmodial slime moulds*. The former go through a phase of living as single cells, that look very like amoebae, and feed by engulfing the bacteria found in rotting wood, dung or damp soil. When a food supply is exhausted, up to 100,000 of these amoebae form into a colony which looks like a single slug-like animal and migrates to a fresh source of bacteria. It then takes on the aspect of a fungus, and forms long-stalked fruiting bodies which release spores. These germinate to release amoebae, which repeat the life cycle. The plasmodial slime moulds are similar in many ways, but have a more complex lifestyle involving sexual reproduction. They form a slimy mass of protoplasm with no internal cell walls, that slowly spreads over the bark or fallen branches of trees.

virus an infectious particle consisting of a 'core' of nucleic acids (DNA or RNA) enclosed in a protein 'shell'. Viruses are acellular, and outside the cell of another organism they remain completely inert, being able to function and reproduce only if they can force their way into a living cell so as to be able to use the cell's system to replicate themselves. In doing so, they may disrupt or alter the host cell's own DNA. The healthy human body reacts to such an invasion by producing an antiviral protein, interferon, which prevents the infection spreading to adjacent cells. Viruses are responsible for causing diseases like canine distemper, chickenpox, common cold, herpes, influenza, measles, rabies, smallpox, yellow fever and many plant diseases. Recent evidence implicates viruses in the development of some forms of cancer. *Retroviruses* are of special interest because they have an RNA genome, and can produce DNA from this RNA, a process which apparently contravenes the central dogma. *Viroids*, discovered in 1971 are even smaller than viruses, a single strand of nucleic acid with no protein coat. They cause stunting in plants and some rare diseases in animals, including humans.

yeast a mass of minute circular or oval vegetable cells about .000085 m/^{1}/$_{3000}$ in in diameter, each of which is a complete plant capable under suitable conditions of reproducing new cells by budding.

Animals

animal one of the two 'kingdoms' of living things, the science of which is zoology, the other being the vegetable kingdom or plants, the science of which is botany.

Animals and plants are fundamentally similar in microscopical structure, being composed of a substance, protoplasm, and the tissues in the more elaborately organized examples of the two kingdoms alike consist primarily of minute particles of protoplasm known as cells. But the overall structure of all the familiar animals and plants is so different that there is no difficulty in distinguishing one from the other. There is also the important physiological difference that animals are capable of living and developing only by the nutritive assimilations of the protoplasmic tissues of other living organisms, plant or animal. Animals are dependent on plants, and must have succeeded them in the evolution of living things. But these differences, both anatomical and physiological, between the more complex and familiar animals and plants break down in the simplest, most primitive forms of animals, the Protozoa, which are so distinct from other animals that

they are given the rank of a sub-kingdom, the rest being assigned to the sub-kingdom Metazoa. Owing to the dying out of formerly existing links, the Metazoa can be classified into a number of primary, definable groups, each of which is known as a phylum, meaning a stock or line of descent; and the classification, or taxonomy, of animals is based on the resemblances such as exist between a whale and a shark and which have been acquired as adaptations to a similar mode of life.

animal classification there are over ten million species of animal in the world. Animals can be readily divided into those with a backbone, the *vertebrates*, and those without, the *invertebrates*. Invertebrates represent some 95% of all animals; they vastly outnumber vertebrates in terms of species also, and they show a greater variety of forms. Classification of the animal kingdom is into phyla (from the Greek word for 'race'). Each phylum is then subdivided into classes, orders, families, genera, and species. The class Mammalia, to which humans belong, numbers less than 5,000 species, and of these, nearly half are rodents and about a quarter are bats. An example of the class Mammalia is the tiger, which belongs to the order Carnivora, family Felidae, is grouped with the lion, leopard, and jaguar in the genus *Panthera*, and is distinguished as a species by the addition of the species name, *Panthera tigris*.

Main Animal Types

amphibian a class of vertebrates (Greek 'double life') which generally spends a gill-breathing larval ('tadpole') stage in fresh water, before becoming an air-breathing adult living on land, returning to the water to breed. Amphibians cannot maintain a temperature much different to their surroundings. They include salamanders, newts, frogs, toads and the tropical worm-like caecilians.

annelid worm segmented worm of the phylum Annelida, which includes earthworms, leeches and marine worms such as lugworms and ragworms. There is a distinct head and the soft body is divided into a number of similar segments shut off from one another by internal partitions. There are no jointed legs or other appendages.

arthropod invertebrate animal with jointed legs and a segmented body with a horny or chitinous casing, the latter being shed periodically and replaced as the animal grows. This definition includes arachnids such as spiders and mites, as well as crustaceans, millipedes, centipedes and insects. They were all formerly placed in the same phylum, Arthropoda, but it is now believed that some groups had a separate origin.

bird warm-blooded, vertebrate animal clothed in feathers, and with its forelimbs transformed into wings. Birds are egg-laying, and feathers and scales originate as epidermal appendages. Except in brain development, they are structurally as highly organized as mammals. Their behaviour is largely instinctive. Yet their body temperature is much than that of mammals, and both physically and mentally they have become highly specialized.

centipede arthropod of the class Chilopoda, having a distinct head, single pair of antennae, and numerous similar segments each bearing a single pair of jointed limbs. Mostly nocturnal and predatory, centipedes have strong 'jaws' with poison fangs to kill insects and worms. Some tropical species reach 30 cm/1 ft, with a bite dangerous to humans.

crustacean one of the class of arthropods that includes crabs, lobsters, shrimps, woodlice, barnacles and many less familiar forms. The external skeleton is made of protein and chitin hardened with lime. Each segment bears a pair of appendages which may be modified as antennae, for feeding, swimming, walking or grasping. Most breathe with gills. There are 30,000+ species, varying from 0.025 cm/0.001 in to 3 m/10 ft across. Most are marine and they are very important in the food-chains of the sea.

echinoderm marine invertebrate which has a basic body structure divided into five sectors. The phylum Echinodermata ('spiny-skinned') includes the starfish, brittlestars, sea-lilies, sea urchins and sea-cucumbers. The skeleton is

external, made of a series of limy plates, and they generally move using tube-feet – small water-filled sacs which can be protruded or pulled back to the body.

fish aquatic vertebrate that breathes using gills. There are three main groups, not very closely related: the jawless fishes (lamprey, hagfish); the sharks and rays; and the bony fishes. In the latter, the majority of living fishes (about 20,000 species), the skeleton is bone, movement is controlled by mobile fins, and the body is usually covered with scales. The gills are covered by a single flap. Many have a swim bladder which the fish uses to adjust its buoyancy. Most lay eggs, sometimes in vast numbers.

flatworm invertebrate of the phylum Platyhelminthes. Some are free-living, but many are parasitic – the tapeworms and flukes. The body is simple and bilaterally symmetrical. The gut has a mouth but no anus or, in tapeworms, is absent. Many are hermaphrodite (male and female), with complex sex organs, the parasitic forms producing large numbers of eggs.

insect arthropod of the class Insecta whose body is divided into head, thorax and abdomen. The head bears one pair of antennae. The thorax bears three pairs of legs, and usually two pairs of wings. More than a million species are known; many more are discovered each year. Size varies from 0.02 cm/0.007 in to 35 cm/1.5 ft. The skeleton is external and made of chitin. The more 'primitive' species (such as cockroaches, bugs) change appearance gradually from hatching to adult. In more 'advanced' species (such as butterflies, flies, beetles) the larva which emerges from the egg is very different from the adult, and between the two is a 'resting' and reorganizing stage, the pupa.

invertebrate any animal without a backbone. More than two million species are known, as against 41,000 species of vertebrates.

jellyfish marine animal of the phylum Cnidaria, with an umbrella-shaped body of semitransparent gelatinous substance fringed

animal classification

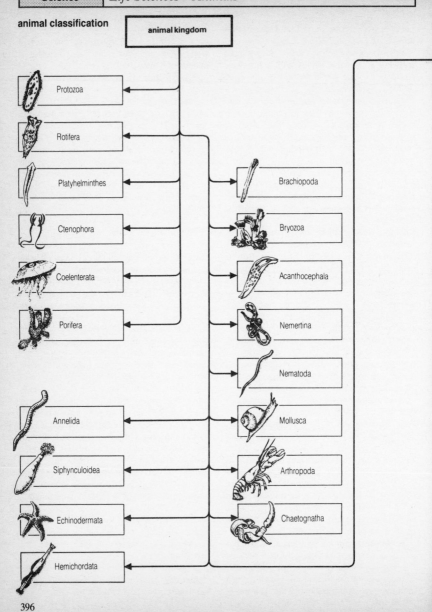

animal kingdom

Protozoa

Rotifera

Platyhelminthes

Ctenophora

Coelenterata

Porifera

Brachiopoda

Bryozoa

Acanthocephala

Nemertina

Nematoda

Annelida

Mollusca

Siphynculoidea

Arthropoda

Echinodermata

Chaetognatha

Hemichordata

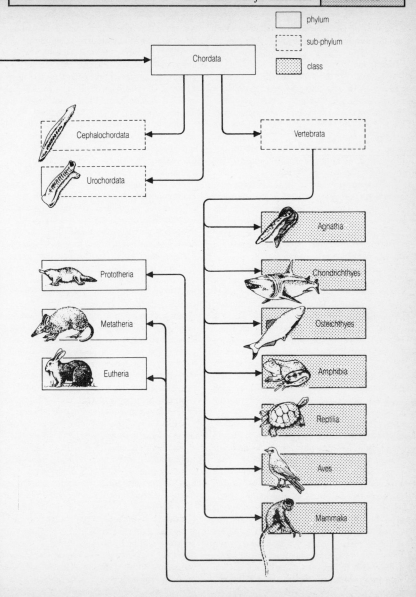

phylum

sub-phylum

class

Chordata

Cephalochordata

Urochordata

Vertebrata

Agnatha

Chondrichthyes

Osteichthyes

Amphibia

Reptilia

Aves

Mammalia

Prototheria

Metatheria

Eutheria

by stinging tentacles. Jellyfish feed on small animals paralysed by these stings. Most move freely, but some are attached by stalks to rocks or seaweed.

mammal vertebrate which suckles its young and has fur or hair, lungs and four-chambered heart. It maintains a constant body temperature in varied surroundings. Most mammals give birth to live young, but the platypus and echidna lay eggs. There are over 4,000 species, adapted to almost every conceivable way of life. The smallest shrew is only 2 gm/0.07 oz, the largest whale up to 200 tonnes.

millipede arthropod of the class Diplopoda, having a distinct head with a pair of short clubbed antennae, and numerous similar segments with two pairs of legs on each. Millipedes live in damp dark places, feeding mainly on rotting vegetation, and some produce a poisonous secretion in defence.

mollusc soft bodied, limbless, and cold-blooded invertebrate, some being marine, although some molluscs inhabit fresh water and a few are terrestrial. Molluscs include shellfish, snails, slugs, and cuttlefish. There is no internal skeleton, but most species have a hard shell covering the body. In some cases, for example the cuttle and squid, the shell is internal. There is a fold of skin, the mantle, which covers the whole body or the back only, and secretes the calcareous substance forming the shell. The lower ventral surface forms the locomotory organ, or foot.

nematode worm unsegmented worm, pointed at both ends, and with a tough smooth outer skin, of the phylum Aschelminthes. Nematodes include some soil and water forms, but a large number are parasites, such as the roundworms and pinworms that live in animals, or the eelworms that attack plant roots. Nematodes are one of the most numerous types of animal.

reptile egg-laying scaly-skinned vertebrate which breathes using lungs and is 'cold-blooded' – needing an outside source of heat to achieve a high body temperature. The main types are tortoises, turtles, crocodiles and alligators, snakes and lizards. The metabolism

is slow, and in some cases (some large snakes) intervals between meals may be months.

rotifer tiny invertebrate, also called 'wheel animalcule' of the Phylum Aschelminthes. Mainly freshwater, some marine, rotifers have a ring of cilia which carries food to the mouth, and also provides propulsion. Smallest of multicellular animals, few reach 0.05 cm/0.02 in.

scorpion arthropod of the class Arachnida, related to spiders. Common in the tropics and sub-tropics, scorpions have a head and crab-like pincers, eight legs, a segmented body, and a long tail ending in a poisonous sting, rarely fatal to humans. Some species reach 15 cm/6 in. They mate after a courtship dance, produce live young, and hunt chiefly at night.

sea anemone invertebrate sea-dwelling animal of the class Cnidaria with a tube-like body attached by the base to a rock or shell. The other end has an open 'mouth' surrounded by stinging tentacles, which capture crustaceans and other small organisms. Sea anemones occur in many beautiful colours, especially in tropical waters.

sea urchin echinoderm, related to starfish, in which the body is globular, heart- or shield-shaped, enclosed by a box armour of limy plates. The spines on the skin may assist in locomotion, or be modified for grasping, as well as giving protection. Urchins graze using five movable teeth surrounding the mouth.

spider arthropod of the class Arachnida, with a cephalothorax (combined 'head-chest'), separated from the abdomen by a narrow waist. There are eight legs, and up to eight eyes. Below the abdomen are the spinnerets from which silk is spun to make the web, although some species stalk their prey. Their fangs inject substances to subdue and digest their prey, the juices of which are then sucked in by the spider.

sponge very simple animal of the phylum Porifera, usually marine. A sponge has a hollow body, its cavity lined by cells bearing flagellae, whose whip-like movements keep water circulating, bringing a stream of food particles. The body walls are strengthened with protein (as in the bath-sponge) or little spikes.

starfish echinoderm with arms radiating from a central body. Usually there are five arms, but some species have more. Starfish are predators, some species using their suckered tube-feet to pull open the shells of bivalve molluscs, then pushing their stomach inside out to surround and digest the animal inside.

vertebrae any animal with a backbone. Vertebrates include mammals, birds, reptiles, amphibians and fishes; in all over 41,000 species.

worm general name for any softbodied, elongated invertebrate. There are many groups of worms, zoologically unrelated, including annelids (such as earthworms), flatworms (such as flukes), and nematodes (roundworms), as well as the marine ribbon-worms (Nemertea).

Plants

plant an organism that carries out photosynthesis, has cellulose cell walls and complex eukaryotc cells and is immobile. However, a few parasitic plants have lost the ability to photosynthesize, but are still considered as plants. Some authorities would also include the single-celled algae, such as *Chlamydomanas* with the plants, although these can move around. On the other hand, some classification schemes exclude all algae, even seaweeds, from the plant kingdom, and put them with the protists. Many of the lower plants (the algae and bryophytes) consist of a simple body or thallus upon which the organs of reproduction are borne. Simplest of all are the threadlike algae, for example, *Spirogyra*, which consist of a chain of cells. The seaweeds (algae) and mosses and liverworts (bryophytes) represent a further development, with their simple, multicellular bodies that have specially modified areas in which the reproductive organs are carried. Higher in the morphological scale are the ferns, clubmosses and horsetails (pteridophytes). Ferns produce leaf-like fronds bearing sporangia on their under-surface in which the spores are carried. The spores are freed and germinate to produce small independent bodies carrying the sexual organs; thus like other pteridophytes, and some seaweeds, has two quite separate generations in its life cycle. The pteridophytes have special supportive water-conducting tissues, which identify them as vascular plants. This group includes all seed plants, that is the gymnosperms (conifers, yews, cycads and ginkgo) and the angiosperms (flowering plants). The seed plants are the largest group, and structurally the most complex. They are usually divided into three parts, root, stem and leaves. Stems grow above or below ground. Their cellular structure is designed to carry water and salts from the roots to the leaves in the xylem, and sugars from the leaves to the roots in the phloem. The leaves manufacture the food of the plant by means of photosynthesis, which occurs in the chloroplasts which they contain. Flowers and cones are modified leaves arranged in groups and enclosing the reproductive organs from which the fruits and seeds result. Plants are autotrophs, that is they make their own food, and are the primary producers in all terrestrial food chains, so that all animal life on land is directly or indirectly dependent on them. As crop plants and animal feed they also supply most human food. They play a vital part in the carbon cycle, removing carbon dioxide from the atmosphere and generating oxygen. The study of plants is known as botany.

plant classification the taxonomy or classification of plants. Originally the plant kingdom included bacteria, diatoms, dinoflagellates, fungi and slime moulds, but these are not now thought of as plants. The unicellular algae, such as *Chlamydomonas*, are often now put with the protists instead of the plants, and some classification schemes even classify the multicellular algae (seaweeds and freshwater weeds) in a new kingdom, the Protoctista,

plant classification

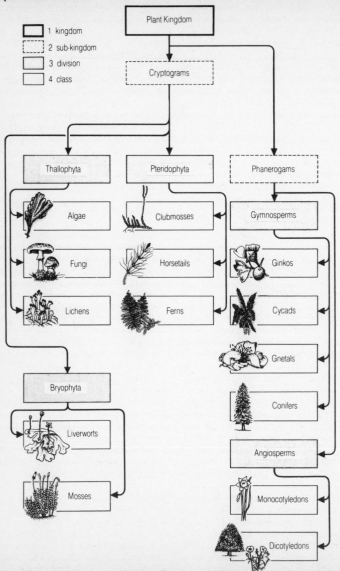

Plant Kingdom

1 kingdom
2 sub-kingdom
3 division
4 class

Cryptograms

Thallophyta

Pteridophyta

Phanerogams

Algae

Clubmosses

Gymnosperms

Fungi

Horsetails

Ginkos

Lichens

Ferns

Cycads

Gnetals

Conifers

Bryophyta

Angiosperms

Liverworts

Monocotyledons

Mosses

Dicotyledons

along with the protists. The groups that are always classified as plants are the bryophytes (mosses and liverworts), pteridophytes (ferns, horsetails and clubmosses) gymnosperms (conifers, yews, cycads and ginkgos) and angiosperms (flowering plants). The angiospersms are split into the monocotyledons (for example, orchids, grasses, lilies) and the dicotyledons (for example, oak, buttercup, geranium and daisy).

The basis of plant classification was established by Linnaeus. Among the angiosperms, it is largely based on the number and arrangement of the flower parts.

photosynthesis the process by which green plants and photosynthetic bacteria and cyanobacteria utilize light energy from the sun to produce food molecules (carbohydrates) from carbon dioxide and water. There are two distinct stages within the process. During the *light reaction* sunlight is used to split water (H_2O) into oxygen (O_2), protons (hydrogen ions, H^+) and electrons. Oxygen is given off as a by-product during the light reaction. The protons and electrons are then used to convert carbon dioxide (CO_2) into carbohydrates (CH_2O) – the *dark reaction* for which sunlight is not required. Photosynthesis is dependent on the ability of chlorophyll to capture the energy of sunlight and use it to split water molecules. Other pigments, such as carotenoids, are also involved in capturing light energy and passing it on to chlorophyll. Photosynthesis by cyanobacteria was responsible for the appearance of oxygen in the earth's atmosphere 2,500 million years ago, and photosynthesis by plants maintains the oxygen level today.

chlorophyll the green pigment present in the majority of plants which is responsible for the absorption of light energy during the light reaction of photosynthesis. It absorbs the red and blue-violet parts of sunlight but reflects the green, thus giving the characteristic colour to most plants. Chlorophyll is found within the chloroplasts, which are present in large numbers especially in the leaves. Cyanobacteria and other photosynthetic bacteria also have

chlorophyll, though of a slightly different type. Chlorophyll is similar in structure to haemoglobin, but with magnesium instead of iron as the reactive part of the molecule.

Main Plant Types

alga simple plant which contains chlorophyll and photosynthesizes, but without true leaves, stems and roots. Most algae are aquatic, commonly called seaweeds, and reproduce usually by spores. Included in the group are minute single-celled organisms such as the freshwater *Chlamydomonas*, simple multicellular forms such as the filamentous *Spirogyra*, and also the larger and more complex wracks, kelps and other seaweeds.

angiosperm flowering plant in which the seeds are enclosed within an ovary, which ripens to a fruit. Angiosperms are divided into monocotyledons and dicotyledons, and include the vast majority of flowers, herbs, grasses, bushes and trees (except conifers).

clubmoss plant of the class Lycopodiales, allied to ferns and horsetails. A larger spore-bearing generation, with leaves and stems with conducting vessels ('veins'), alternates with a small underground sexual generation. Important and numerous about 300 millions years ago, when many grew to tree size, the surviving 100 or so species are all small. The common clubmoss or stag's-horn moss *Lycopodium clavatum* is found on upland heaths.

conifer plant of the class Coniferales, in the gymnosperm group. These are trees or shrubs, often pyramidal in form, with leaves that are 'needles' or scale-like. The 'flowers' are the male and female cones, and pollen is distributed by the wind. The seeds develop in the female cones. Conifers include pines, firs, yews, monkey-puzzles, and larches. Most are evergreen.

cycad primitive flowering plant superficially resembling a fern or palm, but belonging, like conifers, to the gymnosperm group. Cycads also have cones, some being 60 cm/2 ft long. Cycads are known from 200 million years ago, the 80 or so living species in tropical regions being only a small remnant of the group. Some species yield 'sago' from the stem.

dicotyledon angiosperm with two cotyledons (seed-leaves), forming the majority of flowering plants. They generally have broad leaves with net-like veins. Dicotyledons may be small plants such as daisies and buttercups; shrubs; or trees such as oak and beech.

fern plant of the class Filicales, related to horsetails and clubmosses. Ferns are spore-bearing, not flowering, plants, and most are perennial herbs spreading by low-growing roots. The leaves, known as fronds, vary widely in size and shape. Some taller types, tree-ferns, grow in the tropics. There are over 7,000 species, including bracken, an agricultural weed.

ginkgo maidenhair tree *Ginkgo biloba*, is the only surviving representative of the class Ginkgoales of the gymnosperm group. Ginkgos were characteristic of Mesozoic landscapes. *G. biloba* still grows wild in China. The two-lobed leaves are characteristic. It reaches 30 m/100 ft and drops its leaves in winter.

gnetal plant of the small specialized class Gnetales of the gymnosperm group, which includes *Welwitschia mirabilis*, a woody desert plant of southwest Africa, and the shrub *Ephedra*, from which the drug ephedrine is derived.

gymnosperm flowering plant whose seeds are 'naked', that is, not borne within a true fruit as they are in angiosperms. Most gymnosperms have cones. There are four main groups of gymnosperms – conifers, cycads, ginkgos, and gnetals.

horsetail plant of the class Equisetales, related to ferns and clubmosses. There are about 25 living species, bearing their spores on cones at the stem tip. The upright stems are ribbed, and often have spaced whorls of branches. Today they are of modest size, but hundreds, of millions of years ago giant tree-like forms existed.

lichen organism of dual composition, a close association of a fungus and an alga. The alga contributes food material from photosynthesis, the fungus makes the bulk of the body. Lichens can withstand considerable drought. Some, such as 'reindeer moss', have

food value, others are used for dyes, such as litmus, or in medicine.

liverwort plant of the class Hepaticae, allied to mosses. Usually small, liverworts live in damp places and the main sexual generation consists of a 'thallus', which may be flat, green and lobed, like a small leaf, or 'leafy' and moss-like. The spore-bearing generation is smaller, typically 'parasitic' on the thallus, and throws up a capsule from which spores are spread.

monocotyledon angiosperm with a single cotyledon (seed-leaf). Monocotyledons usually have narrow leaves with parallel veins and smooth edges, and hollow or soft stems. Their flower parts are arranged in threes. Most are small plants such as orchids, grasses and lilies, but some, such as palms, are trees.

moss plant of the class Musci, allied to liverworts. Mosses have stems and leaves, but no true roots. The main plant is the sexual generation, the spore-bearing generation growing on it and producing characteristic stalked capsules. Most mosses flourish best in damp conditions.

Biographies

Audubon John James 1785–1851. American naturalist, hunter and wildlife artist. In 1827 he published the first parts of his *Birds of North America*, with a remarkable series of colour plates. Later he produced a similar work on American quadrupeds. The National Audubon Society (originating 1886) has branches throughout the US and Canada for the study and protection of birds.

Banks Sir Joseph 1743–1820. British naturalist and explorer. He accompanied Captain Cook round the world 1768–71, played a leading part in the development of New South Wales, was a principal founder of the Botanical Gardens at Kew, London, introduced new plants into various parts of the world, and was President of the Royal Society from 1778.

Cuvier Georges, baron 1769–1832. French comparative anatomist. In 1798 he produced his *Tableau élémentaire de l'histoire naturelle des animaux*, in which his scheme of classification is outlined. Cuvier was the first to relate the structure of fossil animals to that of their living allies. His great work, *Le Règne animal*, embodies a systematic survey of the animal kingdom.

Darwin Charles Robert 1809–1882. British scientist; founder of the modern theory of evolution, and discoverer of the principle of natural selection. As naturalist of the surveying voyage of HMS *Beagle* 1831–6, he made many observations, especially in South America and the nearby Galapagos Islands. In 1859 he published *On the Origin of Species by Means of Natural Selection* which set out the huge amounts of evidence he had collected to show that evolution had occurred, and explained the principles of natural selection and sexual selection. The book aroused bitter controversy because it did not agree with the literal sense of the Book of Genesis. Darwin himself played little part in the debates, but his *Descent of Man* 1871 added fuel to the theological discussion. Darwin then devoted himself chiefly to botanical studies till his death.

Frisch Karl von 1886–1982. German zoologist, founder with Lorenz of ethology, the study of animal behaviour in the natural environment. Specializing in bees, he discovered how they communicate the location of sources of nectar by 'dances'.

Haeckel Ernst Heinrich 1834–1919. German scientist and philosopher. A supporter of Darwin, he worked for more than 50 years on his own 'recapitulation' theory (that embryonic stages represent past stages in the organism's evolution). Although the theory has been superseded, it stimulated much research in embryology.

Hooke Robert 1635–1703. British experimental physicist and inventor, who furthered the sciences of mechanics and microscopy.

Huxley Thomas Henry 1825–1895. British

scientist, humanist, and agnostic thinker. Following the publication of Darwin's *On the Origin of Species* in 1859, he won fame as 'Darwin's bulldog', and for many years was the most prominent and popular champion of evolution.

Lamarck Jean Baptiste de 1744–1829. French naturalist. He studied medicine and meteorology before turning to botany. His greatest works were his *Philosophie Zoologique* 1809 and the *Histoire naturelle des animaux sans vertèbres* 1815–22. He proposed a theory of evolution based on the now discredited idea that acquired characteristics are inherited.

Leeuwenhoek Anthony van 1632–1723. Dutch anatomist and pioneer microscopist. With the simple (single-lens) microscopes he constructed he was able to observe cells and microorganisms for the first time, and he investigated a great many different subjects, including the structure of the red blood cells, the sperm cells of animals, and yeasts.

Linnaeus Carolus 1707–78. Swedish naturalist and physician, born Carl Linné, but more commonly known by the Latinized version of his name. He travelled extensively in Europe, collecting hundreds of new species, and wrote 14 botanical works, including *Systema Naturae* which contained his system for classifying plants into groups depending on the number of stamens in their flowers. He also devised a system for naming plants and animals, using one Latin (or Latinized) word to represent the genus and a second to distinguish the species. These binomial systems represented the first comprehensive method of identifying and classifying plants.

Lorenz Konrad 1903– . Austrian ethologist. Director of the Max Planck Institute for the Physiology of Behaviour in Bavaria 1961–73, he is known for his studies of animal behaviour.

Mendel Gregor 1822–1884. Austrian monk, abbot of the Augustinian abbey at Bræunn from 1868 and founder of genetics. By experiments with generations of peas in the monastery garden he developed a theory of particulate inheritance, involving dominant

403

and recessive characters. He published his results 1865–9, but his work remained unrecognized until the early 20th century.

Ray John 1627–1705. British naturalist who devised a classification system accounting for nearly 18,000 plant species. It was the first to divide flowering plants into monocotyledons and dicotyledons, with additional divisions made on the basis of leaf and flower characters and fruit types.

Thoreau Henry David 1817–62. US author and naturalist, whose book *Walden, or Life in the Woods* 1854 and many other works showed a close observation of nature from what would now be called an ecological standpoint.

Tinbergen Nikolaas 1907– . Dutch zoologist, specializing in the study of instinctive behaviour. He has had considerable influence in establishing the relatively new science of ethology.

Vries Hugo de 1848–1935. Dutch botanist, who conducted important research on osmosis in plant cells and was a pioneer in the study of plant evolution. His work led to the rediscovery of Mendel's Laws and the formulation of the theory of mutation.

The New Synthesis

genetics the study of inheritance and of genes, which are the units of inheritance. The founder of genetics was Gregor Mendel. From his experiments with plants such as peas he realized that inheritance takes place by means of discrete 'particles', which later came to be called genes. Before Mendel, it had been assumed that the characteristics of the two parents were blended during inheritance, but Mendel showed that the genes remained intact although their combinations change. In the century since Mendel genetics has advanced greatly, first by means of breeding experiments and light-microscope observations (classical genetics), later by means of biochemical and electron-microscope studies (molecular genetics). An important advance was the elucidation of the structure of DNA by Watson and Crick, and the subsequent cracking of the genetic code. These discoveries opened up the possibility of deliberately manipulating genes, or genetic engineering.

molecular biology the study of the molecular basis of life, including the biochemistry of molecules such as DNA, RNA, and proteins, and the structure and function of the various parts of living cells.

biosynthesis the synthesis of organic compounds from simple inorganic ones by living cells. One important biosynthetic reaction is the conversion of carbon dioxide and water to glucose by plants, during photosynthesis. Other biosynthetic reactions produce cell constituents including proteins and fats. Biosynthesis requires energy, and in photosynthesis this is obtained from sunlight, but in most biosynthetic reactions it is supplied by ATP. The term is also used in connection with biotechnology processes.

biotechnology the industrial use of living organisms to produce food, drugs, or other products. Modern processes include fermentation to produce methane and alcohol for fuel from sugar or waste food products; the use of bacteria to remove heavy metals from polluted areas; and the production of protein from oil residues. The most recent advances in biotechnology involve genetic engineering, in which single-celled organisms with modified DNA are used to produce useful substances such as insulin.

genetic engineering the natural course of heredity is interfered with by any breeding programme, but true genetic engineering is direct manipulation of genetic material by biochemical techniques. This is often achieved by introduction of new DNA, ordinarily by means of an infecting virus. This transplantation of genes is used to increase our knowledge of cell function and reproduction, but it can also achieve practical ends, for example, plants grown for food could be given the ability to fix nitrogen, found in some bacteria, and so reduce the need for expensive fertilizers, or simple bacteria may be enabled to produce rare drugs. However, there is a risk that when transplanting genes between different types of bacteria (*Escherichia coli*, which lives in the human intestine, is often used) new and harmful bacteria might be produced, which, on escape from the laboratory, might start an uncontrollable epidemic. One solution, apart from strict safety precautions, is to render the bacteria genetically unable to exist outside the laboratory.

Key Terms

allele an alternative form of a given gene. Thus, blue and brown eyes are determined by different alleles of the gene for eye colour.

base pair the linkage of two base (purine or pyrimidine) molecules in DNA. One base of each pair lies on one of the two strands of the DNA double helix, and one on the other strand, so the base pairs link the two strands, rather like the rungs of a ladder. In DNA, there are four bases: adenine and guanine (purines) and cytosine and thymine (pyrimidines). Adenine always pairs with thymine and cytosine with guanine. Because the pairs are so specific, DNA can replicate itself precisely, by separating the two strands of the helix and forming new strands using the original ones as templates. This is the basis of heredity. When RNA is formed from DNA, base pairs are again used to copy the genetic message, but in RNA another base, uracil, substitutes for thymine.

chromosome a structure in a cell nucleus responsible for the transmission of hereditary characteristics.

clone a group of genetically identical plants or animals. In nature, they are produced by certain types of asexual reproduction, for example, the plantlets that grow from a strawberry runner are genetically identical to the parent individual. By contrast, higher animals and plants normally reproduce sexually, as a result of which their offspring inherit only half of each parent's genes. Interest in generating clones of higher plants and animals has centred on the economic value of perpetuating particularly successful varieties or breeds.

diploid having two sets of chromosomes in each cell. In sexually reproducing species, one set is derived from each parent, the gametes, or sex cells, of each parent being haploid (having only one set of chromosomes) due to meiosis.

DNA deoxyribonucleic acid; a complex two-stranded molecule that contains, in chemically coded form, all the information needed to build, control and maintain a living organism. DNA is a double-stranded nucleic acid that forms the basis of genetic inheritance in all organisms, except for a few viruses that depend on RNA. In eukaryotic organisms, it is organized into chromosomes and contained in the cell nucleus.

By specifying protein sequences, DNA can build a whole organism. All aspects of the functioning of an organism depend on enzymes, and enzymes are proteins also, so DNA controls the rates of protein production also. DNA is 'translated' into protein by means of messenger RNA.

dominance in genetics, the concept that certain characteristics are dominant, that is, they mask the expression of other characteristics, known as recessives. For example if a person has one allele (gene variant) for blue eyes and one for brown eyes, the brown colour will predominate.

enzyme biological catalyst able to convert one chemical to another quickly, without being destroyed itself, for example, those in yeast, used in making bread and alcohol, and those within the human body which digest food, such as pepsin in the stomach. Bulk production of enzymes from bacteria, and increasingly the re-use of pure enzymes bonded to glass, and other materials, underpins the manufacture of, for example, detergents, and low-cost processed cheese. In medicine enzymes may be used to correct disorders of the body's metabolism.

Frankenstein law in the USA, the ruling by the Supreme Court 1980 that new forms of life created in the laboratory may be patented.

gene a unit of inherited material, situated on a strand of nucleic acid (DNA or RNA). In higher organisms, genes are located on the chromosomes. The term 'gene' was first used in 1909 by the Danish geneticist Wilhelm Johannsen to refer to the inherited factor that consistently affects a particular character in an individual that bears it, for example, the gene for eye colour. Also termed a Mendelian gene, after Gregor Mendel, it may have several variants or alleles, each of which specifies a particular form of that character, for example, the alleles for blue eyes or brown eyes. Some alleles show dominance, that is they mask the effect of others, known as recessive alleles.

In the 1940s, it was established that a gene could be identified with a particular length of DNA, which coded for a complete protein molecule, leading to the 'one-gene-one-enzyme' principle. Later it was realized that proteins might be made up of several polypeptide chains, each with a separate gene, so this principle was modified to 'one-gene-one-polypeptide'. However, the fundamental idea remains the same, that genes produce their visible effects simply by coding for proteins; they control the structure of those proteins via the genetic code, as well as the amounts produced and the timing of production. Genes undergo mutation and recombination to produce the variation on which natural selection operates.

genetic code the way in which instructions for building proteins, the basic structural molecules of living matter, are 'written' in the genetic material DNA. This relationship between the sequence of bases, the sub-units in a DNA molecule, and the sequence of amino acids, the sub-units of a protein molecule, is the basis of heredity. The code employs codons of three bases each; it is the same in almost all organisms, except for a few minor differences recently discovered in some bacteria.

genotype the particular set of alleles (variants of genes) possessed by a given organism. The term is usually used in conjunction with phenotype, which is the product of the genotype and all environmental effects.

haploid having one set of chromosomes in each cell. Most higher organisms are diploid, that is they have two sets, but moss plants and many seaweeds are haploid, as are female honey bees (because they develop from eggs that have not been fertilized). *Polyploid* means having more than twice the basic (haploid) number of chromosomes.

heredity the transmission of traits from parent to offspring.

heterozygous having two different alleles of the gene for a given trait. In homozygous organisms, by contrast, both chromosomes carry the same allele. An individual organism will generally be heterozygous for some genes but homozygous for others.

homozygous having two identical alleles of the gene for a given trait. Homozygous individuals always breed true, that is they produce offspring that resemble them in appearance, when bred with a genetically similar individual. Recessive alleles are only expressed in the homozygous condition.

hybrid the offspring from a cross between individuals of two different species, or two inbred lines within a species. In most cases, hybrids between species are infertile and unable to reproduce sexually. In plants, however, doubling of the chromosomes (polyploidy) can restore the fertility of such hybrids. Hybrids between different genera are extremely rare; an example is the leylandii cypress which, like many hybrids shows exceptional vigour, or heterosis. In the wild, a 'hybrid zone' may occur where the ranges of two related species meet.

linkage the association between two or more genes, which tend to be inherited together because they are on the same chromosome. The closer together they are on the chromosome, the less likely they are to be separated by crossing-over (one of the processes of recombination) and they are then described as being 'tightly linked'.

meiosis type of sexual reproduction in which a cell nucleus divides into parts, each containing half of the total number of chromosomes of the original. Two of these unite to form a new and different cell.

mitosis type of asexual reproduction in which the genetic information is reproduced exactly in the new cells, rather than by being split and recombined, as in meiosis.

mutation a change in a particular gene that produces a new variation in a given character of an organism which is thereafter incorporated into the genetic material (DNA) of that organism. This type of change is one of the bases of evolutionary theory. Mutational changes may be spontaneous, or induced, for example by radiation, and may involve the deletion, addition, duplication or inversion of base pairs making up a given segment of DNA. It has been estimated that a given gene will undergo mutation about once in every ten million generations.

peptide a molecule comprising two or more amino acids joined by peptide bonds. A peptide is, generally speaking a much smaller molecule than a protein, but there is no clear dividing line between them. The term peptide is applied to the breakdown products of proteins, to the precursors of proteins, and to hormones such as vasopressin and oxytocin (nine amino acids each). The term 'polypeptide' is used interchangeably with 'peptide' although it generally implies a longer-chain molecule.

phenotype in genetics, the traits actually displayed by an organism. The phenotype is not a direct reflection of the genotype because some alleles are masked by the presence of other dominant alleles. Furthermore, the phenotype is modified by the effects of the environment (for example, poor food stunting growth).

protein a long chain molecule made up of amino acids, joined together by peptide bonds. Proteins are essential to all living organisms. As enzymes they regulate all aspects of metabolism. Structural proteins such as keratin and collagen make up the skin, claws, bones, tendons and ligaments, while muscle proteins produce movement, haemoglobin transports oxygen, and membrane proteins regulate the movement of substances into and out of cells.

For humans, protein is an essential part of the diet.

recessivity in a diploid organism, a recessive allele is one that can only produce a detectable effect on the phenotype of the organism bearing it when both chromosomes carry it, that is, when the same allele has been inherited from both parents, and the individual is homozygous for it. In heterozygous individuals, its effects will be masked by a dominant allele.

replication the production of copies of the genetic material, DNA; it occurs during cell division (mitosis and meiosis).

RNA *ribonucleic acid*. A nucleic acid involved in the construction of proteins from DNA, the genetic material. It is usually single-stranded, unlike DNA, and consists of a large number of nucleotides strung together, each of which comprises the sugar ribose and one of four bases (uracil, cytosine, adenine or guanine). RNA is copied from DNA by the formation of base pairs, with uracil taking the place of thymine. RNA occurs in three major forms, each with a different function in the synthesis of protein molecules. *Messenger RNA* (mRNA) acts as the template for protein synthesis. Each codon (a set of three bases) on the RNA molecule is matched up with the corresponding amino acid, in accordance with the genetic code. This process (translation) takes place in the ribosomes, which are made up of proteins and *ribosomal RNA* (rRNA). *Transfer RNA* (tRNA) is responsible for combining with specific amino acids, and then matching up a special 'anticodon' sequence of its own with a codon or the mRNA. This is how the genetic code is translated.

Although RNA is normally associated only with the process of protein synthesis, it may be the hereditary material itself in some viruses.

sex linkage the tendency for certain characters to occur exclusively, or predominantly, in one sex only. Human examples include red-green colour blindness and haemophilia, both found predominantly in males. In both cases, these characters are recessive and are determined by genes on the X chromosome: since females possess two X chromosomes, any such recessive allele on one of them is likely to be masked by the corresponding allele on the other. In males (who have only one X chromosome paired with an inert Y chromosome) any gene on the X chromosome will automatically be expressed. Colour blindness and haemophilia can appear in females, but only if they are homozygous for these traits, due to inbreeding, for example.

transcription in living cells, the process by which the information for the synthesis of a protein is transferred from the DNA strand on which it is carried to the messenger RNA strand involved in the actual synthesis. It occurs by the formation of base pairs between the DNA molecule and the nucleotides that make up the new RNA strand.

translation in living cells, the process by which proteins are synthesized. During translation, the information coded as a sequence of nucelotides in messenger RNA is transformed into a sequence of amino acids in a peptide chain. The process involves the 'translation' of the genetic code.

Medicine

Medicine and its ever-increasing array of allied sciences, such as pathology (study of cellular disease processes) and epidemiology (study of disease patterns in communities and regions), still have as their focus the prevention, diagnosis, alleviation and cure of disease, both physical and mental. A *medicine* is also any substance used in the treatment of disease. The basis of medicine is anatomy, or the structure and form of the body, and physiology, or the study of the body's functions.

In the West, medicine increasingly relies on new drugs and sophisticated surgical techniques, while diagnosis of disease is more and more by 'non-invasive' procedures such as Computerized Axial Tomography (CAT) scanning. The time and cost of Western-type medical training makes it inaccessible to many parts of the Third World; where health care of this kind is provided, it is often by auxiliary medical helpers trained in hygiene and the administration of a limited number of standard drugs for the prevalent diseases of a particular region. *Complementary* or *alternative medicine* encompasses forms of diagnosis and treatment which stress the use of more natural herbal drugs, and techniques which until recently have been unfamiliar in Western medicine, such as acupuncture, homoeopathy, naturopathy, massage, and osteopathy.

The following pages provide an overview of medical science, including a world survey of major *Diseases and Disorders*, explanations of significant *Medical Terms*, a guide to major *Drug Types*, and a *Chronology* of events in the history of medicine. Psychology is covered in a separate section under the general heading Society.

Diseases and Disorders

AIDS Acquired Immune Deficiency Syndrome a disease marked by weight loss, diarrhoea, swollen glands, and resulting in the destruction of the body's immune system, leaving it vulnerable to infection by viruses and bacteria. It is as yet incurable. Identified 1980, it is caused by a blood-borne virus (HIV, Human Immuno-deficiency Virus). It is transmitted by certain forms of sexual contact; by shared syringes among drug addicts; and by infected blood products. In Britain, AIDS patients in a condition dangerous to others, for example bleeding badly, may be legally detained in hospital under a Public Health Act of 1984.

anaemia medical condition characterized by too few red blood cells or too little haemoglobin (the red oxygen-carrying substance in red blood cells), so that the sufferer becomes quickly tired, faint and breathless. It may result from iron deficiency (as in pregnant women), be linked with rheumatoid arthritis, be the result of nuclear radiation, or inherited. Genetic anaemic diseases include *sickle cell anaemia,* and *pernicious anaemia*, a failure of the stomach to secrete the substances necessary to produce blood from food, which is cured by doses of vitamin B12.

angina or **angina pectoris** (Latin 'tightness of the chest'), may be a sign of a heart disease caused by restricted blood supply to the heart because a coronary artery is narrowed; the pain seems to shoot across the chest and arm, rather than appearing to come from the heart.

arteriosclerosis hardening of the arteries, the thickening and loss of elasticity of the circulatory system. It is associated with ageing and a diet high in saturated fats.

arthritis inflammation of the joints, of which the most widespread form is *rheumatoid arthritis*, which usually begins in middle age in the small joints of the hands and feet, causing a greater or lesser degree of deformity and painfully restricted movement. Aspirin is still the most commonly used alleviating drug. *Osteoarthritis* tends to affect larger joints, such as the knee and hip, so that artificial joints may be used to restore mobility. It appears in later life, especially in those whose joints may have been subject to earlier stress or damage. The disease seems to be influenced by heredity and may be triggered by a virus infection.

asthma recurrent difficulty in inhaling (breathing in) due to the contraction of muscles in the walls of the lungs' breathing passages. It is either allergic in origin, for example a reaction to dust, eggs, milk, the hair or scurf of an animal, or caused by a form of heart disease (*cardiac asthma*) and can be brought on by anxiety.

atherosclerosis thickening of the lining of the arteries, thus hindering blood flow and increasing the risk of heart attack or a stroke by the formation of a blood clot. It is associated with a diet high in animal fats.

bronchitis inflammation of the bronchi (the tubes admitting air to the lungs), usually caused initially by a viral infection (a cold or flu); chronic bronchitis may develop in those exposed to atmospheric pollutants (for example, sulphur dioxide SO_2) or cigarette smoke.

cancer group of diseases resulting in malignant growths or tumours classified as carcinomas, growing from the skin or mucous membrane, and sarcomas, which affect bone, cartilage, and muscle (connective tissue), also including leukaemia (a 'cancer' of the blood). *Production* of cancer cells may be triggered by the activation of genes which are present in normal cells, but which are either dormant or make themselves known at very low levels. Such cells then grow and divide without restriction, forming 'lumps' and sometimes spreading to other parts of the body (metastasizing). Triggering agents include chemical carcinogens, for example asbestos dust, benzpyrene, household chemicals, cigarette-smoking; viruses; radiation, for example

human body

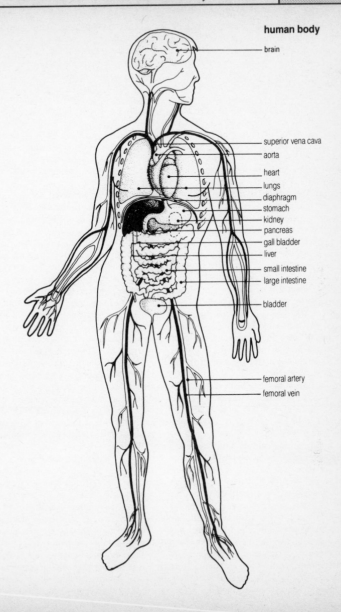

- brain
- superior vena cava
- aorta
- heart
- lungs
- diaphragm
- stomach
- kidney
- pancreas
- gall bladder
- liver
- small intestine
- large intestine
- bladder
- femoral artery
- femoral vein

411

X-rays; family diet and possibly psychological stress. Many experts believe that avoiding such factors would avert more than half of cancers. *Treatment* of cancer includes surgery, radiotherapy, and chemotherapy using cytotoxic drugs which slow or halt cell division. Cancer cells are immortal, so that tumour cells can be grown for ever in culture. The most common cancer sites in men are, in order, the lung, prostate, large intestine, urinary tract, blood (leukaemias) and lymph (lymphomas). The most common cancer sites in women are the breast, large intestine, uterus, lung, blood (leukaemias) and lymph (lymphomas).

cerebral haemorrhage the bursting of a blood vessel in the brain, caused by one or more factors such as a blood clot, high blood pressure combined with hardening of the arteries, chronic poisoning with lead or alcohol, for example; it is popularly known as a *stroke*. It may cause death, or damage parts of the brain and lead to various degrees of paralysis or mental impairment. The effects are usually longterm.

cholera intestinal infection by a bacterium (*Vibrio cholerae*), formerly with a high death rate, much reduced by injections or drinks of saline fluid to prevent dehydration. Transmitted in contaminated water or food, it is still prevalent in many tropical areas.

coronary heart disease heart condition in which the fatty deposits of atherosclerosis form in, and therefore narrow, the coronary arteries which supply the heart muscle. (Latin *corona* 'crown', from their encircling of the heart). These arteries may already be hardened (*arteriosclerosis*). If the heart's oxygen requirements are increased, as during exercise, the blood supply through the narrowed arteries may be inadequate, and the pain of angina results. A heart attack occurs if the blood supply to an area of the heart is cut off, for example because a blood clot (*thrombus*) has blocked one of the coronary arteries. The subsequent lack of oxygen damages the heart muscle (*infarct*), and if a large area of the heart is affected, the attack may be fatal. Coronary heart disease tends to run in families, and is linked to smoking, lack of exercise, and a diet high in saturated (mostly animal) fats which increases the level of blood cholesterol. It is a common cause of death in many developed countries, especially among older men.

dementia a state of mental deterioration accompanied by emotional disturbance. It is usually associated with old age and may be caused by faulty blood supply to the brain. A proportion of younger people showing signs of dementia suffer from *Alzheimer's disease* (loss of brain cells, tangling and distortion of those remaining, and biochemical imbalance). It is as yet untreatable.

diabetes or (*diabetes mellitus*) disease in which a deficiency in the islets of the pancreas gland (which make the hormone insulin) prevents the body using blood sugars properly. In adults it may be controlled by diet and/or insulin; in children it usually needs daily insulin injection. Untreated it causes death in coma.

dysentery infective bleeding and ulceration of the large bowel, causing diarrhoea containing blood and mucus, and usually due to either amoebae or bacillae micro-organisms. Treatment is by drugs, and in the more serious *amoebic dysentery* the amoebae must be killed. It is spread by infected water and foods, and remains common in some tropical areas.

epilepsy disorder of nervous system involving attacks of loss or alteration of consciousness, sometimes with convulsions (fits). It is controlled by anticonvulsant drugs. There are several different forms, and a percentage of young sufferers outgrow the condition.

filariasis collective term for several diseases, prevalent in tropical areas, caused by roundworm (nematode) parasites. Symptoms include blocked and swollen lymph vessels leading to grotesque swellings of the legs and genitals (*Bancroftian filariasis*, *elephantiasis*); and blindness and dry, scaly skin (*onchocerciasis*). These diseases are spread mainly by insects, notably mosquitoes and blackflies.

hepatitis inflammation of the liver. Hepatitis B is a long-term viral disease of the Third World, causing jaundice and linked with liver cancer, but preventable by vaccine. It is carried by the blood and other body fluids; a small proportion of recovered patients become carriers (the virus remains in the liver).

hypertension abnormally high blood pressure, the smooth muscle cells making up the walls of the arteries being constantly contracted. It increases the risk of several illnesses including kidney disorder, stroke, and heart attacks.

leishmaniasis parasitic disease caused by microscopic protozoans (*Leishmania*), prevalent across the tropical countries of the world and transmitted by sandfly midges. Symptoms include ulcerative growths that eat away the nose, mouth and throat; anaemia; and liver and spleen enlargment.

leprosy mainly tropical infectious disease caused by the bacillus *Mycobacterium leprae* which results in broken and bleeding lumps in the skin, skin discoloration, paralysis, shedding of fingers and toes among other symptoms. It is curable by drugs, and currently a vaccine is undergoing trials.

leukaemia form of cancer of the blood, marked by an increase in the white blood cells. Cure or control is by radiotherapy or drugs, especially successful in younger patients.

malaria infectious disease, marked by periodic fever and an enlarged spleen, which affects some 200 million people a year. When a female mosquito of the *Anopheles* genus bites a human with malaria, it takes in with the human blood the malaria parasite (*Plasmodium*). This matures within the insect, and is then transferred when the mosquito bites a new victim. Inside the human body the parasite settles first in the liver, then multiplies to attack the red blood cells, when the symptoms of malaria become evident. In some areas it is resistant to pesticides, but a vaccine is under development. Treatment is by antimalarial drugs.

obesity over-weight, which increases susceptibility to disease, strains the vital organs, and lessens life expectancy; it is remedied by healthy diet and exercise. Results differ in individuals because of variations in the natural rate of the body's metabolic (chemical) processes, and in the structure of fatty tissue itself.

pneumonia inflammation of the lungs, the result of infection by bacteria (expecially pneumococci) or viruses, making breathing difficult. It is treated with antibiotics.

schistosomiasis or **bilharzia** disease contracted by bathing in water containing the snails which act as host to the first larval stage of flukes of the genus *Schistosoma*. When these larvae leave the snail in their second stage of development, they are able to pass through human skin, become sexually mature, and produce quantities of eggs which pass to the intestine or bladder. The human host may die, but before then numerous eggs have passed from the body in urine or faeces to continue the cycle. Some 300 million people are thought to suffer from this disease in tropical countries.

stroke a common name for a cerebral haemorrhage.

trypanosomiasis collection of debilitating long-term diseases caused by infestation with the microscopic single-celled *Trypanosoma*. They include sleeping sickness (*nagana*) in Africa, transmitted by the bites of tsetse flies, and *Chagas' disease* in the Americas, spread by assassin-bugs. Millions of people are affected in warmer regions of the world; the diseases also affect cattle, which form a reservoir of infection.

typhoid fever infectious disease caused by the bacterium *Salmonella typhi* and usually contracted through infected water; there is a temporarily effective vaccine (treatment of the disease itself is by antibiotic drugs). *Paratyphoid fever* caused by *S paratyphi* is a milder form.

Medical Terms

abortion medically, expulsion of the foetus from the womb before it is capable of independent life. It is controversial as a means of birth control (methods include the use of drugs and vacuum aspiration), but was legalized within certain guidelines in the UK in 1967 if carried out during the first 28 weeks of pregnancy. When it happens naturally (spontaneous abortion) it is normally called a *miscarriage*. If induced intentionally it is often called a *termination of pregnancy*.

allergy special sensitivity of the body which makes it react, with an exaggerated response of the natural immune defence mechanism, to the introduction of a harmless foreign substance termed an *allergen*. The person subject to hay fever in summer is allergic to one or more kinds of pollen. Many asthmatics are allergic to certain kinds of dust or to micro-organisms in animal fur or feathers. Others come out in nettle-rash, or are violently sick if they eat shellfish or egg. Drugs may be used to reduce sensitivity or produce tolerance, but there is no universal remedy.

anaesthesia an induced state of insensibility to various feelings such as touch, pressure and pain. Sir Humphry Davy first suggested that nitrous oxide (laughing gas) be used to produce loss of sensation in surgery, and in 1844 Horace Wells, a New England dentist, had a tooth extracted· in this way. Chloroform, used by James Simpson on women in childbirth, received the royal accolade when used by Queen Victoria at the birth of Prince Leopold in 1853. Varied anaesthetics are now given, both general (inducing overall unconsciousness) and local, and there have been experiments with acupuncture and hypnosis. *Epidural anaesthesia* (injection into the space around the membranes covering the spinal cord) is used in childbirth, and increasingly for major abdominal operations; the patient remains conscious, and there is reduced risk of complication, with quicker recovery.

antibody any of the proteins produced in the blood in response to the presence of a bacterium, virus, transplanted organ or other foreign tissue *(antigen)* which attach themselves to the 'invader' (*antigen*) or otherwise help destroy it, a process called the immune reaction.

antigen substance promoting the formation of antibodies by the immune system upon entry into the body. Antigens are derived from proteins and can include harmful viruses, bacteria and protozoa, as well as harmless substances such as grass, pollen, and animal fur that trigger allergies.

arteriography a method of examining the interior of an artery by injecting into it a radio-opaque solution which is visible on an X-ray photograph. Used for the heart's coronary arteries (coronary arteriogram) for example.

auto-immune disease a disorder in which the body's defences are turned against itself, as in rheumatoid arthritis, some types of diabetes, and possibly multiple sclerosis.

biopsy removal of tissue from a living body for the purpose of diagnostic examination.

blood group in 1900 Karl Landsteiner discovered that when the serum of one person's blood was mixed with the red cells of another, agglutination (dangerous clumping) of the red cells may follow. Humans are divided into groups (ABO, Rhesus among others) depending on the ability of their blood to mix with other types. Blood groups are of great importance in transfusions and may be of use in cases of disputed paternity. A Rhesus-positive baby being carried by a Rhesus-negative mother may suffer severe lack of red blood cells (*Rhesus disease*).

blood pressure the pressure, or tension, due to the muscular action of the left side of the heart, which forces the blood out of the left ventricle into the arterial system, acting against the elastic muscular coats of the arteries, which tend to contract and resist the passage of blood. It varies considerably, gives a valuable indication of the condition of a person's health, and is measured in terms of the height in millimetres of a column of mercury which the pressure would support. Normal blood pressure is in the region of 120/80 mm of mercury, the first figure being systolic (as the heart contracts) and the second diastolic (as the heart relaxes between beats). Persistent high blood pressure (hypertension) may be a sign of disease of the arteries. A very high blood pressure, especially when the arteries are hard, brings with it a risk of stroke or kidney disease.

blood test one of a variety of tests made to detect levels of body chemicals, disease or foreign substances such as poisons or alcohol in the blood. Blood tests in commonest use are cell counts, determination of the time taken to coagulate (clot), and the chemical measurement of the major constituents of blood.

Caesarean section the removal of a baby from the womb through an incision in the abdominal wall. Julius Caesar is said to have entered the world in this way.

carrier someone whose body harbours disease-causing organisms (such as typhoid bacteria) but shows no symptoms of the disease. He or she can, however, pass the infection to others.

CAT scan (*Computerized Axial Tomography*). A special X-ray procedure in which the camera 'scans' a body organ, taking hundreds of x-ray pictures from various angles and levels. These are integrated by computer to build up a composite and detailed picture of the organ.

cautery destroying, or fusing, body tissues using heat, electricity, or chemicals. *Cryocautery* employs intense cold; a cautery knife uses heat to seal small blood vessels, so reducing bleeding upon surgical incision.

cervical smear (*PAP smear*) a screening test to detect changes in cells rubbed from the cervix (neck of the womb) that might, without treatment, lead to cancer.

chemotherapy use of drugs and medications to treat illness, especially cancers.

dialysis 'filtering' the blood to remove wastes and impurities, usually as a form of treatment for kidney disease (renal dialysis).

dilatation and curettage (*D and C*) a procedure in which the cervix (neck-shaped entrance of the womb) is widened or dilated, to access the inside of the womb, so that its lining can be scraped away (curettage). It may be carried out to terminate a pregnancy, treat an incomplete miscarriage or discover the cause of heavy menstruation.

electrocardiogram (*ECG*) a recording on a chart of the electrical impulses from the heart, detected by metal sensors attached to the chest, and used to diagnose heart disorders.

electro-encephalogram (*EEG*) a recording on a chart of the electrical discharges of the brain, detected using metal sensors on the scalp, used in diagnosis of brain conditions such as epilepsy.

endoscope a long, telescope-like, usually flexible instrument equipped with a lighting and lens system that enables a doctor to examine, biopsy and photograph the interior of a body cavity.

immunity resistance to infection. It may be *natural* (through the body's natural production of antibodies), *acquired* by the injection of ready-made antibodies (as from horse serum), or *induced* by immunizations, when a harmless version of the infecting organism stimulates antibody production.

mammography a breast X-ray procedure that detects breast cancer at a very early stage.

physiotherapy an aspect of treatment of injury and disease, by physical means such as electrical stimulation, exercise, heat, manipulation, and massage.

psychotherapy the use of psychological methods, chiefly 'talking treatments', against mental disorder. There are many forms, including cognitive therapy and association.

radiotherapy the treatment of disease by radiation from X-ray machines or radio-isotopes. Radiation reduces the activity of dividing cells, and so is especially useful in treating cancer tissue, some non-malignant tumours and some diseases of the skin, and

415

may be used in combination with drugs and surgery. Small irradiating sources may be implanted into the tissue being treated, in an attempt to localize the radiation.

scanning 'non-invasive' examination of body organs to detect abnormalities of structure or functioning. Detectable waves, for example ultrasound, magnetic, or X-rays, are passed through the part to be scanned. Their absorption pattern is recorded, analysed by computer and displayed pictorially on a screen or as a photograph.

screening testing large numbers of apparently healthy people to detect early symptoms of disease.

surgery in medicine, originally the removal of diseased parts or foreign substances from the body. The surgeon now uses not only the scalpel and electric cautery, but beamed high-energy ultrasonic waves, binocular magnifiers for microsurgery, and the intense light energy of the laser. There are many specialized fields, including *cardiac* (heart), *orthopaedic* (bones and joints), *ophthalmic* (eye), *neuro-* (brain and nerves), *thoracic* (chest), and *renal* (kidney) surgery. Modern extensions of the field of surgery include: *microsurgery* for which the surgeon uses a binocular microscope, magnifying 25 times, for example in rejoining a severed limb; *plastic surgery* repair of damaged tissue (for example skin grafts for burns) and restructuring of damaged or deformed parts of the body; also *cosmetic surgery*; *transplant surgery* the transfer of an embryo, genetic material, an organ, tissue, and so on, from one part of the body to another, or to another body.

ultrasound use of high-frequency sound waves to investigate various body organs. Sound waves transmitted through the body are absorbed and reflected to different degrees by different body tissues. By recording the 'echoes' a picture of the different structures being scanned can be built up, such as an image of the unborn baby in the womb.

vaccine modified preparation of viruses, bacteria, and so on, used to inoculate healthy persons, so as to induce the reaction which

produces immunity. Edward Jenner in 1796 first successfully inoculated a child with cow-pox virus to produce immunity to smallpox.

X-rays rays with a short wavelength that pass through most body tissues. Dense tissues such as bone prevent their passage and show up as white areas on X-ray photographs. The chemical barium is opaque to X-rays, and an X-ray photograph (*radiogram*) of the stomach or intestines can be obtained if the patient is first given a 'barium meal' (liquid containing barium). X-rays with very short wavelengths penetrate the tissues deeply, and destroy them: these are used in radiotherapy.

Drug Types

analgesic drug reducing sensitivity to pain, for example cocaine and novocaine for local application; opium and its derivatives morphine and heroin; antipyrine, aspirin, and paracetamol; certain barbiturate drugs. Dangers of addiction may arise.

antacid a substance that neutralizes stomach acid. It may be taken between meals to relieve indigestion and 'heartburn'. Excessive or prolonged need for antacids should be medically investigated.

antibiotic chemical produced by moulds and bacteria which can destroy or prevent the growth of other micro-organisms, mainly bacteria. The older penicillins have in some cases been replaced by cephalosporins, which are used against bacterial diseases, including forms of pneumonia, venereal disease, TB. Most viruses are not affected by antibiotics.

anticoagulant substance that prevents or slows blood clotting.

anticonvulsant drug used to prevent epileptic fits (convulsions or seizures). Although most have some side-effects, in many cases seizures can be completely controlled, after a trial-and-error period, by the right drug.

antidepressant drug prescribed to lift depression. The two main groups of anti-depressants are *tricyclics* and the *monoamine-oxidase inhibitors (MAOIs)*. Both groups take about three to four weeks to show any beneficial effects and both have side-effects. The MAOIs tend to react with other drugs and some foods, and are less often prescribed. Long-term reliance on antidepressives is discouraged.

anti-emetic drug that reduces or removes the feeling of nausea or vomiting.

antifungal drug that acts against fungi, the cause of many skin disorders such as ringworm and athlete's foot.

antihypertensive drug used to lower raised blood pressure. The most widely used are beta blockers and diuretics.

anti-inflammatory substance that reduces the redness, swelling and locally increased temperature of inflammation. The body makes its own anti-inflammatory agents as a part of its natural defence and repair processes. In disease, such drugs as steroids help to suppress unwanted inflammation.

antipsychotic (sometimes called major tranquillizer) drug used to treat the symptoms of severe mental disorder.

antipyretic drug, such as aspirin, used to lower a raised temperature (fever).

antiviral drug that kills viruses or stops them multiplying. They have been some of the most difficult drugs to develop.

barbiturate a type of sleeping pill, now rarely prescribed.

beta blocker drug used to block nerve impulses to special sites (beta receptors) in heart nerves and other body tissues; it reduces the rate of heartbeat and the force of its contractions, and is used to lower raised blood pressure.

bronchodilator drug that causes the airways (bronchi and bronchioles) of the lungs to relax and widen, useful in asthma.

contraceptive drug (or device or technique) that interferes with reproduction by preventing the ripening and release of an egg

cell (ovum), stopping sperm reaching the egg, preventing a sperm fertilizing the egg, or halting implantation of the early embryo in the wall of the womb.

corticosteroid hormonal preparation (now produced synthetically) that reduces inflammation and is also immunosuppressive. Used to treat several disease groups including rheumatoid arthritis, allergies, and some cancers. Over-use causes unpleasant side-effects.

cytotoxic drug that kills or damages cells. Although used specifically to kill the multiplying cells of a tumour, or as an immunosuppressive, it may damage healthy cells as well and therefore have dangerous side-effects.

diuretic drug that rids the body of excess fluid by increasing the output of urine by the kidneys. Used to treat high blood pressure and kidney disease.

hypnotic drug used to induce sleep.

hypoglycaemic drug that lowers the level of glucose sugar in the blood. Diabetics who do not require insulin can control their blood sugar level by diet and hypoglycaemic tablets.

immunosuppressive drug (usually cytotoxic or corticosteroid) that suppresses the body's normal immune reaction to infection or foreign tissue. Used for treating auto-immune diseases (in which the body attacks its own tissues) and to help prevent rejection of organ transplants.

sedative (sometimes called minor tranquillizer) drug with a calming effect. Employed to treat anxiety and, in larger doses, as sleeping drugs. They can cause dependence and should not be taken for long periods.

sleeping pill drug that promotes calmness and sleep. The two main groups are *barbiturates* and the *anti-anxiety (benzodiazepine)* drugs. Benzodiazepines are safer, and have less marked side-effects. However, both groups can cause dependence and should be taken for short periods only.

steroid as a drug, an anti-inflammatory or immunosuppressive agent, usually corticosteroid.

tranquillizer a calming drug, such as an antipsychotic or sedative.

c. 400 BC   Hippocrates recognized disease had natural causes.

c. 200 AD   Galen, the authority of the Middle Ages, consolidated the work of the Alexandrian doctors.

1543   Andreas Versalius gave the first accurate account of the human body.

1628   William Harvey discovered the circulation of the blood.

1768   John Hunter began the foundation of experimental and surgical pathology.

1785   Digitalis used to treat heart disease; the active ingredient was isolated in 1904.

1798   Edward Jenner published his work on vaccination.

1882   Robert Koch isolated the tuberculosis bacillus.

1884   Edwin Klebs, German pathologist, isolated the diphtheria bacillus.

1885   Louis Pasteur produced the rabies vaccine.

1890   Joseph Lister demonstrated antiseptic surgery.

1897   Martinus Beijerinck, Dutch botanist, discovered viruses.

1899   German doctor, Felix Hoffman, developed aspirin; Sigmund Freud founded psychiatry.

1910   Paul Ehrlich synthesized the first specific bacterial agent, salvarsan (cure for syphilis).

1922   Insulin was first used to treat diabetes.

1928   Sir Alexander Fleming discovered the antibiotic penicillin.

1930s   Electro-convulsive therapy (ECT) was developed.

1932   Gerhard Domagk, German bacteriologist and pathologist, began work on the sulphonamide drugs, a kind of antibiotic.

1950s   Major development of antidepressant drugs and also beta blockers for heart disease; Medawar's work on the immune system.

1950–75   Manipulation of the molecules of synthetic chemicals, the main source of new drugs.

1954   Vaccine for polio developed by Jonas Salk.

1960s   Heart transplant surgery began with the work of Christiaan Barnard; new generation of minor tranquillizers called benzodiazepenes was developed.

1971   Viroids, diseasen causing organisms even smaller than viruses, isolated outside the living body.

1978   Birth of the first 'test-tube baby', Louise Brown, on 25 July in England.

1980s   AIDS (Acquired Immune Deficiency Syndrome) first recognized in the USA.

1980   Smallpox declared eradicated by the World Health Organization.

1984   Vaccine for leprosy developed; discovery of the Human Immuno-deficiency Virus (HIV) responsible for AIDS, at the Institut Pasteur in Paris and in the USA.

1987   World's longest-surviving heart transplant patient died in France, 18 years after his operation.

Physics

Physics (sometimes called 'natural philosophy') is a branch of science which is concerned with the ultimate laws which govern the structure of the universe and forms of matter and energy and their interactions. For convenience physics is often divided into branches such as nuclear physics, solid and liquid state physics, electricity, electronics and magnetism, optics, acoustics, heat and thermodynamics.

This section contains an overview of physics. First, *Atomic Physics* deals with the study of matter. Famous physicists, their inventions and discoveries are highlighted in *Biographies*. Brief definitions of *Terms* explain the scientific principles and concepts of various everyday words. Finally, *Landmarks* in physics highlights both the breadth of the subject and its close links with other scientific disciplines.

Atomic Physics

atom the minute separate entity which makes up all matter, and is the tiniest quantity of an element to retain the chemical properties of the element. Atoms range in size fom 10^{-10} (1/10,000,000,000 of a metre) to 4×10^{-10}. This means that they are so small that an atom of tungsten magnified 2,600,000 times (by a field ion microscope), appears as a bright spot not much larger than a pin's head. On this minute scale physicists cannot 'see' in a direct visual sense, but rely on methods such as interpretation of the 'diffraction pattern' produced by electrons 'fired' through a thin specimen of a substance in an 'electron microscope'.

Atoms consist of a very small *nucleus*, only one ten-thousandth the size of the atom. The traditional model has particles of negative electricity called *electrons* moving round the nucleus in orbits which form concentric 'shells'. However, *quantum mechanics*, which looks at particles as 'waves', supplies a newer concept of the atom in which the nucleus is surrounded by 'clouds' of electrons which may assume dumb-bell, cloverleaf, or other shapes. The outermost of these clouds, according to their shape and density, allow the prediction of what chemical reactions are possible and how molecules will combine.

The simplest atom (hydrogen) has only one electron; the most complex naturally occurring (uranium) has 92. The nucleus itself is made up of particles (*protons* and *neutrons*) bound together by the strong nuclear force. Protons have a positive electrical charge and are exactly the same in number as the orbiting electrons, which have an equal but negative charge, so that the two types of particle counterbalance each other. Neutrons are so called because they have no electrical charge. It is the number of protons which is the chief factor in deciding

the kind of atom being dealt with, since the atomic number of an element is simply the number of protons in the nucleus of one atom. By addition or subtraction of protons and electrons, it is possible to fulfil the alchemist's dream, for example to transmute mercury (80 protons) into gold (79 protons), but the cost would be far in excess of the gold produced.

Protons and neutrons (together called *nucleons*) are composed of yet smaller subparticles, *quarks*; electrons, however, are indivisible. In general terms, the so-called elementary particles are quarks and electrons. Quarks have proved difficult to isolate, and may even be, by their very nature, impossible to isolate.

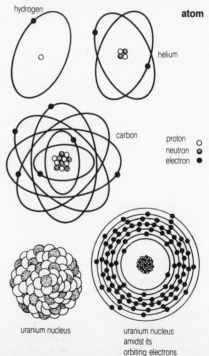

Particles may change from one form to another, and perhaps most important of all in its implications is the fact that their behaviour is not exactly predictable. Physicists (with some exceptions, notably Einstein) accept that it is impossible, even in principle, to fully predict the future behaviour of the particles (for example, simultaneous values of their position and momentum).

particle physics 1932 saw the discovery of a particle, predicted by Dirac, with the mass of an electron, but an equal and opposite charge – the *positron*. This was the first example of an *antiparticle*; it is now believed that almost all particles have corresponding antiparticles. The following year, Pauli argued that a hitherto unsuspected particle must accompany electrons in beta-emission; this so-called *electron-neutrino* interacts with other particles only rarely, so neutrino radiation is extremely penetrating.

particles and fundamental forces by the mid-1930s four fundamental kinds of force had emerged. The *electromagnetic force* acts between all particles with electric charge, and was thought to be related to the exchange between the particles of *photons*, packets of electromagnetic radiation. In 1935, Yukawa suggested that the *strong force* (holding neutrons and protons together in the nucleus) was caused by the exchange of particles with a mass of about a tenth that of a proton; these particles, called *pions*, were found by Powell in 1946. Theoretical work on the *weak force* (responsible for beta radioactivity of the sun) began with Fermi in the 1930s; current theory suggests the exchange during weak interactions of *W* and *Z particles* with masses some 100 times that of the proton. The existence of W and Z particles was confirmed in 1983 at CERN (Conseil Européen pour la Recherche Nucléaire, Geneva). The fourth fundamental force, *gravity*, is experienced by all particles; the projected go-between particles have been dubbed *gravitons*.

leptons, hadrons, and quarks the electron and electron- neutrinos are examples of *leptons* – particles with half-integral spin which 'feel' the weak, but not the strong force. *Hadrons* (particles which 'feel' the strong force) started to turn up in bewildering profusion in experi-ments in the 1950s and 60s. They are classified into *mesons*, with whole-number or zero spins, and *baryons*, with half-integral spins. In 1964 Gell-Mann and Zweig suggested that all hadrons were built from just three types or *flavours* of a new particle with half-integral spin and charge of magnitude either $1/3$ or $2/3$ that of an electron, which Gell-Mann christened the *quark*. Mesons are quark-antiquark pairs (spins either add to 1 or cancel to zero) and baryons are quark triplets. To account for new mesons such as the *psi* the number of quark flavours had risen to six by 1985. In the quark theory, the only truly elementary particles are leptons and quarks. The different types of leptons and quark composites are therefore generally known as *fundamental* or *subatomic particles*.

accelerator a device to bring charged particles (such as protons) up to high kinetic energies, at which they have uses in industry, medicine and in pure physics: when high energy particles collide with other particles the products formed give insights into the fundamental forces of nature. To give particles the energies needed requires many successive applications of a high voltage to electrodes placed in the path of the particles. To save space the particles can be confined to a circular track using a magnetic field.

atomic number the number of electrons, or the positive charge on the nucleus of an atom. The 105 elements are numbered one (hydrogen) to 105 (hahnium) in the Periodic Table.

atomic weight the weight of one atom of an element on a scale where the weight of an oxygen atom is 16.

isotope one of two or more atoms which have the same atomic number, but which contain a different number of neutrons. They may be stable or radioactive, natural or synthetic.

molecule the smallest particle of any substance that can exist in a free state yet still exhibit all the chemical properties of the substance. Molecules are composed of a number of atoms ranging from two atoms in, for example, a hydrogen molecule to many thousands of atoms in the molecules of complex organic substances. The composition of the molecule is determined by the nature of the bonds, probably electric forces, which hold the atoms together. According to the molecular or kinetic theory of matter, molecules are in a state of constant motion, the extent of which depends on their temperature, and they exert forces on one another.

to body tissues, but are especially dangerous if a radioactive substance is ingested or inhaled.

uncertainty principle also called *indeterminacy principle*. A principle established by Heisenberg, giving a theoretical limit to the precision with which an atomic particle's momentum and position can be measured simultaneously: the more accurately the one is determined the more uncertainty there is in the

MAJOR FUNDAMENTAL (SUBATOMIC) PARTICLES

Name	Symbol	Catergory	Mass (electron = 1)	Charge	Spin	Parity
electron	e	lepton	1	−1	1/2	
graviton	g	quantum	0	0	2	
K meson (kaon)	K	meson	988	−1, 0, +1	0	−1
lambda particle	Λ	baryon	2231	0	1/2	+1
muon	μ	lepton	211	−1	1/2	
neutrino	ν	lepton	0	0	1/2	
neutron	n	baryon	1880	0	1/2	+1
omega particle	Ω	baryon	3345	−1	3/2	+1
photon	∝	quantum	0	0	1	−1
pion	π	meson	280	−1, 0, +1	0	−1
proton	p	baryon	1876	+1	1/2	+1
sigma particle	Σ	baryon	2380	−1, 0, +1	1/2	+1
xi particle	Ξ	baryon	2644	−1, 0	1/2	+1

More than one charge in the *Charge* column indicates that there is more than one particle of that type, which differ in charge (there may also be slight differences in mass). Certain particles with a single charge have antiparticles of opposite charge. Thus the positron resembles the electron in every respect except that its charge is +1; similarly, the antiproton has a charge of −1.
Lambda, omega, sigma, and xi particles are known collectively as hyperons.
Baryons and mesons together make up the type termed hadrons.

radioactivity the spontaneous emission of radiation from the nuclei of atoms of certain substances, termed *radioactive*. The radiation is of three main types:
alpha (fast-moving helium nuclei);
beta (fast-moving electrons);
and *gamma* (high-energy highly penetrating protons).
Beta and gamma radiation are both damaging

other. The uncertainty arises because, according to *quantum mechanics*, it is meaningless to speak of a particle's position, momentum, and so on, except as results of measurements, but measuring involves an interaction (such as a photon of light bouncing off the particle under scrutiny), which must disturb the particle, though the disturbance is noticeable only at an atomic scale. The principle implies that one cannot, even in theory, predict the moment-to-moment behaviour of such a system.

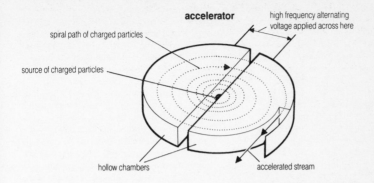

helped to set up CERN at Geneva. His son, *Aage Bohr* (1922–   ), also a physicist, shared a

Nobel prize in 1975 for work on the theory of the atomic nucleus.

Born Max 1882–1970. British physicist, of German origin, who received a Nobel prize in 1954 for fundamental work on quantum mechanics, which explains the properties of atoms and molecules.

Boyle Robert 1627–91. British scientist. He published the seminal *The Skeptical Chymist* 1661; enunciated *Boyle's law*, stating that the product of the pressure and volume of a gas remain constant as long as the temperature remains constant (1662); was one of the founders of the Royal Society.

Cavendish Henry 1731–1810. British physicist. A grandson of the 2nd duke of Devonshire, he devoted his life to scientific pursuits, living in rigorous seclusion at Clapham Common. He discovered the composition of nitric acid and the composition of water. The Cavendish experiment was a device of his to discover the mass and density of the earth.

Chadwick Sir James 1891–1974. British physicist. He studied at Cambridge under Rutherford, and in 1932 discovered the particle in an atomic nucleus which became known as the neutron, because it has no electric charge. In 1935 he was awarded a Nobel prize, and in

Biographies

Angström Anders Jonas 1814–1874. Swedish physicist, who did notable work in spectroscopy and solar physics. After him is named the *Angström unit*, used to express the wavelength of electro-magnetic radiations (light, radiant heat, X-rays). One Angström or Angström unit is one ten-millionth of a millimetre.

Black Joseph 1728–99. Scottish physicist and chemist who in 1754 discovered carbon dioxide (which he called fixed air). In physics, by his investigations (1761) of latent heat and specific heat, he laid the foundation for the work of his pupil, James Watt.

Blackett Patrick Maynard Stuart, Baron Blackett 1897–1974. British physicist. He was awarded a Nobel prize in 1948 for work in cosmic radiation and his perfection of the Wilson 'cloud-chamber'.

Bohr Niels Henrik David 1885–1962. Danish physicist. Nobel prizewinner 1922. In 1952 he

1940 was one of the British scientists reporting on the atom bomb.

Cockcroft Sir John Douglas 1897–1967. British physicist. Born at Todmorden, W Yorkshire, he held an engineering appointment with Metropolitan-Vickers, and took up research work under Rutherford at the Cavendish Laboratory, Cambridge. He succeeded (with Irish physicist Ernest Thomas Sinton Walton 1903–) in splitting the nucleus of the atom for the first time in 1932, and in 1951 they were jointly awarded a Nobel prize.

Curie Marie (born Marya Sklodovska) 1867–1934. Polish chemist, wife of physicist *Pierre Curie* (1859–1906) from 1895. They were awarded the Nobel Prize for Physics (with Becquerel) in 1903 for their work on radioactivity, and in 1911 Marie received the Nobel Prize for Chemistry for her discovery of the elements polonium and radium. She died a victim of the radiation emitted by the chemicals with which she worked. Her daughter and son-in-law, *Irène Joliot-Curie* (1896–1956), and *Frédéric Joliot* (1900–59), received a Nobel prize for chemistry in 1935 for their creation of artificial radioactivity.

de Broglie Louis, 7th duc de Broglie 1892–. French theoretical physicist. In 1929 he was awarded a Nobel prize, having written much from 1924 on quantum theory and having accounted for certain properties of atomic particles in terms of waves, thus laying the foundations of wave mechanics.

Dirac Paul Adrien Maurice 1902–84. British physicist who worked out a version of quantum mechanics consistent with Einstein's special theory of relativity. The existence of the positron, an antiparticle of the electron, was one of its predictions.

Doppler Christian Johann 1803–53. Austrian physicist. He became professor of experimental physics at Vienna, and described the *Doppler effect*, which states that in the same way as the pitch of a sound alters if the body from which it proceeds is moving relatively to a fixed observer, so the light from a moving star varies in colour.

Einstein Albert 1879–1955. German-Swiss physicist who formulated the *theories of relativity* and did important work in radiation physics and thermodynamics. Born at Ulm, in Württemberg, in a Jewish family, he lived with his parents in Munich and then in Italy. In 1913 he took up a specially created post as director of the Kaiser Wilhelm Institute for Physics, Berlin. He received the Nobel Prize for Physics in 1921. After being deprived of his post at Berlin by the Nazis, he emigrated in 1933, to the USA and became professor of mathematics and a permanent member of the Institute for Advanced Study at Princeton, New Jersey. In 1905 he had published his first theory – the *special theory of relativity* – and in 1915 issued his general theory of relativity. His latest conception of the basic laws governing the universe was outlined in his unified field theory made public in 1953.

Fermi Enrico 1901–54. Italian-American physicist who proved the existence of new radioactive elements produced by bombardment with neutrons and discovered nuclear reactions produced by slow neutrons. Born in Rome, he was professor of theoretical physics there from 1926 to 1938, when he settled in the USA. The same year he was awarded a Nobel prize for his discoveries.

Foucault Jean Bernard Léon 1819–68. French physicist who, in 1851, produced the pendulum (named after him) which demonstrates the rotation of the earth on its axis, and was the inventor of the gyroscope.

Frisch Otto 1904–79. Austrian physicist who coined the term 'nuclear fission'. A refugee from Nazi Germany, he worked from 1943 at Los Alamos, then at Cambridge.

Gabor Dennis 1900–79. Hungarian-British physicist, who was awarded a Nobel prize in 1971 for his invention, in 1947, of *holography* (creating three-dimensional images by the use of lasers).

Galileo Galilei 1564–1642. Italian mathematician, astronomer, and physicist, who revolutionized the scientific thinking of his time. In mechanics, Galileo argued convincingly that freely-falling bodies, heavy or light, had the same, constant acceleration (though the story of his dropping cannon balls from the Leaning Tower is probably apocryphal), and that a body moving on a perfectly smooth horizontal surface would neither speed up nor slow down.

Gell-Mann Murray 1929– . American physicist who was awarded a Nobel prize for his work on elementary particles. In 1964 he formulated the theory of the 'quark' as the fundamental constituent of all matter and smallest particle in the universe.

Hahn Otto 1879–1968. West German physical chemist who discovered nuclear fission. With Strassmann 1938 he discovered that uranium nuclei split when bombarded with neutrons, which led to the development of the atom bomb (first used in 1945).

Heaviside Oliver 1850–1925. British physicist whose theoretical work had important implications for radio transmission. His studies of electricity published in *Electrical Papers* 1892 had considerable influence on long-distance telephony. In 1902 he predicted the existence of an ionized layer of air in the upper atmosphere which was verified by Kennelly and was later known as the Kennelly-Heaviside layer (now called the *E layer*). Deflection from it makes possible the transmission of radio signals round the world, which would otherwise be lost in outer space.

Heisenberg Werner Carl 1901–76. German physicist who was an originator of quantum mechanics and the formulator of the uncertainty (indeterminacy) principle that is central to atomic physics.

Helmholtz Hermann Ludwig Ferdinand von 1821–94. German scientist, renowned for his work in thermodynamics. In 1847 he published an epoch-making treatise on the conservation of energy. In his *Doctrine of the Sensations of Tone* 1862 gave a complete study of sound.

Hertz Heinrich 1821–94. German physicist who continued the work of Maxwell in studying electromagnetic waves, preparing the way for radio communication, and showed that their behaviour resembled that of light and heat waves. The unit of frequency, the hertz

(Hz), is named after him.

Joule James Prescott 1818–89. British physicist whose work on the relations between electrical, mechanical, and chemical effects led to the discovery of the first law of thermodynamics (the conservation of energy). He determined the mechanical equivalent of heat (*Joule's equivalent*), and the SI unit of energy, the joule, is named after him.

Kelvin William Thomson, 1st Baron Kelvin 1824–1907. British physicist who pioneered the absolute scale of temperature. His work on the conservation of energy 1851 led to the second law of thermodynamics. Popularly known for his contributions to telegraphy, he developed stranded cables and sensitive receivers, greatly improving transatlantic communications.

Maxwell James Clerk 1831–79. British physicist. His short life was rich in contributions to every branch of physical science, particularly on gases, optics and colour sensation, electricity and magnetism. His theoretical work in the last sphere prepared the way for wireless telegraphy and telephony.

Michelson Albert Abraham 1852–1931. German-born American physicist who became the first American scientist to win a Nobel prize 1907. He invented the Michelson interferometer, made precise measurement of the speed of light, and from 1892 was professor at Chicago. In conjunction with Edward Morley he performed in 1887 the *Michelson-Morley experiment* to detect the motion of the earth through the postulated ether. The failure of the experiment proved the non-existence of the ether (a medium believed to be necessary for the propagation of light) and led Einstein to his theory of relativity.

Newton Sir Isaac 1642–1727. British natural philosopher and mathematician who laid the foundation of physics as a modern discipline. During 1665–6 he formulated the binomial theorem and the differential and integral calculus, dealing with the mathematics of infinitely large numbers and minute changes, and began to investigate the phenomenon of universal gravitation. He was elected Fellow of the Royal Society in 1672, and in 1685 his *universal law of gravitation* was completely expounded as follows: 'Every particle of matter in the universe attracts every other particle with a force whose direction is that of the line joining the two, and whose magnitude is directly as the product of the masses, and inversely as the square of their distance from each other.' His greatest work, *Philosophiae Naturalis Principia Mathematica*, was published in three volumes 1686–7, with the aid of British physicist Edmund Halley (1656–1742). The newton, the unit of force that is now part of the SI system (that is the force required to accelerate a mass of one kilogram by one metre per second) is named after him (unit symbol N).

Ohm Georg Simon 1787–1854. German physicist who promulgated what is known as *Ohm's law*. Ohm's law states that the steady current in a metallic circuit is directly proportional to the constant total electromotive force in the circuit. If a current I flows between two points in a conductor across which the potential difference (voltage) is E, then E/I is a constant (which is known as the resistance between the two points).

Pauli Wolfgang 1900–58. Austrian-American physicist, a Nobel prizewinner 1945 for his work on atomic structure. He originated *Pauli's exclusion principle*, that in a given system no two electrons, protons, neutrons or other particles of half-intergrated spin can be characterized by the same set of quantum numbers. He also predicted the existence of neutrinos.

Planck Max 1858–1947. German physicist who framed the quantum theory 1900. He was awarded the Nobel Prize for Physics in 1918, and became a Fellow of the Royal Society in 1926.

Raman Sir Venkata 1888–1970. Indian physicist who in 1928 discovered what became known as the *Raman effect*: the scattering of monochromatic light when passed through a transparent substance. He was awarded a Nobel prize in 1930 and in 1948 became director of the Raman Research Institute and national research professor of physics.

Rutherford Ernest 1871–1937. New Zealand physicist. A pioneer of modern atomic science, his main researches were in the field of radioactivity, and he was the first to recognize the nuclear nature of the atom. He was awarded a Nobel prize in 1908.

Sakharov Andrei Dmitrievich 1921– . Soviet physicist who is known both as 'the father of the Russian H-bomb' and as an outspoken civil rights campaigner. He protested against Soviet nuclear tests and was a founder of the Soviet Human Rights Committee.

Shockley William 1910– . American physicist who worked with American physicists John Bardeen (1908–) and Walter Houser Brattain (1902–) on the invention of the transistor, that heralded the microelectronics revolution. He was jointly awarded a Nobel prize with them in 1956.

Thomson Sir George Paget 1892–1975. British physicist, son of Sir Joseph Thomson, whose work on interference phenomena in the scattering of electrons by crystals helped to confirm the wave-like nature of particles. He shared a Nobel prize with American physicist Clinton Joseph Davisson (1881–1958) in 1937.

Thomson Sir Joseph John 1856–1940. British physicist who discovered the electron. Educated at Manchester and Cambridge, where he became Cavendish professor of experimental physics 1884–1918, he organized the Cavendish research laboratory which became a world-famous centre of atomic research. His work inaugurated the electrical theory of the atom, and his elucidation of positive rays and their application to an analysis of neon led to the discovery of isotopes, which are different atomic forms of the same chemical element. He was awarded a Nobel prize in 1906.

Volta Alessandro 1745–1827. Italian physicist who pioneered electrical science. Born at Como, he was a professor there and at Pavia. He invented the voltaic pile (the first battery), the electrophorus (an early electrostatic generator) and an electroscope (a device for detecting electric charge). The volt is named after him.

Wheatstone Sir Charles 1802–75. British physicist and inventor. His inventions included the concertina, harmonica, and stereoscope, and he took out the first British patent for the electric telegraph in 1837, with British physicist William Fothergill Cooke (1806–1879). He measured the speed of electric discharge in conductors, and also devised the *Wheatstone bridge* (a special electrical network for measuring resistance).

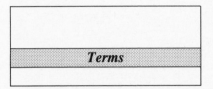

Terms

absolute zero the lowest temperature which could possibly exist, equivalent to −273.1°C when molecules would have no energy. Near this temperature the physical properties of materials change substantially, for example some metals lose their electrical resistance (superconductivity).

absorption has several meanings in science. It most commonly describes the taking up of one substance by another, such as liquid into a solid (like ink into blotting-paper) or a gas into a liquid (like ammonia into water). With pure single substances, the result of such absorption is a uniform solution. In optics, absorption is the phenomenon by which a substance retains radiation of particular wavelengths; for example, a piece of blue glass absorbs all visible light except the wavelengths in the blue part of the spectrum. In nuclear physics, the capture by elements such as boron of neutrons produced by fission in a reactor is also called absorption.

adsorption the taking up of a gas or liquid by the surface of a solid (as activated charcoal, for example, adsorbs gases). It is a phenomenon involving molecular attraction at the surface and should be distinguished from *absorption*.

anode the electrode towards which negative

particles (*anions*) move within a device, such as the cells of a battery, electrolytic cells, diodes.

boiling point for any given liquid, the temperature at which the application of heat raises the temperature of the liquid no further, but converts it to vapour. The boiling point of water under normal pressure is 100°C or 212°F. The lower the pressure, the lower the boiling point and vice versa.

capacitance the ratio of the electric charge on a body to the resultant change of potential. A *capacitor* has a capacitance of one farad when a charge of one coulomb changes its potential by one volt. The farad is an impractically large unit and capacitors normally used in electronic circuits are of the order of millionths of a farad (microfarads) or less.

cathode the electrode towards which positive particles (*cations*) move within a device, such as the cells of a battery, electrolytic cells, diodes.

electric cell

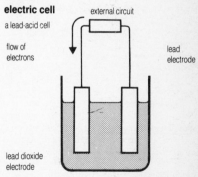

a lead-acid cell

external circuit

flow of electrons

lead electrode

lead dioxide electrode

electrolyte (dilute sulphuric acid)

cell (electric) an apparatus in which chemical energy is converted into electrical energy; the popular name is 'battery', but this should be reserved for a collection of cells in one unit. Electric cells can be divided into: *primary*, which produce electrical energy by chemical action and require replenishing after this action is complete; and *secondary*, or *accumulators*, which are so constituted that the action is reversible, and the original condition can be restored by an electric current. The first battery was made by Volta in 1800.

chain reaction in nuclear physics, a fission reaction which is maintained because neutrons released by the splitting of some atomic nuclei themselves go on to split others, releasing even more neutrons, and so on. Such a reaction can be controlled (as in a nuclear reactor) by using moderators to absorb excess neutrons. Uncontrolled, a chain reaction produces a nuclear explosion (as in an atom bomb).

colour quality or wavelength of light emitted or reflected from an object. Visible white light consists of electro-magnetic radiation of various wavelengths, and if a beam is refracted through a prism, it can be spread out into a spectrum, in which the various colours correspond to the different wavelengths. From high to low wavelengths the colours are red, orange, yellow, green, blue, indigo, violet. When a surface is illuminated, some parts of the white light are absorbed, depending on the molecular structure of the material and the dyes applied to it. A surface that looks red will have absorbed the light from the blue end of the spectrum, but have a high reflection of light from the red, long-wave end. Colours vary in brightness, in hue, and in saturation, that is the extent to which they are mixed with white.

cryogenics science of very low temperatures (approaching absolute zero), including the liquefaction of gases such as nitrogen, helium, hydrogen; and exploitation of special properties produced at these low temperatures, such as the disappearance of electrical resistance (superconductivity).

density measure of the compactness of a substance; its mass per unit volume, measured in kilograms per cubic metre. *Relative density* is the ratio of the density of a substance to that of water at °C.

diffraction the interference phenomena observed at the edges of opaque objects, or discontinuities between different media in the path of a wave train. The phenomena give rise to slight spreading of light into light and dark bands at the shadow of a straight edge. The *diffraction grating* is a device for separating a wave train such as a beam of incident light into its component frequencies (white light results in a spectrum). Sound waves can also be diffracted by a suitable array of solid objects.

diffusion term used in physical chemistry to describe at least three processes: the spontaneous mixing of gases or liquids (classed together as *fluids* in scientific usage) when brought into contact without mechanical mixing or stirring; the spontaneous passage of fluids through membranes; and the spontaneous passage of dissolved materials both through the material in which they are dissolved and also through membranes.

Doppler effect change in the observed frequency of waves due to relative motion between wave source and observer. It is responsible for the perceived change in pitch of an ambulance siren as it approaches and then recedes, and, on a somewhat grander scale, for the shift, towards the red end of the spectrum, of light from distant stars.

dynamics the branch of mechanics that deals with the mathematical and physical study of the behaviour of bodies under the action of forces which produce changes of motion in them.

electric charge the property of some bodies which causes them to exert forces on each other. Two bodies both with positive or negative charges repel each other, while opposite or 'unlike' charged bodies attract each other, since each is in the *electric field* of the other. In atoms, electrons possess a negative charge, and protons an equal positive charge, the unit of charge being the *coulomb* (C). Atoms have no overall charge but can sometimes gain electrons to become negative *ions* or lose them to become positive ions. So-called *static electricity*, seen in such phenomena as the charging of nylon shirts when they are pulled on or off, is in fact the rubbing-on or rubbing-off of electrons from the surface atoms. A flow of charge (such as electrons through a copper wire) constitutes an *electric current*; the flow of current is measured in *amperes*.

electric current the rate of flow of electric charge. Measured in amperes (coulombs per

electromagnetic waves

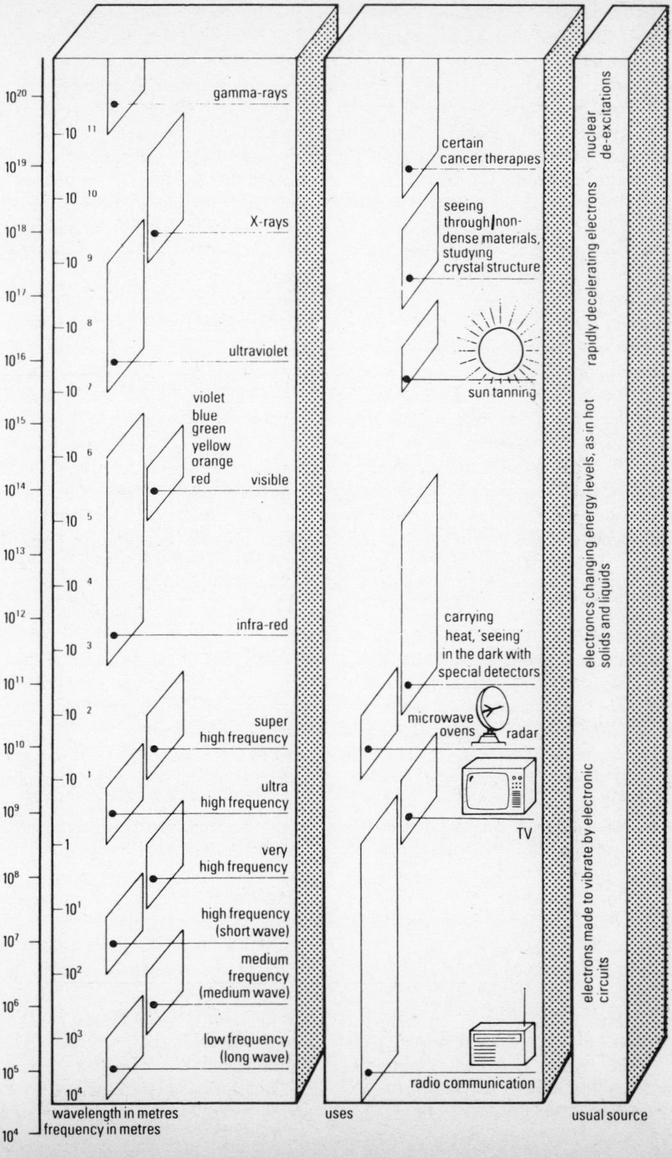

10^{20}
10^{19}
10^{18}
10^{17}
10^{16}
10^{15}
10^{14}
10^{13}
10^{12}
10^{11}
10^{10}
10^{9}
10^{8}
10^{7}
10^{6}
10^{5}
10^{4}
10^{-11}
10^{-10}
10^{-9}
10^{-8}
10^{-7}
10^{-6}
10^{-5}
10^{-4}
10^{-3}
10^{-2}
10^{-1}
1
10^{1}
10^{2}
10^{3}
10^{4}
gamma-rays
X-rays
ultraviolet
violet
blue
green
yellow
orange
red
visible
infra-red
super high frequency
ultra high frequency
very high frequency
high frequency (short wave)
medium frequency (medium wave)
low frequency (long wave)
wavelength in metres
frequency in metres
certain cancer therapies
seeing through non-dense materials, studying crystal structure
sun tanning
carrying heat, 'seeing' in the dark with special detectors
microwave ovens
radar
TV
radio communication
uses
nuclear de-excitations
rapidly decelerating electrons
electrons changing energy levels, as in hot solids and liquids
electrons made to vibrate by electronic circuits
usual source

second).

electrode a conductor by means of which a current passes into or out of a substance, such as the electrodes of an electrolytic cell, an electric furnace, a discharge tube, or a radio valve. Conducting elements separated by an insulating material as in a capacitor (a store of electric charge), are also called electrodes.

electromagnetic field a region of space in which a particle with an electric charge experiences a force. If it does so only when moving, it is in a pure *magnetic field*, if it does so when stationary, it is in an *electric field*. Both can be present simultaneously, as with electromagnets.

electromagnetic waves oscillating electric and magnetic fields travelling together through space at a speed of nearly 300 million metres per second. The (limitless) range of possible frequencies of electromagnetic waves which can be thought of as making up the *electromagnetic spectrum* include radio waves, infrared radiation, visible light, ultraviolet radiation, and X-rays and gamma rays. Dividing 300 million by the frequency (number of cycles per second, or hertz) gives the wavelength of the waves in metres.

electronics the design and application of devices which amplify and switch electrically, without moving parts. The first device was the *thermionic valve* (using electrons moving in a vacuum) on the basis of which electronics developed during the first half of the 20th century to the stage of producing radio, radar, black and white television, and the earliest true computers. *Solid-state* technology, that of the transistor (invented 1949) and multi-transistor circuits in the form of silicon chips, has almost entirely superseded the valve, for reasons of cheapness, compactness, reliability, and low power consumption.

electrostatics the study of electric charges from stationary sources (not currents), for example amber, and lightning.

energy the capacity for doing work. *Potential energy* (PE) is energy deriving from position: thus a stretched spring has elastic PE; an object raised to a height above the earth's surface, or the water in an elevated reservoir, has gravitational PE; a lump of coal and a tank of petrol, together with the oxygen needed for their combustion, have chemical PE (due to relative positions of atoms). Other sorts of PE include *electrical* and *nuclear*. Moving bodies possess *kinetic energy* (KE).

Energy can be converted from one form to another, but the total quantity stays the same (in accordance with the conservation laws that govern many natural phenomena). For example, as an apple falls it loses gravitational PE but gains KE.

entropy in thermodynamics (the study of heat as related to other forms of energy), a parameter representing the state of disorder of a system at the atomic, ionic or molecular level; the greater the disorder, the higher the entropy. Thus the fast-moving disordered molecules of water vapour have higher entropy than those of more ordered liquid water, which in turn have more entropy than the molecules in solid crystalline ice. At absolute zero, the lowest possible temperature ($-273°C/0$ K), when all molecular motion ceases and order is assumed to be complete, entropy is zero.

force that which tends to change the state of rest or the uniform motion of a body in a straight line. It is measured by the rate of change of momentum of the body on which it acts, that is, the mass of the body multiplied by its acceleration $f=ma$.

forces the four fundamental interactions believed to be at work in the physical universe. *Gravity*, which keeps the planets in orbit around the sun, acts between all atomic particles with mass. *Electromagnetic forces*, which stop solids from falling apart, act between all atomic particles with electric charge. In addition to these long-range forces, there are two very short-range forces: the *weak*, responsible for the reactions which fuel the sun, and for the emission of beta particles from certain nuclei; and the *strong*, which binds together the protons and neutrons in the nucleus of atoms. By 1971 a theory was developed which suggested that the weak and electromagnetic forces were linked; experimental support came from observation at CERN in the 1980s. Physicists are now working on theories to unify all four forces.

frequency the number of cycles of a vibration occurring per unit of time. The unit of frequency is the hertz (Hz); 1 Hz = 1 cycle per second, 1 KHz (kilohertz) = 1,000 Hz, 1 MHz (megahertz) = 1,000,000 Hz. Human beings can hear sounds from objects vibrating in the range 20 Hz to 15,000 Hz. Ultrasonic frequencies are above that range.

gravity the force of attraction between an object and the earth because of their masses. According to Newton's law of gravitation, for an object of mass m at a distance d from the centre of the earth of mass M, the force of gravity F equals GmM/d_2, where G is the gravitational constant. According to Newton's second law of motion, F also equals mg, where g is the acceleration due to gravity. Therefore $g = d_2$ and is independent of the mass of the object; at the earth's surface it equals 9.086 m s^{-2} (metres per second per second). In other words, all objects fall to earth with the same acceleration, a fact proved by Galileo's apocryphal experiment of dropping objects off the Leaning Tower of Pisa.

heat a form of energy which, when added to or removed from an object, usually causes a rise or fall in its temperature. Heat always flows from a region of higher temperature to one of lower temperature. Its effect may be simply to raise the temperature, to cause expansion, to melt a solid, to vaporize a liquid, or to increase the pressure of a gas. The *specific heat* of a substance is the ratio of the quantity of heat required to raise the temperature of a given mass of the substance through a given range of temperature, to the heat required to raise the temperature of an equal mass of water through the same range.

There are three ways by which heat may be transferred from one place to another:

convection transmission through a fluid (liquid or gas) by currents, for example when the air in a room is warmed by a fire or radiator, or water is heated in a domestic hot-water system;

conduction heat passing from one part of a medium to neighbouring parts with no visible motion of the medium accompanying the transfer of heat, as when the whole length of a metal rod is heated when one end is held in a fire;

radiation heat transfer by infrared rays. Radiant heat is of the same nature as light. It can pass through a vacuum, travels at the same speed as light, can be reflected and refracted, and does not affect the medium through which it passes.

heat capacity the quantity of heat required to raise the temperature of a substance by one degree. The *specific heat capacity* of a substance is the heat capacity per unit of mass, measured in joules per kilogramme per kelvin (J kg^{-1} K^{-1}).

humidity the quantity of water vapour in a given volume of the atmosphere (*absolute humidity*), or the ratio of the amount of water vapour in the atmosphere to the saturation value at the same temperature (*relative humidity*); at dew-point the latter is 100%. Relative humidity is measured by various types of *hygrometer*.

inductance that property of an electronic circuit or circuit component which when carrying a current is characterized by the formation of a magnetic field and the storage of magnetic energy. It is also a measure of the capability of a circuit or circuit component to store magnetic energy when carrying a current.

kinetics a branch of dynamics dealing with the action of forces producing or changing the motion of a body, as distinguished from *kinematics*, which deals with motion without reference to force or mass.

latent heat heat which changes the state (for example from solid to liquid) of a substance without changing its temperature.

lens a piece of transparent material (such as glass) with two polished surfaces – one concave or convex, and the other plane, concave or convex – to modify rays of light according to the type of lens they traverse. A *convex lens* converges the light and a *concave lens* diverges it. Lenses are essential to spectacles, microscopes, telescopes, cameras, and almost all optical instruments. *Compound lenses* for special purposes are built up from two or more lenses made of glass (or other suitable material) of different refractive index.

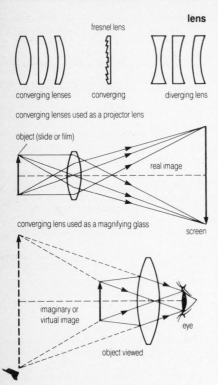

lens

fresnel lens

converging lenses   converging   diverging lens

converging lenses used as a projector lens

object (slide or film)

real image

converging lens used as a magnifying glass

screen

imaginary or
virtual image

eye

object viewed

The image formed by a single lens suffers from several defects or aberrations, notably spherical aberration in which a straight line becomes a curved image, and chromatic aberration in which an image in white light tends to have coloured edges. Aberrations are corrected by the use of compound lenses.

light electromagnetic radiation in the visible range, that is, from about 400 nanometers in the extreme violet to about 770 nanometers in the extreme red. Light is considered to exhibit both particle and wave properties and the fundamental particle or quantum of light is called the *photon*. The speed of light (and of all electromagnetic radiation) in a vacuum is approximately 300 million metres per second or 186,000 miles per second, and is a universal constant denoted by c. This is allegedly the fastest speed in nature, but in 1971 a jet from the galaxy 3C 273 was calculated as travelling at three times this speed, which should be impossible.

magnetism that branch of physics dealing with the properties of *magnets* and *magnetic fields*. Magnetic fields are produced by moving charged particles: in electromagnets electrons flow through a coil of wire connected to a battery; in magnets spinning electrons within the atoms generate the field. Only certain ferromagnetic materials can be made into magnets; this is because forces act between adjacent atoms so that large groups, forming regions or domains, produce fields which reinforce.

Substances differ in degree and kind in their ability to be magnetized (*permeability*). Those substances, like iron, which have very high permeabilities, are said to be *ferromagnetic*. Apart from its universal application to dynamos, electric motors, switch-gear, and so forth, magnetism has become of considerable importance in modern science, including particle accelerators for nuclear research, memory stores for computers, tape recorders, cryogenics (low temperature physics), and investigations of matter and space. Experiments have confirmed that homing pigeons and other animals rely on their perception of earth's magnetic field for their sense of direction, and by 1979 it was suggested that humans to some extent share this sense.

mass the quantity of matter in a body. The British unit of mass is the pound, that is the quantity of matter in a standard platinum cylinder preserved at the standards office at the Board of Trade; in the SI system, now under adoption in Britain, the base unit of mass is the kilogram. Mass determines the acceleration produced in a body by a given force working upon it, the acceleration being inversely proportional to the mass of the body. The mass also determines the force exerted on a body by the gravitational attraction of the earth, although this attraction varies slightly from place to place. At a given place, however, equal masses experience equal gravitational forces, which are known as the weights of the bodies. Masses may, therefore, be compared

magnetism

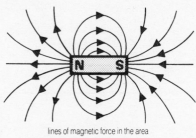

lines of magnetic force in the area
surrounding a bar magnet

by comparing the weights of bodies at the same place, as in a balance.

mechanics the branch of applied mathematics dealing with the motions of bodies and the forces causing them, and also with the forces acting on bodies in equilibrium. It is usually divided into *dynamics* and *statics*. *Quantum mechanics* is the system based on the quantum theory which has superseded Newtonian mechanics in the interpretation of physical phenomena on the atomic scale.

modulation in radio, the intermittent change of frequency, amplitude, and so on, of a radio carrier wave, in accordance with the audio-frequency speaking voice, music, or other signal being transmitted.

momentum of a body, is the product of its mass and its linear velocity; *angular momentum* (of a body in rotational motion) is the product of its moment (turning effect) of inertia and its angular velocity. The momentum of a body does not change unless it is acted on by an external force. The law of conservation of momentum is one of the fundamental concepts

of classical physics. It states that the total momentum of all bodies in a closed system is constant and unaffected by processes occurring within the system.

Newton's laws of motion the three laws that form the basis of Newtonian mechanics. They are:
(1) unless acted upon by a net force, a body at rest stays at rest and a moving body continues moving at the same speed in the same straight line;
(2) a net force applied to a body gives it a rate of change of momentum proportional to the force and in the direction of the force;
(3) when a body A exerts a force on a body B, B exerts an equal and opposite force on A, that is to every action there is an equal and opposite reaction.

optics the scientific study of light and vision, for example shadows cast by opaque objects, images formed in mirrors, and lenses, microscopes, telescopes, and cameras. Light rays are for all practical purposes straight lines, although Einstein has demonstrated that they may be 'bent' by a gravitational field. On striking a surface they are reflected or refracted with some attendant absorption of energy, and the study of these facts is the subject matter of *geometrical optics*.

osmosis the movement of solvent (liquid) through a semipermeable membrane separating solutions of different concentrations. The solvent passes from the dilute solution to the concentrated solution until the two concentrations are equal. Applying external pressure to the solution on the more concentrated side arrests osmosis, and is a measure of the osmotic pressure of the solution. Many cell membranes behave as semi-permeable membranes, and osmosis is an important mechanism in the transport of fluids in living organisms, for example in the transport of water from the roots up the stems of plants. Fish have protective mechanisms to counteract osmosis, which would otherwise cause fluid transport between the body of the animal and the surrounding water (outwards in saltwater fish, inwards in freshwater ones).

photon the smallest 'package', 'particle' or quantum of energy in which light, or any other form of electromagnetic radiation, is emitted.

power the rate of doing work or consuming energy; measured in watts or other units of work per unit time.

quantum theory the theory that many quantities, such as energy, cannot have continuous range of values but only a smaller number of discrete (particular) ones, because they are packaged in 'quanta of energy'.

radiation the emission of radiant energy as particles, waves, sound, and so on.

light or sound waves, when they hit a surface. The *law of reflection* states that the angle of incidence (the angle between the ray and a perpendicular line drawn to the surface) is equal to the angle of reflection (the angle between the reflected ray and a perpendicular to the surface). Thus, rays are reflected at the same angle at which they strike.

refraction the bending of light when it passes from one medium to another, such as from air to glass. Since light travels more slowly in glass than in air, the light bends towards the normal, that is perpendicular, in going from air to glass, but away from the normal when going from glass to air.

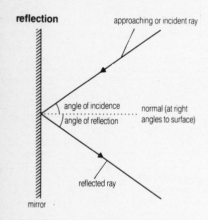

reflection

approaching or incident ray

angle of incidence
angle of reflection

normal (at right angles to surface)

reflected ray

mirror

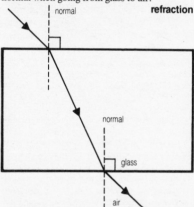

refraction

normal

normal

glass

air

relativity either of two theories propounded by Einstein concerning the nature of space and time, and with far-reaching implications in physics.

The *special theory of relativity* 1905 was devised to simplify the theory of electromagnetism. Starting with the premises that (1) the laws of nature are the same for all observers in unaccelerated motion; and (2) the speed of light is independent of the motion of its source, Einstein showed, for example, that the time interval between two events was longer for an observer in whose frame of reference the events occur in different places than for the observer for whom they occur at the same place. Such 'time dilation' has been confirmed

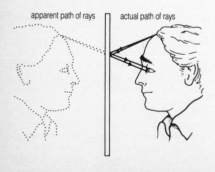

apparent path of rays

actual path of rays

reflection the deflection of waves, such as

434

by experiment and gives a degree of academic respectability to the notion of (forward) time-travel. Einstein's ideas were shown by the German mathematician Hermann Minkowski (1864–1909) to imply that time was in many respects like an extra dimension to space, so physicists now talk of four-dimensional 'space–time'. Einstein showed that for consistency with premises (1) and (2) the principles of dynamics as established by Newton needed modification; the most celebrated new result being the equation $E = mc^2$ which expresses an equivalence between mass (m) and energy (E), c being the speed of light in vacuum.

The *general theory of relativity* 1915 involved a new twist to the concept of space–time; its geometrical properties were to be conceived as modified locally by the presence of a body with mass. A planet's orbit around the sun (as observed in three-dimensional space) arises from its natural trajectory in modified space–time; there is no need to invoke, as Newton did, a force of gravity coming from the sun and acting on the planet. Although since modified in detail, general relativity remains central to modern astrophysics and cosmology; it predicts, for example, the possibility of black holes (small stellar objects collapsing under extreme gravitational force such that light cannot escape from them).

resistance that property of a substance which restricts the flow of electricity through it, associated with the conversion of electrical energy to heat; also the magnitude of this property. A *resistor* is an element whose principal characteristic is resistance, which depends on many factors which may include any or all of the following: the nature of the material, its temperature, dimensions, and thermal properties; degree of impurity; the nature and state of illumination of the surface; and the frequency and magnitude of the current. The practical unit of resistance is the *ohm*.

sound a physiological sensation received by the ear, originating in a vibration (pressure variation in the air), which communicates itself to the air, and travels in every direction, spreading out as an expanding sphere. All sound waves in air travel with a speed which depends on the temperature of the atmosphere; under ordinary conditions this is about 340 m/1,120 ft per second. The pitch of the sound depends on the number of vibrations imposed on the air per second, but the speed is unaffected. The loudness of a sound is dependent primarily on the extent (amplitude) of the to and fro vibration of the air. The lowest note audible to a human being has a frequency of about 26 Hz (vibrations per second), and the highest one of about 18,000 Hz; the lower limit of this range varies little with the person's age, but the upper range falls steadily from adolescence onwards.

spectrum an arrangement in order of magnitude of radiated frequencies of electromagnetic waves, or of the energies of atomic particles. The visible spectrum was first studied by Newton who showed in 1672 that a band of white light (sunlight) passing through a glass prism could be broken into a band of coloured light.

statics the branch of mechanics concerned with the behaviour of bodies at rest and forces in equilibrium, and distinguished from *dynamics*.

thermodynamics the branch of physics dealing with the transfer of heat into other forms of energy, on which is based the study of the efficient working of engines, such as the steam and internal combustion. The three laws of thermodynamics are:
(1) energy can be neither created nor destroyed: heat and mechanical work being mutually convertible;
(2) it is impossible for an unaided self-acting machine to convey heat from one body to another at a higher temperature;
(3) it is impossible by any procedure, no matter how idealized, to reduce any system to the absolute zero of temperature (0 K/−273°C) in a finite number of operations. Put into mathematical form these have widespread applications in physics and chemistry.

transformer a device in which by electromagnetic induction an alternating or intermittent current of one voltage is transformed

435

to another voltage, without change of frequency. A transformer has two coils, a primary for the input, and a secondary for the output, wound on a common iron core. The ratio of the primary to the secondary voltages (and currents) is directly (and inversely) proportional to the number of turns in the primary and secondary coils. It is widely used in electrical apparatus of all kinds and in particular in power transmission where high voltages and low currents are utilized.

ultrasound physical vibrations in matter occurring at frequencies above 20,000 Hz (cycles per second), the approximate limit of human hearing. Propagation of ultrasound in air or other gas is very poor and nearly all practical applications are in liquids or solids. The earliest practical application was to detect submarines during World War I but recently the field of ultrasonics has greatly expanded. The lower frequencies of 20,000–80,000 Hz are mainly used for cleaning in industry and in hospitals. Higher frequencies have been used in the form of pulses to produce echoes as a means of measuring the depth of the sea, to detect flaws in metal, and to show the condition of the foetus and the brain in medicine. High power ultrasound has been used with focusing arrangements to destroy tissue at a depth in the body, and extremely high frequencies of 1,000 MHz (megahertz) or more are used in ultrasonic microscopes.

viscosity the internal friction or resistance to relative motion of the parts of a fluid. Fluids like pitch, treacle, and heavy oils are highly viscous; a perfect fluid would be non-viscous.

wave a pulse or pattern of disturbances which travels through a medium by means of the forces between the particles of the medium. Waves transport energy and show the properties of reflection, refraction, diffraction, and interference. *Sound waves* are longitudinal, that is the particles of the medium (such as air) vibrate to and fro parallel to the direction in which the wave is travelling. *Seismic waves* in the earth's crust include both longitudinal and transverse (at right angles to the direction of propagation) components. *Electromagnetic waves* (such as light) have many of the properties of an ordinary wave, but no medium is needed; the 'disturbance' takes the form of alternating electric and magnetic fields.

work a measure of the result of transferring energy from one system to another to cause an object to move. Thus work W is equal to the product of the force F used and the distance d moved by the object ($W = F \times d$). For example, the work done when a force of 10 newtons moves an object 5 metres against some sort of resistance is 50 newton-metres (= 50 joules). Work should not be confused with *energy* (the capacity to do work, which is also mentioned in joules) or *power* (the rate of doing work, measured in watts).

c. 400 BC	The first 'atomic' theory was put forward by Democritus.
c. 250 BC	Archimedes' principle of buoyancy was established.
1600 AD	Magnetism was described by English physicist and physician William Gilbert (1544–1603).
c. 1610	The principle of falling bodies descending to earth at the same speed was established by Galileo.
1642	The principles of hydraulics were put forward by French mathematician, physicist, and philosopher Blaise Pascal (1623–1662).
1643	The mercury barometer was invented by Italian physicist Evangelista Torricelli (1608–47).
1656	The pendulum clock was invented by Dutch physicist and astronomer Christiaan Huygens (1629–95).
c.1665	Newton put forward the law of gravity, stating that the earth exerts a constant force on falling bodies.
1677	The simple microscope was invented by Dutch microscopist Antoni van Leeuwenhoek (1632–1723).
1690	The wave theory of light was propounded by Huygens.
1704	The corpuscular theory of light was put forward by Newton.
1714	The mercury thermometer was invented by German physicist (Gabriel) Daniel Fahrenheit.
1771	The link between nerve action and electricity was discovered by Italian anatomist and physiologist Luigi Galvani (1737–98).
1795	The metric system was adopted in France.
1798	The link between heat and friction was discovered by American-British physicist Count Benjamin Thomson Rumford (1753–1814).
1800	Volta invented the Voltaic cell.
1808	The 'modern' atomic theory was propounded by British physicist and chemist John Dalton (1766–1844).
1811	Avogadro's hypothesis relating volumes and numbers of molecules of gases was proposed by Italian physicist and chemist Amedeo Avogadro (1776–1856).
1815	Refraction of light was explained by French physicist Augustin Fresnel (1788–1827).
1819	The discovery of electromagnetism was made by Danish physicist Hans Oersted (1777–1851).
1821	The dynamo principle was described by British physicist and chemist Michael Faraday (1791–1867); the thermocouple was discovered by German physicist Thomas Seebeck (1770–1831).
1827	*Ohm's law* of electrical resistance was established by Ohm; Brownian motion resulting from molecular vibrations was observed by British botanist Robert Brown (1773–1858).
1831	Electromagnetic induction was discovered by Faraday.
1842	The principle of conservation of energy was observed by German physician and physicist Julius von Mayer (1814–78).
c.1847	The mechanical equivalent of heat was described by Joule.

1849	A measurement of speed of light was put forward by French physicist Armand Fizeau (1819–96).
1851	The rotation of the earth was demonstrated by Foucault.
1859	Spectrographic analysis was made by German chemist Robert Bunsen (1811–99) and German physicist Gustav Kirchhoff (1824–87).
1861	Osmosis was discovered.
1873	Light was conceived as electromagnetic radiation by Maxwell.
1877	A theory of sound as vibrations in an elastic medium was propounded by British physicist John Rayleigh (1842–1919).
1887	The existence of radio waves was predicted by Hertz.
1895	X-rays were discovered by German physicist Wilhelm Röntgen (1845–1923).
1896	The discovery of radioactivity was made by French physicist Antoine Becquerel (1852–1908).
1897	The electron was discovered by J J Thomson.
1899	Rutherford discovered alpha and beta rays.
1900	Quantum theory was propounded by Planck; the discovery of gamma rays was made by French physicist Paul-Ulrich Villard (1860–1934).
1902	Heaviside discovered the ionosphere.
1904	The theory of radioactivity was put forward by Rutherford and British chemist Frederick Soddy (1877–1966).
1905	Einstein propounded his *special theory of relativity*.
1911	The discovery of the atomic nucleus was made by Rutherford.
1915	Einstein put forward his *general theory of relativity*; X-ray crystallography was discovered by William and Lawrence Bragg.
1922	The orbiting electron atomic theory was propounded by Bohr.
1924	Appleton made his study of the Heaviside layer.
1927	The uncertainty principle of atomic physics was established by German physicist Werner Heisenberg (1901–76).
1928	Wave mechanics was introduced by Schrödinger.
1931	The cyclotron was developed by American physicist Ernest Lawrence (1901–58).
1932	The discovery of the neutron was made by Chadwick; the electron microscope was developed by Soviet-American physicist Vladimir Zworykin (1889–1982).
1933	The positron, the antiparticle of the electron, was discovered by Millikan.
1934	Artificial radioactivity was developed by Frédéric and Irène Joliot-Curie.
1939	The discovery of nuclear fission was made by Hahn and German chemist Fritz Strassman (1902–).
1942	The first controlled nuclear chain reaction was achieved by Fermi.
1956	The neutrino, a fundamental particle, was discovered.
1960	The Mæossbauer effect of atom emissions was discovered by German physicist Rudolf Mæossbauer (1929–); the first maser was developed by American physicist Theodore Maiman (1927–).
1963	Maiman developed the first laser (a term for *l*ight *a*mplification by *s*timulated *e*mission of *r*adiation).

Chemistry

Chemistry is the scientific study of the elements – the way they interact with one another under certain conditions, the properties of the compounds they form, and how, on the one hand, they are the building blocks of all matter, and on the other, are made up of atoms. Nowadays, many aspects of chemistry are closely associated with other scientific disciplines such as atomic physics, astronomy, biology, and mineralogy.

An initial overview of *Key Concepts* presents the three states of matter, atoms and molecules, chemical formulae, and the various branches of chemistry. This is followed by *Inorganic Chemistry*, which is concerned with the elements and all their compounds except those of carbon; a representation of the *Periodic Table of Elements*, which attempts to establish a formal framework from which the properties of elements can be largely determined; and *Organic Chemistry*, which is concerned specifically with the compounds of carbon. Many of the inventors, discoverers, and philosophers associated with the study of chemistry are introduced in the *Biographies*. Finally, the *Chronology* traces the development of the subject from the alchemists, who tried to turn base metals into gold,to the present-day artificial creation of new elements.

Key Concepts

All matter can exist in three states: gas, liquid, or solid. It is composed of minute particles termed *molecules*, and may be further divided into *atoms*. Molecules which contain atoms of one kind only are known as *elements*, while those which contain atoms of different kinds are called *compounds*. The separation of compounds into simpler substances is *analysis*, and the building up of compounds from their components is *synthesis*. When substances are brought together without changing their molecular structure they are said to be *mixtures*. Chemical compounds are produced by a chemical action which alters the arrangement of the atoms in the molecule. Heat, light, vibration, catalyst, radiation or pressure, as well as moisture (for ionization), may be necessary to produce a chemical change.

To facilitate the expression of chemical composition, symbols are used to denote the elements. The symbol is usually the first letter or letters of the English or Latinized name of the element, for example: C, carbon; Ca, calcium; Fe, iron (ferrum). These symbols represent one atom of the element; molecules containing more than one atom are denoted by a subscript figure, as in water, H_2O. In some substances a group of atoms acts as a single atom, and these are enclosed in brackets in the symbol, as in $(NH_2)_2SO_4$, ammonium sulphate. The symbolical representation of a molecule is known as a *formula*. A figure placed before a formula represents the number of molecules of one substance present in another, as in $2H_2O$, two molecules of water. Chemical reactions are expressed by means of equations, as in:

$$NaCl + H_2SO_4 = NaHSO_4 + HCl$$

This equation states the fact that sodium chloride (NaCl) on being treated with sulphuric acid (H_2SO_4) is converted into sodium bisulphate(NaHSO$_4$) and hydrogen chloride (HCl).

Elements are divided into two classes: metals, having lustre, and being conductors of heat and electricity, and non-metals, which usually lack these properties. The *Periodic System*, established by Mendeleyev in 1869, classified elements according to their atomic weights, that is the least weight of the element present in a molecular weight of any of its compounds. Those elements which resemble each other in general properties were found to bear a relation to one another by weight, and these were placed in groups or families. Certain anomalies in this system were removed by classifying the elements according to their atomic number. The latter is the equivalent of the charge on the nucleus of the atom.

Inorganic chemistry deals with the description, properties, reactions, and preparation of the elements and their compounds, with the exception of carbon compounds. *Organic chemistry* is that branch of chemistry which deals with carbon compounds. *Physical chemistry* is concerned with the particular changes which materials may undergo in special circumstances. Physical changes are changes of state only, the properties of the material remaining unaltered. This branch studies in particular the movement of molecules, and the effects of temperature and pressure, especially with regard to gases and liquids.

Inorganic Chemistry

Inorganic chemistry is a major branch of chemistry dealing with the elements and their compounds, except the more complex carbon compounds which are considered in *Organic* *chemistry*. Many types of inorganic com-

COMPOSITION OF THE HUMAN BODY BY WEIGHT

Class	Chemical/element or substance	% body weight
As pure elements or as minerals, salts, and so on	Oxygen	65
	Carbon	18
	Hydrogen	10
	Nitrogen	3
	Calcium	2
	Phosphorus	1.1
	Inorganic molecules	1
	Potassium	0.35
	Sulphur	0.25
	Sodium	0.15
	Chlorine	0.15
	Magnesium, Iron, Manganese, Copper, Iodine, Cobalt, Zinc	Traces
As water and solid matter	Water	60-80
	Total solid material	20-40
As organic molecules	Protein	15-20
	Lipid	3-20
	Carbohydrate	1-15
	Small organic molecules	0-1

pounds exist, the oldest known being acids, bases, and salts. *Acids* usually have a sour taste, change blue vegetable colours (for example litmus) to red, and react with alkalis to form salts. *Alkalis* restore the colours of indicators changed by acids, and react with acids to form salts. All acids contain hydrogen. Acids containing one, two, or three atoms of replaceable hydrogen are called mono-, di-, or tri-basic, respectively. *Salts* are formed by the replacement of the acidic hydrogen by a metal or radical (a group of atoms). If only part of the hydrogen is replaced, an acid salt is formed. A basic salt is usually a compound of a normal salt (in which all the acidic hydrogen is replaced) with excess of base.

Another important group of compounds is the oxides, in which oxygen is combined with another element. Oxides are classified into: (1) *acidic* oxides, forming acids with water; (2)

basic oxides, forming bases (containing the hydroxyl group OH) with water; (3) neutral oxides; and (4) peroxides (containing more oxygen than the normal oxide). Acidic and basic oxides combine to form salts.

Other groups are the compounds of metals with halogens (fluorine, chlorine, bromine, and iodine), called halides (fluorides, chlorides, and so on), and with sulphur (sulphides).

Periodic Table of Elements

The Periodic Table of the elements is a classification of the elements following the statement by Mendeleyev in 1869, that 'the properties of elements are in periodic dependence upon their atomic weight'. There are striking similarities in the chemical properties of the elements in each of the main vertical groups, and a graduation of properties along the horizontal periods. These are dependent on the electronic and nuclear structure of atoms of the elements. The table has been used to predict the existence of as yet unknown transuranic elements.

element one of the 105 known substances, of which 92 occur naturally, which consist of atoms having the same number of protons in their nuclei. Hydrogen and helium were produced in the 'Big Bang'; of the rest, those up to number 56 (iron) are produced by nuclear fusion within the stars, but the more massive, such as lead, uranium, and so on, are produced when an old star explodes and its gravitational energy as it collapses squashes nuclei together. The transuranium elements are artificially made by bombarding uranium with various atomic particles.

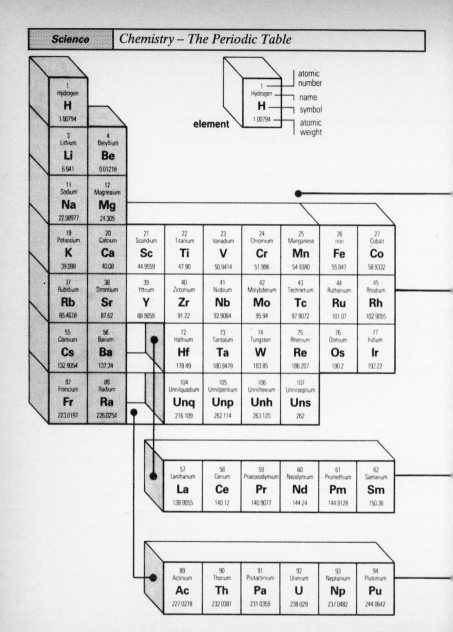

						2 Helium **He** 4.00260

5 Boron **B** 10.81	6 Carbon **C** 12.011	7 Nitrogen **N** 14.0067	8 Oxygen **O** 15.9994	9 Fluorine **F** 18.99840	10 Neon **Ne** 20.179
13 Aluminium **Al** 26.98154	14 Silicon **Si** 28.086	15 Phosphorus **P** 30.97376P	16 Sulphur **S** 32.06	17 Chlorine **Cl** 35.453	18 Argon **Ar** 39.948

28 Nickel **Ni** 58.70	29 Copper **Cu** 63.546	30 Zinc **Zn** 65.38	31 Gallium **Ga** 69.72	32 Germanium **Ge** 672.59	33 Arsenic **As** 74.9216	34 Selenium **Se** 78.96	35 Bromine **Br** 79.904	36 Krypton **Kr** 83.80
46 Palladium **Pd** 106.4	47 Silver **Ag** 107.868	48 Cadmium **Cd** 112.40	49 Indium **In** 114.82	50 Tin **Sn** 118.69	51 Antimony **Sb** 121.75	52 Tellurium **Te** 127.75	53 Iodine **I** 126.9045	54 Xenon **Xe** 131.30
78 Platinum **Pt** 195.09	79 Gold **Au** 196.9665	80 Mercury **Hg** 200.59	81 Thallium **Tl** 204.37	82 Lead **Pb** 207.2	83 Bismuth **Bi** 208.9804	84 Polonium **Po** 209.9871	85 Astatine **At** 209.9871	86 Radon **Rn** 222.0176

63 Europium **Eu** 151.96	64 Gadolinium **Gd** 157.25	65 Terbium **Tb** 158.9254	66 Dysprosium **Dy** 162.50	67 Holmium **Ho** 164.9304	68 Erbium **Er** 167.26	69 Thulium **Tm** 168.9342	70 Ytterbium **Yb** 173.04	71 Lutetium **Lu** 174.97

95 Americium **Am** 243.0614	96 Curium **Cm** 247.0703	97 Berkelium **Bk** 247.0703	98 Californium **Cf** 251.0786	99 Einsteinium **Es** 252.0828	100 Fermium **Fm** 257.0951	101 Mendelvium **Md** 258.0986	102 Nobelium **No** 259.1009	103 Lawrencium **Lr** 260.1054

COMPOSITION OF THE ATMOSPHERE

Air is primarily a mixture of nitrogen, oxygen, and carbon dioxide, but with minute traces of other gases

Gas	Symbol	% Volume	Role
Nitrogen	N	78.08	Cycled through human activities and through the action of micro-organisms on animal and plant waste
Oxygen	O_2	20.94	Cycled mainly through the respiration of animals and plants and through the action of photosynthesis
Carbon dioxide	CO_2	0.03	Cycled through respiration and photosynthesis in exchange reactions with oxygen. It is also a product of burning fossil fuels
Argon	Ar	0.093	
Neon	Ne	0.0018	
Helium	He	0.0005	Chemically inert and with only a few industrial uses
Krypton	Kr	Trace	
Xenon	Xe	Trace	
Ozone	O_3	0.00006	A product of oxygen molecules split into single atoms by the sun's radiation and unaltered oxygen molecules
Hydrogen	H_2	0.00005	Unimportant

Organic Chemistry

Organic chemistry is the chemistry of carbon compounds, particularly the more complex carbon compounds. Many of these are made only by living organisms (for example proteins, carbohydrates), and it was once believed organic compounds could not be made by any other means. This was disproved when Wöhler synthesized urea, but the name 'organic' (that is 'living') chemistry has remained in use. Many organic compounds are derived from oil, which represents the chemical remains of millions of microscopic marine organisms. The basis of organic chemistry is the ability of carbon to form long chains of atoms, branching chains, rings, and other complex structures. In a typical organic compound, each carbon atom forms a bond with each of its neighbouring carbon atoms in the chain or ring, and two more with hydrogen atoms (carbon has a valency of four). Other atoms that may be involved in organic molecules include oxygen and nitrogen. Compounds containing carbon and hydrogen are known as hydrocarbons; those containing carbon, hydrogen and oxygen are carbohydrates. Organic chemistry is largely the chemistry of a great variety of homologous series, in which the molecular formulae, when arranged in ascending order, form an arithmetical progression, for example the *alkanes*, methane CH_4, ethane C_2H_6, propane C_3H_8, butane C_4H_{10}, and so on. The physical properties undergo a gradual change from one member to the next.

Life is carbon-based because of the capacity of carbon atoms to form an almost infinite variety of molecules. Compounds made up of carbon chains are known as *aliphatic*, while those based on rings are *cyclic*.

In inorganic chemistry a specific formula usually represents one substance only, but in organic chemistry it is exceptional for a molecular formula to represent only one substance. Substances having the same molecular formula are called *isomers*, and the relationship is known as *isomerism*. Where substances have the same molecular formula, but differ in their structural formulae, they are called *strucural isomers*, for example chloropropane C_3H_7Cl can have the Cl atom attached to any of the C atoms, giving 1–, 2– or 3– chloropropane. *Spatial isomers*, or *stereo-isomers*, have the same molecular formula, and also the same structural formula, the difference lying in their spatial dispositions. The study of spatial isomers is known as *stereochemistry*.

Hydrocarbons form one of the most prolific of the many organic types; fuel oils are largely made up of hydrocarbons. The most fundamental of organic chemical reactions are oxidation, reduction, hydrolysis, condensation, polymerization, and molecular rearrangement. In living organisms, such changes are often brought about with the help of catalysts called enzymes. This branch of chemistry is generally referred to as *biochemistry*.

COMMON ORGANIC MOLECULE GROUPINGS

Formula	Name	Atomic bonding
CH_3	Methyl	
CH_2CH_3	Ethyl	
CC	Double bond	
CHO	Aldehyde	
CH_2OH	Alcohol	
CO	Ketone	
COOH	Acid	
CH_2NH_2	Amine	
C_6H_6	Benzene ring	

Biographies

Arrhenius Svante August 1859–1927. Swedish scientist, the founder of physical chemistry. Born near Uppsala, he became a professor at Stockholm in 1895, and made a special study of electrolysis. He received the Nobel Prize for Chemistry.

Baekeland Leo Hendrik 1863–1944. American chemist. Born in Ghent, he went to the USA in 1889, and undertook research on photographic materials, inventing Velox paper. His subsequent researches covered the fields of plastics, electro-chemistry, organic chemistry, and electrical insulation. He invented an early type of plastic known as Bakelite.

Bergius Friedrich Karl Rudolph 1884–1949. German research chemist, who received the Nobel Prize for Chemistry in 1931. He invented processes for converting coal into oil, and wood into sugar.

Berzelius Jöns Jakob 1779–1848. Swedish chemist who specialized in the determination of atomic and molecular weights. He invented the system of chemical symbols now in use, discovered several elements and did valuable work on catalysts.

Crookes Sir William 1832–1919. British scientist whose many chemical and physical discoveries included the metal thallium 1861, the radiometer 1875, and Crooke's high vacuum tube used in X-ray techniques.

Curie Marie (born Marya Sklodovska) 1867–1934. Polish chemist, wife of physicist *Pierre Curie* (1859–1906) from 1895. They were awarded the Nobel Prize for Physics (with French physicist Antoine Henri Becquerel) in 1903 for their work on radioactivity, and in 1911 Marie received the Nobel Prize for Chemistry for her discovery of polonium and radium. She died a victim of the radiation emitted by the chemicals with which she worked. Her daughter and son-in-law, *Irène Joliot-Curie* (1896–1956), and *Frédéric Joliot* (1900–59), received a Nobel Prize for Chemistry in 1935 for their creation of artificial radioactivity.

Dalton John 1776–1844. British chemist remembered for his tentative formulation of the atomic theory of chemical composition in *Absorption of Gases* 1805, elaborated in his *New System of Chemical Philosophy* 1808.

Davy Sir Humphry 1778–1829. British chemist. While a laboratory superintendent at Bristol, he discovered the respiratory effects of 'laughing gas' (nitrous oxide) in 1799, and in 1802 became professor at the Royal Institution, London. There he discovered, by electrolysis, the metals sodium, potassium, calcium, magnesium, strontium, and barium. He invented the 'safety lamp' for use in mines where methane was present, in effect enabling the miners to work in previously unsafe conditions.

Faraday Michael 1791–1867. British chemist. He became a laboratory assistant to Sir Humphry Davy at the Royal Institution in 1813, and in 1827 succeeded him as professor of chemistry there. In 1812 he began researches into electricity, and made his first electric

battery. In 1821 he began experimenting on electromagnetism, and ten years later discovered the induction of electric currents and made the first dynamo. Many more discoveries in electricity followed. In 1845 he began a second great period of research in which he discovered what he announced as the magnetization of light.

Fischer Hans 1881–1945. German chemist, who received the Nobel Prize for Chemistry in 1930 for his discovery of haemoglobin in blood.

Gay-Lussac Joseph Louis 1778–1850. French physicist and chemist. Born near Limoges, he became professor of physics at Paris in 1808. In 1804 he made balloon ascents to study the weather. He investigated the physical properties of gases and discovered new methods of producing sulphuric and oxalic acids.

Haber Fritz 1868–1934. German chemist, whose conversion of atmospheric nitrogen to ammonia opened the way for the synthetic fertilizer industry. His study of the combustion of hydrocarbons led to the commercial 'cracking' or fractionating of natural oil into its components, for example diesel, petrol, and paraffin. In electrochemistry he was the first to demonstrate that oxidation and reduction take place at the electrodes; from this he developed a general electrochemical theory. In World War I he worked on poison gas and devised gas masks; he was awarded a Nobel prize in 1918.

Henry William 1774–1836. British chemist. In 1803 he formulated *Henry's law*: when a gas is dissolved in a liquid at a given temperature, the amount (that is the mass) which dissolves is in direct proportion to the gas pressure.

Kekulé Friedrich August 1829–96. German chemist, whose theory (1858) of molecular structure revolutionized organic chemistry. He is most famous for proposing two resonant (co-existing alternative) forms of the benzene ring.

Lavoisier Antoine Laurent 1743–94. French chemist, sometimes called the founder of modern chemistry. He proved that combustion needed only a part of 'air' which he called oxygen. He thereby destroyed the theory of phlogiston (an imaginary 'fire element' released during combustion). With Laplace he showed that water was a compound of oxygen and hydrogen. In this way he established the modern basic rules of chemical combination.

Liebig Justus, Baron von Liebig 1803–73. German chemist, and a major contributor to agricultural chemistry. He introduced the theory of radicals, and discovered chloroform.

Mendeleyev Dmitri Ivanovich 1834–1907. Russian chemist, framer of the Periodic Law which states that the chemical properties of the elements are periodic functions of their atomic weights.

Müller Paul 1899–1965. Swiss chemist, awarded a Nobel prize in 1948 for his discovery of the first synthetic contact insecticide, DDT, in 1939.

Nobel Alfred Bernhard 1833–96. Swedish chemist, inventor of dynamite in 1867. He bequeathed the fortune gained from explosives to found the Nobel prizes.

Pauling Linus Carl 1901– . American chemist, noted for his fundamental work on the nature of the chemical bond, and on the discovery of the helical structure of many proteins. He was awarded the Nobel Prize for Chemistry in 1954. An outspoken opponent of nuclear testing, he received the Nobel Peace Prize in 1962.

Priestley Joseph 1733–1804. British chemist. He discovered oxygen in about 1774 (two yearsw after German chemist Karl Scheele).

Ramsay Sir William 1852–1916. British chemist who, together with physicist Lord Rayleigh, discovered argon in 1894. In 1895 Ramsay manufactured helium, and in 1898 identified neon, krypton, and xenon. With Frederick Soddy he noted the transmutation of radium into helium in 1903, which led to the discovery of the density and atomic weight of radium. He received a Nobel prize in 1904.

Rutherford Ernest 1871–1937. New Zealand physicist. A pioneer of modern atomic science, his main researches were in the field of radioactivity, and he was the first to recognize the nuclear nature of the atom. He was awarded a Nobel prize in 1908.

Soddy Frederick 1877–1956. British physical chemist. After working for Rutherford and Ramsay, he was professor of chemistry at Aberdeen 1914–19 and at Oxford 1919–36. A pioneer of research into atomic disintegration – he coined the term 'isotopes' – he wrote a classic work on radioactivity (*Chemistry of the Radio-Elements* 1912–14), and was awarded a Nobel prize in 1921.

Sutherland Earl Wilbur 1915–74. American physiologist, discoverer of a chemical 'messenger' made by a special enzyme in the wall of cells. Many hormones operate by means of this messenger. He was awarded a Nobel prize in 1971.

Taube Henry 1915– . American chemist, who established the basis of modern inorganic chemistry by his study of the loss or gain of electrons by atoms during chemical reactions. He was awarded a Nobel prize in 1983.

Urey Harold Clayton 1893–1981. American chemist. In 1932 he isolated heavy water and discovered deuterium, receiving a Nobel prize in 1934. He was director of the War Research Atomic Bomb Project, Columbia, 1940–45..

Van 't Hoff Jacobus Henricus 1852–1911. Dutch physical chemist. He explained the 'asymmetric' carbon atom occurring in optically active compounds. His greatest work – the concept of chemical affinity as the maximum work obtainable from a reaction – was shown with measurements of osmotic and gas pressures, and reversible electric batteries. He was the first Nobel prize recipient in 1901.

Werner Alfred 1866–1919. Swiss chemist. He was awarded a Nobel prize in 1913 for his work on valency theory, which explains the chemical properties of an element in terms of the number of electrons orbiting the nucleus of its constituent atoms.

Wöhler Friedrich 1800–82. German chemist who synthesized the first organic compound (urea) from an inorganic compound (ammonium cyanate): it had previously been thought impossible to convert. He also isolated the elements aluminium, beryllium, yttrium, and titanium.

1 AD   Gold, silver, copper, lead, iron, tin, and mercury were known.

1100   Alcohol was first distilled.

1242   Gunpowder introduced to Europe from the Far East.

1540   First known scientific observation and experiment carried out.

1604   Italian mathematician, astronomer and physicist Galileo invented the thermometer.

1620   Scientific method of reasoning expounded by English philosopher Francis Bacon in his *Novum Organum*.

1649   Carbon, sulphur, antimony, and arsenic were known.

1650   Leyden University in the Netherlands set up the first chemistry laboratory.

1660   Law concerning effect of pressure on gas (*Boyle's Law*) was established by English chemist Robert Boyle; definition of the element.

1662   The Royal Society was formed.

1742   Centigrade scale invented.

1746   Lead chamber process developed for manufacturing sulphuric acid; German chemist Andreas Marggraf discovered zinc.

1750   Swedish chemist Axel Cronstedt discovered cobalt and nickel.

1756   Scottish chemist and physicist Joseph Black discovered carbon dioxide.

1772   German chemist Karl Scheele discovered oxygen, two years before Priestley.

1774   Scheele discovered chlorine; Swedish Chemist Johan Gahn discovered manganese; Lavoisier demonstrated his *law of conservation of mass*.

1777   Lavoisier explained burning; sulphur was known to be an element.

1779   Dutch scientist Jan Ingenhousz demonstrated photosynthesis.

1781   English scientist Henry Cavendish showed water to be a compound.

1792   Italian physicist Alessandro Volta demonstrated the electrochemical series.

1793   German chemist Hieronymus Richter demonstrated the *law of equivalent proportions*.

1799   Twenty-seven elements were known.

1800   Volta designed his electric battery.

1801   Dalton demonstrated his *law of partial pressures*.

1803   Dalton expounded his atomic theory.

1807   Sodium and potassium were first prepared by Davy.

1808   Gay-Lussac announced his *law of volumes*.

1811   Publication of Italian physicist Amedeo Avogadro's hypothesis on the relationship of volumes of gases and numbers of molecules to temperature and pressure.

1813   French chemist Bernard Courtois discovered iodine.

1818   Berzelius's atomic symbols were elaborated.

1819   French scientists Henri Dulong and Alexis-Thérèse Petit's *law of atomic heats* was demonstrated.

1820	Danish scientist Hans Christian Oersted demonstrated electromagnetism.
1825	French chemist Antoine-Jeroôme Balard prepared bromine. Matches were invented.
1828	The first organic compounds, alcohol and urea, were synthesized.
1834	Faraday expounded the *laws of electrolysis*.
1836	Acetylene was discovered.
1840	Liebig expounded the carbon and nitrogen cycles.
1846	Scottish chemist Thomas Graham's *law of diffusion* (*Graham's Law*) was expounded.
1849	Fifty-seven elements were known.
1850	Ammonia was first made from coal-gas.
1853	German chemist Robert Bunsen invented his burner.
1858	Cannizzaro's method of atomic weights was expounded.
1862	Haemoglobin was crystallized.
1866	Nobel invented dynamite.
1868	The first plastic substance – celluloid – was made.
1869	Mendeleyev expounded his Periodic Table.
1879	Saccharin was discovered.
1886	French chemist Ferdinand Moissan isolated fluorine.
1894	Ramsay and Rayleigh discovered inert gases.
1897	The electron was discovered by English physicist Sir Joseph Thomson.
1898	The Curies discovered radium.
1905	Einstein's announced his *theory of relativity*.
1912	Vitamins were discovered by British biochemist Gowland Hopkins; British physicist Lawrence Bragg demonstrated that crystals have a regular arrangement of atoms.
1919	Artificial disintegration of atoms by Rutherford.
1920	Rutherford discovered the proton.
1927	British chemist Neil Sidgwick's *theory of valency* was announced.
1928	Vitamin C was crystallized.
1932	Deuterium (heavy water) was discovered; Chadwick discovered the neutron.
1933	British chemist Norman Haworth synthesized Vitamin C.
1942	Plutonium was first synthesized.
1945	The atomic bomb was exploded.
1953	Hydrogen was converted to helium.
1954	Einsteinium and fermium were synthesized.

Mathematics

Mathematics is the science of spatial and numerical relations. The subject is divided into pure mathematics, which includes, as its main divisions, geometry, arithmetic, and algebra, the calculus, and trigonometry; and applied mathematics, which deals with mechanics, the mathematical theories of astronomy, electricity, optics, and thermodynamics. In recent years mathematics has been aided by the computer, a powerful new tool which can create and manipulate mathematical 'models', and everyday arithmetic has been made simpler by the general availability of the electronic pocket calculator.

This section explains, in *Mathematical Terms*, the fundamental concepts, theories, and principles of the subject; in *Geometry and Trigonometry*, the mathematics of the measurement, properties, and relationships of points, lines, angles, surfaces, and angles; and in *Biographies*, the work of important mathematicians. *Mathematical Symbols and Formulae* are presented as a chart at the end of the section.

Mathematical Terms

abacus method of calculating with a handful of counters on a flat surface, used by the Greeks and Romans, and possibly by the builders of Stonehenge. Later types of abacus include those with beads on wires, still used in China. The method has principles in common with the electronic calculator.

algebra method of solving mathematical problems by the use of symbols (letters and signs) when figures are inadequate (the numbers involved may be very large or not known exactly). More advanced algebra is used to work out general problems, for example the equations derived by American physicist Albert Einstein (1879–1955) from his general theory of relativity, and the method of algebraic reasoning first devised by British mathematician George Boole (1815–64) and used in working out the construction of computers.

Arabic numerals the signs 0 1 2 3 4 5 6 7 8 9, which were in use among the Arabs before being adapted by the peoples of Europe during the Middle Ages in place of Roman numerals. They appear to have originated in India, and reached Europe by way of Spain.

arithmetic branch of mathematics that concerns all questions involving numbers, as in counting, measuring, or weighing. Simple arithmetic already existed in prehistoric times. The basic operation of arithmetic is counting. Most arithmetical questions could be answered by counting alone, though with great labour and expenditure of time. Formal calculations allow the same result to be achieved more quickly. The fundamental operations are addition and subtraction, and multiplication and division. Fractions arise naturally in the process of measurement. Decimals are a form of fractions. Powers, that is repeated multiplica-

tion of the same number, are represented by an index, for example $2^5 = $ '2 to the 5th' $= 2 \times 2 \times 2 \times 2 \times 2$. Roots are the reverse of powers. For example, 2 is the 5th root of 32, because $2 \times 2 \times 2 \times 2 \times 2 = 32$. Logarithms form a convenient means of carrying out complicated fundamental arithmetic operations. The essential feature of modern arithmetic is the *place-value* system. The decimal numeral system employs ten numerals (0 1 2 3 4 5 6 7 8 9). In a decimal number, each position has a value ten times that of the position to its immediate right, for example in the number 23 the numeral 3 represents the number 3, but moved one place to the left it would equal three tens. Modern computers operate in base-two, using only two numerals (0 1), known as a binary system. In binary, each position has a value twice as great as the position to its immediate right, so that for example binary 111 is equal to 7 in the decimal system, and 1111 is equal to 15. *modular arithmetic* deals with events recurring in regular cycles, and is used in describing the functioning of petrol engines, electrical generators, and so on. For example in the modulo-twelve system, the answer to a question as to what time it will be in five hours if it is now ten o'clock, can be expressed $10 + 5 = 3$ (that is, $15 - 12$).

base in mathematics, the number of different symbols in a particular number system. Thus our usual (decimal) counting system of numbers has the base 10. In the binary number system, which has only the numbers 1 and 0, the base is 2. A base is also a number which, when raised to a particular power (that is, when multiplied by itself a particular number of times as in $10^2 = 10 \times 10 = 100$), has a logarithm equal to the power i.e., logarithm of 100 to the base 10 is 2.

binomial in algebra, an expression consisting of two terms, such as $a + b$, $a - b$. The *binomial theorem*, discovered by English mathematician and physicist Sir Isaac Newton (1642–1727) and first published in 1676, is a formula whereby any power of a binomial quantity may be found without performing the progressive multiplications.

calculus branch of mathematics that permits the manipulation of continuously varying quantities, applicable to practical problems involving such matters as changing speeds, problems of flight, varying stresses in the framework of a bridge. electrical circuits with varying currents and voltages, and so on. The term is the Latin word for pebble, used in calculations on the abacus. *Integral calculus* deals with the method of summation or adding together the effects of continuously varying quantities. *Differential calculus* deals in a similar way with rates of change. Many of its applications arose from the study of speed. Each of these branches of calculus deals with small quantities which during manipulation are made smaller and smaller, hence both comprise the *infinitesimal calculus*. Differential equations represent complex rates of change and integrals are their empirical solutions. If no known mathematical processes are available, integration can be performed graphically or by a machine, increasingly by computers.

coefficient the number part in front of an algebraic term, signifying multiplication. For example, in the expression $4x^2 + 2xy - x$, the coefficient of x^2 is 4 (because $4x^2$ means $4 \times x^2$), that of xy is 2 and that of x is -1 (because $-1 \times x = -x$). In some algebraic expressions, coefficients are represented by letters called constants, that stand for numbers, for example, in the equation $ax^2 + bx + c = 0$, a, b and c are constants.

complement in set theory within mathematics, the set consisting of the elements within the universal set that are not contained in the designated set. For example, if the universal set is the set of all positive whole numbers and the designated set S is the set of all even numbers, then the complement of S (denoted S') is the set of all odd numbers. In geometry, the complement of an angle is the number of degrees needed to make it a right angle (90°). For example, the complement of 60° is 30° or 60° and 30° are complementary angles. In number theory, the complement of a number is obtained by subtracting it from its base. For example, the complement of 7 in numbers to base ten (the everyday way of counting) is 3.

constant in mathematics, a fixed quantity or one that does not change its value in relation to variables. For example, in the algebraic expression $y^2 = 5x - 3$, the numbers 5 and 3 are constants; so too are a and b in the general equation $ax + b = 0$. In physics, certain quantities are regarded as universal constants that never vary, for example, the speed of light in vacuum, represented by the letter c.

cybernetics science concerned with how systems organize, regulate and reproduce themselves, and also how they evolve and learn. It was founded and named by Norbert Wiener (1894–1964), an American mathematician. The name is derived from the Greek 'steersman'. In the laboratory inanimate objects are created that behave like living systems. Uses range from the creation of electronic artificial limbs to the running of the fully automated factory where decision-making machines operate at up to managerial level.

decimal number a number expressed to the base ten, the number system in ordinary use. Counting is in units (10^0), tens (10^1), hundreds (10^2), thousands (10^3), and so on. Decimal fractions have powers of ten as their denominators, for example, $3/10$, $4/100$, $5/1000$, and so on but are represented by a decimal point followed by the numerator of the fraction preceded if necessary by zeros. For example, the above fractions as decimals are 0.3, 0.04, and 0.005. The use of decimals greatly simplifies addition and multiplication of fractions, though not all fractions can be expressed exactly as a decimal fractions.

differentiation in mathematics, a procedure for finding the rate of change of one variable quantity relative to another. Together, differentation and integration of functions make up calculus.

exponential in mathematics, a function in which the variable quantity is an exponent, that is, an index or power to which another number or expression is raised. For example, $f(x) = ax$ is an exponential function in which a is typically a number, say, 5, and x is the exponent (.1, 0.5, -10, and so on). Such

453

functions are always positive and their values get closer and closer to 0 with increasingly negative values of x. The term 'exponential function' usually refers to $f(x) = ex$, the basis of natural or Naperian logarithms and definitive of many natural phenomena of growth and decay (such as the radioactive decay of various isotopes). In this expression e is an irrational number equal to 2.7283... *Exponential growth* is a form of increase in numbers in which the rate of growth is slow at first but then rises sharply. It applies, for example, to uncontrolled population growth. A graph of population number against time produces a curve that is characteristically rather flat at first but then shoots almost directly upwards.

factorial of a number is the product of all the whole numbers (integers) inclusive between 1 and the number itself. A factorial is indicated by the symbol !. For example, $6! = 1 \times 2 \times 3 \times 4 \times 5 \times 6 = 720$. Zero factorial, $0!$, is defined as 1.

fraction in mathematics, a number that indicates one or more equal parts of a whole (from Latin *fractio* meaning to break), probably arising from the need to break one object into several pieces to share it fairly among several people. The usual way of denoting this is to place below a horizontal line the number of equal parts into which the unit is divided (denominator), and above the line the number of these parts comprising the fraction (numerator); thus $2/3$ or $3/4$. Such fractions are called *vulgar* or *simple fractions*. A *proper fraction* is one in which the numerator is less than the denominator. A combination such as $5/0$ is not regarded as a fraction however (an object cannot be divided into zero equal parts), and mathematically any number divided by 0 is equal to infinity. An *improper fraction* is one in which the numerator is larger than the denominator, for example, $3/2$. An improper fraction can therefore be expressed as a mixed number, for example, $1 1/2$. A *decimal fraction* is one in which the fraction is expressed by figures written to the right of the units figure (which may be 0) after a dot or point (the decimal point), for example 0.04, which is $4/100$.

function in mathematics, a procedure that defines a relationship between quantities, usually variables. For example, in the algebraic expression $y = 4x^3 + 2$, the variable y is a function of the variable x, generally written as $f(x)$. Commonly used in applied mathematics, physics and science generally: for example, the formula $t + 2\pi(l/g)^{1/2}$ shows that for a simple pendulum the time of swing t is a function of its length l and of no other variable quantity (π and g, the acceleration due to gravity, are constants).

geometry branch of mathematics concerned with the properties of space, usually in terms of plane (two-dimensional) and solid (three-dimensional) figures. It probably originated in Egypt, in land measurements necessitated by the periodic inundations of the River Nile, and was soon extended into surveying and navigation. Early geometers were Thales, Pythagoras and Euclid. Analytical methods were introduced and developed by Descartes in the 17th century.

index in mathematics, a number that indicates a function, as in the terms x^2, y^5, and 4^7; the indices are 2, 5, and 7, and indicate respectively $x \times x$; $y \times y \times y \times y \times y$, $4 \times 4 \times 4 \times 4 \times 4 \times 4$. Such terms are multiplied by adding the indices, for example, $x^2 \times x^5 = x^7$; and divided by subtracting the indices, for example, $y^5 + y^3 = y^2$. Any number with the index 0 is equal to 1 for example, $x^0 = 1$ and $99^0 = 1$. Also known as power or exponent. From the latin 'sign, indicator'; plural indices.

integer a positive or negative number. Fractions, such as $1/2$ and 0.35, are known as nonintegral numbers.

interest in finance, a sum of money paid to an investor in return for the loan, usually expressed as percentage per annum. *Simple interest* is interest calculated as a straight percentage of the amount invested. Thus, a sum of £100 invested at 10 per cent simple interest for five years earns £10 a year, giving a total of £50 interest (and at the end of the period the investor receives a total of £150). In *compound interest*, the interest earned over a period of time (for example, per annum) is added to the investment, so that at the end of the next period interest is paid on that total. It is thus a way of paying interest on the accumulated interest. The same sum of £100 invested for five years at 10 per cent compound interest earns a total of £61.05 interest (with £161.05 returned at the end of the period). Generally, for a sum S invested at x per cent simple interest for y years, the total amount returned is $S + xyS/100$. If is it invested at x per cent compound interest for y years, the total amount returned is $S[(100 + x)/100]y$.

logarithm mathematical function that makes the multiplication and division of large numbers simpler by substituting respectively the operations of addition and subtraction. The principle of logarithms is also the basis of the slide rule. With the general availability of the electronic pocket calculator, the need for logarithms has reduced. More formally, a logarithm (or log) is the exponent or index of a number to a specified base. For example, the log of 10 to the base 10 is 1; the log of 100 to the base 10 is 2, because $10^2 = 10 \times 10 = 100$. To multiply 100 by 100 (that is, $10^2 \times 10^2$), the indices are added, giving 10^4. Thus 10^4 or log 10^4 = 10,000. For more difficult calculations, tables of logarithms and antilogarithms are available (usually to the base 10) which show conversions of numbers into logarithms, and vice versa. For example, to multiply 6,560 × 980, one looks up the logarithms of the numbers – 3.8169 and 2.9912 – adds them together (6.8081), then looks up the antilog of this to get the answer (6,428,000).

mathematics the science of spatial and numerical relationships. Many activities in business and commerce make extensive use of mathematics, including accountancy, banking and insurance. Higher mathematics has a powerful new tool in the high-speed electronic computer, which can create and manipulate mathematical 'models' of various systems in science, technology and commerce. Modern methods of teaching arithmetic are sometimes referred to as 'new maths'.

maximum and minimum in mathematics, of a curve representing a function in co-ordinate geometry, where slope changes from positive to negative after reaching a turning point (maximum), or from negative to positive after reaching a turning point (minimum). A tangent to the curve at a maximum or minimum has zero gradient. Maxima and minima can be found by differentiating the function for the curve and setting the differential to zero (the value of the slope at the turning point). For example, differentiating the function for the parabola $y = 2x^2 - 8x$ gives $dy/dx = 4x - 8$. Setting this equal to zero gives $x = 2$, so that $y = -8$ (found by substituting $x = 2$ into the parabola equation). Thus the function has a minimum at the point $(2, -8)$.

mean in mathematics, a specific related term intermediate between the first and last terms of a progression. The simple *arithmetic mean* is the average value of the quantities, that is, the sum of the quantities divided by their number. The *weighted mean* takes into account the frequency of the terms that are summed; it is calculated by multiplying each term by the number of times it occurs, summing the results and dividing this total by the total number of occurences. The *geometric mean* is the corresponding root of the product of the quantities.

number a symbol used in counting or measuring. In mathematics, there are various kinds of numbers. The ordinary numerals, 0, 1, 2, 3, 4, 5, 6, 7, 8, 9, give a counting system which, to the base ten, continues 10, 11, 12, 13, and so on. These are whole decimal numbers (also called cardinals or integers), with fractions represented as $1/4$, $1/2$, $3/4$ and so on, or as decimal fractions (0.25, 0.5, 0.75 and so on). They are also rational numbers. Numbers that cannot be represented as fractions and require symbols, such as $\sqrt{2}$, π and e are irrational: they can be expressed numerically only as the (inexact) approximations 1.414, 3.142 and 2.728 (to three places of decimals) respectively. Number systems can also be devised with bases other than 10. For example, numbers to base two (binary numbers) using only the 0 and 1, produce a series which starts 0, 1, 10, 11, 100, 101, 110, 111. They are commonly used in digital computers to represent the two-state 'in' or 'off' pulses of electricity.

percentage a way of representing a number as a fraction of 100. Thus 45 per cent (or 45%) equals $^{45}/_{100}$, and 45% of 20 is $20 \times {}^{45}/_{100} = 9$. In general, if a quantity x changes to y, the percentage change is $100(x - y)/x$. Thus, if the number of people in a room changes from 40 to 50, the percentage increase is $(100 \times 10)/40 = 25\%$. To express a fraction as a percentage, its denominator must first be converted to 100, for example, $^1/_8 = 12.5/100 = 12.5\%$. The use of percentages often makes it easier to compare fractions that do not have a common denominator.

permutation in mathematics, specified arrangement of a group of objects. In general, the number of permutations of a items taken b at a time is given by $a!/(a - b)!$, where the symbol ! stands for factorial (the product of all the integers (whole numbers) up to and including the number). For example, the number of permutations of four letters taken from any group of six different letters is $6!/2! = (1 \times 2 \times 3 \times 4 \times 5 \times 6)/(1 \times 2) = 360$. The theoretical number of four-letter 'words' that can be made from an alphabet of 26 letters is $26!/22! = 358,800$.

power in mathematics, also called an index or exponent, is written as a superior small numeral. A number or symbol raised to the power 2 is said to be squared (for example, 3^2, x^2) and something raised to the power three is said to be cubed (for example, 2^3, y^3).

probability the likelihood or chance that something will happen, often expressed as 'odds' or, in mathematics, numerically as a fraction. In tossing an unbiased coin the chance that it will land heads is the same as the chance that it will land tails, that is, 1 to 1 or 'evens'; mathematically this probability is expressed as $^1/_2$ or 0.5. The odds against any chosen number coming up on the roll of an unbiased dice are 6 to 1; the probability is $^1/_6$ or 0.1666... If two dice are rolled there are $6 \times 6 = 36$ different possible combinations. The chance that a double (two numbers the same) will come up is only one of these combinations; thus the

probability is $^1/_{36}$ or 0.02777... In general, the probability that n particular events will happen out of a total of m possible events is n/m. A certainty has a probability of 1; an impossibility has a probability of 0.

progression sequence of numbers each formed by a specific relationship to its predecessor: an arithmetical progression has numbers which increase or decrease by a common sum or difference (for example 2, 4, 6, 8); a geometric progression has numbers each bearing a fixed ratio to its predecessor (for example 3, 6, 12, 24), and harmonic progression is a sequence with numbers whose reciprocals are in arithmetical progression, for example 1, $^1/_2$, $^1/_3$, $^1/_4$.

quadratic equation in mathematics a polynomial equation of second degree (that is, an equation containing as its highest power the square of a single unknown variable, such as x^2). The general formula of such equations is $ax^2 + bx + c = 0$, in which a, b, and c are constants and only the coefficient a cannot equal 0. A quadratic equation may have as its solution values of x, two identical values of x, or no real values of x, (that is, the solutions are complex numbers), depending on the value of $b^2 - 4ac$.

reciprocal in mathematics, of a quantity, that quantity divided into 1. Thus the reciprocal of 2 is $^1/_2$ (= 0.5); of 150 is $^1/_{150}$ (= 0.00666666...); of x^2 is $1/x^2$ or x^{-2}.

Roman numerals an old number system using different symbols from today's Arabic numerals (the ordinary numbers 1, 2, 3, 4, 5, and so on). The seven key symbols in Roman numerals as represented today (originally they were a little different) are I (= 1), V (= 5), X (= 10), L (= 50), C (= 100), D (= 500) and M (= 1,000). There is no zero.

scalar quantity in mathematics, any quantity that has magnitude but no direction.

set in mathematics, any collection of defined things, usually denoted by a capital letter and indicated by curly brackets (braces). For example $L = \{$LETTERS OF THE ALPHABET$\}$ represents the set that consists of all the letters of the alphabet. The symbol stands for 'is a member of'; thus pL means that p belongs to the set consisting of all letters, and 4/L means that 4 does not belong to the set consisting of all letters.

simultaneous equations in mathematics, two or more algebraic equations that contain two or more unknown quantities and are simultaneously true. In the simplest case, that of two linear equations with two unknown variables, for example (i) $x + 3y = 6$ and (ii) $3y - 2x = 4$, the solution will be those unique values of x and y that are valid for both equations. One method of solution is first to eliminate one of the variables, whether by substitution, for example, in this case substituting for x in equation (ii) the value $6 - 3y$ obtained by rearranging equation (i); or by multiplying equation (i) by 2 (to give $2x + 6y = 12$) and adding this new equation to equation (ii) to give $9y = 16$, which is easily solved.

slide rule a mathematical instrument having pairs of sliding scales, used for rapid calculations, including multiplication, division, and the extraction of square roots, based on logarithms. Formerly popular with draughtsmen and engineers, it has been largely superseded by the electronic calculator.

square root in mathematics, of a number, another number which when squared (multiplied by itself) equals the given number. For example, the square root of 25 (written $\sqrt{25}$) is 5, because $5 \times 5 = 25$; the square root of 152.2756 is 12.34. As an index, a square root is represented by $\frac{1}{2}$; for example, $16^{1/2} = 4$. Strictly speaking, 16 (and all other numbers greater than zero) has two square roots: $+4$ and -4, because $(-4)^2$ also equals 16. Thus the square root of 16 is written $+4$. Negative numbers (less than 0) do not have square roots that are real numbers. Their roots are represented by complex numbers, in which the square root of -1 is given the symbol i (that is, $i^2 = -1$). Thus the square root of -4 is $+2i$.

statistics the branch of mathematics concerned with the collection and interpretation of data. For meaningful interpretations, there should be a large amount of data to analyse. For example, faced with the task of determin-

ing the mean (average) age of the children in a school, an exact mean could be obtained by averaging the ages of every pupil in the school. A statistically acceptable answer might be obtained by calculating the average based on the ages of a representative sample, consisting say of a random tenth of the pupils from each class. Probability is the branch of statistics dealing with predictions of events. The science has many applications in government, business, industry, and commerce.

topology the branch of geometry which deals with those properties of a figure which remain unchanged even when the figure is transformed, that is bent, stretched, and so on, as for example when a square painted on a rubber sheet is deformed by distorting the sheet. A famous topological problem (studied extensively by the Norwegian mathematician Oystein Ore 1899–) is to provide a proof that only three colours are needed in producing a map, to give adjoining areas different colours. Topology has scientific applications, as in the study of turbulence in flowing fluids.

trigonometry branch of mathematics which solves problems relating to plane and spherical triangles. Its principles are based on the fixed proportions of angles and sides in a right-angled triangle, the simplest of which are the sine, cosine, and tangent (so-called trigonometrical ratios). Using trigonometry it is possible to calculate the lengths of the sides and the sizes of the angles of a triangle as long as one angle and one side are known. It is of practical importance in navigation and surveying and in topics such as simple harmonic motion in physics.

Venn diagram in mathematics, a diagram representing a set or sets and the logical relationships between them. Sets are drawn as circles. An area of overlap between two circles (sets) contains elements that are common to both sets, and thus represents a third set. Circles that do not overlap represent sets with no elements in common (disjoint sets). The method is named after the British logician John Venn (1834–1923).

Geometry and Trigonometry

abscissa in co-ordinate geometry the horizontal or *x* co-ordinate, that is, the distance of a point from the vertical or *y*-axis. For example, a point with the co-ordinates (3,4) has an abscissa of 3.

alternate angles one of a pair of angles that lie on opposite sides of a transversal (a line cutting two other lines). If the two other lines are parallel, the alternate angles are equal.

altitude in geometry, the perpendicular distance from a vertex (corner) of a triangle to the base (the side opposite the vertex). In ordinary terms, the altitude is the height of the triangle.

angle in geometry, the inclination between a pair of lines. Angles are measured in degrees or radians. An angle of 90° (90 degrees) is a right angle. Angles of less than 90° are called *acute angles*; angles of more than 90° but less than 180° are *obtuse angles*. A *reflex angle* is an angle of more than 180° but less than 360°. Angles are measured using a protractor.

arc in geometry, a section of a curve. A circle has two kinds of arcs. An arc that is less than a semi-circle is called a *minor arc*; an arc that is greater than a semi-circle is a *major arc*.

area in geometry, the size of a surface, measured in square units (such as cm² or km²). The area A of a square is the length of side l squared: $A = l \times l = l^2$. For a rectangle, the area is given by $A = l \times b$ where b is the breadth (the shorter side). The area of a triangle is half the length of the base l times the perpendicular height h (altitude): $A = \frac{1}{2}l \times h$; of a parallelogram (a quadrilateral with one pair of sides equal and parallel) is the length times the height (the perpendicular distance between the longer pair of sides): $A = l \times h$; of a circle is π times the square of the radius, r: $A = \pi r^2$. The areas of more complex shapes can often be

found by dividing them into simpler shapes whose areas can be calculated or estimated.

chord in geometry, a straight line joining any two points on a curve. In a circle, the chord that passes through the centre of the circle (the longest chord) is the diameter. In an ellipse (a regular oval), the longest and shortest chords are called the major and minor axes.

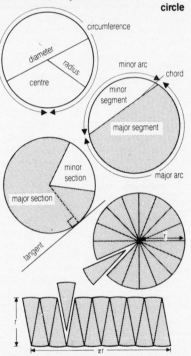
circle

circle path followed by a point which moves so as to keep a constant distance, the *radius*, from a fixed point, the *centre*. The longest distance from one side of a circle to the other, called the *diameter*, is thus twice the radius. The ratio of the distance all the way round the circle – the *circumference* – to the diameter is an irrational number called *pi* (π), roughly equal to 3.14159. A circle of diameter d has a circumference C equal to πd, or $C = 2\pi r$ and an area $A = \pi r^2$. If a circle is divided up by two radii, then the resulting divisions are termed major and minor *sectors*. The area of a circle (πr^2) can be shown by dividing a circle into very thin sectors and reassembling them to make an approximate rectangle.

circumference in geometry, the curved line that encloses a plane figure, for example, a circle or an ellipse. Its length varies according to the nature of the curve, and may be ascertained by the appropriate formula. Thus the circumference of a circle is $2\pi r$, where r is the radius and $\pi = 3.1415927 \dots$ or roughly $^{22}/_7$.

cone in geometry, a solid figure having a plane curve as its base and tapering to a point (the vertex). The line joining the vertex to the centre of the base is called the axis of the cone. A circular cone has a circle as its base; a cone that has its axis at right angles to the base is called a right cone. A circular cone of perpendicular height h and base of radius r has a volume $v = \frac{1}{3}\pi r^2 h$.

conic section curve obtained when a cone is intersected by a plane. Conic sections were first discovered by the ancient Greeks and have been of great importance in mathematics. If the intersecting plane cuts both extensions of the cone it yields a hyperbola; if it is parallel to the side of the cone it produces a parabola. Other intersecting planes produce a circle or an ellipse.

cosine in trigonomentry, a measure of an angle in a right-angled triangle found by dividing the length of the side adjacent to the angle by the length of the hypotenuse (the longest side). It is usually shortened to *cos*.

co-ordinate geometry a system of geometry, also called analytical geometry, in which points, lines, shapes, and surfaces and represented by algebraic expressions. In plane (two-dimensional) co-ordinate geometry, the plane is usually defined by two axes at right angles to each other, the horizontal x-axis and the vertical y-axis, meeting at O, the origin. A point on the plane can be represented by a pair of Cartesian co-ordinates, which define its position in terms of its distance along the x-axis and along the y-axis from O. These distances are

respectively the x and y co-ordinates of the point. Lines are represented as equations; for example, $y = 2x + 1$ gives a straight line, and $y = 3x^2 + 2x$ gives a parabola (a curve). Different lines and curves can be drawn by plotting the co-ordinates of points that satisfy their equations and joining up the points.

cube in geometry, a solid figure whose faces are all squares. It has six equal-area faces and 12 equal-length edges. If the length of one edge is l, the volume of the cube $V = l^3$ and its surface area $A = 6l^2$.

curve in geometry, the locus of a point moving according to specified conditions. The best-known of all curves is the circle, which is the locus of all points equidistant from a given point (the centre). Other common geometrical curves are the ellipse, parabola, and hyperbola, which are also produced when a cone is cut by a plane at different angles.

cycloid in geometry, a curve resembling a series of arches traced out by a point on the circumference of a circle that rolls along a straight line. It has such applications as studying the motion of wheeled vehicles along roads and tracks.

cylinder in geometry, a tubular solid figure with a circular base, ordinarily understood to be a right cyclinder, that is, having its curved surface at right angles to the base. The volume of a cylinder is given by: $V = \pi r^2 h$ where V is the volume, r is the radius, and h is the height. Its total surface area A has the formula: $A = 2\pi r (h + r)$ where A is the total area and $2\pi rh$ is the curved surface area, and $2\pi r^2$ is the area of both ends.

degree in mathematics, a unit of measurement of an angle. Written as°. One complete revolution is 360°. A quarter-turn (90°) is a right angle; a half-turn (180°) is the angle on a straight line.

ellipse a curve joining all points (loci) around two fixed points (foci) so that the sum of the distances from those points is always constant. An ellipse is one of a series of curves known as conic sections; it can also be produced, for example, by imagining a slice taken from a solid cone with an oval base. The diameter passing through the foci is the major axis, and the diameter bisecting this at right angles is the minor axis.

envelope in geometry, a curve that touches all the members of a family of curves. For example, a family of three equal circles all touching each other and forming a triangle (like a clover leaf) has two envelopes: a small circle that fits in the triangular space in the middle, and a large circle that encompasses all three circles.

epicycloid in geometry, a curve resembling a series of arches traced out by a point on the circumference of a circle which rolls around another circle of a different diameter. If the two circles have the same diameter, the curve is a cardioid. Greek mathmaticians thought that planets moved in small circles (epicycles) while completing a large circle (the deferent) round the earth.

equilateral in geometry, of a figure having all sides of equal length. For example, a square and a rhombus are both equilateral four-sided figures. An equilateral triangle, to which the term is most often applied, has all three sides equal and all three angles equal (at 60°).

fractal name given by the French mathematician Benoit Mandelbrod to irregular shapes or surfaces outside the rules of conventional geometry (from Latin *fractus* meaning broken). Sets of curves with such discordant properties were developed by Georg Cantor and Karl Weierstrass. Generated on a computer screen, fractals are used in creating models for geographical or biological processes (for example, the creation of a coastline by erosion or accretion, or the growth of plants). They are also used for computer art, such as that used to illustrate science fiction films by George Lucas.

helix in mathematics, a curve resembling a screw thread. It is generated by a line that encircles a cylinder or cone at a constant angle.

hyperbola in geometry, a curve formed by cutting a right circular cone with a plane so that the angle between the plane and the base is greater than the angle between the base and the side of the cone. A member of the family of curves known as conic sections.

460

locus in mathematics, the path traced out by a moving point. For example, the locus of a point that moves so that it is always at the same distance from another fixed point is a circle; the locus of a point that is always at the same distance from two fixed points is a straight line that perpendicularly bisects the line joining them. From the Latin 'place'.

parabola

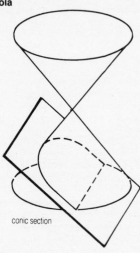

conic section

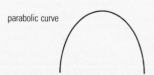

parabolic curve

parabola in mathematics, a curve formed by cutting a right circular cone with a plane parallel to the sloping side of the cone; one of the family of curves known as conic sections. It is a common shape for headlamp reflectors, dish-shaped microwave and radar aerials, and for radiotelescopes. A source of radiation placed at the focus of a paraboloidal reflector is propagated as a parallel beam.

parallelogram in mathematics, a quadrilateral (four-sided plane figure) with opposite pairs of sides equal in length and parallel. In the special cases when all four sides are equal in length, the parallelogram is known as a rhombus, and when the internal angles are right angles, it is a rectangle or square. The diagonals of a parallelogram bisect each other and angles diagonally opposite each other are equal. Its area is the product of the length and the height (the perpendicular distance between the longer pair of sides).

POLYGON

Polygon	number of sides	sum of interior angles (degrees)
triangle	3	180
quadrilateral	4	360
pentagon	5	540
hexagon	6	720
heptagon	7	900
octagon	8	1,080
decagon	10	1,440
duodecagon	12	1,800
icosagon	20	3,240

polygon in geometry, a plane (two-dimensional) figure with three or more sides. Common polygons have their own names, which define the number of sides (for example, triangle, quadrilateral, pentagon). These are all convex polygons, having no interior angle greater than 180°. In general, the more sides a polygon has, the larger the sum of its internal angles and, in the case of a convex polygon, the more closely it approximates to a circle.

polyhedron in geometry, a solid figure with four or more plane faces. Common polyhedra have their own names (for example, pyramid, tetrahedron, cube, cuboid, prism). There are only five types of regular polyhedra (with all faces the same size and shape), as was deduced by early Greek mathematicians; they are the tetrahedron (four equilateral triangular faces), cube (six square faces), octahedron (eight equilateral triangles), dodecahedron (12 regular pentagons) and icosahedron (20 equilateral triangles). The more faces there are on a polyhedron, the more closely it approximates

to a sphere. Knowledge of the properties of polyhedra is important in crystallography and stereochemistry in determining the shapes of crystals and molecules.

prism in mathematics, a solid figure (polyhedron) with two equal polygonal faces (bases) in parallel planes; the other faces being parallelograms, of the same number as there are sides to one of the bases. If these faces are rectangles, it is a right prism. In optics triangular prisms (with triangular bases) are widely used in a variety of intruments including spectroscopes, binoculars, periscopes, and rangefinders, their properties depending on the refractive index of the material of which they are made and the angles at which they are cut.

pyramid

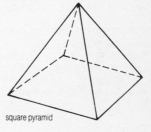

square pyramid

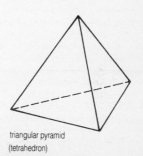

triangular pyramid
(tetrahedron)

pyramid in geometry, a solid figure with triangular side-faces meeting at a common vertex (point) and with a polygon as its base. A pyramid with a triangular base is called a tetrahedron; the Egyptian pyramids have square bases. The volume of a pyramid, no matter how many faces it has, is equal to the area of the base multiplied by one-third of the perpendicular height.

radian in mathematics, an alternative unit to the degree for measuring angles. It is defined as the angle subtended at the centre of a circle by an arc (length of circumference) equal in length to the radius of the circle. There are 2π (approximately 6.284) radians in a full circle or 360°; 1 radian is approximately 57°, and 1° is $\pi/180$ or approximately 0.0175 radians. Radians are commonly used to specify angles in polar co-ordinates.

rectangle a quadrilateral (four-sided figure) with opposite sides equal and parallel, and with right angles (90°) as the internal angles. A rectangle is a special case of a parallelogram. The diagonals of a rectangle bisect each other. Its area A is the product of the length l and breadth b; that is, $A = l \times b$. A rectangle with all four sides equal is a square.

rhombus a diamond-shaped plane figure, a parallelogram with four equal sides (opposite sides are equal in length and parallel) and no internal angle which is a right angle(otherwise it is a square). Its diagonals bisect each other at right angles. The area of a rhombus is equal to the length of a side multiplied by its height (the perpendicular distance between opposite sides).

right-angled triangle a triangle in which one of the angles is a right angle(90°). It is the basic form of triangle for defining trigonometrical ratios (for example, sine, cosine and tangent) and for which Pythagoras' theorem holds true. The longest side of a right-angled triangle is called the hypotenuse; its area is equal to half the product of the other two sides. A triangle constructed on the diameter of a circle with its opposite vertex (corner) on the circumference is a right-angled triangle, a fundamental theorem in geometry first credited to the Greek mathematician Thales (in the 580s BC).

sine in trigonometry, of an angle in a right-angled triangle, the ratio of the length of the side opposite the angle to the length of the

hypotenuse (the longest side). Various properties in physics vary sinsoidally, that is, they can be represented diagramatically by a sine wave (a graph obtained by plotting values of angles against the values of their sines). Examples include simple harmonic motion, such as the way alternating current (AC) electricity varies with time.

sphere in mathematics, a circular solid figure with all points on its surface the same distance from the centre. For a sphere of radius r, the volume $V = {}^{4}/_{3}\pi r^{3}$ and the surface area $A = 4\pi r^{2}$.

tangent in trigonometry, of an angle in a right-angled triangle, the ratio of the length of the side opposite an angle (not the right angle) to the length of the side adjacent to it; a way of expressing the slope of a line. In geometry, a tangent is a straight line that touches a curve and has the same slope as the curve at the point of contact. At a maximum or minimum, the tangent to a curve has zero slope.

tetrahedron

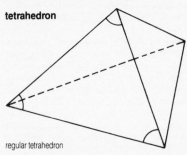

regular tetrahedron

tetrahedron in geometry, a solid figure (polyhedron) with four triangular faces; that is, a pyramid on a triangular base. Tetrahedra are important in chemistry and crystallography in describing the shapes of molecules and crystals; for example, the carbon atoms in a crystal of diamond are arranged in space as a set of interconnected regular tetrahedra.

trapezium in geometry, a four-sided plane figure quadrilateral with two of its sides parallel. If the parallel sides have lengths a and b and the perpendicular distance between them is h

(the height of the trapezium), its area $A = \frac{1}{2}((a + b) \times h)$.

triangle in geometry, a three-sided plane figure. A *scalene triangle* has no two sides equal; an *isosceles triangle* has two equal sides (and two equal angles); and *equilateral triangle* has three equal side (and three equal angles of 60°) A right-angled triangle has one angle of 90°. If the length of one side of a triangle is l and the perpendicular distance from that side to the opposite corner is h (the height or altitude of the triangle), its area $A = \frac{1}{2}l \times h$.

vector any physical quantity that has both magnitude and direction, such as velocity or acceleration of an object, as distinct from a scaler quantity which has magnitude but no direction, such as speed, density, or mass. A vector is often represented geometrically by an arrow on a line of equal length to its magnitude and in technical writing it is denoted by bold (Clarendon) type. Vectors can be added graphically by constructing a triangle of vectors (such as the triangle of forces commonly employed in physics and engineering).

volume in geometry, the space occupied by a three dimensional solid object. A cube, cubois, other prismatic figure or a cylinder has a volume equal to the area of the base multiplied by the perpendicular height. The volume of a sphere is equal to four-thirds of the cube of the radius multiplied by π.

Biographies

al-Khwarizmi Muhammad ibn-Musa 780–c. 850 AD. Arab mathematician who lived and worked in Baghdad and is best known for introducing algorithms (a word based on his name and used for the step-by-step process needed to solve mathematical problems) and for introducing the word algebra (al-jabr) in an adaptation of an earlier Indian text. He com-

piled astronomical tables, put forward Arabic numerals, and pioneered calculation using decimal numbers.

Bernoulli Swiss family of mathematicians: *Jacques Bernoulli* 1654–1705, discovered Bernoullian numbers, a complex series of fractions used in higher mathematics; his brother *Jean Bernoulli* 1667–1748, discovered the exponential calculus; Jean's son *Daniel Bernoulli* 1700–82, made discoveries in hydrodynamics.

Briggs Henry 1561–1630. British mathematician. Savilian professor of geometry at Oxford from 1619, he is best known for his work in constructing the system of logarithms still in popular use.

Descartes René 1596–1650. French mathematician and philosopher. He aimed to express physical sciences in mathematical terms. He founded co-ordinate geometry as a way of defining and manipulating geometrical shapes by means of algebraic expressions. His method of representing points in this system is known as Cartesian co-ordinates in his honour. He was also influential in shaping contemporary theories of astronomy and animal behaviour.

Eratosthenes c. 276–c. 194 BC. Greek geographer and mathematician whose map of the ancient world was the first to contain lines of latitude and longitude. He calculated the earth's circumference, from the N–S distance between Aswan and Alexandria and their difference in latitude (obtained from the midday position of the sun), with an error of less than 320 km/200 mi.

Euclid c. 330–c. 260 BC. Greek mathematician from Alexandria who wrote the *Stoicheia/ Elements* in 13 books, of which nine deal with plane and solid geometry, and four with arithmetic. His main work lay in the systematic arrangement of previous discoveries, and his geometry formed the basis of standard textbooks for over 2,000 years and were still in regular use in English schools in the present century.

Euler Leonhard 1707–83. Swiss mathematician. He developed the theory of differential equations, the calculus of variations, and did important work in astronomy and optics.

463

Fermat Pierre de 1601–65. French mathematician who with Pascal founded the theory of probability and the modern theory of numbers. His *last theorem*, believed to be true, may have been proved by him, but no one else since has succeeded in doing so.

Fibonacci Leonardo c. 1170–c. 1230. Italian mathematician. He published his *Liber abaci* in Pisa in 1202, which led to the introduction of Arabic notation into Europe. From 1960 interest developed in his discovery of the *Fibonacci numbers*, in their simplest form a sequence of numbers in which each number is the sum of its two predecessors (1, 1, 2, 3, 5, 8, 13, and so on). They have unusual characteristics with possible applications in botany, psychology, astronomy. For example, the number of petals and sepals on flowers, the spirals in a spider's web, and the notes in certain scales in music, are all based on such sequences.

Gödel Kurt 1906–78. Austrian-born American mathematical philospher who proved that a mathematical system always contains statements that can be neither proved nor disproved within the system; in other words, as a science mathematics can never be totally consistent and totally complete. He was a friend of Einstein and worked on relativity, constructing a mathematical model of the Universe which made travel back through time theoretically possible.

Lagrange Joseph Louis 1736–1813. French mathematician who presided over the commission that introduced the metric system in 1793. His *Mécanique analytique* 1788 applied mathematical analysis, using principles established by Newton to such problems as the movements of planets when affected by each other's gravitational force.

Lobachevski Nikolai Ivanovich 1792–1856. Russian mathematician, who with the Hungarian Jǎnos Bulyai (1802–60), but independently of him, founded the non-Euclidean geometry in 1829. Lobachevski published the first account of the subject in 1829, but his work went unrecognized until Riemann's system was published.

Lorenz Luwig Valentine 1829–91. Danish mathematician and physicist who developed mathematical formulae to describe various phenomena, such as the relationship between refraction of light and the density of a pure transparent substance, and the relationship between a metal's electrical and thermal conductivity and temperature.

Markov Andrei 1856–1922. Russian mathematician, formulator of the *Markov chain*. This concept holds that a chain of events is governed only by established probability and is uninfluenced by the past history of earlier links in the chain.

Napier John 1550–1617. Scottish mathematician who invented logarithms in 1614, and 'Napier's Bones', an early logarithmic calculating device for multiplication and division.

```
            1
          1   1
        1   2   1
      1   3   3   1
    1   4   6   4   1
  1   5  10  10   5   1
1   6  15  20  15   6   1
1  7  21  35  35  21  7  1
```

Pascal's Triangle

Pascal Blaise 1623–62. French mathematician physicist who is best known for his work on conic sections and (with Fermat) probability theory. Pascal's triangle is an array of numbers in which each is the sum of the pair of numbers above it. Plotted at equal distances along a horizontal axis, the numbers in the rows approximate to the normal (bell-shaped) probability distribution curve which describes the incidence of many natural phenomena; for example, a plot of IQs (intelligence quotient) against numbers of people with a particular IQ gives the bell-shaped graph. In physics, Pascal's chief work concerned fluid pressure and hydraulics. Pascal's principle states that the pressure everywhere in a fluid is the same, so that pressure applied at one point is transmitted equally to all parts of the container. This is the principle of the hydraulic press and jack.

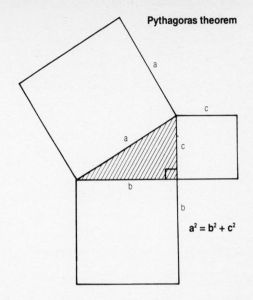

Pythagoras theorem

$$a^2 = b^2 + c^2$$

Pythagoras c. 580–c. 500 BC. Greek mathematician and philosopher who is best-known for the theorem that bears his name. Much of his work concerned numbers, to which he assigned mystical properties. For example, he classified numbers into triangular ones (1, 3, 6, 10,...) which can be represented as a triangular array, and square ones (1, 4, 9, 16,...) which form squares. He also observed that any two adjacent triangular numbers add to a square number (for example, $1 + 3 = 4, 3 + 6 = 9, 6 + 10 = 16,...$). In geometry, Pythagoras' theorem states that in, a right-angled triangle, the square of the hypotenuse (the longest side) is equal to the sum of the square of the lengths of the other two sides. If the hypotenuse is h units long and the lengths of the other sides are a and b, then $h^2 = a^2 + b^2$. This provides a way of calculating the length of any side of such a triangle if the lengths of the other two sides are known.

Riemann Georg Friedrich Bernhard 1826–66. German mathematician whose system of non-Euclidean geometry, thought at the time to be a mere mathematical curiosity, was used by Einstein to develop his General Theory of Relativity.

Rubik Erno 1944– . Hungarian architect, who invented the *Rubik Cube*, a plastic multi-coloured puzzle which can be manipulated and rearranged in only one correct way, but around 43 trillion wrong. Intended to help his students understand three-dimensional design, it became a world craze.

Thales c. 624–c. 547 BC. First important Greek philosophic scientist who in the 6th century BC, at Miletus in Asia Minor, is believed to have made important advances in geometry, particularly regarding angles and triangles.

MATHEMATICAL SYMBOLS AND FORMULAE

Symbols

$a \rightarrow b$	a tending toward b
∞	infinity
lim	limiting value
$a \sim b$	a approximately equal to b
$a \approx b$	a very nearly equal to b
$a = b$	a equal to b
$a \equiv b$	a identical with b (for formulae only)
$a > b$	a greater than b
$a < b$	a smaller than b
$a \gg b$	a much greater than b
$a \ll b$	a much smaller than b
$a \neq b$	
$a \lesseqgtr b$	a not equal to b
$b < a < c$	*a greater than b* and smaller than c
$a \geqq b$	a equal to or greater than b, that is, a at least as great as b
$a \geq b$	
$a \leqq b$	a equal to or smaller than b, that is, a at most as great as b
$a \leq b$	
$b \leqq a \leqq c$	a lying between b and c
$\lvert a \rvert$	absolute value of a; this is always positive, for example $\lvert -5 \rvert = 5$
$+$	addition sign, plus, positive
$-$	subtraction sign, minus, negative
$\times$ or $\cdot$	multiplication sign, times
$:$ or $\div$	division sign, divided by
a+b=c	$a+b$, read as 'a plus b', denotes the sum of a and b. The result of the addition, c, is also known as the sum.
$\int$	indefinite integral
$_a\int^b$	definite integral, or integral between $x = a$ and $x = b$
$a-b=c$	$a-b$, read as 'a minus b', denotes subtraction of b from a.
	$a-b$, or c, is the difference. Subtraction is the opposite of addition.
$a \times b = c$ $ab = c$ $a \cdot b = c$	$a \times b$, read as 'a times b', denotes multiplication of a by b. a and b are the multiplicands or factors; $a \times b$, or c, is the product.
$a:b=c$	$a:c$, read as 'a divided by b', denotes division. a is the dividend, b the divisor; $a:b$, or c, is the quotient. Division is the opposite of multiplication and can also be represented by the fraction $\frac{a}{b}$ or a/b In fractions, a, is the numerator (= dividend), b the denominator (= divisor)
$a^b = c$	a^b, read as 'a to the power b', a is the base, b the exponent
$^b\sqrt{a} = c$	$^b\sqrt{a}$, is the bth root of a, b being known as the root exponent. In the special case of $\sqrt[2]{a} = c$, $\sqrt[2]{a}$ or c is known as the square root of a, and the root exponent is usually omitted, that is, $\sqrt[2]{a} = \sqrt{a}$.
e	base of natural (napierian) logarithms = 2.7182818284....
π	ratio of the circumference of a circle to its diameter = 3.1415925535

Numbers

Between any two real numbers *a* and *b* there can exist only one of the three relationships

$a = b$ or $a > b$ or $a < b$

$a + b = b + a$

$ab = ba$

$(a+b) + c = a + (b+c)$

$(ab)c = a(bc)$

$a(b+c) = ab+ac$

Factorials and Binomial Coefficients

For a positive integer *r* and any real number $n^{(r)}$ represents the products

$n^{(r)} = (n-1)\,(n-2)...(n-r+1)$

where

$n^{(O)} = 1$

by definition

The factorial of a positive integer *n*, symbol *n!*, is defined as

$n! = n(n-1)(n-2)...3 \times 2 \times 1$

where

$O! = 1$

by definition.

Technology

Technology is the practical application of science in industry and commerce. It encompasses not only the use but also the research, design, and development of equipment for such purposes as mining, construction, transport, and energy generation.

This section concentrates on four main areas of technology: *Construction* describes major types of purpose-built structures and their functions; *Telecommunications* looks primarily at the telephone, radio, and television as part of the new science of information technology; *Transport* reviews the main means of travel in the air and on sea, rail, and road; and *Energy* explains the science of the exploitation of renewable and non-renewable resources.

Construction

bridge a construction which provides a continuous path or road over water, valleys, ravines, or above other roads. Bridges may be classified into four main groups:

arch for example Sydney Harbour bridge (steel arch) with a span of 503 m/1,650 ft.

beam or girder as at Rio-Niteroi (1974), Guanabara Bay, Brazil, the world's longest

bridge

continuous box and plate girder bridge: centre span 300 m/984 ft; length 13,900 m/8.7 mi.

cantilever for example Forth rail bridge which is 1,658 m/5,440 ft long and has two main spans, each consisting of two cantilevers.

suspension bridge such as the Humber bridge, the world's longest-span suspension bridge with a centre span of 1,410 m/4,626 ft.

canal an artificial waterway constructed for drainage, irrigation, or navigation.

irrigation canals carry water for irrigation from rivers, reservoirs, or wells, and are carefully designed to maintain an even flow of water over the whole length.

navigation and ship canals constructed at one level between locks, canals frequently link with other forms of waterway – natural rivers, modified river channels, and sea links – to form a waterway system. The world's two major international ship canals are the Suez canal and the Panama canal which provide invaluable short cuts for shipping respectively between Europe and the East and between the east and west coasts of the Americas.

The economy of energy for transporting in such a means of goods transport, where speed is not a prime factor, has encouraged a modern revival of canal transport.

dam a structure built to hold back water, so as to prevent flooding, provide water for irrigation and storage, and to provide hydro-electric power. The world's largest dam is the 10.8 km/6.7 mi long New Cornelia Tailings dam in Arizona, USA, which has a volume of 209 million cu m/274 million cu yds. Like all the biggest dams it is an *earth- and rock-fill dam*, also called an *embankment dam*. Such dams are generally built on broad valley sites. Deep, narrow gorges, however, dictate a concrete dam, the enormous strength of reinforced concrete being able to withstand the enormous water pressures involved. Many concrete dams are triangular in cross-section, with their vertical face pointing upstream. Their sheer weight holds them in position, and they are called *gravity dams*. Some concrete dams, however, are more slightly built in the shape of an arch, with the curve facing upstream. The *arch dam* derives its strength from the arch shape, just as an arch bridge does. A valuable development in arid regions, as in parts of Brazil, is the *underground dam*, where water is stored among sand and stones on a solid rock base, with a wall to ground level, so avoiding rapid evaporation.

tunnel an underground passageway. Tunnelling is an increasingly important branch of civil engineering in mining, transport, and other areas. In the 19th century there were two major advances: the use of compressed air within the tunnel to balance the external pressure of water and of the tunnel shield to support the face and assist excavation. In recent years there have been notable developments in linings, such as concrete segments and steel liner plates, and in the use of rotary diggers and cutters, and of explosives. Famous tunnels include: the world's longest road tunnel, the St Gotthard, Switzerland (1980) 16.3 km/10.1 mi; the world's longest rail tunnel, the Seikan, 1975, under Tsugaru Strait linking Honshu and Hokkaido, Japan, 53.85 km/33.5 mi. A Channel tunnel, or Chunnel, beneath the English Channel was planned as a military measure by Napoleon in 1802. In 1986 a scheme for twin rail tunnels was approved by the French and English governments.

Telecommunications

telecommunications are communications over a distance. The first mechanical telecommunications systems were the *semaphore* and *heliograph* (which used flashes of sunlight). But the forerunner of the modern telecommunications age was the *electric telegraph*. The earliest practicable instrument was invented by Cooke and Wheatstone in Britain in 1837, and used by railway companies, the first public line being laid between Paddington and Slough in 1843.

In the USA Morse invented a signalling code, *Morse code*, which is still used, and a recording telegraph, first used commercially between England and France in 1851. As a result of Hertz's discoveries using electromagnetic waves, Marconi pioneered a *'wireless' telegraph*, ancestor of the radio. He established wireless communication between England and France 1899 and across the Atlantic 1901.

Long-distance voice communication was pioneered in 1876 by Alexander Graham Bell, when he invented the *telephone* as a result of Faraday's discovery of electromagnetism. Today it is possible to communicate with most countries by telephone cable, several hundred simultaneous conversations being carried. However, the chief method of relaying long-distance calls on land is *microwave radio transmission*. The drawback to this is that the transmissions follow a straight line from tower to tower, so that over the sea the system becomes impracticable.

A solution was put forward in 1945 by Arthur C Clarke in *Wireless World*, when he proposed a system of *communications satellites* in an orbit 35,900 km/27,300 mi above the equator, where they would circle the earth in exactly 24 hours, and thus appear fixed in the sky. Such a system is now in operation internationally, operated by Intelsat. The satellites are called geostationary satellites, or synchronous satellites (syncoms). The first to be successfully launched, was *Syncom 2* in Jul 1963. Numbers of such satellites are now in use, concentrated over heavy traffic areas such as the Atlantic, Indian and Pacific Oceans. Telegraphy, telephony, and television transmissions are carried simultaneously by high-frequency radio waves.

In 1980 the Post Office opened its first System X (all electronic, digital) telephone exchange in London, a method already adopted in the USA. Other recent advances include the use of fibre-optic cables consisting of fine glass fibres for telephone lines instead of the usual copper cables. The telecommunications signals are transmitted along the fibres on pulses of laser light. Procedures, technical standards, frequencies, and so on, in telecommunications

radio

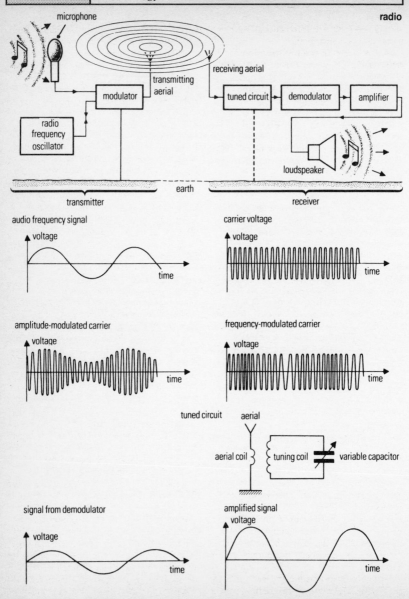

microphone

transmitting aerial

receiving aerial

modulator

tuned circuit

demodulator

amplifier

radio frequency oscillator

loudspeaker

earth

transmitter

receiver

audio frequency signal

voltage

time

carrier voltage

voltage

time

amplitude-modulated carrier

voltage

time

frequency-modulated carrier

voltage

time

tuned circuit

aerial

aerial coil

tuning coil

variable capacitor

signal from demodulator

voltage

time

amplified signal

voltage

time

472

are controlled by the International Telecom-munications Union (ITU).

Milestones in telecommunications

1794 Claude Chappe in France built a long-distance signalling system using semaphore.

1839 Charles Wheatstone and William Cooke devised an electric telegraph in England.

1843 Morse transmitted the first message along a telegraph line in the USA, using his Morse code of signals - short (dots) and long (dashes).

1858 The first transatlantic telegraph cable.

1876 American Alexander Graham Bell invented the telephone.

1877 Edison invented the carbon transmitter for the telephone.

1894 Marconi pioneered wireless telegraphy in Italy, later moving to England.

1900 Fessenden in the USA first broadcast voice by radio.

1901 Marconi transmitted the first radio signals across the Atlantic.

1907 American Charles Krumm introduced the forerunner of the teleprinter.

1920 Stations in Detroit and Pittsburgh began regular radio broadcasts.

1922 The BBC began its first radio transmissions, for the London station 2LO.

1932 The Post Office introduced the Telex in Britain.

1956 The first transatlantic telephone cable was laid.

1962 Telstar pioneered transatlantic satellite communications, transmitting live TV pictures.

1966 Charles Kao in England advanced the idea of using optical fibres for telecommunications transmissions.

1969 Live TV pictures were sent from astronauts on the moon back to earth.

1977 The first optical fibre cable was installed in California.

1986 Voyager 2 transmitted images of the planet Uranus over a distance of some 3,000 million km/2,000 million mi, the signals taking 2 hours 45 minutes to make the journey back to earth.

radio the transmission and reception of radio waves. The theory of electromagnetic waves was first developed by James Clerk Maxwell 1864, given practical confirmation in the laboratory 1888 by Heinrich Hertz, and put to practical use by Marconi, who in 1901 achieved reception of a signal in Newfoundland transmitted from Poldhu in Cornwall.

radio transmission a microphone converts sound waves (pressure variations in the air) into an audio frequency electrical signal. The *oscillator* produces a carrier voltage of high frequency; different stations are allocated different transmitting carrier frequencies. A *modulator* superimposes the audio frequency signal on the carrier. There are two main ways of doing this: *amplitude modulation (AM)*, used for long and medium wave broadcasts in which the strength of the carrier is made to fluctuate in time with the audio signal; in *frequency modulation* (FM), as used for VHF broadcasts, the frequency of the carrier is made to fluctuate. The transmitting aerial emits the modulated electromagnetic waves which travel outwards from it.

radio reception a receiving aerial produces voltages in response to the waves sent out by a transmitter. A *tuned circuit* selects a particular voltage frequency, usually by means of variable capacitor connected across a coil of wire. (The effect is similar to altering the tension in a piano wire, making it capable of vibrating at a different frequency.) The demodulator disentangles the audio signal from the carrier, which is now discarded, having served its purpose. The amplifier boosts the audio signal for feeding to the loudspeaker which produces sound waves.

television the reproduction at a distance by radio waves of visual images.

technology for transmission, a television camera converts the pattern of light it takes in into a pattern of electrical charges. This is scanned line-by-line by a beam of electrons from an electron gun, resulting in variable electrical signals that represent the visual picture. These vision signals are combined with a radio carrier wave and broadcast. The TV aerial picks up the wave and feeds it to the receiver (TV set). This separates out the vision

473

television

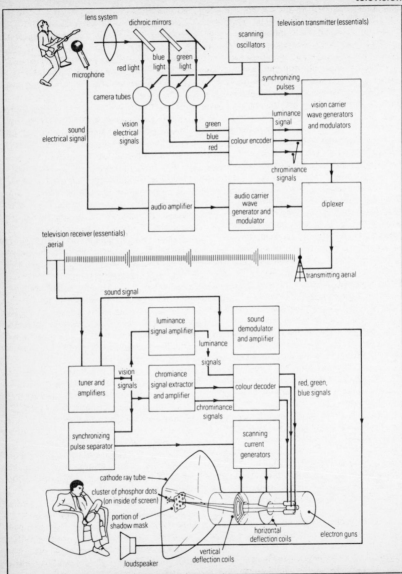

television transmitter (essentials)

lens system
dichroic mirrors
scanning oscillators

red light
blue light
green light

microphone

camera tubes

synchronizing pulses

vision electrical signals

sound electrical signal

green
blue
red
colour encoder

luminance signal

vision carrier wave generators and modulators

chrominance signals

audio amplifier

audio carrier wave generator and modulator

diplexer

television receiver (essentials)
aerial

transmitting aerial

sound signal

luminance signal amplifier

sound demodulator and amplifier

tuner and amplifiers

vision signals

chromiance signal extractor and amplifier

luminance signals

colour decoder

red, green, blue signals

chrominance signals

synchronizing pulse separator

scanning current generators

cathode ray tube
cluster of phosphor dots (on inside of screen)
portion of shadow mask

horizontal deflection coils

electron guns

loudspeaker

vertical deflection coils

signals, which pass to the picture tube, which is a cathode-ray tube. The broad end of the tube, upon which the scene is to appear, has its inside surface coated with a fluorescent material. The vision signals control the strength of a beam of electrons from an electron gun, aimed at the screen and making it glow more or less brightly. At the same time the beam is made to scan across the screen line-by-line, mirroring the action of the gun in the TV camera. The result is a re-creation spot-by-spot, line-by-line of the pattern of light that entered the camera. Twenty-five pictures are built up each second with interlaced scanning (30 in US), with a total of 625 lines (in Europe, but 525 lines in the US and Japan).

colour TV The method of colour reproduction in television uses the principle that any colours can be made by mixing the primary colours red, green, and blue in appropriate proportions. In colour television the receiver reproduces only three basic colours: red, green and blue. It is thus possible to specify the colour which it is required to transmit by sending signals which indicate the amounts of red, green and blue light which are to be generated at the receiver. The three signals are coded into one complex signal which is transmitted as a more or less normal black and white signal, and which produces a satisfactory – or compatible – picture on ordinary black and white receivers. A fraction of each primary red, green and blue signal is added together to produce the normal brightness, or luminance signal. The minimum of extra colouring information is then sent by a subcarrier signal superimposed on the brightness signal. This extra colouring information corresponds to the hue and saturation of the transmitted colour, but without any of the fine detail of the picture. The impression of sharpness is conveyed only by the brightness signal, the colouring being added as a broad colour wash.

Milestones in television

1878 William Crookes in England invented the Crookes tube, which produced cathode rays.

1884 Paul Nipkow in Germany built a mechanical scanning device, the Nipkow disc, a rotating disc with a spiral pattern of holes in it.

1897 Karl Ferdinand Braun, also in Germany, modified the Crookes tube to produce the ancestor of the TV receiver picture tube.

1906 Boris Rosing in Russia began experimenting with the Nipkow disc and cathode-ray tube, eventually succeeding in transmitting some crude TV pictures.

1923 Zworykin in the USA invented the first electronic camera tube, the iconoscope.

1926 Baird demonstrated a workable TV system, using scanning by Nipkow disc.

1928 Baird demonstrated colour TV.

1936 The BBC began regular broadcasting using Baird's system from Alexandra Palace, London.

1940 Experimental colour TV transmission began in the USA, using the modern system of colour reproduction.

1953 Successful colour TV transmissions began in the USA, using the modern system of colour reproduction.

1956 The first videotape recorder was produced in California by the Ampex Corporation.

1962 TV signals were transmitted across the Atlantic via the Telstar satellite.

1970 The first videodisc system was announced by Decca in Britain and AEG-Telefunken in Germany, but it was not perfected until the 1980s.

1975 Sony introduced their videocassette tape recorder system, Betamax, for domestic viewers, six years after their professional U-Matic system; the British Post Office (now British Telecom) announced their Prestel viewdata system.

1978 The BBC and Independent Television introduced the world's first teletext systems, Ceefax and Oracle, respectively.

1979 Matsushita in Japan developed a pocket-sized flat-screen TV set, using a liquid-crystal display (LCD).

video camera a portable television camera that takes 'movie' pictures electronically. It produces an electrical output-signal corresponding to rapid line-by-line 'scanning' of the field of view. The output is recorded on videotape and is played back.

475

video disc a method of recording pictures (and sounds) on disc. The video disc (commercially available from 1978) is chiefly used to provide commercial films for personal viewing. The video disc works in the same way as a compact disc, which records only sounds.

videotape recorder (VTR) a device for recording TV programmes for later viewing, or linked by cable with a video camera. A *camcorder* is a portable videotape recorder with a built-in camera.

Transport

air transport people first took to the air in balloons and began powered flight in airships. But the history of flying is dominated by the aeroplane. The aeroplane is a development of the model glider, first flown by Sir George Cayley (1773–1857) in 1804. But not until the invention of the petrol engine did powered flight become feasible. The Wright brothers in the USA first achieved success, when they flew their biplane *Flyer* on 17 Dec 1903. In Europe, inspired by the Wrights, France led in aeroplane design (Voisin brothers) and Louis Blériot brought aviation much publicity by crossing the Channel in 1909, as did the Reims air races of that year. The first powered flight in England was made by S F Cody in 1908.

The flight of the German Heinkel 178 (1939) ushered in a new era in aviation. It was the first jet plane, propelled not, as all planes before it, with a propeller, but by a jet of hot gases. The first British jet aircraft, the Gloster E.28/39 flew from Cranwell, Lincolnshire, on 15 May 1941, powered by a jet engine invented by Frank Whittle. And today jet planes dominate both military and civilian aviation, although many light planes still use piston engines and propellers for propulsion. The late 1960s saw the introduction of the jumbo jet and the

supersonic airliners, notably the Anglo-French *Concorde*.

aeroplane a heavier-than-air craft supported in flight by fixed wings (aerofoils): it may be unpowered (the glider) or powered, when it is propelled by the reaction from air accelerated rearwards by airscrew(s) (propellers) or jet(s) to overcome the air resistance (drag). Drag depends on frontal area (for example: large, airliner; small, fighter) and shape (drag coefficient); it equals thrust in straight level flight. Less drag (streamlining) means increased speed and lower fuel consumption from given power; less fuel need be carried for a given distance (range) and the aeroplane's weight is reduced.

Aerofoils are so shaped and cambered that air passing above them is speeded up, reducing pressure below atmospheric, while that above is slowed. This produces a vertical force (lift) to support the aircraft's weight. (Lift = weight in level flight.) Minimum weight is thus essential to an efficient aeroplane, requiring a smaller wing which has less drag. Very strong but light aluminium alloys (with copper, magnesium, and so on) are used, and also for the body (fuselage) and where possible for controls and in engines. For supersonic planes special stainless steel and titanium may be used. The thin skin (outer) panels, with ribs and stringers at intervals to prevent buckling, support all flight stresses with no separate structure (semi-monocoque construction). The payload (crew, passengers, bombs, and so on) may be up to one-third all-up weight.

Fastest aeroplane - the Lockheed SR-71, holder of the world air-speed record of 3,529 kph/2,193 mph (over Mach 3.3).

Fastest airliner - Concorde, which can cruise at up to Mach 2.2 (2,333 kph/1,450 mph).

Largest airliner - Boeing 747, which has a wingspan of 59.6 m/195.7 ft and a length of 70.7 m/231.8 ft.

Largest volume aeroplane - the Guppy-201, with a usable volume of 1,104 cu m/39,000 cu ft.

airship essentially a power-driven balloon. All airships have streamlined envelopes or hulls, which contain the inflation gas, and are either non-rigid, semi-rigid or rigid. Count Ferdinand von Zeppelin (1838–1917) was the pioneer of the rigid type, named after him, and used for bombing raids on Britain in World War I. The early airships were vulnerable because they used hydrogen for inflation. It is the lightest gas, but highly flammable. Since World War II, now that large supplies of the non-flammable gas helium are available, there has been renewed interest in airships which cause minimum noise pollution, can lift enormous loads, and are economical on fuel.

balloon bag or envelope of impermeable fabric which rises from the ground when filled with a gas lighter than air. The first successful human ascent was by Pilâtre de Rozier in Paris in Oct 1783 in a hot-air balloon of the type designed by the Montgolfier brothers. Balloons continue in use for sport, and as an economical means of making scientific observations. The first transalantic balloon crossing was made by three Americans (Presque Isle, Maine to Miserey, France) 11–17 Aug 1978.

helicopter an aircraft which achieves both lift and propulsion by means of a rotary wing, or rotor, on top of the fuselage. It can take off and land vertically, move in any direction or remain stationary in the air. Igor Sikorsky in the USA built the first practical single rotor craft in 1939. The rotor of a helicopter has two or more blades, which are of aerofoil cross-section, like an aeroplane's wings. Lift and propulsion are achieved by angling the blades as they rotate.

jet propulsion a method of propulsion in which an object is propelled in one direction by a jet, or stream of gases moving in the other. This follows from Newton's celebrated third law of motion 'to every action, there is an equal and opposite reaction'. The most widespread application of the jet principle is in the jet engine, the commonest kind of aero-engine. The jet engine is a kind of gas turbine. Air, after passing through a forward-facing intake, is compressed by a compressor, or fan, and fed into a combustion chamber. Fuel (usually kerosene) is sprayed in and ignited. The hot gas produced expands rapidly rearwards, spin-

ning a turbine that drives the compressor before being finally ejected from a rearward-facing tail pipe, or nozzle, at very high speed. Reaction to the jet of gases streaming backwards produces a propulsive thrust forwards which acts on the aircraft through its engine-mountings.

rocket a projectile driven through space by the reaction on the rocket of the fast-burning fuel within. Unlike the jet engine, which is also a reaction engine, the rocket engine carries its own oxygen supply to burn its fuel and is totally independent of any surrounding atmosphere. The only form of propulsion available which can function in a vacuum, rockets are essential to the exploration of outer space. Two kinds of rockets are used - one burns liquid propellants, the other solid propellants.

sea transport people have travelled on and across the seas, for various purposes, throughout history. The Greeks and Phoenicians built wooden ships, propelled by oar or sail, to transport themselves and their goods across the sea. The Romans and Carthaginians fought in galleys equipped with rams and rowed by tiers of oarsmen. The oaken ships of the Norsemen were for rough seas, and the fleet of Richard Coeur de Lion was largely of sail. By 1840 iron had largely replaced wood, but fast-sailing clippers survived, built with wooden planks on iron frames. America and Britain made steam experiments as the 19th century opened. The *Comet* appeared in 1812, the Canadian *Royal William* crossed the Atlantic in 1833, and the English *Great Western* steamed from Bristol to New York in 1838. Pettit Smith applied the screw to the *Archimedes* in 1839, and after 1850 the paddle-wheel became obsolete. The introduction of the compound engine and turbine, the latter in 1902, completed the revolution in propulsion until the advent of nuclear-powered vessels after World War II, chiefly submarines.

hovercraft an air-cushion vehicle that rides on a cushion of high-pressure air, free from all contact with the surface beneath. Although hovercraft need a smooth terrain when operating overland, it need not be metalled, and snow and ice present no difficulties, but they are at present best adapted to use on lakes, sheltered coastal waters, river estuaries and swamps.

hydrofoil boat a boat whose hull rises out of the water when it travels at speed. The boat gets its 'lift' from a set of hydrofoils, underwater 'wings' that develop lift in the water in much the same way that an aeroplane wing develops lift in the air.

jetfoil an advanced kind of hydrofoil boat built by Boeing, which is propelled by water jets. It features horizontal fully submerged hydrofoils fore and aft, and has a sophisticated computerized control system to maintain its stability in all waters. Jetfoils have been in service worldwide since 1975.

submarine an underwater ship, especially a warship. An early venture was an underwater boat constructed for King James I by Dutchman Cornelius van Drebbel in 1620. A century and a half later, David Bushness in the USA designed a submarine called *Turtle* for attacking British ships. In both World Wars submarines, from the ocean-going to the midget type, played a vital role. The conventional submarine of this period was driven by diesel engine on the surface and by battery-powered electric motors underwater. The diesel engine also drove a generator that produced electricity to charge the batteries.

In 1954 the USA launched the first nuclear-powered submarine, the *Nautilus*. The modern US nuclear submarine *Ohio*, in service from 1981, is 170 m/560 ft long, displacement about 18,700 tonnes, and carries 24 Trident missiles. As in all nuclear submarines, propulsion is by steam turbine driving a propellor. The steam is raised using the heat given off by the nuclear reactor.

Ship records

The first successful power-driven boat was the *Charlotte Dundas*, built in Scotland in 1801.

The first steam-assisted crossing of the Atlantic was by the US ship *Savannah* in 1819.

The *Great Britain* became the first propeller-driven ship to cross the Atlantic in 1845.

The first steam-turbine driven vessel was Sir Charles Parsons' *Turbinia*, built in 1894.

The largest liner ever was the *Queen Elizabeth*, 83,673 gross tonnes, 314 m/1,031 ft long with a beam of 36 m/118 ft. Launched in 1940, it was gutted by fire in 1972.

The fastest Atlantic crossing by ship was by the US *United States* in 1952, which took 3 days 20 hours 40 minutes to cross between the Ambrose light vessel and the Bishop Rock Light, Isles of Scilly.

The first nuclear-powered ship (as opposed to submarine) was the Russian icebreaker *Lenin*, launched in 1959.

The world's largest ship is the 564,739 tonnes deadweight oil tanker *Seawise Giant*, which is 458 m/1,505 ft long, with a beam of 69 m/226 ft. It was launched in 1979.

Rail transport is by means of a system of parallel tracks laid upon the ground on which vehicles can travel. In the USA and Canada railways made the 19th-century exploitation of the central and western territories possible, and in the USA underpinned the victory of the north in the Civil War, the 'Railway War'. In countries with less developed road systems and large areas of difficult terrain, the railway is still important, as in India (where the British system survives), China, South America (system largely built by British engineers), and the USSR. Electrification, or the use of diesel electric engines, has superseded the steam engine in Britain and other developed countries.

monorail a railway that runs on a single (mono) rail. It was originally invented in 1882 to carry light loads, and when run by electricity was called a telpher. The most successful monorail, the Wuppertal Schwebebahn, has been running in Germany since 1901. It is a suspension monorail, the passenger cars hanging from an arm fixed to a trolley that runs along the rail. Most modern monorails are of the straddle type, the passenger cars running on top of the rail. Straddle-type monorails are often used to transport passengers between terminals at airports, as at Birmingham. This works on the maglev (*mag*netic *lev*itation) principle, supporting the train above the track by magnetic forces.

tramway a city transport system in which wheeled vehicles run along parallel rails, which originated in collieries in the 18th century. The earliest passenger system was in 1832, in New York, and by the 1860s horse-drawn trams plied in London and Liverpool. Trams are now powered either by electric conductor rails below ground or conductor arms connected to overhead wires, but their use on public roads is very limited because of their lack of manoeuvrability. Greater flexibility is achieved with the *trolleybus*, similarly powered by conductor arms overhead, but without tracks. In the 1980s these were in some areas being revived. Both vehicles have the advantage of being non-polluting.

Milestones on the railways

1500s Tramways – wooden tracks along which trolleys ran – were in use in mines.

1804 Richard Trevithick in England built the first steam locomotive and ran it on the track at the Pen-y-darren ironworks in South Wales.

1825 George Stephenson built the first public railway to carry steam trains – the Stockton and Darlington line.

1829 Stephenson designed his locomotive *Rocket*, which trounced its rivals at the Rainhill trials.

1830 Stephenson completed the Liverpool and Manchester Railway, the first steam passenger line; the first American-built locomotive, *Best Friend of Charleston*, went into service on the South Carolina Railroad.

1835 Germany pioneered steam railways in Europe, using *Der Adler*, a locomotive built by Stephenson.

1863 London opened the world's first underground railway.

1869 The first US transcontinental railway was completed at when the Union Pacific and the Central Pacific Railroads met.

1879 Werner von Siemens demonstrated an electric train in Germany; Volk's Electric Railway along the Brighton seafront was the world's first public electric railway.

1883 Charles Lartique built the first monorail, in Ireland.

1885 The trans-Canada continental railway was completed, from Montreal in the east to Port Moody in British Columbia in the west.

1890 The first electric underground railway opened in London.

1912 The first diesel locomotive took to the rails in Germany.

1926 The British steam locomotive *Mallard* set a steam rail speed record of 201 kph/125 mph.

1941 Swiss Federal Railways introduced a gas-turbine locomotive.

1964 Japan National Railways inaugurated the 512 km/320 mi New Tokaido line between Osaka and Tokyo, on which ran the 210 kph/130 mph 'bullet' trains.

1973 British Rail's High Speed Train (HST) set a diesel rail speed record of 229 kph/143 mph.

1979 Japan National Railways' maglev test vehicle attained a speed of 517 kph/321 mph.

1981 France's TGV superfast trains began operation between Paris and Lyons, regularly attaining a peak speed of 270 kph/168 mph.

road transport

bicycle a two-wheeled vehicle powered by pedals. The first pedal-bicycle was invented by the Scotsman Kirkpatrick Macmillan c. 1840, pneumatic tyres being added from 1846, and by 1888 these had been improved by J B Dunlop to boost the cycling craze of the turn of the century. Design changes were then minor until the small-wheeled Moulton bicycle appeared after World War II.

internal combustion engine a heat engine in which fuel is burned inside the engine, contrasting with an external combustion engine like the steam engine in which fuel is burned in a separate boiler. The petrol and diesel engine are both internal combustion engines. They are reciprocating piston engines in which pistons move up and down in cylinders to effect the engine operating cycle. This may be a four-stroke cycle or a two-stroke cycle. Gas turbines, jet and rocket engines are sometimes also considered to be internal combustion engines since they burn their fuel inside their combustion chambers.

motor car a self-propelled vehicle able to be run and be steered on normal roads. The forerunner of the automobile is generally agreed to be

internal combustion engine: the four stroke cycle

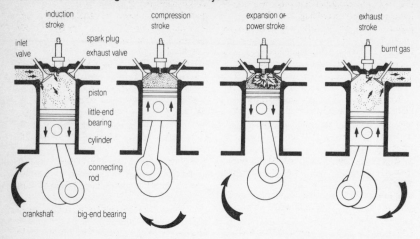

Nicolas-Joseph Cugnot's cumbrous steam carriage 1769, still preserved in Paris.

Another Parisian, Étienne Lenoir, made the first gas engine in 1860, and in 1885 Benz built and ran the first petrol-driven motor car; and Panhard 1890 (front radiator, engine under bonnet, sliding-pinion gearbox, wooden ladder-chassis) and Mercédès 1901 (honeycomb radiator, in-line four-cylinder engine, gate-change gearbox, pressed-steel chassis) set the pattern for the modern car.

A typical modern medium-sized saloon car has a semi-monocoque construction in which the body panels, suitably reinforced, support the road loads through independent front and rear sprung suspension, with seats located within the wheelbase for comfort. It is powered by a petrol engine using a carburettor to mix petrol and air for feeding to the engine cylinders (typically four or six). The engine is usually water cooled. From the engine power is transmitted through a clutch to a four- or five-speed gearbox and thence, in a front-engine rear-drive car, through a drive (propeller) shaft to a differential gear, which drives the rear wheels.

In a front-engine front-wheel drive car, clutch, gearbox, and final drive are incorporated with the engine unit. An increasing number of high-performance cars are being offered with four-wheel drive, with all four wheels being driven. This gives vastly superior roadholding, especially in wet and icy conditions.

motor cycle a two-wheeled vehicle propelled by a petrol engine. Daimler created the first motor cycle, usually called motorbike, when he installed his lightweight petrol engine in a bicycle frame in 1885. The first really successful two-wheel design was devised by Michael and Eugene Werner in France 1901. They adopted the classic motor cycle layout with the engine low down between the wheels. Road races like the Isle of Man TT (Tourist Trophy), established in 1907, helped improve motor cycle design and it soon evolved into more or less its present form.

Milestones in motoring

1769 Nicholas-Joseph Cugnot in France built a steam carriage.

1860 Jean Etienne Lenoir built a gas-fuelled internal combustion engine.

1831 The British government passed the 'Red Flag' Act, requiring a man to precede a 'horseless carriage' with a red flag.

1876 Nikolaus August Otto improved the gas engine, making it a practical power source.

1885 Gottlieb Daimler developed a successful lightweight petrol engine and fitted it to a bicycle to create the prototype of the modern motorbike; Karl Benz fitted his lightweight petrol engine to a three-wheeled carriage to pioneer the motor car.

1886 Gottlieb Daimler fitted his engine to a four-wheeled carriage to produce a four-wheeled motor car.

1891 René Panhard and Emile Levassor established the modern design of cars by putting the engine in front.

1896 Frederick Lancaster introduced epicyclic gearing, which foreshadowed automatic transmission.

1901 The first Mercedes took to the roads. It was the direct ancestor of the modern car; Ransome Olds in the USA introduced mass production on an assembly line.

1906 Rolls-Royce introduced the legendary Silver Ghost, which established the company's reputation for superlatively engineered cars.

1908 Henry Ford also used assembly-line production to manufacture his famous Model T, nicknamed the Tin Lizzie because it used lightweight steel sheet for the body, which looked 'tinny'.

1911 Cadillac introduced the electric starter and dynamo lighting

1913 Ford introduced the moving conveyor belt to the assembly line, further accelerating production of the Model T.

1920 Duesenberg began fitting four-wheel hydraulic brakes.

1922 The Lancia Lambda featured unitary (all-in-one) construction and independent front suspension.

1928 Cadillac introduced the synchromesh gearbox, greatly facilitating gear changing.

1934 Citroën pioneered front-wheel drive in their 2CV model.

1936 Fiat introduce their 'baby' a car, the Topolino, 500 cc.

1938 Germany produced its 'people's car', the Volkswagen 'beetle'.

1948 Jaguar launched the XK120 sports car; Michelin introduced the radial-ply tyre; Goodrich produced the tubeless tyre.

1950 Dunlop announced the disc brake.

1951 Buik and Chrysler in the USA introduced power steering. *1952* Rover's gas-turbine car set a speed record of 243 kph/152 mph.

1954 Bosch introduced fuel-injection for cars.

1957 Felix Wankel built his first rotary petrol engine.

1959 BMC (now Rover) introduced the Issigonis-designed Mini, with front-wheel drive, transverse engine and independent rubber suspension.

1966 California introduced legislation to reduce air pollution by cars.

1972 Dunlop introduced safety tyres, which sealed themselves after a burst.

1980s Lean-burn engines were introduced to improve fuel consumption; electronic ignition and engine controls became widely available; on-board computers were introduced to monitor engine performance, speech synthesizers to issue audible warnings, and wind-tunnel testing to produce body shapes with low drag coefficients; lead-free petrol became widely available.

Energy

The chief direct sources of energy are oil, coal, wood, and gas, and indirectly, electricity produced by the use of such fuels or derived from water power or nuclear fission. Increasing costs and the prospect of exhaustion of coal, oil and gas resources, led in the 1970s to consideration of alternative sources. These included solar power, which provides completely 'clean' energy, wind power, tidal power, and geothermal power. The chief direct sources of energy are oil, coal, wood, and gas, and such animal products as chicken manure; photosynthetic power, produced by the use of simple, fast-reproducing plants as fuel; nuclear power, by fusion rather than fission.

Electricity is generated at power stations at a voltage of about 25,000 volts, which is not a suitable voltage for long-distance transmission. For minimal power loss transmission must take place at very high voltage – up to

electricity generation

coal-fired power station (highly simplified)

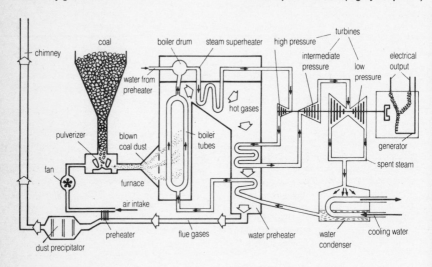

electricity generation and supply electricity is the most useful and most convenient form of energy there is. It can readily be converted into heat and light and used to power machines. Because electricity flows readily through wires, it can be made, or generated, in one place and distributed to anywhere it is needed. Electricity is generated at power stations, where a suitable energy source is made to drive turbines that spin the electricity generators. The generators produce alternating current (AC), and the producing units are generally called turboalternators.

400,000 volts or more. The generated voltage is therefore increased, or stepped-up, by a transformer. The resulting high voltage electricity is then fed into the main arteries of the grid system. This is an interconnected network of power stations and distribution centres covering a large area, sometimes (as in Britain) countrywide, even (as in Europe) from country to country. After transmission to a local substation, the line voltage is reduced by a step-down transformer and distributed by consumers.

geothermal energy either subterranean

hot water pumped to the surface and converted to steam or run through a heat exchanger, or dry steam, directed through turbines to produce electricity.

heat pump machine run by electricity, and so on, on a similar principle to a refrigerator, that is to cool the interior of a building or, conversely, by extracting energy from the atmosphere to give space heating. More than twice as much energy may be transferred as heat as is used to run it.

heat storage means of storing heat for release later. It is usually achieved by using materials which undergo phase changes, for example Glauber's salt, and sodium pyrophosphate, which melts at 7° C. The latter is used to store off-peak heat in the home, the salt being liquefied by cheap heat during the night, and then freezing – to give off heat during the day.

hydroelectric power electricity generated by water power. In a typical hydroelectric power (HEP) scheme water stored in a reservoir, often created by damming a river, is piped into water turbines, coupled to electricity generators. In pumped-storage plants water flowing through the turbines is recycled. A tidal power station is a HEP plant that exploits the rise and fall of the tides. Today about one-fifth of the world's electricity comes from hydroelectric power.

nuclear energy energy from the inner core or nucleus of atoms, as opposed to energy released in chemical processes, which is derived from the electrons surrounding the nucleus.

nuclear fission as in an atom bomb, is achieved by allowing a neutron to strike the nucleus of an atom of uranium-235, which then splits apart to release perhaps two to three other neutrons. If the material is pure uranium-235, a chain reaction is set up when these neutrons in turn strike other nuclei. This happens with great rapidity, resulting in the tremendous burst of energy we associate with the atom bomb. However, the process can be controlled by absorbing excess neutrons in 'control rods' (which may be made of steel alloyed with

boron), and slowing down the speed of those neutrons allowed to act. This is what is done inside a nuclear power plant.

nuclear fusion the process (release of thermonuclear energy by the condensation of hydrogen nuclei to helium nuclei) which occurred in the hydrogen bomb and, as a continuing reaction, in the sun and other stars. It avoids the loss of much of the energy produced which occurs in the original atom bomb, so that it is correspondingly more powerful. Attempts to harness it for commercial power production have so far not succeeded.

reactors there are various types of (fission) reactor in commercial use. In a gas-cooled reactor, a circulating gas under pressure (such as carbon dioxide) removes heat from the core of the reactor, which usually contains natural uranium and has neutron-absorbing control rods made of boron. The Calder Hall reactor is of this type. An advanced gas-cooled reactor (AGR) generally has enriched uranium oxide as its fuel. A water-cooled reactor, such as the steam-generating heavy-water reactor at Winfrith, Dorset, has water circulating through the hot core. The water is converted to steam which drives turbo-alternators for generating electricity. In a pressurized water reactor (PWR) the coolant consists of a sealed system of pressurized heavy water (deuterium oxide), which heats ordinary water to form steam in heat exchangers. The spent fuel from either type of reactor contains some plutonium, which can be extracted and used as fuel for the so-called fast breeder reactor (such as the one at Dounreay, Scotland). This produces more plutonium than it consumes (hence its name) by converting uranium placed in a blanket round the main core. The usual coolant is liquid sodium, a substance that is difficult to handle. A major danger with any type of reactor is the possibility of meltdown, which can result in the release of radioactive material. Problems can also arise over the processing of nuclear fuel and disposal of nuclear waste.

nuclear accidents the most serious have been:
Apr 1986 at Chernobyl (USSR): a leak from a

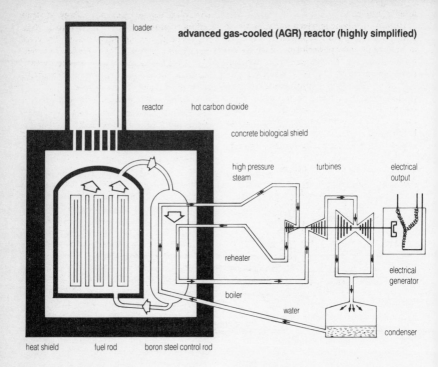

advanced gas-cooled (AGR) reactor (highly simplified)

loader

reactor   hot carbon dioxide

concrete biological shield

high pressure steam   turbines   electrical output

reheater

boiler   water   electrical generator

condenser

heat shield   fuel rod   boron steel control rod

non-pressurized boiling-water reactor, one of the largest in the Soviet Union, caused by overheating. The resulting clouds of radioactive isotopes were traced as far away as Sweden. Vast tracts of land and hundreds of people were contaminated.

1979 at Three Mile Island, Harrisburg, USA: a PWR (*p*ressurized *w*ater *r*eactor) leaked radioactive matter, a leak caused by a combination of mechanical and electrical failure, as well as operator error. In this type of reactor the heat formed by the fission of the uranium is carried away in a sealed and pressurized loop of irradiated water (chiefly 'heavy' water) to steam generators.

1957 at Windscale (now Sellafield), England: fire destroyed the core of a reactor, releasing lethal radioactive fumes into the atmosphere.

solar energy energy derived from the sun's radiation. A solar furnace, such as that built in 1970 at Odeillo in the French Pyrenees, has thousands of mirrors to focus the sun's rays; it produces uncontaminated, intensive heat for industrial and scientific or experimental purposes. Other solar heaters produce less energy and may have industrial or domestic uses. They usually consist of a black (heat-absorbing) panel containing pipes through which air or water is circulated, either by thermal convection or by a pump. Solar energy may also be harnessed indirectly using solar cells, made up of panels of semiconductor material (usually silicon) which generate electricity when illuminated by sunlight. Because of their high cost and low-power output, solar cells have found few applications outside space probes and artificial satellites.

turbine an engine in which steam, water or gas is made to spin a rotating shaft. Turbines are among the most powerful machines. Steam turbines are used to drive generators in power stations and ships' propellers; water turbines spin the generators in hydroelectric power plants; and gas turbines, in the guise of jet engines, power most aircraft, and drive machines in industry. The high-temperature, high-pressure steam for steam turbines is raised in boilers heated by furnaces burning coal, oil or gas, or by nuclear energy. A steam turbine consists of a shaft, or rotor, which rotates inside a fixed casing (stator). The rotor carries 'wheels' consisting of blades, or vanes. The stator has vanes set between the vanes of the rotor, which direct the steam through the rotor vanes at the optimum angle.

windmill a mill with sails or vanes which by the action of wind upon them drive machinery for grinding corn, pumping water, and so on. Windmills were used in the East in ancient times, and in Europe they were first used in Germany and the Netherlands in the 12th century. The main types of windmill are the *'post' mill*, which is turned round a post when the direction of the wind changes, and *'tower' mill* which has a revolving turret on top. It usually has a device (fantail) that keeps the sails pointing into the wind. The energy crisis has led to modern experiments with wind turbines, designed to use wind power on a major scale. Mostly they have a propeller-type rotor mounted on a tall shell tower. The turbine drives a generator for producing electricity. Some wind turbines in the USA have an output of 2 megawatts.

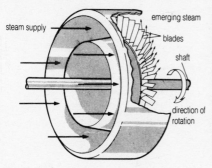

Gazetteer

There are four essential elements in the classic definition of a state, as given by R M MacIver in *The Modern State* 1926: the fact that people have formed an association to create and preserve social order; the fact that the community comprising the state is clearly defined in territorial terms; the fact that the government representing the people acts according to promulgated laws; and the fact that it has the power to enforce these laws.

Today the state is seen as the nation state, or country, so that any community which has absolute sovereignty over a specific area is a state. Although most states are members of the United Nations Organization, this is not a completely reliable criterion: some are not members by choice, as in the case of Switzerland; some have been deliberately excluded, such as Taiwan; and some are members but do not enjoy complete national sovereignty, such as Byelorussia and the Ukraine, both of which form part of the Soviet Union. There will always be debates about whether or not a particular country is a state, but if it has sovereign power to make and enforce laws for the whole of its territory it falls within the definition. Thus the so-called states of the USA, which are to some degree subject to the will of the federal government, are not states in international terms, nor are colonial or similar posessions which, too, are subject to an overriding authority. The simple test is whether or not it has an independent existence in international terms. It can be argued, however, that with the growth of regional, international bodies, such as the European Community, no state now enjoys absolute sovereignty.

Countries of the World

This section, *Countries of the World*, contains up-to-date entries on all of the sovereign states, in alphabetical order. Only countries which exist today are included, and all the countries are listed under their current names; the country known until 1984 as Upper Volta is now Burkina Faso, for example, and Mesopotamia, site of the ancient Sumerian and Babylonian civilizations, is now part of modern Iraq.

The entry for each country lists its full name, its capital, features, exports, currency, population, language, religion, and form of government, and includes a chronology of the most important dates in the history of the country, beginning with the date of its emergence as a unified state or, in the case of more recent countries, with the date of independence. An overview of world history can be found in the History section, and further material on political systems of the world appears in the section on Politics and Government.

Countries of the World

Afghanistan Democratic Republic of
area 636,000 sq km/246,000 sq mi
capital Kabul
towns Kandahár, Herát
features Hindu Kush range (Khyber and Salang passes, and Panjshir Valley, focus of resistance to USSR); Amu Darya, Kabul, and Helmand rivers; Wakhan salient
exports dried fruit, rare minerals, natural gas (piped to USSR), karakul lamb skins, Afghan coats
currency afgháni
population (1985) 15,065,000 (more than 3,000,000 have become refugees since 1979)
language Pushtu

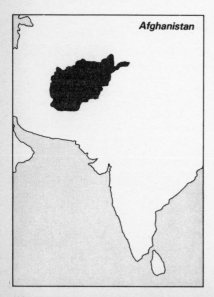

Afghanistan

religion Muslim (80% Sunni, 20% Shi'ite)
government there is a 'puppet regime' (backed by USSR) with Mohammed Najibullah of the People's Democratic (Communist) Party as president of the revolutionary council from 1986 and Sultan Ali Keshtmand as prime minister from 1981.
chronology
1747 Afghanistan became an independent emirate.
1838–1919 Afghan Wars waged between Afghanistan and Britain to counter the threat to British India from expanding Russian influence in Afghanistan.
1919 Afghanistan recovered full independence following Third Afghan War.
1953 General Daud Khan became prime minister and introduced reform programme.
1963 General Daud forced to resign and constitutional monarchy established.
1973 Monarchy overthrown in coup by General Daud Khan.
1978 Daud ousted by Taraki and PDPA in 'Saur Revolution'.
1979 Soviet invasion installed Babrak Karmal in power.
1986 Replacement of Karmal as leader by Dr Najib Ahmadzai : Partial Soviet troop withdrawal.
1987 Afghan government ceasefire offer.

Albania Socialist People's Republic of
exports crude oil, bitumen, chrome, iron ore, nickel, coal, copper wire, tobacco, fruit; there is potential hydroelectric power
currency lek
population (1985) 3,046,000
language Albanian
religion Muslim 70%, although since 1967 Albania is officially a secular state
government under the 1976 constitution Albania is the 'state of the dictatorship of the proletariat'; the unicameral people's assembly is elected by universal suffrage, but real power resides with the first secretary of the communist party (Ramiz Alia from 1985)
chronology
1912 Albania achieved independence from Turkey.

1925 Republic proclaimed.
1928–39 Monarchy of King Zog.
1939–44 Under first Italian and then German rule.
1946 Communist Republic proclaimed under the leadership of Hoxha.
1949 Admitted into Comecon.
1961 Break with Khrushchev's Soviet Union.

Albania

1967 Launch of drive to extinguish religion.
1978 Break with 'revisionist' China.
1985 Death of Enver Hoxha.

Algeria Democratic and Popular Republic of
area 2,381,745 sq km/919,590sq mi
capital Algiers
towns El Djazair, Wahran, Qacentina; ports are Oran, Annaba
features Atlas mountains, Barbary Coast
exports oil, natural gas, iron, wine, olive oil
currency dinar
population (1985) 22,107,000 (75% Arab, 25% Berber)
language Arabic (official); Berber, French
religion Sunni Muslim
government one-party 'irreversible' socialism under National Liberation Front (FLN); presi-

dent is Bendjedid Chadli from 1978, re-elected 1983 and there is a national assembly

Algeria

chronology
1954 War for independence from France led by FLN.
1962 Independence achieved.
1963 Ben Bella elected president.
1965 Ben Bella deposed by military, led by Colonel Houari Boumédienne.
1976 New constitution approved.
1978 Death of Boumédienne.
1979 Bendjedid Chadli elected president. Ben Bella released from house arrest. FLN adopted new party structure.
1981 Algeria helped in securing release of US prisoners in Iran.
1983 Chadli re-elected president.

Andorra Pricipality of
area 465 sq km/190 sq mi
capital Andorre-la-Vella
features set in narrrow valleys of the E Pyrenees
exports main industries tourism and smuggling
currency French franc and Spanish peseta
population (1985) 43,000 (25% Andorrans, 75% immigrant Spanish workers)
language Catalan (official); French, Spanish
religion Roman Catholic

government executive council (head of government Josep Pintat of Argerich from 1985), and legislative general council of the valleys, which elects a 'first syndic'. Traditionally made independent by Charlemagne, Andorra was placed in 1278 under the joint suzerainty of the Count of Foix (his rights now being vested in the president of France) and the bishop of Urgel in Spain, but their powers are nominal.

currency kwanza
population (1985) 7,948,000 (largest ethnic group Ovimbundu)
language Portuguese (official); Umbundu, Kimbundu
religion Roman Catholic 46%, Protestant 12%, Animist 42%
government Marxist executive president (José dos Santos from 1979) and unicameral national assembly; only one political party is permitted.

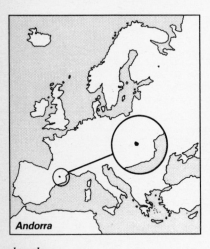

Andorra

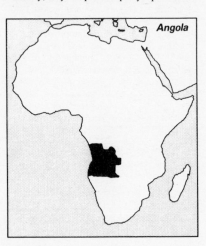

Angola

chronology
1970 Extension of franchise to third generation women and second generation men.
1976 First political party formed.
1977 Franchise extended to first generation Andorrans.
1981 First prime minister appointed by General Council.
1985 Further extensions of the franchise proposed.

Angola People's Republic of
area 1,246,700 sq km/481,350 sq mi
capital and chief port Luanda
towns Lobito and Benguela, also ports
features Kwanza river and the dependency of Cabinda
exports oil, coffee, diamonds, palm oil, sisal, iron ore, fish

chronology
1951 Angola became an overseas province of Portugal.
1956 First independence movement (MPLA) formed.
1961 Unuccessful independence rebellion.
1962 Second nationalist movement (FNLA) formed.
1966 Third nationalist movement (UNITA) formed.
1974 Discussions for independence of Angola started in Lisbon.
1975 Transitional government of independence formed from representatives of MPLA, FNLA, UNITA and Portuguese government. MPLA supported by USSR and Cuba, FNLA by Zaïre and USA, and UNITA by South

Countries of the World | **Gazetteer**

Africa. Angola declared independent. MPLA proclaimed People's Republic under the presidency of Dr Agostinho Neto. FNA and UNITA proclaimed People's Democratic Republic of Angola.

1976 MPLA gained control of most of the country. South African troops withdrawn but Cuban units remained.

1977 MPLA restructured to become MPLA-PT.

1979 Death of Neto, succeeded by José Eduardo dos Santos.

1980 Constitution amended to provide for an elected people's assembly. UNITA guerrillas, aided by South Africa, continued to operate South African raids on SWAPO bases in Angola.

1981 Further South African raids.

1984 Agreement reached on withdrawal of South African troops. The Lusaka agreement.

1985 South African forces 'officially' withdrawn.

1986 Further South African raids into Angola. UNITA continuing to receive South African support.

Antigua and Barbuda The State of

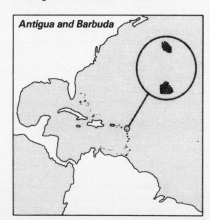

area 280 sq km/108 sq mi, plus Barbuda 50 km/30 sq mi to the north, and Redonda 1 sq km/0.6 sq mi

capital and chief port St John's

features Antigua is the largest of the Leeward Islands, Redonda is uninhabited

exports sea island cotton, rum

currency East Caribbean dollar

population (1985) 80,000

language English

religion Christian

government governor general and house of representatives (prime minister from 1976 Vere C Bird, Labour).

chronology

1967 Antigua and Barbuda became an associated state within the Commonwealth, with full internal independence.

1971 Progressive Labour Movement (PLM) won the general election by defeating the Antigua Labour Party (ALP).

1976 The PLM called for early independence but the ALP urged caution. The ALP won the general election.

1980 Constitutional conference to discuss independence.

1981 Full independence.

1984 ALP won a decisive victory in the general election.

Argentina Republic of

area 2,780,000 sq km/1,073,000 sq mi

capital Buenos Aires

towns Rosario, Córdoba, Tucumán, Mendoza, Santa Fé; ports are La Plata and Bahía Blanca

features Andes, Aconcagua; rivers Paraná and Colorado; Gran Chaco, Pampas, Tierra del Fuego

exports beef, livestock, cereals, wool, tannin, groundnuts, linseed oil, minerals (coal, copper, molybdenum, gold, silver, lead, zinc, barium, uranium), and the country has huge resources of oil, natural gas, and hydroelectric power

currency austral

population (1985) 7,451,000 (mainly of Spanish or Italian origin, only about 30,000 American Indians surviving)

language Spanish

religion Roman Catholic (state supported)

government senate and house of deputies, and a president (Raul Alfonsín of the Radical party

493

from 1983) elected by popular vote, through electoral colleges.

Argentina

chronology

1816 Achieved independence from Spain.

1946 Juan Perón elected president, supported by his wife 'Evita'.

1952 'Evita' Perón died.

1955 Perón overthrown and civilian administration restored.

1966 Coup brought back military rule.

1973 The Perónist party won the presidential and congressional elections. Perón returned from exile in Spain as president, with his third wife, 'Isabelita', as vice-president.

1974 Perón died. Succeeded by 'Isabelita'.

1976 Coup resulted in rule by a military junta led by General Jorge Videla. Constitution amended, congress dissolved and hundreds of people, including Señora Perón, detained.

1976–78 Ferocious campaign against left-wing elements. The start of the 'dirty war'.

1978 Videla retired. Succeeded by General Roberto Viola, who promised a return to democracy.

1981 Videla died suddenly. Replaced by General Leopoldo Galtieri.

1982 With a deteriorating economy, Galtieri sought popular support by ordering an invasion of the British-held Falkland Islands. After losing the short war, Galtieri was removed and replaced by General Reynaldo Bignone.

1983 A military commision of inquiry placed the blame for the Falklands defeat on Galtieri and his junta. Amnesty law passed and 1853 democratic constitution revived. General elections resulted in the Union Civica Radical party, led by Dr Raul Alfonsín, winning the presidency and a narrow majority oin the chamber of deputies. Alfonsín instituted an immediate and drastic shake-up of the armed forces.

1984 A Commission on the Disappearance of Persons (CONADEP) reported on over 8,000 people who had disappeared during the 'dirty war' of 1976–83.

1985 A deteriorating economy forced Alfonsín to seek help from the IMF and introduce a harsh austerity programme.

1986 Unsuccessful attempt on Alfonsín's life.

Australia The Commonwealth of

area 7,704,441 sq km/2,974,693 sq mi

capital Canberra

towns Adelaide, Alice Springs, Brisbane, Darwin, Melbourne, Perth, Sydney

features the world's driest continent; Great Australian Desert, Great Barrier Reef, Great Dividing Range, Darling river and the Murray system, Lake Eyre, Nullarbor Plain; unique animals include kangaroo, koala, numbat, platypus, wombat, Tasmanian devil and 'tiger'; budgerigar, cassowary, emu, kookaburra, lyre bird, black swan, and such deadly insects as the bulldog ant and funnel web spider

exports cereals,'meat and dairy products; wool (30% of world production) fruit, wine, nuts, sugar, and honey; minerals include bauxite (world's largest producer), coal, iron, copper, lead, tin, zinc, opal, mineral sands, and uranium; machinery and transport equipment

currency Australian dollar

population (1985) 15,345,000, (95% British, 3% other Europeans, 1.5% Aborigines)

language English
religion Anglican 36%, other Protestant 25%, Roman Catholic 33%
government Australia is a federal commonwealth (within the Commonwealth) with a governor-general, representing the sovereign of the UK, senate and house of representatives, all six states (New South Wales, Queensland, South Australia, Tasmania, Victoria, Western Australia) having equal representation in the former, but proportional representation in the latter; the federal prime minister (since 1983) is Bob Hawke. Each state (except Queensland) has a governor and parliament of two houses, and the cabinet is headed by a premier. Australia also comprises the Australian Capital Territory, and the self-governing Northern Territory.

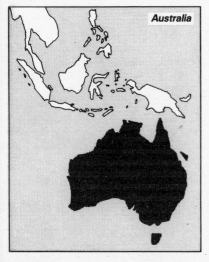

Australia

chronology
1966 Sir Robert Menzies resigned, after being Liberal prime minister for 17 years, and was succeeded by Harold Holt.
1968 John Gorton became prime minister, following Holt's death in a swimming accident.
1971 Gorton defeated on a confidence vote and succeeded by William McMahon, heading a Liberal-Country Party coalition.
1972 Coalition broke up and Gough Whitlam became prime minister, leading a Labour government.
1974 Labour re-elected under Whitlam, but without a majority in the Senate.
1975 Senate blocked the government's financial legislation and, with Whitlam declining to resign, he was dismissed by the governor-general, who invited Malcom Fraser to form a Liberal-Country Party caretaker government. The action of the governor-general, Sir John Kerr, was widely criticized.
1977 Sir John Kerr resigned.
1980 Coalition returned with a still smaller majority.
1983 Australian Labour Party, returned to power under Bob Hawke, immediately convened a meeting of employers and unions to seek a consensus on economic policy to deal with growing unemployment.
1984 Labour returned, with a reduced majority, in an early general election.

Austria Republic of (German *Österreich*)
area 83,850 sq km/32,375 sq mi
capital Vienna
towns Graz, Linz, Salzburg, Innsbruck
features Austrian Alps (including Zugspitze and Brenner and Semmering passes), Vienna Plain, River Danube; Hainburg, the largest primeval rain forest left in Europe, now under threat from a dam
exports minerals, manufactured goods
currency Schilling
population (1985) 7,451,000
language German
religion Roman Catholic 90%
government there is a popularly elected non-executive president and a National Assembly of two chambers: Nationalrat (chancellor from 1986 Franz Vranitzky, a Socialist), and Bundesrat. There are three political parties: Socialist Party (SPO), People's Party. and Freedom Party.
chronology
1918 Hapsburg rule ended, republic proclaimed.

1938 Incorporated into German 'Reich' by Hitler.

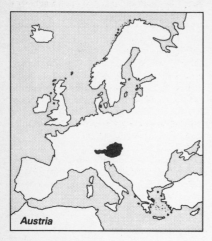

Austria

1945 1920 constitution reinstated and SPO-OVP coalition formed.
1955 Allied occupation ended and the independence of Austria formally recognized.
1966 OVP in power with Josef Klaus as chancellor.
1970 SPO formed a minority government, with Bruno Kreisky as chancellor.
1983 SPO hegemony ended. Kreisky resigned and was replaced by Fred Sinowatz, leading an SPO-FPO coalition.
1986 Dr Kurt Waldheim elected president. Sinowatz resigned and was succeeded by Franz Vranitzky. SPO-FPO coalition ended. In the November general election no party won an overall majority and Vranitzky formed a 'grand-coalition' of the SPO and the OVP, with the OVP leader, Alois Mock, as vice-chancellor. Sinowatz denounced the coalition as a betrayal of socialist principles and resigned his SPO chairmanship.

Bahamas Commonwealth of the
area 13,935 sq km/5,380 sq mi
capital Nassau on New Providence
features comprises 700 coral islands and about

496

1,000 cays, only 30 of which are inhabited
exports cement, pharmaceuticals, petroleum products, crawfish, rum, pulpwood; over half the islands' employment comes from tourism
currency Bahamian dollar
population (1985) 230,000
language English
religion Christian
government under the constitution of 1973 there is a governor-general, senate and house of assembly (prime minister from 1967 Lynden O Pindling).

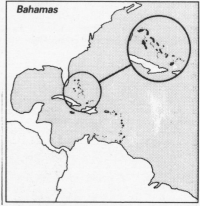

Bahamas

chronology
1964 Internal self-government attained.
1967 First national assembly elections.
1968 Progressive Liberal Party increased its majority.
1972 Progressive Liberal Party increased its majority again. Constitutional conference to discuss full independence.
1973 Full independence achieved.
1977 Progressive Liberal Party increased its majority again.
1982 Progressive Liberal Party returned with reduced majority.
1983 Allegations of drug trafficking by government ministers.
1984 Deputy prime minister and two cabinet ministers resigned. Pindling denied any per-

sonal involvement and was endorsed as Party leader.

Bahrain

area 600 sq km/400 sq mi
capital Manama on the largest island (also called Bahrain) of the 33 in the group
towns oil port Mina Sulman
features a causeway 25 km/15 mi long (1985) links Bahrain to the mainland of Saudi Arabia; Sitra island is a communications centre for the lower Gulf, and has a satellite tracking station; there is a wildlife park featuring the oryx on Bahrain, and most of the south of the island is preserved for the ruling family's falconry
exports oil and natural gas
currency Bahrain dinar
population (1985) 431,000 (two-thirds are nationals)
language Arabic, Farsi
religion Muslim (Shi'ite 60%, Sunni 40%)
government the emir from 1961 is Sheikh Isa bin Sulman Al-Khalifa 1933– ; administration is by a cabinet, chosen by the emir, and his power is virtually absolute

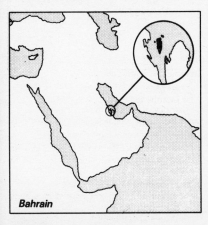

Bahrain

chronology
1816 Under British protection.
1968 Britain announced its intention to withdraw its forces. Bahrain joined, with Qatar and the Trucial States, a Federation of Arab Emirates.
1971 Qatar and the Trucial States left the Federation and Bahrain became an independent state.
1973 New constitution adopted, with an elected national assembly.
1975 Prime minister resigned and national assembly dissolved. Emir and his family assumed virtually absolute power.
1986 Gulf University established in Bahrain. Causeway built linking Bahrain to Saudi Arabia.

Bangladesh People's Republic of

area 143,000 sq km/55,000 sq mi
capital Dhaka

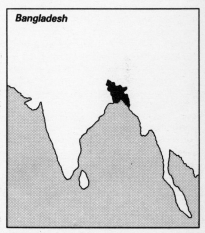

Bangladesh

towns ports Chittagong, Khulna
features Bangladesh is an alluvial plain, part of the Ganges-Brahmaputra river system; it has an annual rainfall of 2,540 5 mm/100 in; some 75% of the land is less than 3 m/10 ft above sea level and tidal waves, triggered by the cyclones common in the area, as well as tidal surges, can cause devastation additional to river water flooding
exports jute (50% of world production), tea
currency taka
population (1985)101,408,000

language Bangla (Bengali)

religion Sunni Muslim 85% (there is a unique system of using imams as 'worker-priests'), Hindu 14%

government a unicameral parliamentary system, with a president (General Hossain Ershad from 1983).

chronology

1947 Formed into eastern province of Pakistan following partition of British India.

1970 Half a million killed in flood disaster.

1971 Independent Bangladesh emerged under-leadership of Sheikh Mujib ur-Rahman following civil war.

1975 Assassination of Sheikh Mujib. Martial law imposed.

1976–77 Major-General Zia ur-Rahman assumed power.

1978–79 Elections held and civilian rule restored.

1981 Assassination of Major-General Zia.

1982 Lieutenant-General Ershad assumed power in army coup. Martial law imposed.

1986 Elections held. Martial law ended.

Barbados

areà 430 sq km/166 sq mi

capital Bridgetown

features subject to hurricanes; most easterly island of the W Indies

exports sugar and rum, oil

currency Barbados dollar

population 252,000 (1985)

language English

religion Christian

government a governor-general, senate and house of assembly (Prime Minister Errol Barrow from 1986).

chronology

1951 Universal adult suffrage introduced. The Barbados Labour Party (BLP) won the general election.

1954 Ministerial government established.

1955 Democratic Labour Party (DLP) formed.

1961 Full internal self-government. DLP, led by Errol Barrow, in power.

1966 Barbados achieved full independence within the Commonwealth. Barrow became the new nation's first prime minister.

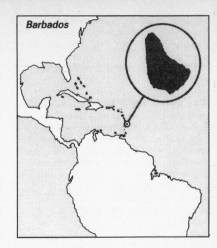

Barbados

1971 DLP re-elected.

1972 Diplomatic relations with Cuba established.

1976 BLP, led by 'Tom' Adams, returned to power.

1981 BLP re-elected.

1983 Barbados suported US invasion of Grenada.

1985 Adams died suddenly. Bernard St John became prime minister.

1986 DLP, led by Barrow, returned to power.

1987 Barrow died 1 Jun.

Belgium Kingdom of

area 30,513 sq km/11,779 sq mi

capital Brussels

towns Ghent, Liège, Charleroi, Bruges, Mons, Blankenburghe, Knokke; ports are Antwerp, Ostend, Zeebrugge

features Ardennes; rivers Scheldt and Meuse

exports iron and steel, textiles, manufactured goods, petrochemicals

currency Belgian franc

population (1985) 9,858,000 (comprising Flemings (of Germanic origin) and Walloons (a Celtic people who came under Roman rule), the latter were formerly predominant, but are now outnumbered by the former) *language* in the north (Flanders) Flemish (a Dutch dialect, known as Vlaams) 57%, in the south (Wallonia) Walloon (a French dialect which is almost a separate language) 30%, with 11% bilingual, and German (eastern border); all are official

religion Roman Catholic

government Belgium is a constitutional monarchy, and the senate and chamber of representatives are elected by proportional representation.

Belgium

chronology

1830 Belgium became an independent kingdom.

1914 Invaded by Germany.

1940 Again invaded by Germany.

1948 Belgium became founder member of Benelux Customs Union.

1949 Belgium became founder member of Council of Europe.

1951 Leopold III abdicated in favour of his son, Baudouin.

1952 Belgium became founder member of European Coal and Steel community (ECSC).

1957 Belgium became founder member of the European Community (EEC).

1971 Steps towards regional autonomy taken.

1972 German-speaking members of the cabinet included for the first time.

1973 Linguistic parity achieved in government appointments.

1974 Separate regional councils and ministerial committees established.

1977 Coalition government, led by Leo Tindemans (CVP) established.

1980 Open violence over language divisions. regional assemblies for Flanders and Wallonia and a 3–member executive for Brussels created.

1981 Short-lived coalition led by Mark Eyskens (CVP) was followed by the return of Martens.

1985 Martens formed his 6th coalition.

Belize

area 22,965 sq km/8,867sq mi

capital Belmopan

towns port Belize City

features half the country is forested, much of it high rain forest

exports sugar, citrus, rice, lobster tails

currency Belize dollar

population (1985) 166,400 (including Maya minority in the interior)

language English (official), but Spanish is widely spoken

religion Roman Catholic 60%, Protestant 35%, Hindu and Muslim minorities

government there is a governor-general, a senate and a house of representatives (prime minister from 1984 Manuel Esquivel, United Democratic Party).

chronology

1862 Belize became a British colony.

1954 Constitution adopted, providing for limited internal self-government. General election won by People's United Party led by George Price.

1964 Full internal self-government granted.

1965 Two-chamber national assembly introduced, with Price as prime minister.

1970 Capital moved from Belize City to Belmopan.

1975 British troops sent to defend the frontier with Guatemala.
1977 Negotiations undertaken with Guatemala but no agreemeent reached.

Belize

1980 UNO called for full independence.
1981 Full independence achieved. Price became prime minister.
1984 PUP and Price defeated in general election. UDP, led by Manuel Esquivel, formed the government. Britain reaffirmed its undertaking to defend the frontier.
1985 New talks with Guatemala proved inconclusive.

Benin People's Republic of
area 112,600 sq km/43,480 sq mi
capital Porto Novo
towns Abomey, Natitingou; chief port Cotonou
features coastal fishing villages on stilts
exports cocoa, groundnuts, cotton, palm oil
currency CFA franc
population 4,005,000 (1984)
language French official; local dialects
religion Animism 65%; Christianity 17%; Islam 13%
government unicameral National Revolutionary Assembly of 336 People's Commissioners established under the Marxist-Leninist constitution of 1977; President Ahmed Kerekou came to power by a coup in 1972.

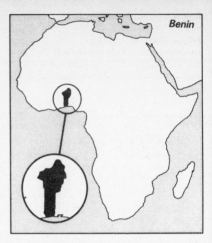

Benin

chronology
1851 Under French control
1958 Became self-governing dominion within the French Community
1960–72 Acute political instability, with switches from civilian to military rule
1972 Military regime established by General Mathieu Kerekou
1974 Kerekou announced that the country would follow a path of 'scientific socialism'. Name of country changed from Dahomey to Benin
1977 Return to civilian rule under a new constitution
1980 Kerekou formally elected President by the National Revolutionary Assembly
1984 Kerekou re-elected

Bhutan Kingdom of
area 46,600 sq km/18,000 sq mi
capital Thimphu
features occupies southern slopes of the Himalayas, and is cut by valleys of tributaries of the Brahmaputra
exports timber, minerals
currency ngultrum; also Indian currency
population (1985) 1,286,000

language Dzongkha (a Tibetan dialect), Nepali and English (all official)
religion Mahayana Buddhist
government democratic monarchy (King Jigme Singye Wangchuck 1955–, succeeded 1972), with a national assembly, two-thirds elected.

Bhutan

chronology
1865 Trade treaty with Britain signed.
1907 First hereditary monarch installed.
1910 Anglo-Bhutanese treaty signed.
1945 Indo-Bhutan Treaty of Friendship signed.
1952 King Jigme Dorji Wangchuk installed.
1953 National assembly (Tsogdu) established.
1959 4,000 Tibetan refugees given asylum.
1968 King established first cabinet.
1972 King died and was succeeded by his son, Crown Prince Jigme Singye Wangchuk.
1979 Tibetan refugees told to take up Bhutanese citizenship or leave. Most stayed.
1983 Bhutan became a founder member of the South Asian Regional Co-operation organisation (SARC).

Bolivia Republic of
area 1,098,000 sq km/424,000 sq mi
capital La Paz (seat of government), Sucre (legal capital and seat of judiciary)
towns Santa Cruz, Cochabamba
features Andes, and Lakes Titicaca and Poopó
exports tin (second largest world producer), other non-ferrous metals, oil, gas (piped to Argentina), agricultural products
currency peso boliviano
population (1985) 6,195,000; (Quechua 25%, Aymara 17%, Mestizo 30%, European 14%)
language Spanish (official); Aymara, Quechua
religion Roman Catholic, (state recognized)
government executive president Víctor Paz Estenssoro 1907– of the National Revolutionary Movement from 1985; senate and chamber of deputies.

Bolivia

chronology
1825 Independence achieved.
1952 Dr Víctor Paz Estenssoro (MNR) elected president.
1956 Dr Hernan Siles Zuazo became president.
1960 Estenssoro returned to power.
1964 Army coup led by vice-president.
1966 General Barrientos became president.
1967 Uprising, led by 'Che' Guevara, put down with US help.

501

1969 Barrientos killed in air crash, replaced by vice-president Siles Salinas. Army coup deposed him.

1970 Army coup put General Torres Gonzalez in power.

1971 Torres replaced by Colonel Banzer Suarez.

1973 Banzer promised a return to democratic government.

1974 An attempted coup prompted Banzer to postpone elections and ban political and trade union activity.

1978 Elections declared invalid after allegations of fraud.

1980 More inconclusive elections followed by another coup, led by General Garcia. Allegations of corruption and drug trafficking led to cancellation of US and EEC aid.

1981 Garcia forced to resign. Replaced by General Torrelio Villa, who promised to fight corruption and return to democratic government.

1982 Torrelio resigned. Replaced by military junta led by General Vildoso. Because of worsening economy, Vildoso asked congress to install a civilian administration. Dr Siles Zuazo chosen as president.

1983 Economic aid from US and Europe resumed.

1984 New coalition government formed by President Siles. Attempted abduction of president by right-wing officers. The president undertook a five-day hunger strike as an example to the nation.

1985 President Siles Zuazo resigned. Election result inconclusive. Dr Víctor Paz Estenssoro, at the age of 77, chosen by Congress.

Botswana Republic of
area 575,000 sq km/222,000 sq mi
capital Gaborone
features larger part of Kalahari Desert, including Okovango Swamp, remarkable for its wildlife
exports diamonds, copper, nickel, and meat
currency pula
population (1985) 1,068,000 (80% Bamangwato, 20% Bangwaketse)
language English (official); Setswana,

(national)
religion Christian (majority)
government executive president (Quett Masire from 1980), national assembly and advisory house of chiefs.

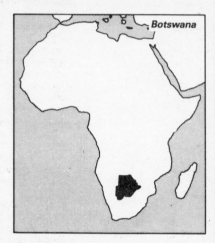

Botswana

chronology
1885 Became a British protectorate.
1960 New constitution created a legislative council.
1963 End of high commission rule.
1965 Capital transferred fron Mafeking to Gaborone. Internal self-government granted. Seretse Khama, leader of BDP, elected head of government.
1966 Full independence achieved. New constitution came into effect. Name changed from Bechuanaland to Botswana. Sir Seretse Khama elected president.
1980 Sir Seretse Khama died and was succeeded by Vice-President Dr Quett Masire.
1984 Masire re-elected.
1985 South African raid on Gaborone.

Brazil Federal Republic of
area 8,512,000 sq km/3,286,000 sq mi
capital Brasilia
towns São Paulo; ports are Rio de Janeiro, Belo Horizonte, Recife, Porto Alegre,

Salvador
features Amazon Basin, Mount Roraima, and
enormous energy resources, both hydroelectric (Itaipú dam on the Paraná, and
Tucurui, on the Tocantins) and nuclear (uranium ores); Xingu National Park
exports coffee, sugar, cotton; textiles and
motor vehicles; iron, chrome,ʼ manganese,
tungsten and other ores, as well as quartz
crystals, industrial diamonds
currency cruzado (introduced 1986; value 100
cruzeiros, the former unit)
population (1985) 135,000,000 (including
200,000 Indians, survivors of 5,000,000,
especially in Rondonia and Mato Grosso,
mostly living on reserves)

Brazil

language Portuguese; there are 120 Indian
languages
religion Roman Catholic 89%; Indian faiths
government under the 1969 constitution a president, enabled to legislate by decree on economic or national security questions (José
Sarney, who as vice-president succeeded
Neves 1985), indirectly elected by an electoral
college. There is pressure for direct presidential elections.
chronology
1822 Brazil became an independent empire,
ruled by Dom Pedro, son of the refugee King
João VI of Portugal.
1889 Monarchy abolished and republic
established.
1891 Constitution for a federal state adopted.
1930 Dr Getulio Vargas became president.
1945 Vargas deposed by the military.
1946 New constitution adopted.
1950 Vargas returned to office.
1954 Vargas committed suicide.
1956 Juscelino Kubitschek became president.
1960 Capital moved to Brasilia.
1961 João Goulart became president.
1964 Bloodless coup made General Castelo
Branco president. He assumed dictatorial
powers, abolishing free political parties.
1967 New constitution adopted. Branco succeeded by Marshal da Costa e Silva.
1969 Da Costa e Silva resigned because of ill-
health and a military junta took over.
1974 General Ernesto Geisel became
president.
1978 General Baptista de Figueiredo became
president.
1979 Political parties legalized again.
1984 Mass calls for a return to fully democratic
government.
1985 Tancredo Neves became first civilian
president for 21 years. Neves died and was
succeeded by the vice-president, José Sarney.

Brunei
area 5,800 sq km/2,226 sq mi
capital (and chief port) Bandar Seri Begawan
features 75% of the area is forested; the
Limbang valley splits Brunei in two, and its
cession to Sarawak in 1890 is disputed by
Brunei
exports liquefied natural gas (world's largest
producer) and oil, but both expected to be
exausted by 2000 AD
currency Brunei dollar
population (1985) 232,000 (of Malaysian
origin); 50,000 Chinese (few granted
citizenship)
language Malay, (official); English

religion Muslim
government independent sultanate (Sultan Sir Hassanal Bolkiah Mu'izzadin Waddaulah from 1967, prime minister from 1984). There is a cabinet.

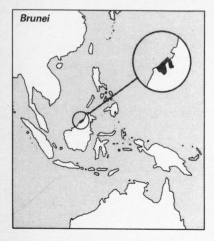

chronology
1888 Brunei became a British protectorate.
1941–45 Occupied by the Japanese.
1959 Written constitution made Britain responsible for defence and external affairs.
1962 Sultan began rule by decree.
1963 Proposal to join Federation of Malaysia abandoned.
1967 Sultan abdicated in favour of his son, Sir Hassanal Bolkiah Mu'izzadin Waddaulah.
1971 Brunei given internal self-government.
1975 UN resolution called for independence for Brunei.
1984 Full independence achieved, with Britain maintaining a small force to protect the oil and gas fields.
1985 A 'loyal and reliable' political party legalized.
1986 Sultan's father died..

Bulgaria People's Republic of
area 110,840 sq km/42,796 sq mi
capital Sofia

504

towns Plovdiv, Rusé; Burgas and Varna are Black Sea ports
features Balkan mountains, Black Sea coast
exports textiles, chemicals, non-ferrous metals, timber, minerals, machinery
currency lev
population (1985) 8,947,000 (including 800,000 ethnic Turks now subjected to compulsory assimilation)
language Bulgarian, Turkish
religion Eastern Orthodox Christian 90%, Sunni Muslim 10%, but the latter faith is discouraged
government under the 1971 constitution the council of state (chairman Todor Zhivkov) is elected by the unicameral national assembly, itself popularly elected. Real power lies with the Politburo, also headed by Zhivkov.

chronology
1908 Bulgaria became a kingdom independent of Turkish rule.
1944 Soviet invasion of German-occupied Bulgaria.
1946 Monarchy abolished and Communist-dominated People's Republic proclaimed.
1947 Soviet-style constitution adopted.
1949 Death of Georgi Dimitrov.

1954 Election of Todor Zhivkov as BCP general secretary.

1971 Constitution modified : Zhivkov elected president.

1985–86 Large-scale administrative and personnel changes effected under Soviet stimulus.

Burkina Faso 'Republic of Honest Men', formerly Republic of Upper Volta

area 274,000 sq km/106,000sq mi

capital Ouagadougou

towns Bobo-Doiulasso

features landlocked plateau, savannah country; headwaters of the river Volta

exports cotton, groundnuts, livestock, hides and skins

currency CFA franc

population (1985) 6,773,931

language French (official); there are about 50 native languages

religion Animist 53%, Sunni Muslim 36% Roman Catholic 11%

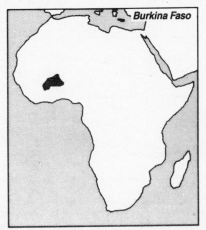

Burkina Faso

government a mainly civilian government was overthrown by a military coup in 1983 led by Captain Thomas Sankara, the then prime minister, who became president, with a council

of ministers.

chronology

1958 Became a self-governing republic within the French Community.

1960 Full independence achieved, with Maurice Yameogo as the first president.

1966 Military coup, led by Colonel Lamizana. Constitution suspended, political activities banned and a supreme council of the armed forces established.

1969 Ban on political activities lifted.

1970 Referendum approved a new constitution leading to a return to civilian rule.

1974 After experimenting wiith a mixture of military and civilian rule, General Lamizana reassumed full power.

1977 Ban on political activities removed. Referendum approved a new constitution based on civilian rule.

1978 Lamizana elected president.

1980 Lamizana overthrown in a bloodless coup led by Colonel Zerbo.

1982 Zerbo ousted in a coup by junior officers. Major Ouédraohgo became president and Captain Thomas Sankara prime minister.

1983 Sankara seized complete power and set up a National Revolutionary Council (CNR).

1984 Upper Volta renamed Burkina Faso.

Burma Socialist Republic of the Union of

area 678,000 km/261,789 sq mi

capital (and chief port) Rangoon

towns Mandalay, Karbe

features over half is forested; rivers Irrawaddy and Chindwin

exports rice, rubber, jute, teak; varied minerals; jade, rubies, sapphires

currency kyat

population (1985) 36,919,000

language Burmese

religion Hinayana Buddhist; Christian and animist minority

government under the constitution of 1973, Burma is a one-party socialist republic, with a president (General San Yu) and council of state, elected by the people's assembly.

chronology

1886 United as province of British India.

1937 Became crown colony in the British

Commonwealth.
1942–45 Occupied by Japan.
1948 Granted independence from Britain. Left the Commonwealth.

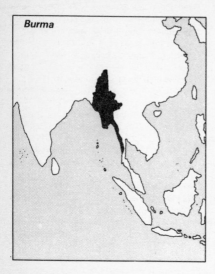

Burma

1962 General Ne Win assumed power following army coup.
1973–74 Adoption of presidential style, 'civilian' constitution.
1975 Formation of opposition National Democratic Front..

Burundi Republic of
area 27,834 sq km/10,747 sq mi
capital Bujumbura
towns Kitega
features Lake Tanganyika, Great Rift Valley
exports coffee, cotton, tea; nickel; hides, livestock; there are also 500 million tonnes of peat reserves in the basin of the Akanyaru river
currency Burundi franc
population (1985) 4,673,000 (of whom 15% are the Nilotic Tutsi, still holding most of the land and political power, and the remainder the Bantu Hutu. An unsuccessful Hutu rebellion in the early 1970s led to 150,000 Hutu deaths)
language Kirundi (a Bantu language) and

506

French, (official); Kiswahili
religion Roman Catholicism over 50%; with a Sunni Muslim minority
government president (Colonel John Baptiste Bagaza) appointed by the supreme military council

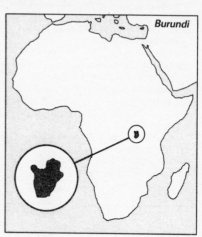

Burundi

chronology
1962 Separated from Ruanda-Urundi, as Burundi, and given independence, as a monarchy under King Mwambutsa IV.
1966 King deposed by his son Charles, who became Ntare V, and was himself deposed by his prime minister, Captain Michel Micombero, who declared Burundi a republic.
1972 Ntare V killed, allegedly by the Hutu tribe. Large-scale massacres of Hutus by the rival Tutsi tribe, of which Micombero was a member.
1973 Micombero made president and prime minister.
1974 Union for National Progress (UPRONA) declared the only legal political party, with the president as its secretary-general.
1976 Army coup deposed Micombero. Colonel Jean-Baptiste Bagaza appointed president by Supreme Revolutionary Council.
1977 President promised a return to civilian

rule and a five-year plan to stamp out corruption and secure social justice.

1981 New constitution adopted, providing for a national assembly.

1984 Bagaza elected president with over 99% of the votes cast..

Cameroon United Republic of country of W Africa

area 474,000 sq km/183,580 sq mi

capital Yaoundé

towns chief port Douala

features Mount Cameroon 4,070 m/13,352 ft, an active volcano on the coast, W of the Adamawa Mountains. Desert in the far N in the Lake Chad basin, dry savannah plateau in the intermediate area, and in the south dense tropical rainforest

products cocoa, coffee, bananas, cotton, timber, rubber, ground nuts. Gold and aluminium are mined

currency CFA franc

population (1985) 9,737,000

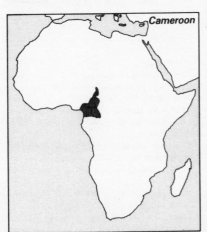
Cameroon

language French and English in pidgin variations (official), but there has been some discontent with the emphasis on French; there are 163 indigenous peoples with many African languages

religion Roman Catholic 35%, animist 25%, Muslim 22%, Protestant 18%

government there is an executive president, (Paul Biya from 1982) and national assembly, both elected for five years; only one political party is allowed.

chronology

'1884 Under German rule.

1916 Captured by Allied Forces in World War I.

1922 Divided between Britain and France.

1946 French and British Cameroons made UN Trust Territories.

1960 French Cameroon became the independent Republic of Cameroon. Ahmadou Ahidjo elected president.

1961 Northern part of British Cameroon merged with Nigeria and southern part joined the Republic of Cameroon to become the Federal Republic of Cameroon.

1965 Ahidjo re-elected president.

1966 A one-party regime was introduced.

1970 Ahidjo re-elected.

1972 New constitution made Cameroon a unitary state.

1973 New national assembly elected.

1975 Ahidjo re-elected.

1982 Ahidjo resigned and was succeeded by Paul Biya.

1983 Biya began to remove his predecessor's supporters and was accused by Ahidjo of trying to create a police state. Ahidjo went into exile in France.

1984 Biya re-elected and defeated a plot to overthrow him.

1985 UNC changed its name to RPDC.

Canada Dominion of

area 9,975,223 sq km/3,851,809 sq mi, including freshwater lakes

capital Ottawa

towns Toronto, Montreal, Vancouver, Winnipeg, Edmonton, Quebec, Hamilton, Calgary

features St Lawrence Seaway, Mackenzie river; Great Lakes; Arctic Archipelago; Rocky Mountains; Great Plains or Prairies; Canadian Shield

exports wheat; timber, pulp and newsprint; fish, especially salmon; furs (ranched fox and mink exceed the value of wild furs); oil and natural gas; aluminium, asbestos, coal, copper, iron, nickel; motor vehicles and parts, industrial and agricultural machinery, fertilizers

currency Canadian dollar

population (1985) 25,399,000 (including 300,000 American Indians, of whom 75% live on over 2,000 reserves in Ontario and the four Western Provinces; some 300,000 Métis (people of mixed race) and 19,000 Inuit (or Eskimo), of whom 75% live in the NW Territories) Over half Canada's population lives in Ontario and Quebec.

language English, French, (both official) (about 70% speak English, 20% French, and the rest are bilingual); there are also N American Indian languages and the Inuit Inuktitut

religion Roman Catholic 40%, Protestant 35%;

Canada

government Canada is a federal union (within the Commonwealth) of 10 provinces (Alberta, British Columbia, Manitoba, New Brunswick, Newfoundland, Nova Scotia, Ontario, Prince Edward Island, Quebec, and Saskatchewan) and two territories (the Yukon Territory and Northwest Territories), the latter comprising

508

more than-one third of Canada with an average population density of 0.1 per sq mi.

federal government the Queen is represented by a governor-general, who acts as chief of state, and there is a senate of 104 members (appointed until age 75) and house of commons of 264 members elected by universal suffrage for five years (Prime Minister Brian Mulroney from 1984). The chief parties are the Progressive Conservative, Liberal, and New Democratic.

provincial government the Queen is represented by a lieutenant-governor in each province, appointed by the governor-general; and there is an executive council and a legislative assembly (Quebec having an additional legislative council). The provinces enjoy sovereign authority in all local matters.

territories each has a resident commissioner appointed by the federal government, the latter retaining control over all natural resources, and is represented by a single member in the Senate and House of Commons. There is support for increased autonomy or adoption of provincial status, and claims by the native peoples for control of land were under negotiation in 1983.

chronology

1957 Progressive Conservatives returned to power after 36 years in opposition.

1963 Liberals re-elected under Lester Pearson.

1968 Pearson suceeded by Pierre Trudeau.

1972 Trudeau re-elected.

1974 Trudeau re-elected.

1979 Joe Clark, leader of the Progressive Conservatives, formed a minority government. Trudeau announced his intention to retire.

1980 Clark defeated on budget proposals. Trudeau reconsidered his retirement decision. Liberals, under Trudeau, returned with a large majority.

1982 Canada Act removed Britain's last legal control over Canadian affairs.

1983 Clark replaced as leader of the Progressive Conservatives by Brian Mulroney.

1984 Trudeau retired and was succeeded, as Liberal leader and prime minister, by John

Turner. Progressive Conservatives won the general election by a large majority and Brian Mulroney became prime minister.

Cape Verde Republic of

area 4,033 sq km/1,557.5 sq mi

capital Praia

features archipelago of 10 islands 565 km/350 mi W of Senegal, strategically important because it dominates the western shipping lanes

exports bananas, coffee

currency Cape Verde escudo

population (1985) 312,000 (including some 100,000 Angolan refugees)

language Creole dialect of Portuguese

religion Roman Catholic 80%

government Executive President (Aristides Pereira from 1975) and one-party national assembly.

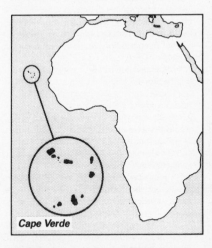

Cape Verde

chronology

1974 Moved towards independence transitional Portuguese-Cape Verde government.

1975 Full independence achieved. National people's assembly elected. Aristedes Pereira, secretary-general of the African Party for the Independence of Portuguese Guinea and Cape Verde (PAIGC), became the first president.

1980 Constitution adopted, providing for eventual union with Guinea-Bissau

1981 Union with Guinea-Bissau abandoned and the constitution amended. PAIGC became PAICV. Pereira re-elected.

Central African Republic

area 625,000 sq km/240,000 sq mi

capital Bangui

features most of the country is on a plateau, with rivers flowing N and S. The N is dry and there is rain forest in the SW

exports diamonds, uranium, coffee, cotton, and timber

currency CFA franc

population (1985) 2,664,000

language Sangho, French (both official)

religion Animist over 50%; Christian 35%, both Catholic and Protestant; Muslim 10%

government from 1981 a Military Committee for National Recovery, headed by General André Kolingba; all political parties were suspended, but a new constitution was in preparation in 1985.

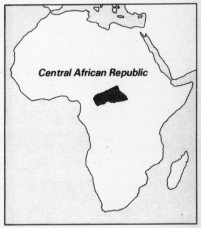

Central African Republic

chronology

1960 Central African Republic achieved independence from France with David Dacko elected president.

509

1962 The Republic made a one-party state.

1965 Dacko ousted in a military coup led by Colonel Bokassa.

1966 Constitution rescinded and national assembly dissolved.

1972 Bokassa declared himself president for life.

1976 Bokassa made himself emperor of the Central African Empire.

1979 Bokassa deposed by Dacko following violent repressive measures by the self-styled emperor, who went into exile.

1981 Dacko deposed in a bloodless coup, led by General André Kolingba, and an all-military government established.

1983 Clandestine opposition movement formed .

1984 Amnesty for all political party leaders announced. President Mitterrand of France paid a state visit.

1985 New constitution, with some civilians in the government, promised.

1986 General Kolingba re-elected.

1986-87 Bokassa tried and condemned to death.

Chad Republic of
area 1,284,000 sq km/495,753.5 sq mi

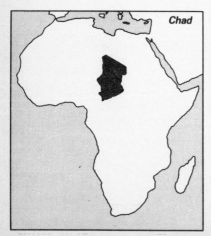
Chad

capital N'djamena

features Lake Chad, Sahara Desert

exports cotton; meat, livestock, hides and skins; there are resources of bauxite, uranium, gold, oil

currency CFA franc

population (1985) 5,036,000

language French (official); Arabic

religion Muslim (north); Christian, Animist (south)

government in 1982 Hissène Habré (1942–) became president, first head of a united country since 1965, and backed by Egypt, Sudan, and USA.

chronology

1960 Independence from France achieved, with François Tombalbaye as president.

1963 Violent opposition in the Muslim north, led by the Chadian National Liberation Front (Frolinat), backed by Libya.

1968 Revolt quelled with French help.

1975 Tombalbaye killed in coup led by army chief of staff, Felix Malloum, who appealed for national reconciliation. Frolinat continued its resistance.

1978 Malloum tried to find a political solution by bringing the former Frolinat leader, Hissène Habrè, into his government but they were unable to work together.

1979 Malloum forced to leave the country. An interim government (GUNT) was set up under the presidency of General Goukouni. Habré continued his opposition with his Army of the North (FAN).

1981 Habré was now in control of half the country, forcing Goukouni to flee to Cameroon and then Algeria, where, with Libyan support, he set up a 'government in exile'.

1983 Habré's regime recognized by OAU but in the north Goukouni's supporters, with Libyan help, fought on. Eventually a ceasefire was agreed, effectively dividing the country into two halves either side of latitude 1° north.

1984 Libya and France agreed a simultaneous withdrawal of forces.

1985 Fighting between Libyan-backed and French-backed forces intensified in what had become a divided nation.

Chile Republic of
area 741,765 sq km/286,400.5 sq mi
capital Santiago
towns Concepción, Vina del Mar, Temuco; ports are Valparaiso, Antofagasta, Arica, Iquique
features Andes mountains, Lake Titicaca, Atacama desert; includes Easter Island, Juan Fernandez Island, and half of Tierra del Fuego
exports copper, iron, nitrate (Chile is the chief mining country of S America); paper and pulp
currency peso
population (1985) 12,042,000 (the majority *mestizo*, of mixed American Indian and Spanish descent)
language Spanish
religion Roman Catholic
government under the 1980 constitution, Pinochet was to remain president for 10 years, the National Congress was dissolved, and all political parties were banned.

Chile

chronology
1964 Christian Democrats formed government under Eduardo Frei.
1970 Dr Salvador Allende became the first democratically elected Marxist president. He embarked on an extensive programme of nationalization and social reform.
1974 Government overthrown by the military, led by General Augusto Pinochet. Allende killed. Policy of repression began during which all opposition was put down and political activity banned.
1980 Constitution paving the way for democratic government by 1989 was announced.
1983 Growing opposition to the regime from all sides, with outbreaks of violence.
1987 Elections promised for 1990.

China People's Republic of. In Chinese: *Zhonghua Renmin Gonghe Guo.*
area 9,569,700 sq km/3,694,000.5 sq mi
capital Beijing (Peking)
towns Chongqing (Chungking), Shenyang (Mukden), Wuhan, Nanjing (Nanking), Harbin; ports Tianjin (Tientsin), Shanghai, Qingdao (Tsingtao), Lüda (Lü-ta), Guangzhou (Canton)
features rivers Huang He (Yellow River), Chang Jiang (Yangtze-Kiang), Xi Jiang (Si Kiang); Great Wall of China; Kongur Shan
exports tea; livestock and animal products; textiles (silk and cotton); oil, minerals (China is the world's largest producer of tungsten), chemicals; light industrial goods
currency yuang
population (1985) 1,037,588,000 (of whom the majority are Han (ethnic Chinese); the 67 million of other groups (including Tibetan, Uigur, and Zhuang) live in border areas). By 2000AD the population is estimated to be 2,000,000,000, hence the encouragement of late marriage and restriction of births (preferably to a single child) by penalties such as deduction of 'workpoints' (which affects the income of the couple's commune). There is also an Overseas Chinese community of some 24,000,000.
language Chinese
religion officially atheist, but traditionally Taoist, Confucianist, and Buddhist; Muslim 13,000,000; Catholic 3–6,000,000 (divided between the 'patriotic' church established 1958, and the 'loyal' church subject to Rome);

511

Protestant 3,000,000

government under the 1982 constitution there is a president (from 1983 Li Xiannnian 1905–1), and a national people's congress, both elected for five years. The latter chooses the prime minister (Zhao Ziyang) who heads a state council of ministers, appointed on his recommendation. Since 1980 there have been elected people's governments in the 29 provinces, autonomous regions, and special municipalities. Both central and local government is now freer from Communist Party control, though the Party (General Secretary Zhao Ziyang) remains powerful. Deng Xiao-ping continues to be influential in promoting a mixed economy: state, collective, and individual enterprise now being allowed. In 1984 an identity card system, for all over 16, was introduced, issued by the Minister of Public Security.

China

chronology
1949 People's Republic of China proclaimed by Mao Zedong.
1954 Soviet–style constitution adopted.
1956–7 Hundred Flowers Movement encouraged criticism of the government.
1958–60 Great Leap Forward commune

experiment to achieve 'true communism'.
1960 Withdrawal of Soviet technical advisors.
1962 Sino-Indian border war.
1962–65 Economic recovery programme under Liu Shaoqi; Maoist 'Socialist Education Movement' rectification campaign.
1966–68 Great Proletarian Cultural Revolution and overthrow of Liu Shaoqi.
1969 Ussuri river border clashes with Soviet Union.
1970–76 Reconstruction of party-state system under Mao and Zhou Enlai.
1971 Death of Lin Biao. Entry into United Nations.
1972 President Nixon visited Beijing.
1975 New state constitution. Unveiling of Zhou's 'Four Modernizations' programme.
1976 Death of Zhou Enlai and Mao Zedong, appointment of Hua Guofeng as prime minister and CCP chairman. Deng in hiding. 'Gang of Four' arrested.
1977 Rehabilitation of Deng Xiaoping.
1979 Economic reforms introduced. Diplomatic relations opened with United States. Punitive invasion of Vietnam.
1980 Zhao Ziyang appointed prime minister.
1981 Hu Yaobang succeeded Hua as CCP chairman. Imprisonment of 'Gang of Four'.
1982 New state constitution adopted.
1984 'Enterprise management' reforms for industrial sector.
1986 Student demonstrations for democracy.
1987 Dismissal of Hu Yaobang as CCP leader.

Colombia Republic of
area 1,139,000 sq km/456,500 sq mi
capital Bogotá
towns Medellin, Cali, Bucaramanga; ports are Barranquilla, Cartagena
features Andes mountains
exports emeralds (world's largest producer), coffee (2nd largest world producer), bananas, cotton, meat, sugar, oil, skins and hides
currency peso
population (1985) 29,347,000 (mainly of mixed Spanish-American Indian descent)
language Spanish
religion Roman Catholic
government executive president (Virilio Barco

Varges from 1986) and senate and house of representatives, directly elected for four years; conflict between the Liberal and Conservative parties was ended in 1957 by the formation of a National Front sharing power which successfully blocked the National Popular Alliance opposition. Colombia remains a democracy, though guerrilla activity and terrorism continue.

Colombia

chronology
1903 Full independence achieved. Conservatives in power.
1930 Liberals returned to power.
1946 Conservatives in power.
1948 Left-wing mayor of Bogotá assassinated. Widespread outcry.
1949 Start of near civil war, 'La Violencia', during which 280,000 people died.
1957 Hoping to halt the violence, Conservatives and Liberals agreed to form a National Front, sharing the presidency.
1970 National Popular Alliance (ANAPO) formed as a left-wing opposition to the National Front.
1974 National Front accord temporarily ended.
1975 Civil unrest because of disillusionment with the government.

1978 Liberals, under Julio Turbay, revived the accord and began an intensive fight against drug dealers.
1982 Liberals maintained their control of Congress but lost the presidency. The Conservative president, Belisario Betancur, attempted to end the violence by granting left-wing guerrillas an amnesty, freeing political prisoners and embarking on a large public works programme.
1984 Minister of Justice assassinated by, it was suspected, drug dealers. Campaign against them was stepped up.
1986 Liberal, Virgilio Barco Vargas elected president by a record margin.

Comoros Federal Islamic Republic of
area 2,170 sq km/838 sq mi
capital Moroni
features comprises islands of Grand Comore, Anjouan, Maheli.
exports copra, vanilla, cocoa, sisal, coffee, cloves, essential oils

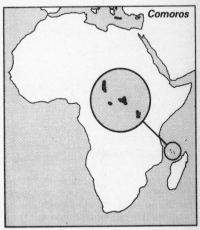

Comoros

currency CFA franc
population (1985) 469,000
language French, Arabic (official); Comorian (Swahili dialect)
religion Muslim (official)

513

government under the 1978 constitution an executive president (Ahmed Abdallah Abderemane), and a unicameral federal assembly.

chronology

1975 Independence achieved, but with Mayotte a reluctant member of the new federal state. Ahmed Abdallah elected president.

1976 Abdallah overthrown by Ali Soilih.

1978 Soilih killed by mercenaries working for Abdallah. Islamic republic proclaimed and Abdallah elected president.

1979 The Comoros became a one-party state. Powers of the federal government increased.

1984 Abdallah re-elected.

1985 Constitution amended to make Abdallah head of government as well as head of state.

Congo People's Republic of the

area 342,000 sq km/132,000 sq mi

capital Brazzaville

towns chief port Pointe Noire

features Zaïre (Congo) river on the border; half the country is rain forest

exports timber, potash, petroleum

currency CFA franc

population (1985) 1,798,000 (chiefly Bantu)

language French (official)

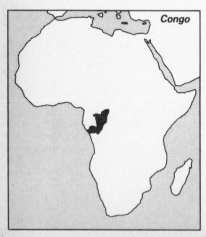

Congo

religion Animist 50%, Christian 48%

government under the 1979 constitution there is an executive president (Denis Sassou-Nguesso from 1979) and people's national assembly; since 1969 the Parti Congolais de Travail (PCT) has been the sole political party.

chronology

1960 Achieved full independence from France, with Abbe Youlou as the first president.

1963 Youlou forced to resign. New constitution approved, with Alphonse Massamba-Débat as president.

1964 The Congo became a one-party state.

1968 Military coup, led by Captain Marien Ngouabi, ousted Massamba-Débat.

1970 A Marxist state, the People's Republic of the Congo, was announced, with the Congolese Labour Party (PCT) as the only legal party.

1977 Ngouabi assassinated. Colonel Yhombi-Opango became president.

1979 Yhombi-Opango handed over the presidency to PCT, who chose Colonel Denis Sassou-Ngessou as his successor.

1984 Sassou-Ngessou elected for another five-year term.

Costa Rica Republic of

area 50,997 sq km/19,690 sq mi

capital San José

towns ports Limón, Puntarenas

features highest literacy rate in Latin America; there has been no standing army since the civil war of 1948–49

exports coffee, bananas, cocoa, sugar

currency colone

population (1985) 2,644,000 (including 1,200 Guaymi Indians)

language Spanish

religion Roman Catholic

government executive president (Oscar Arias Sanchez from 1986) elected for four years, and a legislative assembly.

chronology

1949 New constitution adopted. National army abolished. José Figueres, co-founder of the National Liberation Party (PLN) was elected president. He embarked on an ambitious socialist programme.

1953 Figueres re-elected.
1958–73 Mainly Conservative administrations returned.
1974 PLN regained the presidency and returned to socialist policies.
1978 Rodrigo Carazo, Conservative, elected president. Sharp deterioration in the state of the economy.

1982 Luis Alberto Monge of the PLN elected president. Harsh austerity programme introduced to rebuild the economy. Pressure from the United States to abandon its neutral stance and condemn the Sandinista regime in Nicaragua.
1983 Policy of neutrality reaffirmed.
1985 Following border clashes with Sandinista forces, a US-trained anti-guerrilla guard was formed.
1986 Oscar Arias Sanchez won the presidency on a neutralist platform.

  Cuba Republic of
area 114,524 sq km/44,200 sq mi
capital Havana
features largest of the West Indian islands; US base (on perpetual lease since 1934) at Guantánamo Bay (Gitmo), and Soviet base at Cienfuegos

exports sugar (largest producer after USSR), tobacco, coffee; iron, copper, nickel
currency Cuban peso
population (1985) 10,105,000 (plus 125,000 refugees from the Cuban port of Mariel, hence *marielitos* in USA); 66% are of Spanish descent, and a large number are of African origin
language Spanish
religion Roman Catholic 45%
government under the constitution of 1976 there is a an executive president (Fidel Castro) and council of ministers, and the Communist Party prevails.

chronology
1902 Cuba achieved independence.
1933 Fulgencia Batista seized power.
1944 Batista retired.
1952 Batista seized power again to begin an oppressive regime.
1953 Fidel Castro led an unsuccessful coup against Batista.
1956 Castro led a second unsuccessful coup.
1959 Batista overthrown by Castro. 1940 constitution replaced by a 'Fundamental Law', making Castro prime minister, his brother, Raul, his deputy and Che Guevara his No.3.
1960 All US businesses in Cuba appropriated

515

without compensation.

1961 US broke off diplomatic relations and sponsored an unsuccessful invasion, the 'Bay of Pigs' episode. Castro announced that Cuba had become a communist state, with a Marxist-Leninist programme of economic development.

1962 Cuba expelled from the Organization of American States (OAS). Soviet atomic missiles removed from Cuba at US insistence.

1965 Cuba's sole political party renamed Cuban Communist Party (PCC). With USSR help, Cuba began to make considerable economic and social progress.

1972 Cuba became a full member of the Moscow-based Council for Mutual Economic Assistance (CMEA).

1976 New socialist constitution approved and Castro elected president.

1976–81 Castro became involved in extensive international commitments, assisting Third World countries, particularly in Africa.

1982 Cuba joined other Latin American countries in giving moral support to Argentina in its dispute with Britain.

1983 Castro criticized the US invasion of Grenada.

1984 Castro tried to improve US-Cuban relations by discussing the exchange of US prisoners in Cuba with Cuban 'undesirables' in the US.

Cyprus Mediterranean island, divided between the southern Republic of Cyprus (Greek *Kypros*), and the Turkish Republic of Northern Cyprus (Turkish *Kibris*).

area 9,251 sq km/3,572 sq mi, 40% in Turkish hands

capital Nicosia (divided between the Greeks and Turks)

towns ports of Paphos, Limassol, and Larnaca (Greek); and Morphou, and ports Kyrenia and Famagusta (Turkish)

features Attila Line; two British military enclaves on the S coast. at Episkopi (which includes RAF Akrotiri) and Dhekelia

exports citrus, grapes, Cyprus sherry, potatoes; copper, pyrites

currency Cyprus pound

population (1985) 665,600 (Greek Cypriot 80%, Turkish Cypriot 20%)

language Greek and Turkish (official); English

religion Greek Orthodox, Sunni Muslim

government **Greek** president (Spyros Kyprianou from 1977; re-elected 1983) and house of representatives, *Turkish* president (Rauf Denktash from 1976) and legislative assembly.

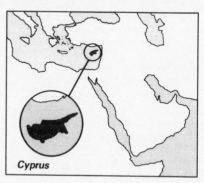

Cyprus

chronology

1955 Guerrilla campaign for *enosis*, or union with Greece, started by Archbishop Makarios and General Grivas.

1956 Makarios and enosis leaders deported.

1959 Compromise agreed and Makarios returned to be elected president of an independent Greek-Turkish Cyprus.

1960 Full independence achieved, with Britain retaining its military bases.

1963 Turks set up their own government in northern Cyprus. Fighting broke out between the two communities. UN peacekeeping force installed.

1971 Grivas returned to start a guerrilla war against the Makarios government.

1974 Grivas died.

1975 A military coup deposed Makarios, who fled to Britain. Nicos Sampson appointed president. Turkish army sent to northern Cyprus to confirm the Turkish Cypriots' control. The military regime in southern Cyprus collapsed and Makarios returned. Northern Cyprus declared itself the Turkish Federated State of Cyprus (TFSC), with Rauf Denktas as president.

1977 Makarios died and was succeeded by Spyros Kyprianou.

1981 UN sponsored peace talks failed.

1983 An independent Turkish Republic of Northern Cyprus (TRNC) was proclaimed but was recognized only by Turkey.

1984 Further UN peace proposals rejected.

1985 Summit meeting between Kyprianou and Denktas failed to reach agreement.

Czechoslovakia Solialist Rupublic of
area 127,895 sq km/49,381 sq mi
capital Prague
towns Brno, Bratislava, Ostrava

Czechoslovakia

features Carpathian Mountains, rivers Morava, Labe (Elbe), Vltava (Moldau); divided by valley of the Morava into the western densely populated area with good communications, and the eastern sparsely populated, comparatively little-developed Slovak area
exports machinery, timber, ceramics, glass, textiles
currency koruna
population (1985) 15,502,000 (60% Czech, 30% Slovak, with Hungarian, Polish, German, Russian, and other minorities)
language Czech and Slovak (official)

religion Roman Catholic with Protestant minority
government president (from 1975 Gustav (Husak) and a federal assembly comprising a chamber of the people (two to one Czech majority) and chamber of the nations (half Czech half Slovak)
chronology
1945 Liberation of Czechoslakia.
1948 Communists assumed power in coup and new constitution framed.
1968 'Prague Spring' experiment with liberalization ended by Soviet invasion
1969 Czechoslovakia became a federal state. Husak elected CCP leader.
1977 Emergence and suppression of 'Charter 77' human rights movement.
1985-86 Criticism of Husak rule by new Soviet leadership

Denmark Kingdom of
area 43,075 sq km/16,631 sq mi
capital Copenhagen
towns Åarhus, Odense, Åalborg, Esbjerg, all ports

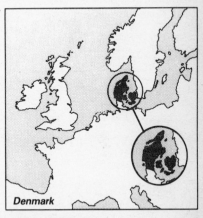
Denmark

features comprises the peninsula of Jylland/Jutland, plus the islands of Sjaelland, Fünen, Lolland, Bornholm, etc.; there are sand dunes and lagoons on the W coast and long inlets on the E

exports bacon, dairy produce, eggs, fish, mink pelts; car and aircraft parts, electrical equipment, textiles

currency krone

population (1985) 5,105,000

language Danish (official)

religion Lutheran

government constitutional monarchy (Queen Margrethe II from 1972), with a unicameral Folketing (parliament) elected by proportional representation. The Social Democrats are the largest party: prime minister Poul Schlter, coalition, from 1982.

chronology

1940–45 Occupied by Germany.

1945 Iceland's independence recognized.

1947 Frederik IX succeeded Christian X.

1948 Home rule granted for Faeroe Islands.

1949 Became a founder member of NATO.

1953 Major revision of the constitution.

1960 Joined EFTA.

1972 Margrethe II became Denmark's first queen for nearly 600 years.

1973 Left EFTA and joined EEC.

1979 Home rule granted for Greenland.

1985 Strong non-nuclear movement in evidence.

Djibouti Republic of

area 23,000 sq km/8,880 5 sq mi

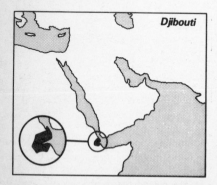

capital and chief port Djibouti; population 150,000

exports acts mainly as a transit port for Ethiopia

currency Djibouti franc

population (1985) 297,000 (Issa 40%, Afar 35%, Arab 25%)

language Somali, Afar, French, Arabic

religion Sunni Muslim

government president (Hassan Gouled Aptidon from 1977) plus a chamber of deputies.

chronology

1977 Full independence achieved. Hassan Gouled elected president.

1979 All political parties combined to form the People's Progress Assembly (RPP).

1981 New constitution made RPP the only legal party. Gouled re-elected. Treaties of friendship signed with Ethiopia, Somalia, Kenya, and Sudan.

1984 Policy of neutrality reaffirmed.

Dominica Commonwealth of

area 750 sq km/290sq mi

capital Roseau, with a deepwater port

features largest of the Windward Islands; of great beauty, it has mountains of volcanic origin rising to 1,620 m/5,315 ft

exports bananas, coconuts, citrus, lime and bay oil

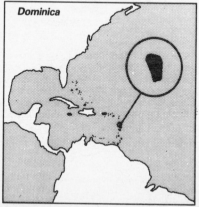

currency East Caribbean dollar, pound sterling, French franc

population (1984) 74,000 (mainly black African

in origin, but with a small Carib reserve of c.500)

language English (official), but the Dominican *patois* still reflects earlier periods of French rule

religion Roman Catholic 80%

government non-executive president, with a part-elected, part-nominated house of assembly (prime minister from 1980 Eugenia Charles, Freedom Party, re-elected 1985)

chronology

1978 Dominica achieved full independence within the Commonwealth. Patrick John, leader of the Dominica Labour Party (DLP), elected prime minister.

1980 Dominica Freedom Party (FDP), led by Eugenia Charles, won a convincing victory in the general election.

1981 Patrick John was implicated in a plot to overthrow the government.

1982 John tried and acquitted.

1985 John retried and found guilty. Regroupinng of left-of-centre parties resulted in the new Labour Party of Dominica (LPD). DFP, led by Eugenia Charles, re-elected.

Dominican Republic

area 48,430 sq km/18,700 sq mi

Dominican Republic

capital Santo Domingo

features Pico Duarte 3,174 m/10,417 ft, highest point in the Caribbean islands

exports sugar, gold, coffee, ferro-nickel

currency peso

population (1985) 6,614,000

language Spanish (official)

areligion Roman Catholic

government under the constitution of 1966, there is an executive president (Joaquín Balaguer from 1986), senate and house of representatives.

chronology

1930 Military coup established the dictatorship of Rafael Trujillo.

1961 Trujillo assassinated.

1962 First democratic elections resulted in Juan Bosch, founder of the Dominican Revolutionary Party (PRD) becoming president.

1963 Bosch overthrown in military coup.

1966 New constitution adopted. Joaquín Balaguer, leader of the Christian Social Reform Party (PRSC) became president.

1970 Balaguer re-elected.

1974 Balaguer re-elected.

1978 PRD returned to power, with Silvestre Antonio Guzmán as president.

1982 PRD re-elected, with Jorge Blanco as president.

1985 Blanco forced by IMF to adopt austerity measures to save the economy.

1986 PRSC returned to power, with Joaquín Balaguer re-elected president.

Ecuador Republic of

area 301,150 sq km/116,270 5 sq mi

capital Quito

towns Cuenca; chief port Guayaquil

features Andes mountains, which are divided by a central plateau, or Valley of the Volcanoes, including Chimborazo, and Cotopaxi, which has a large share of the cultivable land and is the site of the capital; untouched rainforest of the Amazon basin with a wealth of wild life; Ecuador is crossed by the Equator, from which it derives its name; Galapagos Islands

exports bananas, cocoa, coffee, sugar, rice, balsa wood, fish

currency sucre

population (1985) 9,378,000

language Spanish (official); Quechuan, Jivaroan
religion Roman Catholic
government under the 1979 constitution, there is a president (Léon Febres Cordero from 1984; right-wing Social Christian Party (PSC)), and single-chamber elected congress.
chronology
1830 Ecuador became an independent republic.
1930–48 Great political instability.

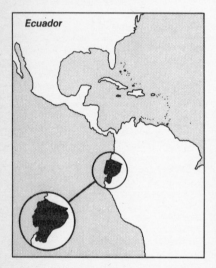

Ecuador

1948–55 Liberals in power.
1956 First Conservative president for 60 years.
1960 Liberals returned, with José Velasco as president.
1961 Velasco deposed and replaced by the vice-president.
1963 Military junta installed.
1968 Velasco returned as president.
1972 A coup put the military back in power.
1978 New democratic constitution adopted.
1979 Liberals in power but opposed by right-and left-wing parties.
1982 Deteriorating economy provoked strikes, demonstrations and a state of emergency.

1983 Austerity measures introduced.
1985 No party with a clear majority in the national congress. Febres Cordero narrowly won the presidency for the Conservatives.

Egypt Arab Republic of
area 1,000,000 sq km/386,198 sq mi
capital Cairo
towns Gîza; ports Alexandria, Port Said
features River Nile; Aswan High Dam and Lake Nasser; Sinai; remains of Ancient Egypt (Pyramids, Sphinx, Luxor, Karnak, Abu Simbel, El Faiyum)
exports cotton and textiles
currency Egyptian pound
population (1985) 49,000,000
language *ancient* survives to some extent in Coptic, used in the rituals of the Coptic Church, and written in a modified Greek alphabet; *modern* Arabic

Egypt

religion *ancient* owing to development from local deities, a consistent theology was never developed, but beliefs were less primitive than animal-headed gods suggest (they were often emblematic, in the same way that Christ is represented as a lamb), and there was also the concept of a single deity; *modern* Sunni Muslim 95%; Coptic Christian 5%

government under the constitution of 1971, Egypt is a ' democratic socialist state', with an executive president (Hosni Mubarak from 1981), nominated by a popularly elected people's assembly and confirmed by plebiscite for a six-year term.

chronology
1914 Egypt became a British protectorate.
1936 Independence recognized. King Fuad succeeded by his son, Farouk.
1946 Withdrawal of British troops except from Suez Canal Zone.
1952 Farouk overthrown by the army in a bloodless coup.
1953 Egypt declared a republic, with General Neguib as president.
1956 Neguib replaced by Colonel Gamal Nasser. Nasser announced nationalization of Suez Canal; Egypt attacked by Britain, France and Israel. Ceasefire agreed because of US intervention.
1958 Short-lived merger of Egypt and Syria as United Arab Republic (UAR). Subsequent attempts to federate Egypt, Syria and Iraq failed.
1967 Six Days War with Israel ended in Egypt's defeat and Israeli occupation of Sinai and the Gaza Strip.
1970 Nasser died suddenly and was succeeded by Anwar Sadat.
1973 Attempt to regain territory lost to Israel led to fighting and a subsequent ceasefire was arranged by US Secretary of State, Henry Kissinger.
1977 Dramatic visit by Sadat to Israel to address the Israeli parliament was criticized by Egypt's Arab neighbours.
1978 Camp David talks in the United States resulted in a treaty between Egypt and Israel. Egypt expelled from the Arab League.
1981 Sadat assassinated and succeeded by Hosni Mubarak.
1983 Relations between Egypt and the Arab world showed signs of improvement, with only Libya and Syria maintaining a trade boycott.
1984 Mubarak's party won an overwhelming victory in the people's assembly elections.

El Salvador Republic of

area 21,393 sq km/8,236 sq mi
capital San Salvador
features smallest and most thickly populated Central American country
exports coffee, cotton
currency colón
population (1985) 4,981,000 (mainly of Spanish-Indian extraction, including some 500,000 illegally in the USA)
language Spanish
religion Roman Catholic

El Salvador

government executive president (José Napoleón Duarte 1980–82, and from 1984; Christian Democrat) and legislative assembly.
chronology
1961 The Conservative Party (PCN) won an overwhelming victory in the national assembly.
1972 Allegations of human rights violations and growth of left-wing guerrilla activities. PCN candidate, General Carlos Romero, elected president.
1979 A coup replaced Romero with a military-civilian junta.
1980 Archbishop Oscar Romero assassinated. Country on verge of civil war.
1981 The Mexican and French governments recognized the guerrillas as a legitimate politi-

521

cal force but the USA actively assisted the government in its battle against them.
1982 Assembly elections boycotted by left-wing parties and held amid considerable violence.
1983 New constitution adopted.
1984 Presidential election won by the Christian Democrat (PDC) candidate, José Duarte.
1985 PDC won a convincing majority in the national assembly.
1986 Duarte sought a negotiated settlement with the guerrillas.

Equatorial Guinea Republic of
area 28,100 sq km/10,852 sq mi
capital Malabo
features comprises mainland Rio Muni, plus the small islands of Corisco, Elobey Grande and Elobey Chico, and Bioko Island (formerly Fernando Po) together with Pagalu Island (formerly Annobon).
exports cocoa, coffee, bananas, timber
currency ekuele
population (1985) 350,000

religion nominally Christian, mainly Catholic, but in 1978 Roman Catholicism was banned
government executive president (Lieutenant Colonel Teodoro Obiang Nguema Mbasogo from 1979, confirmed in office for seven years from 1982) with cabinet and national assembly.
chronology
1968 Achieved full independence from Spain. Francisco Macias Nguema became first president, soon assuming dictatorial powers.
1979 Macias overthrown aand replaced by his nephew, Teodoro Obiang Nguema Mbasogo, who established a military regime. Macias tried and executed.
1982 Obiang elected president for another seven years. New constitution, promising a return to civilian government, adopted.

Ethiopia Republic of (formerly also known as *Abyssinia*)
area 1,000,000 sq km/395,000 sq mi
capital Addis Ababa
towns Asmara (capital of Eritrea), Dire Dawa; ports are Massawa, Assab

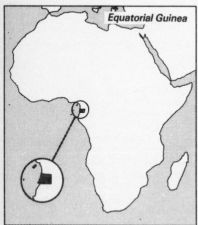

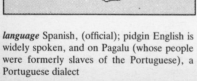

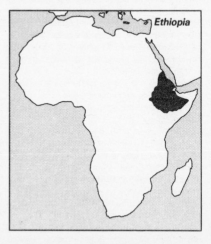

language Spanish, (official); pidgin English is widely spoken, and on Pagalu (whose people were formerly slaves of the Portuguese), a Portuguese dialect

features Danakil and Ogaden deserts, Blue Nile; ancient remains at Aksum, Gondar, Lalibela among other places; only African country to retain its independence during the

colonial period
exports coffee, pulses, oilseeds, hides and skins
currency birr
population (1985) 42,266,418 (Oromo 40%, Amhara 25%, Tigre 12%, Sidama 9%)
language Amharic (official); Tigre, Galla, Arabic
religion Christian (Ethiopian Orthodox Church, which has had its own patriarch since 1976) 50%, Sunni Muslim 50%
government Unitary Socialist one-party state, with a Provisional Military Administrative Council (The Derg) established 1974 (chairman Lieutenant Colonel Mengistu Haile Mariam).
chronology
1974 Haile Selassi deposed and replaced by a military government led by General Teferi Benti. Ethiopia declared a socialist state.
1977 Teferi Benti killed and replaced by Colonel Mengistu Haile Mariam.
1984 The Workers' Party of Ethiopia (WPE) declared the only legal party.
1986 Country in the throes of worst famine for more than a decade. Western aid sent and internal resettlement programmes undertaken. Draft of new constitution for the People's Democratic Republic of Ethiopia published.

Fiji
area 18,272 sq km/7,055 sq mi
capital Suva on Viti Levu
features comprises some 800 islands (about 100 inhabited), the largest being Viti Levu (10,386 sq km/400 sq mi) and Vanua Levu (5,535 sq km/2,137 sq mi); Nadi airport is an international Pacific staging place
exports sugar, coconut oil, ginger, timber, canned fish; tourism is important
currency Fiji dollar
population (1985) 700,000 (44% Fijian, holding 80% of the land communally, and 50% Indians introduced in the 19th century to work the sugar crop)
language English, (official); Fijian, Hindi
religion Hindu 50%; Methodist 44%
government there is a senate and house of representatives, headed by a prime minister,

and a governor-general who represents Queen Elizabeth II of Britain

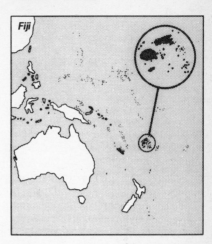

chronology
1970 Full independence achieved. Ratu Sir Kamisese Mara elected as first prime minister.
1977 Alliance Party formed a coalition in a hung parliament and then won an inconclusive majority.
1982 Alliance Party returned to power.
1987 Dr Bauvadra (Fijian Labour Party) elected prime minister of coalition government. He was deposed by a military coup (14 May) led by Lieutenant-Colonel Sitiveni Rabuka.

Finland Republic of
area 337,050 sq km/130,125 5 sq mi
capital Helsinki
towns Tampere, and the port of Turku
features one third is within the Arctic Circle; Saimaa Canal; it includes the Åland Islands
exports metal, chemical and engineering products (icebreakers and oil rigs); paper, timber, and textiles; fine ceramics, glass, and furniture
currency Finnish mark
population (1985) 4,908,000
language Finnish, Swedish, (official); Lapp
religion Lutheran 90%
government executive elected president

(Mauno Koivisto from 1982) and unicameral parliament (Prime Minister Kalev Sorsa from 1982, Social Democratic Party, SDP)

Finland

chronology
1917 Independence declared.
1939 Defeated by USSR in 'Winter War'.
1941 Joined Hitler in invasion of USSR.
1944 Concluded separate armistice with Allies.
1948 Finno-Soviet Pact of Friendship, Co-operation and Mutual assistance signed.
1977 Trade treaty with EEC signed. Trade agreement with USSR signed.

France Republic of
area (including Corsica) 551,553 sq km/212,960 sq mi
capital Paris
towns Lyon, Lille, Bordeaux, Toulouse, Nantes, Strasbourg; ports are Marseille and Nice
features rivers Seine, Loire, Garonne, Rhône, Rhine; mountain ranges Alps, Massif Central, Pyrenees, Jura, Vosges, Cévennes Vosges; Ardennes, Auvergne, Dordogne, Riviera
exports fruit (especially apples), wine, cheese; cars, aircraft, chemicals, jewellery, silk, lace; tourism is very important
currency franc
population (1985) 55,166,000 (including 4,500,000 immigrants, chiefly from Portugal, Algeria, Morocco and Tunisia; immigration policy was tightened from 1974)
language French (regional languages include Breton)
religion mainly Roman Catholic (not recognized by State); Muslim 2,000,000; Protestant 750,000
government under the Fifth Republic there is an executive president (François Mitterrand from 1981) elected for seven years, who presides over the Council of Ministers and appoints the prime minister (from 1986 Jacques Chirac 1932–1). There is also a senate (indirectly elected) and a directly elected national assembly (five-year term). The chief parties are: Socialist (Mitterrand); Rassemblement pour la République (RPR neo-Gaullist, Chirac); Union pour la Démocratie Française (UDF Giscardian); National Front (rightist, Jean-Marie Le Pen); Communist (Marais). The right-wing victory in the general election of 1986 led for the first time to a combination of Socialist president and neo-Gaullist prime minister.

In local government there has been devolution under Mitterrand, and the 22 *régions* have from 1984 directly elected councils headed by a president (with the powers of a former regional prefect); each of the 96 *départements* in turn has an elected general council with a president who has taken over most of the powers of the former prefect, the latter (renamed 'commissioner of the republic') now deals only with public order; the departments are subdivided into *communes* with a municipal elected council headed by a mayor.

chronology
1944–46 De Gaulle provisional government.
1946 Commencement of Fourth Republic.
1954 Independence granted to Indochina.
1956 Moroccan and Tunisian independence.
1957 Entry into EEC.
1958 Recall of De Gaulle following 'Algeria crisis'. Constitution approved for Fifth Republic.
1962 Algerian independence granted.
1966 French withdrawal from NATO military command.

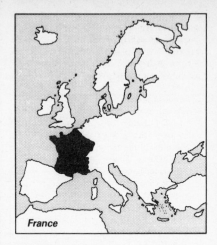

France

Léon Mba became the first president.
1964 Attempted coup by rival party foiled with French help. Mba died and was succeeded by his protégé, Albert-Bernard Bongo.

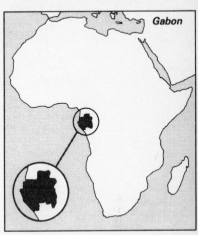

Gabon

1968 'May events' crisis.
1969 De Gaulle resigned following referendum defeat. Pompidou became president.
1974 Giscard elected president.
1981 Mitterrand elected Fifth Republic's first Socialist president.
1983–84 Economic policy U-turn.
1986 'Right coalition' Assembly victory. Co-habitation experiment, Socialist president and right-wing prime minister.

Gabon Republic of.
area 266,700 sq km/103,000.5 sq mi
capital Libreville
features Gabon river; Schweitzer hospital at Lambaréné
exports petroleum; manganese, iron, uranium; timber
currency CFA franc
population (1985) 988,000
language French (official); Bantu
religion Animist 60%; Roman Catholic 35%; small Muslim minority
government executive president (Omar Bongo from 1976), and unicameral national assembly; the Democratic Party is the only party allowed.
chronology
1960 Independence from France achieved.

1968 One-party state established.
1973 Bongo re-elected; converted to Islam, he changed his first name to Omar.
1979 Bongo re-elected.
1986 Bongo re-elected..

Gambia Republic of the
area 11,000 sq km/4,000 sq mi
capital Banjul
features Gambia river; the republic is surrounded on three sides by Senegal, and is the smallest state in Black Africa
exports groundnuts, palm oil, fish
currency dalasi
population (1985) 751,000
language English (official)
religion Muslim 70%, with Animist and Christian minorities
government executive president (Sir Dawda Jawara from 1970) elected for five years, and house of representatives
chronology
1965 Achieved independence as a constitutional monarchy within the Commonwealth,

525

with Dawda K Jawara as prime minister.
1970 Declared itself a republic, with Jawara as president.

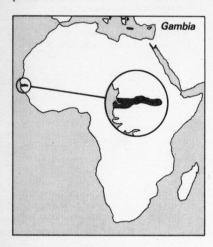

Gambia

1972 Jawara re-elected.
1977 Jawara re-elected.
1981 Attempted coup foiled with the help of Senegal. Plans announced for a merger with Senegal.
1987 Jawara re-elected

Germany (East) German Democratic Republic
area 108,180 sq km/41,768 sq mi
capital East Berlin
towns Leipzig, Dresden, Karl-Marx-Stadt, Magdeburg; chief port Rostock
features Harz mountains, Erzgebirge, Fichtelgebirge, Thüringer Wald; rivers Elbe, Oder and Neisse; many lakes, including Müritz
exports lignite; rare minerals (uranium, cobalt for example); coal, iron, and steel; fertilizers; plastics
currency GDR Mark
population (1985) 16,686,000
language German
religion Protestant 80%; Catholic 11%
government under the 1968 constitution there is a chairman (Erich Honecker from 1976) of the council of state, the latter being elected by the

elected people's chamber of 500 deputies. The Socialist Unity Party (SUP) or Communist Party is the only party permitted. For local government, to obliterate old associations, the country is divided into 14 *Bezirke* (districts), named after their chief towns.

East Germany

chronology
1949 The German Democratic Republic established as an independent state.
1953 Riots in East Berlin suppressed by Soviet troops.
1961 The Berlin Wall erected to stem flow of refugees.
1964 Treaty of Friendship annd Mutual Assistance signed with Soviet Union.
1971 Erich Honecker elected Socialist Unity Party leader.
1973 Basic Treaty ratified, normalizing relations with Federal Republic.
1975 Friendship Treaty with Soviet Union renewed for 25 years.

Germany (West) Federal Republic of
area 248,651.5 sq km/95,984 sq mi
capital Bonn
towns West Berlin, Cologne, Munich, Essen, Frankfurt-am-Main, Dortmund, Düsseldorf; ports Hamburg, Kiel, Cuxhaven, Bremerhaven
features rivers Rhine, Weser, Elbe, Danube;

Black Forest, Alps

exports machine tools (world's leading exporter); cars and commercial vehicles, electronics, industrial goods, textiles, chemicals, iron and steel; wine

currency Deutsche Mark (DM)

population (1985) 60,950,000 (including 4,400,000 'guest workers' (*Gastarbeiter*), of whom 1,600,000 are Turks; the rest are Yugoslavs, Italians, Greeks, Spanish, and Portuguese

language German

religion Protestant 49%; Roman Catholic 47%

government under the constitution of 1949, there is a non-executive federal president (Richard von Weizsächer from 1984), and a parliament of two houses, the upper (*Bundesrat*) consists of delegates from the states (*Länder*) into which West Germany is subdivided, and the lower (*Bundestag*), the cabinet being headed by the federal chancellor (Helmut Kohl from 1982).

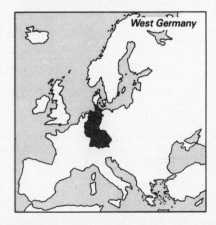

West Germany

chronology

1945 German surrender and division into four (American, French, British, Russian) occupation zones.

1948 Berlin crisis.

1949 Establishment of Federal Republic under the 'Basic Law' Constitution with Adenauer as chancellor.

1954 Grant of full sovereignty.

1957 Entry into EEC. Recovery of Saarland.

1959 SPD's Bad Godesberg conference.

1961 Construction of Berlin Wall.

1963 Retirement of Chancellor Adenauer.

1969 SPD gained power under Brandt.

1972 Basic Treaty with East Germany.

1974 Resignation of Brandt.

1982 Withdrawal of FDP from federal coalition. Kohl new chancellor.

Ghana Republic of

area 238,537 sq km/92,100 sq mi

capital Accra

towns Kumasi, and ports Sekondi-Takoradi, Tema

features river Volta; traditional kingdom of Ashanti

exports cocoa, coffee, timber; gold, diamonds, manganese and bauxite

currency cedi

population (1985) 13,004,000

language English (official)

religion Christian 43%; Animist 38%; Muslim 12%

government under the constitution of 1979, a president elected for a four-year term (Head of State Flight Lieutenant Jerry Rawlings since 1982), a council of state, and a parliament forbidden to introduce a one-party regime.

chronology

1957 Independence achieved, within the Commonwealth, with Kwame Nkrumah as president.

1960 Ghana became a republic and a one-party state.

1966 Nkrumah deposed and replaced by General Joseph Ankrah.

1969 Ankrah replaced by Akwasi Afrifa who initiated a return to civilian government.

1972 Another coup placed General Acheampong at the head of a military government.

1978 Acheampong deposed in a bloodless coup led by Frederick Akuffo.

1979 Another coup by junior officers put Flight Lieutenant Jerry Rawlings in power.

1980 Return to civilian rule.

1981 Rawlings seized power again, complaining

about the incompetence of previous governments.

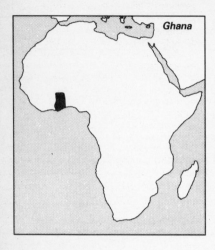

Ghana

Greece (Hellenic Republic)
area 131,944 sq km/50,944 sq mi
capital Athens
towns Thessaloniki, Patras, Larisa, Heraklion – all are ports
features include a large number of islands, notably Crete, Corfu and Rhodes; Corinth canal; Mount Olympus; archaeological sites; there are US military bases at Hellenikon, Nea Makri (both near Athens), and (on Crete) at Souda Bay near Iraklion
exports tobacco, fruit (including currants) and vegetables, olives and olive oil, textiles
currency drachma
population (1985) 9,921,000
language Greek
religion Greek Orthodox Christian 97%
government under the constitution of 1975 there is a president (Christos Sartzetakis from 1985), elected by a unicameral parliament (prime minister from 1981 Andreas Papandreou, Panhellenic Socialist Movement (PASOK; opposition leader Constantine Mit-

528

sotakis, New Democracy Party). Under Papandreou a programme of devolution from the ministries to the nomarchs (equivalent of the French prefects) and local councils of the nomoi (regions) was begun, and he planned removal of presidential checks on the government's executive power.

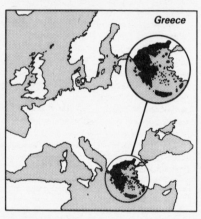

Greece

chronology
1946 Civil war broke out between royalists and communists. Communists defeated.
1949 Monarchy re-established with Paul as king.
1964 King Paul succeeded by his son, Constantine.
1967 Army coup removed the king and Colonel George Papadopoulos became prime minister.
1973 Republic proclaimed, with Papadopoulos as president.
1974 Constantine Karamanlis recalled to lead a government of National Salvation. New Democracy Party (ND), won a decisive general election victory. Restoration of the monarchy rejected by a referendum.
1975 New constitution adopted, making Greece a republic.
1977 ND re-elected.
1980 Karamanlis resigned as prime minister and was elected president.
1981 Greece became a full member of the EEC.

Panhellenic Socialist Movement (PASOK) won the general election, making Andreas Papandreou Greece's first Socialist prime minister.

1983 Five–year defence and economic cooperation agreement signed with the USA. ten–year economic cooperation agreement signed with USSR.

1985 PASOK re-elected.

Grenada southernmost of the Windward Islands.

area (including the Grenadines, notably Carriacou) 344.5 sq km/133 sq mi

capital St George's

features smallest independent nation in the western hemisphere

exports cocoa, nutmeg, bananas, mace

currency East Caribbean dollar

population (1984) 113,000

language English

religion Roman Catholic

government governor-general and 15–member parliament (prime minister from 1984 Herbert Blaize 1918–   of the New National Party).

Grenada

chronology

1974 Full independence achieved, with Eric Gairy elected prime minister.

1979 Gairy was removed in a bloodless coup led by Maurice Bishop. Constitution suspended

and a People's Revolutionary Government (PRG) established.

1982 Relations with the US and Britain deteriorated as ties with Cuba and USSR strengthened. Reported fears of a US invasion were strongly discounted.

1983 After Bishop's attempt to improve relations with the US, he was overthrown by left-wing opponents. A coup established a Revolutionary Military Council (RMC) and Bishop and some of his colleagues were executed. The US, accompanied by troops from some other Eastern Caribbean countries, invaded Grenada, overthrowing the RMC. The 1974 constitution was reinstated.

1984 The newly-formed New National Party (NNP) won 14 of the 15 seats in the house of representatives and its leader, Herbert Blaize, became prime minister.

Guatemala Republic of

area 108,889 sq km/42,042 sq mi

capital Guatemala City

towns Quezaltenango, Puerto Barrios (naval base)

features earthquakes are frequent

exports coffee, bananas, cotton

currency quetzal

population (1985) 8,346,000 (American Indians 54%, *mestizos*, of mixed American Indian and Spanish descent, 42%)

language Spanish

religion Roman Catholic

government single-chamber national assembly, directly elected for a five-year term. Head of state and head of government from 1986 Mario Vinicio Cerezo, of the Christian Democratic Party.

chronology

1954 Colonel Carlos Castillo became president, following a US-backed coup.

1957 Castillo assassinated and succeeded by General Miguel Ydígoras.

1963 Military coup made Colonel Enrique Peralta president.

1965 New constitution adopted.

1966 Cesar Méndez elected president.

1970 National Liberation Movement (MLN) candidate, Carlos Araña, elected president.

1974 General Kjell Laugerud (MLN) became president. Widespread political violence.
1978 General Fernando Romeo became president.

1981 Growth of anti-government guerrilla movement.
1982 General Angel Anibal became president. An army coup installed General Ríos Montt as head of a junta and then as president. Political violence continued.
1983 Montt removed in a coup led by General Mejía Victores.
1985 New constitution adopted. Guatemalian Christian Democratic Party (PDCG) won the Congressional elections, with Vinicio Cerezo elected president.

Guinea Republic of
area 245,860 sq km/95,000 sq mi
capital Conakry
towns Labe, N'Zerekore, Kankan
features Fouta Djallon, area of sandstone plateaux, cut by deep valleys
exports coffee, rice, palm kernels; alumina, bauxite, diamonds
currency sily
population (1985) 5,597,000 (chief peoples being Fulani 40%, Mandingo 25%)
language French (official)
religion Muslim 62%; Christian 15%; tribal

35%
government president (Brigadier-General Lansana Conté from 1984) heading a collectively responsible committee of the armed forces.

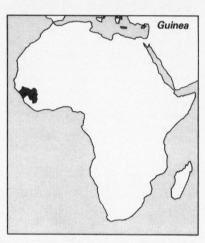

French colony from 1888, Guinea became independent in 1958, with Ahmed Sékou Touré 1922–84 as absolute president 1958–84. On his death, the armed forces denounced his 'bloody and ruthless dictatorship', and themselves assumed control. The national assembly and the one permitted political party were dissolved.
chronology
1958 Full independence from France achieved. Sékou Touré elected president.
1977 Strong opposition to Touré's policies of rigid Marxism forced him to accept the return of a mixed economy.
1980 Touré returned unopposed for a fourth seven-year term of office.
1982 New constitution adopted.
1984 Touré died. A bloodless coup established a military committee for national recovery, with Brigadier-General Lansana Conté at its head.
1985 Attempted coup against Conté foiled.

Guinea-Bissau
area 36,125 sq km/14,000 sq mi
capital and chief port Bissau
features include the archipelago of Bijagos
exports rice, coconuts, peanuts; fish; salt
currency peso
population (1985) 860,000
language Crioulo, Cape Verdean dialect of Portuguese
religion Muslim 40%; Christian 4%
government executive head of state (Major João Vieira from 1980) with a council of state, national people's assembly and eight regional councils. The African Party for the Independence of Guinea and Cape Verde (PAIGC) is the only political party.

- Guinea-Bissau

chronology
1956 African Party for the Independence of Guinea and Cape Verde (PAIGC) formed to secure independence from Portugal.
1973 Two-thirds of the country declared independent, with Luis Cabral as president of a state council.
1974 Portugal recognized independence of Guinea-Bissau.
1980 Cape Verde decided not to join a unified state. Cabral deposed amd João Vieira became chairman of a council of revolution.
1981 PAIGC confirmed as the only legal party, with Vieira as its secretary-general.
1982 Normal relations with Cape Verde restored.
1984 New constitution adopted, making Vieira head of government as well as head of state.

Guyana Co-operative Republic of
area 210,000 sq km/83,000 sq mi
capital and port Georgetown
features Mount Roraima; Kaietur National Park including Kaietur Fall on the Potaro (tributary of Essequibo) 250 m/ 822 ft (five times height of Niagara)
exports sugar, rice, rum, timber, diamonds
currency Guyana dollar

Guyana

population (1985) 768,000 50% E Indians (introduced to work the sugar plantations after the abolition of slavery), 30% Negro; 5% Amerindian
language English (official); Hindi
religion Christian 57%; Hindu 33%; Sunni Muslim 9%
government executive president Desmond Hoyte from 1985, and national assembly elected for five years by proportional representation. Divisions are racial; the People's National Congress (PNC) black people; People's Progressive Party (PPP), led by Cheddi Jagan, E Indian.
chronology

1953 Assembly elections won by the People's Progressive Party (PPP), supported mainly by Indian descendants

1961 Internal self-government granted.

1966 Full independence achieved.

1970 Guyana became a republic within the Commonwealth.

1980 New constitution adopted, making the president both head of government and head of state. Forbes Burnham, PNC leader, became the first executive president.

1985 Burnham died and was succeeded by PNC colleague, Desmond Hoyte.

Haiti Republic of (French *Haïti*)

area 27,740 sq km/10,710 sq mi

capital Port-au-Prince

features only French-speaking republic in the Americas; the island of La Tortuga off the N coast was formerly a pirate lair; US military base at Môle St Nicolas, the nearest point to Cuba

exports coffee, sugar, sisal, cotton, cocoa, rice

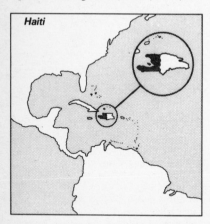

Haiti

of Jean-Claude Duvalier, power is now in the hands of a joint military and civil council, headed by General Henry Namphy.

chronology

1804 Independence from France achieved.

1957 Dr François Duvalier (Papa Doc) elected president.

1964 Duvalier pronounced himself president for life.

1971 Constitution amended to allow the president to nominate his successor. Duvalier died and was succeeded by his son, Jean-Claude (Baby Doc).

1986 Duvalier deposed and replaced by General Henri Namphy, as head of a governing council.

Honduras Republic of

area 112,088 sq km/43,227.5 sq mi

capital Tegucigalpa

towns San Pedro Sula; ports Henecan (on Pacific), La Ceiba

features 45% forested, and with areas still unexplored

exports coffee, bananas, timber (including mahogany, rosewood)

Honduras

currency lempira

population (1985) 5,762,000

language French (official, spoken by the bourgeoisie); créole, spoken by 90% black majority

religion Roman Catholic (official, but opposed to the regime)

government following the departure in Feb 1986

currency lempira/peso

population (1985) 4,499,000 (90% mestizo, 10% Indians, Europeans)

language Spanish

religion Roman Catholic
government executive president (José Azcona del Hoyo from 1986) elected for a four-year term, and unicameral congress of deputies.
chronology
1838 Honduras achieved independence.
1980 After more than a century of mostly military rule, a civilian government was elected, with the leader of the Liberal Party of Honduras (PLH), Dr Roberto Suazo, as president. The commander-in-chief of the army, General Gustavo Alvarez, nevertheless retained considerable power.
1983 Close involvement with the United States in providing naval and air bases and allowing Nicaraguan counter-revolutionaries to operate from Honduras.
1984 Alvares ousted in a coup led by junior officers, resulting in a review of policy towards the United States and Nicaragua.
1985 José Azcona (PLH) elected president.
   Hungary Hungarian People's Republic
area 93,000 sq km/35,920 sq mi
capital Budapest
towns Miskolc, Debrecen, Szeged, Pécs
features Great Hungarian Plain; Bakony Forest; rivers Danube, Tisza; Lake Balaton
exports machinery, vehicles, chemicals, textiles
currency forint
population (1985) 10,644,000 (Magyar 92%; Gypsy 3%; German 2.5%). A Hungarian minority in Romania is the cause of some friction between the two countries
language Hungarian (or Magyar), one of the few languages of Europe with non-Indo-European origins. It is grouped with Finnish and Estonian in the Finno-Ugrian family
religion Roman Catholic 50%; other Christian denominations 50%
government there is a parliament and presidential council, of which the chairman is head of state, but real power rests with the Communist politburo (from 1956 Head of Hungary Socialist workers Party, János Kádár).
chronology
1946 Republic proclaimed.
1949 Soviet style constitution adopted.
1956 'Hungarian National Rising' workers'

demonstrations in Budapest, democratization reforms by Nagy overturned by Soviet tanks, Kádár installed as HSWP leader.

1968 Economic decentralization reforms.
1983 Competition introduced into elections.
   Iceland Republic of
area 103,000 sq km/ 39,758 sq mi
capital Reykjavik
features active volcanoes (Hekla was once thought the gateway to Hell), geysers, hot springs, lava fields, and new islands being created offshore (Surtsey in 1963); subterranean hot water heats Iceland's homes
exports cod and other fish products
currency krona
population (1985) 241,000
language Icelandic, the most archaic Scandinavian language, in which some of the finest sagas were written.
religion Evangelical Lutheran
government there is a president (Vigdís Finnbogadóttir from 1980), and parliament (Althing) of two houses, the oldest parliament in the world
chronology
1944 Independence from Denmark achieved.
1949 Joined NATO and the Council of Europe.
1953 Joined the Nordic Council.
1976 'Cod War' with the United Kingdom.

533

1979 Iceland announced a 200 mile exclusive fishing zone.

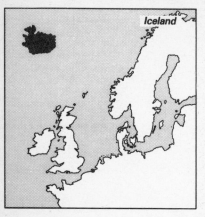

1983 Steingrimur Hermannsson appointed to lead a Progressive-Independence Party coalition.

India Republic of (Indian *Bharat*)
area 3,208,274 sq km/1,175,410 sq mi
capital New Delhi
towns Bangalore, Hyderabad, Ahmedabad; ports Calcutta, Bombay, Madras, Kanpur, Pune, Nagpur
features comprises 23 states and eight union territories (Andaman and Nicobar Islands, Arunachal Pradesh, Chandigarh, Dadra and Nagar Haveli, Delhi, Lakshadweep, Pondicherry, and Goa, Daman and Diu); rivers Ganges, Indus, Brahmaputra; Deccan, Himalayas; Taj Mahal; cave paintings (Ajanta); one of the world's most advanced communities in communications via satellite TV (weather forecasting, agricultural information, and education)
exports tea, coffee, fish; iron ore; leather, textiles, polished diamonds
currency rupee
population (1985) 767,681,000
language Hindi, (official), English and 14 other recognized languages: Assamese, Bengali, Gujarati, Kannada, Kashmiri, Malayalam, Marathi, Oriya, Punjabi, Sanskrit, Sindhi, Tamil, Telugu, Urdu
religion Hindu 80%; Sunni Muslim 10%; Christian 2.5%; Sikh 2%
government executive president elected for five years by members of parliament and the state assemblies (Rajiv Gandhi from 1984), council of states (Rajya Sabha) and house of the people (Lok Sabha).

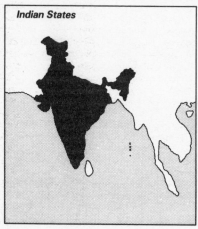

chronology
1947 Independence achieved from Britain.
1950 Federal Republic proclaimed.
1962 Border skirmishes with China.
1964 Death of prime minister Nehru.
1965 Border war with Pakistan over Kashmir.
1966 Indira Gandhi became prime minister.
1971 War with Pakistan leading to creation of Bangladesh.
1975–77 'State of Emergency' proclaimed.
1977–79 Janata government in power.
1980 Indira Gandhi returned in landslide victory.
1984 Assassination of Indira Gandhi. Rajiv Gandhi returned with record majority.

Indonesia Republic of
area 1,925,000 sq km/741,000 sq mi
capital Jakarta

Indonesia

1942 Occupied by Japan. Nationalist government established in power.

1945 Japanese surrender. Nationalists declared independence under Sukarno.

1949 Formal transfer of Dutch sovereignty.

1950 Unitary constitution established.

1963 Western New Guinea (Irian Jaya) ceded by Holland.

1965–6 Attempted Communist coup: General Suharto emergency administration.

1967 Sukarno replaced as president by Suharto.

1976 Annexation of E Timor.

Iran Islamic Republic of (until 1935 *Persia*)
area 1,648,000 sq km/636,000 sq mi
capital Tehrán
towns Esfahán, Meshed, Tabriz, Shiraaz, Ahwaz; chief port Abadan
features Elburz and Zagros mountains; Lake Rezayeh; Dasht-Ekavir Desert; ruins of Persepolis
exports carpets, cotton textiles, metalwork, leather goods; oil and petrochemicals
currency rial

towns ports Surabaya, Semarang
features world's largest Islamic state; comprises 1,400 islands, including the greater part of the Sunda Islands to the west of the Moluccas, both the *Greater Sundas* (including Java and Madura, part of Kalimantan/Borneo, Sumatra, Sulawesi and Belitung) and the *Lesser Sundas/Nusa Tenggara* (including Bali, Lombok, Sumba, Timor), as well as Malaku/Moluccas and part of New Guinea (Irian Jaya)
exports coffee, rubber, palm oil and coconuts, tin, tea, tobacco; oil and liquid natural gas
currency **rupiah**
population (1985) 173,103,000 (including 300 ethnic groups)
language Indonesian, closely allied to Malay
religion Muslim 90%; Buddhist, Hindu and Pancasila (a secular cult official ideology)
government there is an executive president (General Suharto from 1967), and a house of representatives; the people's consultative assembly (theoretically with supreme power) meets about every five years.
chronology
17th century Dutch rule established.

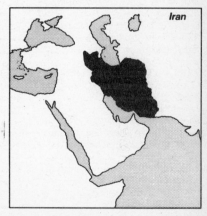

Iran

population (1985) 45,191,000 (including minorities in Azerbaijan, Baluchistan, Khuzestan (Arabistan) and Kurdistan)
language Farsi, Kurdish, Turk, Arabic, English, French

religion Shi'ite Muslim (official)
government under the 1979 constitution there is an executive president (Muslim and eligible for re-election once) and a one-chamber legislative assembly, both elected for four years, but a council of guardians ensures that all laws conform to Islam, and power is ultimately in the hands of the religious leader, the Ayatollah Ruhollah Khomeini.
chronology
1946 British, American and Russian forces left Iran.
1951 Oilfields nationalized by prime minister Mohammed Mussadeq.
1953 Mussadeq deposed and the Shah Mohammad Reza Pahlavi took full control of the government.
1975 The Shah introduced a single party system.
1978 Opposition to the Shah organized from France by Ayatollah Khomeini.
1979 The Shah left the country and Khomeini returned to create an Islamic state. Students seized US hostages in Tehran.
1980 Start of Gulf war against Iraq.
1981 American hostages finally released.
1984 Egyptian peace proposals rejected.
1985 Gulf war fighting intensified. UN Secretary-General's peace moves were unsuccessful.
1987 Further intensification of the war.

Iraq Republic of
area 444,000 sq km/172,000 sq mi
capital Baghdad
towns Mosul and port of Basra
features rivers Tigris and Euphrates; reed architecture of the marsh Arabs; sites of Eridu, Babylon, Nineveh, Ur, Ctesiphon
exports dates (80% of world supply); wool; oil
currency Iraqi dinar
population (1985) 15,507,000
language Arabic (official)
religion Shi'ite Muslim 60%; Sunni Muslim 30%; Christian 3%
government under the 1970 constitution there is a Revolutionary Command Council, which elects the president (Saddam Hussein from 1979); the only legal political party is the National Progressive Front (alliance of the socialist Ba'ath Party and Kurdish parties)

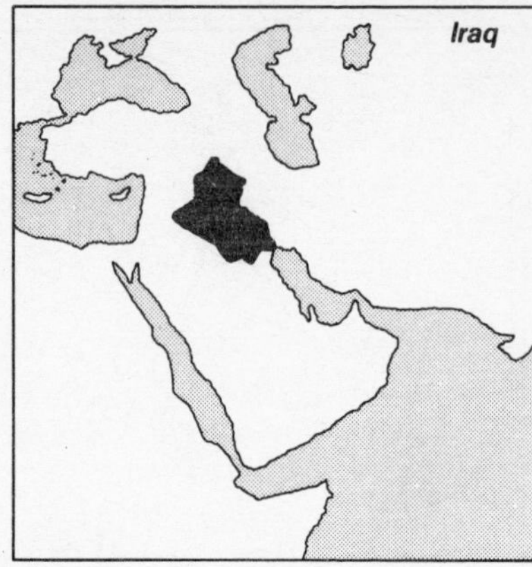

chronology
1920 Iraq became a British League of Nations protectorate.
1921 Hashemite dynasty established, with Faisal as king.
1958 Monarchy overthrown and Iraq became a republic.
1968 Supreme power vested in a Revolutionary Command Council (RCC), with General al-Bakr as its chairman and head of state and head of government.
1979 Al-Bakr replaced by Saddam Hussain.
1980 New constitution adopted, providing for an elected national assembly. Gulf War between Iraq and Iran broke out.
1987 Fighting in the war intensified.

Ireland Republic of (Irish ***Éire***)
area 68,892 sq km/26,601 sq mi
capital Dublin
towns Cork, Dun Laoghaire, Limerick, Waterford, all ports
features Bog of Allen, source of domestic and national power; rivers Shannon, Liffey, Boyne; Magillicuddy's Reeks, Wicklow Mountains; Lough Corrib, lakes of Killarney; Galway Bay and Aran Islands; heavy rainfall
exports livestock, dairy products; Irish whis-

key; micro- electronic components and assemblies; mining and engineering products, chemicals, tobacco, clothing. Tourism is important.

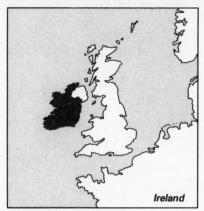

Ireland

population (1985) 3,588,000
language Irish and English (both official)
religion Roman Catholic
government under the constitution of 1937, a nominal president, with a senate (Seanad Éireann), and house of representatives (Dáil Éireann) elected by proportional representation. The prime minister (Taoiseach) is Charles Haughey (from February 1987), of the Fianna Fáil party; the opposition party is Fine-Gael.
chronology
1921 Anglo-Irish Treaty resulted in creation of the Irish Free State (Southern Ireland), granted dominion status within the Commonwealth, and the secession from it of Northern Ireland.
1937 Eire established as an independent state.
1949 Eire left the Commonwealth and became the Republic of Ireland.
1973 Fianna Fáil defeated after 40 years in office. Liam Cosgrave formed a coalition government.
1979 Fianna Fáil returned to power, with Charles Haughey as prime minister.
1981 Garret FitzGerald formed a Fine Gael/Labour Party coalition.

1983 New Ireland Forum formed, but rejected by the British government.
1985 Anglo-Irish Agreement signed.
1986 Protests by Ulster Unionists against the Agreement.
1987 General election won by Charles Haughey; Garret FitzGerald resigned as Fine Gael leader.

Israel State of
area 20,770 sq km/8,017 sq mi (as at 1949 armistice)
capital Jerusalem (not recognized by the United Nations)
towns ports Tel Aviv/Jaffa, Haifa, Eilat; Bat-Yam, Holon, Ramat Gan, Petach Tikva, Beersheba
features coastal plain of Sharon between Haifa and Tel Aviv noted since ancient times for fertility, River Jordan, Dead Sea, Lake Tiberias, Negev Desert, Golan Heights; historic sites, Jerusalem, Bethlehem, Nazareth; Masada, Megiddo, Jericho; caves of the Dead Sea scrolls

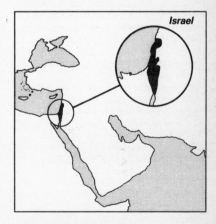

Israel

exports citrus and other fruit, avocados, chinese leaves; fertilizers, plastics, petrochemicals, textiles; electronics (military, medical, scientific, industrial), electro-optics, precision instruments and aircraft and missiles
currency shekel

population (1985) 4,128,000 (including c. 750,000 Arabs as Israeli citizens and over 1 million Arabs in the occupied territories); under the Law of Return 1950, 'every Jew shall be entitled to come to Israel as an immigrant', those from the East and E Europe are *Ashkenazim*, and from Spain, Portugal, Arab N Africa, are *Sephardim* (over 50% of the population is now of Sephardic descent). An Israeli-born Jew is a *Sabra*; c. 500,000 Israeli Jews are resident in the USA
language Hebrew and Arabic (official); Yiddish, European and West Asian languages
religion Israel is a secular state, but the predominant faith is Judaism; the Arabs practise Sunni Islam
government president, single chamber parliament (Knesset), elected for four years (Prime Minister Yitzhak Shamir from 1986)
chronology
1948 Independent State of Israel proclaimed with Ben Gurion as president.
1963 Ben Gurion resigned and was succeeded by Levi Eshkol leading a coalition.
1964 Palestine Liberation Organization (PLO) founded with the aim of overthrowing the State of Israel.
1967 Israel victorious in the Six Day War.
1968 Israel Labour Party formed led by Mrs Golda Meir.
1969 Golda Meir became prime minister.
1974 Yom Kippur War. Golda Meir succeeded by Itzhak Rabin heading a coalition.
1977 Menachem Begin elected prime minister. Egyptian president addressed the Knesset.
1978 Camp David talks.
1979 Egyptian-Israeli agreement signed.
1982 Israel pursued PLO fighters into Lebanon.
1983 Agreement reached for withdrawal from Lebanon.
1984 Government of National Unity formed.
1985 Israeli prime minister had secret talks with King Hussein of Jordan.

Italy Republic of
area 301,245 sq km/116,300 sq mi
capital Rome
towns Milan, Turin; ports Naples, Genoa, Palermo, Bari, Catania
features Maritime Alps, Dolomites, Apennines; rivers Po, Adige, Arno, Tiber, Rubicon; lakes Como, Maggiore, Garda; Europe's only active volcanoes, Vesuvius, Etna, Stromboli; islands of Sicily, Sardinia, Elba, Capri, Ischia; enclave of the Vatican
exports wine, fruit and vegetables; textiles (Europe's largest silk producer), leather goods, motor vehicles, electrical goods, chemicals, marble (Carrara), sulphur and mercury, iron and steel
currency lira
population (1985) 57,116,000
language Italian, derived from Latin
religion Roman Catholic 90%

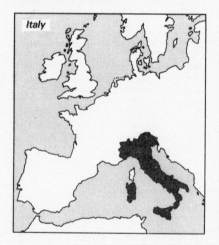

government under the constitution of 1947 there is a non-executive president, and a senate (elected for six years) and chamber of deputies elected for five years. There are 20 regions, all with their own parliaments, but five have special autonomous status: Friuli-Venezia Giulia, Sardinia, Sicily, Trentino-Alto-Adige and Valle d'Aosta
chronology
1946 Monarchy replaced by a republic.
1948 New constitution adopted.

1954 Trieste returned to Italy.

1976 Communists proposed the establishment of a broad-based, left-right government, the 'historic compromise'. Idea rejected by the Christian Democrats.

1978 Christian Democrat Aldo Moro, architect of the historic compromise, kidnapped and murdered by Red Brigades terrorists.

1983 Bettino Craxi became the Socialist leader of a broad coalition government.

1987 Craxi resigned, inconclusive election resulted in further attemts to form a coalition.

Ivory Coast Republic of (officially *Côte d'Ivoire since 1986*)

area 322,463 sq km/127,000 sq mi

capital Abidjan

towns Bouakeé

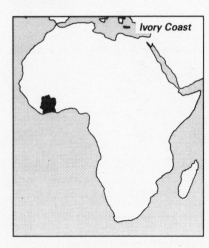

Ivory Coast

features combination of tropical rain forest (diminishing as it is exploited) in the south, and savannah in the north

exports coffee, cocoa, timber, petroleum

currency CFA franc

population (1985) 10,090,000

language French (official)

religion Animist 65%; Muslim 24%; Christian 11%

government executive president (Félix Houphouët-Boigny from 1960), and single chamber national assembly; there is only one legal party.

chronology

1958 Achieved internal self-government.

1960 Achieved full independence, with Félix Houphouët-Boigny as president of a one-party state.

Jamaica

area 11,525 sq km/4,411 sq mi

capital Kingston

towns Montego bay, Spanish Town, St Andrews

features Blue mountains (so-called because of the haze over them, and famous for their coffee); partly undersea remains of the pirate city of Port Royal, destroyed by an earthquake in 1692

exports sugar, bananas, bauxite, rum, coffee, coconuts, liqueurs, cigars

currency Jamaican dollar

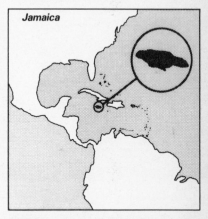

Jamaica

population (1985) 2,366,000 (a mixture of several ethnic groups)

language English; Jamaican creole

religion Protestant 70%; Rastafarianism

government under the 1962 constitution a governor-general, an elected house of representatives and a nominated senate. The prime minister (Edward Seaga from 1980; re-elected

539

1983) heads the Labour Party, the left-wing People's National Party, (Michael Manley) is in opposition

chronology

1959 Granted internal self-government.

1962 Achieved full independence, with Sir Alexander Bustamente as prime minister.

1967 Jamaica Labour Party re-elected.

1972 Michael Manley (PNP) appointed prime minister.

1976 PNP re-elected.

1980 JLP elected, with Edward Seaga as prime minister.

1983 JLP re-elected.

Japan (Japanese *Nippon*)

area 370,000 sq km/142,680 sq mi

capital Tokyo

towns Fukuoka, Kitakyushu, Kyoto, Sapporo; ports Osaka, Nagoya, Yokohama, Kobe, Kawasaki

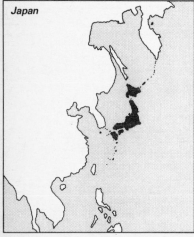

Japan

features comprises over 1,000 islands, of which the chief are Hokkaido, Honshu, Shikoku, Kyushu

exports televisions, cassette and video recorders, radios, cameras, computers, robots, and other electronic and electrical equipment; cars and other vehicles, ships; iron and steel; chemicals, textiles

currency yen

population (1985) 120,731,000

language Japanese (official); English is widely spoken. Japanese is related to Korean, is tonal and builds up words by adding simple words together to form compounds; it is written in a modified system of ideographs borrowed from the Chinese in the 3rd century, and a later simplified system (kana) has never replaced it; it has many borrowings from other languages, especially Western ones. The Japanese put their family names first, e.g. Nakasone Yasuhiro

religion Shinto; Buddhist; Christian (minority)

government headed by the emperor (Hirohito since 1926), a constitutional monarchy since 1947, and the parliament has a house of councillors and house of representatives (prime minister from 1982 Nakasone, re-elected 1986), both popularly elected. The chief parties are the Liberal Democrats (LDP), in power almost continuously since World War II, and the Democratic Socialists (DSP).

chronology

1945 Japanese surrender. Allied control commission in power.

1946 Framing of 'Peace Constitution'.

1952 Full sovereignty regained.

1955 Formation of Liberal Democratic Party.

1972 Ryukyu Islands regained.

1974 Resignation of Prime Minister Tanaka over Lockheed bribes scandal.

1982 Election of Yasuhiro Nakasone as Liberal Democratic Party (LDP) president and prime minister.

1986 Nakasone re-elected

Jordan The Hashemite Kingdom of

area 98,000 sq km/38,000 sq mi

capital Amman

towns Aqaba, the only port

features Dead Sea, River Jordan, archaeological sites, e.g. Jerash, Roman forum

exports potash, phosphates, citrus

currency Jordanian dinar

population (1985) 2,668,000 (including Palestinian refugees)

language Arabic

religion Sunni Muslim

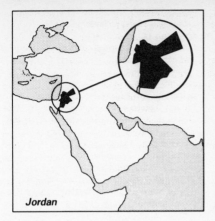

Jordan

government constitutional monarchy (King Hussein since 1952); the lower house of parliament is elected by universal suffrage (Prime Minister Zaid Rifai from 1985), the upper is nominated by the king, who can also dissolve parliament.

chronology

1946 Achieved full independence as Transjordan.

1949 New State of Jordan declared.

1953 Hussain ibn Talai became King of Jordan.

1958 Jordan and Iraq formed Arab Federation which ended when the Iraqi monarchy was deposed.

1982 Hussain tried to mediate in Arab-Israeli conflict.

1985 Hussain put forward a framework for a Middle East peace settlement. Secret meeting between Hussain and Israeli prime minister.

Kampuchea People's Republic of
area 181,000 sq km/71,000 sq mi
capital Phnom Penh
towns Battambang, and the seaport Kompong Som
features Mekong river; ruins of Angkor
exports rubber, rice
currency Kampuchean riel
population (1985) 6,249,000
language Khmer (official); French

religion Theravada Buddhist
government under the 1981 constitution there is an executive president (Heng Samrin), with a council of state, council of ministers, and national assembly. World governments are divided on the question of recognition, and the United Nations still recognizes the Sihanouk regime.

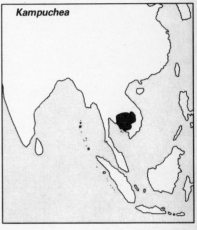

Kampuchea

chronology

1863–1941 Vietnam became a French protectorate.

1941–45 Occupied by the Japanese.

1946 Recaptured by France.

1953 Granted full independence.

1970 Prince Sihanouk overthrown by American-backed Lon Nol.

1975 Lon Nol overthrown by Khmer Rouge.

1978–79 Vietnamese invasion and installation of Heng Samrin government.

1982 Formation of tripartite resistance coalition.

Kenya Republic of
area 583,000 sq km/224,960 sq mi
capital Nairobi
towns Kisumu and the port of Mombasa
features Great Rift Valley, Mt Kenya, Lake Nakuru (flamingos), Aberdare National Park

(includes Treetops Hotel, where Elizabeth II heard that she had succeeded to the throne), the Masai Mara National Park (which forms part of the same ecosystem as Tanzania's Serengeti); Tsavo National Park, Nairobi National Park, Malindini Marine Reserve, Lake Turkana (Rudolf), Olduvai Gorge

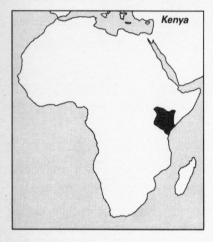

Kenya

exports coffee, tea, sisal, pineapples
currency Kenya shilling
population (1985) 20,194,000 (with one of the world's fastest growth rates; the dominant ethnic group is the Kikuyu)
language Swahili, but English is in general use
religion indigenous religions with Christian and Muslim minorities
government president (Daniel arap Moi; re-elected 1983) and unicameral national assembly; it is a one-party state of the Kenya African National Union (KANU), but competition for seats allows a democratic element.
chronology
1950 Mau Mau campaign began.
1953 Jomo Kenyatta imprisoned.
1956 Mau Mau campaign defeated.
1963 Granted independence, with internal self-government and Kenyatta as prime minister.
1964 Established as a republic, within the

Commonwealth, with Kenyatta as president.
1978 Death of Kenyatta. Succeeded by Daniel arap Moi.
1982 Attempted coup against Moi foiled.
1983 Moi re-elected.

Kiribati Republic of
area 655 sq km/253 sq mi
capital and port Tarawa
features comprises 33 Pacific islands: the Gilbert, Phoenix and Line Islands, and Banaba (Ocean Island)
exports copra
currency Australian dollar
population (1985) 61,000
language English and Gilbertese (official)
religion Christian, both Roman Catholic and Protestant.

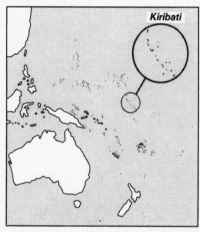

Kiribati

government there is an executive president or Beretitenti (Ieremia Tabai from 1979), with a unicameral legislature.
chronology
1977 Gilbert Islands granted internal self-government.
1979 Achieved full independence, within the Commonwealth, as the Republic of Kiribati, with Ieremia Tabai as president.
1982 Tabai re-elected.

542

1983 Tabai re-elected.

Korea Democratic People's Republic of (*North Korea*)
area 121,250 sq km/46,815 sq mi
capital Pyongyang

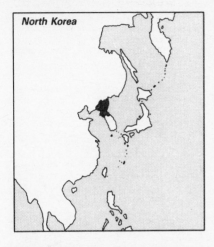

features the richest of the two Koreas in mineral resources
exports coal, iron, copper, textiles, chemicals
currency won
population (1985) 20,082,000
language Korean
religion traditionally Buddhist and Confucianism
government under the constitution of 1972, there is an executive president (Kim Il Sung, who also heads the all-powerful Communist Party Central Committee) and supreme people's assembly.
chronology
1948 Democratic People's Republic of Korea formed.
1950 North Korea invaded South to begin Korean War.
1953 Armistice agreed to end Korean War.
1961 Friendship and mutual assistance treaty signed with China.
1972 New constitution, with executive presi-

dent, adopted.
1983 Four South Korean cabinet ministers assassinated in Rangoon (Burma) by North Korean army officers.

Korea Republic of (*South Korea*)
area 99,999 sq km/38,450 sq mi
capital Seoul
towns Taegu, and the ports of Pusan and Inchon
features before 1945 mainly agricultural, but with US aid became a 'workshop of Asia'
exports steel, ships, chemicals, electronics, textiles, plastics
currency won

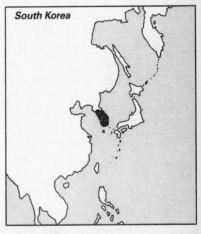

population (1985) 42,643,000
language Korean
religion traditionally Buddhist and Confucianism
government executive president (General Chun Doo-Hwan from 1980), and national assembly
chronology
1948 Republic proclaimed.
1950–53 War with North Korea.
1960 President Syngham Rhee resigned following unrest.
1962 Military coup by General Park Chung-

Hee. Industrial growth programme.

1979 Assassination of resident Park.

1980 Military coup by General Chun Doo-Hwan. He subsequently became president.

Kuwait the State of

area 19,000 sq km/7,400 sq mi

capital Kuwait (also chief port)

features oil revenues make it one of the world's best equipped states in public works, medical and educational services

exports oil

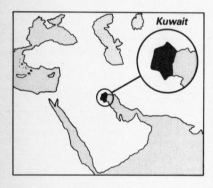

currency Kuwait dinar

population (1985) 1,710,000 40% Kuwaitis; some 30% are Palestinians

language Arabic

religion Sunni Muslim, with Shiah minority

government ruler HH Sheikh Jaber al-Ahmad al-Sabah 1928–1, who acceded in 1977, with an elected national assembly.

chronology

1961 Achieved full independence, with Sheikh Abdullahh al-Salem al-Sabah as emir.

1965 Sheikh Abdullah died and was succeeded by his brother, Sheikh Sabah.

1967 Sheikh Sabah died and was succeeded by Crown Prince Jaber.

Laos People's Democratic Republic of

area 235,700 5 sq km/91,000 sq mi

capital Vientiane

towns Luang Prabang, the former royal capital

features Mekong river, hydroelectric power

being exported to Thailand; Plain of Jars, where a prehistoric people carved stone jars large enough to hold a person; used to be known as the Land of a Million Elephants

exports tin, teak (worked by elephants)

currency kip

population (1985) 42,643,000

language Lao

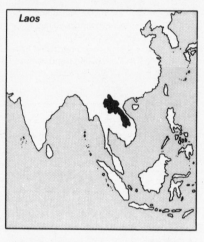

religion traditionally Theravada Buddhist

government president (Prince Souphanouvong from 1975) and national assembly

chronology

1893–1945 Laos became a French Protectorate.

1945 Temporarily occupied by Japan.

1946 Retaken by France.

1950 Granted semi-autonomy in French Union.

1954 Full independence achieved.

1960 Right-wing government seized power.

1962 Coalition government established; civil war continued.

1973 Vientiane ceasefire agreement.

1975 Communist dominated republic proclaimed.

Lebanon Republic of

area 10,400 sq km/3,400 sq mi

capital Beirut, also a port

towns Tripoli, Tyre, (all ports) and Sidon
features few of the celebrated cedars of
Lebanon remain; Mt Hermon; Chouf Mountains; archaeological sites at Baalbeck, Byblos,
Tyre; until the civil war, the financial centre of
the Middle East
exports citrus and other fruit, and industrial
products to Arab neighbours
currency Lebanese pound
population (1985) 2,619,000 (including 350,000
Palestinian refugees, many driven out, killed in
fighting or massacred 1982–5)
language Arabic (official); French and English
religion Christian (Maronite and Orthodox)
40%; Muslim (Shi'ite 33%, Sunni 24%) 57%;
Druze 3%

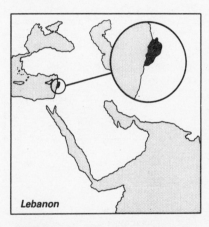

government president (always a Maronite
Christian: Amin Gemayel from 1982), who
appoints the prime minister (always a Sunni
Muslim), and an elected national assembly,
always presided over by a Shi'ite Muslim.
chronology
1944 Full independence achieved.
1964 Palestine Liberation Organization (PLO)
founded in Beirut.
1975 Outbreak of civil war between Christians
and Muslims.
1976 Ceasefire agreed.
1978 Israel invaded south Lebanon in search of

PLO fighters. International peace keeping
force established. Fighting broke out again.
1979 Part of south Lebanon declared an 'independent free Lebanon'.
1982 Bachir Gemayel became president, but
assassinated before he could assume office.
Amin Gemayel became president.
1983 Agreement reached for the withdrawal of
Syrian and Israeli troops, but not honoured.
1984 Most of international peace keeping force
withdrawn.
1985 Lebanon nearing a state of anarchy, with
many foreigners being taken hostage.
1987 Syrian army enter Beirut; Prime Minister
Rashid Karami assassinated.
   Lesotho Kingdom of
area 30,346 sq km/11,716 sq mi
capital Maseru
features Lesotho is an enclave within South
Africa
exports wool, mohair; diamonds

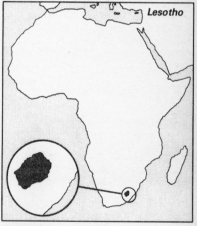

currency loti
population (1985) 1,512,000
language Sesotho and English (official)
religion Christian 70% (Roman Catholic 40%)
government constitutional monarchy
(Moshoeshoe II from 1960), with a senate
(comprising chiefs and members nominated by
the king) and elected national assembly.

545

chronology
1966 Basutoland achieved full independence, within the Commonwealth, as the Kingdom of Lesotho. The Basotho National Party (BNP) in power, with Chief Leabua Jonathan as prime minister.
1975 BNP members attacked by the Lesotho Liberation Army (LLA), with South African encouragment.
1986 South Africa imposed a border blockade, forcing the deportation of 60 African National Congress members. General Justin Lechanya elected prime minister.

Liberia Republic of
area 112,820 sq km/43,548 5 sq mi
capital Monrovia
features nominally the world's largest merchant navy because minimal controls make Liberia's a 'flag of convenience'
exports iron ore, rubber, diamonds; coffee, cocoa, palm oil
currency Liberian dollar
population (1985) 1,512,000 (95% belonging to the indigenous peoples)
language English (official)
religion Muslim 20%; Christian 15%; traditional 65%

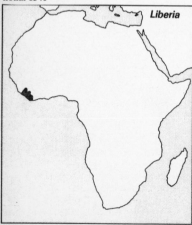

government military head of state (Samuel K Doe from 1980), pending return to civilian rule

under the 1984 constitution (executive president, senate, and house of representatives) by elections in Oct 1985. These elections were won by Samuel Doe, though opposition critics claim this was fraudulently done
chronology
1847 Founded as an independent republic.
1944 William Tubman elected president.
1971 Tubman died and was succeeded by William Tolbert.
1980 Tolbert assassinated in a coup led by Samuel Doe, who suspended the constitution and ruled through a People's Redemption Council (PRC).
1984 New constitution approved. National Democratic Party of Liberia (NDPL) founded by Doe.
1985 NDPL won decisive victory in general election. Unsuccessful coup against Doe.

Libya (Socialist People's Libyan Arab *Jamahiriyah* – or 'state of the masses')
area 1,780,000 sq km/680,000 sq mi
capital Tripoli

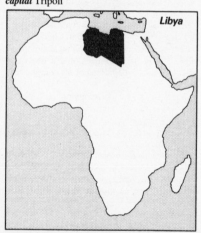

towns the ports of Benghazi and Misurata
features Gulf of Sirte, Libyan Desert; rock paintings of c. 3000 BC in the Fezzan; Roman city sites of Leptis Magna, Sabratha among others; the plan to pump water from below the Sahara to the coast risks rapid exhaustion of a

largely non-renewable supply
exports oil, natural gas
currency Libyan dinar
population (1985) 3,752,000 (including 500,000 foreign workers)
language Arabic
religion Sunni Muslim
government local people's congresses send officials to a general people's congress (1,000 members), which meets bi-annually for a week; this appoints the general people's committee, of which the secretary is prime minister, but Khaddhafi, the 'leader of the Revolution' is effective ruler.
chronology,
1942 Achieved independence as the United Kingdom of Libya, under King Idris.
1969 King deposed in a coup led by Colonel Muammar al-Khaddhafi. Revolution Command Council (RCC) set up and the Arab Socialist Union (ASU) proclaimed the only legal party.
1972 Proposed federation of Libya, Syria and Egypt abandoned.
1980 Proposed merger with Syria abandoned. Libyan troops began fighting in Chad.
1981 Proposed merger with Chad abandoned.
1986 US bombing of Khaddhafi's headquarters, following allegations of his complicity in terrorist activities.

Liechtenstein Principality of
area 160 sq km/62 sq mi
capital Vaduz
features only country in the world to take its name from its reigning family; most highly industrialized country
exports microchips, precision engineering, processed foods, postage stamps; easy tax laws make it an international haven for foreign companies and banks
currency Swiss franc
population (1985) 27,000 (33% foreign)
language German
religion Roman Catholic
government constitutional monarchy (from 1984, Prince Hans Adam 1945–1), which can call and dismiss parliament, and appoints the prime minister on the advice of the unicameral

parliament of 15 members.
chronology
1938 Prince Franz Josef II came to power.
1984 Vote extended to women in national elections.

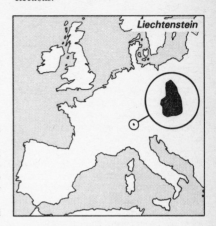

Luxembourg Grand-Duchy of
area 2,586 sq km/999 5 sq mi

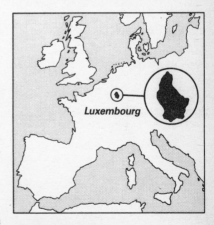

capital Luxembourg
features River Moselle; part of the Ardennes (Oesling)

exports iron and steel, chemicals, synthetic textiles; banking is very important; Luxembourg is economically linked with Belgium
currency Luxembourg franc
population (1985) 366,000
language French (official); local Letzeburgesch; German is also spoken
religion Roman Catholic
government executive power is held by Grand Duke Jean 1921–1 (from 1964), who also shares legislative power with the chamber of deputies
chronology
1948 With Belgium and the Netherlands, formed the Benelux customs union.
1958 Benelux became economic union.
1961 Prince Jean became acting head of state on behalf of his mother, the Grand Duchess Charlotte.
1964 Grand Duchess Charlotte abdicated and Prince Jean became grand duke.

   Madagascar Democratic Republic of.
area 594,000.5 sq km/228,500 sq mi
capital Antananarivo;
towns chief port Toamasina
features one of the last places in the world to be inhabited, it evolved in isolation with unique animals, for example the lemur, now under threat from destruction of the forests
exports coffee, sugar, spice, textiles
currency Malagasy franc
population (1985) 9,941,000
language Malagasy (of the Malayo-Polynesian family) (official); French and English
religion Animist 50%; Christian 40%; Muslim 10%
government under the constitution of 1975 there is an executive president (Lieutenant Commander Didier Ratsiraka from 1975; re-elected in 1983), and senate and house of assembly.
chronology
1960 Achieved full independence, with Philibert Tsiranana, leader of the PSD (Social Democratic Party), as president.
1972 Army took control of the government.
1975 Martial law imposed under a national military directorate. New constitution proclaimed the Democratic Republic of

Madagascar, with Didier Ratsiraka as president.

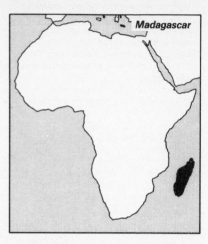

1976 Front-Line Revolutionary Organization (AREMA) formed.
1977 National Front for the Defence of the Malagasy Socialist Revolution (FNDR) became the sole legal political organization.
1983 Ratsiraka re-elected.

   Malawi Republic of.
area 117,000 sq km/47,950sq mi
capital Lilongwe
towns Blantyre-Limbe
features Lake Malawi; Livingstonia National Park on the Nyika Plateau in the N, rich in orchids, arthropods, elephants; Shiré Highlands, noted for tea and tobacco, and rising to 1,750 m/5,800 ft
exports tea, tobacco, cotton, groundnuts, sugar
currency kwacha
population (1985) 7,056,000
language English (official); Chichewa
religion Christian 50%; Muslim 30%
government there is an executive president (Hastings Banda from 1966) and parliament, which may include any number of nominated members in addition to those elected. The Malawi Congress Party is the only permitted

political party.
chronology
1964 Nyasaland achieved independence, within the Commonwealth, as Malawi.
1966 Became a one-party republic, with Hastings Banda as president.
1971 Banda was made president for life.
1977 Banda started a programme of moderate liberalization.

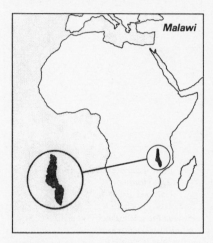

Malawi

language Malay (official, usually written in Arabic characters); in Sarawak English is also official
religion Muslim (official)
government head of state (federation) (Mahmud Iskander from 1984). The head of state is elected from among their number by the nine rulers of the Malay states for five years; a senate, and an elected house of representatives (prime minister from 1981 Mahathir bin Mohamed).

Malaysia

Malaysia
area 331,500 sq km/128,000 sq mi
capital Kuala Lumpur
towns Kuching in Sarawak and Kota Kinabalu in Sabah
features comprises W Malaysia (the nine Malay States – Perlis, Kedah, Johore, Selangor, Perak, Negri Sembilan, Kelantan, Trengganu, Pahang; plus Penang and Malacca); and E Malaysia (Sarawak and Sabah); 75% of the area is forested
exports pineapples, palm oil; rubber, timber; petroleum (Sarawak), bauxite
currency ringgit
population (1985) 15,467,000 (Malaysian 47%; Chinese 34%; Indians, Pakistanis 9%, and indigenous peoples (Dayaks, Ibans) of E Malaysia 10%)

chronology
1963 Formation of Federation of Malaysia.
1965 Secession of Singapore from Federation.
1969 Anti-Chinese riots in Kuala Lumpur.
1971 Launch of Bumiputra 'new economic policy'.
1981 Election of Dr Mahathir bin Mohamad as prime minister.

Maldives Republic of
area 298 sq km/115 sq mi
capital Malé
features comprises some 2,000 coral islands,

only about 200 being inhabited
exports coconuts and copra, and bonito (fish related to tunny). Tourism is important
currency Maldivian rupee
population (1985) 182,000
language Divehi (related to Sinhalese)
religion Sunni Muslim

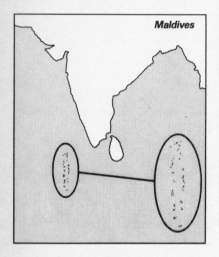

government executive president (Maumoon Abdul Gayoom from 1978), with a cabinet and house of representatives; no political parties are allowed.
chronology
1953 Originally a sultanate, the Maldive Islands became a republic within the Commonwealth.
1954 Sultanate restored.
1965 Achieved full independence outside the Commonwealth.
1968 Sultan deposed and a republic reinstated with Ibrahim Nasir as president.
1978 Nasir retired and was replaced by Maumoon Abdul Gayoom.
1982 Rejoined the Commonwealth.
1983 Gayoom re-elected.
Mali Republic of
area 1,204,000 sq km/465,000 sq mi

capital Bamako
features Niger river; includes part of the Sahara; the old town of Timbuktu
exports cotton, groundnuts, livestock
currency Mali franc
population (1985) 7,908,000

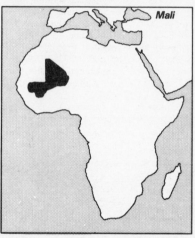

language French (official); Bambara
religion Sunni Muslim 65%; Animist 35%
government executive president (General Moussa Traoré from 1969, with extensions) elected once only for six years, with a council of ministers, and national assembly elected for three years. There is only one political party, the Democratic Union of the Mali People (UDPM).
chronology
1959 With Senegal, formed the Federation of Mali.
1960 Became the independent Republic of Mali, with Mobido Keita as president.
1968 Keita replaced in an army coup by Moussa Traoré.
1974 New constitution made Mali a one-party state.
1976 New national party, the Malian People's Democratic Union, announced.
1983 Agreement between Mali and Guinea, for

eventual political and economic integration signed.

Malta Republic of
area 316 sq km/122 sq mi
capital Valletta
features includes the island of Gozo 67 sq km/26 sq mi and Comino 2.5 sq km/1 sq mi; large commercial dock facilities
exports vegetables, knitwear, hand-made lace, plastics, electronic equipment
currency Maltese pound
population (1985) 355,000
language Maltese (related to Arabic, with Phoenician survivals and influenced by Italian)
religion Roman Catholic

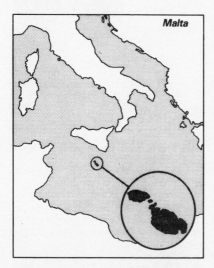
Malta

government president and house of representatives, elected by proportional representation (prime minister from 1987 Dr Edward Adami).
chronology
1942 Awarded the George Cross.
1955 Dom Mintoff (Malta Labour Party) became prime minister.
1956 Referendum approved proposal for integration with the United Kingdom. Proposal

opposed by the Nationalist Party.
1958 MLP rejected the integration proposal.
1962 Nationalists elected, with Borg Olivier as prime minister.
1964 Achieved full independence, within the Commonwealth. Ten–year defence and economic aid treaty with Britain signed.
1971 Mintoff re-elected.
1972 Seven-year NATO agreement signed.
1974 Became a republic.
1976 Mintoff returned, with a reduced majority.
1981 Mintoff re-elected.
1984 Mintoff retired and was replaced by Mifsud Bonnici as prime minister and MLP leader.
1987 Bonnici defeated in election by Dr Edward Adami (Nationalist Party).

Mauritania Islamic Republic of
area 1,030,000 sq km/419,000 sq mi
capital Nouakchott
features mainly forms part of the Sahara Desert
exports iron ore, fish
currency ougiya
population (1985) 1,656,000 (30% Arab Berber, 30% black Africans, 30% Haratine (descendants of black slaves, who remained slaves till 1980)
language Arabic (official); French
religion Sunni Muslim
government president and prime minister (Colonel Maaouya Ould Sidi Ahmed Taya from 1981) and national assembly.
chronology
1960 Achieved full independence, with Mauritanian People's Party leader, Motar Ould Daddah, as president.
1975 Western Sahara ceded by Spain. Mauritania occupied the southern part and Morocco the rest. Polisario Front formed in Sahara to resist the occupation by Mauritania and Morocco.
1978 Daddah deposed in bloodless coup and replaced by Mohamed Khouni Ould Haidalla. Peace agreed with Polisario Front.
1984 Haidalla overthrown by Maaouya Ould Sid; Ahmed Taya. Polisario regime formally recognized. Diplomatic relations with

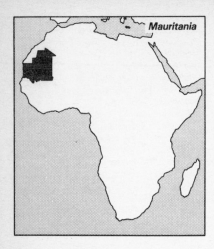

Mauritania

Mauritius Socialist Movement, pledged to make Mauritius a republic within the Commonwealth. Assembly refused to make Mauritius a republic. Ramgoolam appointed governor-general. Jugnauth formed a new coalition government.

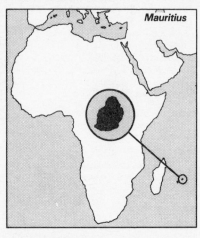

Mauritius

Morocco broken.

1985 Relations with Morocco restored.

Mauritius State of

area 1,865 sq km/720 sq mi; the island of Rodrigues is part of Mauritius and there are several small island dependencies

capital Port Louis

features geologically part of Gondwanaland, it has unusual wildlife including the dodo, flying fox, lemur, and ostrich. There are no poisonous snakes

exports sugar, knitted goods; tourism is increasingly important

currency Mauritius rupee

population (1985) 1,024,900

language English (official); Creole French

religion Hindu 45%; Christian 30%; Muslim 15%

government governor-general (Sir Veerosomy Ringadoo from 1986) and legislative assembly

chronology

1968 Achieved full independence, within the Commonwealth, with the Mauritius Labour Party leader, Seewoosagur Ramgoolam, as prime minister.

1982 Aneerood Jugnauth prime minister.

1983 Jugnauth formed a new party, the

1986 Veerosomy Ringadoo appointed governor general.

Mexico United States of

area 1,979,650 sq km/763,944 sq mi

capital Mexico City

towns Guadalajara, Monterrey; port Veracruz

features frontier of 2,000 miles with USA; resorts Acapulco, Mexicali, Tijuana; the two Sierra Madres; Baja California; volcanoes, for example Popocatepetl; archaeological sites of pre-Spanish period

exports silver, gold, lead, uranium; oil and natural gas (to USA); traditional handicrafts; fish and shellfish

currency peso

population (1985) 79,662,000 (a minority are *criollos* of Spanish descent, 12% are American Indian, and the majority are of mixed descent; 50% of the total are under 20 years of age)

language Spanish (official); Indian languages include Nahuatl, Maya, and Mixtec

Mexico

exports some light industry, but economy depends on tourism and gambling
currency French franc
population (1985) 28,000
language French
religion Roman Catholic
government a hereditary monarchy (Prince Rainier III), with elected national and communal Councils

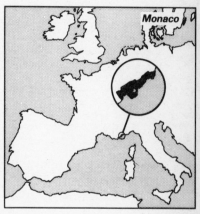

Monaco

religion Roman Catholic
government federal republic of 31 states and a federal district; executive president (Miguel de la Madrid Hurtado from 1982) elected for six years by popular vote, who cannot be re-elected; with senate and chamber of deputies. The Partido Revolucionario Institucional (Institutional Revolutionary Party, (PRI)) has dominated every election since 1930.
chronology
1821 Mexico achieved independence from Spain.
1846–48 Mexico at war with USA.
1848 Maya Indian revolt suppressed.
1863 Maximilian of Austria proclaimed emperor.
1917 New constitution introduced, designed to establish permanent democracy.
1983–4 Financial crisis.
1985 PRI returned to power. Earthquake in Mexico City.

Monaco Principality of
area 1.5 sq km/O.575 sq mi
capital Monaco-Ville (population 1,500)
town Monte Carlo, noted for its film festival, motor races, and casino
features surrounded to landward by French territory, it is being expanded by filling in the sea; aquarium and oceanographic centre

chronology
1861 Became an independent state, under French protection.
1918 France given a veto over succession to the throne.

Mongolian People's Republic
area 1 560,000 sq km/600,000 sq mi
capital Ulan Bator
towns Darkhan, Choybalsan
features Altai Mountains, part of Gobi Desert
exports meat and butter, varied minerals, furs
currency tugrik
population (1985) 1,893,000
language Khalkha Mongolian (official), Chinese, Russian
religion formerly Tibetan Buddhist Lamaist; suppressed in the 1930s
government Great People's Assembly elected for four years by universal suffrage (the chair-

man of the presidium is head of state); the Communist party is the only political party.
chronology
1911 Outer Mongolia gained autonomy from China.
1924 People's Republic proclaimed.
1946 China recognized Outer Mongolia's independence.
1966 20–year friendship, co-operation and mutual assistance pact signed with Soviet Union. Deterioration in relations with China.

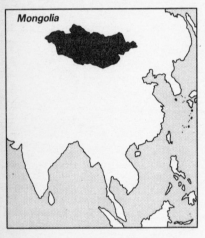

1986 Soviet troop numbers reduced and Outer Mongolia's external contacts broadened.

Morocco Kingdom of
area 458,730 sq km/166,000 sq mi
capital Rabat
towns Marrakesh, Fez, Kenes; ports are Casablanca, Tangier
features Atlas Mountains; Ceuta (from 1580), Melilla (from 1492), and three small coastal settlements are held by Spain; a tunnel across the Strait of Gibraltar to Spain was proposed in 1985
exports dates, figs; cork, wood pulp; canned fish; phosphates; tourism is important
currency dirham
population (1985) 23,117,000
language Arabic (official); French, Spanish

religion Sunni Muslim
government constitutional monarchy (Hassan II), with a unicameral legislature elected two-thirds directly and one-third indirectly through electoral colleges.
chronology
1956 Achieved independence from France as the Sultanate of Morocco.
1957 Sultan restyled King of Morocco.

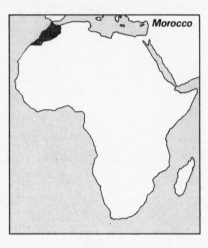

1960 Hassan II came to the throne.
1972 Major revision of the constitution.
1975 Western Sahara ceded by Spain to Morocco and Mauritania.
1976 Guerrilla war in the Sahara by the Polisario Front. Sahrawi Arab Democratic Republic (SADR) established in Algiers. Diplomatic relations between Morocco and Algeria broken.
1979 Mauritania signed a peace treaty with Polisario.
1983 Peace formula for the Sahara proposed by the Organization of African Unity (OAU) but not accepted by Morocco.
1984 Hassan signed an agreement for co-operation and mutual defence with Libya.

Mozambique People's Republic of
area 784,960 sq km/303,070 sq mi

capital and chief port Maputo
towns other ports Beira, Nacala
features rivers Zambezi, Limpopo
exports sugar, cashews, tea, cotton, copra, sisal
currency escudo
population (1985) 13,638,000 (mainly indigenous Bantu peoples; Portuguese (formerly 250,000) 50,000)

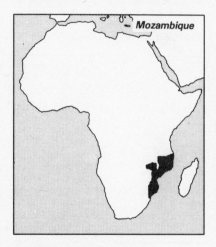
Mozambique

Nauru Republic of
area 21 sq km/8 sq mi
products phosphates
currency pound sterling
population (1985) 8,000 (mainly Polynesian)
language Nauruan, English
religion Protestant 45%
government head chief and executive president (Hammer DeRoburt 1968–1976, and from 1978) and parliament of 18 members.

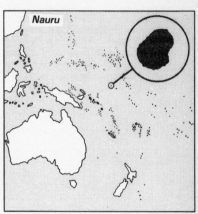
Nauru

language Portuguese (official)
religion Animist 69%; Roman Catholic 21%; Muslim 10%
government executive president (Joaquim Chissano from 1986), council of ministers and elected people's assembly. Frelimo (the Marxist liberation front, Frente de Libertação de Moçambique) is the sole political party.
chronology
1962 Frelimo established.
1975 Full independence achieved as a socialist republic, with Samora Machel as president, and Frelimo as the sole legal party.
1983 Re-establishment of good relations with Western powers.
1984 Nkomati Accord signed with South Africa.
1986 Machel killed in air crash, and succeeded by Joaquim Chissano.

chronology
1888 Annexed by Germany.
1920 Administered by Australia, New Zealand and UK until independence, except 1942–45, when occupied by Japan.
1968 Full independence achieved, with 'special member' Commonwealth status. Hammer DeRoburt elected president.
1971 DeRoburt re-elected.
1973 DeRoburt re-elected.
1976 Bernard Dowiyogo elected president.
1978 DeRoburt returned to power.
1983 DeRoburt re-elected.
1986 Hung parliament.
Nepál
area 141,400 sq km/54,600 sq mi
capital Káthmándu
features Mt Everest, Mt Kanchenjunga

exports jute, rice, timber
currency Nepalese rupee
population (1985) 16,480,000 (mainly known by the name of the predominant clan, the Gurkhas; the Sherpas are a Buddhist minority of northeast Nepál)
language Nepáli
religion Hindu, with Buddhist minority
government constitutional monarch, King Birendra (1946–) from 1972, who still appoints a number of members to the non-party national parliament (panchayat) elected indirectly by a rising succession of village/town, district, and zone panchayats, by universal suffrage

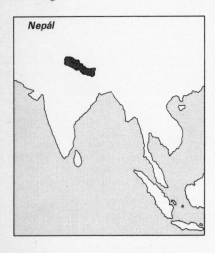

chronology
1768 Nepál emerged as a unified kingdom.
1846–1951 Ruled by the Rana family.
1951 Monarchy restored.
1959 Constitution created elected legislature.
1960–1 Parliament dissolved by king and political parties banned.
1980 Constitutional referendum held following popular agitation.
1981 Direct elections held to national assembly.
1983 Overthrow of monarch-supported prime minister.

1986 New assembly elections return a majority opposed to panchayat system.

Netherlands Kingdom of the (including the Netherlands Antilles), popularly referred to as *Holland*
area 34,000 sq km/13,020 sq mi
capital Amsterdam
towns The Hague (seat of government); chief port Rotterdam
features almost completely flat; rivers Rhine, Schelde (*Scheldt*), Maas; Ijsselmeer (formerly the Zuider Zee); Frisian islands

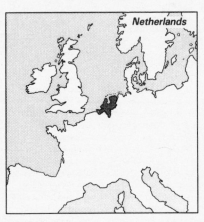

exports dairy products, flower bulbs, vegetables, petro-chemicals, electronics
currency guilder
population (1985) 14,481,000 (including 300,000 Eurasians of Dutch-Indonesian origin absorbed 1949–64 from the former colonial possessions of Indonesia, East Indies, New Guinea, and Suriname)
language Dutch
religion Roman Catholic 35%; Protestant 28%
government under the revised constitution of 1972, there is a constitutional monarch (Beatrix) of the House of Orange, and a parliament of two chambers, the upper elected for six years by the provincial council, and the lower elected for four years by proportional representation (prime minister from 1982 Rudolph

Lubbers (Christian Democratic Appeal), at the head of a centre-right coalition)

chronology

1940–44 Occupied by Germany during World War II.

1947 Joined Benelux Union.

1948 Queen Juliana succeeded Queen Wilhelmina to the throne.

1949 Founder member of NATO.

1958 Joined European Community.

1980 Queen Juliana abdicated in favour of her daughter Beatrix.

New Zealand

area 268,675 sq km/103,736 sq mi

capital Wellington

towns Hamilton, Palmerston North, Christchurch, Dunedin; ports Wellington, Auckland

features comprises North and South Islands, Stewart and Chatham Islands. On *North Island* besides Ruapehu, at 2,797.5 m/ 9,175 ft, the highest of three active volcanoes, there are the geysers and hot springs of the Rotorua district, Lake Taupo (616 5 sq km/238 sq mi), source of Waikato river, and NE of the lake, Kaingaroa state forest, one of the world's largest planted forests. On *South Island* are the Southern Alps and Canterbury Plains, famous for sheep

exports lamb and beef, wool and leather, dairy products and other processed foods; kiwi fruit became a major export crop in the 1980s; seeds and breeding stock; timber, paper, pulp; light aircraft

currency New Zealand dollar

population (1985) 3,271,000 (including 270,000 Maoris and 60,000 other Polynesians; the whites are chiefly of British descent)

language English (official); Maori (the Lange government pledged to give it official status)

religion Protestant 50%; Roman Catholic 15%

government under the amended constitution of 1947, there is a governor-general appointed by the Crown, aided by an executive council, and a unicameral legislature, the house of representatives (Prime Minister David Lange from 1984, Labour), elected for three years, which includes four Maori members.

chronology

1947 Full independence within the Commonwealth confirmed by the New Zealand parliament.

New Zealand

1972 National Party government replaced Labour Party, with Norman Kirk as prime minister.

1974 Kirk died and was replaced by Wallace Rowling.

1975 National Party returned, with Robert Muldoon as prime minister.

1978 National Party re-elected, with a reduced majority.

1984 Labour Party returned under David Lange.

1985 Non-nuclear defence policy created disagreements with France and the United States.

Nicaragua Republic of

area 148,000 sq km/57,150 sq mi

capital Managua

towns chief port Corinto

features largest state of Central America, and most thinly populated; lakes Nicaragua and Managua

exports coffee, cotton, sugar

currency cordoba

population (1985) 2,232,000 (70% *mestizo*; 15% Spanish descent; 10% Indian or black)

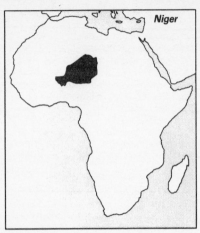

assembly. President from 1974 Colonel Seyni Kountché.

language Spanish (official)
religion Roman Catholic
government constituent assembly elected in 1984; president from Jan 1985 Daniel Ortega Saavedra.
chronology
1962 Sandinista National Liberation Front (FSLN) formed to fight Somoza regime.
1979 Somoza government ousted by FSLN.
1982 Subversive activity against the government promoted by the US. State of emergency declared.
1985 Denunciation of Sandinista government by US President Reagan. FSLN won big victory in assembly elections.
1987 New constitution came into effect.

Niger Republic of
area 1,187,000 sq km/459,000.5 sq mi
capital Niamey
features part of the Sahara Desert and subject to Sahel droughts
exports groundnuts; livestock; gum arabic; tin, uranium
currency CFA franc
population (1985) 6,491,000
language French (official); Hausa, Djerma
religion Sunni Muslim 85%; Animist 15%
government a presidential system based on that of the USA, but with a single-chamber national

chronology
1960 Achieved full independence from France with Hamani Diori elected president.
1965 Diori re-elected.
1970 Diori re-elected.
1974 Diori ousted in an army coup led by Seyni Kountché.
1977 Co-operation agreement signed with France.

Nigeria Federal Republic of
area 924,000 sq km/357,000 sq mi
capital Lagos
towns chief port Lagos; administrative headquarters Abuja; Ibadan, Ogbomosho, Kano; ports Port Harcourt, Warri, Calabar
features river Niger; harmattan (a dry wind from the Sahara)
exports petroleum (richest African country in oil resources); cocoa, groundnuts, palm oil, cotton, rubber, tin
currency naira
population (1985) 102,783,000 (of three main ethnic groups, Yoruba in the west, Ibo in the east, and Hausa-Fulani in the north)
language English (official); Hausa, Ibo,

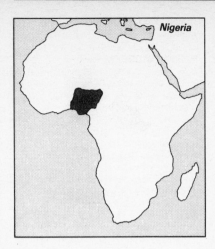

Nigeria

area 324,220 sq km/125,065.5 sq mi
capital Oslo
towns Bergen, Trondheim and Stavanger
features beautiful fjords, including Hardanger and Sogne, the longest 185 km/115 mi and deepest 1,245 m/4,080 ft; forests and glaciers cover 25%; Midnight Sun and Northern Lights; great resources of hydroelectric power; dependencies in the Arctic (Svalbard and Jan Mayen) and in the Antarctic (Bouvet and Peter I Island, and Queen Maud Land)

Norway

Yoruba
religion Sunni Muslim in the north, Christian in the south
government supreme military council headed by Major-General Ibrahim Babangida who became head of government in a bloodless military coup in 1985, and a federal executive council which acts as a cabinet.
chronology
1960 Achieved full independence within the Commonwealth.
1963 Became a republic, with Nnamdi Azikiwe as president.
1966 Military coup, followed by a counter-coup led by General Yakubu Gowon. Slaughter of many members of the Ibo tribe in the north.
1967 Declaration of an independent state of Biafra by the military governor of the eastern region, Colonel Chuk Wuemeka Odumegwu-Ojukwu. Outbreak of civil war.
1970 Surrender of Biafra and end of civil war.
1975 Gowon ousted in a bloodless coup led by General Muhammadu Buhari.
1985 Buhari replaced in a bloodless coup led by Major-General Ibrahim Babangida, who promised to return to civilian rule.
Norway Kingdom of

exports petrochemicals from North Sea oil and gas; paper, wood pulp, furniture; iron ore and other minerals; hightech goods, for example gas turbines, TV sets; sports goods; fish
currency krone
population (1985) 4,152,000
language Riksmlzal (formal Dano-Norwegian) and Landsmåal (based on the local dialects of Norway)
religion Evangelical Lutheran (endowed by state)
government constitutional monarchy (Olav V), with a parliament (Storting) elected for four years (prime minister from 1986 Ms Harlem Brundtland)
chronology
1814 Became independent from Denmark.
1905 Links with Sweden ended.

1940–45 Occupied by Germany.
1949 Joined NATO.
1952 Joined Nordic Council.
1957 King Haakon VII succeeded by his son, Olav V.
1960 Joined EFTA.
1972 Accepted into membership of the European Community but application withdrawn, following a referendum.

Oman Sultanate of
area 212,000 sq km/82,000 sq mi
capital Muscat
towns Salalah in Dhofar (the barren southern province)
features Jebel Akhdar highlands, plateau reaching to the edge of the 'Empty Quarter'; including Kuria Muria islands; Masirah Island is used in aerial reconnaissance of the Arabian Sea and Indian Ocean

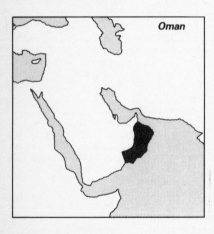

Oman

chronology
1951 Muscat and Oman achieved full independence as the Sultanate of Oman. Treaty of friendship with Britain signed.
1970 After 38 years rule, Sultan Said bin Taimur overthrown in a bloodless coup, and replaced by his son Qaboos bin Said.

Pakistan Islamic Republic of
area 803,900 sq km/310,400 sq mi; one-third of Kashmir is under Pakistani control
capital Islamabad
towns Karachi (largest city and port), Lahore
features the 'five rivers' (Indus, Jhelum, Chenab, Ravi and Sutlej), feeding one of the world's largest irrigation systems; Khyber Pass; sites of the Indus Valley civilization
exports cotton textiles, rice, leather, carpets
currency Pakistan rupee
population (1985) 99,199,000 (66% Punjabi, 13% Sindhi)
language Urdu and English (official); Punjabi

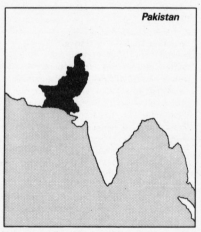

Pakistan

exports oil, dates, silverware
currency Omani rial
population (1985) 1,228,000
language Arabic
religion Sunni Muslim
government Sultan Qaboos bin Said is himself prime minister, legislating by decree, with the aid of a cabinet and (from 1981) a consultative assembly.

religion Sunni Muslim 75%; Shi'ite Muslim 20%; Hindu 4%
government executive president (Zia ul-Haq from 1978) heading a national security council, which was established 1985 to increase the presidential powers; at the same time parlia-

ment also assembled (Prime Minister Mohammad Khan Junjo).

chronology
1947 Pakistan formed following partition of
India.
1956 Proclaimed a republic.
1958 Military rule imposed by General Ayub
Khan.
1969 Power transferred to General Yahya
Khan.
1971 Assembly elections held; secession of East
Pakistan (Bangladesh). Following civil war,
power was transferred to Zulfiqar Ali Bhutto.
1977 Bhutto overthrown in military coup by
General Zia ul-Haq. Martial law imposed.
1979 Bhutto executed.
1981 Opposition Movement for Restoration of
Democracy formed. Islamization process
pushed forward.
1985 Non-party elections held, amended constitution adopted, martial law and ban on
political parties lifted.
1986 Agitation for free elections launched by
Benazir Bhutto.

Panama Republic of
area 76,614 sq km/31,293 sq mi
capital Panama City
towns Cristóbal, Balboa, Colón
features Panama Canal; Barro Colorado Island
in Gatun Lake (the reservoir which supplies
the canal), a tropical forest reserve since 1923;
Smithsonian Tropical Research Institute
exports bananas, petroleum products; copper
from one of the world's largest deposits;
shrimps
currency balboa
population (1985) 2,180,000
language Spanish
religion Roman Catholic
government executive president (from 1985
Eric Arturo Del Valle; Democratic Revolutionary Party, (PRD)) and legislative assembly
chronology
1903 Became independent from Colombia.
1974 Agreement to negotiate a full transfer of
the Panama Canal from the United States to
Panama.
1977 US-Panama Treaty, transferring the

Canal to Panama, with the United States
guaranteeing its protection and an annual
payment.

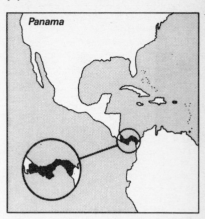

1984 Nicolas Ardito Barletta of the Democratic
Revolutionary Party (PRD) elected president.
1985 Barletta resigned to be replaced by Eric
Arturo Dell Valle.

Papua New Guinea
area 462,000 sq km/178,260 sq mi
capital Port Moresby
features wholly within the tropics, with a rainfall up to 200 in a year; rare birds of paradise,
the world's largest butterfly, orchids
exports copra, coconut oil, palm oil, tea;
copper
currency kina
population (1985) 3,326,000 (including
Papuans, Melanesians, Pygmies, and various
minorities)
language English (official); Pidgin
religion Protestant 33%; Roman Catholic 18%;
local faiths
government governor-general, and unicameral
house of assembly; prime minister Michael
Somare from 1982.
chronology
1883 Annexed by Queensland, and soon
became known as the Australian Territory of
Papua.

561

1884 North East New Guinea annexed by Germany.

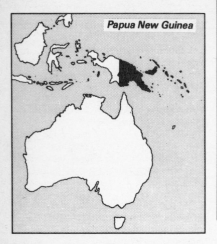

Papua New Guinea

Paraguay

1914 North East New Guinea occupied by Australia.

1921–42 Held as a League of Nations mandate.

1942–45 Occupied by Japan.

1975 Achieved full independence, within the Commonwealth, with Michael Somare as prime minister.

1980 Sir Julius Chan, leader of the People's Progress Party, became prime minister.

1982 Somare returned to power.

1985 Somare challenged by deputy prime minister, Payas Wingti, who later formed a new, five-party coalition government.

Paraguay Republic of

area 406,752 sq km/157,042sq mi

capital Asunción

town port Concepción

features Paraná and Paraguay rivers; Itaipú dam on border with Brazil; Chaco

exports cotton, soybeans, timber, tung oil, maté

currency guaraní

population (1985) 3,989,000 (95% of mixed Guaraní Indian-Spanish descent)

language Spanish (official), spoken by 4%; Guaraní 50%; remainder bilingual

religion Roman Catholic

government executive president, elected for five years (Alfredo Stroessner from 1954,) and parliament of two houses

chronology

1811 Independent from Spain.

1865–70 At war with Argentina, Brazil and Uruguay. Much territory lost.

1932–35 Much territory won from Bolivia during the Chaco War.

1954 General Alfredo Stroessner in power. He has since been re-elected six times, despite increasing opposition and accusations of human rights violations.

1984–87 Speculation increased about Stroessner's successor; some favour an eighth term, with his son succeeding him, others would prefer him to retire in 1988, when he will be 76. The general himself is reported to favour staying on.

Peru Republic of

area 1,332,000 sq km/514,060 sq mi

capital Lima, including port of Callao

towns Arequipa, Iquitos, Chiclayo

features Andes mountains, Lake Titicaca, Peru Current, Atacama Desert; monuments of the Chimu and Inca civilizations
exports coffee; alpaca, llama and vicuna wool; fishmeal; lead, copper, iron, oil

Peru

currency sol
population (1984) 19,698,000 46% American Indian, mainly Quechua and Aymara; 43% of mixed Spanish–American Indian descent
language Spanish, Quechua, (both official)
religion Roman Catholic
government executive president (Alan García Pérez from 1985), senate and chamber of deputies
chronology
1824 Achieved independence from Spain, the last South American country to do so.
1902 Boundary dispute with Bolivia settled.
1927 Boundary dispute with Colombia settled.
1942 Boundary dispute with Ecuador settled.
1948 Army coup, led by General Manuel Odria, installed a military government.
1963 Return to civilian rule, with Fernando Belaunde as president.

1968 Return of military government in a bloodless coup, by General Juan Velasco.
1975 Velasco replaced, in a bloodless coup, by General Morales Bermudez.
1980 Return to civilian rule, with Fernando Belaunde as president.
1981 Boundary dispute with Ecuador renewed.
1985 Belaunde succeeded by Social Democrat, Alan Carcía Perez.

Philippines Republic of the
area 300,000 sq km/115,700 sq mi
capital Manila (on Luzon)
towns Quezon City
ports Cebu, Davao (on Mindanao) and Iloilu
features comprises over 7,000 islands, with volcanic mountain ranges traversing the main chain north to south, and 50% of the area still forested. The largest islands are *Luzon* 108,172 sq km/41,765 sq mi (site of Clark Field, US air base, and Subic Bay, US naval base) and *Mindanao* 94,227 sq km/36,381 sq mi, which has the active volcano Apo (2,855 m/9,369 ft) and mountainous rain forest; others include Samar, Negros, Palawan, Panay, Mindoro, Leyte, Cebu and the Sulu group
exports sugar, copra and coconut oil; timber; iron ore and copper concentrates
currency peso
population (1985) 56,808,000 (93% Malaysian)
language Filipino (based on the Malay dialect, Tagalog), but English and Spanish are in common use
religion Roman Catholic 84%; Protestant 9%; Muslim 5%
government Corazón Aquino (born 1933) heads a government set up in 1986, following the deposition of President Marcos after many years of increasingly despotic government.
chronology
1542 Named the Philippines by Spanish explorers.
1565 Conquered by Spain.
1898 Ceded to the United States.
1935 Grant of internal self-government.
1942–5 Japanese occupation.
1946 Independence granted.
1965 Ferdinand Marcos elected president.
1983 Murder of Benigno Aquino.

563

1986 Overthrow of Marcos by Corazón Aquino's 'people's power' movement.

Philippines

1987 New constitution approved,sweeping victory for Aquino coalition in elections.

Poland People's Republic of
area 312,600 sq km/120,600 sq mi
capital Warsaw
towns Lódź, Kraków, Wroclaw, Poznań, Katowice, Bydgoszcz; Gdánsk, Szczecin

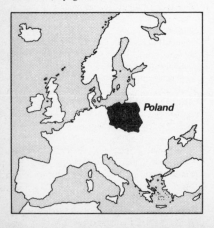

Poland

features comprises part of the great plain of Europe; Vistula, Oder and Neisse rivers
exports coal, softwood timber, chemicals
currency zloty
population (1985) 37,160,000
language Polish, a Slavonic language
religion Roman Catholic 93%
government under the modified constitution of 1976, the nominal head of state is the chairman of the council of state, elected by the Sejm (parliament), itself elected by universal suffrage. Real power lies with the first secretary of the politburo (General Wojciech Jaruzelski from 1981, who is also minister of defence).
chronology
1939 German invasion and occupation.
1944 Germans driven out by Russian force.
1945 Polish boundaries re-drawn.
1947 Communist people's republic proclaimed.
1956 Pozon riots. Gomulka installed as Polish United Workers' Party (PUWP) leader.
1970 Gomulka replaced by Gierek.
1980 Emergence of Solidarity free trade union following Gdansk disturbances.
1981 Imposition of martial law by General Jaruzelski.
1983 Ending of martial law.
1984 Amnesty for political prisoners.

Portugal Republic of
area 91,631 sq km/34,861 sq mi (including Azores and Madeira)
capital Lisbon
towns Coimbra; and the ports Oporto, Setúbal
features rivers Minho, Douro, Tagus
exports port wine, olive oil, resin, cork
currency escudo
population (1985) 10,046,000
language Portuguese, one of the Romance languages, ultimately derived from Latin.
religion Roman Catholic
government president (Dr Mario Soares from 1986), a corporative chamber and national assembly (prime minister from 1985 Aníbal Cavaco e Silva, Social Democrat).
chronology
1928–68 Personal rule of prime minister Antonio de Oliveira Salazar.

Portugal

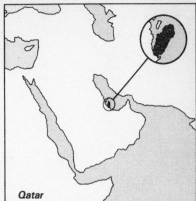

Qatar

1968 Salazar succeeded by Marcello Caetano.

1974 Caetano removed in a military coup, led by General Antonio Ribeiro de Spinola. Spinola was then replaced by General Fransisco da Costa Gomes.

1976 New constitution, providing for a gradual return to civilian rule, adopted. Minority government appointed, led by Socialist Party leader, Mario Soares.

1978 Soares resigned.

1980 Francisco Balsemão formed a centre-party coalition, following two and a half years of political instability.

1982 Draft of new constitution approved, reducing the powers of the presidency.

1983 PS–PSD (Socialist Party–Social Democratic Party) coalition government formed.

1985 PSD minority government formed, with Cavacoe Silva as prime minister.

1986 Mario Soares elected first civilian president for 60 years.

Qatar State of

area 11,437 sq km/4,250 sq mi

capital and chief port Doha

towns Dukhan, centre of oil production

features negligible rain and surface water, so that only 3% is fertile, but irrigation allows self-sufficiency in fruit and vegetables; rich oil discoveries since World War II

exports oil and natural gas, petrochemicals, fertilizers, iron and steel

currency Qatar riyal

population (1985) 301,000 (mainly in Doha)

language Arabic

religion Sunni Muslim

government Sheikh Khalifa bin Hamad al-Thani (born 1930) from 1972, when he deposed his cousin and introduced reforms

chronology

1970 Constitution adopted, confirming the emirate as an absolute monarchy.

1971 Achieved full independence. New Treaty of Friendship with Britain signed.

1972 Emir Sheik Ahmad replaced in a bloodless coup, by his cousin, Crown Prince Sheikh Khalifa.

Romania or **Rumania** Socialist Republic of

area 237,500 sq km/91,699 sq mi

capital Bucharest

towns Brasov, Timisoara, Cluj, Iasi; ports are Galati, Constanta, Sulina

features Carpathian Mountains, Transylvanian Alps, river Danube, Black Sea coast; especially rich in mineral springs

exports petroleum products and oilfield equipment, electrical goods, cars (largely to Com-

munist countries)
currency leu

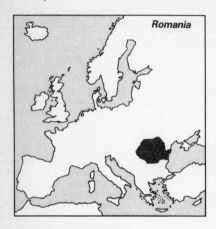

Romania

population (1985) 22,734,000 (including 400,000 Germans)
language Romanian, a Romance language descended from that of Roman settlers, though later modified by Slav influences
religion Romanian Orthodox Church (linked with the Greek Orthodox)
government grand national assembly, which sits only briefly, and a state council, headed by the president (Nicolae Ceausescu from 1967, who is also general secretary of the Communist party, with which real power rests).
chronology
1944 Pro-Nazi Antonescu government overthrown.
1945 Communist-dominated government appointed.
1947 Boundaries redrawn. King Michael abdicated and People's Republic proclaimed.
1949 New constitution adopted. Joined Comecon.
1952 New Soviet-style constitution.
1955 Romania joined Warsaw Pact.
1958 Russian occupation forces removed.
1965 Succession of Georghiu-Dej by Ceausescu. New constitution adopted.
1974 Post of president of the republic created.

1985–86 Winters of austerity and power cuts.
   Rwanda or *Ruanda* Republic of
area 26,338 sq km/10,169 sq mi
capital Kigali
features part of lake Kivu; volcanic mountains, highest peak Mt Karisimbi 4,507 m/14,786 ft; Kagera river (whose headwaters are the source of the Nile) and National Park
exports coffee, tea, pyrethrum, tin and tungsten
currency Rwanda franc
population (1984) 5,650,000 (Hutu 90%; Tutsi 9%)

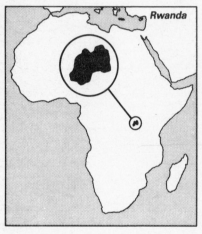

Rwanda

language Kinyarwanda (a Bantu language) and French
religion Christian (mainly Catholic) 54%; Animist 45%; Muslim 1%
government executive president (Juvenal Habyarimana from 1973) and national development council.
chronology
1962 Rwanda achieved full independence as the Republic of Rwanda, with Gregoire Kayibanda as president.
1962–65 Tribal warfare between the Hutu and the Tutsi.
1972 Renewal of tribal fighting.

1973 Kayibanda ousted in a military coup led by Major-General Juvenal Habyarimana.
1978 New constitution approved.

St Christopher (St Kitts)-Nevis federal state comprising two islands in the Caribbean Lesser Antilles
area 261 sq km/100 sq mi
capital Basseterre (on St Kitts)

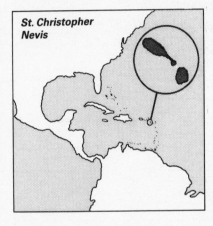

towns Nevis (chief town of Nevis)
features St Kitts was the first of the British West Indian islands to be colonized
exports sugar and molasses, cotton; tourism is important
currency East Caribbean dollar
population (1985) 47,000
language English
religion Christian
government governor-general appointed by the British monarch; there is a prime minister (Kennedy Simmonds from 1983) heading a conservative coalition from 1980, and a national assembly (nine members) for both islands on St Kitts, and a separate assembly on St Kitts.
chronology
1967 St Christopher, Nevis and Anguilla were granted internal self-government, within the

Commonwealth, with Robert Bradshaw, Labour party leader, as prime minister.
1970 Nevis Reformation Party (NRP) formed.
1971 Anguilla left the federation.
1978 Bradshaw died and was succeeded by Paul Southwell.
1979 Southwell died and was succeeded by Lee L Moore.
1980 People's Action Movement–NRP coalition government, led by Kennedy Simmonds.
1983 St Christopher and Nevis achieved full independence within the Commonwealth.
1984 PAM–NRP coalition re-elected.

St Lucia
area 616 sq km/238 sq mi
capital Castries
features second largest of the Windward group; mainly tropical forest

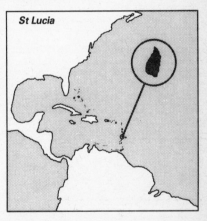

exports bananas, cocoa, copra; tourism is important
currency East Caribbean dollar
population (1985) 122,000
language English
religion 90% Roman Catholic
government governor-general, senate, house of assembly (prime minister from 1982 John Compton).
chronology
1967 Granted internal self-government as a

West Indies Associated State.
1979 Achieved full independence within the Commonwealth, with John Compton, leader of the United Workers' Party (UWP), as prime minister. Allan Louisy, leader of the St Lucia Labour Party (SLP), replaced Compton as prime minister.
1981 Louisy resigned and was replaced by Winston Cenac. George Odlum left the SLP to form the Progressive Labour Party (PLP).
1982 Compton returned to power at the head of a UWP government.

St Vincent and the Grenadines
area 389 sq km/150 sq mi, including N Grenadines 44 sq km/17 sq mi
capital Kingstown
features Mustique, one of the Grenadines, is an exclusive holiday resort
exports bananas, arrowroot, copra
currency East Caribbean dollar
population (1985) 102,000

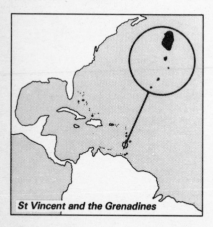

St Vincent and the Grenadines

language English
religion Christian (Methodist, Anglican, Roman Catholic)
government governor-general and house of assembly (prime minister James Mitchell from 1984, centrist New Democratic Party)
chronology
1969 Granted internal self-government.

568

1974 Achieved full independence within the Commonwealth, with Milton Cato as leader of the St Vincent Labour Party (SVLP).
1984 James Mitchell, leader of the New Democratic Party (NDP), won a surprising victory and replaced Cato as prime minister.

Samoa Western
area 2,842 sq km/1,097 sq mi
capital Apia on Upolu
features comprises islands of Savai'i and Upolu, with two smaller islands and islets; mountain ranges on the main islands; huge lava flows on Savai'i which cut down the area available for agriculture

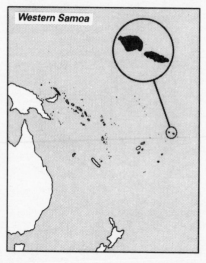

Western Samoa

exports copra, bananas, cocoa; tourism is important
currency tala
population (1985) 160,000
language English and Samoan (official)
religion Christian
government head of state, eventually to be elected for five years (Malietoa Tanumafili II, sole head for life from 1962); legislative assembly (prime minister from 1982 Va'ai Kolone).
chronology

1962 Achieved full independence within the Commonwealth, with Fiame Mata'afa Mulinu'u as prime minister.

1975 Mata'afa died and was succeeded by Tupuola Taisi Efi, the first non-royal prime minister.

1979 New opposition party formed, the Human Rights Protection Party (HRPP).

1982 HRPP won the general election and Va'ai Kolone became prime minister, but was replaced the same year by Tupuola Efi. Tupuola Efi then resigned when the assembly failed to approve his budget and was replaced by the new HRPP leader, Tufilau Eti Alesana.

1985 The HRPP won the general election and Tufilau Eti continued as prime minister. He later resigned over his budget proposals and the Head of State erfused to call a general election, iniviting Va'ai Kolombe to return to lead the government.

San Marino Most Serene Republic of
area

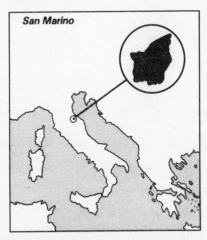

58 sq km/22.5 sq mi
capital San Marino
features completely surrounded by Italian territory; one of the world's smallest states
exports wine, ceramics, paint
currency Italian lira

population (1985) 22,300
language Italian
religion Roman Catholic
government legislative great and general council, and an executive state congress, headed by two bi-annually elected regents
chronology
1962 Treaty with Italy signed, recognising its independence and providing for its protection.
1947–78 Governed by a series of left-wing coalitions.

São Tomé e Principe Democratic Republic of
area 964 sq km/372 sq mi
capital São Tomé
features comprises the two main islands and several smaller ones
exports cocoa, copra
currency dobra
population (1985) 105,000

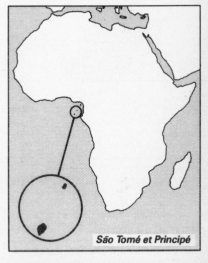

language Portuguese
religion Roman Catholic
government executive president and people's assembly, president from 1975 Manuel Pinto da Costa; only one party is allowed.

569

chronology
1973 Granted internal self-government.
1975 Achieved full independence, with Manuel Pinto da Costa as president.
1984 Formally declared itself a non-aligned state.

Saudi Arabia Kingdom of
area 2,400,000 sq km/927,000 sq mi
capital Riyadh
towns Mecca, Medina, and the ports of Jidda and Dammam
features Nafud desert in the north, and the Rub' al Khali ('Empty Quarter') in the south, area 650,000 sq km/ 250,000 sq mi
exports oil
currency rial

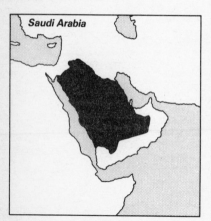

population (1985) 11,152,000
language Arabic
religion Sunni Muslim, with a Shi'ite minority in the east under the influence of Ayatollah Khomeini
government the king (Fahd ibn Abdul Aziz from 1982) heads the council of ministers as prime minister; there is no formal constitution.
chronology
1953 King Faisal died and was succeeded by his eldest son, Saud.
1964 King Saud forced to abdicate and was succeeded by his brother, Faisal.

1975 King Faisal assassinated by a nephew and succeeded by his half-brother, Khalid.
1982 King Khalid died suddenly of a heart attack and was suceeded by his brother Crown Prince Fahd, who had effectively been ruling the country for some years because of King Khalid's ill health.

Senegal Republic of
area 197,000 sq km/76,000.5 sq mi
capital and chief port Dakar
towns Thies, Kaolack
features river Senegal; The Gambia forms an enclave within it
exports ground nuts, cotton; fish; phosphates

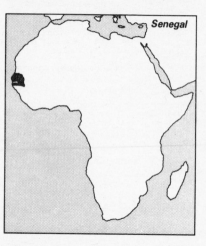

currency CFA franc
population (1985) 6,485,000
language French (official)
religion Muslim 80%; Christian 10% (chiefly Roman Catholic); Animist 10%
government executive president (Abdou Diouf from 1981) with a government council and national assembly. There is a multi-party system.
chronology
1960 Achieved full independence, with Léopold Sedar Senghor, leader of the Sengalese Progressive Union (UPS), as

president.
1966 UPS declared the only legal party.
1976 UPS reconstituted as the Sengalese Socialist Party (PS). Abdou Diouf nominated as Senghor's successor.
1980 Senghor retired and was succeeded by Diouf. Troops sent to defend The Gambia.
1981 Military help again sent to the Gambia.
1982 Confederation of Senegambia came into effect.
1983 Diouf re-elected. Post of prime minister abolished.

Seychelles
area 404 sq km/156 sq mi
capital Victoria on Mahé
features comprises two distinct island groups, one concentrated, the other widely scattered, totalling well over 100 islands and islets; the unique 'double coconut'
exports copra, cinnamon; tourism is important
currency Seychelles rupee
population (1985) 66,000

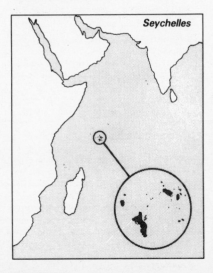

Seychelles

government there is an executive president (France – Albert René from 1977) with a council of ministers and people's assembly.
chronology
1970 Constitutional conference in London on future status of Seychelles. James Mancham, leader of the Seychelles Democratic Party (SDP), argued for full independence, while France-Albert René, leader of the Seychelles People's United Party (SPUP), favoured full integration with the UK.
1975 Internal self-government granted.
1976 Full independence achieved, as a republic within the Commonwealth, and Mancham as president.
1977 René ousted Mancham in an armed coup and took over the presidency.
1979 New constitution adopted, making the SPUP, restyled the Seychelles People's Progressive Front (SPPF), the only legal party.
1981 Attempted coup by South African mercenaries thwarted.
1984 René re-elected.

Sierra Leone Republic of
area 73,325 sq km/27,925 sq mi
capital Freetown

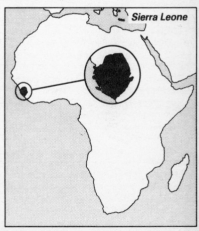

Sierra Leone

language Creole, spoken by 95%, English and French (all official)
religion Christian (Roman Catholic 90%)

towns Bo, Kenema, Makeni

571

features coastal mangrove swamps with hot and humid climate (3,500 mm/138 in rainfall annually)

exports palm kernels, cocoa, coffee, ginger; diamonds, bauxite, rutile

currency leone

population (1985) 3,883,000

language English (official); local languages

religion Muslim 60%; Animist 30%

government under the constitution of 1978, it is a one-party state (All People's Congress: APC), with an executive president (Major-General Joseph Saidu Momoh from 1985) and a house of representatives.

chronology

1961 Achieved full independence, as a constitutional monarchy within the Commonwealth, with Sir Milton Margai, leader of the Sierra Leone People's Party (SLPP), as prime minister.

1964 Sir Milton succeeded by his half brother Albert Margai.

1967 General election results disputed by the army who set up a National Reformation Council and forced the governor-general to leave.

1968 Another army revolt made Siaka Stevens, leader of the All-People's Congress (APC), prime minister.

1971 New constitution adopted, making Sierra Leone a republic, with Stevens as president.

1978 APC declared the only legal party. Stevens sworn in for another seven- year term.

1985 Stevens retired at the age of 80and was succeeded by Major-General Joseph Momoh.

Singapore Republic of

area 581.5 sq km/225.6 sq mi

capital Singapore City in the S of the island, a major world port and financial centre, founded by Stamford Raffles (commemorated by a museum)

features comprises Singapore Island (joined to the mainland by a causeway across the Strait of Johore) and 54 small islands; temperature ranges only between 2°–3°C/7°–8°F

exports electronics, petroleum products, rubber, machinery, vehicles

currency Singapore dollar

population (1985) 2,556,000 (Chinese 75%; Malay 14%; Tamil 7%)

language Malay, Chinese, Tamil and English (all official)

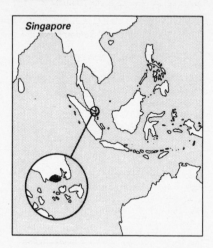
Singapore

religion Buddhist, Taoist, Muslim, Hindu, Christian

government there is a president (Wee Kim Wee from 1985) and unicameral parliament (prime minister from 1959 Lee Kuan Yew)

chronology

1918 Singapore leased to British East India Company.

1958 Placed under Crown rule.

1942 Invaded and occupied by Japan.

1945 Japanese removed by British forces.

1959 Independence granted from Britain: Lee Kuan Yew became prime minister.

1963 Joined new Federation of Malaya.

1965 Left Federation to become independent republic.

1985 Wee Kim became president.

Solomon Islands

area 29,785 sq km/11,500 sq mi

capital Honiara on Guadalcanal

features comprises the southern islands of the Solomon Islands the archipelago including the largest, Guadalcanal (area 4,000 sq km/2,500 sq mi), Malaita, San Cristobal, New Georgia, Santa Isabel, Choiseul; mainly mountainous and forested, with rivers ideal for hydroelectric power

exports palm oil, copra, rice, timber

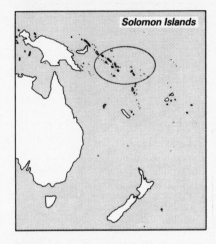

Solomon Islands

currency Solomon Island dollar

population (1985) 267,000 (the majority Melanesian)

language English (official)

religion Christian

government constitutional monarchy with Elizabeth II of Britain as head of state; governor-general and unicameral parliament (prime minister from 1984 Sir Peter Kenilorea).

chronology

1978 Achieved full independence, within the Commonwealth, with Peter Kenilorea, leader of the Solomon Islands United Party (SIUP), as prime minister.

1981 Solomon Mamaloni, leader to the People's Progressive Party (PPP), replaced Kenilora as prime minister.

1984 Kenilora returned to power, heading a coalition government.

Somalia Democratic Republic of

area 700,000 sq km/270,000 sq mi

capital Mogadishu

towns Hargeisa, Kismayu, port Berbera

features one of the world's poorest countries; many of the people are nomadic raisers of livestock

exports livestock, skins, hides, bananas

currency Somali shilling

population (1985) 7,595,000 (including 1,000,000 refugees from W Somalia)

language Somali (national language); Arabic (also official); Italian, English

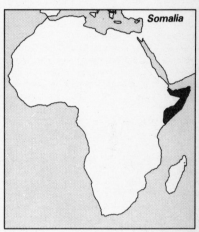

Somalia

religion Sunni Muslim

government under the 1979 constitution there is an executive president (Major-General Mohamed Siad Barre from 1969) nominated by the Revolutionary Socialist Party (the only legal party) and elected by the people's assembly, elected by popular vote.

chronology

1960 Achieved full independence.

1963 Border dispute with Kenya, diplomatic relations with the UK broken.

1968 Diplomatic relations with the UK restored.

1969 Following the assassination of the president, the army seized power. Major-General Mohamed Siad Barre suspended the constitution and set up a Supreme Revolutionary

Council.

1978 Defeated in eight months war with Ethiopia.

1979 New constitution for a socialist one-party state adopted.

1987 Barre re-elected.

South Africa Republic of (Afrikaans *Republiek van Suid Afrika*)

area 1,223,181 sq km/433,678 sq mi

capital Cape Town (legislative), Pretoria (administrative)

towns Johannesburg, Bloemfontein; ports Cape Town, Durban, Port Elizabeth, East London

features Drakensberg Mountains, Table Mountain; Limpopo and Orange rivers; the Veld and the Karroo; part of Kalahari Desert; Johannesburg gold mines and Kimberley diamond mines

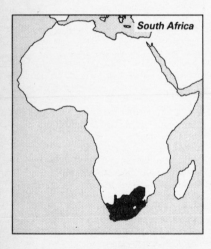

South Africa

exports maize, sugar, wool, fruit, gold, platinum (world's largest producer), diamonds

currency rand

population (1985) 42,465,000 (68% black, of whom the largest nations are the Zulu, Xhosa, Sotho and Tswana, 18% white, 10% coloured, and 3% Asiatic)

language Afrikaans and English (both official); various Bantu languages

religion organized on colour lines, most whites belonging to the Christian Nederduits Gereformeerde Kerk/Dutch Reformed Church; Anglican, Methodist, and Catholic, these three last also having non-white congregations

government executive president, chosen by an electoral college drawn from the three houses of parliament (P W Botha, National Party, from 1984), and a president's council (white, coloured and Indian); black affairs are vested in the president (the Black National States being held to give them self-government). Under the constitution of 1984, parliament comprises three houses: house of assembly (white), house of representatives (coloured), and house of delegates (Indian), which legislate each for their own affairs: general legislation having to pass all three houses. Blacks are excluded from direct participation in government, and are systematically segregated from whites under a policy of apartheid.

chronology

1948 Apartheid system of racial discrimination initiated by National Party (NP) leader, Daniel Malan.

1958 Malan succeeded as prime minister by Hendrik Verwoerd.

1960 African National Congress (ANC) banned and its leader Nelson Mandela, imprisoned.

1961 South Africa withdrew from the Commonwealth and became a republic.

1966 Verwoerd assassinated and succeeded by B J Vorster.

1977 Death in custody of Steve Biko.

1978 Vorster resigned and was replaced by Pieter W Botha.

1982 Andries Treurnicht left NP to found extreme right-wing party, the Conservative Party of South Africa (CPSA).

1984 New constitution adopted, giving representation to Coloureds and Indians.

1985 Growth of violence in Black townships. Commonwealth heads of government appointed the Eminent Persons Group (EPG) to investigate the possibility of South Africa's removing apartheid and thus avoiding the need to impose sanctions.

1986 EPG reported that there were no signs of relaxation and a limited package of measures was agreed. US Congress voted to impose sanctions. Some major multinational companies announced that they were closing down their South African operations. State president Botha announced that there would be a general election in 1987.

Spain
area 504,879 sq km/194,883 sq mi

Spain

capital Madrid
towns Bilbao, Valencia, Saragossa, Murcia; and the ports Barcelona, Seville, Málaga
features includes Balearic and Canary Islands, and Ceuta and Melilla; rivers Ebro, Douro, Tagus, Guadiana, Guadalquivir; Iberian Plateau (Meseta); Pyrenees, Cantabrian Mountains, Andalusian Mountains, Sierra Nevada
exports citrus, grapes, pomegranates, vegetables, wine (especially sherry), olive oil, tinned fruit and fish; iron ore, cork; cars and other vehicles; leather goods; ceramics
currency peseta
population (1985) 38,829,000
language Spanish (Castilian, official), but regional languages are recognized within their own boundaries (Basque, Catalan, Galician, Valencian, and Majorcan are the chief examples)
religion Roman Catholic (there are restrictions on the practice of Protestantism)
government under the constitution of 1978, Spain is a parliamentary monarchy (Juan Carlos from 1975), with a *Cortes Generales* comprising congress of deputies (prime minister from 1982 Felipe González, Socialist Party) elected by proportional representation, and elected senate. There are 17 regions which have a degree of devolved power with their own elected assemblies: Andalusia, Aragón, Asturias, Balearic Islands, Canary Islands, Cantabria, Castile-La Mancha, Castille-Léon, Catalonia, Estremadura, Euskadi (Basque Country), Galicia, La Rioja, Madrid, Murcia, Navarre, Valencia.
chronology
1947 General Franco announced a return to the monarchy after his death, with Prince Juan Carlos as his successor.
1975 Franco died and was succeeded by King Juan Carlos I as head of state.
1978 New constitution adopted with Adolfo Suárez, leader of the Democratic Centre Party, as prime minister.
1981 Suárez resigned and was succeeded by his deputy, Calvo-Sotelo. Attempted military coup thwarted.
1982 Socialist Workers' Party (PSOE), led by Felipe González, won a sweeping electoral victory. Basque separatist organization (ETA) stepped up its terrorist campaign.
1985 ETA's campaign spread to holiday resorts.
1986 Referendum confirmed NATO membership. Spain joined the European Community. PSOE, under González, re-elected.

Sri Lanka Democratic Socialist Republic of
(former name *Ceylon*
area 65,000 sq km/25,332 sq mi
capital and chief port Colombo
towns Kandy; and the ports of Jaffna, Galle, Negombo, Trincomalee
features Adam's Peak; ruined cities of Anuradhapura, Polonnaruwa

1983 Tamil terrorist violence escalated.

Sudan The Democratic Republic of
area 2,500,000.5 sq km/967,500 sq mi
capital Khartoum
towns Omdurman, Juba; chief port Port Sudan
features River Nile, Sudd swamp
exports cotton, gum arabic, sesame, groundnuts, durra
currency Sudanese pound
population (1985) 22,972,000, Arab-speaking and Muslim in the north (70%), and speakers of African languages in the south
language Arabic (official); English

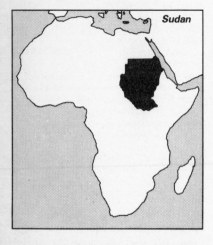

Sudan

religion Sunni Muslim in the north, Animist in the south, with a Christian minority
government elections in April 1986 were won by Umma (a moderate Islamic Party), headed by Sadiq-el-Mahdi. The new government consists of Umma merged with the Democratic Union Party, with Sadiq-el-Mahdi as Prime Minister.
chronology
1955 Civil war between the Muslim north and non-Muslim south broke out.
1956 The Sudan achieved independence as a republic.
1958 Military coup replaced the civilian government with a Supreme Council of the Armed

Forces.
1964 Civilian rule reinstated.
1969 Coup led by Colonel Gaafar Mohammed Nimeri established a Revolutionary Command Council (RCC) and the country's name was changed to the Democratic Republic of the Sudan.
1970 Agreement in principle on the union with Egypt.
1971 New constitution adopted, Nimeri confirmed as President, and the Sudanese Socialist Union (SSU) declared to be the only legal party.
1972 Proposed Federation of Arab Republics, comprising Sudan, Egypt and Syria abandoned. Addis Ababa conference proposed autonomy for southern provinces.
1974 National assembly established.
1983 Nimeri re-elected amid growing opposition to his social, economic and religious policies.
1985 Nimeri deposed in a bloodless coup led by General Swar al-Dahab, who set up a Transitional Military Council (TMC), and announced that he would hand over power to a civilian government within a year.
1986 More than 40 political parties fought the general election with none obtaining a clear majority. A coalition government was formed and the Assembly was charged with producing a new constitution.

Suriname Republic of
area 163,265 sq km/63,250.5 sq mi
capital Paramaribo
features Surinam river
exports bauxite, rice, citrus; timber
currency Surinam guilder
population (1985) 395,000, including Creole, Chinese, Hindu, and Indonesian peoples
language Dutch, English (official)
religion Christian 35%, Hindu 25%, Muslim 17%
government National Military Council (headed by Lt-Colonel Desi Bouterse from 1982); a national assembly was appointed 1985 to draft a new constitution.
chronology
1954 Granted internal self-government as

576

Dutch Guiana.

1975 Achieved full independence with Dr Johan Ferrier as president and Henck Arron, leader of the Suriname National Party (NPS), as prime minister.

1980 Arron's government overthrown in an army coup but President Ferrier refused to recognize the military regime and appointed Dr Henk Chin A Sen to lead a civilian administration. Army replaced Ferrier with Dr Chin A Sen.

1982 Army, led by Lieutenant-Colonel Desi Bouterse, seized power, setting up a Revolutionary People's Front.

1985 Ban on political activities lifted and the leaders of the traditional parties invited to participate in government.

Swaziland Kingdom of
area 17,400 sq km/6,704.5 sq mi
capital Mbabane
features landlocked enclave between South Africa and Mozambique; Mount Kilimanjaro; Serengeti National Park
exports sugar, citrus; timber, asbestos, iron ore
currency lilangeni

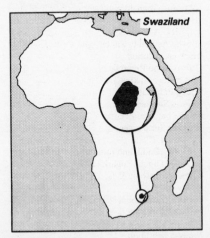

Swaziland

population (1985) 636,000
language English; Swazi 90% (both official)

religion Christian, both Protestant and Catholic
government the king (Mswati III from 1986) nominates part of both senate and house of assembly, the rest being elected by an electoral college.
chronology
1967 Granted internal self-government.
1968 Achieved full independence from Britain, within the Commonwealth, as the Kingdom of Swaziland, with King Sobhuza II as head of state.
1973 The King suspended the constitution and assumed absolute powers.
1978 New constitution adopted.
1982 King Sobhuza died and his place was taken by one of his wives, Dzeliewe, until his son, Prince Makhosetive, reached the age of 21.
1983 Queen Dzeliewe ousted by another wife, Ntombi.
1984 Following a royal power struggle, it was announced that the Crown Prince would become king at the age of 18.
1986 Crown Prince formally invested as King Mswati III.

Sweden Kingdom of
area 449,700 sq km/173,629.5 sq mi
capital Stockholm
towns Göteborg, Malmö, Uppsala, Norrköping, Vasteras
features many lakes, for example Väner, Vätter, Mälar, Hjälmar; islands of Öland and Gaotland; large herds of wild elk
exports aircraft, cars, domestic equipment, ballbearings, drills, missiles, electronics; petro-chemicals; textiles; furnishings, ornamental glass
currency krona
population (1985) 8,348,000 (including 1,200,000 post-war immigrants from Finland, Turkey, Yugoslavia, Greece)
language Swedish, one of the Scandinavian division of Germanic languages
religion Christian (Evangelical Lutheran)
government under the 1975 constitution the powers of the monarchy (Carl XVI Gustaf from 1973) are nominal, and the Salic law was

577

abrogated 1980, so that Crown Princess Victoria, born 1977, is first in line to succeed. The unicameral parliament (Riksdag) is elected by proportional representation (Prime Minister Olof Palme, Social Democrat, was assassinated 1986 and has been replaced by his former deputy, Ingmar Carlsson).

chronology
12th century United as an independent nation.
1397–1520 Under Danish rule.
1914–45 Neutral in both World Wars.
1951–76 Social Democratic Labour Party in power.
1969 Olof Palme became Social Democratic Labour Party leader and prime minister.
1971 Constitution amended, creating a single chamber parliament.
1975 King's constitutional powers reduced.
1976 Thorbjörn Fälldin, leader of the Centre Party, became prime minister, heading their centre-right coalition.
1982 Social Democrats, led by Palme, returned to power.
1985 Social Democrats won the largest number of seats in parliament and formed a minority government, with communist support.
1986 Olof Palme murdered in Stockholm. Ingvar Carlsson became prime minister and leader of the Social Democratic Labour Party.

578

Switzerland (Swiss Confederation)
area 41,288 sq km/15,941 sq mi
capital Bern(e)
towns Zürich, Geneva, Lausanne; river port Basel
features most mountainous country in Europe (Alps and Jura mountains); winter sports area of the upper valley of the river Inn (Engadine); lakes Maggiore, Lucerne, Geneva, Constance
exports electrical goods, chemicals and pharmaceuticals, watches, precision instruments, confectionery; banking, insurance and tourism are important
currency Swiss franc
population (1985) 6,457,000
language German 69%; French 20%; Italian 10% (all official); Romansch 1%
religion Roman Catholic 50%; Protestant 48%
government federal assembly of two houses, a directly elected national council, and council of states (two members chosen by each of the 26 cantons); the assembly elects the executive federal council, and the president, who holds office for only one year.

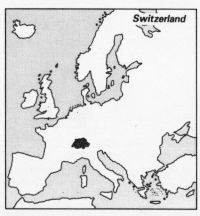

chronology
1648 Became independent of the Holy Roman Empire.
1798–1815 Helvetic Republic established by French Revolutionary armies.

1847 Civil war resulted in greater centralization.

1971 Women given the vote in federal elections.

1984 First female cabinet minister appointed.

1986 Referendum rejected a proposal for membership of UNO.

Syria (Syrian Arab Republic)
area 186,000 sq km/72,000 sq mi
capital Damascus
towns Aleppo, Homs, Hama; chief port Lattakia
features Mount Hermon, Golan Heights; river Euphrates; Crusader castles (Krak des Chevaliers); Phoenician city sites (Ugarit)
exports cotton, oil, cereals, phosphates
currency Syrian pound

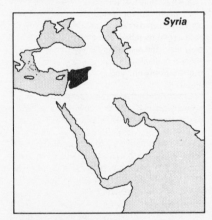

Syria

population (1985) 10,535,000
language Arabic (official)
religion Sunni Muslim, but the ruling minority is Alawite, an Islamic sect; also Druze, again an Islamic sect
government executive president, who must be Muslim (General Hafez el Assad from 1970) and an elected people's council; the ruling Ba'ath party is socialist.
chronology
1946 Achieved full independence from France.
1958 Merged with Egypt to form the United Arab Republic (UAR).
1961 UAR disintegrated.
1967 Six-Day War resulted in the loss of territory to Israel.
1971 Following a bloodless coup, Hafiz al-Assad became president.
1973 Israel consolidated its control of the Golan Heights following the Yom Kippur War.
1976 Substantial numbers of troops committed to the civil war in Lebanon.
1983 President Assad suffered a heart attack but recovered.
1984 Presidents Assad and Gemayel approved a plan for government of national unity in Lebanon.
1985 Assad secured the release of US hostages held in an aircraft hijacked by an extremist Shi'ite group.

Taiwan island (formerly Formosa) off the coast of the People's Republic of China. Forms (with nearby islands) the Republic of China
area 36,000 sq km/14,000 sq mi
capital Taipei
towns ports Keelung, Kaohsiung
features include Penghu Island (Pescadores), Jinmen (Quemoy) and Mazu (Matsu)
exports with US aid, Taiwan is highly industrialized: textiles, petrochemicals, steel, plastics, electronics
currency Taiwan dollar
population (1985) 19,117,322, 89% Taiwanese, 11% mainlanders whose dominance causes resentment
language Mandarin Chinese *religion* officially atheist, but traditional religions are Taoist, Confucianist, and Buddhist
government there is a president (Chiang Kai-shek's son Chiang Ching-kuo from 1978; re-elected 1984) and National Assembly, elected in 1947 with indefinite life; a small number of elected native Taiwanese were admitted in 1972; ruling party Kuomintang.
chronology
1683 Taiwan (Formosa) annexed by China.
1895 Ceded to Japan.
1945 Recovered by China.
1949 Nationalist government fled to Taiwan

following Chinese revolution.
1954 American-Taiwanese mutual defence treaty.
1971 Expulsion from United Nations.

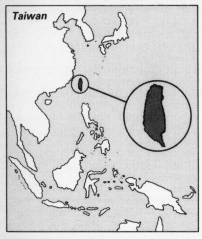

1972 Commencement of legislature elections
1975 President Chaing Kai-shek died; succeeded by Chiang Ching-Kuo.
1979 Diplomatic relations severed with the USA and security pact annulled.
1986 First opposition party to Kuomintang formed.

Tanzania United Republic of
area 942,580 sq km/373,700 sq mi
capital Dodoma
towns chief port Dar es Salaam
features comprises the islands of Zanzibar, and nearby Pemba; Mount Kilimanjaro, called 'shining mountain', because of the snow and glaciers which crown it (Kibo, an extinct volcano and its highest peak, is the highest mountain in Africa 5,895 m/19 340 ft); parts of Lakes Victoria and Tanganyika; Serengeti National Park, and the Olduvai Gorge; Ngorongoro Crater 14.5 km/9 mi across and 762 m/2,500 ft deep
exports coffee, cotton, sisal, cloves from Zanzibar, tea, tobacco
currency Tanzanian shilling
580

population (1985) 21,701,000
language Kiswahili, English (both official)

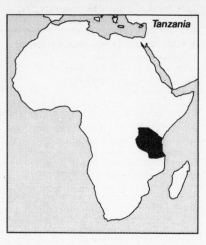

religion Muslim 35%, Christian 35%, traditional 30%
government executive president and Commander-in-Chief of the armed forces (Ali Hassan Mwiinyi from 1985) and single-chamber national assembly. Julius Nyerere remained influential as chairman of the only permitted political party (Chama Cha Mapinduzi (CCM), 'Revolutionary Party'). Zanzibar has a limited degree of autonomy, but rule by decree was introduced in 1964.
chronology
1961 Tanganyika achieved full independence, within the Commonwealth, with Julius Nyerere as prime minister.
1962 Tanganyika became a republic, with Nyerere as president.
1964 Tanganyika and Zanzibar became the United Republic of Tanzania, with Nyerere as president.
1967 East African Community (EAC) formed. Arusha Declaration.
1977 CCM proclaimed the only legal party. EAC dissolved.
1979 Tanzanian troops sent to Uganda to help

the Uganda National Liberation Front overthrow the president Idi Amin.
1984 Nyerere announced his retirement. Prime
Minister Edward Sokoine killed in a road
accident.
1985 Ali Hassan Mwiinyi elected president..
   Thailand The Kingdom of
area 514,000 sq km/198,247 sq mi
capital and chief port Bangkok
towns Chiangmai
features rivers Chao Phraya, Mekong, Sal-
ween; tools and weapons from the Bronze Age
exports rice, sugar; rubber, teak; tin (fifth
largest producer), rubies, sapphires
currency baht

Thailand

population (1985) 51,546,000, Thai 75%, Chinese 14%
language Thai and Chinese, both official
religion Buddhist
government under the 1978 constitution, a
constitutional monarch (Bhumibol Adulyadej
from 1946); and national assembly comprising
senate appointed by the king on the recommendation of the prime minister (General
Prem Tinsulanonda from 1980; re-elected
1983), and a house of representatives elected
by universal suffrage.

chronology
1782 Siam absolutist dynasty commenced.
1896 Anglo-French agreement recognized
Siam as independent buffer state.
1932 Constitutional monarchy established.
1939 Name of Thailand adopted.
1941–4 Japanese occupation.
1946 Military seized power in coup.
1973–4 Military government overthrown:
democratic constitution adopted.
1976 Military re-assumed control.
1978 New constitution promulgated.
1980 General Prem Tinsulandonda assumed
power inaugurating an era of civilian
government.
   Togo W African Republic of
area 56,000 sq km/21,850 sq mi

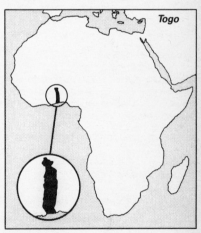
Togo

capital Lomé
features two savanna plains, divided by a range
of hills which runs NE–SW. There are rich
mineral deposits (phosphates, bauxite, marble, iron ore, limestone); there are dry plains,
forest, and arable land with plantations of
cotton, cassava, coffee, and cocoa palms
exports cocoa, coffee, coconuts, copra; phosphate, bauxite
currency CFA franc

581

population (1985) 3,023,000

language French (official); many local languages

religion traditional 60%, Muslim 20%, Christian 20%

government executive president (General Gnassingbé Eyadéma 1937–1) from 1967 and unicameral national assembly; the Rassemblement du Peuple Togolais is the only legal political party.

chronology

1960 Achieved full independence as the Republic of Togo, with Sylvanus Olympio as president.

1963 Olympio ousted and killed in a military coup. Nicolas Grunitzky became president.

1967 Grunitzky replaced by General Gnassingbé Eyadéma, in a bloodless coup.

1973 The Assembly of Togolese People (RPT) formed as the only legal political party.

1979 New constitution adopted. Eyadéma re-elected.

Tonga or *Friendly Islands*

area 748 sq km/289 sq mi

capital Nuku'alofa on Tongatpu

features comprises three groups of islands in the SW Pacific, mostly coral formations, but the western are actively volcanic

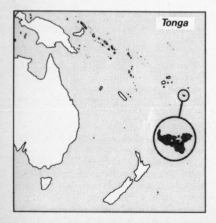

Tonga

currency Tongan dollar or pa'anga

582

population (1985) 103,000

language Tongan and English

religion Wesleyan 47%, Roman Catholic 14%, Free Church of Tonga 14%, Mormon 9%, Church of Tonga 9%

government constitutional monarch, Taufa'ahau Tupou IV (1918–) who in 1965 succeeded his mother, Queen Salote, remembered in the UK for her 1952 visit for the coronation of Elizabeth II; and legislative assembly (Prime Minister Prince Tu'pelehake, younger brother of the king).

chronology

1965 Death of Queen Salote who was succeeded by her son, Prince Tupout'a who took the title King Tupou IV.

1970 Achieved full independence within the Commonwealth..

Trinidad and Tobago Republic of

area Trinidad 4,828 sq km/1,864 sq mi and Tobago 300 sq km/116 sq mi

capital Port of Spain

towns San Fernando

features comprises the two main islands, and some smaller ones; Pitch Lake is a self-renewing source of asphalt and was used by Raleigh when repairing his ships

exports angostura bitters, first blended from herbs as a stomach remedy in 1824, and now used to season food and fruit, and flavour 'pink' gin; asphalt, natural gas and oil

currency Trinidad and Tobago dollar

population (1985) 1,186,000 (equally divided between those of African and Indian descent)

language English (official), Hindi, French, Spanish

religion Roman Catholic 33%, Protestant 14%, Hindu 25%, Muslim 6%

government president, (Ellis Clarke), from 1976. Senate and house of representatives (Prime Minister Arthur Robinson of the National Alliance from 1986).

chronology

1956 The People's National Movement (PNM) founded.

1959 Granted internal self-government, with PNM leader, Eric Williams, as Chief Minister.

1962 Achieved full independence, within the

Commonwealth, with Williams as prime minister.

1976 Became a republic, with Ellis Clarke as president and Williams as prime minister.

giba from 1957, for life from 1974), and national assembly, directly elected for five years

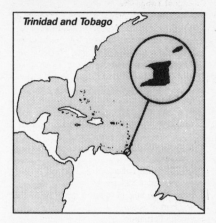

Trinidad and Tobago

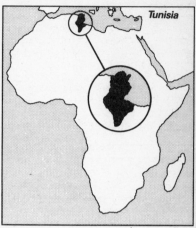

Tunisia

1981 Williams died and was succeeded by George Chambers with Arthur Robinson, leader of the Trinidad and Tobago National Alliance, Leader of the Opposition.
1982 The National Alliance became the National Alliance for Reconstruction (NAR).
1986 NAR defeated PNM in the general election and Arthur Robinson became prime minister.

Tunisia Republic of
area 164,000 sq km/63,300.5 sq mi
capital and chief port Tunis
towns other ports Sfax, Sousse, Bizerta
features fertile island of Jerba, linked to the mainland by a causeway, and identified with the island of the lotus-eaters; Shott el Jerid salt lakes; holy city of Kairouan, ruins of Carthage
exports oil, phosphates, iron ore
currency dinar
population (1985) 7,259,000
language Arabic, official; French
religion Sunni Muslim, with a politically active fundamentalist opposition to the government, Jewish and Christian minorities
government executive president (Habib Bour-

chronology
1955 Granted internal self-government.
1956 Achieved full independence as a monarchy, with Habib Bourguiba as Prime Minister.
1957 Monarchy abolished and Tunisia became a republic with Bourguiba as president.
1959 New constitution adopted.
1975 Bourguiba made president for life.
1985 Diplomatic relations with Libya severed. Israeli raid on PLO headquarters near Tunis.

Turkey Republic of
area 730,350 sq km/301,300.5 sq mi
capital Ankara
towns Istanbul and Izmir, also chief ports
features Bosporus and Dardanelles; Anatolian plateau, Taurus Mountains in SW (highest peak Kaldi Dağ 3,734 m/12,251 ft); mountains on the Aicenian/Iranian border Mnt Ararar, rivers Kizil, Irmak, including and the sources of the Euphrates and Tigris. Archaeological sites include Catal Hüyük, Ephesus, and Troy; the still surviving rock villages of Cappadocia, and historic towns (Antioch, Iskenderun,

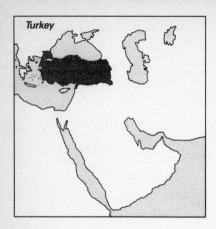

Turkey

Tarsus).

exports cotton and yarn, hazelnuts, citrus, tobacco, dried fruit, chromium ores

currency Turkish lira

population (1985) 50,661,000 85% Turkish, 12% Kurdish

language Turkish, official (it is related to Mongolian, but is written in the Western Latin script), Kurdish Arabic

religion Sunni Muslim

government executive president (General Kenan Evren from 1982) re-elected for seven years by the grand national assembly (elected 1983 with strictly 'vetted' candidates), with a civilian presidential council (the former military national security council). Prime minister from 1983 Targut Ozal.

chronology

1950 First free elections won by the Democratic Party (DP), whose leader, Adnan Menderes became prime minister.

1960 Government overthrown in military coup and Menderes executed.

1961 New constitution adopted with Cemal Gursel as president.

1965 Justice Party (JP), led by Suleman Demirel, in power.

1971 Army forced Demirel to resign.

1973 Civilian rule returned under Bulent

Ecevit.

1974 Turkish troops sent to protect the Turkish community in Cyprus.

1975 Demeril returned at the head of a right-wing coalition.

1978 Ecevit returned with another coalition, in the face of economic difficulties and factional violence.

1979 Demeril returned but violence grew.

1980 Army took over and set up a National Security Council (NSC), with Bulent Ulusu as prime minister. There followed a period of harsh repression of political activists.

1982 New constitution adopted.

1983 Political activity legalized again, with old parties dissolved and reformed under new names. Motherhood Party (ANAP) won the assembly elections and its leader, Turgut Ozal, became prime minister.

1987 Ban lifted on opposition parties. Turkey applied to join European Community.

Tuvalu South West Pacific State of

area 24.6 sq km/9.5 sq mi

capital Funafuti

features the name means 'cluster of eight' islands (there are actually nine, but one is very small)

exports phosphates, copra, handicrafts, stamps

currency Australian dollar

population (1985) 8,580, mainly Polynesian

language Tuvaluan and English

religion Christian, chiefly Protestant

government Governor-General and parliament of 12 members, which elects a prime minister (Tomasi Puapua from 1981) and the majority of the cabinet.

chronology

1978 Achieved full independence within the Commonwealth with Toaripi Lauti as prime minister.

1981 Lauti replaced by Tomasi Puapua.

1985 Puapua re-elected.

1986 Islanders rejected proposal for republican status.

Uganda Republic of

area 236,000 sq km/93,980.5 sq mi

capital Kampala

towns Jingar, M'Bale, Entebbe

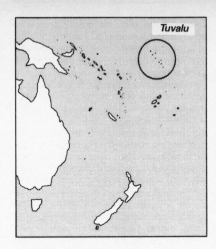

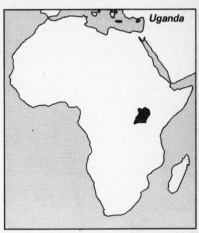

minister.

1963 Proclaimed a federal republic, with King Mutesa II as president.

features Ruwenzori Range; national parks: Murchison Falls, Queen Elizabeth, Kidepo and Lake Mboro; Owen Falls, a cataract on the White Nile where it leaves Lake Victoria (a dam supplies hydroelectricity for Uganda and Kenya)

exports coffee, cotton, tea, and copper

currency Uganda shilling

population (1985) 14,689,000 comprising several ethnic groups: the largest are the Baganda (Buganda), from whom the name of the country comes; others include the Langi and Acholi, and there are a few surviving pygmies

language English (official); Ki-Swahili is a lingua franca

religion Christian 50%, Animist 45%, Muslim 5%

government President Museveni of the National Resistance Movements heads a new government in Kampala, with Dr Sampson Kisseka as prime minister. The NRM is gradually ousting from power General Okello and the former Ugandan army.

chronology

1962 Achieved independence within the Commonwealth, with Milton Obote, leader of the Uganda People's Congress (UPC), as prime

1966 King Mutesa ousted in a coup led by Obote, who ended the federal status and became executive president.

1969 All opposition parties banned after an assassination attempt on Obote.

1971 Obote overthrown in an army coup led by Major–General Idi Amin, who established a ruthlessly dictatorial regime, expelling thousands of Ugandan Asians.

1978 After heavy fighting, Amin was forced to leave the country.

1979 A provisional government was set up with Yusuf Lule as president. Lule was replaced by Godfrey Binaisa.

1980 Binaisa overthrown and a military commission made preparations for a return to an elected government. UPC won the general election and Milton Obote returned to power.

1985 After years of opposition, mainly by the National Revolutionary Army (NRA) and uncontrolled indiscipline in the regular army, Obote was ousted by Brigadier Basilio Okello, who entered a power-sharing agreement with the NRA leader, Yoweri Museveni.

1986 Agreement ended and Museveni became president, heading a broad-based coalition government.

Union of Soviet Socialist Republics (USSR)

area 22,274,700 sq km/8,647,250 sq mi

capital Moscow

towns Kiev, Tashkent, Kharkov, Gorky, Novosibirsk, Minsk, Sverdlovsk, Kuibyshev, Chelyabinsk, Dnepropetrovsk, Tbilisi; ports Leningrad, Odessa, Baku, Archangelesk, Murmansk, Vladivostok, Vostochny, Rostov

features Ural and Caucasus mountains, and part of the Pamirs and Altai mountains; Karakum Desert; Black, Caspian and Aral Seas.

U.S.S.R.

exports cotton, timber; iron and steel, non-ferrous metals, electrical equipment, machinery, arms; oil and natural gas and their products; asbestos, gold, manganese. The USSR has 58% of world coal reserves; 59% of oil; 41% iron; 88% manganese; 54% potassium salts; 30% phosphates (55% of trade is with Communist countries)

currency rouble

population (1985) 277,504,000 (two-thirds living in towns, and of 125 different nationalities); 52% ethnic Russians; 17% Ukrainians

language Slavic (Russian, Ukranian, Byelorussian, Polish), Altaic (Turkish, etc.), other Indo-European, Uralian, Caucasian

religion 'freedom of conscience' is guaranteed under the constitution, but religious belief is discouraged and considered incompatible with party membership (17,500,000 members); the largest Christian denomination is the Orthodox Church (30,000,000); but the largest religious sect is Sunni Muslim (40,000,000), making the USSR the 5th largest Muslim nation; Jews 2,500,000

government under the constitution of 1977, the USSR comprises 15 republics, and (for smaller national groupings), autonomous republics, regions, and areas. The highest organ of government is the Supreme Soviet of two chambers elected for five years: the Soviet of the Union (one deputy for every 300,000 population) and of Nationalities (32 deputies from each constituent republic; 11 from each autonomous republic; five from each autonomous regions, and one from each national area). The Supreme Soviet elects the council of ministers, chaired by the prime minister, and also the presidium, chaired by the state president (Andrei Gromyko from 1985). No one can stand as a candidate in any election without Communist Party approval. The inner cabinet of the party is the Politburo (general secretary from 1985, Mikhail Gorbachev), which controls the entire system. Each constituent and autonomous republic also has its own Supreme Soviet, and local government is run by district, town, and village soviets.

chronology

1941–45 'Great Patriotic War'.

1949 Creation of Council for Mutual Economic aid (Comecon).

1953 Death of Stalin. Removal of Beria. 'Collective leadership' in power.

1955 Creation of Warsaw Pact.

1956 Khrushchev's February 'secret speech'. Hungarian uprising.

1957–58 Ousting of 'anti-party' group and Bulganin.

1960 Sino–Soviet rift.

1962 Cuban missile crisis.

1964 Khrushchev ousted by new 'collective leadership'.

1968 Brezhnev doctrine. Invasion of

Czechoslovakia.

1969 Sino–Soviet border war.

1972 Salt I agreement.

1975 Helsinki Accord.

1977 New state constitution. Brezhnev elected president.

1979 Salt II. Soviet invasion of Afghanistan.

1980 Kosygin replaced as prime minister by Tikhonov.

1980–81 Polish crisis.

1982 Deaths of Suslov and Brezhnev. Yuri Andropov new CPSU leader.

1984 Chernenko succeeded Andropov.

1985 Gorbachev succeeded Chernenko. Gromyko appointed president. Reagan–Gorbachev Geneva Summit.

1986 Gorbachev's power consolidated at 27th Party Congress. Chernobyl nuclear disaster. Reagan–Gorbachev Reykjavik 'mini-summit'.

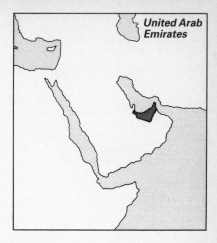

United Arab Emirates (UAE) federation of the emirates of Abu Dhabi, Ajman, Dubai, Fujairah, Sharjah, Umm al Qaiwain, Ras al Khaimah

total area 83,000 sq km/32,000 sq mi

towns chief town Abu Dhabi; chief port Dubai

features linked by their dependence on oil revenues

exports oil and natural gas

currency UAE dirham

population (1985) 1,283,000, 10% being nomadic

language Arabic (official); Farsi, Hindi, and Urdu are spoken by immigrant oilfield workers from Iran, India, and Pakistan

religion 90% Moslem; Christian, Hindu

government the federation is headed by a supreme council of the seven rulers which appoints a council of ministers, and there is an elected national council with no executive powers. The president is Sheikh Zayed (Abu Dhabi) and the vice-president is Sheikh Rashid (Dubai).

chronology

1952 Trucial Council established.

1971 Federation of Arab Emirates came into being but was later dissolved. Six of the Trucial States formed the United Arab Emirates, with the ruler of Abu Dhabi, Sheikh Zayed, as

president.

1972 The seventh state joined.

1976 Sheikh Zayed threatened to relinquish presidency unless progress towards centralization became more rapid.

1985 Diplomatic and economic links with the USSR and with China established.

United Kingdom (UK) a kingdom in N Europe consisting of England, Scotland, Wales, and Northern Ireland. It was formed as the United Kingdom of Great Britain and Ireland in 1801, becoming the United Kingdom of Great Britain and Northern Ireland after the formation of the Irish Free State in 1922

area 94,226 sq mi/244,044 sq km

capital London

towns Birmingham, Leeds, Sheffield, Manchester, Edinburgh, Bradford; Glasgow, Liverpool, Bristol, Newcastle-upon-Tyne, Cardiff are also ports

features rolling landscape, becoming increasingly mountainous towards the north and in Scotland, Grampian mountains and in Wales (Snowdon). The climate is characteristically milder than N Europe, due to the Gulf Stream, with considerable rainfall. No point is further than 120 km from the sea; indented coastline with various small islands.

Rivers: Thames, Severn

United Kingdom

exports agricultural (cereals, rape, sugar beet, potatoes) meat and meat products, poultry, dairy products; electronic and telecommunications equipment; engineering equipment and scientific instruments; North Sea oil and gas, petrochemicals, pharmaceuticals, fertilizers; film and television programmes; tourism is important

currency pound sterling

population (1985) 56,423,000

religion mainly Christian (Church of England and other Protestant sects with Roman Catholic minority); Jewish, Muslim minorities

language English, Welsh, Gaelic

government there is no written constitution. The Queen (Elizabeth II from 1952) is a constitutional monarch, and is also head of the Commonwealth. There is a parliament of two houses, with Northern Ireland, Scotland, and Wales sending members in proportion to their populations; local government is through county/district councils. Metropolitan counties to administer main conurbations were set up in 1972 and abolished 1986.

chronology

BC

Old Stone Age Remains at Cheddar Caves, Somerset; Kent's Cavern, Torquay.

New Stone Age Long barrows.

Bronze Age Round barrows.

c. 1800 Invasion of the Beaker people who began Stonehenge.

c. 450 Iron Age began.

400 Celtic invasion.

55 and 54 Julius Caesar's raiding visits.

43 AD Roman conquest began.

1st century Romans prevented by Picts from penetrating far into Scotland.

407 Roman withdrawal, but partial reoccupations c. 417–27 and c. 450.

5th–6th centuries Christianity introduced into Scotland from Ireland.

5th–7th centuries Anglo-Saxons overran all England except Cornwall and Cumberland, forming independent kingdoms, for example Northumbria, Mercia, Kent, Wessex.

c. 450–600 Wales became chief Celtic stronghold to the west as a result of the Saxon invasions of southern Britain.

c. 597 St Augustine converted England to Christianity.

829 Egbert of Wessex accepted as overlord of all England.

878 Alfred ceded N and E England to the Danish invaders though keeping them out of Wessex.

9th century Kenneth MacAlpin united the kingdoms of Scotland.

1066 Norman Conquest of England.

11th–12th centuries Continual pressure on Wales from across the English border (resisted notably by Llewelyn I and II).

1171 Henry II established a colony in Ireland.

1215 King John was forced to sign Magna Carta.

1266 Scotland gained Hebrides from Norway at Treaty of Perth.

1277 Edward I of England was accepted as overlord by the Welsh.

1284 Edward I completed conquest of Wales begun by the Normans.

1292 Scottish throne granted by Edward I (attempting to annex Scotland) to John Baliol.

1295 Model Parliament set up in England.

1297 The Scots under Wallace defeated England at Stirling Bridge.

1314 Robert Bruce defeated the English at Bannockburn.

1328 Scottish independence was recognized by England.

1338–1453 Hundred Years War with France enabled English parliament to secure control of taxation, and, by impeachment, of the king's choice of ministers.

1348–9 Black Death raged in England.

1350–1400 Welsh nationalist uprisings against the English, the most notable of which was that led by Owen Glendower (1359–1415).

1371 The first Stuart king of Scotland, Robert II.

1381 Social upheaval in England led to Peasants' Revolt, brutally repressed.

1399 Richard II deposed by the English parliament for absolutism.

1455–85 Wars of the Roses.

1497 Henry VII ended the power of the feudal nobility with the suppression of the Yorkist revolts.

1513 James IV of Scotland killed at Battle of Flodden.

1529 Henry VIII became head of the English church.

1536–43 Acts of Union united England and Wales after conquest.

1568 Mary Queen of Scots fled to England.

1578 James VI took over government of Scotland.

1587 Mary Queen of Scots beheaded.

1588 Spanish Armada attempted unsuccessfully to invade England.

1603 James I united the English and Scottish crowns; parliamentary dissidence increased.

1638 Scottish rebellion against England.

1642–52 Civil War in England between royalists and parliamentarians, resulting in victory for parliament.

1649 Charles I executed and the Commonwealth set up.

1651–60 Oliver Cromwell conquered Scotland.

1653 Cromwell appointed Lord Protector.

1660 Restoration of Charles II.

1685 Monmouth rebellion.

1688 William of Orange invited to take the throne as William III; flight of James II.

1689 Jacobites defeated at Killiecrankie.

1692 Massacre of Glencoe, Scotland.

1707 Act of Union between England and Scotland under Queen Anne.

1721 Walpole unofficially the first prime minister under George I.

1783 Loss of the N American colonies.

1800 Act of Ireland united Britain and Ireland.

1832 Great Reform Bill became law.

1846 Repeal of Corn Laws by Robert Peel.

1848 Chartists movement formed.

1867 Second Reform Bill introduced by Disraeli and passed.

1906 Liberal victory: programme of social reform.

1911 Powers of House of Lords curbed.

1914 Irish Home Rule Bill introduced.

1916 Lloyd George became prime minister.

1920 Home Rule Act incorporated the northeast of Ireland (Ulster) into the United Kingdom of Great Britain and Northern Ireland.

1921 Ireland, except for Ulster, became a dominion (Irish Free State, later Eire, 1937).

1924 First Labour government led by Ramsay Macdonald.

1926 General Strike.

1931 National government; unemployment reached 3,000,000.

1940 Churchill became head of coalition government.

1945 Labour government under Attlee; birth of Welfare State.

1951 Conservatives defeated Labour.

1961 Britain applied unsuccessfully to join EEC.

1964 Labour victory under Wilson.

1967 Second unsuccessful application to join EEC.

1970 Conservatives under Heath defeated Labour.

1972 Parliament prorogued in Northern Ireland; direct rule from Westminster began.

1973 Britain joined EEC.

1974 Three-day week; coal strike; Wilson replaced Heath.

1976 Defeat of Devolution Bills.

1977 Liberal-Labour pact.
1979 Victory for Conservatives under Thatcher.
1981 Formation of Social Democrat Party; riots in inner cities.
1982 Unemployment over 3,000,000 for the first time since the 1930s.
1984–5 Coal strike, the longest in British history.
1986 Abolition of metropolitan counties.
1987 General election resulted in third successive victory for Conservative leader Margaret Thatcher.

United States of America (USA)

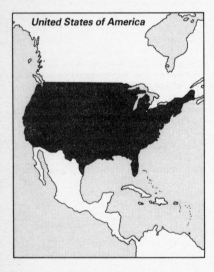

area 9,500,000 sq km/3,536,855 sq mi
capital Washington DC
towns largest cities, New York, Los Angeles, Chicago, Philadelphia, Detroit, San Francisco-Oakland, Washington, Dallas-Fort Worth, Houston, Boston, Nassau-Suffolk, St Louis, Pittsburgh, Baltimore, Minneapolis-St Paul, Atlanta, all metropolitan areas over two million population
currency US dollar
regions the 50 states and District of Columbia
590

(seat of federal government) are usually divided into 10 regions by physical, historical, and economic criteria
Border States Arkansas, Kentucky, Maryland, Missouri, Tennessee, West Virginia *area* 622,045 sq km/240,172 sq mi *economy* called the Border States because they separate the traditional differing economic areas, and tend to a balance of agriculture and industry *population* 19,224,424.
Mid Atlantic States Delaware, New Jersey, Pennsylvania;
area 143,035 sq km/55,226 sq mi; *economy* traditionally industrial with the vast coal, iron and steel area of Pittsburg, but with other industries and agriculture becoming important; *population* 19,826,000.
The Midwest Illinois, Indiana, Michigan, Ohio, Wisconsin;
area 642,998 sq km/248,282 sq mi; *economy* agricultural, with Wisconsin the premier dairying state of the USA, but with important industries based on the iron ores of Michigan, especially the automobile industry of Chicago/Detroit; *population* 41,769,750
Mountain States Arizona, Colorado, Idaho, Montana, Nevada, New Mexico, Utah, Wyoming;
area 2,237,699 sq km/863,885.5 sq mi; *economy* traditionally based on ranching and mining, but irrigation has increased agricultural production, and Arizona is now the leading cotton state; vast mineral resources include coal (50% of US recoverable reserves); oil (larger reserves than Alaska); uranium (90% of US production); gold (70% US production); silver (50% US production); 50% of the land and 80% of *population* 11,368,330.
New England Connecticut, Maine, Massachusetts, New Hampshire, Rhode Island, Vermont;
area 172,516 sq km/66,608 sq mi; *economy* agriculture and forestry predominate; but industry and tourism are also important; *population* 12,350,000.
New York;
area 128,400 sq km/49,576 sq mi; *economy* industrially the second most important state;

population 17,557,300.

Pacific States Alaska, California, Hawaii, Oregon, Washington;
area 251,180 sq km/96,981 sq mi; *economy* varied as the location of the states, from the tropical crops of Hawaii to the coal, oil, and natural gas of northern Alaska; Oregon is the leading US timber state, Washington also mainly rural, but diversifying; *population* 31,796,869, of which nearly 24 million are in California, the most populous US State.

The Prairie States Iowa, Kansas, Minnesota, Nebraska, North Dakota, South Dakota
area 1,159,194 sq km/447,561 sq mi; *economy* agriculturally the most important area, Kansas being the premier US wheat state, and Iowa (95% under cultivation) being the wealthiest agricultural state, Nebraska also being very important; North Dakota now also has oil, South Dakota is the second largest US gold producer, and Minnesota mines 60% of US iron ore; *population*12,266,600

The South Alabama, Florida, Georgia, Louisiana, Mississippi, North Carolina, South Carolina, Virginia;
area 1,009,790 sq km/389,869 sq mi; *economy* traditional agriculture is being overtaken by industrialization, Louisiana a leading oil state, Georgia producing kaolin and 30% of the world's phosphate; *population* 40,160,000.

The South West Oklahoma, Texas;
area 873,495 sq km/ 337,258 sq mi; *economy* traditionally the realm of the cowboy, it has oil, with Texas supplying one-third of US needs, and agriculture is being extended by dairy farming; *population* 17,273,650.

population (1985) 238,631,000, the ethnic minorities include 26,500,000 black, and about 20 million Hispanic; one million American Indians (50% concentrated in Arizona, California, New Mexico, North Carolina, Oklahoma)
language English; largest minority language Spanish
religion 73 million Protestant; 50 million Roman Catholic; six million Jewish; four million Eastern orthodox
government under the constitution of 1787, the states are self-governing, but general taxation, foreign affairs, and control of the armed forces are in the hands of the federal government. Executive power is vested in the president, elected every four years by popularly elected electors for each state (equal to the number of senators and representatives it has in Congress); he or she is eligible for two terms only. The Cabinet, of heads of executive departments, is chosen by the president subject to Senate confirmation, but its members have far less power than their British equivalents, and may not be members of the legislature. Legislative power rests with the two Houses of Congress: the Senate comprises two members for each state, elected for six years, one third re-elected every two years; the House of Representatives comprises 435 members, states being represented in proportion to their population, elected every two years.

chronology
1565 First permanent European settlements made (in what later became the USA) by Spain in Florida.
1585–86 First English settlement made in Virginia by settlers sent out by Raleigh.
1607 First permanent English settlement at Jamestown, Virginia.
1620 Pilgrim Fathers landed at Plymouth.
1664 New Amsterdam, founded by the Dutch, taken by the English and renamed New York.
1775 The Thirteen Colonies rose against the British home government.
1776 Declaration of Independence.
1783 Treaty of Paris: Britain recognized independence of the Thirteen Colonies.
1787 US constitution drawn up.
1789 Washington elected as first president.
1803 Louisiana Purchase.
1812–14 War of 1812 with England, arising from commercial disputes caused by Britain's struggle with Napoleon.
1819 Florida purchased from Spain.
1823 Monroe Doctrine.
1835 Texas proclaimed independence from Mexico.
1836 The Alamo.
1841 First wagon-train left Missouri with emi-

grants for California.

1842 Oregon Trail opened up settlement of the state.

1846–8 Mexican War resulted in cession to USA of Arizona, California, Colorado (part), Nevada, New Mexico, Texas, Utah.

1846 Mormons, under Brigham Young, founded Salt Lake City.

1848 California gold rush.

1859 John Brown seized US Armoury at Harpers Ferry.

1860 Lincoln elected president.

1861–5 Civil War.

1865 Slavery abolished.

1865 Assassination of Lincoln.

1867 Alaska bought from Russia.

1890 Battle of Wounded Knee, the last major battle between American Indians and US troops.

1898 War with Spain ended with the Spanish cession of Philippines, Puerto Rico, and Guam; also agreed that Cuba be independent.

1898 Hawaii annexed.

1903 Panama declared independent with US support and signed treaty for Panama Canal.

1917–18 USA entered World War I.

1929 Wall Street crash.

1933 F D Roosevelt's New Deal put into force.

1941–5 Pearl Harbor precipitated US entry into World War II.

1945 Death of Roosevelt. Truman assumed the presidency.

1949 US backing given to Taiwan.

1950–53 American involvement in Korean war. McCarthy investigations.

1952 Eisenhower elected president.

1960 J F Kennedy elected president.

1961 Bay of Pigs incident.

1963 Assassination of J F Kennedy. Johnson assumed the presidency.

1964–8 'Great Society' civil rights and welfare measures.

1964–73 US involvement in Vietnam war.

1968 Nixon elected president.

1972 Nixon re-elected; Salt-I arms limitation talks.

1973–4 Watergate scandal.

1974 Nixon resigned as president; replaced by Gerald Ford.

1975 Final US withdrawal from Vietnam.

1976 Carter elected president.

1978 Energy bill passed. Camp David summit.

1979 US-Chinese diplomatic relations normalised. Salt-II talks.

1979–80 Iranian hostage crisis. 'Carter doctrine' proposed following Soviet invasion of Afghanistan.

1980 Reagan elected president. Republicans gained Senate majority.

1983 US invasion of Grenada.

1984 Landslide Reagan presidential victory.

1985 Reagan-Gorbachev Geneva summit.

1986 Tax reform bill. Reagan-Gorbachev 'mini-summit'. Republicans lost Senate majority. 'Iran-Contragate' scandal.

Uruguay Oriental Republic of

area 196,945 sq km/72,180 sq mi

capital Montevideo

features smallest of the South American republics; rivers Negro and Uruguay

exports meat and meat products; leather and wool; textiles

currency nuevo peso

population (1985) 2,936,000, mainly of Spanish and Italian descent, also Mestizo, Mulatto and Negro

language Spanish

religion Roman Catholic 60%

government president (Julio Maria Sanguinetti Cairolo from 1985), senate and chamber of deputies

chronology

1956 The Blanco party in power, with Jorge Pacheco Areco as president.

1972 The Colorado Party returned, with Juan Maria Bordaberry Aronceno as president.

1976 Bordaberry deposed by the army and Dr Aparacio Méndez Manfredini became president.

1984 Violent anti-government protests after 10 years of repressive rule.

1985 Agreement reached between the army and political leaders for a return to constitutional government. Colorado Party narrowly won the general election and Dr Julio Maria Sanguinetti became president.

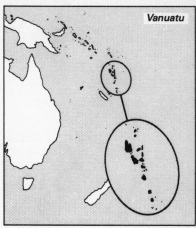

delayed independence but it was achieved, within the Commonwealth, in the following month, with Father Walter Lini, Vanuaaku Party (VP), as Prime Minister.

1986 A government of National Accord established under President Sanguinetti's leadership.

Vanuatu Republic of

area 14,750 sq km/5,700 sq mi

capital Vila on Efate

features comprises about 70 islands, the chief including Espiritu Santo, Malekala, and Efate; there are three active volcanoes

exports copra, fish, coffee; tourism is important

currency vatu

population (1985) 140,000, 90% Melanesian

language Bislama (Pidgin), English, French, all official.

religion Anglican 14%; Presbyterian 40%; Roman Catholic 16%; Animist 15%

government there is a president, and representative assembly (Prime Minister Father Walter Lini from 1980), and national council of chiefs

chronology

1975 Representative Assembly established.

1978 Government of National Unity formed, with Father Gerard Leymang as Chief Minister.

1980 Revolt on the island of Espiritu Santo

1983 VP re-elected, with Father Lini continuing as Prime Minister.

Vatican City State

area 0.4 sq km/109 acres

features forms an enclave in the heart of Rome, including Vatican Palace, official residence of the Pope; the basilica and square of St Peter's; also includes a number of churches in and near Rome; the Pope's summer villa at Castel Gandolfo

currency issues its own coinage, which circulates together with that of Italy

population (1985) 1,000

language Italian

religion Roman Catholic

government the Pope has absolute legislative, executive, and judicial powers, but delegates the government to a commission

chronology

1947 New Italian Constitution confirmed the sovereignty of the Vatican City State.

1978 John Paul II became the first non-Italian Pope for more than 400 years.

1984 Catholicism no longer the Italian state religion.

1969 Dr Rafael Caldera became the first Social Christian Party President.

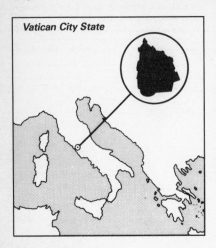

Venezuela Republic of
area 912,068 sq km/352,150 sq mi
capital Caracas
towns Barquisimeto, Valencia, and the port of Maracaibo
features Lake Maracaibo, River Orinoco, Angel Falls; unique flora and fauna; annual rainfall over 7,600 mm/300 in
exports coffee, cocoa; timber; oil, aluminium, iron ore, petrochemicals
currency bolívar
population (1985) 17,317,000, 70% mestizos, but including 32,000 American Indians
religion Roman Catholic
language Spanish (official), Indian languages 2%
government under the 1958 constitution there is an executive president (Jaime Lusinchi, Democratic Action Party (AD), from 1984) and senate and chamber of deputies, all elected for five years
chronology
1961 New Constitution adopted, with Romulo Betancourt as president.
1964 Dr Raúl Leoni became president.

1974 Carlos Pérez Rodriguez, of the (AD), became president.
1979 Dr Luis Hierrera, of the Social Christian Party (COPEI), became president.
1984 AD won both the presidential and the congressional elections and Dr Jaime Lusinchi became president. He tried to solve the nation's economic problems through a social pact between the government, trade unions, and business, and by rescheduling the national debt..

Vietnam The Socialist Republic of
area 336,000 sq km/129,000 sq mi
capital Hanoi
towns ports Ho Chi Minh City (formerly Saigon), Da Nang, and Haiphong
features Red river and Mekong deltas, where cultivation and population are concentrated; Vietnam ranks third among world Communist powers
exports rice, rubber; coal, iron, apatite
currency dong
population (1985) 60,492,000; c. 750,000 refugees, the majority ethnic Chinese, left the country 1975–9, some settling in SW China, others fleeing by sea (directly or via China), the 'boat people', to Hong Kong, and elsewhere

Vietnam

towns Ta'iz, and chief port Hodeida
features hot moist coastal plan, rising to
plateau (known in classical times as *Arabia
felix* because of its fertility)
exports cotton, coffee, grapes

North Yemen

language Vietnamese, of uncertain origin, but
tonal, in the same way as Chinese and Thai
religion traditionally Buddhist and Taoist
government there is a 12–member Council of
State (the country's collective presidency)
elected from the National Assembly, elected
by direct adult suffrage for a five year term, but
power rests with the Communist Party (general
secretary Nguyen Van Linh from 1986).
chronology
1945 Japanese removed from Vietnam.
1946 Commencement of Vietminh war against
French.
1954 France defeated at Dien Bien Phu. Vietnam divided along 17th parallel.
1964 United States entered Vietnam war.
1973 Paris ceasefire agreement.
1975 Saigon captured by North.
1976 Socialist Republic of Vietnam
proclaimed.
1978 Admission into Comecon. Invasion of
Kampuchea.
1979 Sino–Vietnamese border war.
1986 Retirement of 'old guard' leaders..
Yemen, North *(Yemen Arab Republic)*
area 195,000 sq km/75,000 sq mi
capital San'a

currency riyal
population (1985) 6,159,000
language Arabic
religion Sunni Muslim 50%; Shiah Muslim
50%
government executive president (Colonel Ali
Abdullah Saleh from 1978) and assembly.
chronology
1962 North Yemen declared the Arab Republic
of Yemen (YAR), with Abdullah al-Sallal as
president. Civil war broke out between royalists and republicans.
1967 Civil war ended with the republicans
victorious. Sallal deposed and replaced by a
Republican Council.
1971–72 War betwen South Yemen and YAR.
Both sides finally agreed to a union but the
agreement was not kept.
1974 Ibrahim al-Hamadi seized power and a
Military Command Council was set up.
1977 Hamadi assassinated and replaced by
Ahmed ibn Hussein al-Ghashmi.
1978 Constituent People's Assembly appointed
and the Military Command Council dissolved.

595

Ghashmi killed by an envoy from South Yemen and succeeded by Ali Abdullah Saleh. War broke out again between the two Yemens.
1979 Ceasefire agreed with, again, a commitment to a future union.
1983 Saleh re-elected president for a further 5–year term.
1984 Joint committee on foreign policy for the two Yemens met in Aden.

Yemen, South *(People's Democratic Republic of Yemen)*
area 160,000 sq km/62,000 sq mi
capital Aden (used by the USSR as a naval base)
features less fertile than North Yemen; it includes the islands of Perim (in the strait of Bab-el-Mandeb, at the southern entrance to the Red Sea), Socotra, and Kamaran

South Yemen

exports cotton goods, coffee
currency Yemeni dinar
population (1985) 2,209,000
language Arabic
religion Sunni Muslim 91%
government president and secretary general of the socialist party and supreme people's council, president Haydar Abu Bakr al-Attas, from 1986.
chronology
1967 People's Republic of Southern Yemen

founded.
1970 Country renamed the People's Democratic Republic of Yemen (PDRY), led by the Marxist National Front Party (NF).
1972 War with the Yemen Arab Republic (YAR).
1978 YAR president killed by a bomb carried by a PDRY envoy. Yemen Socialist Party (YSP) formed as a 'Marxist-Leninist vanguard party'. War between YAR and PDRY.
1979 Ceasefire aagreed and YAR and PDRY agreed to move towards eventual union.
1983 Joint Yemen Council established.
1985 Ali Nasser elected president but deposed after his personal guards had killed three of his party opponents.
1986 Hayder Abu Bakr al-Attas became president and secretary-general of the YPS Political Bureau..

Yugoslavia Socialist Federal Republic of
area 255,874 sq km/98,740 sq mi
capital Belgrade
towns Zagreb, Skopje, Ljubljana; ports Split and Rijeka
features constituent republics of Bosnia-Hercegovina, Croatia, Kosovo, Macedonia, Montenegro, Serbia, Slovenia, Vojvodina; River Danube; scenic Dalmatian coast and Dinaric Alps; Lake Shkodër
exports machinery, electrical goods, chemicals
currency dinar
population (1985) 23,124,000 including Serbs 36%; Croats 20%; Muslims 9%; Slovenes 8%; Albanians 7%; Macedonians 6%
language individual national languages have equality, but Serbo-Croat is the most widespread
religion Orthodox (Serbs); Roman Catholic (Croats); Muslim (50% in Bosnia)
government legislative assembly of two houses (federal chamber, and chamber of republics and provinces); direct election has been replaced by a complex delegational system. A collective state presidency of nine (representing the republics and provinces), has one of its members elected annually as head of state, from 1986 Sinan Hasani.
chronology

1917 Creation of Kingdom of the Serbs, Croats and Slovenes.

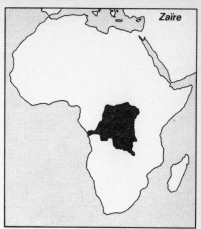

1929 Name of Yugoslavia adopted.

1941 Invasion by Germany.

1945 Communist Federal Republic formed under leadership of Tito.

1948 Split with Soviet Union.

1953 Self-management principle enshrined in constitution.

1961 Formation of Non-Aligned Movement under Yugolavia's leadership.

1974 New constitution adopted.

1980 Death of Tito. Collective Leadership assumed power.

Zaïre Republic of

area 2,345,000 sq km/895,000 sq mi

capital Kinshasa

towns Kananga, Lubumbashi, Kisangani; ports, Matadi, Boma

features Zaïre river; lakes: Tanganyika, Mobutu Sese Seko, and Edward; Ruwenzori mountains

exports palm oil, coffee, tea, rubber, timber; copper, cobalt (80% of world output), zinc, cadmium, industrial diamonds

currency zaïre

population (1985) 30,505,000

language French (official); Swahili, Lingala

religion 70% Christian; 10% Muslim

government under the constitution of 1978, there is a directly elected president (Mobutu from 1965) and unicameral legislature; only one party, the Popular Revolutionary Movement (MPR) is permitted

chronology

1960 Achieved full independence as the Republic of the Congo. Civil war broke out between the central government and Katanga province.

1963 Katanga war ended.

1967 New constitution adopted.

1970 Joseph-Desire Mobutu elected president.

1972 Country became the Republic of Zaïre, with the Popular Movement of the Revolution (MPR) the only legal political party.

1977 Mobutu re-elected.

1984 Mobutu re-elected.

Zambia Republic of

area 752,620 sq km/290,586.5 sq mi

capital Lusaka

towns Kitwe, Ndola, Kabwe, Chipata, Livingstone

features Zambezi river, Kariba Dam

exports copper, emeralds, tobacco

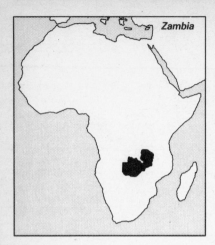
Zambia

area 390,600 sq km/150,820 sq mi
capital Harare
towns Bulawayo, Gweru, Kwekwe, Mutare, Hwange
features Hwange National Park, part of Kalahari Desert
exports tobacco, citrus, tea, coffee; gold and silver
currency Zimbabwe dollar
population (1985) 8,678,000; Shona 80%; Ndbele (in Matabeleland, who are descendants of Zulus who in the early 19th century conquered the Shona) 20%; before independence there were c.275,000 Europeans; in 1985 c.100,000

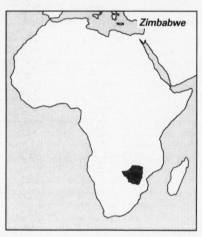
Zimbabwe

currency kwacha
population (1985) 6,832,000
language English, (official); the majority speak Bantu languages
religion mainly Animist, 21% Roman Catholic, also Protestant, Hindu and Moslem minorities
government from 1972 a one–party state (United National Independence Party: UNIP). There is an executive president (Kenneth Kaunda from 1964), and the central committee of the party has precedence over the National Assembly. In 1982 Kaunda planned to adopt 'scientific socialism' as the country's political philosophy.
chronology
1964 Achieved full independence, within the Commonwealth, as the Republic of Zambia, with Kenneth Kaunda as president.
1972 UNIP declared the only legal party.
1976 Support for the Patriotic Front in Rhodesia declared.
1980 Unsuccessful coup against President Kaunda.
1983 Kaunda re-elected president.
1985 Kaunda elected chairman of the Front Line States.
  Zimbabwe Republic of

598

language English, (official); Shona, Ndbele, Nyanja
religion Christian
government under the 1980 constitution there is a non-executive president, Senate and House of Representatives (prime minister from 1980 Robert Mugabe, ZANU (PF)), one-fifth European.
chronology
1961 Zimbabwe African People's Union (ZAPU) formed, with Joshua Nkomo as leader.

1962 ZAPU declared illegal.

1963 Zimbabawe African National Union (ZANU) formed, with Robert Mugabe as secretary-general.

1964 Ian Smith became prime minister. Nkomo and Mugabe imprisoned.

1965 ZANU banned. Smith declared unilateral independence.

1966–8 Abortive talks between Smith and UK prime minister Harold Wilson.

1974 Nkomo and Mugabe released. Geneva conference agreed a date for constitutional independence.

1979 Smith produced a new constitution and established a government with Bishop Abel Muzorewa as prime minister. New government denounced by Nkomo and Mugabe. Con-ference in London agreed independence arrangements (Lancaster House Agreement).

1980 Full independence achieved, with Robert Mugabe as prime minister.

1981 Rift between Mugabe and Nkomo.

1982 Nkomo dismissed from the cabinet and left the country temporarily.

1984 ZANU–People's Front (PF) Party Congress agreed to create a one-party state at some time in the future.

1985 Relations between Mugabe and Nkomo improved. ZANU–PF increased its majority in the general election and Mugabe continued as prime minister.

1986 Joint ZANU–PF rally held amid plans for merger.

Index